BUSINESS ECONOMICS
and
INDIAN BUSINESS ENVIRONMENT

BUSINESS ECONOMICS
and
INDIAN BUSINESS ENVIRONMENT

[B.Com. General]

[New Syllabus: 2010-11]

Debes Mukherjee

Former Teacher-in-Charge
St Paul's C. M. College, Kolkata

New Central Book Agency (P) Ltd

LONDON

DELHI KOLKATA PUNE HYDERABAD ERNAKULAM

REGD. OFFICE
8/1 Chintamoni Das Lane, Kolkata 700 009, India
email: ncbapvtltd@eth.net

OVERSEAS OFFICE
27 Catherine Court, Chase Road, Southgate, London, N14 4RB

EXPORT OFFICE
212 Shahpur Jat, New Delhi 110 049
email: ncbaexp@ncbapvtltd.com

BRANCHES

208B Peacock Lane, Shahpur Jat
New Delhi 110 049
email: ncbadel@ncbapvtltd.com

House No. 3-1-315, 1st Floor
Nimboliadda, Kachiguda, Hyderabad 500 027
email: ncbahydb@ncbapvtltd.com

Shop Nos. 3 & 4, Vinayak Towers
681/B Budhwar Peth, Appa Balwant Chowk
Pune 411 002
email: ncbapune@ncbapvtltd.com

GSS Shopping Complex, 1st Floor
Opposite College Post Office, Convent Road
Ernakulam 682 035
email: ncbaernk@ncbapvtltd.com

BUSINESS ECONOMICS AND INDIAN BUSINESS ENVIRONMENT

First Published: 2003, Reprinted: 2004, With Additions: 2007, 2008
Second Edition [Thoroughly Revised and Updated]: July 2009
With Additions: September 2010

PUBLISHER AND TYPESETTER
New Central Book Agency (P) Ltd
8/1 Chintamoni Das Lane, Kolkata 700 009

PRINTER
New Central Book Agency (P) Ltd
Web-Offset Division, Dhulagarh, Sankrail, Howrah

COVER DESIGNER
Ankit

COVER PRINTER
Biswanath Studio, Kolkata

TECHNICAL EDITOR
Subas Maitra

PROJECT COORDINATORS
Prabhat Jas, Tarun Dey, Swapan Sarkar

ISBN: 81-7381-438-4

Price: Rs 250.00

Contents

BUSINESS ECONOMICS

INDIAN BUSINESS ENVIRONMENT

APPENDICES

Preface

The University of Calcutta has been consistently changing Commerce syllabi in the light of changing business environment. Economics or so to say, Business Economics has seen some changes in the new B.Com. (General) Course. For instance, in Module I (call it Microeconomic Theory) of Paper 1.5 Economics—1, some fundamental tools of Business Economics, such as, graphs, functions, schedules, etc., have been added in this new syllabus. In Module II (call it Indian Economic Environment), barring concepts of economic growth and development, critical issues of unemployment, poverty and income distribution, inflationary trends, parallel economy, rural credit, food security, etc., have been incorporated. This edition addresses all these changes. As study of Indian business environment demands always up-to-date facts and figures, the current edition is filled with the latest statistics drawn from reliable sources.

My word of thanks go to those people who have made these changes in this book possible in the quickest possible time.

5 September 2010 **Debes Mukherjee**

New Gems Cooperative Housing Society Ltd
8 S. N. Chatterjee Road
Kolkata 700 038
Phone: (033) 2407 1715
e-mail: dmbmpmcm@rediffmail.com

Preface to the Second Edition

Revision of this book was long overdue. I regret my inability to make a thorough revision of the book earlier because of some unavoidable factors. However, the present edition is a thoroughly revised version. For the benefit of the students, some of the chapters have been recast while an entire chapter on 'Problems of Growth and Role of Government' has been deleted as the topic was not included in the syllabus. Deficiencies that the book had in the previous edition have been removed.

Some of the new issues that remained uncovered in the earlier edition have been incorporated in this edition. These are: National Policy on Farmers 2007, Mid-term Appraisal of the Tenth Plan, Eleventh Five Year Plan (2007-12), Trade and Development; GATT vs WTO, etc. Above all, data relating to Indian Business Environment have been updated with the aid of the latest available information. While incorporating data, recent trends and developments in the Indian economy as well as the policy measures adopted by the Government have been analysed so that the student community is benefitted largely.

The current edition makes a change in the question pattern in accordance with the changes suggested by the University of Calcutta.

Suggestions and criticisms from all quarters will be appreciated which will help the author to make the book error-free in the subsequent editions.

I express my sincere thanks to all who helped me in this endeavour in various ways.

1 July 2009 **Debes Mukherjee**

Preface to the First Edition

Since preface is deemed to be "the soul of the book", I have ignored the biblical advice: "It is a foolish thing to make a long prologue." New syllabus of the 21st century looks at the economic issues rather in a different setting. One may call it modern economics. And to carry out this message, I prefer to write a somewhat long preface to highlight the essential features of this book.

Almost after a lapse of 50 years, the demand for a uniform pattern of syllabus all over India at the undergraduate level has been met under the guidance of the University Grants Commission. The syllabus meant for BCom course of the Universities of Calcutta, Kalyani, etc., follows the UGC curriculum with minor additions and omissions. The current text aims at meeting the needs of the students of all the universities of West Bengal as also other universities of different States and Union Territories of the country.

The present title *Business Economics and Indian Business Environment* is an accessible approach to the world of economics that essentially involves hard choices. For the understanding of the subject, no prior knowledge of economics is essential. However, one has to learn a simple and usable body of economics at this undergraduate economics course. Keeping this in mind, the book has been divided into two parts: 'Business Economics' and 'Indian Business Environment'. The first part focusses on the core of microeconomics. Indeed, the heart of business economics is microeconomics. It provides an analysis of decision-takers, like firms and consumers. The book begins with What to produce, How to produce, and For Whom to produce. It provides an overview of demand and supply forces—both of commodities and resources. This then naturally leads to market structure. An attempt has been made to cover all the salient market forms to have knowledge of management decisions concerning pricing of a product and the volume of output. The order of discussion has been made logical so that an understanding of basic ideas of business economics (or microeconomics) becomes clear and coherent.

From abstract theorisation, we then move on to the real world of Indian macroeconomic environment. Macroeconomics is the study of the economy as a whole. Unless students are exposed to abstract theories, a basic understanding of macroeconomy will remain incomplete. To fill this gap, a unique portrait of the Indian economy has been made in the second part of the book. An attempt has been made here to emphasise the links between economic theory and Indian macroeconomic issues. Strengths and weaknesses of Indian agriculture, industry, etc., have been sketched out for a period till date since independence. The book places emphasis on various problems of growth like unemployment, poverty, etc., during the plan period. The author firmly believes that the study of Indian economics always demands the use of up-to-date facts and figures. The present title has been enriched with the latest information and statistics.

We are living in a global capitalist system in which national identities are difficult to assign. Chapter 16 is concerned with the international business environment in the light of 'globalisation'. Globalisation has brought tremendous change in the nature of competition. This has been greatly facilitated by international economic institutions like the IMF, World Bank, WTO, etc. so as to create a global capitalist order. Will it bring prosperity to India? This chapter tries to give an answer to this million-dollar question.

How to confront short questions of 2 marks each is a matter of concern to students. Taking into account this serious matter, another chapter (Chapter 17) called 'Short Questions and Answers' has been added at the end of the book.

The author, however, does not claim any originality in writing such a textbook, particularly when one has to travel along the contours of a syllabus structured by the appropriate authorities. The author hopes that the students and the readers of this book will be able to understand today's economic environment from this simple and readable text. Remember, this is not a text meant for teachers and specialists of the subject—but for students. However, a new book always requires to be 'introduced' to the students by the teachers.

Over the last 30 years of teaching, I have been greatly benefitted from stimulating and productive advice, comments and suggestions from quite a large number of people including my classroom students. I sincerely acknowledge their 'contributions'. Recently, I organised a 'Summer School of Economics' at my own college for 10 + 2 students to help them to pursue Economics Honours at the undergraduate level. Really, I owe my gratitude to these 'infant' students of Economics since teaching in these classes were indeed challenging, and stimulating. I must thank the Second Year BSc Economics Honours students of St Paul's College—Sri Arindam Maiti and Saumit Das—who helped me a lot in the preparation of the contents of the book. I express my sincere thanks to the publisher Sri Amitabha Sen of New Central Book Agency (P) Ltd, who always provides an inspiring support and encouragement in writing books.

However, I request everyone to send their valuable suggestions for the improvement of the treatise. This is where the 'services' of teachers and specialists an author badly needs.

1 August 2003 **Debes Mukherjee**

New Syllabus

(2010-11)

UNIVERSITY OF CALCUTTA

Paper 1.5: Economics—I (100 Marks)

Module—I (50 Marks)

MICROECONOMIC THEORY

Unit—I : INTRODUCTION

Economics—Scope and subject-matter. Distinction between Economics and Business Economics. Tools required—Functional relationships, schedules, graphs, concept of slope and its measurement, etc. Resources—Scarcity and efficiency—Production Possibility Frontier—Its shifting.

Unit—II: BASICS OF DEMAND AND SUPPLY

The concept of demand and demand function—Derivation of Individual demand curve and Market demand curve—Shifting of the demand curve—The supply function and the supply curve—Derivation of individual supply curve and market supply curve—Shifting of the supply curve—Determination of equilibrium price.

Unit—III: THEORY OF CONSUMER BEHAVIOUR

Cardinal analysis—Law of diminishing marginal utility—Consumer surplus; Ordinal approach—Indifference curve analysis—Budget line—Consumer Equilibrium—Income consumption curve and price consumption curve—Hicksian decomposition of price effect into substitution effect and income effect—Demand curve for normal, inferior and Giffen goods.

Concept of Elasticities of demand—Measurement of various elasticities of demand—Distinction between slope of a demand curve and the elasticity of demand—Elasticity of supply—Measurement.

Unit—IV: THEORY OF PRODUCTION

Production Function—The Law of variable proportions—Relationships among TP, AP, and MP; Concept of Isoquant and Isocost—Finding the optimal employment of inputs—Ridge lines: The economic region of production—Output expansion path and homogeneous production function.

Unit—V: THEORY OF COST

Cost analysis—Different concepts—Accounting and Economic costs, Opportunity cost. Private and social costs : Short run and long run costs.

Unit—VI: MARKET FOR COMMODITIES

Revenue concepts under different market conditions: TR, AR, MR and relationship among AR, MR, and elasticity of demand.

Perfect competition—Short run and long run equilibrium—Supply curve in the short run (shutdown and breakeven point concepts). Monopoly—Short run and long run equilibrium—Concept of Price discrimination. Monopolistic competition, Oligopoly Market—Short run and long run equilibrium.

Unit—VII: FACTOR PRICE DETERMINATION

Theory of Wage Determination—Backward bending supply curve of labour: Determination Rent, Profit and Interest rate.

Module—II (50 Marks)

INDIAN ECONOMIC ENVIRONMENT

Unit—I: INDIAN BUSINESS ENVIRONMENT

Concepts: Economic Growth and Development; Meaning of Underdeveloped Economy: Basic Characteristics of Indian economy. **(Marks–5)**

Unit—II: OVERVIEW OF INDIAN ECONOMIC TRENDS **(Marks–10)**

National Income: Concept—Methods of measurement of national income in Indian economy—Trend of National Income and per capita income—Trend in structural composition of national income. Trend in occupational structure. Trends in Saving and Investment in Indian economy.

Unit—III: ISSUES IN INDIAN ECONOMY

Problems of Growth: Unemployment, Poverty, Inequality in Income distribution, inflation. Concept of Parallel economy.

Unit—IV: PROBLEMS AND POLICIES OF INDIAN ECONOMY **(Marks–15)**

(A) Basic features of Indian agriculture: Low productivity; Land reform, Green Revolution: Rural Credit: Agricultural Marketing; Impact of New Agricultural Policy (NAP) on Indian Agriculture with special reference to Food Security.

(B) Industrial development during plan period: Industrial sickness; Industrial Policies in the Pre-reform and Post-reform period in 1991.

Unit—V: INDIAN ECONOMIC PLANNING **(Marks–10)**

Concepts of Economic Planning; Objectives and achievements of Indian Five-year Plans (Plan period I to XI).

Old Syllabus

UNIVERSITY OF CALCUTTA

PAPER II: BUSINESS ECONOMICS AND BUSINESS ENVIRONMENT (100 MARKS)

GROUP A: BUSINESS ECONOMICS (60 MARKS)

1. **INTRODUCTION:** Basic Problems of an Economy; Working of Price Mechanism and Resource Allocation.
2. **BASICS OF DEMAND AND SUPPLY:** Elasticity of Demand—Concept and Measurement; Price, Income and Cross Elasticity; Average Revenue; Marginal Revenue.
3. **CONSUMER OPTIMISATION:** Indifference Curve Approach; Derivation of Individual Demand Curve; Price Effect, Income Effect, Substitution Effect.
4. **THEORY OF PRODUCTION:** Production Function; Law of Variable Proportions; Isoquants; Economic Regions and Optimum Factor Combination; Expansion Path; Returns to Scale; Internal and External Economies and Diseconomies.
5. **THEORY OF COSTS:** Short Run and Long Run Cost Curves—Traditional and Modern Approaches.
6. **MARKET STRUCTURES AND OPTIMISATION OF FIRM AND INDUSTRY**
   (a) **Perfect Competition:** Profit Maximisation and Equilibrium of Firms and Industry: Short Run and Long Run Supply Curves; Price and Output Determination.
   (b) **Monopoly:** Determination of Price under Monopoly; Equilibrium of Firm; Comparison between Perfect Competition and Monopoly; Price Discrimination.
   (c) **Monopolistic Competition:** Meaning and Characteristics; Price and Output Determination under Monopolistic Competition; Product Differentiation; Selling Costs.
   (d) **Oligopoly:** Characteristics; Cournot Model; Kinked Demand Curve Model.
7. **FACTOR PRICING:** Marginal Productivity Theory; Determination of Rent, Wage, Interest and Profit.

GROUP B: BUSINESS ENVIRONMENT (40 MARKS)

1. **INDIAN BUSINESS ENVIRONMENT:** Components and Features.
2. **INDIAN ECONOMIC TRENDS SINCE INDEPENDENCE:** Concept of National Income and Its Sectoral Composition; Structural Changes; Savings and Investment.
3. **INDIAN AGRICULTURE:** Performance; Problems and Prospects; Economic Reforms and Indian Agriculture.
4. **INDUSTRIAL DEVELOPMENT IN INDIA:** Trends; Problems and Prospects; Economic Reforms and Indian Industry; Foreign Direct Investment and Foreign Collaboration in Indian Industries.
5. **INDIAN FIVE YEAR PLANS:** Objectives, Achievements and Failures.
6. **INTERNATIONAL ENVIRONMENT:** An Overview of International Trading Environment; Trends in World Trade and the Problems of Developing Countries; Foreign Trade and Economic Growth; International Economic Institutions—GATT, WTO, World Bank, IMF.

BUSINESS ECONOMICS

1

INTRODUCTION TO BUSINESS ECONOMICS

1.1. INTRODUCTION

Prof. Samuelson once remarked economics as the 'queen of social sciences'. Today, economics is hailed as 'the superpower of the social sciences'—possibly because it influences greatly the lives of people, *albeit* the ordinary public. Even hardcore scientists and non-economists can never dismiss economics. Abstract economic theories may be dull and uninteresting to them. These theories may not fit the real world. But their practical applications bear testimony to the fact that economics exercises powerful influence on our daily lives. To perform effectively and responsibly as citizens, politicians, bureaucrats and administrators, workers in a firm/farm, trade unionists, NGO workers, consumers, scientists, doctors, and, hence, all people need to know some economics.

Understanding the role of government against the backdrop of market economy and the challenges of globalisation that a country experiences today are the two most important reasons why people study economics, says Nobel Prize winning economist P. A. Samuelson. He adds further : "All your life—from cradle to grave and beyond—you will run up against the brutal truths of economics. As a voter, you make decisions on issues—on the government deficit, on taxes on free trade, on inflation and unemployment—that cannot be understood until you have mastered the rudiments of this subject."

In fact, economists borrow from many other disciplines. Today, we find an interdisciplinary approach in economics and cross-fertilisation of ideas. One can use economics to learn how to make better decisions. That is why we— including the non-economists, confront mind-boggling questions and often make observations. Such questions and observations arise from our daily lives.

Since economics affects our daily lives, one must understand why the real world is such and not the other way around. Since economics is a study of how individuals, firms and governments within our society make choices, we begin this chapter by asking questions about our economic observations drawn from our own experiences, media reports, books of history, political science and, various other branches of sociology.

Following questions are relevant in this book :

- Why is the price of petrol, diesel going up?
- Why does share price fluctuate?
- Why does tuition fee in educational institutions rise now?
- Why does a computer engineer earn more than a Ph.D degree-holder professor?
- Why does a firm or a government office go for computerisation?
- Why does general price level rise in some years and fall in some other?
- Why is health care spending less compared to the needs of the Indian society?
- Why are so many Indians unemployed?
- Why do many Indians live below the poverty line?
- Would India be able to achieve a 10 p.c. growth rate in the Eleventh Plan (2007-12)?
- While making economic decisions, how should emphasis be given to make our land environment-friendly?
- Does Internet service affect economic organisation?
- Should we go for more liberalisation, privatisation and globalisation to make the Indian economy a developed one?
- And many such questions.

Thus, economics is not all about money—as it is believed by many. It is not a 'bread-and-butter science'. This idea is indeed a common fallacy based on misunderstandings about economics. We study economics to answer all the aforesaid questions. While searching answers for these questions, economists travel to other branches of knowledge hitherto kept reserved for those branches. This is what may be called 'economic imperialism'. As a result, the borders between economics and other branches of social science, criminology, epidemiology, etc., have virtually vanished. So, the subject-matter of economics has undergone a revolutionary change. That is why it is said "Economists are venturing far beyond their own ivory towers.".

1.2. DEFINITION OF ECONOMICS

Before entering the intricacies of economic theory, we should understand what business economics is. Business economics or managerial economics is the application field of economic theories, mainly microeconomic theories. So, before defining business economics, we must say something about economics.

The English word economics is derived from the ancient Greek word *oikonomia*—meaning the management of a family or a household. It is thus clear that the subject economics was first studied in ancient Greece. What was the study of household management to Greek philosophers like Aristotle (384-322 BC) was the "study of wealth" to the mercantilists in Europe between the sixteenth and eighteenth centuries. Economics, as a study of wealth, received great support from the Father of economics, Adam Smith, in the late eighteenth century.

Since then, the subject has travelled a long and this Greek or Smithian definition serves our purpose no longer. Over the passage of time, the focus of attention has been changed. As a result, different definitions have evolved. These definitions can conveniently be grouped into three : (i) Smith's Wealth definition; (ii) Marshall's Welfare definition; and (iii) Robbins' Scarcity definition.

1.2.1. Adam Smith's Wealth Definition

The formal definition of economics can be traced back to the days of Adam Smith (1723-90)— the great Scottish economist. Following the mercantilist tradition, Adam Smith and his followers regarded economics as a science of wealth which studies the process of production, consumption and accumulation of wealth. His emphasis on wealth as a subject-matter of economics is implicit in his great book—*'An Inquiry into the Nature and Causes of the Wealth of Nations'* or, more popularly known as *'Wealth of Nations'*—published in 1776. According to Smith: "The great object of the Political Economy of every country is to increase the riches and power of that country." Like the mercantilists, he did not believe that the wealth of a nation lies in the accumulation of precious metals like gold and silver. To him, wealth may be defined as those goods and services which command value-in-exchange. Economics is concerned with the generation of the wealth of nations. Economics is not to be concerned only with the production of wealth but also the distribution of wealth. The manner in which production and distribution of wealth will take place in a market economy is the Smithian 'invisible hand' mechanism or the 'price system'. Anyway, economics is regarded by Smith as the 'science of wealth.'

Other contemporary writers also define economics as that part of knowledge which relates to wealth. John Stuart Mill (1806-73) argued that economics is a science of production and distribution of wealth. Another classical economist Nassau William Senior (1790-1864) argued "The subject-matter of the Political Economics is not Happiness but Wealth." Thus, economics is the science of wealth. However, the last decade of the nineteenth century saw a scathing attack on the Smithian definition and in its place another school of thought emerged under the leadership of an English economist, Alfred Marshall (1842-1924).

Criticisms : Following are the main criticisms of the classical definition :

- This definition is too narrow as it does not consider the major problems faced by a society or an individual. Smith's definition is based primarily on the assumption of an 'economic man' who is concerned with wealth-hunting. That is why critics condemned economics as 'the bread-and-butter science'.
- Literary figures and social reformers branded economics as a 'dismal science', 'the Gospel of Mammon' since Smithian definition led us to emphasise on the material aspect of human life, i.e., generation of wealth. On the other hand, it ignored the non-material aspect of human life. Above all, as a science of wealth, it taught selfishness and love for money. John Ruskin (1819-1900) called economics a 'bastard science.' Smithian definition is bereft of changing reality.
- The central focus of economics should be on scarcity and choice. Since scarcity is the fundamental economic problem of any society, choice is unavoidable. Adam Smith ignored this simple but essential aspect of any economic system.

1.2.2. Marshall's Welfare Definition

Alfred Marshall in his book *'Principles of Economics'* published in 1890 placed emphasis on human activities or human welfare rather than on wealth. Marshall defines economics as "a study of men as they live and move and think in the ordinary business of life." He argued that economics, on one side, is a study of wealth and, on the other, is a study of man. Emphasis on human welfare is evident in Marshall's own words: "Political Economy or Economics is a study of mankind in the ordinary business of life; it examines that part of individual and social action which is most closely connected with the attainment and with the use of the material requisites of well-being." Thus, "Economics is on the one side a study of wealth; and on the other and more important side, a part of the study of man." According to Marshall, wealth is not an end in itself as was thought by classical authors; it is a means to an end—the end of human welfare. This Marshallian definition has the following important features :

- Economics is a social science since it studies the actions of human beings.
- Economics studies the 'ordinary business of life' since it takes into account the money-earning and money-spending activities of man.
- Economics studies only the 'material' part of human welfare which is measurable in terms of the measuring rod of money. It neglects other activities of human welfare not quantifiable in terms of money. In this connection A. C. Pigou's (1877-1959)—another great neo-classical economist—definition is worth remembering. Economics is "that part of social welfare that can be brought directly or indirectly into relation with the measuring rod of money."
- Economics is not concerned with "the nature and causes of the Wealth of Nations." Welfare of mankind, rather than the acquisition of wealth, is the object of primary importance.

Criticisms : Though Marshall's definition of economics was hailed as a revolutionary one, it was criticised on several grounds. They are :

- Marshall's notion of 'material welfare' came in for sharp criticism at the hands of Lionel Robbins (later Lord) (1898-1984) in 1932. Robbins argued that economics should encompass 'non-material welfare' also. In real life, it is difficult to segregate material welfare from non-material welfare. If only the 'materialist' definition is accepted, the scope and subject-matter of economics would be narrower, or a great part of economic life of man would remain outside the domain of economics.
- Robbins argued that Marshall could not establish a link between economic activities of human beings and human welfare. There are various economic activities that are detrimental to human welfare. The production of war materials, wine, etc., are economic activities but do not promote welfare of any society. These economic activities are included in the subject-matter of economics.
- Marshall's definition aimed at measuring human welfare in terms of money. But 'welfare' is not amenable to measurement, since 'welfare' is an abstract, subjective concept. Truly speaking, money can never be a measure of welfare.
- Marshall's 'welfare definition' gives economics a normative character. A normative science must pass on value judgments. It must pronounce whether a particular economic activity is good or bad. But economics, according to Robbins, must be free from making value

judgment. Ethics should make value judgments. Economics is a positive science and not a normative science.

- Finally, Marshall's definition ignores the fundamental problem of scarcity of any economy. It was Robbins who gave a scarcity definition of economics. Robbins defined economics in terms of allocation of scarce resources to satisfy unlimited human wants.

1.2.3. Robbins' Scarcity Definition

The most accepted definition of economics was given by Lord Robbins in 1932 in his book *'An Essay on the Nature and Significance of Economic Science'*. According to Robbins, neither wealth nor human welfare should be considered as the subject-matter of economics. His definition runs in terms of scarcity : "Economics is the science which studies human behaviour as a relationship between ends and scarce means which have alternative uses." From this definition, one can build up the following propositions :

- Human wants are unlimited; wants multiply—luxuries become necessities. There is no end of wants. If food were plentiful, if there were enough capital in business, if there were abundant money and time—there would not have been any scope for studying economics. Had there been no wants there would not have been any human activity. Prehistoric people had wants. Modern people also have wants. Only wants change—and they are limitless.
- The means or the resources to satisfy wants are scarce in relation to their demands. Had resources been plentiful, there would not have been any economic problems. Thus, scarcity of resources is the fundamental economic problem to any society. Even an affluent society experiences resource scarcity. Scarcity of resources gives rise to many 'choice' problems.
- Since the prehistoric days one notices constant effort of satisfying human wants through the scarcest resources which have alternative uses. Land is scarce in relation to demand. However, this land may be put to different alternative uses. A particular plot of land can be either used for jute cultivation or steel production. If it is used for steel production, the country will have to sacrifice the production of jute. So, resources are to be allocated in such a manner that the immediate wants are fulfilled. Thus, the problem of scarcity of resources gives rise to the problem of choice. Society will have to decide which wants are to be satisfied immediately and which wants are to be postponed for the time being. This is the choice problem of an economy. Scarcity and choice go hand in hand in each and every economy : "It exists in one-man community of Robinson Crusoe, in the patriarchal tribe of Central Africa, in medieval and feudalist Europe, in modern capitalist America and in Communist Russia."

In view of this, it is said that economics is fundamentally a study of scarcity and of the problems to which scarcity gives rise. Thus, the central focus of economics is on opportunity cost and optimisation.

This scarcity definition of economics has widened the scope of the subject. Putting aside the question of value judgement, Robbins made economics a positive science. By locating the basic problems of economics — the problems of scarcity and choice — Robbins brought economics nearer to science. No wonder, this definition has attracted a large number of people into Robbins' camp. The American Nobel Prize winner in Economics in 1970, Paul Samuelson, observes : "Economics is the study of how men and society choose, with or without the use of money, to employ scarce productive resources which could have alternative uses, to produce various commodities over time, and distribute them for consumption, now and in the near future, among various people and groups in society."

Criticisms : This does not mean that Robbins' scarcity definition is faultfree. His definition may be criticised on the following grounds :

- In his bid to raise economics to the status of a positive science, Robbins deliberately downplayed the importance of economics as a social science. Being a social science, economics must study social relations. His definition places too much emphasis on 'individual' choice. Scarcity problem, in the ultimate analysis, is the social problem—rather an individual problem. Social problems give rise to social choice. Robbins could not explain social problems as well as social choice.
- According to Robbins, the root of all economic problems is the scarcity of resources, without having any human touch. Setting aside the question of human welfare, Robbins committed a grave error.
- Robbins made economics neutral between ends. But economists cannot remain neutral between ends. They must prescribe policies and make value judgments as to what is good for the society and what is bad. So, economics should pronounce both positive and normative statements.
- Economics, at the hands of Robbins, turned to be a mere price theory or microeconomic theory. But other important aspects of economics like national income and employment, banking system, taxation system, etc., had been ignored by Robbins.

Conclusion : The science of political economy is growing and its area can never be rigid. In other words, the definition must not be inflexible. Because of modern research, many new areas of economics are being explored. That is why the controversy relating to the definition of economics remains and will remain so in the future. It is very difficult to spell out a logically concise definition. In this connection, Mrs. Barbara Wotton's remarks may be noted : 'Whenever there are six economists, there are seven opinions !'

Despite these, Cairncross' definition of economics may serve our purpose : "Economics is a social science studying how people attempt to accommodate scarcity to their wants and how these attempts interact through exchange." By linking 'exchange' with 'scarcity', Prof. A. C. Cairncross has added another cap to economics. However, this definition does not claim any originality since scarcity—the root of all economic problems—had been dealt with elegantly by Robbins. That is why, Robbinsian definition is more popular : Economics is the science of making choices. Modern economics is a science of rational choice or decision-making under conditions of scarcity.

1.3. DEFINITION OF BUSINESS ECONOMICS OR MANAGERIAL ECONOMICS

The teaching of economics is, thus, an abstract theorisation with little connection to business But theoretical models of economics are to be applied in business areas. Once theoretical models of economics are applied in business, the gap between economics and business gets minimised. The branch of managerial economics or business economics has established links between business and economics. Business economics is, thus, an applied economics. Economics is the study of human beings (e.g., consumers, firms) in producing and consuming goods and services in the midst of scarcity of resources. Managerial or business economics is an applied branch of organising and allocating a firm's scarce resources to achieve its desired goals.

Managerial economics or business economics is economics applied in decision-making. Business economics, thus, interweaves economic principles and business. Business managers apply economic laws and principles while presenting business problems and their ways of solutions. Thus, business economics can be defined as the application of economic analysis to business problems faced by an enterprise. It provides a link between economic theory and the decision sciences in the analysis of managerial decision-making. It relies heavily on traditional economics and decision sciences.

Identification of the problems and the solving of the problems are the two crucial elements of decision-making of a business firm. Business economists help business managers in making sound business decisions. Business success, in fact, greatly depends on appropriate business decisions. However, appropriate decision-making is not an easy job in this changing world. On the basis of past knowledge and experience, business managers take business decisions and make future plans. But decision-makers are constrained by the 'uncertainty' of the real world where changes occur either in a hidden way or in an open way. In this changing but uncertain world, an accurate decision-making is impossible even if talents of top quality business economists are employed. It is due to this uncertainty, prediction or estimation relating to the volume of sales of a product, cost of production, profit, etc., is more likely to be imperfect. In other words, against the backdrop of uncertainty and a changing world, business managers will have to anticipate changes so that the impact of unfavourable situations becomes insignificant. Thus, business decision-making is an art. Cultivation of this art is made through economic principles. In this sense, managerial economics is an applied economics. It is concerned with the application of economic concepts and analytical tools to the process of decision-making of a business enterprise.

Thus, managerial economics or business economics is a special branch of economics that bridges the gap between abstract economic theory and managerial practice. Through a process of application of the principles, concepts and tools of economics to solve the managerial problems of a business enterprise business economists have greatly minimised the problem of uncertainty arising in business.

[An Illustration of the Relationship Between Economic Theory and Business—Machlup's Overtaking Analogy]

The application field of economic theory is popularly known as business economics or managerial economics. Can economic theory be applied in business practice efficiently? Fritz Machlup, in answering this question, gave an analogy between the behaviour of a motorist deciding whether or not to overtake on a two-lane highway and the behaviour of a profit-maximising firm. Overtaking decision of the motorist involves construction of a very complex set of equations. While overtaking, the motorist must have a knowledge about the weight, power, speed of the vehicle being driven, the condition of the road, weather, information about the number of vehicles plying on the highway, and a set of assumptions about the behaviour and objectives of other drivers. Unfortunately, even the most expert and cautious drivers do not have all these information. But the model-builder makes such unrealistic assumptions. Under the circumstance, the decision of overtaking in a two-lane highway seems to be next to impossible. In reality, all the drivers overtake dozens of times every day. Such overtaking decisions are deemed to be 'correct' only if accidents are not met with.

If we compare this behavioural overtaking decision of a motorist with that of the behaviour of a profit-maximising firm, we will reach the same conclusion. A profit-maximising firm assumes that it has perfect information about costs and revenue conditions. But that too is an unrealistic assumption. Still they assume such and are always guided by profit-maximising motive. "Like the driver taking the decision to overtake, managers 'behave' as if they had the relevant information, in which case they will behave like the profit-maximising model and that model will be a good predictor of their behaviour."[1]

1. Howard Davies—*Managerial Economics for Business, Management and Accounting*; ELBS (1991)

1.4. CHARACTERISTICS OF BUSINESS ECONOMICS

Business economics is essentially concerned with the various decisions of a business enterprise. The unit of study of business economics is the firm. Thus, managerial economics studies decision-making behaviour of a firm or an industry. Microeconomics takes into account the behaviour of smaller economic agents, such as a firm or a consumer or an input owner. It deals with the operation of a consumer, a firm involving the determination of price of a commodity, revenue, costs and, hence, profit levels, etc. Managerial economics is, thus, essentially microeconomic in character as it has its origin in theoretical microeconomics. Profs. H. C. Petersen and W. C. Lewis suggest that managerial economics should be thought of as applied microeconomics. It is an application of that part of microeconomics focusing on those topics which are of great interest and importance to business managers. These topics include theories of demand, production and cost, profit-maximising model of the firm, optimal prices and advertising expenditures, government regulation, etc. Managerial economics is concerned with finding optimal solutions to business decision problems.

Secondly, economic concepts and principles of the 'theory of firm' are employed in business economics. Thus, in business economics, the main emphasis is given upon the firm, the environment in which the firm finds itself, and the business decision which firms have to take. In this sense, managerial economics is narrower in scope than pure economic theory.

Thirdly, broadly there are two main branches of economics—'positive' economics and 'normative' economics. Positive economics deals with 'description' while normative economics deals with 'prescription'. By building up propositions on the basis of a set of assumptions, positive economics tries to explain economic phenomenon. Normative economics comments on the desirability of that phenomenon and suggests policy measures. Value judgments are, thus, pronounced in normative economics. In the words of Profs. Mote, Paul and Gupta : "Managerial economics is a part of normative economics as its focus is more on prescribing choice and action and less on explaining what has happened. Managerial economics draws on positive economics by utilising the relevant theories as a basis for prescribing choices."

Fourthly, business economics not only seeks to investigate and analyse how and why businesses behave as they do but also the implictions of their actions and policies for the industry in which they operate and, finally, for the economy as a whole. In this business environment, both internal and external factors work. Business economics seeks to analyse various internal and external constraints that businesses experience in their process of growth and survival, draw conclusions as to how and why businesses behave as they do. "Business economics therefore focuses on the issues relevant to a business and its operations, and to the business environment." Thus, business economics is considered as applied economics. It casts away abstract economic theories. Managerial economists look at practical applications of theoretical models.

Finally, business economics is essentially microeconomic in character. In other words, macroeconomic theory has less relevance for managerial economics. Truly speaking, business economics should also deal with a wider environment—the macroeconomy. Macroeconomics is concerned with the behaviour of the economic system in totality. It studies the determination of aggregate national income, level of employment, general price level, the international balance of payments, etc. It is true that aggregating economic trends or external economic factors do not directly affect business decisions of a firm. But what is true is that changing macroeconomy not only influences aggregate or national income but also the demand for the product of a business firm. Efficient business managers must have awareness as well as keenness of studying and explaining macroeconomic environment. In this sense, business economics cannot be devoid of macroeconomics.

1.5. SUBJECT-MATTER AND SCOPE OF BUSINESS ECONOMICS

We have already said that managerial economics or business economics is applied microeconomics employed for the purpose of facilitating decision-making and forward planning. As far as decision-making and forward planning are concerned, one has to face the following problems:

Problem of resource allocation seems to be a pressing problem for any organisation. Resources are not plentiful. A firm has to organise scarce resources efficiently so that optimal outcomes are obtained. Such resource allocation problem includes production programming, transportation problem, etc. Non-optimal organisation of resources may spell disaster to any organisation.

Inventory and queuing are important problems to any firm. A firm has to hold an optimal level of stocks of raw materials and finished product so that business uncertainties can be minimised. Business managers must decide an optimal level of inventories. Such decisions are taken by firms after considering demand and supply conditions. Since forward planning by management is essential, a firm must make decisions—whether new machines are to be installed or more professionals are to be employed. As most of the decisions cannot be implemented simultaneously, the firm manager must make a trade-off between decisions. Taking a particular decision out of a variety of decisions is known as queuing problem. A manager places or queues alternative decisions and picks up a right one.

Price fixation is another interrelated problem connected with decision-making. A firm has to take up a right pricing decision.

Finally, the decision-maker faces investment problems for a variety of reasons. Truly speaking, any forward planning by management involves investment problems which are by nature knotty. Investment problems boil down to the problems of allocating resources over time. A firm has to make decision about the volume of investment. It must decide where to invest, when to invest. It must know the sources of funds, etc.

Anyway, business economics is concerned with decision-making and forward planning.

The scope of business economics (both micro and macro variety) is a wider one since it "uses the logic of Economics, Mathematics and Statistics to provide effective ways of thinking about business decision problems." In view of this saying of Prof. D. C. Hague, we can argue that there are links between managerial economics and management science. In fact, the boundaries between the two subjects are not clear-cut but overlapping.

Managerial economics is largely an applied branch of microeconomics. Its macroeconomic content is not to be belittled. It uses the methods and techniques of microeconomics mostly in the field of management. As Haynes and William Warren state: "The relation of managerial economics to economic theory (of either the micro or macro variety) is much like that of engineering to physics, or of medicine to biology or bacteriology. It is the relation of an applied field to the more fundamental but more abstract basic discipline from which it borrows concepts and analytical tools." It is to be pointed out here that measurement without theory may lead to false precision and diagnosis while theory without measurement can hardly be operationally useful.

Now we are in a position to explain the scope of business economics. By scope of (business) economics we mean the field of the subject, the boundaries that delimit and delineate the topics to be addressed. Determination of the scope of the subject includes: (i) definition of the subject, (ii) subject matter of business economics, (iii) is business economics a positive or a normative science?

In this section of discussion, we are interested in knowing the field or area of the subject. Since business economics is thought of as applied microeconomics, the scope of business economics includes :

- analysis, estimation and forecasting of consumer demand for a product;
- analysis of cost and output;
- determination of price of a commodity, work policy and business strategies of a business enterprise;
- long-run planning decisions of a firm that studies capital budgeting and capital management.

Managerial economics now includes 'operations research'—a mathematical technique to solve business problems.

Fig. 1.1 Economics, Business Management and Business Economics

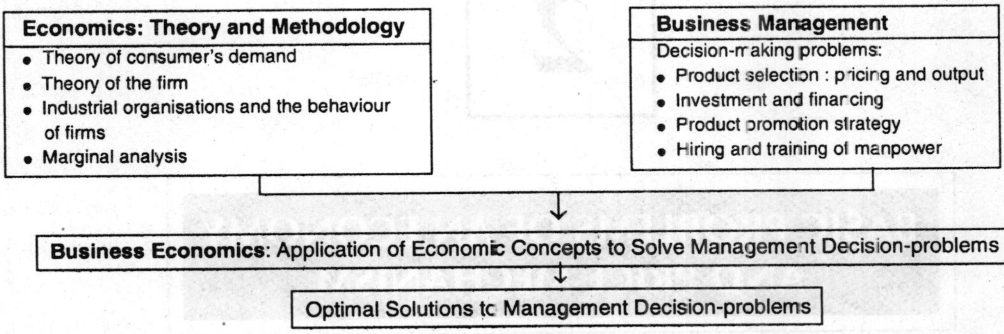

Finally, we must say that there is a great deal of linkages between managerial economics and other disciplines and fields of study. It uses the logic of economics, mathematics and statistics. Managerial economics is related to management science or the decision sciences. Management science is concerned with techniques for improvement of decision-making. Business economics is related to accounting. Accounting is essentially concerned with recording and analysing the financial activities of a business firm. To quote Prof. D. C. Hague: "The main task of management accounting is now seen as being to provide the sort of data which managers need if they are to apply the idea of managerial economics to solve business problems correctly; accounting data are also to be provided in a form so as to fit easily into the concepts and analysis of managerial economics." In view of the relationship between managerial economics and other disciplines, it may be called an art, and not a science. Though an art, decision-making in this uncertain world has become more perfect. Better choices, better prediction, etc., are likely to emerge because of the interaction among basic disciplines.

Thus, it is clear from the above discussion that managerial or business economics helps managers of firms, administrators of non-profit and profit-making hospitals, schools, colleges and universities to recognise how economic forces affect organisations. It applies economic theory and methods to business and administrative decision-making in both profit and non-profit sector. Business economics links economic concepts with quantitative methods to develop tools for managerial decision-making. Business economics, thus, intends to bridge the gap that exists between economics and business management theory. This process is illustrated in Fig. 1.1.

Thus, business economics is closely linked with many disciplines (such as marketing, finance, management accounting, management science etc. in a business curriculum)

QUESTIONS (WITH ANSWER-HINTS)

Long Questions (16 marks)

1. Briefly explain the popular definitions of economics.
   Ans. 1.2.-1.2.3.
2. What is business economics? What are its essential characteristics?
   Ans. 1.3 and 1.4.
3. Give a brief account of the subject-matter and scope of business economics.
   Ans. 1.5.

Medium-sized Questions (8 marks)

1. Give an idea about Lionel Robbins' definition of economics.
   Ans. 1.2.3.
2. Mention major characteristics of business economics.
   Ans. 1.4.
3. Discuss the subject-matter of business economics.
   Ans. 1.5.

2

BASIC PROBLEMS OF AN ECONOMY AND PRICE MECHANISM

2.1. FUNDAMENTAL ECONOMIC PROBLEMS ARISING OUT OF SCARCITY

Economics is a social science that tries to explain the economic basis of human societies. The basis or the central focus of every human society is scarcity and choice. In truth, scarcity is the fundamental economic problem faced by all individuals and societies since there is no affluence, no abundance, no plenty. Here we want to identify the nature of economic problems of any society.

No economy is free from fundamental economic problems. Even the richest nation of the world experiences alternating crises. Why? The answer is scarcity. Scarcity must not be confused with poverty. It is faced by all—both rich and poor. "Scarcity is a fact of life just as is gravity. And just as physicists did not invent gravity, economists did not invent scarcity." If everyone had enough money to purchase anything in the world, or if every business had all the resources in sufficient quantities so that all goods are available in right quantity or if every society moves on a higher growth path as it advances, then there would have been no need to study economics and, hence, there would have been no economic problems. Unfortunately, such a utopian state did never exist; nor does it exist in the present. In future too, no such happy state will ever emerge.

An author remarked : "It exists in one-man community of Robinson Crusoe, in the patriarchal tribe of Central Africa in medieval and feudal Europe, in modern capitalist America and in Communist Russia."

This is because of the fact that resources to satisfy growing needs of people are limited in nature. Human wants are virtually limitless. As time progresses or as society advances, wants change. Luxuries become necessities. This means that the wants of people don't cease only its character undergoes a change. Wants range from personal affairs to matters of worldwide urgency. Once the bare necessities are fulfilled, an individual may demand such goods that provide comfort to him. In fact, there is no limit to the wants of an individual or of a society.

But the means of fulfilling the variety of societal wants are limited, so that the goods and services themselves are scarce. In other words, resources are scarce in relation to wants of all consumers, firms and govermental bodies. Scarcity does not refer to non-availability of resources in the physical sense. Here scarcity means availability in amounts less than sufficient to satisfy all wants or desires. Had resources been plentiful there would not have been any economic problems. Unfortunately, resources are scarce since the dawn of recorded history. It is a central problem of today's world and it will continue to be so in future. Anyway, what is important in the economic life of any society is the interaction between scarce resources and the unlimited wants.

Since resources are limited in quantity, choices have to be made. Scarcity and choice go hand in hand, choosing is necessary against the backdrop of limited resources. In the absence of scarcity, the study of economics would be entirely useless. Economics is the study of making choices as resources are limited in quantity—when such resources are used to produce one good, they cannot be used to produce another good. Hence the choice. A society has to allocate its scarce resources among the competing and unlimited wants. In the process of allocation of resources, an economy has to make a large number of choices. There are at least five fundamental categories of choice that a society addresses.

2.1.1. Five Categories of Choice

In a world of scarce resources, it is impossible to ignore making choices. That is to say, scarcity demands choices of many types. There are five questions or five main categories of choice that summarise fundamental economic problems:

- What goods and services are to be produced and in what quantities? This is called the 'allocation problem'.
- How are these goods and services to be produced? This is called the 'production problem'.
- For whom are these goods and services to be produced? This is called the 'distribution problem'.

In short, these problems are called the **'WHAT', 'HOW' and 'FOR WHOM'.**

These three problems can be presented in the form of a table.

Table 2: 1 Three Basic Economic Problems (Questions)

From the standpoint of a country as a whole	From the standpoint of a firm/industry
WHAT goods and services are to be produced? (Allocation problem)	The product decision
HOW these goods and services are to be produced? (Production problem)	The hiring and firing of workers, purchase of required inputs, capital budgeting decision, etc.
FOR WHOM these goods are to be produced? (Distribution problem)	The market segmentation decision i.e. assigning of marketing fields where products would be sold.

In addition to these trio, we have two other problems that require to be addressed here :

- Are the country's scarce resources being fully utilised or are some of them remaining idle? This is the problem of 'resource utilisation'.
- Is the productive capacity of an economy growing or remaining static over time? This is the problem of 'economic growth'.

The first three questions are studied under the heading microeconomics while the last two fall under macroeconomics.

The first question is concerned with the allocation of scarce resources among alternative uses. Given the problem of scarcity, a society has to decide first what type of goods and services should be produced. Such decisions must be based on the needs of the society. Not all goods and services are demanded by the people. Goods and services that are of pressing needs are to be produced immediately. There are some goods whose demand can be postponed for a temporary period. Further, given the problem of scarcity, not all the goods and services can be produced in right quantities that a society demands. Hence, the economy must set the target of production in accordance with the needs of the society. Anyway, this decision is connected with the allocation of scarce resources among the competing human wants. For example, if a society decides to produce more nuclear bombs, given the problem of scarcity, it must give up the production of another commodity, say, wheat. Thus, a "*trade-off*"—a phrase commonly used by economists—is involved.

It may not be irrelvant to point out here that this allocation problem or the decision of 'what to produce' is examined in 'microeconomics'.

The second question relates to the technique of production. There are a variety of methods to produce goods and services. Usually, there are two techniques of production to produce a commodity in certain amount : they are labour-intensive technique and capital-intensive technique. Normally, production of simple, unsophisticated consumer goods requires labour-intensive technique of production, while production of iron and steel demands capital-intensive method of production. But, strict adherence to these rules is neither possible nor desirable. Therefore, the choice of a right technique of production is crucial since output has to be maximised or cost of production has to be minimised. It is suggested that a country must choose that technique of production that can produce goods and services in the least possible cost manner.

The third problem is connected with the problem of distribution of goods and services among the various members of the society. Given the resource constraint, an economy cannot produce enough goods for all the members of a society. Thus, distribution is of great importance. The economy must specify the mechanism by which goods and services already produced is distributed. Clearly, the distribution of the given output is settled by the purchasing power of the demanders. People with high income have the largest purchasing power. Thus, we are interested in determining the incomes or prices of different input services.

The fourth problem is connected with the utilisation of resources. We know that a society does not have adequate resources to produce every kind of goods that people want, even if these resources are efficiently utilised. But a free enterprise capitalistic economy may exhibit unemployment or underemployment of resources, men and machines may remain idle. This means wastage of resources. A capitalist economy can never utilise its resources fully. Resources remain involuntarily unemployed there. This causes national output to decline. In other words, actual production falls short of the target or anticipated output. This is really a problem of macroeconomics. (Lord) John Maynard Keynes

(1883-1946) in the 1930s searched the causes for unemployment of resources and made suggestions, in his magnum opus *'The General Theory of Employment, Interest and Money' (1936)*, to control unemployment, depression mainly through government action.

The fifth problem is associated with the problem of economic growth. An economy must grow over time. It remains static if national income, investment, employment, price level, etc. grow at the same rate year after year. No economy is static. Every economy tries to achieve a higher growth rate—hitherto not attained—through technological improvement and other means.

Every economy, irrespective of its nature, must face these problems. There is no escape route to avoid all these problems since scarcity and choice are at the heart of any economic activity. All the economies—primitive economy, feudal economy, customary economy, capitalist economy, socialist economy or mixed economy—address these problems.

It may be added here that the first three questions are concerned with the allocation of scarce resources, production and distribution of goods and services or income among the members of the society. Since we are basically concerned with the market economy, these basic questions are solved by price mechanism. These questions are handled under the heading "Microeonomics" or "Price Theory". The last two questions are addressed in "Macroeconomics."

2.1.2. Illustrating Economic Problems : The Production Possibility Curve

Now we will illustrate these central economic problems in terms of a diagram. A curve—called the production possibility frontier (PPF)—will be used here to show how choice is made among scarce economic alternatives.

Every society has to decide what goods and services to produce, how to produce, and for whom to produce — given the stock of resources. Let us consider a hypothetical economy where all resources — land, labour, capital and organisation —are used to produce two goods, food and clothing. Various possible combinations of output of these two goods can be represented by the production possibility curve (PPC). A PPC (or a PPF) shows all the possible combinations of two goods which a country can produce if available resources are fully and efficiently employed. This is illustrated in Fig. 2.1.

The production of food is measured on the vertical axis and the production of cloth is measured on the horizontal axis. OA amount of food can be produced with all its resources fully employed, if no cloth is produced. On the other hand, if the country decides to produce cloth only using all available resources fully, it can produce maximum OB amount of cloth; no food will be produced. But with the existing stock of resources and the level of technology, a country produces combinations of both the goods. If all the different output combinations of the two goods— food and cloth —are joined together, we get the curve AB. AB is the PPC or PPF.

The PPC or PPF itself describes the production or the supply side of the economy. All points on the PPC represent combinations of food and cloth that a country can produce, given the full employment of the country's resources and technology. If a country should decide to raise cloth output (from OC_1 to OC_2) then the curve AB shows that this can be achieved only by reducing food output (from OF_1 to OF_2). The reduced output of food is the opportunity cost of

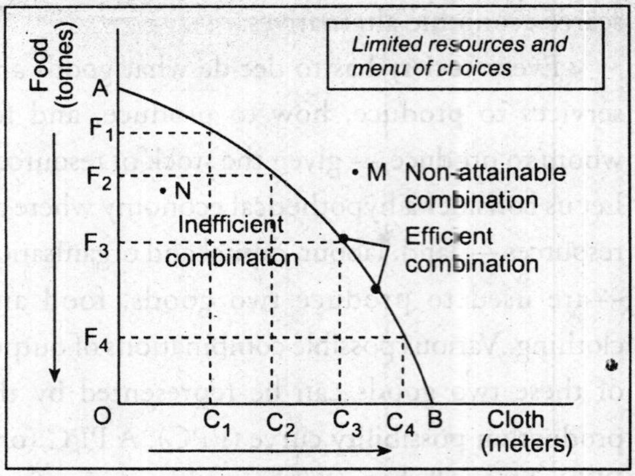

Fig. 2.1 : Production Possibility Frontier

producing more cloth output. The quantity of food that is sacrificed is called the opportunity cost of producing more cloth. The PPC, thus, shows that each increase in the output of one good involves a sacrifice or decrease in the production of another good.

As scarcity always involves choices, economists say that 'there cannot be free lunch'. One may indeed get 'lunch' without paying any price! Your office, after remarkable performance may provide today's 'lunch' to all the staff. Even then, there is a 'cost' to someone—ultimately to the society in which we live. An economy unarguably faces resource scarcity that can be used for producing other commodities. In other words, in making the 'lunch' available, either we sacrifice production of food for more cloth output or we sacrifice cloth output for production of additional unit of food output. This sacrifice is called 'opportunity cost' by economists. To get more of one commodity, we need to sacrifice the opportunity of getting another commodity.

Now, we can say that the PPC illustrates scarcity and choice. It can explain the **What, How** and **For Whom** problems that an economy faces.

PPC shows the maximum production of two goods with given resources. If the society decides to have more cloth output, it will lie closer to point B. If the society plans to produce more foodgrains, it will be nearer to point A. How much food and cloth output will be produced using the available resources greatly depends on the demand for these two items. Production will be made in accordance with the demands for the products. Any production combination below or inside the curve AB is attainable, but it represents an inefficient use of resources. Point N suggests that, as the resources are not fully and efficiently utilised, the society enjoys fewer outputs. Consider point M that lies outside the PPC. This is an impossible combination as the nation does not have enough resources to produce those quantities of food and cloth. Thus, the PPC describes what goods and services are to be produced, and in what quantities. All points on the PPC describe that society's resources are optimally utilised. As these points on the curve represent maximum amount that can be produced with full employment of resources, these points describe efficient combinations.

The PPC highlights the second problem—the problem of choosing appropriate technique of production. All kinds of technique do not produce the same level of output. Some techniques are more efficient than others in the sense that the former produces large quantities at lower costs. If a technique of production is deemed to be inefficient, resources will not be fully or optimally utilised. Inefficient techniques result in lower output. Point N on the PPC describes inefficient outcomes—given the resources available in the economy. If a technique of production is an efficient one, the society will then stay on the curve AB. However, the choice of a certain technique of production crucially depends on the availability of resources. In a labour-abundant country, a labour-intensive technology may be chosen while, in a capital-rich country, a capital-intensive technology may be recommended. However, such clear-cut decision may not be advisable at face value. Other relevant factors must be taken into account while selecting a right technique of production.

However, the PPC cannot describe the 'for whom to produce' problem directly.

Let us talk about the fourth problem. Whether an economy's resources are fully utilised or not can be read from the PPF. Any point inside the AB curve indicates lower volume of outputs of both food and cloth compared to points on the curve AB. Point N indicates inefficient use of resources or a failure to use all the resources that are available. In other words, lesser outputs are available inside the PP curve because of under-utilisation of resources.

The fifth problem can also be explained in terms of PPF. If a country stays on the curve AB drawn in Fig. 2.1 then the productive capacity of the society becomes static. As a result, the problem of scarcity gets magnified more and more as time progresses. Thus, it cannot move to point M of Fig. 2.1. What is required is the increase in production and productivity so that the scarcity

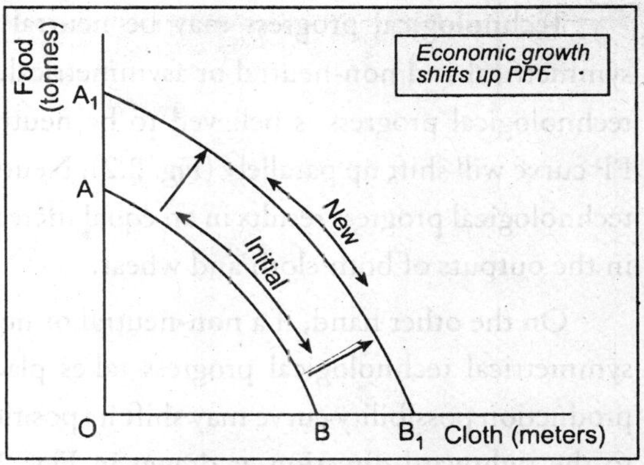

Fig. 2.2 : Shifting of the PPF

problem can be lessened. This means the shifting of the PPC outwards. There are three main ways through which an economy's capacity to produce can be raised. These are : (i) growth of capital stock, (ii) improvement in technology, and (iii) population.

With given stock of resources, an economy has the production potential represented by the curve AB in Fig 2.2. Suppose, capital accumulation takes place. As a result, the AB curve will shift out to A_1B_1 indicating larger output of food and cloth. Similarly, improvement in technology as well as a rise in labour force consequent upon the population growth will shift the entire curve to the rightward direction. However, there is no reason to believe that the PPC will shift parallely in the upward direction.

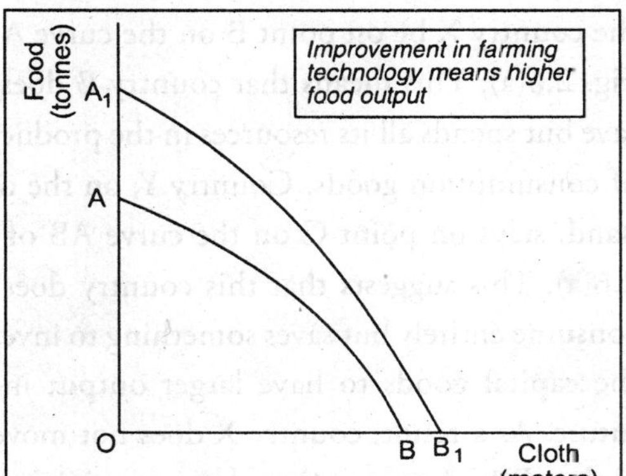

Fig. 2.3 : Shifts of PPC

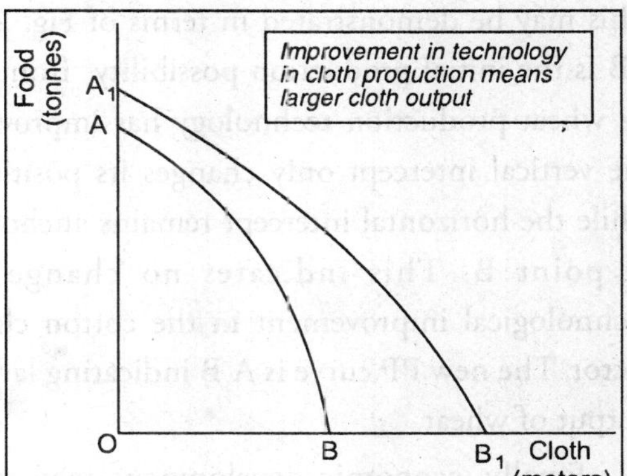

Fig. 2.4 : Shifts of PPC

Technological progress may be neutral or symmetrical and non-neutral or asymmetrical. If technological progress is believed to be neutral, PP curve will shift up parallely (Fig. 2.2). Neutral technological progress results in an equal increase in the outputs of both cloth and wheat.

On the other hand, if a non-neutral or non-symmetrical technological progress takes place, production possibility curve may shift its position to the rightward direction as drawn in Figs 2.3 and 2.4. An improvement in farming technology shifts PP curve from AB to A_1B_1 more along the food axis (Fig. 2.3). Since technological improvement does not take place in cloth production, B_1 lies rather close to point B. Fig. 2.4 demonstrates that technological improvement has taken place in cloth production. AB has shifted to A_1B_1 indicating greater availability of cloth output.

It may happen that technological progress may take place only in the production of wheat, rather than cloth. Because of the introduction of HYV seeds in wheat production, Indian agriculture witnessed some sort of revolution, called green revolution or, more specifically wheat revolution, in the early 1970s. As a result, wheat output increased substantially during this time. This may be demonstrated in terms of Fig. 2.5. AB is the initial production possibility frontier. As wheat production technology has improved, the vertical intercept only changes its position, while the horizontal intercept remains anchored at point B. This indicates no change in technological improvement in the cotton cloth sector. The new PP curve is A_1B indicating larger output of wheat.

Finally, economic development may take place due to increase in the output of capital goods.

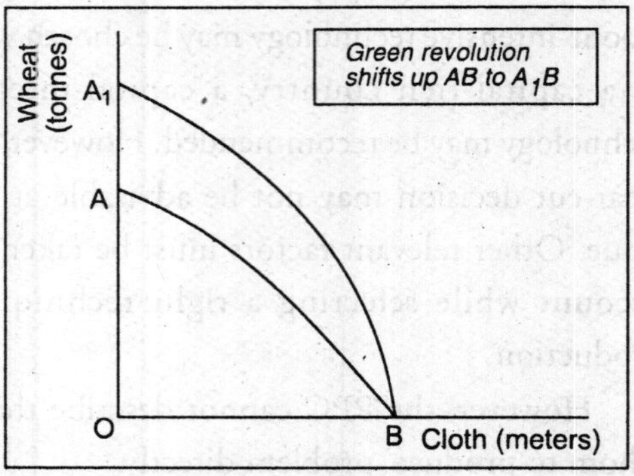

Fig. 2.5 : Non-symmetrical Technical Change and Shifts of PPC

This means that a country has to make a choice between consumer goods and capital goods. How quicker the economic development will be depends on how much investible resources are utilised for the production of capital goods (that helps in raising future consumption) and for the production of consumption goods (that maximises present consumption). If a country attaches more importance to the production of consumption goods, its economic development will be slower. If greater importance is given to future consumption, i.e., production of capital goods, a country will experience a higher growth rate. Thus, capital formation is an important source of economic growth. This is shown in Fig. 2.6.

Let us assume that there are two countries, X and Y whose initial PP curves are identical. Let the country X be on point B on the curve AB of Fig. 2.6(a). This means that country B does not save but spends all its resources in the production of consumption goods. Country Y, on the other hand, stays on point C on the curve AB of Fig. 2.6(a). This suggests that this country does not consume entirely but saves something to invest in the capital goods to have larger output in the future. As a result, country X does not move on higher PPC but stays on the same AB in Fig. 2.6(b). Since country Y sacrificies a part of its

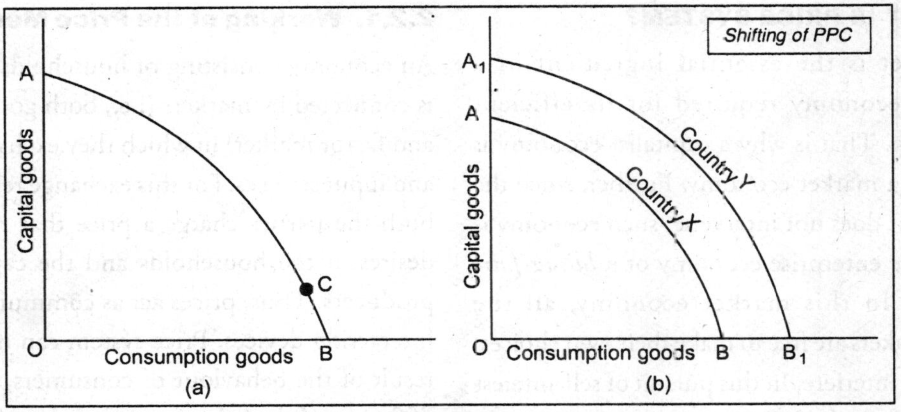

Fig. 2.6 : Capital Formation and PPC

present consumption, its PP curve takes an outward move and shifts to A_1B_1. The new A_1B_1 curve reflects that country Y produces more of both consumption and capital goods in future. Thriftiness has caused PP to shift upward. This indicates economic growth.

2.1.3. Shape of the PPC

The production possibility frontier is a bowed out curve or concave from above. This shape is due to the operation of the law of diminishing returns or the law of increasing opportunity cost, that is the sacrifice of a next-best alternative. A small increase in food output indicates a reduction in the output of cloth. The fall in food output is the opportunity cost of a larger cloth output. However, a society's food output increases because the inputs required for cloth production are transferred to food production. Now, more and more employment of resources in food output will result in a decline in its marginal productivity. This means an increase in cost. Hence another name of the law of diminishing returns is the law of increasing opportunity cost.

Consider point A on the curve AB of Fig. 2.1. If the nation decides to produce OC_1 amount of cloth, it should sacrifice AF_1 amount of food output. Production of more cloth demands an additional F_1F_2 amount of food output to be sacrificed, and so on. As the society decides to produce more cloth, it will have to sacrifice food output. It is clear from the figure that gradually marginal product of input needed for food production declines. This indicates $F_3F_4 > F_2F_3 > F_1F_2$. In other words, the rate of substitution between food and cloth is diminishing and, hence PP curve is concave to the origin.

If PP curve becomes a straight line, it will reflect a fixed rate of substitution between food and cloth. In other words, for a straight line PP curve, the opportunity cost remains unchanged. This is the case of constant opportunity cost.

The slope of the PP curve drawn in Fig. 2.1 is $\frac{OA}{OB}$. It measures the opportunity cost in terms of food of producing 1 extra metre of cloth. The slope of the PP curve is often called marginal rate of transformation (MRT) of food into cloth or of cloth into food. For a straight line PP curve, MRT is unchanged and, for a convex PP curve, the slope i.e., MRT increases and, hence, the opportunity cost increases.

2.2 WHAT IS PRICE SYSTEM?

Market is the essential ingredient of a capitalist economy required for its efficient functioning. That is why a capitalist economy is also called a market economy. Further, since the government does not intervene, such economy is called a free enterprise economy or a *laissez-faire* economy. In this market economy, all the decisions-takers are free to make their own choices; no one will interfere. In this pursuit of self-interest and general good of all, every economic agent or unit (i.e., households and firms) is guided by a hidden hand or 'invisible hand'. The 'invisible hand' mechanism, as designated by Adam Smith, operates due to the free play of competition.

The price system is one in which all economic decisions are taken through the medium of prices which are, by nature, self-adjusting and self-correcting—though every decision-taker acts selfishly. As there is no central regulating authority, decisions are taken by invisible hand or price system. Though millions of people (both households and firms) act selfishly, they are led as if by an 'invisible hand' to achieve the best results of the economy. The decisions of what, how and for whom to produce are determined by demand and supply conditions of commodities and input services. Thus, the price mechanism serves as a connecting or communicating mechanism between the two economic agents of a capitalist society: households and firms. Prices that are determined by the interaction of households and firms in goods market and in factors market are called freely (market) determined prices; as governmental control is conspicuously absent in a market economy. Changes in prices are caused by changes in demand and supply conditions.

2.2.1. Working of the Price Mechanism

An economy consisting of households and firms is connected by markets (i.e., both goods market and factor market) in which they exchange goods and input services. For this exchange relationship, both the parties charge a price that reflects the desires of the households and the capacities of producers. Thus, prices act as communicating or interacting devices. Price system can now be the result of the behaviour of consumers, behaviour of firms and the behaviour of markets (i.e., goods market and input market). We know that there are millions of people who make independent decisions relating to consumption and production through the medium of price system. Firms in a market economy operate in product markets to sell their produces and in factor markets to buy or hire input services. "The price system embraces both types of markets and broadly operates so as to ensure that resources are allocated in accordance with consumer demand."

Prices serve messages on demand and production. Suppose, because of flood the state of West Bengal experiences a fall in the output of onion. This will induce people to reduce their consumption of onion since supplies are inadequate. People may be knowing from media that this year fewer quantities of onion would be available in the market. If the information supplied by the media does not reach to all onion buyers of the country, how will they learn it? The answer is the price system. Onion buyers will find a rise in the price of onion in the markets. Thus price, rather than the media, gives effective message to buyers and producers. Buyers are supposed to buy less of it since it is now more scarce. Higher price of onion is an incentive to grow more onions to the farmers in the next year.

A similar question may be raised and answered in the same way. Why do computer specialists earn more than physicists? Why is the rate of interest charged by the village moneylenders higher than the rate of interest charged by the commercial banks? The simple answer to all these questions relating to the factor market is that price is determined by demand and supply forces. A change in price is also caused by changes in demand and or in supply.

Again, price does not only act as a signalling device, but also provides incentives to firm and households to change their production and consumption plans. In this sense, price acts as an incentive provider. If more of a commodity is demanded (may be due to a rise in income of the consumers, or a fall in output due to recession, or flood or drought) relative to its supply, its price will rise. This will cause profits of producers to rise. Profit now acts as an incentive to other firms to join and produce the commodity that gives larger profits. In addition, firms will divert resources from the production of low-priced commodity to the production of high-priced profit-yielding commodity. As now production—and, hence, supply, of the commodity rises, its price falls, profit declines and it will continue until the demand-supply equality is restored. Similar sequence may be obtained if supply falls short of demand for a commodity. In this way, the price system brings together both the goods markets and factor markets. As these markets are interlinked, each propels the other. This working of the price mechanism has been shown in Fig. 2.7.

For the sake of simplicity, we consider here only good 'X' and one input, 'labour'. It can be applied to any number of goods and inputs. Here D_X represents demand for good X, S_X refers to supply of goods X, D_L demand for labour, S_L supply of labour, W wage or price of labour. The above figure shows how the price system results in a reallocation of resources in response to signals given by consumers about their changes in the demand for commodity. This, in turn, affects the prices of inputs in the input markets. Changes in the prices of inputs bring about changes in the prices of product as well as in the demand pattern of consumers through the price system. "In this way the *price system* acts, as it were, like a marvellous computer, registering people's preferences for different goods, transmitting these preferences to firms, moving resources to produce the goods, and deciding who shall obtain the final products." (Jack Harvey : *Modern Economics*).

Fig. 2.7 : Price Mechanism

2.2.2. Conditions Required for Price Mechanism to Play Its Role

Price mechanism provides the link between households and firms or provides the focus for interactions between buyers and sellers. We have seen that prices provide (i) information, and (ii) incentives. However, its efficient functioning is subject to many conditions. In other words, price system can allocate resources in an automatic way if certain conditions are fulfilled:

- **Perfect competition in both product and factor markets:** With perfect competition in product and factor markets, the price system may operate successfully along the lines sketched above. Perfect competition refers to a market situation where there are innumerable number of sellers and buyers and no single buyer or seller can influence the price of the commodity or input services. Every buyer and seller behaves as a price-taker. Thus, in perfect markets, price differences are quickly eliminated and the market participants choose on the basis of price.
- **Perfect knowledge :** Buyers and sellers have perfect knowledge and information upon which decisions are taken by them. This means that both the buyers and the sellers know well in advance the prices being charged in the product market and factor market. Based on this knowledge and information every participant in the markets, i.e., both consumers and firms, make plan accurately. For instance, if some firms in an industry earn excess profit, not only the existing firms but also the would-be producers know what profits are being earned by the existing firms. Just knowing it is not enough. Having gathered this knowledge, the producers can take future plans and programmes.

  Whenever these two conditions—perfect markets and perfect knowledge—are met then a single price for both commodities and resources will prevail in the market.
- **Free entry :** Successful functioning of price mechanism requires that there must be freedom of entry of new firms into the industry. Whenever some firms get abnormal profit, new firms have the full freedom to enter this business. If it is not allowed, the existing firms may influence the price to suit their own requirements. As new firms enter the industry, abnormal profit is eliminated. On the other hand, if the demand for a product declines, some firms might experience loss. Their loss will induce marginal firms to leave the industry. Thus, the freedom of entry and exit allows profit motive to function. It is to be kept in mind that such entry and exit can be effective only if there is perfect knowledge.

Let us put this free entry and exit condition in the following way. In an imperfect market (say, monopoly, monopolistic competition or oligopoly) there are restrictions to enter or leave product markets and the factor markets in response to profit opportunities. Suppose, the market for good X is characterised by monopoly—a market dominated by one seller. A monopolist need not raise output for good X in the midst of a rising demand for it. Rather, he will exploit this situation of excess demand by raising the price of the commodity and will thus enjoy some abnormal profits. No one is allowed to enter this business. The monopolist is not required to demand more factor inputs to meet increased consumer demand. All these suggest that the price system cannot work if there are barriers to entry and exit; there may arise a situation of high prices and excess profit—thereby leading to the exploitation of buyers of a commodity and suppliers of input services.

- **Perfect mobility of inputs :** Inputs must be perfectly mobile and uniformly available to all firms. If there is a change in the demand for a product and if firms decide to meet the consumers' demand, they must transfer input resources from this line of production to another line. If resources are not channellised from the unprofitable lines of production to the profitable ones, it will surely bring losses to the firm. Thus, perfectly free entry and perfect mobility of inputs bring markets into equilibrium so that excess profit and losses get eliminated. Not only should inputs be mobile but they should also be available to all firms so that shortages of input services do not stop production.

Thus, in the absence of individual or government control, price mechanism under perfect competition operates automatically. But we must recognise that this price system is an idealised simplification—similar to the concepts of vacua and frictionless motors in physics.

2.2.3. Price Mechanism and What, How and For Whom

Now, it is time to solve out the fundamental economic problems arising out of the scarcity of resources of an economy. Here the solutions to the basic problems will be presented in terms of a free market economy where the price system seems to be the best guide.

The price system is a system when crucial economic decisions of WHAT, HOW and for WHOM to produce are not consciously taken by individual consumers and firms but through the medium of prices.

The decision of 'What to produce' is determined by preferences of the consumers. Information about consumers' tastes and preferences is signalled to the producers. The price of a commodity provides such information displayed by money 'votes'. This means that consumers cast their 'votes' for commodities by spending their money. Commodities having greater preference must have higher prices. If consumers prefer to purchase more synthetic cloth instead of cotton cloth, the price of the former will rise. Retail cloth merchants will now place more 'orders' of synthetic cloth to the wholesalers who will ultimately put their 'orders' on the cloth manufacturers. This sequence of events propelled by price rise of synthetic cloth will provide a signal to the producers that it is profitable for them to produce more synthetic cloth. Consequently, producers will shift their resources from cotton cloth production to synthetic cloth production and will demand more resources required for the synthetic cloth production. Price of input resources will rise because of increase in demand for it among producers or, to encourage the suppliers of input services, firms will pay higher prices for inputs so that consumers' demand can be met. Thus, prices act as signal from the consumers to the input suppliers that more synthetic cloth need to be produced. If firms do not respond to consumers' preferences they will have to suffer losses. Remember that prices are

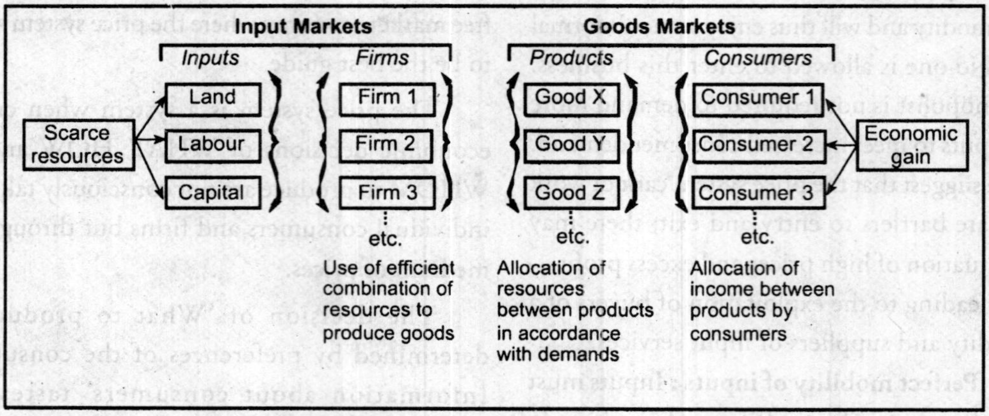

Fig. 2.8 : Exchange Mechanism in a Market : Demand and Supply

signals that reflects tastes and preferences of the consumer..

The answer to the question 'How goods are produced' depends also on the price system. Producers will select a technique of production that yields minimum cost. Obviously, choice of a technique of production depends on the volume of goods to be produced and on the price of inputs. An efficient technique of production is that in which costs are the lowest: Costs of production are mainly governed by the prices of input resources which are determined by demand and supply conditions. A shortage of an input causes its price to rise. As capital is scarce its price is high and as labour is abundant its price is low. Thus, producers have an incentive to use low-priced input services. Or firms have the tendency to use more labour and less capital. A different combination of labour-capital will now emerge. It is, thus, the demand for and supply of input resources which determine their prices and, hence, influence the input combinations. It is the price mechanism that helps society to conserve scarce resources.

The final question 'For whom to produce' also depends on prices (or incomes) which are determined by demand for and supply of factors of production. Greater the income higher is the propensity to consume. We know that households are input owners. Those inputs are supplied to the firms to earn incomes. Obviously, incomes of input owners depend on (i) the volume of ownership of factor services, and (ii) the prices of factors. Assuming the distribution of the ownership of factor services as given, incomes depend on prices of input services which are determined by demand and supply conditions. Since the supply of computer engineers is low compared with their demand, computer engineers earn more incomes than other people. Doctors generally earn more 'prices' or incomes as their supplies are less compared with their demands. On the other hand, an unskilled worker earns lower wages since their supplies are high relative to demand. Factor incomes, in turn, affect consumption demand. People with higher incomes can buy high-priced commodity while people with lower-incomes can afford to buy cheaper varieties of commodities. Thus, factor incomes govern the distribution of commodities among the members of the society.

The interaction between buyers and sellers

in the output market and input market determines basic decisions of **what, how** and **for whom**. The price system embraces both types of market and functions in such a way that resources are allocated in accordance with the demands made by consumers.

Thus, it is clear from the foregoing discussion that the price system is an economic system in which prices play a key role in allocating input resources, outputs, and incomes. It is the price system that guides the economy's decision of **what, how** and **for whom to produce** in the absence of any central authority. The interaction of demand and supply forces determine the market prices of commodities of all kinds and resources.

Fundamental decisions relating to what, how, and for whom are determined in a market economy by the interaction of buyers and sellers in the product market and in the input market. This is shown in Fig. 2.8 where firms act as producing units and operate in the goods market as the sellers of the good and in the input markets as the buyers of resources. Likewise, consumers act as consuming units and operate in the goods market as the buyers of goods; and in the input markets as the sellers of inputs.

Thus, the price mechanism serves as a connecting or communicating mechanism between private consumers and producers. Such price system has been described by Adam Smith as 'the invisible hand' because it coordinates decentralised decision-taking of millions of consumers and producers.

QUESTIONS (WITH ANSWER-HINTS)

Long Questions (16 marks)

1. What are the basic economic problems faced by an economy?

   Ans. 2.1. and 2.1.1.

2. How do you explain fundamental economic problems in terms of the production possibility curve?

   Ans. 2.1.1 and 2.1.2.

3. What is a production possibility curve? Explain its shape. Why and when does it shift outward?

   Ans. 2.1.2 and 2.1.3.

4. What is price mechanism? How does it operate in a free market economy?

   Or

   What is meant by price mechanism? Explain how price mechanism solves the basic problem of a capitalist economy. (C.U. 2008)

   Ans. 2.2 and 2.2.1.

Medium-sized Questions (8 marks)

1. Discuss the resource allocation mechanism of a market system.

   Ans. 2.2.1.

2. What is price mechanism? Point out the conditions required for price mechanism to play its role effectively.

   Ans. 2.2 and 2.2.2.

3. How does price mechanism solve basic economic problems?

   Or

   What are the three roles of price?

   Ans. 2.2 and 2.2.3.

3

THE BASICS OF DEMAND AND SUPPLY

3.1. INTRODUCTION

Every market has a demand side and a supply side. In a market economy, one is often asked how prices are determined. In a market economy, demand and supply determine the price. To be more specific, price of a commodity, say a personal computer, is determined when its demand and supply are equal to each other. By the same way, price of any input is determined by its demand and supply. Thus, for any market (say, a commodity market or an input market) we face three elements — demand element (that describes the behaviour of a consumer), supply element (that describes the behaviour of a firm) and market equilibrium (that describes how consumers and firms interact in the market). In this chapter, we will concentrate on the fundamentals of demand and supply and, finally, elasticities of demand and supply.

3.2. MEANING OF DEMAND

In ordinary language, by demand for private consumption goods we mean desire for goods and services. But, simple desire does not constitute demand in economics. In economics, demand for a commodity must be backed by purchasing power of the consumer. So, by demand we mean 'effective demand'. To fulfil the desire of a commodity, the consumer must have the capacity to buy it as well as the desire to buy it.

In microeconomics, we use the term 'consumers' to refer to those who also buy goods and services for their own consumption. We use the term 'households' to refer to a group of consumers. The 'demand' for a commodity refers to the desired purchase of a commodity by a consumer or a group of consumers, i.e., the quantity of a good that consumers want to buy per period (say an hour, or a day, or a week, or a month, or even a year).This kind of demand may be called 'direct demand' as distinct from 'derived demand'. Note that input demand is called derived demand. This has been disussed in Chapter 10.

3.2.1. Law of Demand

Demand for a commodity always depends on the price of that commodity. Demand has no meaning unless it is related to time. Thus, demand for anything at a given price is the amount of it which will be bought per unit of time at that price.

The law of demand establishes the functional relationship between the price of a commodity and the quantity demanded for it. Other things remaining the same, i.e., *ceteris paribus*, (such as, constancy in money income of the consumer, tastes and preferences of the consumer, price of related goods, etc.), a consumer will demand more of a commodity if its price falls, or vice versa. Thus, the law of demand establishes an inverse relationship between the demand for a commodity and its price. This demand function is usually expressed in terms of the following equation:

$$\overset{\uparrow}{D_X} = f(\underset{\downarrow}{P_X}),\ \textit{ceteris paribus}$$

This function presented in the language of mathematics is a shorthand way of saying that demand for good X is only a function of the price (P) of good X and other price and non-price variables, *ceteris paribus*. As $P_X \downarrow D_X \uparrow$ or as $P_X \uparrow D_X \downarrow$.

Besides own price, demand for a commodity depends on many other factors. Thus, when we examine the relationship between price and the quantity demanded for a commodity we assume that all other determinants of quantity demanded (stated above) remain unchanged. Holding all these constant is known as the *ceteris paribus* assumption, implying that 'other things being equal'. We then vary the price of X and study how it affects the quantity of X demanded. Thereafter, we hold the own price constant and vary other variables one by one (i.e., one at a time). This enables us to understand the importance of each variable on demand. After doing this, we can aggregate the separate influences of two or more variables to find out what would happen if two, three or more variables affecting demand change at a time—as is seen in reality.

3.2.2. Illustrating the Law of Demand

If we hold all other variables that influence demand for a commodity constant, the quantity demanded for a commodity will vary inversely with its price. This relation holds true in case of almost all the commodities that we buy. This is known as the law of demand. This is shown by the arrowheads given in demand equation. This can be read as $P_X \uparrow D_X \downarrow$ or $P_X \downarrow D_X \uparrow$.

Table 3.1 illustrates the law of demand. It shows the relation between price and the quantity demanded of a particular commodity, say, X. Column (i) in Table 3.1 shows the different quantities of X that a hypothetical consumer, say, Mr. A, would be ready to buy at five different prices. This table is known as the demand schedule. The demand schedule for a commodity of an individual is a catalogue of different amounts of the commodity that he or she will buy at different prices. It is a table of prices and the corresponding quantities demanded for a good. It shows, for example, that at a price of Rs. 3.00 per kg, his quantity demanded is 8 kg per week; at a price of Rs. 2.00 his quantity demanded is 12 kg per week and so forth. Each price-quantity combination is indicated by a reference point such as a, b, c, ... etc. This schedule establishes the inverse relationship between price and demand for X.

Table 3.1. : Mr. A's Demand Schedule for good X

Reference Point (in Fig. 3.1)	Price (Rs. per kg) (i)	Quantity Demanded (kg per week) (ii)
a	3.50	6
b	3.00	8
c	2.50	10
d	2.00	12
e	1.50	15

We can easily present the data of Table 3.1 in the form of a graph. This is done in Fig. 3.1, where we measure price on the vertical axis and quantity on the horizontal axis.

Point 'a' shows that when price is Rs. 3.50 the quantity demanded is 6 kgs. Point 'b' shows that when price is Rs. 3.00 the quantity demanded is 8 kgs. Other points represent three other price-

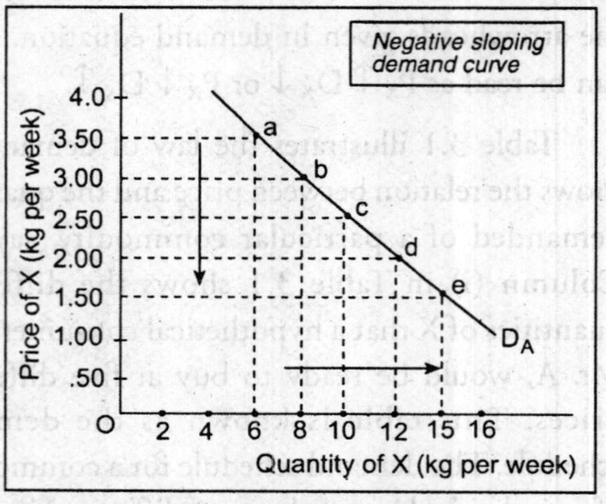

Fig. 3.1: Individual Demand Curve

quantity combinations (originally shown in Table 3.1).

Picturisation of the demand schedule gives us a demand curve. A demand curve is, thus, a graph of the demand schedule. By connecting all the points we get a continuous line. This may be called the demand line for X of Mr. A represented by D_A in Fig. 3.1. The demand schedule is specific in nature because it shows only five possible combinations of price and quantity.

The demand curve, on the other hand, is more general in nature because it shows not only these five but various other possible combinations of price and quantity as well. In other words, the demand curve shows various other quantities of X that will be demanded by Mr. A at various other prices, i.e., at all intermediate prices. For example, by the demand curve we can find out how much of X will be demanded at a price of Rs. 1.75. In order to find it out we have to locate the price Rs. 1.75 on the vertical axis and find out a point which corresponds to this price on the demand curve. We then draw a perpendicular line from that point to find the associated quantity at that price. It is possible to do this for any price. For example, when price is Rs. 1.75 the quantity demanded is 14 kg per week. The demand curve describes the complete relationship between the price of a commodity and the quantity demanded of the same. It is a graph that shows the quantity one buyer will buy at every possible price.

The demand curve in Fig. 3.1 illustrates the law of demand which states that the quantity demanded for a commodity increases when its price falls. The converse is also true : the quantity demanded falls when price rises. Thus, there is a negative (inverse) relation between price and quantity. They move in opposite directions. If one increases the other falls.

3.2.3. Why does the Demand Curve Slope Downwards?

Why do people buy more of a commodity when its price falls? Alfred Marshall explained negative sloping demand curve in terms of a celebrated law in economics : the law of diminishing marginal utility. Modern economists argue that the law of demand has to be explained in terms of 'income effect' and 'substitution effect' of a price change. Thus, the negative sloping demand curve is to be explained in terms of the above-noted three reasons. We explain below each of them :

• **Diminishing MU** : The *first* one is the law of diminishing marginal utility. It is said that this law governs the purchase plan of a consumer. It states that more and more consumption of a commodity will cause its marginal utility to decline. So, marginal utility curve is also downward sloping. A consumer gets maximum satisfaction when the price of a commodity is equal to its marginal utility (i.e., $P = MU$). So long as price remains below marginal utility (i.e., $P < MU$) this equilibrium (equality) condition breaks down. In such a situation, a consumer buys more of that commodity to re-establish the equality between price and marginal utility. Thus, this law suggests that a fall in price leads to a greater demand, and a rise in price causes demand to fall.

- **Income effect** : The *second* reason is the income effect. When the price of a commodity falls (or rises) the real income of the consumer increases (or decreases). However, the money income remains constant. Suppose a consumer buys four kilograms of fish daily, and spends for it Rs. 600. Now, if price of fish falls to Rs. 140 per kilogram, he is supposed to spend now Rs. 560. So, there occurs a gain of Rs. 40 following a fall in its price. Now, he can purchase more fish. This effect thus testifies the law of demand.

- **Substitution effect** : *Thirdly,* substitution effect is another reason. When the price of a commodity falls, the substitutes of that commodity become costlier to the buyer; example: tea and coffee are substitute goods. When price of tea falls coffee becomes expensive or tea becomes cheaper than coffee. In such a situation, our consumer will spend more on tea and less on coffee. On the other hand, if price of tea rises, a consumer will buy more coffee.

All these three factors jointly explain the negative sloping demand curve.

3.2.4. Demand Schedule and Market Demand Curve

To arrive at the market demand we add together the demands of all individual consumers. For the purpose of illustration, let us take a simple case where there are only two consumers—Mr. A and Mr. B. Table 3.2 is a market demand schedule. The information given in this table is plotted on Fig. 3.2 which shows the market demand curve. This is derived by adding up the two demand curves, i.e., of A and of B shown separately.

Table 3.2 : Individual and Market Demand Schedules

Price (Rs. per kg)	Quantities Demanded		
	Mr. A (kg per week)	Mr. B (kg per week)	Market Demand (kg per week) (Mr. A + Mr. B)
(i)	(ii)	(iii)	(iv) = (ii) + (iii)
3.00	15	18	33
3.20	14	16	30
3.40	12	14	26
3.60	9	10	19
3.80	5	7	12
4.00	3	5	8

We may first deal with the market demand schedule. This is obtained by adding the quantity demanded by Mr. A and Mr. B at each price. We thus arrive at a total quantity demanded in column (iv). At a high price, say Rs. 4 per kg, Mr. A demands less than B. Anyway, both individuals demand less (more) when price is more (low). Thus, like individual demand schedules, market demand schedule exhibits inverse relationship between price and quantity demanded. It is to be kept in mind that to derive market demand schedule, we add horizontally all the individual demand schedules.

- **Market Demand Curve** : The market demand curve for X, shown in Fig. 3.2, is constructed by plotting the market demand schedules in column (iv) of Table 3.2. In fact, it is derived by adding horizontally the demand curves

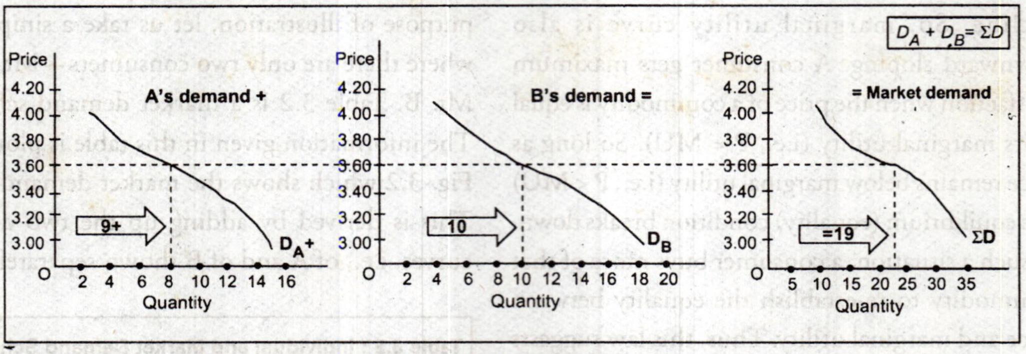

Fig. 3.2 : Derivation of a Market Demand Curve

of the two (representative) buyers. Look at Fig. 3.2. By taking a common price on each curve, and adding the corresponding quantities, we find the total quantity demanded at each price. For example, at a price of Rs. 3.00 per kg, the figure tells us that Mr. A will demand 15 kg while Mr. B will demand 18 kg. This makes a total of 33 kg which is plotted as the total market demand associated with a price of Rs. 3.00 per kg. Thus, the market demand curve is derived by adding up horizontally the demand curves of individual consumers. Like the individual demand curve, market demand curve is also negatively sloped.

In theory, we draw the market demand curve by horizontally adding up the demand curves of individual consumers. But, in practice, we rarely obtain market demand curves by summing up the demand curves of millions and millions of individual consumers. Instead, we form an idea about market demand by observing total quantities directly.

3.3. EXCEPTIONS TO THE LAW OF DEMAND

The law of demand simply states that the quantity demanded of a commodity varies in the opposite direction to its own price. This is usually observed in case of most goods that we buy. But there are certain exceptions to this law. The following five exceptions bear relevance in this context:

- **Speculative demand** : In a speculative market (such as the stock market) a rise in the price of a commodity (such as share) creates impression among buyers that its price will rise further. So people start buying more of the commodity when its price rises.[1] This is not truly an exception to the law of demand in the sense that the demand curve here is not upward sloping. Hence, there is no movement along it from left to right. In fact, in a speculative market we see a shift of a normal downward sloping demand curve—people buy more at the same price. Some economists wrongly refer to this as an exception because they get confused between two issues—movement along a demand curve and shift of the demand curve.

- **Snob appeal:** People sometimes buy certain commodities like diamond at high prices not due to their intrinsic worth but for a different reason. The basic object is to display their riches to the other members of the community to which they themselves belong. This is known as snob appeal, which induces people to purchase items of conspicuous consumption. This is a genuine

1. A price fall creates a similar type of behaviour—people become eager to sell more when price falls. It is because a price fall creates the feeling among people that price will fall further.

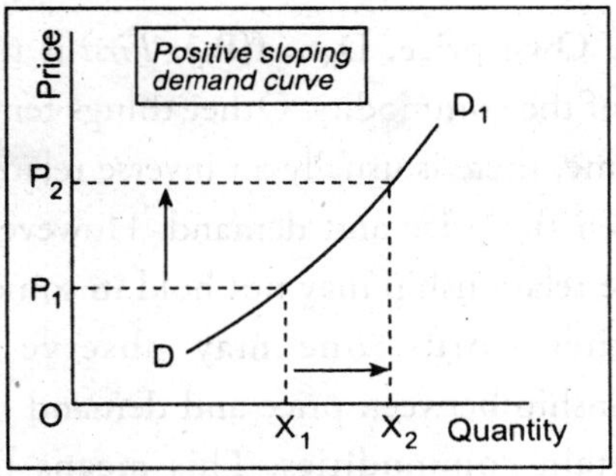

Fig. 3.3: Exceptional Demand Curve

exception to the law of demand. The demand curve for such an item will be upward sloping (Fig. 3.3). Thus, if, the price of diamond falls, people will buy less of it. In a word, purchasers value diamond and other costly items because of their prices and because of the psychic satisfaction that they derive from it.

- **Using price as an index of quality :** There are many instances when buyers behave in an "irrational" manner in the sense that price is related to the quality of a product. Most consumers do not have the capacity or technical knowledge to examine the physical properties of a product (such as reliability, durability, economy, etc.) as in the case of an item such as a motor car or a VCR. So, in the absence of other information, price is taken as an index of quality. Thus, a high-priced car is more valued than a low-priced one. A costly book is often considered to be more useful by a student than a cheap title. In such cases, the demand curve may be upward sloping. This argument is not a new one. This applies to our previous case where we referred to commodities having snob appeal. So this point really reinforces the previous one.[1]

[1] In this context, the following comments from Lipsey and Harbury bear relevance : "Note that the above argument applies only to consumers who incorrectly assume that quality has changed because price has changed.... If the quality of the good does not change then it is not quite the same good and its demand curve will shift. Thus, the observation that a fall in price is accompanied by a fall in quantity demanded of a good whose quality has changed is not an observation of two points on the positively sloped demand curve. Instead, it represents two points on two different demand curves."

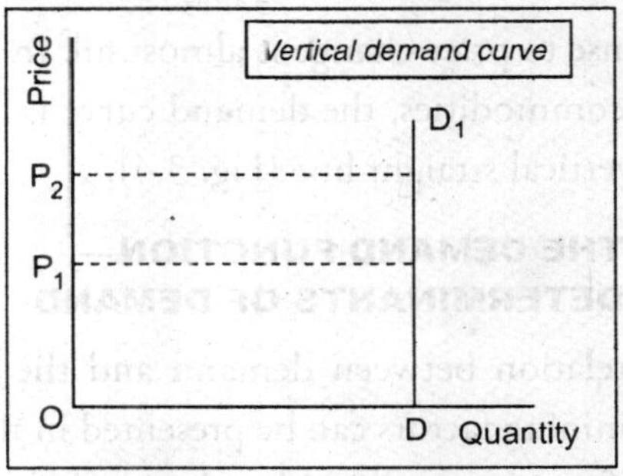

Fig. 3.4: Exceptional Demand Curve

- **Giffen goods :** A 'Giffen good' is a special variety of inferior goods. Sir Robert Giffen (1837-1910) of Scotland observed in the 19th century that poor people spend the major proportion of their income on a staple item, viz., potato. If the price of this good rises they will become so poor that they will be found to spend less on other items and buy more potatoes in order to get a minimum diet and keep themselves alive. For such goods, the demand curve will be upward sloping, looking like the supply curve of Fig. 3.3. Note this is very exceptional and potatoes that we consume should be viewed as normal good, rather than 'Giffen goods'.

- **Possibility of future rise in prices :** If a consumer anticipates that the price of a commodity will rise in future he will purchase more of that commodity now. Thus, the consumer will purchase more—even if present price is high.

In all the cases mentioned above, the demand curve DD_1 exhibits positive slope as shown in Fig. 3.3. At a price OP_1, a consumer demands OX_1 of a commodity. As its price rises to OP_2, demand also rises to OX_2. Thus, the law of demand breaks down.

- **Highly essential goods :** Finally, in case of certain highly essential items such as life-saving drugs, people buy a fixed quantity at all possible prices. Heart patients will buy the same quantity of 'Sorbitrate' whether price is high or low. Their response to price change is almost nil. In cases of such commodities, the demand curve is likely to be a vertical straight line (Fig. 3.4).

3.4. THE DEMAND FUNCTION— DETERMINANTS OF DEMAND

The relation between demand and the various determining factors can be presented in the form of a function called the demand function. Following are, therefore, the main determinants of demand :

$$D_X = f(P_X, P_a...P_C, M, T, E, S, A, Q_X, G, E_n)$$

where $P_a...P_C$ represents prices of related goods, i.e., substitute and complementary to good X;

M represents income;

T represents tastes and preferences of the consumers;

E represents anticipation regarding future change in price;

S represents climatic condition;

A represents advertisement;

Q_X represents quality of good X;

G represents government policy; and

E_n represents environmental concern.

Let us explain all these (both price and non-price) determinants of demand :

- **Own price, $D_X = f(P_X)$:** *First* is the own price of the commodity. Other things remaining the same, there is usually an inverse relationship between the price and demand. However, such inverse relationship may not hold in some cases. In other words, one may observe direct relationship between price and demand in cases of certain commodities. This means that an increase in price leads to an increase in demand.

- **Prices of related goods, $D_X = f(P_a...P_C)$:** *Secondly*, demand for a commodity depends on the prices of related goods, such as substitute goods and complementary goods. For substitute or competitive goods, one finds a direct relationship. Whenever there is an increase in the price of tea, its substitute, i.e., coffee's, demand tends to rise. Again, two products often 'go together'. This means that these products complement each other. Car and petrol are considered as complementary goods. If price of petrol per litre rises, demand for car declines. Thus, in this case, we find an inverse or negative relationship.

In Fig. 3.5, we have shown how demand for a commodity changes when price of related goods changes. In Fig. 3.5(a), we measure quantities of substitute goods on the horizontal axis, say coffee, and price of another goods, say tea, on the vertical axis.

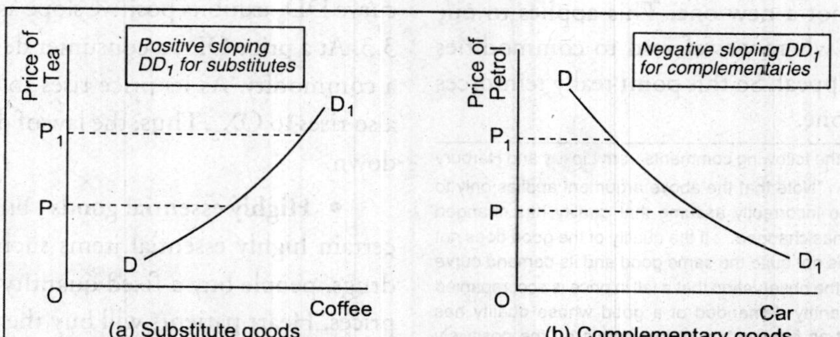

Fig. 3.5: Demand Curves for Substitute and Complementary Goods

As price of tea rises from OP to OP_1, coffee becomes cheaper and as a result its demand rises. That is why demand curve for substitute goods is positive sloping indicating a direct relationship between price and demand.

In Fig. 3.5(b), we measure quantities of car on the horizontal axis while price of its complementary, say petrol, is measured on the vertical axis. If price of petrol declines from OP_1 to OP, there will be a tendency on the part of the people to buy more cars. In view of this, demand curve is negative sloping for complementary goods indicating inverse relationship between price and quantity demanded.

- **Income $D_X = f(M)$:** *Thirdly,* income is another determinant of demand for a commodity. There are some commodities whose demand increases as money income of a consumer rises. However, a consumer may not necessarily behave in this way. He may buy less of a commodity when his money income rises. Such a commodity is called 'inferior' commodity.

In Fig. 3.6, we have drawn income-demand curve that shows the relationship between income and demand of a good. As income rises from OM_1 to OM_2, demand for ordinary food item goes up. Thus, it is a normal good. If income increases beyond OM_2, its demand will fall. As ordinary food item becomes less attractive at a higher income, it is then called inferior good.

- **Taste, $D_X = f(T)$:** *Fourthly,* taste and preference of the consumer is another factor that determines the demand for a commodity. A consumer dictated by his own tastes wears dhoti and another consumer wears trousers. If a consumer shows preference for dhoti instead of trousers, his demand curve would shift to the right

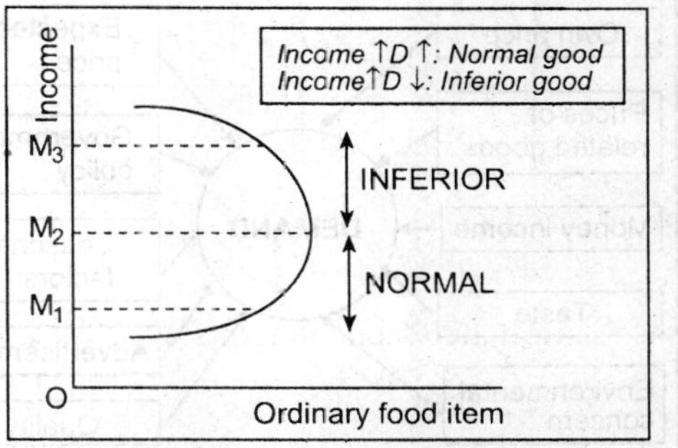

Fig. 3.6: Income-Demand Curve

and a decreasing preference for dhoti would shift the demand curve to the left. The greater the shift in taste and preferences, the larger is the shift of the demand curve either in the rightward or in the backward direction. In fact, taste and preference is an element that considers non-monetary determinants of demand (e.g., modern style).

- **Expected price, $D_X = f(E)$:** *Fifthly,* expectation of a consumer regarding the future change in the price of a commodity may lead to a change in the demand for a commodity. Demand for automobiles in India has gone down in recent times because buyers expect a further fall in its price in the near future.

- **Seasonal factors, $D_X = f(S)$:** *Sixthly,* climatic conditions also influence the demand for a commodity. Demand for woollen garments rise during winter, while ice-cream has a larger demand during summer.

- **Advertisement, $D_X = f(A)$:** *Seventhly,* advertisement has an important bearing on the demand for a commodity. A consumer is often provoked to buy a commodity merely by its advertisement propaganda.

- **Quality, $D_X = f(Q_X)$:** *Eighthly,* quality and design of a product also exerts influence on quantity demanded. Consumer attaches importance to the quality of product while buying.

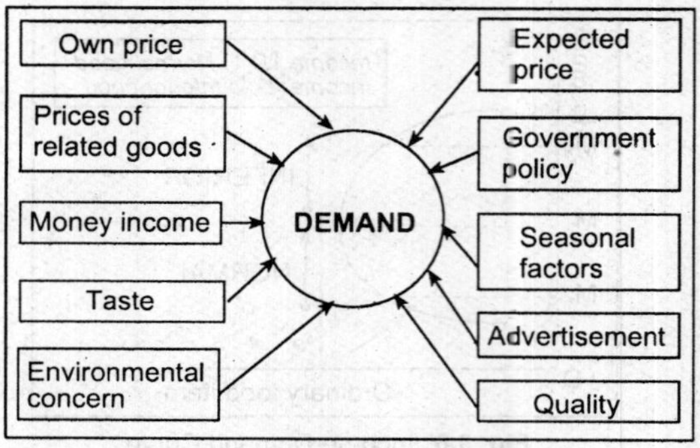

Fig. 3.7: Determinants of Demand

A good quality product should have a greater demand. Whenever the quality of a product suffers, buyers reduce their purchases and switch over to other related products whose quality is still not inferior.

- **Government policy, $D_X = f(G)$:** *Ninthly*, demand for a commodity is also influenced by the policy of the government. Government, by imposing tax on a commodity, may curtail consumption of that commodity. Wine will be demanded less if taxes on it are increased. Similarly, government may encourage the consumption of a commodity by providing subsidy on it. People buy commodities at a cheaper price from shops run by the government.

- **Environmental concern, $D_X = (E_n)$:** *Finally*, warming and pollution are causing heavy damage to our environment. People are demanding more eco-friendly atmoshphere. Such environment-consciousness has an important bearing on the demand for a commodity. For instance, motor car emits carbon dioxide (CO_2) in large quantities causing aggravation of many health problems. Now if people decide to buy bicycle more instead of motor cars, there will be a shift in demand.

All these determinants have been shown in a summary form in Fig. 3.7.

These are the factors that influence the demand for a commodity of a consumer. However, own price of the commodity seems to be the most important determinant of demand. To isolate the various determinants of demand and to study the relationship between demand and own price of the commodity, economists make use of *'ceteris paribus'* clause. To explain the constancy of demand determinants other than the own price of the commodity, we put a bar sign over them. Thus, the demand function becomes

$$\downarrow D_X = f(\uparrow P_X, \bar{P}_a \ldots \bar{P}_C, \bar{M}, \bar{T}, \bar{E}, \bar{S}, \bar{A}, \bar{Q}_X, \bar{G}, \bar{E}_n)$$

3.5. CHANGE IN QUANTITY DEMANDED AND CHANGES IN DEMAND

Economists often draw a distinction between change in quantity demanded of a commodity and change in its demand. In this context, we may note that the word 'demand' is a broad term. It refers to the whole demand curve of a commodity. The demand curve shows the relationship between the price of a commodity and the quantity demanded of the same on the assumption that all other variables affecting demand remain constant. However, the term quantity demanded is a narrow term. It refers to a particular point on the curve. Now, by looking at a demand curve we can see the effect of a change in price on quantity demanded. If price rises the quantity demanded of a commodity falls, and if price falls, the quantity demanded of the same rises. The effects of such price changes are shown by movements along the same demand curve from left to right or right to left. Such movements show change in the quantity demanded for a commodity. These movements are sometimes described as extensions or contractions of demand. If price falls there is a downward movement to the right. This is known as an extension of demand. On the other hand, a contraction of demand refers to an upward movement along the same demand curve from right to left in response to a rise in price.

If, on the other hand, there is a change in any other factor (except the own price of the commodity under consideration), the demand curve will shift to a new position. This implies that at a given price, a larger or a smaller quantity of the commodity will be demanded. This is known as a change in demand. Such a change occurs when there is a change in income of buyers or in its distribution, or in the prices of related goods (substitutes and complements), in people's expectations or in other non-economic factors. A change in demand is usually referred to as a change in the conditions of demand. For example, when most people in India get bonus at the time of festival they buy more sweets even though prices of sweets remain the same.

These two concepts can be explained with the help of Table 3.3.

Table 3.3 : Movements and Shifts in Demand

(1) Price of X	(2) Demand for X (increase)	(3) Demand for X (original)	(4) Demand for X (decrease)
Rs. 6	12	10	8
Rs. 5	15	13	10
Rs. 4	20	15	13

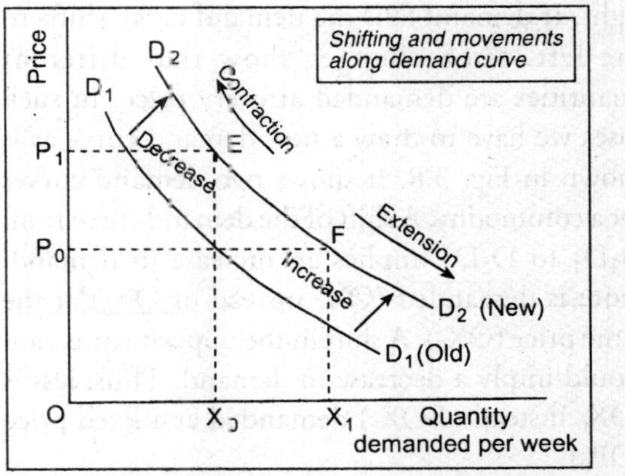

Fig. 3.8: Change in Demand vs Change in Quantity Demanded

Comparing column (3) with columns (2) and (4), one can explain change in demand. When price of X, say, is Rs. 6 per unit, then its initial demand is 10 units. Assuming price at Rs. 6, demand may increase to 12 units or decrease to 8 units. This then is a situation of change in demand.

Thus, in the above table, column-wise movement refers to a change in demand.

On the other hand, at a price of Rs. 6, initial demand is 10 units. If price falls to Rs. 5 then demand will increase to 15 units, and so on. Such a movement is known as a change in quantity demanded. It refers to the movement up and down along a given demand schedule. In other words, row-wise movement refers to a change in quantity demanded.

Changes in demand are of two types. If demand increases the demand curve shifts to the

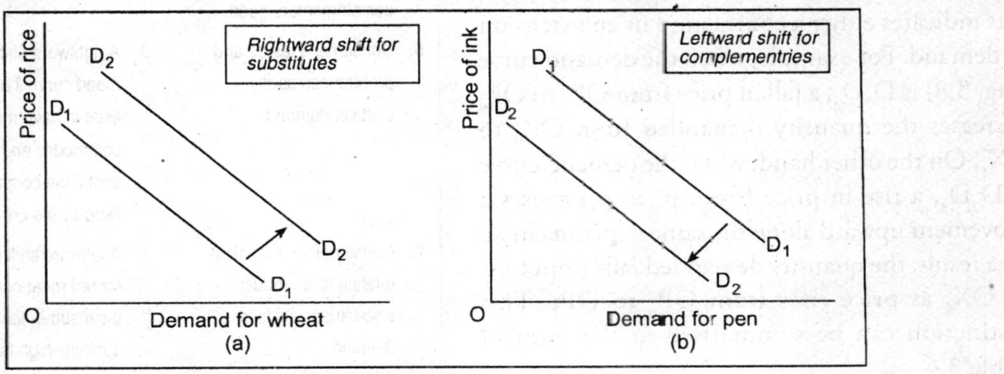

Fig. 3.9: Shifts of the Demand Curve

right. If demand falls the demand curve shifts to the left. Such changes show that different quantities are demanded at every price. In such cases we have to draw a new demand curve as is shown in Fig. 3.8. It shows two demand curves for a commodity. A shift of the demand curve from D_1D_1 to D_2D_2 implies an increase in demand; more is demanded (OX_1 instead of OX_0) at the same price (OX_0). A shift in the opposite direction would imply a decrease in demand. Thus, less is (OX_0 instead of OX_1) demanded at a fixed price (OP_0)

We know that demand curve shifts its position when all the determinants of demand, except the own price of the commodity change. An increase in money income, for example, shifts up demand curve from D_1D_1 to D_2D_2.

The demand curve also shifts up from D_1D_1 to D_2D_2 in Fig. 3.9(a). This is because wheat and rice are substitute goods. As price of rice declines demand for wheat declines, and vice versa. Because of the increase in the price of rice, demand for wheat rises and the demand curve shifts up from D_1D_1 to D_2D_2.

But in the case of complementary goods, like pen and ink, demand curve shifts backwards. As price of ink declines demand for pen rises, or, as price of ink rises demand for pen falls. That is why demand curve moves downward from D_1D_1 to D_2D_2 in Fig. 3.9(b).

A change in quantity demanded for a commodity resulting from a change in its own price will lead to a movement along the curve itself; this indicates either a contraction or an extension of demand. For example, when the demand curve (Fig. 3.8) is D_2D_2, a fall in price from OP_1 to OP_0 increases the quantity demanded from OX_0 to OX_1. On the other hand, when the demand curve is D_2D_2, a rise in price (from p_0 to p_1) causes a movement upward along the same demand curve. As a result, the quantity demanded falls from OX_1 to OX_0 as price rises from OP_0 to OP_1. This distinction can be summarised in the form of Table 3.4.

Table 3.4 : The Terminology of Demand Curves

Change	Terms Used to Describe the Change
(A) A change in the price of the good causes a MOVEMENT ALONG a demand curve	
1. Price of the good rises.	1. *A decrease, fall or reduction in the quantity demanded.*
2. Price of the goods falls.	2. *An increase, or a rise in the quantity demanded.* An extension of demand.
(B) A change in any of the other influences causes a SHIFT of a demand curve	
1. A rise in income, if the good is a normal one. A fall in income, if the good is an inferior one.	1. *A rightward,* upward or northeasternly shift of the demand curve.
2. A rise in the price of a substitute item.	2. *An increase in demand.*
3. A fall in the price of a complementary good. A change in tastes in favour of the good.	3. An improvement in the conditions of demand.
4. A fall in income if the good is normal. A rise in income if the good is inferior.	4. A *leftward,* downward or southwesternly *shift of the demand curve.*
5. A fall in the price of a substitute item. A rise in the price of a complementary good.	5. *A decrease in demand.*
6. Consumer's tastes and preferences cause shifts in demand	6. A rightward shift of the demand curve if a consumer likes to have more of a commodity and a leftward shift if the commodity is not liked by the consumer.
7. Consumer's information relating to a product also causes shifts in demand.	7. A leftward shift in demand for red meat occurs when a consumer learns that it contains high fat.

3.6. ELASTICITY OF DEMAND

The law of demand indicates the direction of change in quantity demanded to a change in price. It states that when price falls, demand rises. But, how much the quantity demanded rises (or falls) following a certain fall (or rise) in prices cannot be known from the law of demand. That is to say, how much quantity demanded changes following a change in the price of a commodity can be known from the concept of elasticity of demand.

In Fig. 3.10, we have drawn two demand curves for good X and good Y. Both these curves are negative sloping. Let us assume that prices of both goods X and Y are P_{X_1} and P_{Y_1} (note that $P_{X_1} = P_{Y_1}$). At price OP_{X_1}, a consumer demands OX_1 and at price OP_{Y_1}, OY_1 is demanded. Now if prices of both X and Y decline by an identical amount to OP_{X_2} and OP_{X_2}, quantity demanded for X and Y rises from OX_1 to OX_2 and from OY_1 to OY_2, respectively. But the change in quantity demanded for good X is greater than the change in quantity demanded for Y. This means that good X is more sensitive or responsive to a change in its price than good Y. This is called elasticity of demand.

By elasticity of demand, we normally mean price elasticity of demand. (Price) elasticity of demand measures the degree of responsiveness of quantity demanded following a change in own price of the commodity, holding money income and prices of related goods constant. (Price) elasticity of demand is the relative difference in the dependent variable (here, quantity) divided by the relative difference in independent variable (here, price). Alternatively, it is defined as the absolute value of the ratio of percentage change in quantity demanded to a percentage change in price. Thus, the elasticity of demand is a relative concept. The formula for calculating elasticity of demand is :

$$E_p = \frac{\text{proportional changes in quantity demanded}}{\text{proportional changes in price}}$$

$$= \frac{\text{\% changes in quantity demanded}}{\text{\% changes in price}}$$

$$E_p = \left|\frac{\Delta Q / Q}{\Delta P / P}\right| = \left|\frac{\Delta Q}{\Delta P} \cdot \frac{P}{Q}\right|$$

The vertical lines in the formula denote that we take the absolute value of the ratio and ΔP and ΔQ denote the changes in price and quantity.

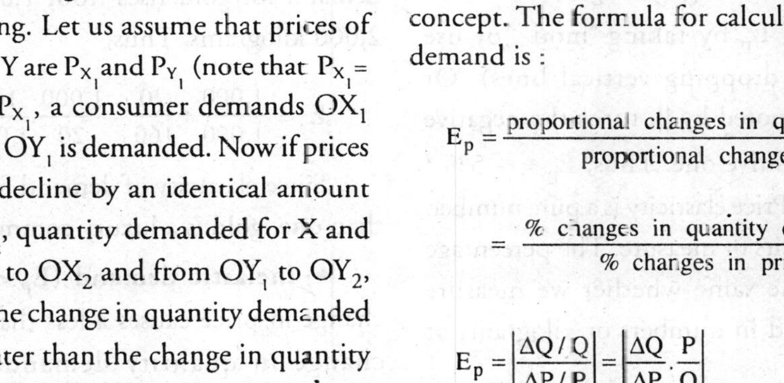

Fig. 3.10: Responsiveness of Product Demand

Since both price and quantity move in opposite direction, E_p must always be a negative number.

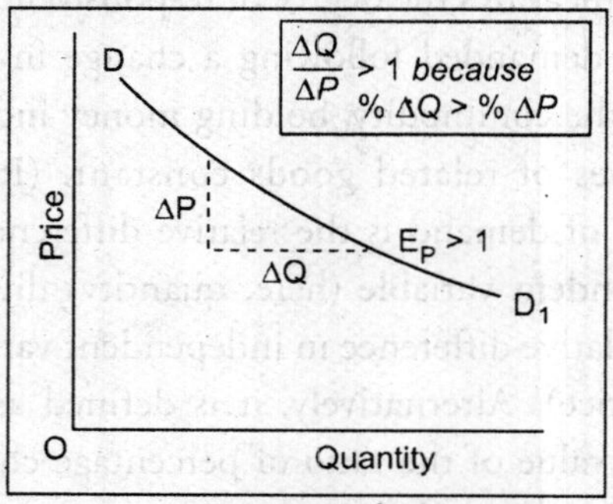

Fig. 3.11 : Elastic Demand

Normally, we drop the negative sign and take the absolute value of E_p by taking 'mod' (or use negative sign by dropping vertical lines). Or absolute value, denoted by ||, turns the negative number into a positive one. Thus, $E_p = |-5\% / 2\%| = |-2.5| = 2.5$. Price elasticity is a pure number, independent of units of measure. The percentage change will be the same whether we measure quantity demanded in numbers or kilograms or litres.

3.6.1. Types of Own (Price) Elasticity of Demand

For all types of commodities, the rate of change of quantity demanded to a change in own price is not uniform. For some commodities, demand is said to be more responsive to price changes compared to other commodities. That is why there are various types of elasticities of demand. They are of the following five types :

- **Elastic demand** ($E_p > 1$): Demand is said to be elastic if the change in price causes a more than proportionate change in quantity demanded. A 10 p.c. change in price causes quantity demanded to change by more than 10 p.c. In other words, if E_p is greater than one, demand is said to be elastic (Fig. 3.11). Normally, demand is elastic for luxury goods.

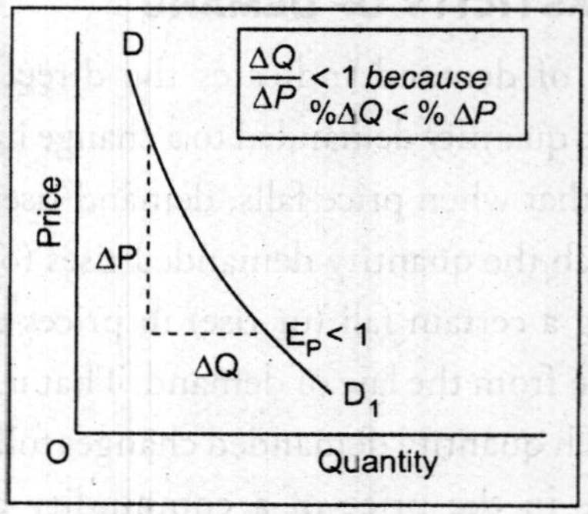

Fig. 3.12 : Inelastic Demand

Assume that let the price of gold per gm declines from Rs. 160 to Rs. 140. As a result, demand for gold rises from 1,000 kilograms to 2,000 kilograms. Thus,

$$E_p = \frac{1,000}{1,000} \div \frac{20}{160} = \frac{1,000}{20} \cdot \frac{160}{1,000} = 8$$

Since elasticity of demand for gold is greater than one, gold is a luxury commodity.

- **Inelastic demand** ($E_P < 1$): When the change in price causes a less than proportionate change in quantity demanded, demand is inelastic. A 10 p.c. cut in price may cause quantity demanded to fall by, say, 1 p.c. Thus, demand is said to be inelastic (or $E_P < 1$), shown in Fig. 3.12. Usually, demand is inelastic for necessary goods.

Suppose that following a drop in the price of wheat from paisa 40 to paisa 20 per kilogram demand for wheat rises from 1,600 kilograms to 2,000 kilograms. This means

$$E_P = \frac{400}{1,600} \div \frac{20}{40} = \frac{400}{20} \cdot \frac{400}{1,600} = 0.5$$

Then, wheat has an inelastic demand since $E_P < 1$ and wheat is a necessary good

- **Unit elasticity of demand** ($E_p = 1$) : When the change in price causes the same proportionate change in quantity demanded, demand has unit elasticity. A 10 p.c. decline in price will lead to an

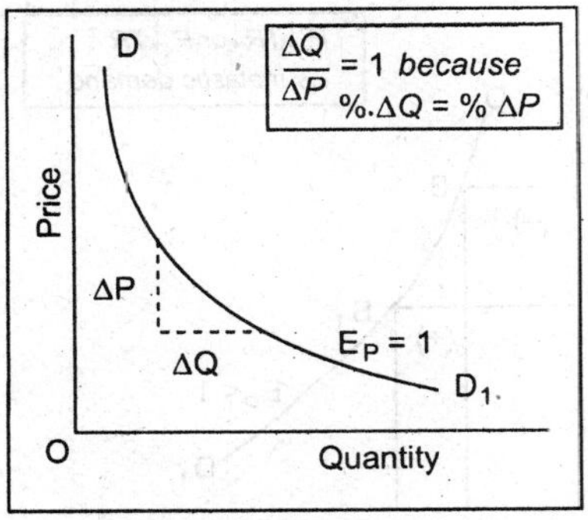

Fig. 3.13: Unitary Elastic Demand

exactly 10 p.c. increase in quantity demanded. Then $E_p = 1$ (Fig. 3.13).

Suppose that the price of a commodity declines from Rs. 200 to Rs. 100 per kilogram. as a result demand for that commodity rises from 400 kilograms to 800 kilorams. Thus,

$$E_p = \frac{400}{400} \div \frac{100}{100} = \frac{400}{100} \cdot \frac{100}{400} = 1$$

- **Perfectly elastic demand ($E_p = \infty$):** When a slight change in price causes a fantastic change in quantity demanded, the value of elasticity of demand tends to be infinity—and the demand is said to be infinitely or perfectly elastic. In this case, the demand curve (DD_1) becomes parallel to the horizontal axis (Fig. 3.14). Under perfectly competitive market, the demand curve for a product of an individual firm becomes perfectly elastic.

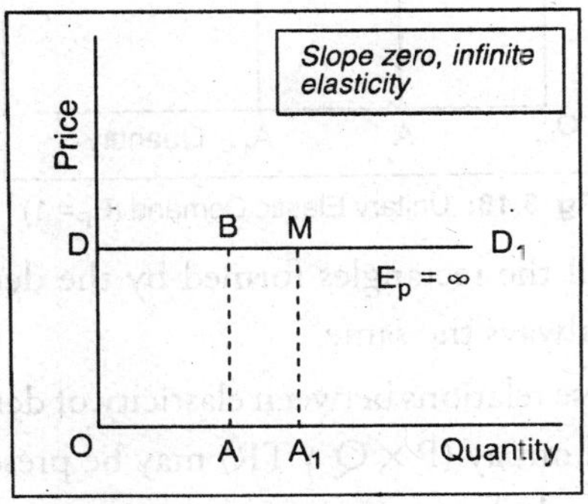

Fig. 3.14: Perfectly Elastic Demand

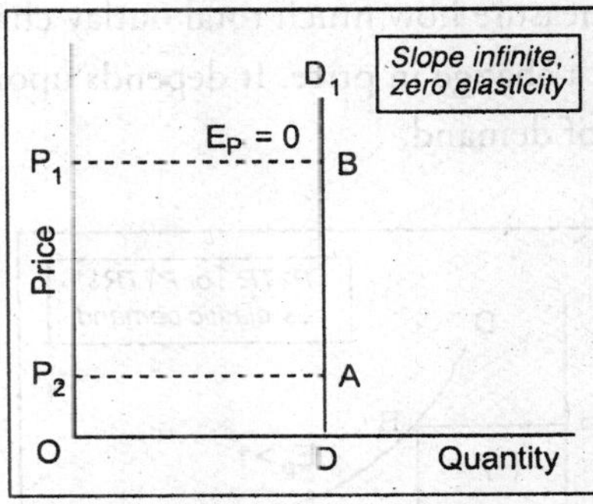

Fig. 3.15: Perfectly Inelastic Demand

- **Perfectly inelastic demand (E_p= 0):** If quantity demanded becomes completely unresponsive to price changes, the coefficient tends to be zero. In this case, whatever the price, even if it is zero, quantity demanded will remain fixed at a particular level. The demand curve, thus, becomes parallel to the vertical axis (Fig. 3.15) and demand is said to be completely (perfectly) inelastic.

Thus, elasticity of demand varies from zero to infinity.

3.7. MEASUREMENT OF ELASTICITY OF DEMAND

There are three methods of measuring elasticity of demand. These are : (a) total outlay (revenue) method; (b) point elasticity method, and (c) arc elasticity method. All these methods are described below.

3.7.1. Elasticity and Total Revenue or Total Outlay Method

Marshall offered the method of total revenue or total outlay for estimating elasticity of demand. What the sellers receive from the sale of commodities is called total expenditure or outlay of buyers. There is no difference between total revenue and total outlay since what is spent by buyers is received as income by sellers. Thus, total outlay/revenue is the price multiplied by the quantity purchased, i.e., TR = P × Q. Here we want to measure how much total outlay changes following a change in price. It depends upon the elasticity of demand.

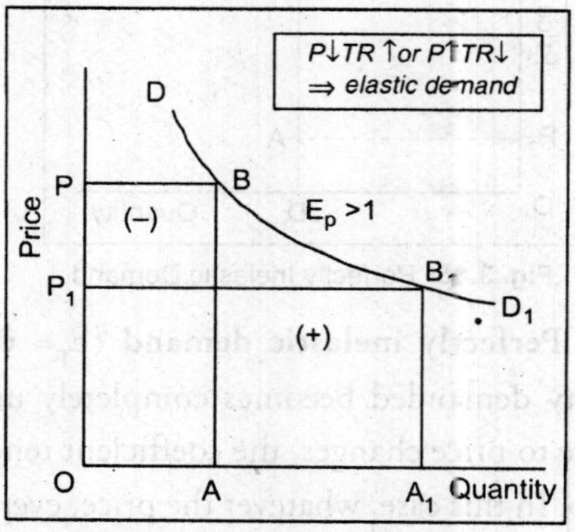

Fig. 3.16: Elastic Demand ($E_p > 1$)

• **Elastic demand** : Suppose, price declines (rises). As a result, total expenditure rises (falls). Under the circumstance, the value of elasticity of demand becomes greater than one. In Fig. 3.16, we have drawn a demand curve having a value greater than one. At a price OP, OA is demanded. Thus, the total expenditure equals OP × OA = rectangle OPBA. As price drops to OP_1, quantity demanded rises to OA_1. Now, the total expenditure becomes $OP_1 \times OA_1$ = rectangle $OP_1B_1A_1$.

Since rectangle $OP_1B_1A_1$ > rectangle OPBA, demand is said to be elastic. Remember : When price and total outlay move in opposite direction, demand for the product becomes elastic.

• **Inelastic Demand** : If the total outlay falls when price falls, or if total outlay rises when price rises, then demand is said to be inelastic (i.e., E_p<1). In Fig. 3.17, initial total outlay is OP × OA = rectangle OPBA. Now, if price falls, total outlay becomes $OP_1 \times OA_1$ = rectangle $OP_1B_1A_1$. Fig. 3.17 suggests that the rectangle

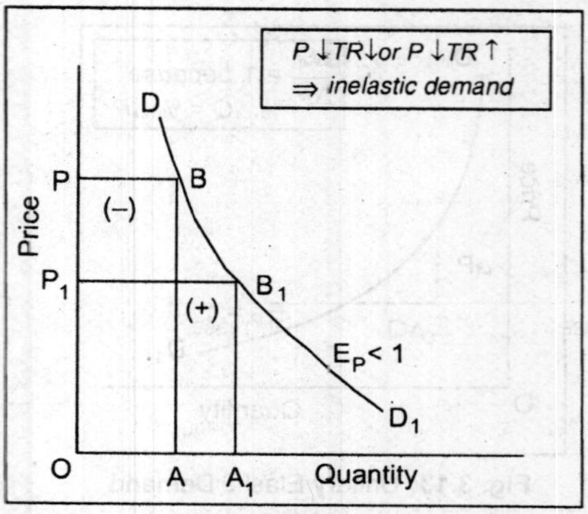

Fig. 3.17: Inelastic Demand ($E_P < 1$)

OPBA is larger than the rectangle $OP_1B_1A_1$. Hence, demand is inelastic.

• **Unitary elastic** : Irrespective of variations in demand and price, if the total outlay does not change, then demand is unit elastic (i.e., $E_p = 1$). In Fig. 3.18, we see that, at price OP, total outlay is rectangle OPBA. When price declines to OP_1 total outlay becomes the area $OP_1B_1A_1$. Since rectangle OPBA = rectangle $OP_1B_1A_1$, demand is said to have a unitary elasticity. The demand curve then looks like a rectangular hyperbola since the

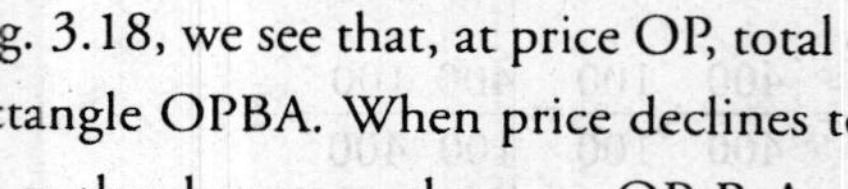

Fig. 3.18: Unitary Elastic Demand (E_P= 1)

area of all the rectangles formed by the demand curve is always the same.

These relations between elasticity of demand and total outlay (P × Q = TR) may be presented here in a tabular form:

Table 3.5 : Elasticity and TR

Change in price	E_p	Change in TR	Nature of the good
Increase	$E_p > 1$	Decrease	Luxury
Decrease	$E_p > 1$	Increase	
Increase	$E_p < 1$	Increase	Necessary
Decrease	$E_p < 1$	Decrease	
Increase	$E_p = 1$	No change	—
Decrease	$E_p = 1$	No change	

The relationship between elasticity and total outlay can also be explained in terms of Fig. 3.19 where we measure price of the commodity on the vertical axis and the total outlay on the horizontal axis. Here ABCD is the total outlay curve. In the segment AB, demand is inelastic ($E_p < 1$), because price and total outlay move in the same direction. Demand is said to be elastic ($E_p > 1$) in the region CD since price and total outlay move in opposite directions. As total outlay remains invariant when price changes in the region BC, the demand is unitary elastic.

3.7.2. Point Elasticity Method of Measurement

When the change in price is infinitesimally small, Marshallian method may not provide an accurate estimate of elasticity of demand. In that case, a geometrical method may be employed. This

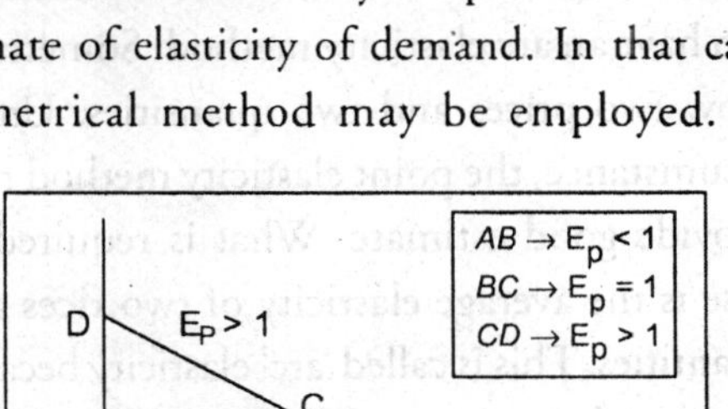

Fig. 3.19: Total Outlay Curve and Elasticity of Demand

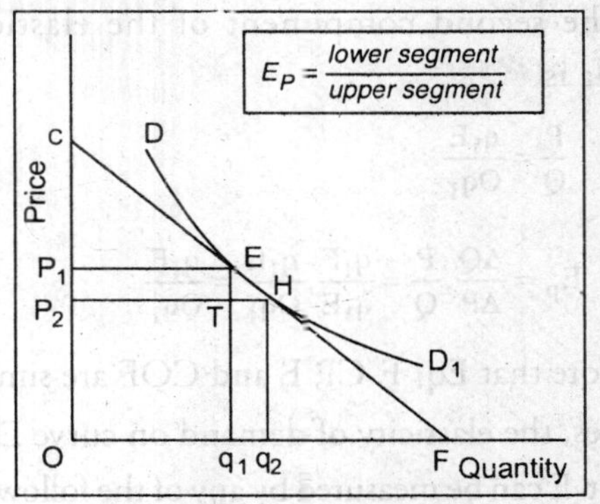

Fig. 3.20: Point Elasticity

method aims at measuring elasticity of demand at a particular point on a demand curve. So long, we tried to calculate elasticity over a certain area or segment of a demand curve and the terms elastic, inelastic and unitary elastic have been applied to the whole demand curve. However, such is not true. It may happen that the demand for a product can be elastic in one price range and inelastic in another. In fact, the degree of elasticity varies from one price range to another. So, it is better to calculate elasticity at a particular point on a demand curve to have an accurate estimate. This is explained in terms of Fig. 3.20.

Here, demand curve is DD_1. To measure elasticity of demand at point E, we have drawn a straight line CF tangent to DD_1 at point E. Points E and H are very close to each other. As price declines from OP_1 to OP_2, quantity demanded rises from Oq_1 to Oq_2. The formula for elasticity of demand is :

$$E_p = \frac{\Delta Q}{Q} \div \frac{\Delta P}{P}$$

The slope of the demand curve

$$\frac{\Delta P}{\Delta Q} = \frac{q_1E}{q_1E}$$

$$\therefore \frac{\Delta Q}{\Delta P} = \frac{q_1F}{q_1E}$$

The second component of the elasticity formula is

$$\frac{P}{Q}=\frac{q_1E}{Oq_1}$$

$$\therefore\ E_p=\frac{\Delta Q}{\Delta P}\cdot\frac{P}{Q}=\frac{q_1F}{q_1E}\cdot\frac{q_1E}{Oq_1}=\frac{q_1F}{Oq_1}$$

Note that Eq_1 F, CP, E and COF are similar triangles, the elasticity of demand on curve DD_1 at point E can be measured by any of the following ratios of distances :

$$E_p=\frac{q_1F}{Oq_1}=\frac{P_1O}{P_1C}=\frac{EF}{EC}$$

Thus, elasticity of demand at point E on a curvilinear demand curve DD_1 is approximately equal to

$$\frac{EF}{EC}=\frac{\text{lower segment of the demand curve}}{\text{upper segment of the demand curve}}$$

On the basis of this method of measurement, one can estimate the elasticity of demand on a linear demand curve, show in Fig. 3.21.

Here, DD_1 is a linear demand curve. Elasticity of demand varies from point to point on a demand curve. At point O, the elasticity of demand is $\frac{PD_1}{PD}$. As the distance between PD_1 and PD is the same, it is unit elastic (i.e., $E_p = 1$). As we move downwards along the curve DD_1 from the

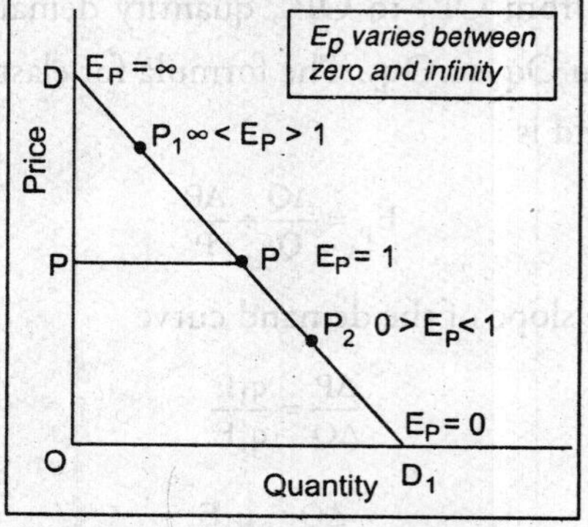

Fig. 3.21: Elasticity of Demand

midpoint, say point P_2, elasticity declines. At P_2, it is inelastic (i.e., $0 > E_p < 1$) since $P_2D_1 < P_2D_1 < P_2D$. At point D, elasticity is zero since $\frac{0}{DD_1}$ is equal to zero. Further, as we move upwards from the mid point, elasticity increases. At P_1, it is elastic (i.e., $\infty < E_p > 1$) since $P_1D_1 > P_1 D$. On the other hand, at point D, it is infinite since $\frac{DD_1}{0}$ is equal to infinity. Thus, at lower prices, it is inelastic and, at higher prices, it is elastic.

Thus, elasticity of demand on a straight line demand curve varies from zero to infinity.

3.7.3 ARC ELASTICITY METHOD

For very small movements in price and quantity, point elasticity method is an appropriate one. In other words, point elasticity method measures (price) elasticity of demand at a particular point on the demand curve. However, if price change is somewhat of a larger magnitude then geometrical method may give misleading estimate. To avoid this problem, elasticity is measured over an arc of the demand curve. In other words, when we intend to estimate (price) elasticity of demand over some portion (i.e., the arc) of the demand curve, we then have an arc elasticity method. Sometimes we know two prices and two quantities. Under the circumstance, the point elasticity method may not provide good estimate. What is required in this case is the average elasticity of two rices and two quantities. This is called 'arc' elasticity because it measures the average elasticity on an arc of demand curve.

Suppose we have the following information about two prices and quantities :

Price (P)	Demand (Q)
Rs. 60.00 (P_1)	400 (Q_1)
Rs. 50.00 (P_2)	800 (Q_2)

Here changes in both price and quantity are much larger. Using old price (P_1) and old quantity (Q_1), one finds the value of elasticity of demand as :

$$E_p = \frac{\Delta Q}{\Delta P} \cdot \frac{P_1}{Q_1} = -\frac{400}{10} \cdot \frac{60}{400} = -6.0$$

When new price (P_2) and new quanity (Q_2) are taken into account, the coefficient becomes

$$E_p = \frac{\Delta Q}{\Delta P} \cdot \frac{P_2}{Q_2} = -\frac{400}{10} \cdot \frac{50}{800} = -2.5$$

Thus, estimation of elasticity in accordance with the formula for point elasticity method gives vastly different results. In other words, since elasticity of demand varies depending on the base, one should consider average price and average quantity demanded to calculate eleasticity of demand. That is to say, we want to measure average elasticity over an arc of the demand curve (i.e., mid-point or average, price quantity)

$$E_{arc} = -\frac{\Delta Q}{\left(\frac{Q_1 + Q_2}{2}\right)} \div \frac{\Delta P}{\left(\frac{P_1 + P_2}{2}\right)}$$

$$= -\frac{\Delta Q}{\left(\frac{Q_1 + Q_2}{2}\right)} \times \frac{\left(\frac{P_1 + P_2}{2}\right)}{\Delta P} = -\frac{\Delta Q}{\Delta P}\left(\frac{P_1 - P_2}{Q_1 - Q_2}\right)$$

In our above example, the arc elasticity s

$$E_{arc} = -\frac{400}{10} \cdot \frac{60 + 50}{400 + 800} = -\frac{400}{10} \cdot \frac{110}{1200} = -3.66$$

In terms of Fig. 3.22, we want to compute arc price elasticity of demand over the arc AB of the demand curve DD_1. In other words, we want to mesure elasticity between points A and B. The above formula measures arc elasticity over the straight line AB. To do so, we have to take the average of prices (OP and OP_1) and average of

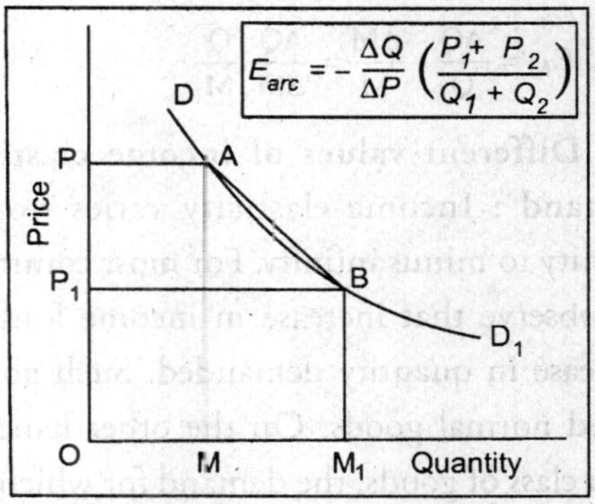

Fig. 3.22: Arc Elasticity

quantities (OM and OM_1) Greater the convexity of the demand curve between A and B, or greater the divergence between points A and B, One obtaints almost perfect estimate of elasticity. Or greater the concavity of the demand curve between points A and B, the poorer approximation of measurement of arc elasticity. As we go on making the price change smaller and smaller, the arc of the demand curve may vanish or converge to a points. So, as special case of arc elasticity, the concept of point elasticity becomes relevant.

3.8 INCOME ELASTICITY OF DEMAND

The concept of elasticity of demand can be broadened to measure the response of quantity demanded to any of the factors affecting the market demand for a commodity. Besides the price of the commodity under consideration, we have also to know how changes in income and in the price of other commodities affect elasticity of demand.

As incomes rise consumers normally increase their demands for most of the commodities they consume. The responsiveness of demand to changes in income is measured by using the concept of income elasticity of demand. It is denoted by E_M and is expressed as :

$$E_M = \frac{\%\text{ change in quantity demanded}}{\%\text{ change in income}}$$

$$E_M = \frac{\Delta Q}{Q} + \frac{\Delta M}{M} = \frac{\Delta Q}{\Delta M} \cdot \frac{Q}{M}$$

Different values of income elasticity of demand : Income elasticity varies from plus infinity to minus infinity. For most commodities we observe that increase in income leads to an increase in quantity demanded. Such goods are called normal goods. On the other hand, there are a class of goods, the demand for which falls as income rises. Such goods are called inferior goods. Normal goods have positive income elasticity; inferior goods have negative elasticity. The boundary between the two is zero income elasticity, corresponding to the case where a change in income leaves quantity demanded unchanged.

Fig. 3.23 shows the relationship between income and quantity demanded for the three types of goods. Good A is a normal good (or non-inferior good) with positive income elasticity of demand ($0 < E_M < 1$) (D_A curve). A normal good or a non-inferior good is one whose coefficient of income elasticity is positive but less than one. One may also call such normal good a necessary good. E_M is positive because income and demand move in the same direction. Its coefficient is less than one because a change in income causes a smaller change in quantity demanded. If $E_M > 1$, then

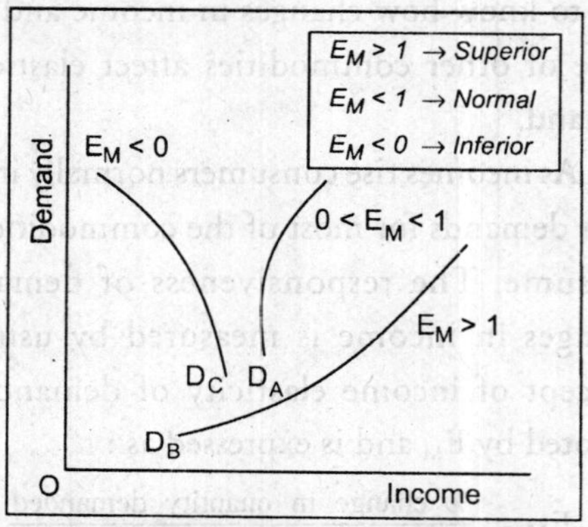

Fig. 3.23: Categories of Income Elasticity

good is said to be a luxury one (D_B curve). Further, there are some goods whose demand falls as income rises. In other words, if income and demand move in opposite direction then $E_M < 0$ and such commodity is called inferior commodity (D_C curve). These three types of commodity showing negative, positive but less than one, and positive elasticity have been shown in Fig. 3.23.

The boundary between positive and negative elasticities is zero income elasticity ($E_M = 0$). If quantity demanded remains invariant consequent upon a change in money income, then E_M becomes equal to zero.

3.9. CROSS-ELASTICITY OF DEMAND

Cross-elasticity of demand is the degree to which the demand for one commodity responds to a change in the price of another commodity.

The formula for measuring the coefficient of cross elasticity of demand is :

$$E_{XY} = \frac{\text{\% change in quantity demanded for Y}}{\text{\% change in price of X}}$$

$$E_{XY} = \frac{\frac{\Delta Q_Y}{Q_Y}}{\frac{\Delta P_X}{P_X}} = \frac{\Delta Q_Y}{\Delta P_X} \cdot \frac{P_X}{Q_Y}$$

Cross-elasticity of demand may be positive or negative, depending on the relationship between the two commodities. If the commodities are substitutes cross-elasticity will be positive, i.e., a rise in the price of the first commodity will cause an increase in the demand for the other commodity.

Fig. 3.24 shows the relationship between P_X and demand for substitute good, Y. If X and Y are substitutes then the quantity demanded for Y is directly related to the price of X. If they are complements, then quantity demanded for Y is

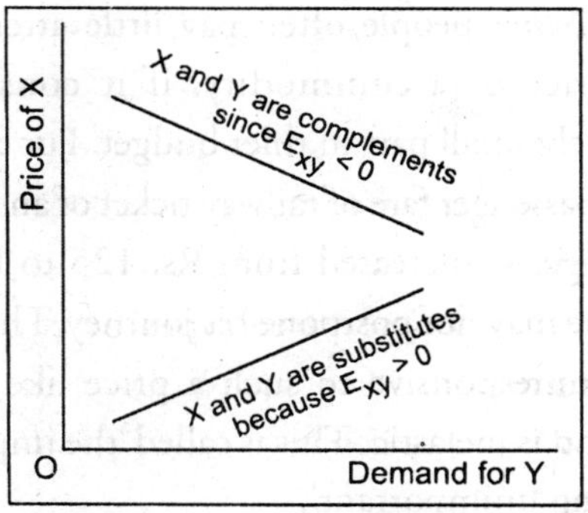

Fig. 3.24 : Cross-elasticity of Demand

inversely related to the price of X. Thus, for substitute goods, cross-elasticity of demand becomes positive and for complementary goods it is negative. If goods X and Y are not related either way (say, good X is a calculator while good Y is trousers) then the value of cross-elasticity of demand becomes zero.

3.10. FACTORS DETERMINING ELASTICITY OF DEMAND

There are various factors on which elasticity of demand depends :

Firstly, it depends on the nature of the commodity. Commodities which are supposed to be essential or critical to our daily life must have an inelastic demand, since price change of these items do not bring about a greater change in quantity demanded. But luxury goods have an elastic demand. Demand for these goods can be quickly reduced when their prices rise. When their prices fall, consumers demand them in larger quantities. However, whether a particular commodity is a necessary or a luxury one depends on income, tastes and preferences of the consumer. A particular good may be necessary to someone having an inelastic demand. Same commodity may be elastic to another consumer. For instance, owning a TV may be a luxury item to a low income person. But the same may be bought as an essential item by a rich person.

Secondly, commodities having large number of substitutes must have an elastic demand. Some products, such as Horlicks, Complan, Viva, Maltova, Milo, etc., have quite a large number of close substitutes. A change in the price of, say, Horlicks, the prices of other substitutes remaining constant, will lead a consumer to substitute one

Table 3.6 : Elasticities and Formulae

Concept	Symbol	Formula	Sign	Size	Nature of the good
Price elasticity	E_P	$\frac{\%\text{ change in } Q}{\%\text{ change in } P} \cdot \frac{P}{Q}$	-ve	$E_M > 1$ Elastic	Luxury
		or $(\Delta Q/\Delta P).(P/Q)$		$E_P < 1$ Inelastic	Necessary
Income elasticity	E_M	$\frac{\%\text{ change in } Q}{\%\text{ change in } M} \cdot \frac{M}{Q}$	+ve	$E_M > 1$ Elastic	Luxury
		or $(\Delta Q/\Delta M).(M/Q)$		$E_M < 1$ Inelastic	Necessary
				$E_M < 0$	Inferior
Cross-elasticity	E_{XY}	$\frac{\%\text{ change in } Q_X}{\%\text{ change in } P_Y} \cdot \frac{P_Y}{Q_X}$	+ve	$E_{XY} > 0$	Complement
		or $\left[\frac{\Delta Q_Y}{\Delta P_X}\right] \frac{P_X}{Q_Y}$	–ve	$E_{XY} < 0$	Substitutes

beverage for another. If price of Horlicks goes down, buyers will demand more of it and less of its substitutes. Conversely, demand is fairly inelastic in the case of those commodities which do not have a large number of substitutes.

Thirdly, there are some commodities which can be used for a variety of purposes. For example, electricity. If price per unit of electricity consumed falls, people will reduce their consumption of its substitutes (e.g., coal, gas, etc.,) and increase the consumption of electricity. Coefficient of price elasticity of demand in this case must be greater than one. On the other hand, when a commodity is used only for one or two purposes, a price change will have less effect on its quantity demanded and, therefore, demand will be inelastic.

Fourthly, there are some commodities consumed out of habits and conventions which have an inelastic demand. Even in the face of rising prices of those commodities or falling income, people will consume those (such as, cigarette). For this reason, price elasticity as well as income elasticity of demand for this type of commodity is inelastic. Further, gold ornaments are used in the marriage ceremony rather out of convention, though gold prices are rising. When gold is used in this way, its demand becomes inelastic.

Fifthly, shorter the time, lower will be the elasticity of demand. This is because in the short run, satisfactory substitutes of a product may not be available. Thus, demand for a product in the short run usually becomes inelastic. Such a commodity will be elastic in the long run when close substitutes may be produced. Thus, the response of quantity demanded to a change in price will tend to be greater (smaller), the longer (shorter) the time-span considered. In the long run, there is enough time for adjustments to be made following a change in price.

Sixthly, people often pay little attention to the price of a commodity, if it constitues a relatively small part in thier budget. For example, if the passenger fare of railway ticket of an irregular passenger is increased from Rs. 125 to Rs. 130, then he may not postpone his journey. This means he is unresponsive to such a price like and his demand is inelastic. This is called 'the importance of being unimportant'.

Finally, durable commodities have an elastic demand. If the price of these goods rise, people will spend less on these goods. On the other hand, following a fall in price of durable commodities (e.g., refrigerator) people demand more. In the case of non-durable commodities we have an elastic demand.

3.11. IMPORTANCE OF THE CONCEPT OF ELASTICITY OF DEMAND

The concept of elasticity of demand has both theoretical and practical value. The concept may be used in understanding as well as tackling various economic problems :

- **Price determination :** Use of the concept of elasticity of demand is required in the price determination of a commodity under different market conditions. Under perfect competition, in the short run in which supply is absolutely inelastic, price depends upon the elasticity of demand. If demand suddenly falls—supply remaining fixed—prices will fall, and if demand suddenly rises prices will rise as output cannot be increased. Again, the stability of prices also depends on the elasticity of demand and elasticity of supply. If either the demand or the supply is elastic, fluctuations in prices will be within narrow limits. Further, if the demand for an agricultural commodity is inelastic, increased production may spell disaster to the economic condition of farmers. So the government can accept measures to save the plight of the farmers.

A monopoly seller must have a knowledge relating to the elasticity of demand for his product while determining price of his commodity. A monopolist will produce a commodity in the range of his demand curve where demand is said to be elastic. He will never produce in the range of his demand curve where demand is inelastic. Obviously, price determination of the monopoly product will be governed by the elasticity of demand.

- **Wage determination** : The concept of elasticity of demand is employed in wage determination. Wages, in modern days, are determined through the process of collective bargaining. Trade union will be successful in raising the wage rate provided labour demand is deemed to be inelastic. This is because of the fact that the degree of substitution between labour and other labour-substituting inputs is less. Trade union becomes cautious in demanding higher wage rates when demand for labour is said to be elastic. Under the circumstance, employer may be forced to employ more machines (assumed to be a cheaper input) than labour.

Anyway, this concept may be employed in analysing the problems connected with changes in the conditions of supply. Economists are interested in knowing the effect on employment in the software industry following a rise in the wages of workers engaged in this industry. We can answer this question in terms of Fig. 3.25.

Here DD is the rather inelastic demand curve whereas demand curve D_1D_1 is an elastic one. Both these demand curves intersect the supply curve, SS, at point E. Thus, the equilibrium price is OP and equilibrium quantity demanded and supplied is OC.

Let there be an increase in wages of workers in the computer industry. Consequently, supply curve for computer will shift left to S_1S_1 and price will rise to OP_2 if demand curve is assumed to be DD and to OP_1 if demand curve is D_1D_1. However, output contracts more in the case of

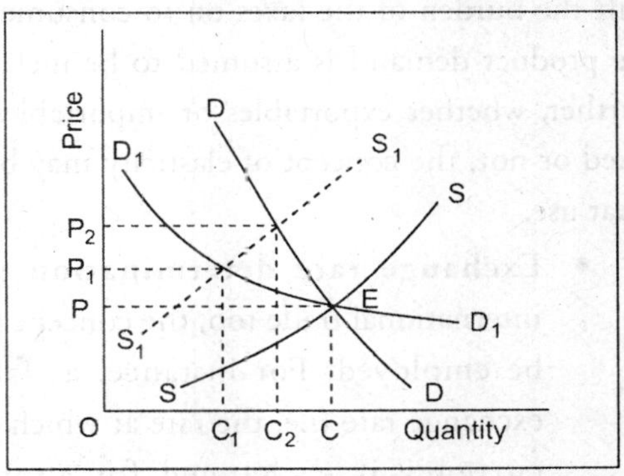

Fig. 3.25 : Demand for and Supply of Comptuer

elastic demand (from OC to OC_1). If demand is inelastic, output will shrink less (from OC to OC_2).

"The general rule is that where demand is elastic, a change in supply will cause the quantity sold to change rather than price; where demand is inelastic, price changes rather than the quantity sold. Thus a trade union will find it more difficult to obtain a wage increase for its members without creating unemployment where the elasticity of demand for the product made is high." *(Jack Harvey's Modern Economics)*

- **Policy determination:** The concept of elasticity of demand is of great importance to a Finance Minister. While imposing tax or raising the existing tax rates, the Finance Minister must have a sufficient knowledge of the elasticity of demand for the taxed commodity. If the demand for the product is inelastic, the purpose of the tax, i.e., revenue-earning, will be served. That is why taxes are mostly imposed or rates of taxes are raised in the case of inelastic demand.

Again, the concept may be used in the determination of incidence of a tax. It is easier to shift the burden of the taxes on to consumers if the product demand is assumed to be inelastic. Further, whether exportables or importables be taxed or not, the concept of elasticity may be of great use.

- **Exchange rate determination** : In international trade too, the concept may be employed. For instance, as far as exchange rate (i.e, the rate at which one currency is exchanged for another currency) determination is concerned, the concept of elasticity of demand is of great importance. The concept of elasticity of demand is used to justify whether devaluation of a currency is a right step in curing balance of payment problems of a country. Devaluation is expected to correct the balance of payments disequilibrium if the sum of the elasticities of demand for export and import exceed unity.

In international trade theory, within the limits set by the comparative costs, the terms of trade will also depend on the elasticity of demand of each country for the goods of other countries.

In fine, elasticity of demand is a concept which has much applicability as far as business decision-making is concerned and is, therefore, of much importance in modern economics. In fact, most businessmen should try to form as precise an idea of elasticity as possible. The concept of elasticity of demand is useful in business decision-making because "it is a convenient shorthand way of expressing the effects of price change on demand for a commodity and as such it is relevant to price fixing."

3.12. SUPPLY

Supply is the quantity of a good which is offered for sale at a given price at a particular time. "The amount of a product that firms are able and willing to offer for sale is called the quantity supplied."

Supply is a desired flow. It measures how much firms are willing to sell and not how much they actually sell. It is to be remembered that the firms may not supply the entire amount of a commodity that they produce per period of time. Supply may exceed or fall short of production. Supply in a particular year is the total production plus-minus stocks of the commodity.

3.12.1. Law of Supply and the Supply Curve

The functional relationship between price and quantity supplied presented in mathematical language is usually expressed in the following way :

$$\underset{\downarrow}{\overset{\uparrow}{S}}_X = f\left(\underset{\downarrow}{\overset{\uparrow}{P}}_X\right), \textit{ceteris paribus}$$

where S_X is the supply of good X and P_X is the price of good X, holding other variables constant. There exists a direct or positive relationship between price and quantity supplied. The law of supply states that, *ceteris paribus,* as the price of a commodity rises (falls), its supply rises (falls).

When this price-quantity relationship is plotted on a graph we get a supply curve that slopes upwards.

- **The Supply Curve** : Thus, the law of supply can be explained by drawing a supply curve for a commodity. To do this, we now illustrate the relationship between price and quantity supplied with hypothetical data for a producer of good X. The data can be presented either in the form of a schedule or a graph. Table 3.7 shows the supply schedule of good X.

Table 3.7 : A Producer's Supply Schedule of X

Reference point	Price (Rs. per kg)	Quantity supplied (in kg)
t	4	0
u	8	30
v	12	60
w	16	90
x	20	120
y	24	150
z	28	180

The supply schedule shows the relationship between quantity supplied and price. It is a numerical tabulation that lists some prices and shows the quantity that will be offered for sale at each price. Our supply schedule suggests that nothing would be offered for sale when price is Rs. 4 per kg. If price rises to Rs. 8 per kg, 30 kg will be supplied. If price rises to Rs. 12, 60 kg will be supplied, and so forth. Each price-quantity combination is shown by a reference letter such as t, u, v, etc. for the sake of convenience.

The data presented in Table 3.7 can be presented in the form of a graph as in Fig. 3.26. Both Table 3.7 and Fig 3.26 give the same information. In fact, Fig 3.26 is a graphical representation of Table 3.7. Note that supply curve is a graph of the supply schedule.

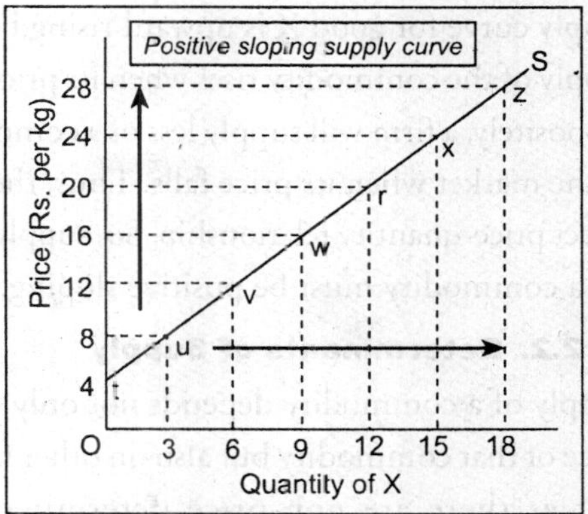

Fig. 3.26 : Supply Curve

The supply curve does not start from the origin. It starts from point t. In other words, the supply curve has positive intercept. It cuts the vertical axis at a positive price. The implication is that there must exist a positive price for any quantity of a commodity to be offered at all. If price is less than this nothing will be offered for sale. In this context Alfred Marshall referred to the reservation price of a commodity. In Fig 3.26 a price greater than Rs. 4 per kg is essential to produce and offer any output of X. If price were less than Rs. 4 per kg the minimum cost per unit could not be covered and output (quantity supplied) would be zero.

The smooth line through points t to z is the producer's supply curve. Like the demand curve, it is also the locus of alternative price-quantity combinations. It shows the different quantities offered for sale at seven different prices as also at all intermediate prices. For example, from Fig. 3.26 we can find out how much will be offered for sale at a price of Rs. 22 per kg. All we have to do is to locate the price on the vertical axis, draw a horizontal line from this point which cuts the supply curve at a particular point and then draw a perpendicular from that point. This point here indicates that when price is Rs. 22 per kg, the quantity offered for sale is 135 kg. Note that the supply curve for good X is upward rising because supply of the commodity rises when its price rises. Oppositely, a firm will supply less of a commodity in the market when its price falls. Thus, there is a direct price-quantity relationship. So, supply curve for a commodity must be positive sloping.

3.12.2. Determinants of Supply

Supply of a commodity depends not only on the price of that commodity but also on other factors. Just as there are non-price determinants of demand, there are non-price determinants of supply. Thus the supply function may now be expressed as

$S_X = f(P_X, P_a \ldots P_C, P_L \ldots P_0, T, S_t\, O, G)$

$P_X \rightarrow$ own price of good x,

$P_a \ldots\ldots P_C$ prices of related goods,

$P_L \ldots P_0$ prices of inputs,

$T \rightarrow$ time

$S_t \rightarrow$ the state of technology,

$O \rightarrow$ objectives of the firm,

$G \rightarrow$ taxes, subsidies and regulation.

Now, we will explain all these determinants of supply in brief.

- **Own price, $S_X = f(P_X)$** : *First,* the most important factor that influences the supply of a commodity is its own price. And the relationship between supply and own price is a direct one.

- **Prices of related goods, $S_X = f(P_a \ldots P_C)$:** *Secondly,* supply of any commodity largely depends not only on own price of the commodity but also on the prices of its substitute and complementary goods. If market price of wheat rises, the jute farmers would be interested in wheat production so that in the next season they can increase the supply of wheat. On the other hand, in the case of joint product, a rise in the market price of mutton will increase the quantity of leather supplied.

- **Prices of inputs, $S_X = f(P_X \ldots P_0)$:** *Thirdly,* price of inputs is also an important determinant of supply. If the price of an input (say, wage bill) rises, the cost of production will surely increase. Consequently, profit will tend to decline. Seeing an unprofitable situation, a firm will reduce the supply of a commodity and will try to switch to the production of another commodity which is still not unprofitable.

- **Time, $S_X = f(T)$:** *Fourthly,* in the short run usually the supply of a commodity (mainly perishable good) is unresponsive to price change. But in the long run, the supply of a commodity tends to be more flexible or fluctuating in response to the changing situation. For non-reproducible goods, the supply becomes highly inelastic.

One can now suggest that the supply of a commodity also depends on its nature. For instance, the supply of non-perishable goods responds more than the perishable goods when their prices change.

- **Technology, $S_X = f(S_t)$:** *Fifthly,* the state of art or the technology has an important bearing on the supply of a commodity. As newer and modern technologies are employed in a concern, production and costs of production tend to rise. This results in a change in quantity supplied.

- **Firm's objectives, $S_X = f(O)$** : *Sixthly,* the nature of a firm's objectives also affect the supply decisions. Firms can have different goals. Usually, profit maximisation is the most fundamental objective of a firm. Modern business firms aim at maximisation of sales revenue rather than profit. Supply of a commodity under these two broad objectives is likely to be different. Thus, the supply

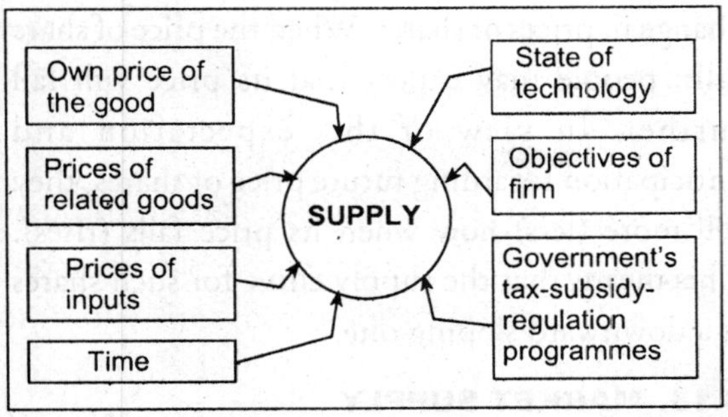

Fig. 3.27 : Determinants of Supply

of a commodity depends on the goals or objectives of a firm. Changes in these objectives of the firms will lead to a change in quantity supplied.

- **Government policy, $S_X = f(G)$:** *Finally*, by imposing taxes on firms, the government can affect the supply of a commodity. The government may ask business firms to pay taxes for polluting the atmosphere or for meeting government services on education, health, etc. As these taxes increase costs, firms reduce supplies. Similarly, subsidies may be given to firms so that they can produce goods needed by the society. Often new firms are encouraged to produce some goods (e.g., software) by giving subsidies to these goods or by reducing taxes. Further, government may use its regulatory device (e.g., industrial licensing) to control the activities of business firm. This affects supply.

All these determinants of supply have been represented in a diagrammatic form (Fig. 3.27).

3.12.3. Why is Supply Curve Upward Sloping?

The law of supply expresses the relationship between the price of a commodity and its quantity supplied. The relationship between price and quantity supplied is a positive one. As price rises, supply rises. Thus, the law of supply can be stated in the following way : Other things remaining the same, the quantity of any commodity that firms will produce and offer for sale is directly related to the own price of the commodity; lower (higher) is the price, the lesser (larger) is the quantity supplied. Thus, the supply curve will slope upwards.

The supply curve is usually positive sloping because of the following reasons :

First, the supply curve is positive sloping due to the operation of the law of diminishing marginal returns or law of increasing cost. If we increase variable inputs beyond certain point, their marginal productivity will tend to decline while costs of employing more and more inputs will tend to rise. Under the circumstance, unless prices are not increased, sellers will not be interested in offering their products in the market for sale. Thus, at a high price, a larger quantity is supplied.

Secondly, producers produce with the hope of getting maximum profit. When price rises, profit per unit of the commodity sold becomes larger. As production becomes profitable, more production and, hence, more of that is supplied in the market. As profit becomes lower at a low price, supply of the commodity tends to become low.

3.12.4. Exceptions to the Law of Supply

However, there are certain exceptions to the law of supply. Following exceptions are worth mentioning in this context :

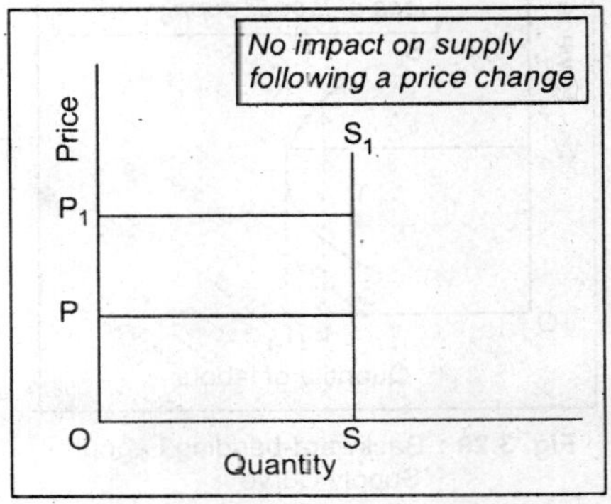

Fig. 3.28 : Vertical Supply Curve

First, the supply curve of rare goods (such as the art work of a dead painter) or non-reproducible goods is a vertical straight line. An unchanged quantity is offered for sale at all possible prices. In this case, the supply curve becomes perfectly inelastic. Land is also completely inelastic in supply. This is shown in Fig. 3.28. SS_1 supply curve shows that whatever the price of the commodity or land (even if it is zero), supply of the commodity or land is always OS.

Secondly, the law of supply breaks down in the case of labour supply curve. In Fig. 3.29, labour supply curve is backward bending due to the operation of income effect and substitution effect of wage rate changes. Below the wage rate OW_1, as wage rate rises supply of labour tends to rise. Here substitution effect is stronger than income effect. But beyond OW_1 wage rate, any rise in it will cause labour to work less and will induce him to take more leisure. Thus, income effect becomes stronger than the substitution effect. As a result, the supply curve of labour becomes backward bending.

Thirdly, if firms anticipate that the product prices will fall much in the near future, they will sell more now just to clear their stocks of goods. Such possibility may arise in the short run.

Finally, the supply curve may be negative sloping in the share market. As share market is characterised by uncertainty, people anticipate the change in prices of shares. When the price of share falls, people may expect that its price will fall further. In view of this expectation and anticipation regarding future price of shares, they sell more (less) now when its price falls (rises). This means that the supply curve for such shares is a downward sloping one.

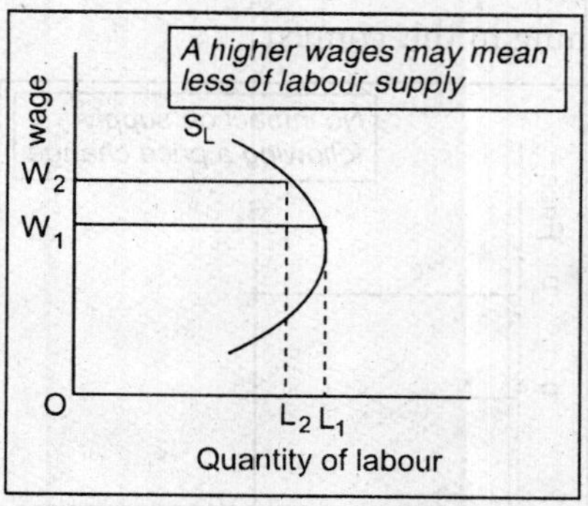

Fig. 3.29 : Backward-bending Labour Supply Curve

3.13. MARKET SUPPLY

To get total or market supply, we have to add the supplies of all the producers of a product. Thus, the market supply of a good is the sum of quantities of that good that individual firms are willing to offer for sale at a given time period. Suppose there are two producers of X in an area, viz. A and B. Both of them supply at the same point of time.

We show the supply schedule and the supply curve of the first producer, i.e., A, in Table 3.7 and Fig. 3.26. These are reproduced in Table 3.8 and Fig. 3.30. But Table 3.8 and Fig. 3.30 contain additional information. In Table 3.8, we also show the supply schedule of another producer, viz. B. Similarly, in Fig. 3.30 we draw the supply curve of B. Here we assume that the minimum price at which B can offer a positive quantity (i.e., Rs. 8) is higher than required by A (i.e., Rs. 4).

Table 3.8 : Individual and Market Supply Schedules

Price (Rs. per kg)	QUANTITIES SUPPLIED		
	Producer A (kg per month)	Producer B (kg per month)	Market Supply (kg per month) (ii + iii)
(i)	(ii)	(iii)	(iv)
4	0	0	0
8	30	0	30
12	60	15	75
16	90	30	120
20	120	45	165

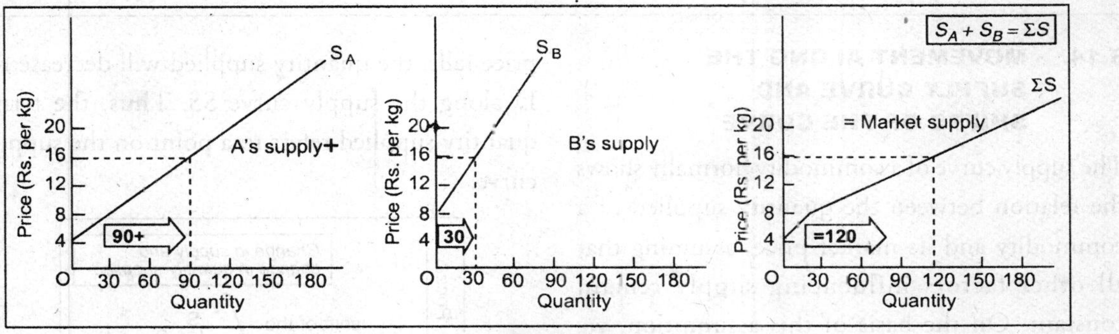

Fig. 3.30 : Derivation of a Market Supply Curve

The market supply is derived simply by adding the quantities supplied at each price by the two producers. Thus, we see that when the market price of X is Rs. 8, producer A offers a positive quantity (viz., 30 kg), but producer B offers nothing. So market supply is the same as individual supply (i.e., the amount offered by producer A). Producer B is less efficient than producer A, i.e., B's cost per unit is higher than that of A. So at this low price (Rs. 8 per kg) producer B is not willing to offer good X for sale in the market. However, as price rises to Rs. 12 per kg, producer A offers 60 kg and producer B, 15 kg. Market supply is, therefore, 75(= 60 + 15) kg. At each price the market supply is the sum of the quantities offered by A and B as Table 3.8 indicates.

The market supply curve, shown in Fig. 3.30, is arrived at by adding up the supply curves of the two producers. (It would, however, be obtained straightway by plotting the information contained in columns (i) and (iv) in Table 3.8). S_A is the supply curve of producer A and S_B is that of B. Both these curves are upward rising. Thus, the market supply curvè is the horizontal addition of the individual supply curve. Thus, when the market price is Rs. 16 per kg, the market supply is 120 kg, which is the sum of supplies of 90 kg and 30 kg of the two producers, respectively. If we repeat the same exercise for other prices we get a number of points. The locus of all such points is the market supply curve 'ΣS'. If we assume that there are 100 producers of X and all are alike in all respects then each of them would offer the same quantity at all possible prices. In this case the market supply curve would be a 100-fold extension of a single firm's supply curve. Like the supply curve of an individual firm, the market supply curve also slopes upward from left to the right.

To sum up, the supply of any commodity per given period of time at any given price depends on the cost incurred in producing it. It may be noted that both the individual firms and the industry, as a whole, will be influenced by changes in prices. In the industry, if price increases, this will increase the level of profit. Consequently, new firms will enter the industry while existing firms will increase their own outputs. On the other hand, if price falls we would expect firms to supply less of a commodity.

Once we understand this relationship between price and the quantity supplied, our first law of supply becomes reasonably obvious. It states that more will tend to be supplied at a higher price than at a lower price and this generalisation is demonstrated by an upward sloping supply curve.

3.14. MOVEMENT ALONG THE SUPPLY CURVE AND SHIFTS OF THE CURVE

The supply curve of a commodity normally shows the relation between the quantity supplied of a commodity and its market price, assuming that all other factors influencing supply remain constant. On the basis of this assumption, we consider movement along the same supply curve from left to right (or from right to left). But, in practice, we observe that other factors do not remain constant over time. If there is a change in another variable, holding own price constant, the whole supply curve will shift to a new position. So economists find it necessary to draw a distinction between a movement along the supply curve and a shift of the entire curve.

A movement along the same curve implies that a larger (smaller) quantity of a commodity is being supplied at a lower (higher) price. Such movements imply that different quantities are being offered for sale at different prices, *ceteris paribus*. Thus, if all the determinants of supply, except the own price of the commodity, remain constant then we have a change in quantity supplied. This is also called movement along the same supply curve caused by a change in the product's own price, Symbolically

$$S_X = f(P_X, \bar{P}_a \ldots\ldots \bar{P}_C, \bar{P}_L \ldots\ldots \bar{P}_O, \bar{T}, \bar{S}_t, \bar{O}, \bar{G})$$

The bar signs over heads of all the variables, except P_X , indicates that those variables are constant.

A movement along a supply curve occurs when a change in own price of a commodity causes a change in the quantity supplied. This may be explained in terms of Fig. 3.31. At the price OP, let PA be the supply of a commodity. If price rises, the quantity supplied will increase to M and, if price falls, the quantity supplied will decrease to D along the supply curve SS. Thus, the term quantity supplied refers to a point on the supply curve.

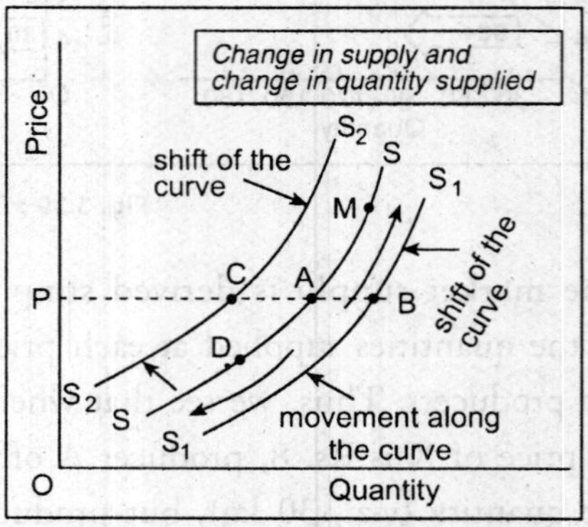

Fig. 3.31 : Shifts of the Supply Curve

On the other hand, there occurs a shift in supply when any of the determinants of supply, except the own price, i.e. non-price determinants, changes. This means that the supply curve shifts bodily due to a change in something other than the product price. Symbolically,

$$S_X = f(\bar{P}_X, P_a \ldots\ldots P_C, P_L \ldots\ldots P_O, T, S_t, O, G)$$

Here P_X is fixed.

A shift of the supply curve implies that a different quantity is being offered for sale at a particular given price, as Fig. 3.31 shows. As the supply curve shifts from SS to S_1S_1 the quantity offered for sale at price OP goes up from PA to PB. Such shifts occur due to changes in one or more of the *ceteris paribus* assumptions and are known as changes in the conditions of supply.

If one of the determinants of supply—except own price—change, the supply curve may shift backward or forward. At a price OP, the quantity supplied is PA. Now, if taxes are imposed on the article, the supply curve will shift from SS to S_2S_2, thereby reducing supply from PA to PC, even price of the good in question is kept at OP. On the other hand, assume that the price of raw materials declines. This causes SS curve to shift to the rightward direction to S_1S_1 and the supplier now supplies PB, a larger quantity than PA.

It is interesting at this stage to provide a few illustrations of the causes of shifts of supply curves as also to explain the directions of shifts. Table 3.7 summarises the main causes of such shifts and indicates their direction.

Table 3.9 : THE TERMINOLOGY OF SUPPLY CURVES

Change	Terms Used to Describe the Change
(A) A change in the price of the good causes a MOVEMENT ALONG a supply curve	
1. Price of the good rises.	1. An increase or rise in the quantity supplied.
2. Price of the good falls.	2. A decrease, fall or reduction in the quantity supplied.
(B) A change in any of the other influences causes a SHIFT of a supply curve.	
1. A rise in the price of a substitute product.	1. A rightward, downward or south-easternly shift of the supply curve.
2. A fall in the price of a factor of production.	2. An increase in supply.
3. An improvement in the state of technology (a rise in productivity).	3. An improvement in the conditions of supply
4. A fall in the price of a substitute product.	4. Rightward, downward or north-westernly shift of the supply curve.
5. A rise in the price of a factor of production.	5. A decrease in supply.
6. A deterioration in the state of technology (a fall in productivity).	6. A deterioration in the conditions of supply.
7. A change in objective of a firm : from profit maximisation to sales maximisation.	7. A rightward shift of supply curve.

3.15. ELASTICITY OF SUPPLY

The law of supply indicates the direction of change—if price goes up, supply will increase. But how much supply will rise in response to an increase in price cannot be known from the law of supply. To quantify such change we require the concept of elasticity of supply that measures the extent of quantities supplied in response to a change in price.

Elasticity of supply measures the degree of responsiveness of quantity supplied to a change in own price of the commodity. It is also defined as the percentage change in quantity supplied divided by percentage change in price. It can be calculated by using the following formula :

$$E_S = \frac{\%\text{ change in quantity supplied}}{\%\text{ change in price}}$$

Symbolically,

$$E_S = \frac{\Delta Q}{Q} \div \frac{\Delta P}{P} = \frac{\Delta Q}{\Delta P} \times \frac{P}{Q}$$

Since price and quantity supplied, in usual cases, move in the same direction—the coefficient of E_S is positive.

3.15.1. Types of Elasticity of Supply

For all the commodities, the value of E_S cannot be uniform. For some commodities, the value may be greater than or less than one. Like elasticity of demand, there are five cases of E_S:

- **Elastic supply ($E_S > 1$)** : Supply is said to be elastic when a given percentage change in price leads to a larger change in quantity supplied. Under this situation, the numerical value of E_S will be greater than one but less than infinity. SS_1 curve of Fig.3.32 exhibits the elastic supply.

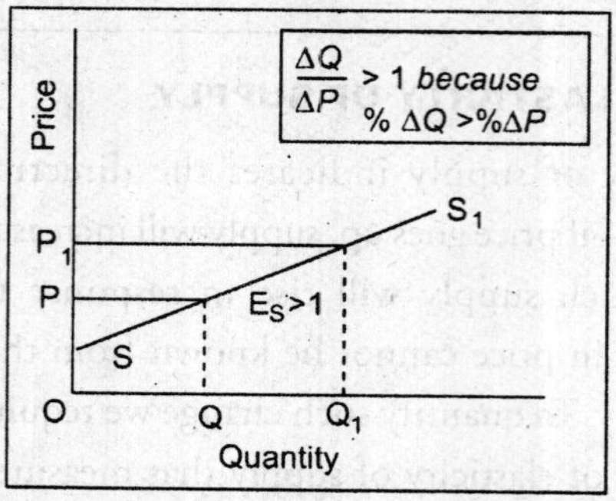

Fig. 3.32 : $E_S > 1$

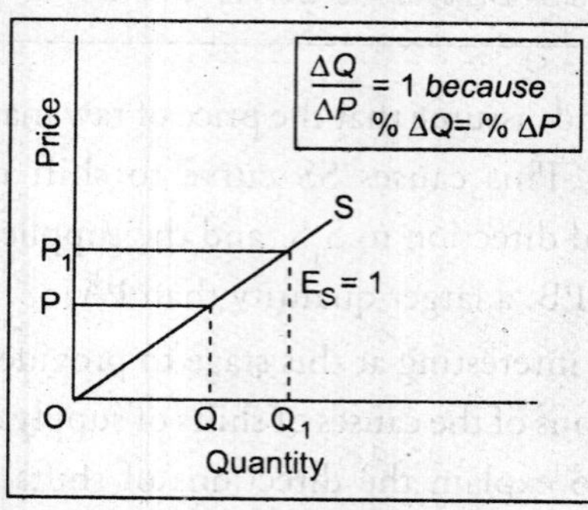

Fig. 3.34 : $E_S = 1$

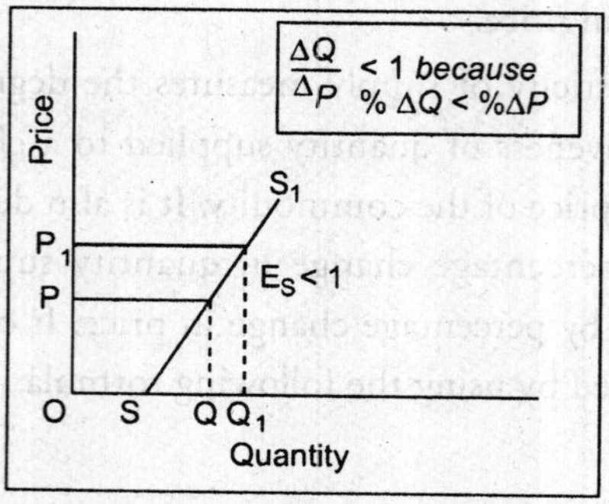

Fig. 3.33 : $E_S < 1$

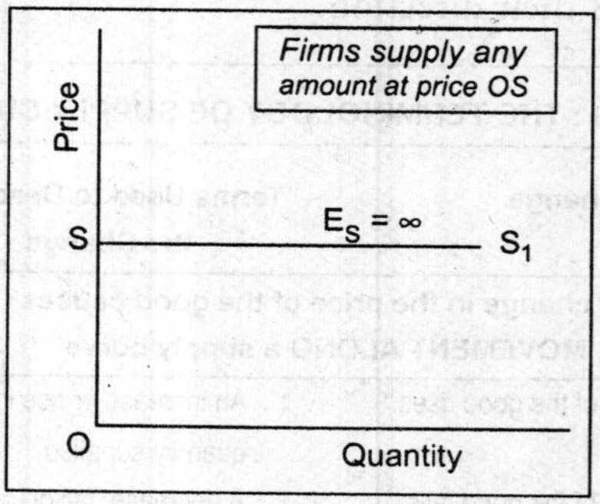

Fig. 3.35 : $E_S \rightarrow \infty$

Here quantity supplied changes by a larger magnitude than does price.

- **Inelastic supply ($E_S < 1$)**: Supply is said to be inelastic when a given percentage change in price causes a smaller change in quantity supplied. Here the numerical value of elasticity of supply is greater than zero but less than one. Fig. 3.33 depicts inelastic supply curve where quantity supplied changes by a smaller percentage than does price.

- **Unitary elasticity of supply ($E_S = 1$)**: If price and quantity supplied change by the same magnitude, then we have unitary elasticity of supply. Any straight line supply curve passing through the origin, such as the one shown in Fig. 3.34, has an elasticity of supply equal to 1. This can be verified in this way. For any straight line positively-sloped supply curve drawn through the origin, the ratio of P/Q at any point on the supply curve is equal to the ratio ΔP/ΔQ. Note that ΔP/ΔQ is the slope of the supply curve while elasticity is $\left(1/\frac{\Delta P}{\Delta Q} = \frac{\Delta Q}{\Delta P}\right)$.

Thus, in the formula $\left(\frac{\Delta Q}{\Delta P} \cdot \frac{P}{Q}\right)$, the two ratios cancel out each other.

- **Perfectly elastic supply ($E_S = \infty$)**: The numerical value of elasticity of supply, in exceptional cases, may reach up to infinity (∞).

The supply curve SS_1 drawn inFig. 3.35 has an elasticity of supply equal to infinity. Here the supply curve has been drawn parallel to the horizontal axis. The economic interpretation of this supply curve is that an unlimited quantity will be offered for sale at the price OS. If price slightly drops down below OS, nothing will be supplied.

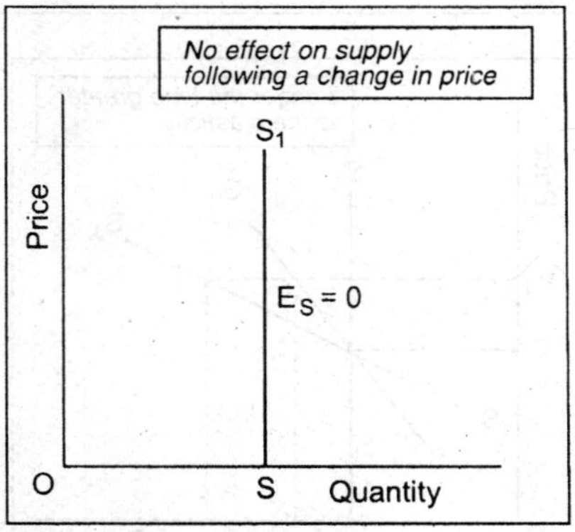

Fig. 3.36 : $E_S = 0$

• **Perfectly inelastic supply ($E_S = 0$)** : Another extreme is the completely or perfectly inelastic supply or zero elasticity. SS_1 curve drawn in Fig. 3.36 illustrates the case of zero elasticity. This curve shows that, whatever the price of the commodity—it may even be zero, the quantity supplied remains unchanged at OS. This sort of supply curve is conceived when we consider the supply curve of land from the viewpoint of a country, or the world, as a whole.

One important point to note here. Any straight line supply curve that intersects the vertical axis above the origin has an elasticity of supply greater than one (Fig. 3.32). Elasticity of supply will be less than one if the straight line supply curve cuts the horizontal axis on any point to the right of the origin, i.e., the quantity axis (Fig. 3.33).

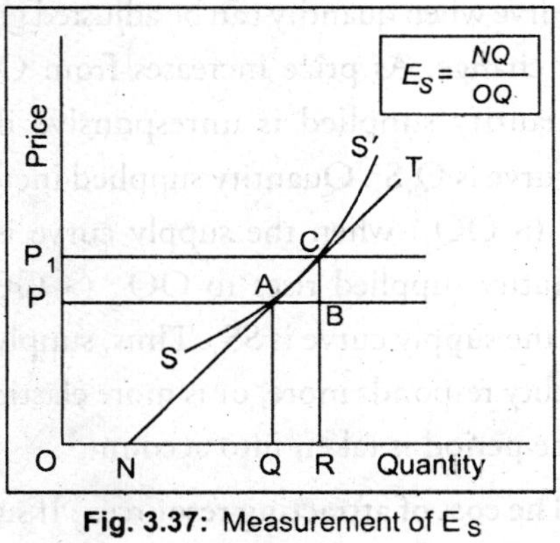

Fig. 3.37: Measurement of E_S

3.16. MEASUREMENT OF ELASTICITY OF SUPPLY

Here we will measure the elasticity of supply at a particular point on a given supply curve. This is shown in Fig. 3.37 where SS′ is the supply curve. To measure the elasticity of supply at a particular point on the curve SS′, we have drawn a straight line NT in such a way that it touches SS′ curve at points A and C. As these two points lie very close to each other, the slope of the supply curve as well as the slope of the NT line are the same. Following is the formula :

$$E_S = \frac{\Delta Q}{\Delta P} \cdot \frac{P}{Q} = \frac{AB}{BC} \times \frac{QA}{OQ}$$

Triangles ABC and NQA are similar triangles.

Thus, we can write $\frac{NQ}{QA}$ instead of $\frac{AB}{BC}$.

Therefore,

$$E_S = \frac{NQ}{QA} \times \frac{QA}{OQ} = \frac{NQ}{OQ}$$

As the figure suggests NQ<OQ, the coefficient of elasticity of supply is less than one, i.e., inelastic.

If the NT straight line passes through the origin, the elasticity of supply becomes unity, and if it passes through the price or vertical axis, the coefficient will be greater than one, i.e., elastic.

3.16.1. Determinants of Elasticity of Supply

Here we are concerned with certain factors which affect elasticity of supply, viz., the nature of the good, the definition of the good, the relevance of the time period, and so on.

• **The nature of the good :** As with demand elasticity, the most important determinant of elasticity of supply is the availability of substitutes. In the context of supply, substitute goods are those to which factors of production can most easily be transferred. For example, a farmer can easily move from growing wheat to producing jute. Of course, mobility of factors is very important for such substitution. As a general rule, the more easily the factors can be transferred from the production of one good to that of another, the greater will be the elasticity of supply.

Further, since durable goods can be stored for a long time, its elasticity of supply is very high. But for non-durable goods and persishable goods elasticity of supply tends to be less.

• **The definition of the commodity :** As in the case of demand, elasticity of supply also depends on the definition of the commodity. The more narrowly a commodity is defined, the greater is its elasticity of supply. For example, it is easier for a tailor to transfer resources from producing red skirts to green skirts than from skirts to men's trousers.

• **Time:** Time also exerts considerable influence on the elasticity of supply. Supply is more elastic in the long run than in the short run. The reason is easy to find out. The longer the time period, the easier it is to shift resources among products, following a change in their relative prices. This is usually true in case of most agricultural commodities, because of the natural time lag between planting and harvesting of crops. In agriculture, production plans have to be made months or even years ahead and they cannot be altered quickly.

Manufacturing industries, on the other hand, can usually adjust their output upwards or downwards fairly quickly in response to changing conditions in the market. Extractive industries come somewhere between the two : various types of mining, oil production and forestry can only alter their production plans slowly and, therefore, at any given time, have relative inelastic supply conditions.

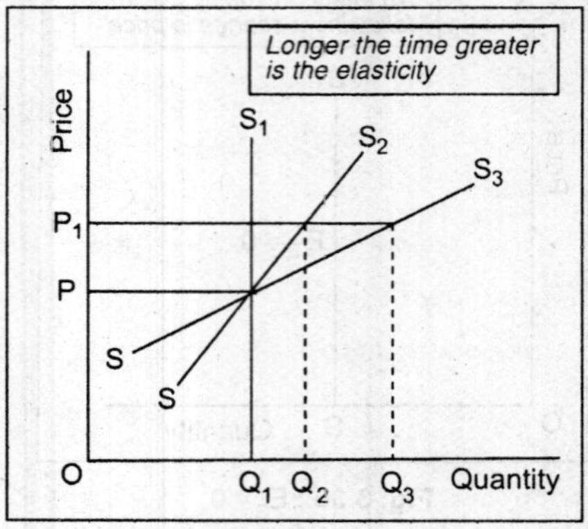

Fig. 3.38 : Elasticity and Time

Fig. 3.38 shows how time influences supply of a commodity. If a very short period or momentary period is considered, the supply curve will be perfectly inelastic (Q_1S_1 curve), where quantity supplied does not change, even if price changes. In the short run, some degree of elasticity is found since supply can be adjusted to price change (SS_2 curve). SS_3 curve is a rather long run supply curve when quantity can be adjusted greatly to price change. As price increases from OP to OP_1, quantity supplied is unresponsive if the supply curve is Q_1S_1. Quantity supplied increases to OQ_2 (> OQ_1) when the supply curve is SS_2 and quantity supplied rises to OQ_3 (> OQ_2 > OQ_1) if the supply curve is SS_3. Thus, supply of a commodity responds more, or is more elastic, if a long time period is taken into account.

• **The cost of attracting resources :** If supply is to be increased it is necessary to attract resources from other industries. This usually involves raising the prices of these resources. As their prices rise, cost of production also increases. So supply becomes relatively inelastic. If these resources can be obtained cheaply then supply is likely to be relatively elastic. These considerations become very important at times of full employment when the only available factors of production are those which can be attracted from other industries and uses.

- **The level of price** : Elasticity of supply is also likely to vary at different prices. Thus, when the price of a commodity is relatively high, the producers are likely to be supplying near the limits of their capacity and would, therefore, be unable to make much response to a still higher price. When the price is relatively low, however, producers may well have surplus capacity which a higher price would induce them to use.

3.17. PRICE DETERMINATION

Here we will see how the interaction of demand and supply forces determine equilibrium price in a perfectly competitive market or industry. By equilibrium we mean a state of balance in which two opposing forces come into operation. An equilibrium is a state of rest from which there is no tendency to change the system. Market equilibrium occurs where demand and supply balance each other—there is no difference between these two opposing forces and, hence, these are at rest.

Fig. 3.39 shows the normal-shaped market demand and market supply curves. When the demand curve DD and supply curve SS intersect we obtain equilibrium price and equilibrium quantity. Equilibrium price is OP* and equilibrium quantity is OQ*. At this price, the amount that the sellers are willing to sell in the market is exactly matched by the amount that the buyers are willing to buy. At this price, both the parties are satisfied. Neither buyer nor seller is willing to disturb this situation.

The equilibrium price OP* — defined by the intersection of demand and supply curves — is also called the "market-clearing price", since at this price, excess supply and excess demand are zero. This can be explained in the following way. If price is higher than OP*, say OP_1, buyers are willing to buy P_1M, while sellers are willing to sell a large quantity P_1N. Thus, there is an excess supply or temporary surplus to the tune of MN in the market. Sellers are dissatisfied. As a result, there will be downward pressure on price (following competition among sellers). Price will continue to decline until OP* is reached. Similarly, at a price lower than OP*, say OP_2, there occurs an excess demand or temporary shortage in the market to the extent of HF. Here buyers are dissatisfied. Now competition among buyers will lead to an upward pressure in price. It will rise till OP* is reached. Thus, OP* is equilibrium price or market-clearing price. Or all other prices except OP* are disequilibrium prices.

It is to be kept in mind that a market economy does not require economists or any government agencies or producers and consumers to clear the market.

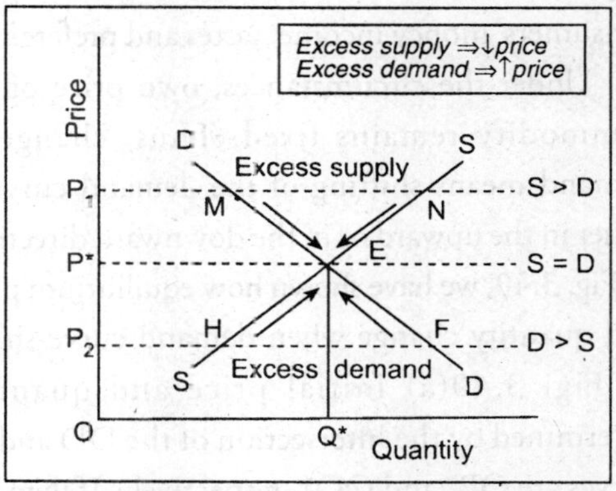

Fig. 3.39: Equilibrium in a Competitive Market

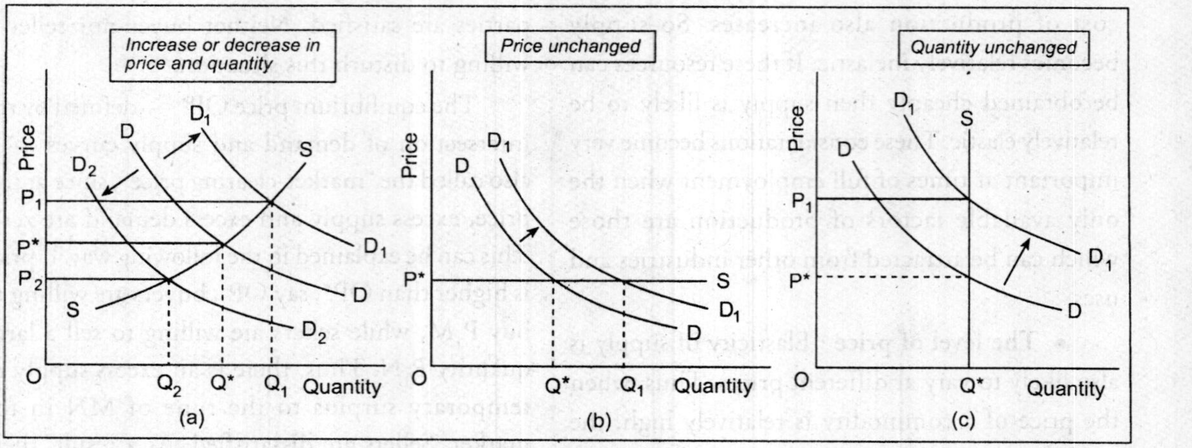

Fig. 3.40: Change in Equilibrium : Change in Demand

3.17.1. Change in Equilibrium Price-Quantity

Under perfect competition, equilibrium occurs at that point where demand equals supply. That does not mean that this equilibrium price will rule for all the time. In fact, equilibrium situation will undergo a change if there is a change in demand or a change in supply. Here we will exanine the effects of changes in demand and supply on the equilibrium price and quantity. By changes in demand and supply we mean shifting of the demand and the supply curves, respectively.

• **Change in Demand** : Change in demand implies increase in demand following a change in consumers' money income, tastes and preferences, etc. Under the circumstances, own price of the commodity remains fixed. Thus, change in demand means shifting of the demand curve—either in the upward or in the downward direction. In Fig. 3.40, we have shown how equilibrium price and quantity change when demand curve shifts. In Fig. 3.40(a) initial price and quantity determined by the intersection of the DD and SS curves are OP* and OQ*, respectively. If demand increases, the demand curve will shift to D_1D_1 and the new equilibrium price will rise to OP_1 and quantity demanded and supplied will increase to OQ_1. Similarly, when the demand curve shifts downward to D_2D_2, prices and quantity decline to OP_2 and OQ_2, respectively.

In Fig. 3.40(b), the supply curve has been assumed to be perfectly elastic. Initial equilibrium price and quantity are represented by OP* and OQ*, respectively. Now, an increase or decrease in demand will not cause equilibrium price (OP*) to change. An increase in demand will only cause the equilibrium quantity to rise to OQ_1.

If the supply curve is drawn perfectly inelastic as in Fig. 3.40(c), an increase in demand will cause price to rise to OP_1. The equilibrium quantity will remain the same (OQ*).

• **Change in Supply** : By change in supply, we mean shifting of the supply curve. If supply increases (or decreases), the supply curve will shift rightward (or leftward). In Fig. 3.41(a), OP* is the initial equilibrium price and OQ* the equilibrium quantity. Now, suppose supply increases and the new supply curve S_1S_1 intersects the demand curve. As a result, equilibrium price drops to OP_1 and the equilibrium quantity

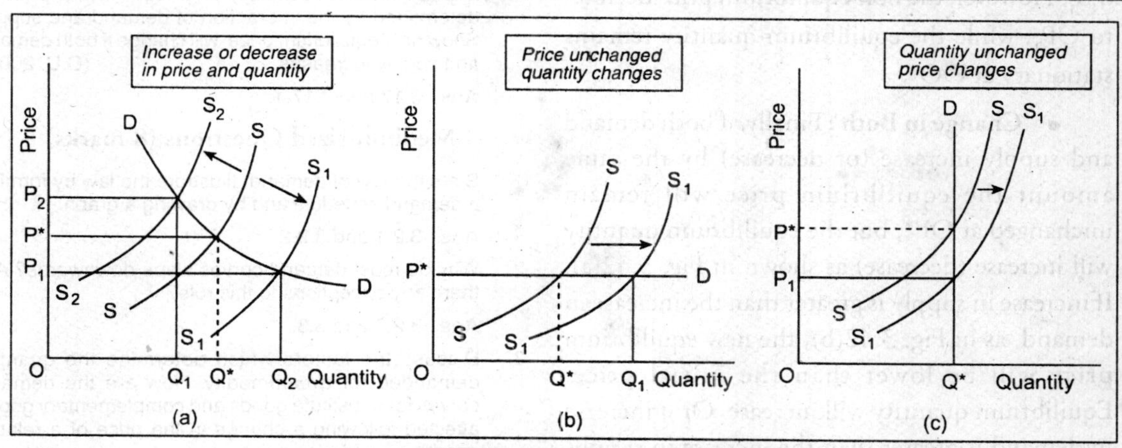

Fig. 3.41: Change in Equilibrium : Change in Supply

demanded and supplied increases to OQ_2. Similarly, a fall in supply results in an opposite effect.

In Fig. 3.41(b) intersection between perfectly the elastic demand curve and the SS supply curve determines equilibrium price OP* and equilibrium quantity OQ*. As supply increases, the supply curve shifts to S_1S_1. As a result, equilibrium quantity rises to OQ_1, but the equilibrium price remains unchanged at OP*. In Fig. 3.41(c), a perfectly inelastic demand curve has been drawn. Initial equilibrium price and quantity are OP* and OQ*, respectively. Increase in supply means shifting of the supply curve to

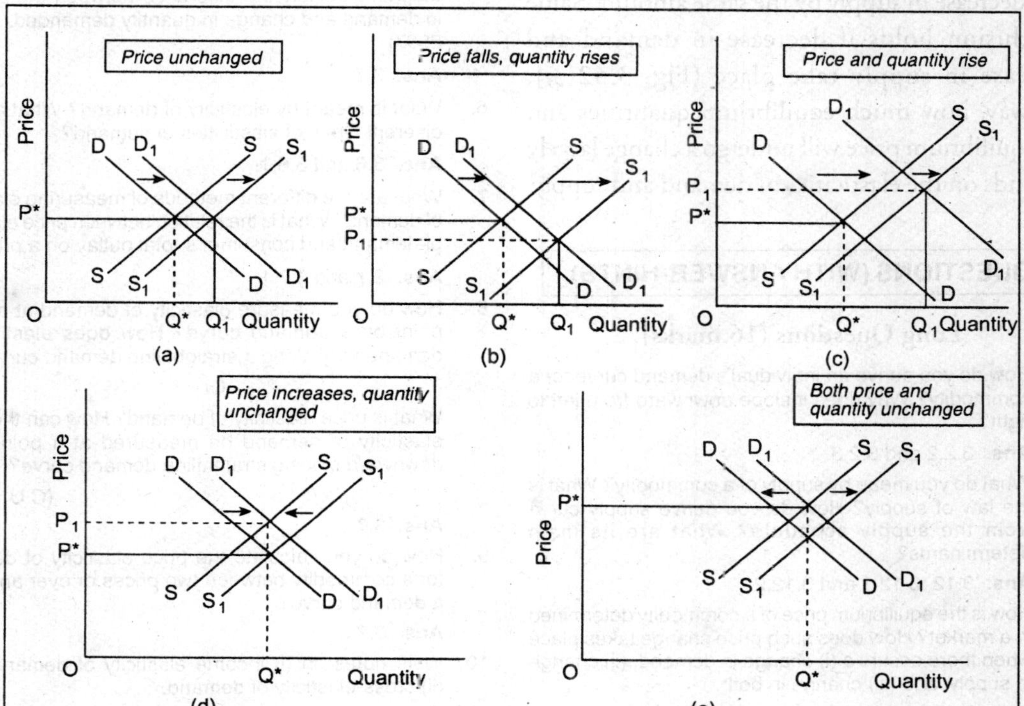

Fig. 3.42: Change in Equilibrium : Change in Both

S_1S_1. However, the new equilibrium price declines to OP_1, while the equilibrium quantity remains stationary at OQ*.

• **Change in Both :** Finally, if both demand and supply increase (or decrease) by the same amount the equilibrium price will remain unchanged at OP*, but the equilibrium quantity will increase (decrease) as shown in Fig. 3.42(a). If increase in supply is greater than the increase in demand, as in Fig. 3.42(b), the new equilibrium price will be lower than the initial price. Equilibrium quantity will increase. Or if increase in demand is greater than the increase in supply, as in Fig. 3.42(c), the equilibrium price and the equilibrium quantity will be higher than the initial situation.

Increase in demand and decrease in supply will lead to an increase in price [Fig. 3.42(d)], but the equilibrium quantity may increase or decrease. However, the equilibrium quantity will remain unchanged at OQ* if increase in demand is offset by a decrease in supply by the same amount. Same conclusion holds if decrease in demand and increase in supply take place (Fig. 3.42(e)]. Anyway, how much equilibrium quantities and the equilibrium price will undergo a change largely depends on the elasticities of demand and supply.

QUESTIONS (WITH ANSWER-HINTS)

Long Questions (16 marks)

1. How do you derive an individual's demand curve for a commodity? Why does it slope downward from left to right?

   Ans. 3.2.2 and 3.2.3.

2. What do you mean by supply of a commodity? What is the law of supply? How do you derive supply curve from the supply schedule? What are its main determinants?

   Ans. 3.12, 3.12.1 and 3.12.2.

3. How is the equilibrium price of a commocity determined in a market? How does such price change takes place when there occurs a (i) change in demand, (ii) change in supply, and (iii) change in both.

   Ans. 3.17 and 3.17.1.

4. Explain diagrammatically how equilibrium price is determined by the interaction of demand and supply. Show how equilibrium price will change if both demand and supply increases (C.U. 2008)

   Ans. 3.17 and 3.17.1.

Medium-sized Questions (8 marks)

1. State the law of demand. Illustrate the law by forming a demand schedule and by drawing a graph.

   Ans. 3.2.1 and 3.2.2.

2. Why do most demand curves slope downwards? Are there any exceptions to this rule?

   Ans. 3.2.3 and 3.3.

3. Discuss the factors which determine the quantity demanded for a commodity. How are the demand curves for substitute goods and complementary goods affected following a change in the price of a related good?

   Ans. 3.4.

4. Distinguish between individual demand and market demand. How do you derive market demand curve for a commodity?

   Ans. 3.2.4.

5. Distinguish between a change in demand and a change in quantity demanded—noting the causes of each. Illustrate your answer with examples and graph.

   Or

   For what reasons does a demand curve shift? Explain diagrammatically the difference between the change in demand and change in quantity demanded. (C.U. 2007)

   Ans. 3.5.

6. What is meant by elasticity of demand? What are the different types of elasticities of demand?

   Ans. 3.6 and 3.6.1.

7. What are the different methods of measuring elasticity of demand? What is the relation between price elasticity of demand and consumer's total outlay on a product?

   Ans. 3.7 and 3.7.1.

8. How do you measure elasticity of demand at a given point on a demand curve? How does elasticity of demand vary along a straight line demand curve?

   Or

   What is price elasticity of demand? How can the price elasticity of demand be measured at a point on a downward sloping straightline demand curve? (C.U. 2008)

   Ans. 3.7.2.

9. How do you calculate the price elasticity of demand for a commodity between two prices or over an arc of a demand curve?

   Ans. 3.7.3.

10. Write notes on (i) income elasticity of demand, and (ii) cross-elasticity of demand.

    Ans. (i) 3.8 and (ii) 3.9.

11. What is price elasticity of demand? Explain the factors on which elasticity of demand depends.

    Ans. 3.6 and 3.10.

12. Discuss the importance of the concept of elasticity of demand.

    Ans. 3.11.

13. What is the law of supply? Why is supply curve upward rising? Are there any exceptions?

    Ans. 3.12.1 and 3.12.3 and 3.12.4.

14. How do you derive the market supply curve for a commodity?

    Ans. 3.13.

15. Make a distinction between a change in supply and a change in quantity supplied.

    Ans. 3.14.

16. What is elasticity of supply? What are the different types of such elasticity?

    Ans. 3.15 and 3.15.1.

17. What do you mean by elasticity of supply? How do you measure elasticity of supply at a given point of a supply curve? What are the determinants of elasticity of supply?

    Ans. 3.15., 3.16 and 3.16.1.

4

PREFERENCE THEORY OF DEMAND

4.1. INTRODUCTION : CARDINAL AND ORDINAL APPROACHES TO DEMAND ANALYSIS

There are two approaches in economic literature that explain the negative sloping demand curve. *First* is the Marshallian utility or cardinal approach, and *second* is the modern or ordinal approach.

Alfred Marshall (1842-1924)—the great neo-classical economist—refined the utility approach initially developed by W. S. Jevons, K. Menger, and L. Walras independently. Marshall just perfected their analyses.

A consumer consumes a commodity because it has the capacity to satisfy his wants. The term 'utility' refers to this want-satisfying power. According to Marshall, 'utility' obtained from the consumption of a commodity can be measured in cardinal numbers, just as we can measure the day temperature or body temperature. Utility can be measured in cardinal numbers, like 1, 2, 3, etc. Marshall called it 'utils'. Though utility is an abstract as well as subjective concept, its measurement involves complications. In order to avoid complications, Marshall suggested that utility is to be measured cardinally in money terms, i.e., money spent on buying a commodity. Suppose, a consumer buys a commodity at a price of Rs. 10. Thus, his total utility is equal to Rs. 10. Hence the name cardinal approach to demand analysis.

Modern economists like Sir J. R. Hicks and R. G. D. Allen argued in the 1930s that utility, being a psychological concept, can never be measured in cardinal numbers. Utility is intrinsic in character which is not quantifiable. Further, utility varies from person to person. Hence, utility is a relative as well as a subjective concept hardly amenable to measurement. If it can be measured, it can be measured in ordinal numbers, like I, II, III, etc. Different levels of utility derived from the consumption of commodities can only be ranked or ordered. A consumer can only rank or order his preference pattern. He cannot say that commodity A gives utility to the extent of 10 and commodity B to the extent of 12. He can only compare A and B and say that B is preferable to A. But how much utility is obtained from A or from B cannot be quantified by the consumer.

Hence the name ordinal approach to demand analysis.

In explaining his cardinal approach, Marshall used the law of diminishing marginal utility. Modern economists, on the other hand, invented the tool of indifference curve to explain the consumer behaviour.

However, economists are constantly searching a better theory to explain consumer behaviour. A new technique was discovered by P. A. Samuelson in 1939 in this direction. His analysis came to be known as 'revealed preference approach.'

4.2. CARDINAL APPROACH TO DEMAND ANALYSIS

A utility function may be defined as the descriptive statements that relates satisfaction to the consumpion of (private) goods and services. It can be written as

Utility = f (goods, services)

By utility we mean want-satisfying power of a commodity. Such power exists in material things. Anyway, a commodity is demanded because it has utility. Negative sloping demand curve is often explained in terms of utility analysis.

According to Marshall, utility derived from a commodity can be measured in cardinal numbers like 1, 2, 3, etc., just as we can measure the temperature of human body. Marshall intended to measure utility by an imaginary unit called 'util'. Utility is an abstract concept and its units are arbitrary. Further, he suggested the measurement of utility obtained from a commodity in terms of money. When a consumer spends Rs. 5 to buy a kilogram of potato it means his utility equals 5. Hence the name cardinal measurement of utility.

4.3. LAW OF DIMINISHING MARGINAL UTILITY

Total Utility (TU) and Marginal Utility (MU) : Total Utility (TU) refers to the total satisfaction or total benefit derived from the *entire* consumption of a commodity. Normally, greater the volume of consumption, greater is the level of total satisfaction. This means that the total utility function reflects the quantitative relationship between the satisfaction yielded by a good and its rate of consumption. We are assuming that utility is measured in terms of util. Table 4.1 shows the volume of TU obtained by an individual from the consumption of tea. Table 4.1 or utility schedule reflects the taste and preferences of a tea drinker. It tells us that as the consumer drinks more and more cups of tea, his TU rises. For the first cup of tea he gets utility of 20 utils, for the second 38 utils, and so on. However, when the consumer consumes the fifth cup of tea his TU remains unchanged at 70 utils. Drinking of the sixth cup of tea causes a decline in TU.

Table 4.1 : Law of Diminishing Marginal Utility

Number of cups of tea	TU	MU
0	0	
		20 (= 20 – 0)
1	20	
		18 (= 38 – 20)
2	38	
		17 (= 55 – 38)
3	55	
		15 (= 70 – 55)
4	70	
		0 (= 70 – 70)
5	70	
		– 5 (= 65 – 70)
6	65	

Marginal utility (MU) means change in TU following a change in the consumption of the commodity.

$$\text{Marginal utility} = \frac{\text{change in total utility}}{\text{change in the quantity of a good}}$$

MU, thus, is an addition to or subtraction from TU. In other words, MU is the difference in TU arising from a change in the use of the *last* unit of the commodity. Table 4.1 states that an individual gets utility of 55 utils from the third cup and 70 utils from the fourth cup of tea. So his MU becomes 15 utils. Thus, MU for the fourth cup is the difference in TU from the fourth and the third cups of tea. Or MU for the n-th unit of a good is the difference between the TU of the n-th unit and the n-1th unit, i.e., the previous unit :

$$MU_n = TU_n - TU_{n-1}$$

- **Law of Diminishing MU** : One of the fundamental laws relating to the tastes and preferences of the consumer is the law of diminishing MU and not TU. Whenever a particular commodity is consumed, its desiredness, i.e., marginal utility to a consumer, on an average, tends to decline. Marshall called this "familiar and fundamental tendency of human nature". The law can be stated in the following way :

Other things remaining the same (i.e., money income, tastes and preferences, prices of goods, etc. remain unchanged), the more one consumes a commodity, his MU will eventually decline. Or more and more consumption of a commodity will cause MU to decline ultimately. The rate of decline may not be uniform for all commodities. What is true is that the tendency of diminishing MU will ultimately arrive. This law can be stated in Marshall's own words :

"The additional benefit which a person derives from a given increase of a stock of a thing diminishes with every increase in the stock that he already has."

The above table suggests that as consumption of tea rises, TU also rises. Our consumer gets more and more satisfaction as he drinks tea; but his MU gradually declines. When TU is maximum, MU becomes zero (i.e., for the fifth cup of tea). This means extra consumption of tea adds less and less to his TU. In other words, the rate of increase in TU declines. If the consumer decides to drink the sixth cup of tea his TU will fall and MU will become negative. In other words, our consumer, in this situation, gets dissatisfaction or disutility. This tendency of a consumer relating to his consumption of a commodity is known as the 'law of diminishing marginal utility'. The law of diminishing marginal utility says something about "all you can eat" special. It is quite likely that an individual will stop eating once MU from eating food is zero. At this point total utility is maximum. Consumption beyond this will cause TU to decline and distaste for food will grow in the minds of the consumer.

The relationship between TU and MU can be summarised in the following form :

If TU	then MU
• increases at a diminishing rate	• declines
• is maximum	• is zero
• declines	• becomes negative

This law can be illustrated with the help of a diagram. In Fig. 4.1 we measure cups of tea consumed on the horizontal axis and both TU and MU of tea on the vertical axis.

The figure suggests that the TU curve gradually rises, reaches a peak, and from there it declines. On the other hand, the MU curve gradually declines. When OX_5 units of tea are consumed, TU becomes maximum and MU

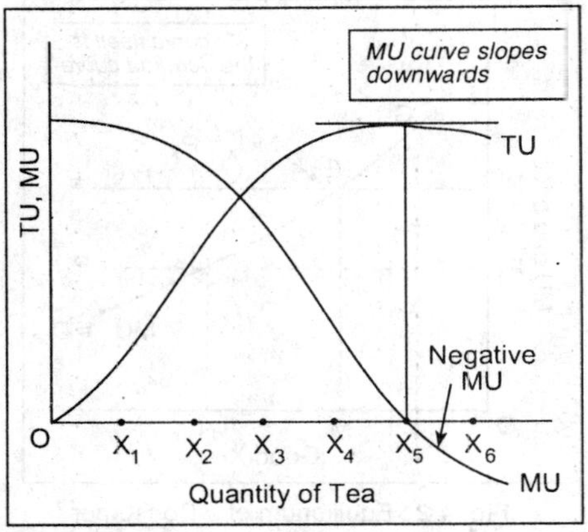

Fig. 4.1: Law of Diminishing Marginal Utility

becomes zero. To understand this, we have drawn a tangent at the highest point of the TU curve. As the tangent is parallel to the horizontal axis the TU is maximum. Remember that the slope of the TU curve is the MU. The slope of the TU at its maximum point is zero. So the MU must be zero. If a consumer consumes OX_6 units of tea his TU will decline and MU will be negative. Here the MU curve cuts the horizontal axis indicating disutility. Anyway, the tendency of the MU curve to slope downwards from left to right is suggestive of the law of diminishing MU.

Assumptions behind the law : The Marshallian law of diminishing MU will come into operation provided certain assumptions are made :

- utility derived from a commodity is cardinally measurable;
- marginal utility derived from a commodity tends to diminish;
- marginal utility of money remains constant;
- money income, tastes and preferences, prices of substitute and complementary goods, etc. remain unchanged.

Exceptions : Obviously, if any of the assumptions do not hold, the law may not be operative.

Exceptions to this law are :

First, utility, being a psychological concept, cannot be measured in cardinal numbers. It varies from person to person and from place to place.

Secondly, like commodities, MU of money may also diminish. It does not remain invariant to a consumer when his stock of money changes. More and more purchase of commodities means fall in stock of money. In such a situation, the MU of money should rise. When stock of money rises the MU of money should decline.

Thirdly, the law may not be applicable in the case of articles of hobby. Usually, a postal stamp collector has an unending appetite for additional stamps. Naturally, the law of diminishing MU for this commodity does not hold then.

Fourthly, the law of diminishing MU may not hold if a consumer gets very little quantity of a commodity. For a thirsty man, drops of water consumed in several doses may not exhibit the law of diminishing MU.

Despite these limitations, the law usually holds. In other words, the above-noted exceptions are not true exceptions to this law. The law can be postponed for the time being but the law of diminishing MU is more likely to appear eventually. The law appears to be an empirical one. That is why this law can explain the law of demand.

4.3.1. Derivation of Demand Curve from Marginal Utility Curve

By equilibrium, we mean a state of balance or rest. The basic objective of a consumer is the maximisation of satisfaction from the consumption of goods. A consumer reaches equilibrium when he gets maximum satisfaction or maximum total utility. After getting maximum utility a consumer does not find any interest in changing his consumption pattern. He, thus, comes to a rest.

The concept of marginal utility is employed to explain the equilibrium of a consumer. The marginal utility curve is also employed to derive the demand curve for a commodity. Before describing the equilibrium of a consumer in a single commodity framework, we must assume the following :

- utility is cardinally measurable;
- marginal utility of a commodity diminishes but marginal utility of money remains constant;
- price of the commodity, money income, etc., do not change;
- our representative consumer acts rationally in the sense that he is neither an extravagant nor a miser.

The tastes and preferences of the consumer are represented by the marginal utility (MU) curve, which is negative sloping in character. Given the limited money income and the product price, the rational consumer sets out to maximise his 'net' utility. Net utility is the difference between marginal utility obtained from a commodity and the price sacrificed to have this commodity. His net utility becomes maximum when marginal utility (measured in money units) equals the price of the product. Thus, the condition for equilibrium of a consumer for good X is reached when $MU_X = P_X$.

A consumer spends his given money income in such a way that the marginal utility of the last unit purchased is equal to the price of the product.

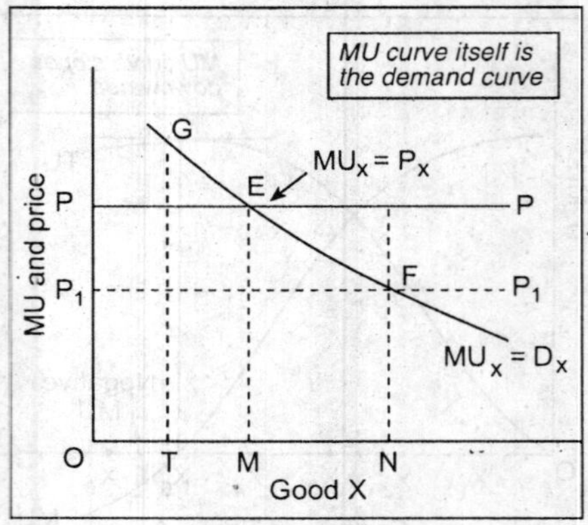

Fig. 4.2 : Equilibrium of a Consumer

If $MU_X \neq P_X$, the consumer will go on either consuming more or less until equality is restored. Clearly, a consumer can increase his total utility by purchasing more or less as long as the value he places on each additional unit exceeds or falls short of the amount he must pay. In Fig. 4.2, we have drawn MU curve for good X which exhibits the law of diminishing MU. We measure quantities of good X on the horizontal axis and price as well as MU obtained from X on the vertical axis. To explain constancy in price we have drawn PP line as parallel to the horizontal axis. At this given price, the consumer is at liberty to buy any amount he likes. As long as MU_X exceeds P_X, it is profitable to purchase more of X. Suppose, our consumer buys OT of X. Since $MU_X > P_X$, the consumer can increase his utility by purchasing more of X. It will continue until point E is reached where $MU_X = P_X$. At this point, the consumer reaches equilibrium and gets maximum satisfaction by buying OM units of good X. Similarly, when the consumer purchases ON of good X, his sacrifice is larger than the utility obtained, i.e., $P_X > MU_X$. So, a consumer will reduce his purchases in order to maximise net utility until the point E is reached. Thus, E is the equilibrium point where our consumer gets highest satisfaction.

• **Derivation of a Demand Curve :** Now we will derive a demand curve showing price-quantity relationship. When the consumer consumes one commodity, the marginal utility schedule itself for this commodity is the demand curve. We know that a consumer—with his limited money income and given price of the product—will go on purchasing a commodity to obtain the greatest satisfaction until the marginal utility for the commodity is equal to its price. This is shown in Fig. 4.2 where E is the initial equilibrium point. Now by varying the price, we can derive another set of equilibrium points to obtain a demand curve.

In Fig. 4.2 our consumer demands OM of good X when its price is OP. Note that, corresponding to this amount of consumption, $MU_X = P_X$. If price of X falls to OP_1, a new equilibrium point—F—is obtained. Corresponding to point F, the consumer purchases a larger quantity of X, i.e., ON. This means that at a lower price, a larger quantity is demanded. Thus, the MU_X curve itself is the demand curve for X which is inclined negatively throughout the length. So, we can conclude that the demand curve for a normal good is negatively sloped due to the operation of the law of diminishing marginal utility.

4.3.2. Deficiencies of Marshallian Utility Analysis

The two important laws of economics—the law of diminishing marginal utility and the principle of substitution—have been derived from the Marshallian cardinal utility analysis. These two laws explain negative sloping demand curve. However, in the 1930s, the Marshallian utility analysis came in for sharp criticisms and, as a result, some new theories developed. The main criticisms against this utility approach are :

• **Unrealistic assumptions :** *First,* Marshall's utility analysis is based on some unrealistic assumptions. For instance, Marshall assumed that utility derived from a commodity can be measured in cardinal numbers. But, modern economists like Profs. J. R. Hicks and R. G. D. Allen had suggested that utility, being a psychological concept, can never be measured in cardinal numbers. Actually, there is no measuring rod to measure utility derived from the consumption of a commodity. According to them, utility can be measured in ordinal numbers. This means that the consumer is capable of comparing different levels of utility. A consumer can say that a particular commodity gives him a higher or lower level of satisfaction than another commodity. Of course, he cannot quantify the level of satisfaction. As the law of demand is based on Marshall's utility analysis, the explanation of the law of demand seems to be inaccurate.

• **MU of Money can never be constant :** *Secondly,* Marshall's assumption of constant marginal utility of money is another unrealistic assumption. And this is the most crucial assumption of the utility theory. According to Marshall, utility from a good can be measured in terms of money. To measure utility (in cardinal numbers) in terms of money, marginal utility of money must remain invariant. But, like commodities, marginal utility of money also diminishes when stock of money rises. If it is so, measurement of utility in terms of money seems to be irrational.

• **No formal Distinction between Income and Substitution Effect** : *Thirdly,* because of the constancy in the marginal utility of money, Marshall could not distinguish between income effect and substitution effect of a price change. We know that a change in the price of a commodity results in two types of changes : one is the income effect and another is the substitution effect. Marshall considered only the substitution effect and ignored the income effect. Because of constancy in the marginal utility of money, Marshall ignored income effect. As Marshall considered only substitution effect, his demand curve is always negative sloping. In other words, Marshall could not explain Giffen paradox for which the law of demand does not hold.

Because of these criticisms, Marshallian utility analysis fell into disrepute. In the 1930s, Hicks and Allen introduced an alternative theory known as ordinal utility theory or indifference theory which is an improvement over Marshall's cardinal utility theory.

4.4. ORDINAL APPROACH : INDIFFERENCE CURVE

Modern economists like Hicks and Allen have rejected the cardinal measurement of utility. On the other hand, their approach is known as ordinal approach. A consumer can rank his preference out of various commodity bundles. That is to say, utility, though not measurable, is comparable. If a consumer is presented with a number of various combination (say, A, B, C) of two goods, he can rank them in a scale of preferences. A consumer can say that A is preferable to B or B to A. But he can't say that from A he gets maximum satisfaction of 10 units.

• **Meaning of Indifference Curve** : In Fig. 4.3 (a), we measure good X on the horizontal

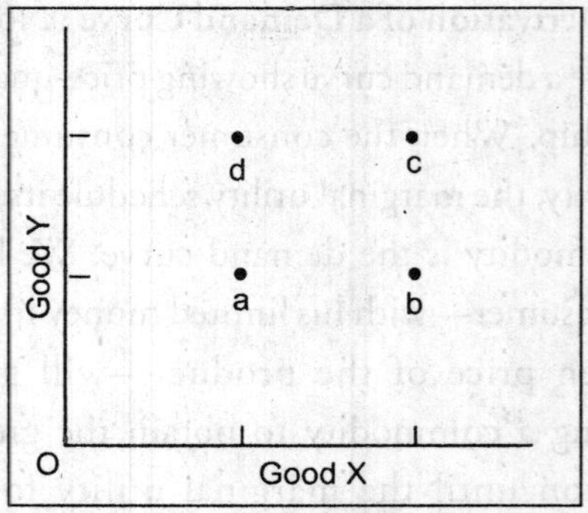

Fig. 4.3(a) : Combinations of X and Y

axis and good Y on the vertical axis. a, b, c and d are four combinations of X and Y. All these combinations may be either preferred by the consumer or a consumer may be indifferent among these combinations.

Rationality assumption states that more is always preferred to less. Thus, 'c' is preferred to 'a', 'b' or 'd' since c suggests larger combinations of X and Y. Likewise, 'd' is preferred to 'a'. But, we are not sure whether 'd' is preferred to 'b' or 'b' is preferred to 'd'. If no preference is observed between 'd' and 'b', we can assume that the consumer is indifferent between combinations 'd' and 'b'. Connecting these two points, we obtain indifference curve shown in Fig. 4.3(b). Before describing this figure, we use Table 4.2 to derive indifference curve.

Table 4.2 : Combinations of X and Y

Combination	Good X	Good Y
A	1	6
B	2	3
C	3	2
D	4	$1\frac{1}{2}$

Suppose, a consumer purchases various combinations of goods X and Y shown in Table 4.2. Our consumer gets the same level of satisfaction from X and Y whether he purchases

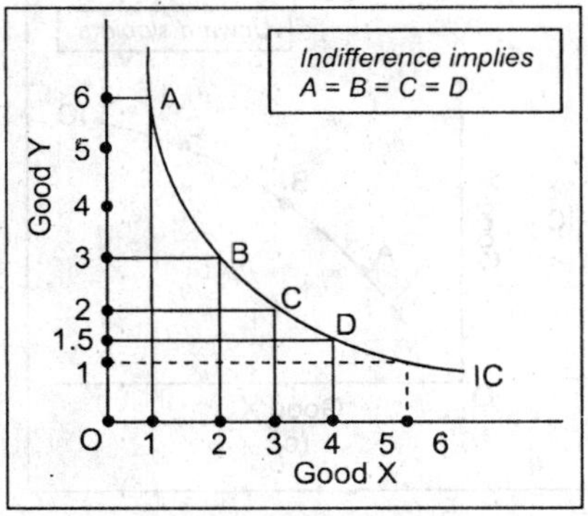

Fig. 4.3(b) : Indifference Curve

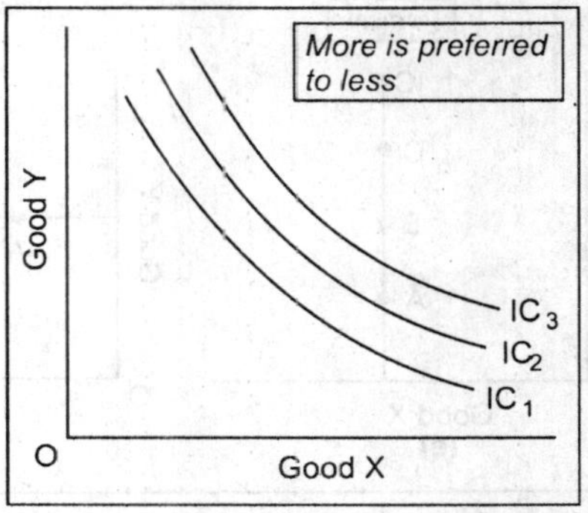

Fig. 4.4 : Indifference Map

combination A or B or C or D. To him, all such combinations give the same level of satisfaction. That is why he is indifferent between different combinations.

This table can be represented with the help of Fig. 4.3(b) where we measure goods X and Y on the horizontal and vertical axis, respectively. Point A on the curve IC denotes 1 unit of X and 6 units of Y. Point B denotes 2 units of X and 3 units of Y. Similarly, points C and D denote the use of more X and less Y. By joining these points we get a curve known as the indifference curve, IC. Our consumer is indifferent between all these points. He can't say which point is giving him the maximum satisfaction. All the points give him the same level of satisfaction. Thus, an indifference curve represents various combinations of goods X and Y that yield the same amount of satisfaction to the consumer. As he cannot say which combination of the two goods gives him the highest satisfaction, he is, therefore, indifferent between the combinations. Hence the name indifference curve.

4.4.1. Indifference Map

A set of indifference curve plotted on a graph is called an indifference map. A consumer is indifferent on an indifference curve and not between two indifference curves. Higher indifference curve represents higher level of satisfaction.

A consumer can have more of both the goods if he experiences, say, an increase in income. In Fig. 4.4, an indifference map has been drawn. IC_1 is the lower order indifference curve. IC_2 is the higher order indifference curve that contains more of X and Y. Thus, IC_2 is preferable to IC_1. By the same logic, IC_3 is preferable to IC_2. That is to say, $IC_3 > IC_2 > IC_1$. An indifference map consists of more than one indifference curve. In other words, an indifference map is a family of indifference curves.

4.4.2. Characteristics of Indifference Curve

An indifference curve has three important properties :

- **An indifference curve must slope downwards from left to the right.**

Proof : It is clear from Fig. 4.3(b) that if the consumer travels from point A to B, he tends to consume more of X and less of Y. Similarly, the consumer purchases more of X and less of Y if he moves from point B to C or from C to D. This must be so if the level of satisfaction is to remain

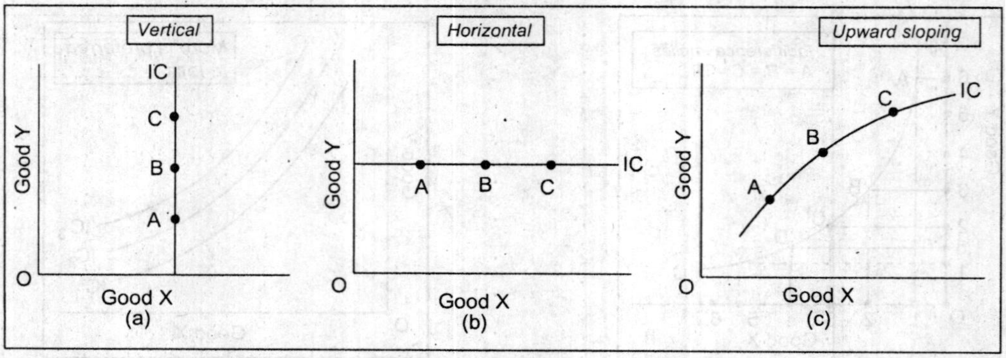

Fig. 4.5 : Unlikely Shapes of Indifference Curve

the same on an indifference curve. Thus, an indifference curve must have a negative slope.

Proof of this negatively sloped indifference curve can also be made with the help of the Fig. 4.5. In Fig. 4.5(a), IC is drawn parallel to the vertical axis indicating that, as a consumer moves from A to B, to C, his consumption of Y rises while that of X remains the same. The consumer is indifferent between having more or less of the commodity X. Thus, X is a neuter good. In Fig. 4.5(b), as IC is parallel to the horizontal axis, the consumption of X rises and that of Y remains unchanged. By the same logic, good Y is a neuter good. To have a negatively sloped indifference curve, consumption of one good must increase while that of another must decline. Further, indifference curve can never be upward rising as shown in Fig. 4.5(c). As a consumer moves from A to B, to C, his consumption of both X and Y rises. This shape of indifference curve is also ruled out. Thus, indifference curve must be downward sloping.

- **An indifference curve is convex to the origin. Or it is concave from above.**

Proof : An indifference curve is convex to the origin because of diminishing marginal rate of substitution between two goods, X and Y, (MRS_{XY}). Marginal rate of substitution of X for Y represents the amount of Y which the consumer gives up for an additional unit of X so that his satisfaction remains intact. As the rate of substitution diminishes, the curve must be convex to the origin. This has been explained with the help of Fig. 4.6.

If a consumer moves from D to C, he sacrifices Y and takes up more X. It means that the loss of satisfaction caused by giving up Y_1Y_2 of Y equals the gain in satisfaction due to the increase in good X by X_1X_2. Thus, the rate of substitution is :

$$\frac{OY_1 - OY_2}{OX_2 - OX_1} = \frac{DE}{EC}$$

Similarly, if he moves from C to B, the rate of substitution becomes :

$$\frac{OY_2 - OY_3}{OX_3 - OX_2} = \frac{CF}{FB}$$

However, $\frac{DE}{EC} > \frac{CF}{FB}$. This means that initially the consumer was prepared to sacrifice more of Y for X. But, as he slides down the curve, his stock of Y diminishes and stock of X increases. This suggests that he is willing to give up less and less of Y for a given increment in X. Thus, the

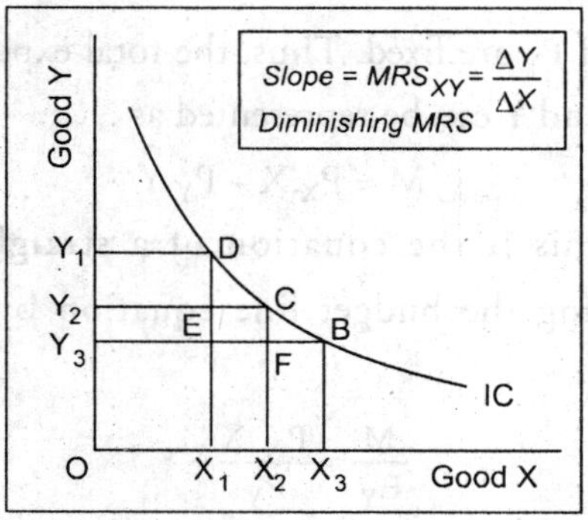

Fig. 4.6 : Convex Indifference Curve

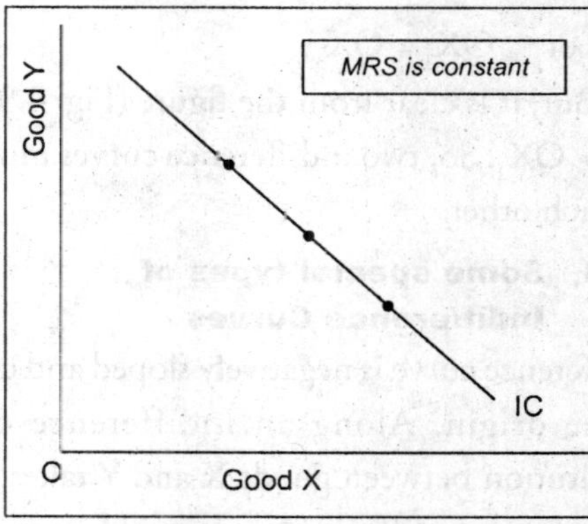

Fig. 4.7 : Straight line Indifference curve

marginal rate of substitution of X for Y (MRS_{XY}) falls as the consumer possesses more of X and less of Y. So, an indifference curve must be convex to the origin.

It is to be remembered that the slope of an indifference curve is MRS. The slope is $-\frac{\Delta Y}{\Delta X}$. Thus the slope is negative.

Anyway, if the indifference curve is steep (flat) MRS will be high (low). If two goods are perfect substitutes, then the indifference curve would be a straight line (Fig. 4.7) and MRS would be constant. For complementary goods, the indifference curve becomes L-shaped (Fig. 4.8).

On the other hand, an indifference curve can never be concave to the origin since the rate of substitution becomes increasing.

- **No two indifference curve can touch or intersect each other.**

Proof : If two curves intersect each other we will get an absurd result. This is shown in Fig. 4.9 where IC_1 and IC_2 have cut each other at point 'c'. Points a and c lie on IC_2 and points 'b' and 'c' lie on IC_1. As points 'a' and 'c' lie on IC_2 these two points must represent the same level of satisfaction, that is

$$OX_1 + OY_1 = OX_2 + OY_2 \quad .....(i)$$

Similarly, from points c and b on IC_1, we get

$$OX_1 + OY_1 = OX_3 + OY_2 \quad .....(ii)$$

As the L.H.S. of (i) and (ii) are the same, it follows, that

$$OX_2 + OY_2 = OX_3 + OY_2$$

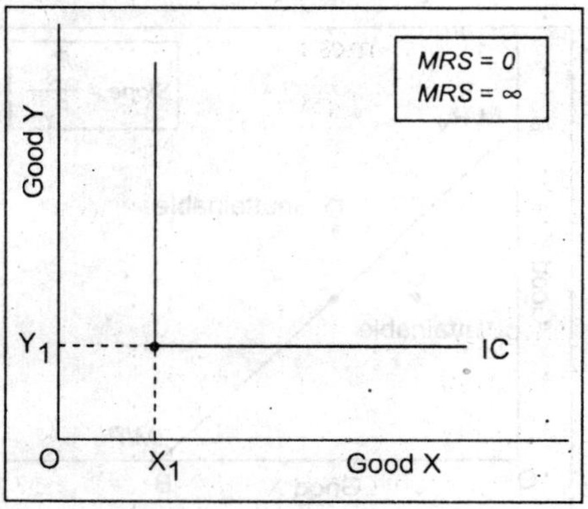

Fig. 4.8 : L-shaped Indifference Curve

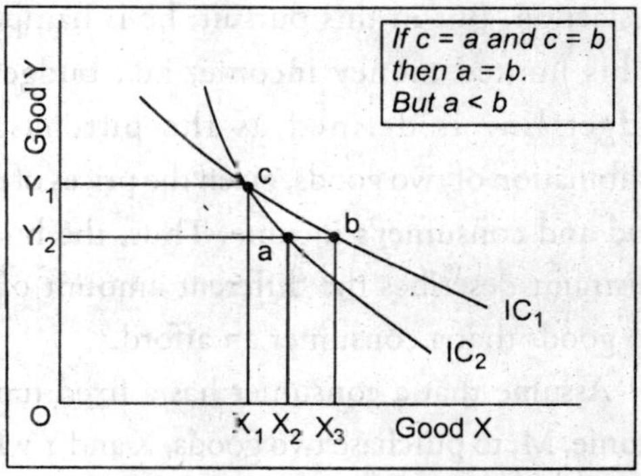

Fig. 4.9 : Non-intersecting Indifference Curve

or $OX_2 = OX_3$

But, it is clear from the figure (Fig. 4.9) that $OX_3 > OX_2$. So, two indifference curves must not cut each other.

4.4.3. Some special types of Indifference Curves

Indifference curve is negatively sloped and convex to the origin. Along an indifference curve, substitution between goods X and Y takes place. However, an indifference curve will be negatively sloped but a straight line if two goods are considered as perfect substitutes (e.g., tea and coffee). This is shown in Fig. 4.7.

This IC indicates that an individual wants to give up the same amount of good Y (say, two cups of tea) for each additional unit of good X (say one cup of coffee). There the slope of the indifference curve, MRS_{XY}, is constant.

For complementary goods, IC is L-shaped (Fig. 4.8). Always, a fixed proportion of the two goods will be consumed. Example : right shoe and left shoe, pen and ink, etc. Here, always OX_1 of X and OY_1 of Y will be consumed by the consumer. One cannot have more of X and less of Y or more of Y and less of X.

4.5. BUDGET LINE

A consumer always tries to maximise his satisfaction. But in this pursuit, he is hampered by his limited money income, i.e., budget. A budget line is defined as the purchasable combination of two goods, given the prices of each good and consumer's income. Thus, the budget constraint describes the different amount of the two goods that a consumer an afford.

Assume that a consumer has a fixed money income, M, to purchase two goods, X and Y whose prices are P_X and P_Y respectively. Also assume that P_X and P_Y are fixed. Thus, the total expenditure on X and Y can be represented as

$$M = P_X.X + P_Y.Y$$

This is the equation of a straight line. Dividing the budget line equation by P_Y we obtain,

$$\frac{M}{P_Y} = \frac{P_X.X}{P_Y} + Y$$

Subtracting $\frac{P_X.X}{P_Y}$ from both sides of this equation, we obtain the value of Y

$$Y = \frac{M}{P_Y} - \frac{P_X.X}{P_Y}$$

Similarly, solving for X, we get

$$X = \frac{M}{P_X} - \frac{P_Y.Y}{P_X}$$

Here M/P_Y is the vertical intercept of the equation. It shows the maximum purchasable amount of Y, if no unit of X is bought. This is represented by the distance OA in Fig. 4.10. Similarly, M/P_X is the horizontal intercept. It shows the maximum purchasable amount of X, if no Y is bought. This is represented by OB.

Thus, A and B are two extreme points. By joining these two points we obtain the budget line AB that shows purchasable combinations of goods

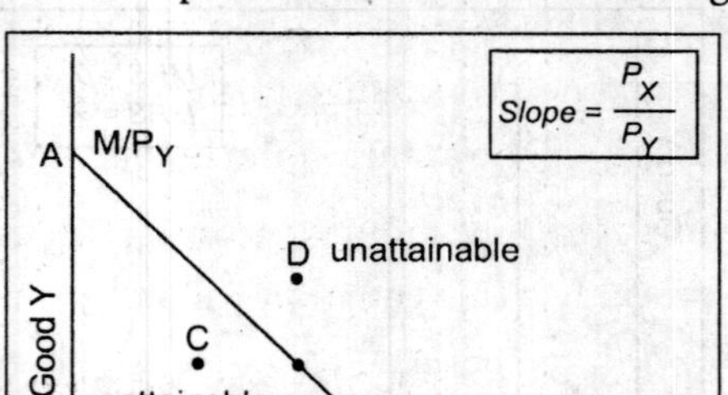

Fig. 4.10 : Budget Line

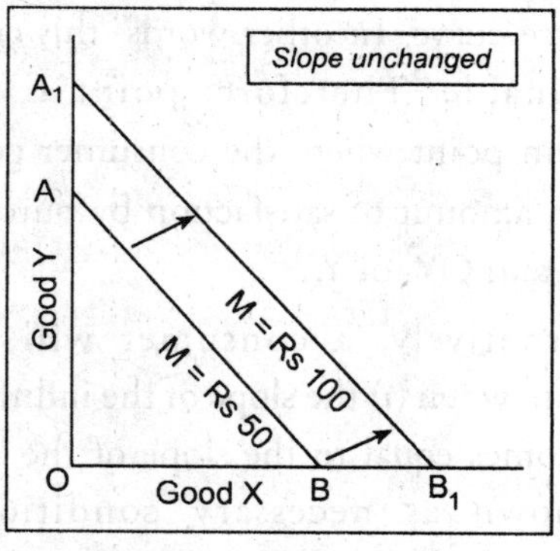

Fig. 4.11 : Shifts in Budget Line

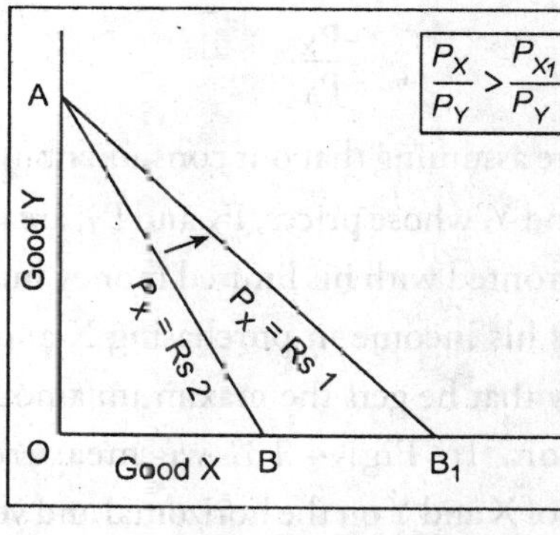

Fig. 4.12 : Change in Slope

X and Y where the whole of income is spent. Thus, AB is a straight downward sloping line. The consumer cannot go beyond the line AB since money income will not permit him to do so (point D).

Thus, the budget constraint describes the different bundles of two goods that a consumer can buy.

Since the line AB has a negative slope, its slope is represented by the price ratio of goods X and Y,

$$= \frac{-\text{amount of } Y}{(+)\text{amount of } X} = -\frac{(M/P_Y)}{(M/P_X)}$$

$$\text{Slope} = -\frac{OA}{OB} = -\frac{P_X}{P_Y}$$

The position and slope of the budget line depends on money income and prices of two goods. In other words, if there is a change in money income or a change in the prices of any good, there will be a shift in the budget line.

Suppose, only money income is doubled. Now the budget line equation will be :

$$2M = X.P_X + Y.P_Y$$

This results in an upward shifting of the budget line. Prior to the increase in money income, budget line was AB in Fig. 4.11. After the increase in money income, new budget line becomes A_1B_1. As there is a parallel shift of the budget line, its slope remains unchanged.

Let us assume that price of X falls. AB is the initial budget line. Its slope is P_X/P_Y. Now, if price of X falls from Rs. 2 to Re. 1, the budget line shifts to AB_1. Since the line AB is steeper than AB_1, the slope of the budget line AB (P_X/P_Y) is g r e a t e r than the slope of the budget line AB_1 (P_{X1}/P_Y) [Fig. 4.12].

4.6. CONSUMER'S EQUILIBRIUM

A consumer will be in equilibrium when he gets maximum satisfaction from the consumption of various commodities. One can show the point of satisfaction of the consumer with the aid of indifference curve and budget line. An indifference curve represents the combinations of two goods that yield the same level of satisfaction to the consumer. However, in attaining maximum satisfaction, a consumer is constrained by his (a) fixed and limited money income, and (b) the prices of the commodities that he buys.

We will establish the consumer's equilibrium position with the help of the indifference curve and the budget line. A budget line represents combinations of two goods that can be purchased if the entire money income is spent. Its slope is the price ratio, i.e.,

$\frac{P_X}{P_Y}$

We are assuming that our consumer buys two goods X and Y, whose prices, P_X and P_Y, are given. He is confronted with his limited money income. He spends his income in purchasing X and Y in such a way that he gets the maximum amount of satisfaction. In Fig. 4.13, we measure the quantities of X and Y on the horizontal and vertical axes, respectively. AB is the initial budget line or consumption possibility line. The consumer, in fact, travels on the line AB. He cannot go beyond the budget line as his money income will not permit him to do so. We have drawn a family of indifference curves, represented by IC_1, IC_2, and IC_3.

A consumer will be in equilibrium when his budget line is tangential to the highest attainable indifference curve. In terms of Fig. 4.13, IC_1 crosses the budget line at points C and D. As IC_1 is a lower-order indifference curve, it must not represent highest satisfaction. So the consumer will climb on to a new and higher indifference curve, IC_2. This new curve touches the budget line at point E. As IC_3 lies outside the budget line the consumer cannot climb up to the higher

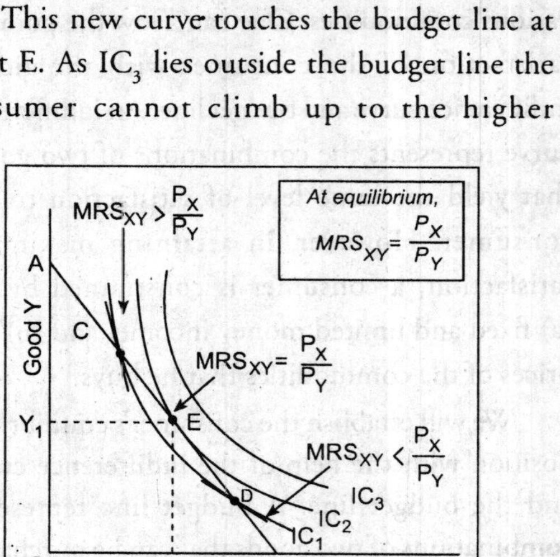

Fig. 4.13 : Consumer's Equilibrium

indifference curve. In other words, this curve is not attainable. Therefore, point E is the equilibrium point where the consumer gets the maximum amount of satisfaction by purchasing OX_1 of X and OY_1 of Y.

Alternatively, a consumer will be in equilibrium when (i) the slope of the indifference curve becomes equal to the slope of the budget line (known as necessary condition or, mathematically, first-order condition); and (ii) the indifference curve is convex to the origin at the point of tangency (known as sufficient condition or second-order condition). The slope of the indifference curve is the marginal rate of substitution between X and Y. Symbolically, it is MRS_{XY}. Again, the slope of the budget line is nothing but the price ratio of the two commodities.

Symbolically, it is $\frac{P_X}{P_Y}$.

Our consumer is in equilibrium at point E since $MRS_{XY} = \frac{P_X}{P_Y}$. At points C and D, the slopes of the two curves are unequal.

At point C, $MRS_{XY} > \frac{P_X}{P_Y}$. The consumer will now travel along the budget line from point C toward E. This means that the consumer is willing to sacrifice more Y to have larger quantities of X. As he does this, his satisfaction increases without spending additional money. In the process, he reaches point E on IC_2 and gets maximum satisfaction.

The opposite is true at point D where $MRS_{XY} < \frac{P_X}{P_Y}$. So the consumer, in order to get higher satisfaction, will go on purchasing more of

Y and less of X, of course, without incurring additional expenses. Anyway, the optimum point is reached at point E where the indifference curve is tangential to the budget line.

Thus, points C and D cannot be equilibrium points. Point E is the equilibrium point as

$$MRS_{XY} = \frac{P_X}{P_Y}$$

$$\text{Or } MRS_{XY} = \frac{MU_X}{MU_Y} = \frac{P_X}{P_Y}$$

So, the necessary condition for equilibrium is fulfilled. Sufficient condition requires that the indifference curve must be convex to the origin at the point of tangency. Since these two conditions are fulfilled at point E, our consumer is in equilibrium at that point. This is called 'interior' solution where a consumer buys both the goods.

4.6.1. Consumer's Equilibrium with Concave Indifference Curve— A Corner Solution

It is the shape of the indifference curve that determines the location of consumer's equilibrium. We know that an indifference curve is negatively sloped and convex to the origin. A consumer would reach equilibrium and would consume positive quantities of both the goods, and hence, would obtain 'interior solution' provided indifference curve is convex to the origin. This is known as sufficient condition or second-order condition for equilibrium. Necessary condition or the first-order condition states that the slope of the budget line, $\frac{P_X}{P_Y}$, is equal to the slope of the indifference curve MRS_{XY}. If one of these two conditions is violated, a consumer may not get 'interior solution'. Rather, he will experience a 'corner solution' and will end up with the zero consumption of one of the two commodities. When does a consumer get 'corner solution'?

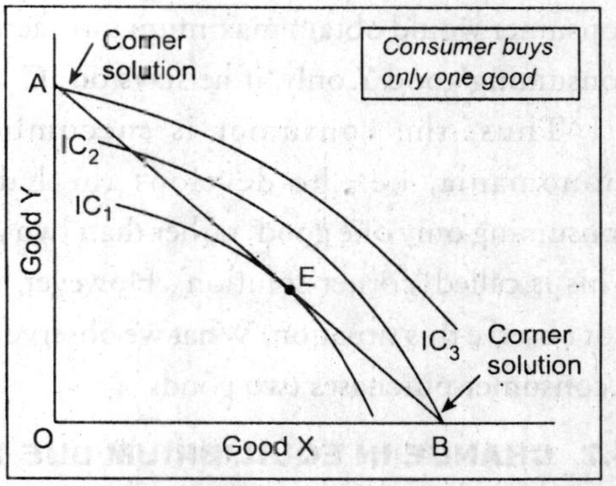

Fig. 4.14 : Concave Indifference Curve and Equilibrium

Suppose a consumer faces a concave-shaped indifference curve. Hence the sufficient condition for equilibrium is violated. At the point of tangency between the budget line and concave-shaped indifference curve, a consumer would not be able to maximise his satisfaction.

As usual, point E of Fig. 4.14 is the point of tangency between the budget line, AB, and the indifference curve, IC_1. IC_1, being a lower-order indifference curve, yields lower level of satisfaction. In other words, though at point E, $MRS_{XY} = \frac{P_X}{P_Y}$, our consumer gets smaller satisfaction since IC_1 is a lower-order indifference curve. So the consumer will try to climb up to a higher indifference curve, IC_2 or IC_3. If he decides to start along the budget line AB from point E towards the right he will reach point B on IC_2 or if he moves from point E towards A he will land at point A on IC_3. The consumer would be maximising his satisfaction at point B if he likes to stay on IC_2. Under the circumstance, our consumer would be maximising satisfaction by consuming good X only. Similarly, at point A, the consumer would obtain maximum satisfaction by consuming good Y only, if he stays on IC_3.

Thus, the consumer is succumbed to monomania, i.e., he develops the habit of consuming only one good, rather than two goods. This is called 'corner solution'. However, we do not observe this situation. What we observe is that a consumer purchases two goods.

4.7. CHANGE IN EQUILIBRIUM DUE TO CHANGE IN MONEY INCOME

The equilibrium of a consumer is explained when the following two conditions are fulfilled. These are : (i) the slope of the indifference curve is equal to the slope of the budget line; and (ii) the indifference curve must be convex to the origin. Further, in developing the equilibrium condition, we assume that the money income and the prices of the two goods that a consumer purchases remain fixed. Now, if one of these variables (such as money income, price of one good) change, the equilibrium of a consumer would also undergo a change.

Here we will examine the impact of a change in money income on the demand for both the goods X and Y, while the prices of X and Y remain constant. This is illustrated in terms of Fig. 4.15-4.17.

An increase in money income, holding all prices constant, leads to a parallel outward shift in the budget line. In Fig. 4.15, AB is the initial budget line and the initial equilibrium point is E_1 on IC_1 where the consumer consumes OX_1 of X and E_1X_1 of Y. As money income rises, the budget line AB shifts to the right in a parallel manner. This new price line is tangential to the indifference curve IC_2 at point E_2. Corresponding to this equilibrium point E_2, the consumer buys more of X and more of Y. By the same logic, E_3 is another equilibrium point when the budget line is A_2B_2. This new equilibrium point or optimal consumption bundle suggests larger consumption of both X and Y.

By joining all the tangency points or the equilibrium points we get a curve known as income consumption curve (ICC) or income expansion path (IEP) since this curve depicts the relationship between changes in the consumer's income and his demand. The locus of successive equilibrium points is called the income consumption curve which shows the quantities

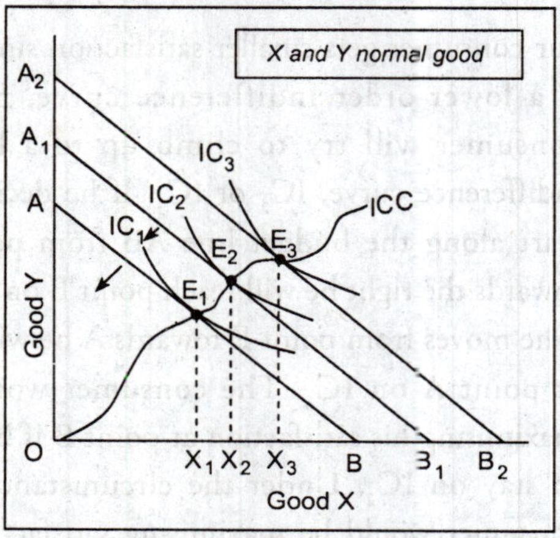

Fig. 4.15 : Income Consumption Curve and Income Effect

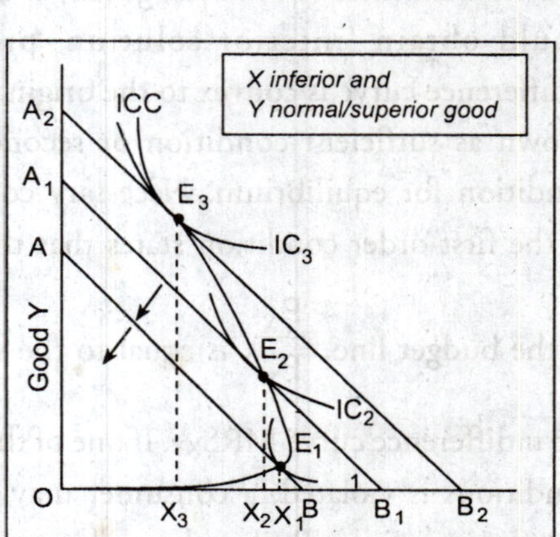

Fig. 4.16 : ICC and Negative Income Effect

of X and Y demanded at different income levels. This income consumption curve or expenditure consumption curve traces out 'income effect' which shows the reaction of the consumer to income changes. Income effect may be positive or negative. In Fig. 4.15, income effect is positive since the consumer purchases more of both X and Y when money income rises. Thus, goods X and Y are normal or superior goods. A normal good is one whose income effect is positive. As income consumption curve is upward sloping, income effect is positive for both the goods X and Y.

However, there is no guarantee that a consumer will always behave in the manner as described in Fig. 4.15. It may happen that a consumer might purchase less of a commodity even if his money income rises. This is shown in Fig. 4.16 where the income consumption curve is backward bending. This means that as money income rises, our consumer purchases less of X but more and more of Y. Thus, for good X, income effect is negative, and for good Y, it is positive. Thus, good X is an inferior good. An inferior good is one for which income effect is negative. However, since income effect for good Y is positive, good Y is called normal or superior good. Truly speaking, good Y may be called an ultra-superior good. Thus, it is clear that the two goods cannot be inferior at the same time—if one good becomes inferior the other must be normal or superior. However, the two goods can be normal or superior at the same time.

In Fig. 4.17, we have drawn a forward-falling ICC. This figure suggests that as income rises demand for Y decreases while that of X rises. Thus, the income effect of good Y is negative and that for good X is positive. In other words, good Y becomes inferior while good X becomes a normal

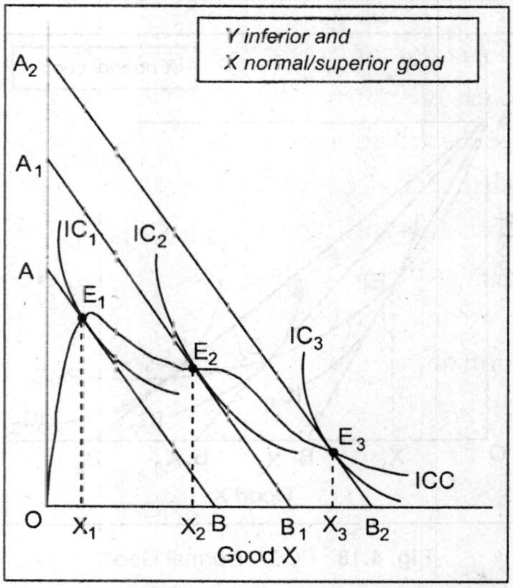

Fig. 4.17 : ICC and Income Effect

or superior good. Or following our definition, good X can be labelled as an ultra-superior good. So, the two goods cannot be inferior at the same time.

4.7.1. Change in Equilibrium Due to Change in Price

Let us now consider the effect of a change in price of good X on equilibrium, holding money income and price of good Y constant. The change in equilibrium following a change in the price of the commodity is called price effect.

As before, the initial equilibrium point is E_1 where the budget line AB (before the change in price of X) is tangential to the indifference curve, IC_1 in Fig. 4.18. Now, let the price of X fall and the budget line shift to AB_1. The new point of equilibrium is E_2. Further decline in P_X leads to a shift in the budget line and, hence, the equilibrium point to E_3.

By joining all these equilibrium points, we get a curve known as the price consumption curve (PCC) drawn in Figs. 4.18 and 4.19. Price

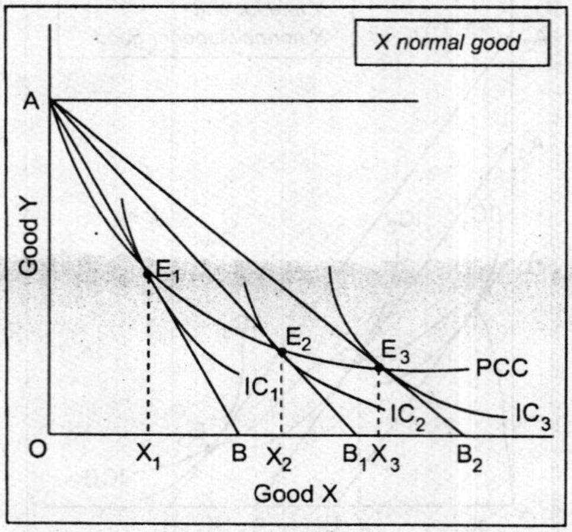

Fig. 4.18 : PCC—Normal Good

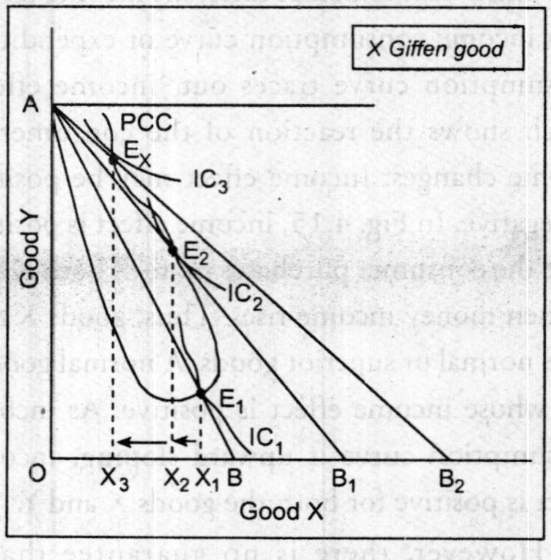

Fig. 4.19 : PCC—Giffen Case

consumption curve traces out price effect which may be positive or negative. In Fig. 4.18, price consumption curve is negative sloping indicating that as P_X falls, its demand rises. However, Fig. 4.19 illustrates backward-bending price consumption curve. This curve demonstrates that, as P_X falls, its demand falls. So, the price effect is positive. Thus, good X is to be called a Giffen good.

4.8. CONSTRUCTION OF DEMAND CURVE FROM PRICE CONSUMPTION CURVE

The demand curve for a commodity shows what different quantities will be purchased at different prices, other things remaining the same. Such demand curve may be derived either from the Marshallian utility approach or from the indifference curve analysis. Whatever the approach we adopt, the demand curve for a normal good is negative sloping. The process of deriving the demand curve from the indifference map is illustrated below.

Let us assume that a consumer purchases good X from his limited money income. In the upper part of Fig. 4.20, we have drawn price consumption curve (PCC). In the upper panel, the horizontal axis measures quantities of X while the vertical axis measures money income instead of the usual practice of measuring another good, say Y. Here the money income may be treated as a composite good whose price is assumed to be constant. Further, indifference curve drawn here shows combinations of two goods X and money income (or a composite good) that give the same level of satisfaction.

Suppose, a consumer has a money income of OA. With this given income he purchases different quantities of X at different prices. With income OA, the consumer can purchase maximum OB amount of X. Thus, AB is the initial budget line. As the line AB is tangential to IC_1 at point E_1 the consumer reaches equilibrium there. If price of X falls, the budget line would shift to AB_1 and new equilibrium would be achieved at point E_1. E_3 is another equilibrium point when the budget line is AB_2 following a decline in the price of X. By connecting all these equilibrium points E_1, E_2 and E_3 we get price consumption curve (PCC). This curve shows various quantities of X that a consumer is willing to purchase at various prices but does so indirectly through total expenditure

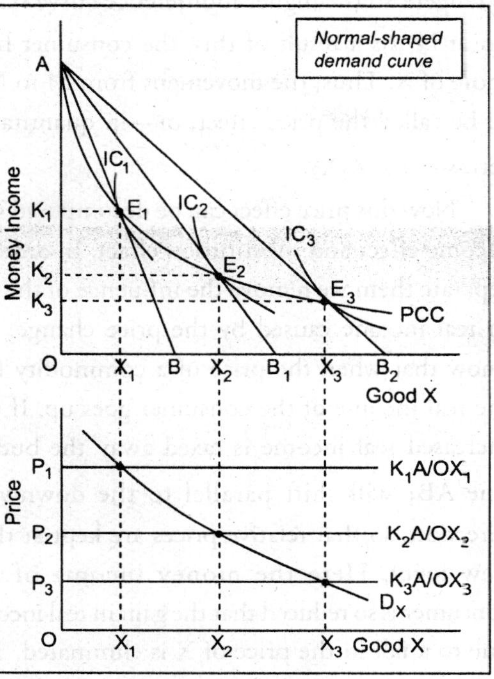

Fig. 4.20 : PCC and Negative Sloping Demand Curve

incurred on this commodity. To derive the price of X that is charged in the market, we have to divide the total expenditure on X by the respective quantities of X that the consumer would purchase.

Suppose, the initial equilibrium point is E_1 and the equilibrium quantity that is purchased is OX_1. This means that the consumer, out of his total money income OA, spends K_1A to purchase OX_1 of X. Thus, the price of X per unit becomes K_1A/OX_1. This price is shown as OP_1 in the bottom part of the figure (Fig. 4.20). Similarly, at equilibrium point E_2, the consumer spends AK_2 to buy OX_2 of X. Thus, the price per unit of X is OP_2 (= K_2A/OX_2), shown in the lower part of the figure. Likewise, we find out the price at point E_3. As the consumer spends AK_3 to buy OX_3 amount of X, the price per unit comes to AK_2/OX_3 or OP_3. This has been shown in the lower part. Thus, the consumer purchases OX_1 at a price OP_1, OX_2 at a price OP_2 and OX_3 at a price OP_3.. By joining these equilibrium quantities we obtain the price-demand curve, D_X, as a negative sloping curve. This means that, as price of X falls, demand for X rises. Thus, good X is a normal or superior good. Anyway, for a Giffen good, the demand curve would be positive sloping.

4.9. PRICE EFFECT = SUBSTITUTION EFFECT + INCOME EFFECT : NORMAL GOOD

The effect on the quantity demanded of a change in its own price is called the price effect. This shows the total effect of price change. Change in price, in general, exerts two influences on quantity demanded. These two are income effect and the substitution effect. When the price of 'X' falls the real income (purchasing power) of the consumer goes up. A consumer thinks that his income has gone up but money income is held constant. With the increased real income the consumer can purchase more of a commodity—this is the income effect of price change which may be positive or negative. If the consumer purchases more of a commodity following an increase in real income (due to a fall in the price of commodity) income effect is said to be positive. It will be negative when a consumer purchases less of a commodity following a fall in real income.

Secondly, when the price of a commodity falls the relative price changes. When price of 'X' falls, 'X' becomes cheaper and 'Y' dearer. A consumer will always prefer cheaper commodity for dearer commodity. This is known as substitution effect. The substitution effect, thus, reflects the tendency for a consumer to substitute one good for another when there is a change in relative price of two goods. The substitution effect measures the effect of changes in relative price of any commodity,

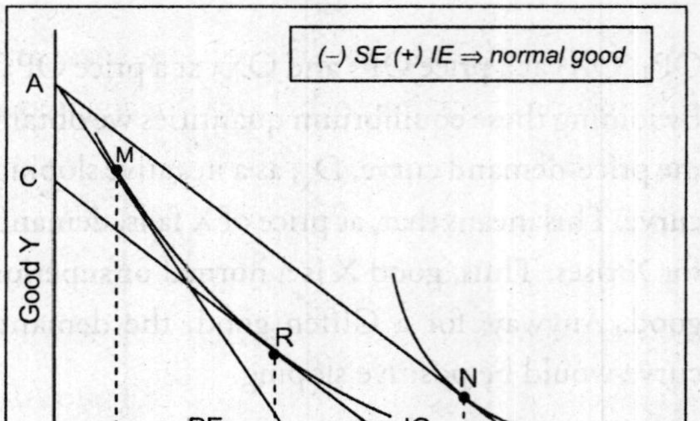

Fig. 4.21 : PE = SE + IE (Normal Good)

holding the real income constant. By constancy in real income we mean that the money income and the relative prices are so changed that the consumer stays on the same indifference curve, thereby giving the same level of satisfaction after the change in price. Thus, the price effect is the resultant of two effects—the income effect and the substitution effect. These two effects of a fall in price can now be explained in terms of Fig. 4.21.

In Fig. 4.21, AB is the initial budget line and M is the initial point of equilibrium. Corresponding to this equilibrium point, our consumer purchases OX_1 of OX. Now the price of X falls and the budget line shifts to AB_1 which is tangent to the higher indifference curve IC_2 at point N. As a result of this, the consumer buys more of X. Thus, the movement from M to N is to be called the price effect, or—in quantitative terms—it is X_1X_2.

Now this price effect can be decomposed into income effect and substitution effect. In order to separate them we remove the influence of the rise in real income caused by the price change. We know that when the price of a commodity falls the real income of the consumer goes up. If this increased real income is taxed away the budget line AB_1 will shift parallel to the downward direction, so that relative prices are kept at their new level. Here the money income of the consumer is so reduced that the gain in real income due to a fall in the price of X is eliminated. The relative price is no longer given by the slope of the line AB but by the slope of the line CD. We have drawn the imaginary budget line CD parallel to AB_1. The budget line is, thus, shifted to the left in such a way that it becomes tangent to the initial indifference curve IC_1 at R. The movement from M to R along the same indifference curve, IC_1, measures the substitution effect of price change. Here, as X is cheaper and Y is dearer, our consumer buys more of X and less of Y. Thus, in quantitative terms, X_1X_3 is the substitution effect. Substitution effect is always negative—due to which the consumer buys more of X when its price falls.

Now, we return the consumer's increased money income which had been taxed away earlier. The budget line shifts parallel to AB_1 and the consumer climbs up to a higher indifference curve IC_2 and equilibrium occurs at point N. The movement from R to N is, thus, the income effect which enables the consumer to buy more of X, that is, X_3X_2. Here, the price effect is negative. As per our diagram :

$$PE = X_1X_2$$
$$SE = X_1X_3$$
$$IE = X_3X_2$$
$$\therefore \quad X_1X_2 = X_1X_3 + X_3X_2$$

Generally, these two effects operate in the same direction, so that a fall in the price of a commodity causes the consumer to buy more of it. In other words, as positive income effect and negative substitution effect work in the same direction, the demand for X rises when its price falls. Here, X is a normal good or a superior good since the income effect is positive.

Demand curve for a normal good has been drawn in the lower panel of the figure. Let us assume that the initial price of X is OP_1 in accordance with the original budget line AB. At this price the consumer buys OX_1. When the price of X drops to OP_2 the budget line shifts to AB_1. Quantity demanded rises to OX_2. Now, by joining the points T and S, we get a negative sloping demand curve. Thus, X is a normal good.

4.10. PE = SE + IE : NON-GIFFEN INFERIOR GOOD

In case of an inferior good, the income effect is negative since demand for it tends to decline as income rises. However, the substitution effect for any good is always negative. Thus, for an inferior good, both income effect and substitution effect are negative but negative substitution effect outweighs negative income effect. That is why the demand curve for an inferior good is also negative sloping, rather than positive sloping. In other words, an inferior good (defined in this sense) is not a Giffen good.

In Fig. 4.22 we show the income effect and substitution effect of a price change for an inferior good. AB is the initial budget line and IC_1 is the initial indifference curve. E is the initial equilibrium point. At this point, our consumer buys OX_1 of X and EX_1 of Y. Now, suppose price of X is reduced such that the budget line shifts to AB_1 and the consumer reaches equilibrium at point E_1 on IC_2. The total price effect is, thus, X_1X_2 which can be split into substitution effect and income effect.

To examine the substitution effect first, we have drawn an imaginary budget line CD in such a way that it touches the initial indifference curve

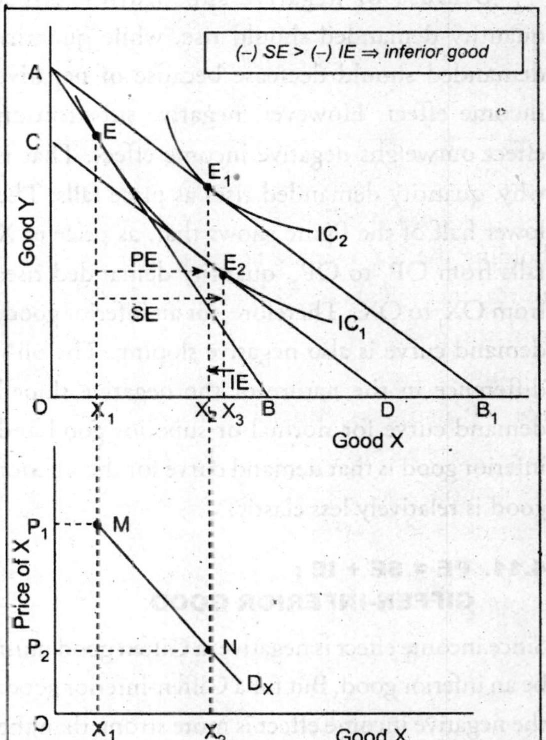

Fig. 4.22 : PE = SE + IE (Inferior Good)

(IC_1) so that the satisfaction remains unchanged. This occurs at point E_2. Thus, the movement from E to E_2 along the same indifference curve is the substitution effect or, in quantitative terms, X_1X_3.

The movement from E_2 to E_1 describes income effect. [If an income consumption curve is drawn, it will take a backward turn]. Income effect is, thus, negative, since quantity demanded has decreased from OX_3 to OX_2. Since income effect is negative, the product in question is an inferior one.

Thus, $PE = X_1X_2$

$SE = X_1X_3$

$IE = X_3X_2$

Because of negative substitution effect quantity demanded should rise, while quantity demanded should decrease because of negative income effect. However, negative substitution effect outweighs negative income effect. That is why, quantity demanded rises as price falls. The lower half of the figure shows that, as price of X falls from OP_1 to OP_2, quantity demanded rises from OX_1 to OX_2. Therefore, for an inferior good, demand curve is also negative sloping. The only difference in the nature of the negative sloped demand curve for normal or superior good and inferior good is that demand curve for the inferior good is relatively less elastic.

4.11. PE = SE + IE : GIFFEN-INFERIOR GOOD

Since income effect is negative, a Giffen good must be an inferior good. But for a Giffen-inferior good, the negative income effect is more strong than the negative substitution effect. As a result, the demand for a Giffen good rises (falls) when its price rises (falls). In other words, the demand curve becomes positive sloping. This is shown in Fig. 4.23.

According to this figure,

$PE = X_1X_2$

$SE = X_1X_3$

$IE = X_3X_2$

As usual, substitution effect (i.e., the movement along the same indifference curve) is negative and is measured by the distance X_1X_3. Negative substitution effect causes quantity demanded to rise (fall) when price falls (rises). Here, the commodity is an inferior one since income effect is negative. It is due to the negative income effect, the quantity demanded falls (rises) when real income rises (falls). Note that the negative income effect is much more strong than

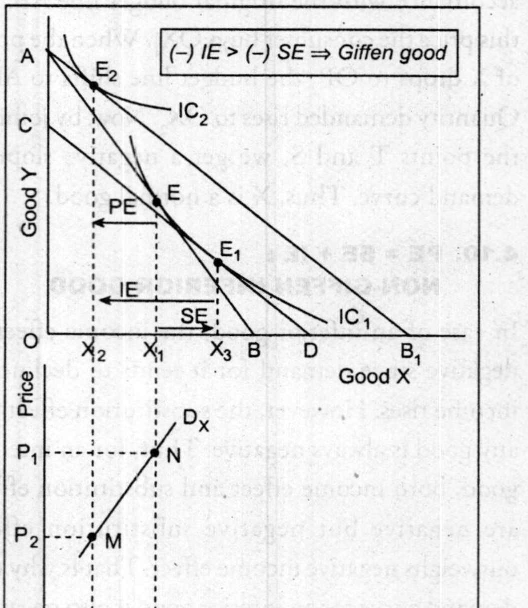

Fig. 4.23 : PE = SE + IE (Giffen Good)

the negative substitution effect. Hence, the good is a Giffen-inferior one. Anyway, demand curve is, thus, positive sloping. As price falls, demand falls and, as price rises, demand rises.

Remember that all Giffen goods are inferior goods but all inferior goods are not Giffen goods. Inferior good is an income phenomenon while Giffen good is a price phenomenon that violates the law of demand. In fact, Giffen good, not inferior good, is a bona fide exception to the law of demand.

4.12. ACHIEVEMENTS OF INDIFFERENCE CURVE ANALYSIS

Despite pouring 'old wine in a new bottle', the introspective ordinal approach is superior in many respects to Marshall's approach.

Marshall believed in cardinal measurability of utility. A consumer can measure the utility derived from a commodity in cardinal numbers just as one can measure the temperature of a day or of a human body. Not only that, Marshall assumed that utilities are additive and comparable. This assumption follows from independent utility functions which state that the utility obtained from a commodity is a function of that commodity alone. This amounts to saying that the utility from a pen is a function of the pen alone, not of ink. So this theory does not take into account the substitute or complementary goods.

On these points, modern writers like Hicks and Allen strongly differ. They argue that utility—being a psychological concept—can never be measured in cardinal numbers. What an individual can do is the ordering of the state of preferences. That is why this approach is known as ordinal approach. How much utility a consumer gets from the consumption of a commodity cannot be quantified. He can at best say that this commodity is preferable to that of another commodity. He can state his preference pattern. That is why their approach is also known as preference approach.

Between the two analyses, the modern approach is more realistic. Marshallian approach emphasises too much on psychological aspect. Assumptions of this approach are restrictive and unrealistic. But indifference curve assumes too little. And assumptions are less restrictive. In this sense, we find a touch of reality in indifference-preference analysis.

Secondly, one of the fundamental assumptions of the utility approach is the constancy in the marginal utility of money, though for a commodity, marginal utility must be diminishing. However, like commodity, marginal utility for money should also diminish. Marshall—assuming constancy in the marginal utility of money—ignored income effect of a price change. Change in price, in general, has two effects. One is the income effect and another is the substitution effect. Assuming constancy in the marginal utility of money, Marshall could not split price effect into income effect and substitution effect. Ignoring income effect due to constancy in the marginal utility of money, Marshall could not explain Giffen Paradox which is suggestive of positive sloping demand curve. In Marshall's analysis, it is due to this that demand curve is always negative sloping. On the other hand, Hicksian analysis, though it implicitly assumes diminishing marginal utility for a commodity, rejects constancy in the marginal utility of money. And, it is due to this indifference curve could explain Giffen paradox satisfactorily with the aid of the concept of (negative) income effect.

Thirdly, another contribution of this approach is the establishment of a better criteria for the classification of goods into substitutes and complements. Marshall could not explain the issue of substitute and complementary commodities since he assumed 'independent' utility function. This means that utility of a commodity is a function of that commodity alone. As against this, ordinalists have given detailed analysis of interrelated goods.

Fourthly, the methodology of the modern theory has proved a framework for measuring consumer's surplus which has an important bearing on welfare economics. This helps in deciding government policy.

Fifthly, it has been criticised that the concept of MRS engineered by Hicks-Allen is simply the new name of the concept of marginal utility. However, this criticism is not tenable because the concept of MRS is based on comparability of utilities of two commodities and not their measurability. In this connection, Prof. Tapas Majumdar's remark is worth noting. If we do not assume that marginal utilities are measurable even in principle, we can still have the marginal rates of substitution which is another distinct advantage of the ordinal formulation. Thus, the replacement of the principle of diminishing marginal utility by the principle of diminishing marginal rate of substitution is not a mere translation. It is a positive change in the theory of consumer's demand.

Thus, undoubtedly, indifference curve analysis is an improved approach over the Marshallian approach

4.13. INDIFFERENCE CURVE VS. UTILITY APPROACH

The utility theory was the first theory of the role of tastes in consumption. At the hands of Marshall, the utility theory got its full maturity with the discovery of the concept of 'margin' in economics. However, the theory went into disrepute in the 1930s when Profs. Hicks and Allen came out with a new tool, popularly known as indifference curve. At a first glance, the two theories appear to be radically different from each other. For instance, the former relies on the cardinal measurement of utility derived from a commodity. On the contrary, and quite rightly, the indifference approach talks about measurability of utility in an ordinal sense. But, on a close scrutiny, one finds a great deal of similarities between the two approaches. These are :

- **Similarities**

Firstly, both the approaches assumed that their consumers behave rationally. They behave rationally so as to maximise their utility or satisfaction. Marshall used the term utility. But Profs. Hicks and Allen preferred the term 'satisfaction' instead of 'utility'. What is important to us is that what 'utility' with Marshall is 'satisfaction' with Hicks.

Secondly, so far as equilibrium condition of the consumer is concerned, both the approaches believe in the proportionality rule. In Marshall's analysis, a consumer reaches equilibrium when the ratios of the marginal utilities of various commoditis, say X and Y, are equal to their price ratio of two goods. Symbolically,

$$\frac{MU_X}{MU_Y} = \frac{P_X}{P_Y}$$

In indifference curve analysis, a consumer reaches equilibrium when the slope of the indifference curve, MRS_{XY}, is equal to the slope of the budget line, $\frac{P_X}{P_Y}$. Symbolically,

$$MRS_{XY} > \frac{P_X}{P_Y}$$

It is worth noting here that there is a relationship between marginal rate of substitution (MRS) and marginal utility (MU). As a consumer moves along an indifference curve his consumption of one good, say Y, decreases, while that of another good, say X, rises. When the consumer sacrifices Y, his marginal utility for Y becomes $+ \Delta Y \times MU$ of Y. But as consumption of X increases his MU for X becomes $- \Delta X \times MU$ of X. Since, on an indifference curve, satisfaction remains unchanged, decline in utility must be compensated by an increase in utility. That is,

$$-\Delta Y.MU_Y = + \Delta X.MU_X$$

$$\text{Or} \quad -\frac{\Delta Y}{\Delta X} = \frac{MU_X}{MU_Y}$$

$-\frac{\Delta Y}{\Delta X} = \frac{MU_X}{MU_Y}$ is the slope of the indifference curve which is nothing but MRS_{XY}. So, one can write

$$MRS_{XY} = \frac{MU_X}{MU_Y}$$

So the equilibrium condition for both the approaches is the same :

$$MRS_{XY} = \left(\frac{MU_X}{MU_Y}\right) = \frac{P_X}{P_Y}$$

In indifference curve analysis, $\frac{MU_X}{MU_Y}$ has been substituted for MRS_{XY}.

Thirdly, both the approaches employ the method of introspection. Utility approach is labelled as "introspective cardinalism" while indifference analysis is labelled as "introspective ordinalism". Utility analysis is based on introspection. Like the utility analysis, indifference approach is also rooted in the introspectively derived ordinal utility functions of the consumers. To this extent, this approach is also subjective. In view of this, Prof. Tapas Majumdar said : "That the basic methodological approach of Hicks-Allen is the same as in the Marshallian marginal utility hypothesis; it is, that is to say, mainly introspective."

Forthly, both the approaches implicitly or explicity assume diminishing marginal utility derived from a commodity. However, dimisnishing marginal utility is explicity recognised in utility analysis. The concept of diminishing marginal utility is implicit in Hicks-Allen analysis. In this analysis, an indifference curve becomes convex to the origin because of diminishing MRS. and MRS, is equivalent to $\frac{MU_X}{MU_Y}$. Law of diminishing MU and the law of diminishing MRS are the two sides of the same coin.

Thus, what is clear from the above discussion is that there are striking similarities—rather than striking differences—between the two approaches. Indifference curve analysis has simply substituted new concepts and equations in place of psychological or subjective concept of utility. It has simply changed the garb without altering the basic premise. In view of this, Prof. Robertson thinks that the indifferences curve technique is just an 'old wine in a new bottle'.

QUESTIONS (WITH ANSWER-HINTS)

Long Questions (16 marks)

1. What do you mean by indifference curve? What is an indifference map? Discuss the properties of an indifference curve.

   Ans. 4.4, 4.4.1, and 4.4.2.

2. Explain the condition of a consumer's equilibrium in terms of indifference curve analysis.

   Or

   A consumer may not reach equilibrium if his indifference curve cuts the budget line.

   Ans. 4.6.

3. Discuss the characteristics of an indifference curve. How would you explain the consumer's equilibrium under indifference curve analysis? (C.U. 2008)

   Ans. 4.4.2, and 4.6.

4. How is an income consumption curve derived? Now define a normal good and an inferior good using income consumption curve. Can both the goods be inferior at the same time?

   Ans. 4.7.

5. When the price of a good changes two effects come into operation—substitution effect and income effect. Using these concepts, derive demand curves for (a) a normal good, (b) an inferior good, and (c) a Giffen good.

   Ans. (a) 4.9, (b) 4.10, (c) 4.11.

Medium-sized Questions (8 marks)

1. What do you mean by total utility and marginal utility? Explain the law of diminishing marginal utility. Point out the limitations of this law.

   Ans. 4.3.

2. State the law of diminishing marginal utility. What are the assumptions behind this law? What are its exceptions?

   Ans. 4.3.

3. At equilibrium of a consumer, marginal utility derived from a commodity must equal its price. Explain.

   Or

   How do you use the law of diminishing marginal utility to derive a normal-shaped demand curve for a commodity?

   Ans. 4.3.1.

4. Point out the deficiencies of marginal utility analysis.

   Ans. 4.3.2.

5. What is a budget line? How is it constructed? How do you distinguish between shifts in the budget line following a change in money income and a change in the price of one of the two goods?

   Ans. 4.5.

6. Construct an indifference curve with concave shape. Now draw a budget line and show equilibrium of a consumer.

   Ans. 4.6.1.

7. Derive price consumption curve for both normal and Giffen goods.

   Ans. 4.7.1.

8. How do you derive a demand curve from the price consumption curve?

   Ans. 4.8.

9. Show that the price effect is the sum total of income effect and substitution effect. (C.U. 2007)

   Ans. 4.9.

10. Point out the achievements of indifference curve analysis.

    Ans. 4.12

11. Point out the similarities and dissimilarities between indifference curve analysis and utility analysis.

    Ans. 4.13

5

THEORY OF PRODUCTION

5.1 INTRODUCTION

We have considered the demand side of the market forces in chapters three and four. There is another element of market forces—the forces of supply. The supply side is indeed concerned with the behaviour of producer or firm just as consumer behaviour is studied to understand demand side. The theory of production and cost (cost function is derived from production function) is central to the economic management of a firm. The starting point of the theory of production is the technology of production of a firm. This technology describes relationship between inputs and output. This relationship or the production function governs the level of production. Output is a function of inputs. In the short run, output behaviour is governed by the levels of non-proportional returns. Here we keep some inputs fixed. In the long run, inputs are subject to change. Output is then governed by the law of returns to scale. Reasons of constant, increasing and falling returns to scale have been discussed. The chapter ends with the discussion of isoquant or production indifference curve—the counterpart of indifference curve of a consumer.

5.2 IMPORTANCE OF THE THEORY OF PRODUCTION

The theory of production is at the heart of business economics. That is why its importance is great. *First,* the cost theory is a derived theory—it is derived from the production theory. Cost has great relevance in the determination of price of a commodity.

Secondly, the theory of production may be used in the determination of rewards of an input. The basis of input demand theory is the theory of production.

5.3 PRODUCTION FUNCTION

The key concept in the theory of production is the production function. The word 'function' in mathematics expresses the relationship between dependent and independent variables. Or a function shows a cause and effect relationship. The production function shows the technological or engineering relationship between inputs (independent variables or cause) and output (dependent variable or effect).

Using one-output and two-input function, the relationship between output and inputs is summarised in the following form:

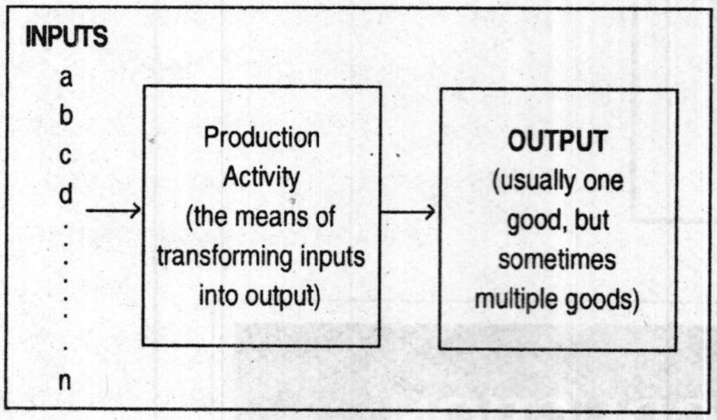

$$\text{Output} = f(\text{input}_1, \text{input}_2)$$

$$\text{Or} \quad Q = f(L, K)$$

where Q denotes the quantity of output produced and L and K denote the respective quantities of labour and capital used. By using L and K in a production process, one obtains output (Q). The technician or the engineer of an establishment describes the production process in terms of variables such as pressure, density and horse power. The economists' production function incorporates the engineering technology. Production engineers tell us how many units of L and K are used to yield a given output by using a particular process of production. Which particular production process (out of various alternatives) will be chosen by the firm depends on the prices of inputs and output that are bought and sold in the market place. Thus, a production function, being a technical one, presents physical combinations only. In brief, a production function is a graph, or a table or an equation showing the maximum output that can be produced with the help of inputs.

To the economists, production function is something more. A production function shows costs for using inputs and revenues for output sold. As the production function is given in the form of a table showing physical combinations of different inputs to obtain certain unit of output, it is not within the domain of economics. Economists are concerned not with the physical combinations but with the costs, revenue, output behaviour in response to changes in inputs used, etc. Whenever there is a change in input usage in a production process, output changes. Why does output change in this way or that way is studied by economists through production function. Consequently, different laws governing output are obtained.

The form of production function of an establishment is determined by the state of technology whose size depends on the time span. This means that a short run production function is different from a long period production function. To understand the difference, let us define short run and long run.

5.4 TIME HORIZONS: SHORT RUN AND LONG RUN

Short run is that time period when a firm cannot change all its inputs. In the short run, some inputs are held fixed and some are variable. Inputs which are not subject to change are called fixed inputs (like land, machine, etc.). Inputs whose use can be varied are called variable inputs (like casual labour, raw materials, etc.).

Long run is that period of time when no inputs are held fixed. Long period of time will enable a firm to change even its size or scale of production. In the long run, there are no fixed inputs. All inputs are variable in the long run.

However, the actual length of time, under the heading either short run or long run, does not refer to a calendar time. It varies from firm to firm or from industry to industry.

Consequent upon this definition, one obtains both short run and long run production function. A short run production function assumes fixity in all inputs except one or two. On the other hand, a long run production function assumes all inputs are variable. Using functional notation, we have the following short run production function form:

$$Q = f(L, \overline{K})$$

where L is a variable input and K is a fixed input. To explain fixity of input K, we have used bar sign on the head of K.

Production in the short run is subject to the law of variable proportions while production in the long run is subject to the laws of returns to scale.

5.5 LAW OF VARIABLE PROPORTIONS

A firm increases output in the short run by varying only variable inputs. Thus, the firm's production function becomes

$$Q = f(L, K, \overline{O})$$

In this production function, inputs K and O are assumed to be constant.

Now for different values of labour (L), we get different values of output (Q). The relation between L and Q are usually expressed in terms of 'total product' (TP) of labour. In addition, this concept of production function gives us concepts of 'average product' (AP) and 'marginal product' (MP) or marginal physical product (MPP) or incremental product.

A firm increases its level of production in the short run by making changes in input-mix Here we want to learn the returns to a variable input. Changes made in input-mix and their impact on output are studied under a celebrated law in economics: the law of diminishing returns or the law of variable proportions or the law of non-proportional returns.

Statement of the law: This law states that if we go on increasing more and more of a variable input, the amount of other inputs held constant, the returns to the variable input become non-proportional : it may first show increasing returns, then constant for a while and, eventually diminishing returns. In short, as additional units of a variable input are added to a given amount of fixed input, ultimately average and marginal products of the variable input will decline. Before explaining the non-proportional returns to the variable input, we must know the meanings of TP, AP and MP.

- **TP:** Different values of a variable input, given a specified amount of the fixed input, will give us different values of output during a given period of time. Total output is usually called the total product (TP).
- **AP:** The average product of an input is the total product divided by the number of variable input needed to produce this output. It is the output per unit of the input used. In symbols

$$AP = \frac{TP}{L}$$

AP initially rises, then reaches a maximum, and declines thereafter.

- **MP:** The marginal product is the change in total output resulting form a change in the use of variable input. In other words, it is the addition to the total product consequent upon a change in the employment of input. Symbolically,

$$MP = \frac{\Delta TP}{\Delta L}$$

Or $$MP = TP(L) - TP(L-1)$$

MP is thus the difference in total product of the L-th unit and the (L-1)th unit of production.

Thus the returns to the variable input are non-proportional: we first obtain increasing stage where TP, AP and MP rise. Then we have diminishing stage where TP increases at a slower

Table 5.1: Law of Variable Proportions

Units of variable input	TP	AP $(= \frac{TP}{L})$	MP $(= \frac{\Delta TP}{\Delta L})$	
1	4	4	4	Stage I
2	10	5	6	
3	21	7	11	
4	40	10	19	
5	55	11	15	Stage II
6	60	10	5	
7	63	9	3	
8	64	8	1	
9	63	7	−1	Stage III

rate and AP and MP decline. Ultimately, we have a negative stage when TP declines and MP becomes negative. These increasing, diminishing and negative stages of production can be explained with the help of an arithmetic example and figure.

Table 5.1 suggests that as the number of labour employed increases from 1 to 4 along with some fixed inputs, TP increases at an increasing rate and hence AP and MP rise. This is because of the fact that as variable input increases, better utilisation of fixed inputs occurs thereby causing TP to rise at an increasing rate. This stage is thus known as the stage of increasing returns or Stage I.

Now if more labour is added diminishing returns to this variable input will set in. Increase in the number of labour from 5 to 8 causes TP to rise but at a diminishing rate. As a result, AP and MP decline. This stage has been christened as the diminishing stage of production or the Stage II.

Finally, total productivity of labour now tends to decline gradually because of the fixity of fixed inputs. In other words, more employment of labour along with the fixed inputs results in an optimum utilisation of fixed inputs. Once this stage of optimum utilisation occurs, any increase in labour will cause its productivity to decline. Once the 9th unit of labour is employed TP declines from 64 to 63 units. As a result, MP becomes negative. This stage is characterised as the negative stage or the Stage III.

Graphical treatment: Now, we use graph to explain the law of variable proportions. In Fig. 5.1, we measure units of variable input (i.e., labour) on the horizontal axis, and TP, AP and MP on the vertical axis.

Consider first the TP curve. As labour is increased relative to the fixed inputs, TP curve rises rapidly, reaching its maximum slope at point F. Up to point F, TP rises at an increasing rate. Thereafter TP starts to decline. A typical TP curve thus shows that it rises initially slowly, then more rapidly, and then more slowly again, until it finally reaches a maximum and begins to decline. Note that points below the TP curve are inefficient and points above the TP curve are unattainable. In this sense, TP curve has the similarity with the production possibility curve that separates the attainable as well as efficient output levels from those of unattainable levels of output. Points on the TP curve are thus efficient. MP is the slope of the TP curve. Thus the maximum slope of TP (i.e., point F) must correspond to the maximum on the MP (point R). Once the employment of labour crosses this point, TP increases at a diminishing rate. When OT unit of labour is employed AP becomes maximum.

Beyond OT unit of labour employed, TP continues to rise, of course, at a diminishing rate, and reaches maximum at point K. Here the slope of TP becomes zero and, hence, MP becomes zero (corresponding to ON volume of labour employed).

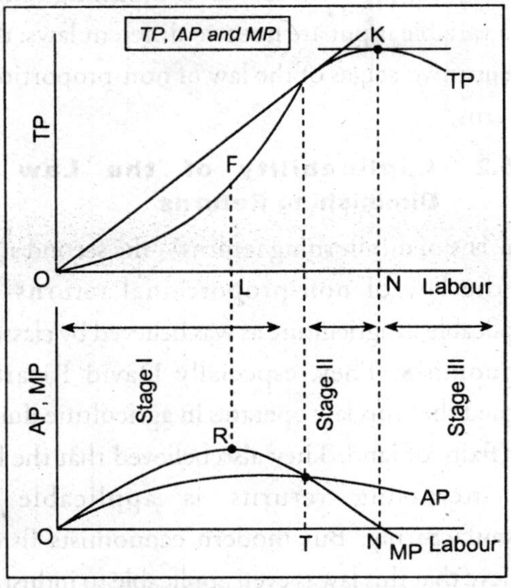

Fig. 5.1: Law of Variable Proportions

Beyond ON, if labour is employed, TP will decline and MP will become negative.

The relations among TP, AP and MP are used to define three stages of production.

Stage I is known as the stage of increasing returns where TP increases at an increasing rate and hence AP and MP rise. However, MP exceeds AP throughout this stage.

Stage II is called diminishing stage since both AP and MP decline, but are positive. This is the most crucial stage as far as the decision to produce is concerned.

Stage III is called the stage of negative returns where TP declines and MP becomes negative.

The above discussion will help us to show (i) the relationship between AP and MP and (ii) the three stages of production in a nutshell.

First, the relationship between AP and MP:

If MP > AP, AP will rise as labour increases.

If MP < AP, AP will decline as labour increases, and when MP = AP, then AP is at a maximum.

Now the nature of three stages of production:

Stage I: MP > 0, AP is rising. Thus, MP > AP — increasing stage;

Stage II: MP > 0, but AP is falling. Thus, MP < AP but TP is increasing because MP > 0 —diminishing stage.

Stage III: MP < 0 and TP is falling — negative stage.

Now a pertinent question: Out of the three stages, where will the firm produce? It is argued that no rational profit-maximising firm would produce either in stage I or in Stage III. A sensible producer would always produce in Stage II where both AP and MP of the variable input (here labour) are positive.

In Stage I, though AP of the variable input increases, MP of the fixed input is negative. In this stage, fixed input is used in large proportion relative to the small doses of the variable input. There does not occur optimum utilisation of the fixed input. As a result, its MP becomes negative. Similarly, stage III is characterised by negative marginal returns of the variable input. Here the variable inputs are combined in large proportion with the fixed input. If the variable inputs are cost-free, even then the firm would not be dare enough to produce in this stage, though MP of the fixed input is positive. As MP of the fixed input is negative in stage I, and MP of the variable input is negative in stage III, a rational producer would never operate in these two stages. These two stages are known as "stages of economic absurdity" or "economic nonsense." Optimum utilisation of both fixed and variable inputs takes place only in stage II. In other words, all the inputs are used in right or economical manner in this stage. That is why, in this stage, the APs and MPs of both fixed and variable inputs are positive but diminishing. Production must occur in stage II.

5.5.1. Explanation of Increasing Diminishing Returns

In stage I, the fixed input is abundant relative to the variable input. This kind of defective input-mix results in an underutilisation of fixed inputs. As the number of variable inputs rises, fixed input tends to get combined with the variable inputs in an economical manner, thereby leading to an increase in productivity of the fixed inputs. Probably, this is due to the fact that fixed inputs are generally indivisible. Indivisibility of the fixed inputs coupled with the rising numbers of variable inputs cause output to rise greatly due to the better utilisation of the fixed inputs. Hence, indivisibility of fixed inputs is the first cause for the increasing returns. *Secondly,* as more and more variable inputs are employed, their efficiency tends to rise, because specialisation or the so-called division of labour takes place. As a result, AP and MP of the variable inputs rise or average and marginal costs of variable inputs decline. Thus, the stage of increasing returns to a variable input is also known as the stage of diminishing cost.

Thereafter, a time comes when defective input combination gives place optimum combination of fixed and variable inputs. Now, if more variable inputs are added then, again, input combination becomes inefficient. Now, we have abundant variable inputs relative to indivisible fixed input. As indivisible fixed input is used in wrong proportion with the abundant variable input, average and marginal returns must diminish. Further, there is a limit to specialisation beyond which it cannot be increased. As a result, costs of production tend to rise. Thus, the stage of diminishing returns may be called the stage of increasing cost.

Finally, one point must be pointed out here. It is argued that the law of increasing returns to a variable input or the law of diminishing returns to a variable input are not two different laws; they are just two stages of the law of non-proportional returns.

5.5.2. Applicability of the Law of Diminishing Returns

The law of diminishing returns—the second stage of the law of non-proportional returns—is applicable in agriculture as was believed by classical economists. They, especially David Ricardo, argued that this law operates in agriculture due to the fixity of land. They also believed that the law of increasing returns is applicable to manufacturing. But modern economists firmly believe that this law is even applicable to industrial production as well as other fields of production. For example, building construction, mining, fishing are other activities which are subject to diminishing returns in the ultimate analysis. Application of modern technology may postpone the appearance of the law of diminishing returns for the time being. Ultimately, the law will set in. That is why this law is a universal one.

5.6. LAW OF RETURNS TO SCALE

When a firm changes all its inputs in the same proportion then we can say that there occurs a change in the scale of production. The study of changes in output following a change in the scale of production results in a "law of returns to scale" which has to be distinguished from the "law of returns to a variable input" obtainable in the short run. A firm can change its scale of operation only if a sufficiently long time is allowed. Thus, the "law of returns to scale" forms the subject-matter of long run production function.

We will now describe returns to scale with the help of a table and graph. For simplicity's sake, we assume that there are two inputs—labour and capital. Table 5.2 shows how output changes when these inputs are used in certain fixed ratio.

Table 5.2: Returns to Scale

Labour	Capital	Total output	Increase in the rate of output	Nature of returns to scale
1	1	4	4	
2	2	10	6	IRS
3	3	18	8	
4	4	28	10	
5	5	38	10	CRS
6	6	48	10	
7	7	58	10	
8	8	65	7	
9	9	70	5	DRS
10	10	74	4	

This table suggests that the firm initially experiences IRS when it expands output, after then CRS, and finally DRS. Fig. 5.2 also illustrates how does change in scale occur as output changes. Now we will trace out causes behind each stage of returns to scale.

If all inputs are increased by the same proportion, keeping factor proportions unaltered, then there occurs an increase in scale. The percentage increase in output due to one per cent increase in all inputs determines the returns to scale. Suppose, one-output three-variable :nput production function is given by

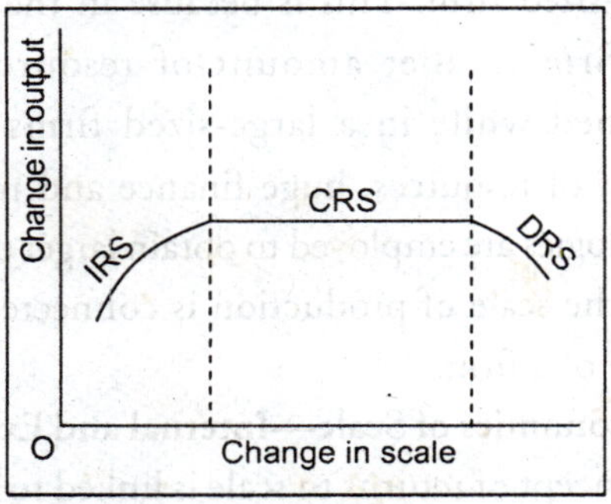

Fig. 5.2: Stages of Returns to Scale

$$Q = f(L, B, K)$$

Now, if all these inputs are exactly doubled then output may be doubled. If so, then returns to scale are said to be constant. Suppose, all L, B, K inputs are increased by 3, then output will also increase by 3, i.e.

$$3Q = f(3L, 3B, 3K)$$

If doubling or trebling of inputs cause output to increase by more than 3, then we have increasing returns to scale. And, returns to scale are said to be decreasing when doubling of inputs results in turning out an output less than that.

As firms increase the scale of production, initially the increase in output is subject to increasing returns, then constant returns and, finally, diminishing returns to scale. Initially, if we increase all the inputs by one percentage point, output will increase by more than one per cent. Then we have the stage of increasing returns to scale (IRS). Now, if the rate of increase in output remains constant following a one per cent increase in input then we have the stage of constant returns to scale (CRS). Later on, the firm experiences diminishing returns to scale (CRS). The firm experiences even diminishing returns to scale (DRS) as scale of production rises.

If	Then
1. Percentage change in TC < percentage change in Q	Economies of scale (decreasing LAC) (IRS)
2. Percentage in TC = percentage change in Q	No economies of scale or CRS (constant LAC)
3. Percentage change in TC > percentage change in Q	Diseconomies of scale or DRS (rising LAC)

5.6.1. Explanation of IRS

Size of a firm is the most proximate cause of the emergence of IRS. As the size of a firm increases, returns to scale becomes increasing. One large-sized factory seems to be more efficient than two small-sized firms. If the diameter of a pipe is doubled, flow from it will be more than double. Similarly, a double-decker bus can carry twice the number of passengers as does a single-decker bus at a slightly higher total cost. Thus, the economy of increased dimensions argue for IRS.

Secondly, the technical and/or managerial indivisibility also explains IRS. Some of the factors are large and lumpy since these do not come in small bits. For example, one cannot install half a blast furnace! A large-sized firm can use these lumpy and indivisible factors most efficiently. Lumpiness is the only source of economies of large scale production.

Thirdly, indivisibility of inputs and specialisation are interrelated. With the increase in size, this is also called increased 'division of labour' that follows from Adam Smith's famous pin-factory case. The degree of specialisation tends to rise. As a result, efficiency and productivity of an input will rise.

Due to the interplay of these factors, large scale firm enjoys economies of production—both internal and external. Economies of large scale production, therefore, lie behind the existence of IRS.

5.6.2. Explanation of CRS

It is true that IRS does not last long. Thus, returns to scale must not be rising. At best, it can be constant. CRS states that if all inputs are doubled, output will also be doubled. But it is argued that the phenomenon of CRS is a very temporary one. If all inputs are doubled then what is there to prevent output from being doubled? There are two reasons behind this situation. Scarcity of some inputs and indivisibility of some inputs are the two causes behind DRS, rather than CRS. So, we can oppositely argue that if these two elements do not operate then one would obtain CRS. Remember that under CRS, economies and diseconomies of scale cancel each other and as a result, long run average cost becomes constant.

5.6.3. Explanation of DRS

DRS is supposed to set in once the firm oversteps the limit of expansion. Continuous increase in all inputs and, hence, expansion in the size of a firm beyond a certain point lead to the emergence of DRS. One of the reasons behind the occurrence of DRS is the managerial inefficiency since there are limits to the efficient functioning of management. As the size of the firm increases, inefficiency tends to rise and diseconomies of large scale production become stronger than the economies of scale. Again, DRS may appear due to the exhaustion of fixed natural resources or physical constraints of inputs. There is no guarantee that the coal production will be doubled if the size of coal mine is doubled because the stock of coal on the earth is not plentiful in amount. This will surely raise cost of production.

5.7. ECONOMIES OF SCALE OF PRODUCTION

Scale of production refers to the size of a firm. A small-sized firm yields lower output compared to a large-sized firm. This is because in the small-sized firm smaller amount of resources are combined while in a large-sized firms larger amount of resources, huge finance and modern technologies are employed to obtain larger output. Thus, the scale of production is connected with the size of a firm.

Economies of Scale—Internal and External: The concept of returns to scale is linked to that of economies of scale. A firm may experience economies of scale if costs per unit of output fall as the scale of production increases. Thus, by economies of scale we mean advantages in large scale production. It also refers to the factors which cause average cost of production to decline as output rises or scale of production increases. A firm enjoys economies of scale when doubling of output causes costs to become less than double. As the size of a firm grows it enjoys certain economies of scale.

Marshall classified these economies of scale into two groups: internal economies and external economies.

Internal economies of production arise when the benefits or advantages of a firm's expansion are enjoyed by the firm itself. Thus, internal economies accrue only to the individual firm by its own organisational ability and effort. These internal advantages reaped by the firm enable it to lower its average cost of production as its scale of production increases. These are called internal because the scale economies are within the control of the firm.

On the other hand, external economies arise when an increase in a firm's production produces favourable effects on other firms. In other words, benefits of increased production spread on other firms in the industry or in the region. Such economies arise because the development of an industry leads to the development of ancillary services or benefit to all firms. Thus, external economies are available to all firms in the industry irrespective of their sizes. These are called external because the scale economies are outside the control of the firm.

These two economies of scale result in a falling average cost as output rises. But there are some adverse repercussions on a firm or on other firms. Such adverse or unfavourable effects are termed as diseconomies of large scale production. Economies of scale enjoyed by a firm or other firms within the industry or in a particular locality will sooner or later be replaced by diseconomies of large scale production when average cost of producing a commodity, instead of declining, tends to rise. Likewise, there are internal and external diseconomies. Diseconomies of scale are not to be confused with diminishing returns.

Types of Internal Economies: Internal economies result from various factors. These are: (i) technological economies, (ii) marketing economies, (iii) financial economies, (iv) managerial economies, and (v) risk-distribution economies.

Technological economies:

- *Increased specialisation* : One of the most important sources of internal economies is technology. Large firms can use specialised and highly efficient machinery (often called 'dedicated machinery') along with specialised labour. If the production process is split into a number of various stages, machines can be designed specially for each stage. That is why large scale production or mechanised production means mass production. Large firms can arrange for specialisation of both labour and machines. The division of labour or specialisation itself can result in higher productivity.
- *Factor indivisibility*: Factor indivisibility is another source of technological economies enjoyed internally by a firm. Some factors are indivisible or lumpy in character. These cannot

be installed in fraction or in smaller units. Steel production requires installation of blast furnace having high fixed costs. If large scale operations are to be made in steel factory it should employ indivisible items. It will be grossly inefficient if small quantities of steel are produced with this blast furnace. Obviously, a large firm will then be able to achieve lower costs.

- *Economies of increased dimensions*: Doubling the length, breadth and the height of a cube, the surface area increases four times and the volume increases eight times of the original. This simple mathematical principle is suggestive of economies of increased dimensions. Large firms often reap economies of increased dimensions than small firms. This results in lower costs. If the dimension of a container increases, the cubic capacity increases more than proportionately. If the diameter of a water-pipe is increased then the discharge of water will be larger than its diameter. A double-decker bus carries more passengers than a single-decker bus, yet no extra cost is required. Again, when a firm doubles its sales, it is not at all needed to double its inventory expenditures. This is called economies of increased dimensions.
- *Principle of multiples*: Usually, the production process of a large firm involves the use of different types of machinery having different capacities. Some of them can produce small quantities while some others large quantities of output, thus, achieving a high utilisation rate. In other words, efficient as well as optimum utilisation of machines is possible since large firms can afford to make use of multiple machines. Further, production may be multi-stage. For example, car component suppliers remain closely linked to car manufacturers. Once these are conducted on a large scale, it becomes cost effective.
- *Use of by-products*: A large firm can utilise its by-product or save the waste materials. A big factory like that of Tata's can use its smoke emanating from its factory site to produce articles like tar, naptha, etc. A small firm is always at a disadvantageous position. A large sugar factory can produce alcohol as a by-product.
- *Research and development* : It is only the large firms that can conduct its own research and development programme so that newer and improved techniques of production are developed.

▲ **Marketing economies:** A large firm can reap substantial economies in the purchase and sale of goods and raw materials. As large firms purchase raw materials in bulk quantities, they can obtain the same at a wholesale cheaper price, or at a favourable discount. As far as sale or distribution of a product of a large firm is concerned, it appoints expert or specialist sellers as well as expensive but more cost-effective advertising. Advertisements attract more customers and, hence, lead to increased volume of sales.

▲ **Financial economies:** A large firm can secure business finance easier as it has huge assets. Because of its reputation, the shares of large firms are sold easily. Again, investors enjoy greater confidence in buying shares, debentures and other securities of a large firm. Further, large firms obtain loans from banks and other agencies at favourable rates because of their long-standing reputation and influence.

▲ **Managerial or administrative economies:** It is the size of large firms that enable them to use more advanced and specialised management techniques. Different departments may enjoy specialist management personnel. Managerial economies can now be secured by the delegation of functions to each specialist. This is known as functional specialisation or horizontal division of labour. In other words, this is really applying division of labour in the field of management.

▲ **Risk-distribution economies:** A business always involves uncertainty and, hence, risk. Through diversification of output, markets, sources of supply, a large firm can withstand any adverse conditions emanating from a particular product or market. In other words, a large firm can spread its risks and the loss in one market consequent upon a decline in demand may be offset by the gain in another market. Thus, large firms are less vulnerable to risks involved in business. A small firm is exposed to large risks since it cannot distribute risk among different products or markets because of the absence of diversification.

Types of external economies: Like internal economies, external economies can also be grouped into three: (i) economies of concentration or localisation, (ii) economies of information, and (iii) economies of disintegration.

- *Economies of concentration*: It may happen that a particular area(s) often specialise in the production of particular products due to the availability of various inputs required for production. If a particular area is endowed with a variety of resources including infrastructural facilities, industries tend to flock in such areas. In other words, more and more industries get concentrated in these geographical areas leading to a decline in average costs of all firms.

  It is often said that Bangalore is the Silicon Valley of Asia as its growth in this part is phenomenal. The computer software firms in Bangalore share external economies from their close proximity to each other forms. All enjoy the benefits of a pool of highly skilled staff, shared traning programmes, better transport links, etc.

  External economies may also be related to a trade association which may provide trade information as well as market trends. It may organise trade fair or various marketing facilities that may not be exploited lay a single firm.

- *Economies of information*: All the firms, particularly the bigger ones, in a geographical area may cooperate in the realm of research and development. The R and D wing of the modern large firms provide valuable information relating to a business through its trade and technical journals. Other firms benefit from the dissemination of information for which no direct costs are incurred by these firms. Thus, average costs of production decline.

- *Economies of disintegration*: When an industry develops many specialised firms get established specialising in particular stages of the production process. This is called disintegration which results in increased efficiency.

5.7.1. Diseconomies of Scale

Economies of scale can never be unlimited. As a result, expansion beyond a certain point will not cause average costs to decline. Instead, it will rise as the firm expands. In other words, when the size of a firm becomes large, possibilities for economies get exhausted and diseconomies set in.

There are five important internal causes of diseconomies of scale :

- **Technical diseconomies:** The size of the firm may hurt itself. Technologically, it is not wise always to use more and more complex machinery which itself is expensive.

- **Marketing diseconomies**: We know that division of labour or specialisation is limited by the extent of the market. If the market is narrow, continual expansion in size may not be cost-effective. Transport costs may shoot up if raw materials or finished products are required to be transferred in distant markets.

- **Financial diseconomies :** Growth of large firms is often hampered due to financial constraint. Sometimes, it may fail to secure necessary amount of finance from the market, particularly if the firm's financial credibility is lost or damaged. Same is true in the share market. Often a large firm fails to secure necessary finances through sale of shares and debentures.

- **Managerial disconomies:** As the size of a firm increases, administrative problem as well as coordinating problem may emerge due to the growth of bureaucracy or a minute division of managerial labour. In a large-sized firm, managerial functions become increasingly difficult to perform effectively since more and more layers of administrators and executives are added with the expansion in size. Here Parkinson's Second Law comes into effect which states: "Subordinates multiply at a fixed rate, regardless of the amount of work produced!"

These are internal diseconomies of large scale production. Diseconomies of scale may also be external. Because of localisation of industries in a locality, there occurs the problem of traffic congestion or pollution. In view of these problems of large scale production, modern governments also support the growth of small firms. The philosophy of 'small is beautiful' works.

5.8. TWO VARIABLE INPUTS—ISOQUANT OR ISOPRODUCT CURVE

So far we have concentrated our attention to one variable input: labour. Now we say that to produce a commodity we need two variable inputs. Further, we assume that these two inputs are substitutable throughout the production process. One can represent these two substitutable inputs production functions in a diagram and obtain a curve called isoquant or isoproduct curve or production indifference curve, which is similar to indifference curve in the consuming sector.

Modern economists analyse the theory of production in terms of isoquant. Isoquant is a concept similar to indifference curve popularised by J. R. Hicks and R. G. D. Allen.

Meaning: The Greek word 'iso' means 'equal' or 'same' Thus, an isoquant or 'iso' product curve is a curve along which output is the same. For the sake of analysis, we are assuming that our producer employs two inputs—labour (L) and capital (K). A firm can produce a certain amount of a commodity by employing different combinations of labour and capital. When this information is plotted on a graph paper, we obtain an isoquant. A particular level of output may be obtained if the following combinations of labour and capital are utilised :

Table 5.3 : Alternative Combinations of Inputs for Producing a Given Output (50 units)

Combination	Labour (L)	Capital (K)	Marginal Rate of Technical Substitution ($MRTS_{KL}$)
A	1	15	
			1 : 5
B	2	10	
			1 : 3
C	3	7	
			1 : 2
D	4	5	
			1 : 1
E	5	4	

The above table tells us that to produce 50 units of output, the producer can choose 1 unit of labour and 15 units of capital (i.e., combination A). However, if he chooses combination B or C or D or E, the same volume of output will be obtained. Thus, he is indifferent about what

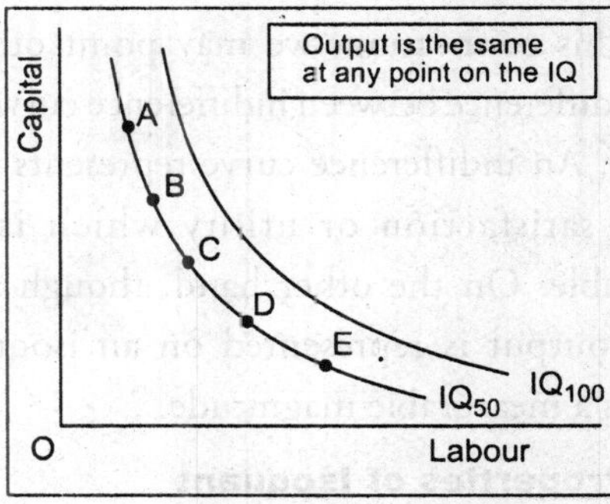

Fig. 5.3: Isoquant

combination of inputs to choose. Whatever the combination he chooses, firm's output level remains fixed at 50 units. If we plot this information on a graph paper, we will obtain production indifference curve or equal output curve, as shown in Fig. 5.3.

In Fig. 5.3, labour is measured along the horizontal axis and capital is measured along the vertical axis. We have drawn an isoproduct curve represented by a curve IQ_{50}. Point A on IQ_{50} represents just one possible combination of labour and capital which can be used to produce 50 units of output. Point B is another possible combination of labour and capital to produce the same level of output. But at point B, more labour and less capital is used. Points C, D and E have similar meanings. Now by joining these points we get an isoquant. Each and every point on an isoquant represents the same level of output.

Thus, an isoquant represents different combinations of two inputs, i.e., labour and capital that yield the same level of output. An isoquant is a contour line showing different combinations of inputs that are physically capable of producing a given amount of output.

A family of isoquants is called isoquant map. Higher-order isoquant represents higher level of output. By employing more labour and capital, a firm can produce larger output. Thus, IQ_{100} lies above IQ_{50}.

In this connection, we may point out the primary difference between indifference curve and isoquant. An indifference curve represents same level of satisfaction or utility which is not quantifiable. On the other hand, though same level of output is represented on an isoquant, output is a measurable magnitude.

5.8.1. Properties of Isoquant

Like an indifference curve in the consumer plane, a production indifference curve or an isoquant has the following properties:

- An isoquant normally slopes downward from left to right. Or it has a negative slope.
- An isoquant is convex to the origin.
- No two isoquants can intersect each other.

We consider these properties in turn.

An isoquant is negatively sloped: As we move along an isoquant the amount of one input must increase while that of another must decline. If both labour and capital yield positive marginal products, then increasing the number of labour while holding the number of capital constant would increase output. So, if we want to maintain a constant level of output when the quantity of labour (or capital) is increased, the quantity of capital (or labour) must decrease. This implies a negatively sloped isoquant. In other words, downward slope suggests that both the inputs have positive marginal products.

An isoquant is convex to the origin: Isoquant analysis assumes that the two inputs needed for producing a given level of output are substitutes, though not perfect substitutes. Thus, isoquant is convex to the origin because of the diminishing "marginal rate of technical substitution between labour and capital" ($MRTS_{K \text{ for } L}$ or $MRTS_{L \text{ for } K}$).

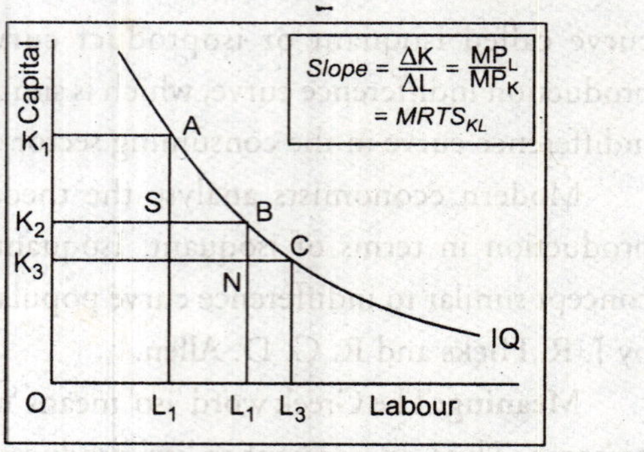

Fig. 5.4: Convex-shaped Isoquant

The rate at which one input is substituted for another is called the MRTS. Consider the hypothetical example shown in Table 5.1. Suppose our producer moves along an isoquant from the combination represented by A to the combination B. We want to learn how many units of capital will have to be sacrificed to get one additional unit of labour. The answer is, clearly, 5. The ratio of 5 to 1 is called the MRTS. Now, if the producer moves from B to C combination, the MRTS would be 3 to 1. Thus, with larger quantities of labour and smaller quantities of capital to produce a level of output of, say, 50 units, the MRTS, continuously declines. It is due to the diminishing MRTS an isoquant becomes convex to the origin. The Table 5.1 suggests that the MRTS (1 : 5 > 1 : 3 >1 : 2 >1 : 1) is declining.

Fig. 5.4 explains convexity of an isoquant. Let us choose points A, B and C on an isoquant. If production occurs at A, the firm would use OK_1 units of capital and OL_1 units of labour. As we move from point A to B, less capital and more labour are required to produce the given level of output. This amounts to saying that labour is substituted for capital. The rate at which labour is substituted for capital (i.e., MRTS) is

$$\frac{OK_1 - OK_2}{OL_1 - OL_2} = \frac{AS}{SB}$$

Similarly, for movements from B to C, the MRTS is

$$\frac{OK_2 - OK_3}{OL_1 - OL_3} = \frac{BN}{NC}$$

Since, $\frac{AS}{SB} > \frac{BN}{NC}$, one can say that MRTS is diminishing and isoquant is convex to the origin. The slope of an isoquant is MRTS. Diminishing MRTS is expressed graphically by the flattening of the slope of the isoquant.

One important point is to be noted here. MRTS is related to the marginal products of two inputs. We have seen that as MRTS declines labour is substituted for capital. In other words,

$$MRTS_{K \text{ for } L} = -\frac{\Delta K}{\Delta L}$$

Since, $\left(\frac{\Delta K}{\Delta L}\right)$ is the slope of an isoquant (note the negative sign), the MRTS is given by the slope of an isoquant. And, MRTS is equal to the ratio of marginal product of labour (MP_L) to the marginal product of capital (MP_K). If we move along an isoquant, the reduction in one unit of capital must be compensated by the increase in labour input. Reduction of capital input means fall in output and increase of labour means rise in output. Fall in output must cancel out the increase in output, so that output level along an isoquant remains fixed. The reduction in output following the reduction in the use of capital input is—$\Delta K.MP_K$. The increase in output consequent upon an increase in labour input is $\Delta L.MP_L$. Along an isoquant, decrease in output should exactly match increase in output. That is,

$$-\Delta K.MP_K = \Delta L.MP_L$$

$$\text{or } -\frac{\Delta K}{\Delta L} = \frac{MP_L}{MP_K} = MRTS_{K \text{ for } L}$$

If isoquants were concave to the origin, the MRTS between two inputs would be increasing one, rather than a diminishing one.

Isoquants cannot intersect: We do not find any necessity to prove this property here as we did so in connection with the consumer indifference curve. The same logic can be applied here.

5.9. RIDGE LINES: ECONOMIC REGION OF PRODUCTION

An isoquant represents combinations of two inputs that yield the same level of output. However, not all points of an isoquant are relevant for production. Such points may be called infeasible points. One should consider only feasible portions of an isoquant. This is because of the fact that no rational producer will produce where marginal product of an input is either zero or negative. If the isoquant is backward bending and upward sloping marginal product of any input will be negative, and, hence, this portion of isoquant may be considered as economically non-sensible region of production. Only the negatively sloped segment of the isoquant is relevant for production or economically feasible.

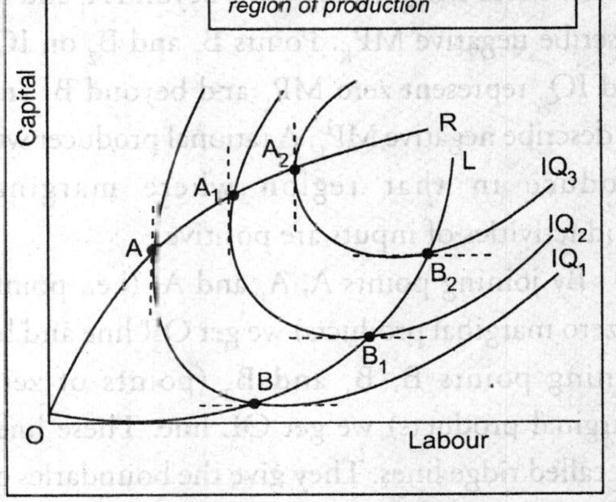

Fig. 5.5 : Isoquant Map and Feasible Region of Production

This is shown in Fig. 5.5 where we have drawn three isoquants showing different levels of output for different labour-capital combinations. This diagram separates economic region of production from uneconomic region of production. Region in which marginal products of all inputs are positive constitutes economic region of production. Or the region in which input substitution takes place may be called economic region of production. In an uneconomic region, as marginal product of an input becomes either zero or negative, the question of input substitution does not arise. Production in such region is, for obvious reasons, unprofitable or infeasible.

At point A on IQ_1, the firm employs certain units of labour and capital. Since the tangent to IQ_1 at point A is parallel to the vertical axis, marginal product of capital (MP_K) is zero. If more capital is used, marginal product of capital should be negative. In other words, beyond point A, MP_K is negative. At point B on IQ_1, MP_L is zero and beyond point B on IQ_1, MP_L is negative. Thus points between A and B represent positive marginal productivities of both labour and capital. Here substitution between two inputs takes place. Similarly, points A_1 and A_2 on IQ_2 and IQ_3 describe zero MP_K while points beyond A_1 and A_2 describe negative MP_K. Points B_1 and B_2 on IQ_1 and IQ_2 represent zero MP_L and beyond B_1 and B_2 describe negative MP_L. A rational producer will produce in that region where marginal productivities of inputs are positive.

By joining points A, A_1 and A_2 (i.e., points of zero marginal products) we get OR line and by joining points B, B_1 and B_2 (points of zero marginal products) we get OL line. These lines are called ridge lines. They give the boundaries of the economic region of production where input substitution takes place. Any points on isoquants outside the upper ridge line OR and lower ridge line OL constitute uneconomic region of production. Production must take place inside the ridge lines. Note that ridge lines separate the relevant (i.e., negatively sloped) from the irrelevant portions (i.e., povitively sloped) of the isoquants.

5.10. ISOCOST LINE

We have not discussed till now the costs incurred by a firm to produce a given level of output. The cost of production is the sum of all outlays on purchasing inputs required to produce. Such cost information can be available from the isocost line similar to budget line obtained in the theory of consumer behaviour. An isocost line shows various combinations of two inputs—labour and capital—that can be bought for a given amount of expenditure.

Let us assume that a typical firm uses two inputs, L and K, whose prices are P_L (or, w) and P_K (or, r). These input prices (w and r) are given to the producer. Let 'C' be the total cost of production for employing different units of L and K.

We can represent all these information in terms of a straight line equation:

$$C = (P_L.L) + (P_K.K)$$

$$C = w.L + r.K$$

If the firm decides to purchase input K only, then solving for K, we obtain

$$r.K = C - w.L$$

Dividing both sides by r, gives

$$\frac{C}{r} - \frac{W}{r}.L$$

If the firm spends 'C', which is given and 'r' is the price of capital then $\frac{C}{r}$ denotes the maximum amount of capital that can be bought. Thus, $\frac{C}{r}$ is the vertical or ordinate intercept, if capital is measured on the vertical axis of a diagram. The second-term, i.e., $\frac{w}{r}$ is the slope of the line or price ratio of the two inputs which is negative.

Similarly, if entire 'C' is spent on buying labour, then the firm can purchase maximum amount of labour by the following amount.

Solving for L, one obtains :

$$L = \frac{C}{w} - \frac{r}{w}.K$$

Here $\frac{C}{w}$ represents maximum amount of labour that can be bought. If labour is measured on the horizontal axis then $\frac{C}{w}$ will represent horizontal intercept. As usual, $\frac{r}{w}$ is the slope of the equal cost line.

If we plot all these information on a graph paper, we obtain isocost line, as shown in Fig. 5.6. We measure labour on the horizontal axis and capital on the vertical axis. Point B on the horizontal axis represents the maximum purchasable amount of labour with a given monetary outlay, if no capital is bought. In terms of equation, point B is nothing but $\frac{C}{w}$, the horizontal intercept. Similarly, point A shows the maximum purchasable amount of capital if no labour is bought. Thus, point A is $\frac{C}{r}$, the vertical intercept. However, a firm purchases both of the two inputs. Between points A and B, there are innumerable purchasable combinations of labour and capital. Now, if all these purchasable combinations of inputs are joined together, we would obtain isocost line (AB). Thus, an isocost line represents alternative combinations of labour and capital that may be purchased for a given

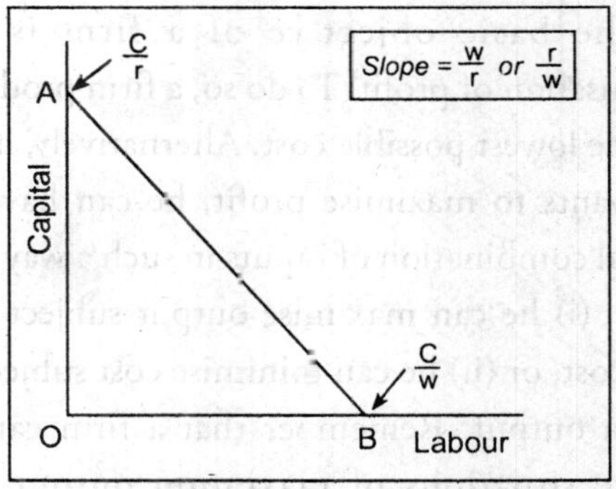

Fig. 5.6: Isocost Line

monetary outlay. An increase in monetary outlay would cause isocost line to shift to the upward direction. Conversely, there will be an inward shift of the isocost line if monetary outlay declines. These lines are called isocost or equal cost lines since costs remain the same throughout a particular line.

The slope of an isocost line is the negative of the price ratio. Thus, the slope of an isocost line AB is $-\frac{OA}{OB}$.

We know that $OA = \frac{C}{r}$. and $OB = \frac{C}{w}$.

Therefore,

$$-\frac{OA}{OB} = -\frac{C}{r} / \frac{C}{w} = -\frac{C}{r} . \frac{w}{C} = -\frac{w}{r} = \frac{P_L}{P_K}$$

Whenever there is a parallel shifting of the isocost line following a change in total expenditure then the slope of the isocost line would remain the same. However, a change in the relative input price will cause a change in the slope of the isocost line.

5.11. EQUILIBRIUM OF A FIRM: OPTIMUM COMBINATION OF INPUTS

After knowing the concepts of isoquant and isocost line, one must find out the optimal combination of resources. In other words, a firm should choose a correct or optimal combination of resources.

The basic objective of a firm is the maximisation of profit. To do so, a firm produces with the lowest possible cost. Alternatively, if the firm wants to maximise profit, he can have an optimal combination of inputs in such a way that either : (i) he can maximise output subject to a given cost, or (ii) he can minimise cost subject to a given output. Remember that a firm cannot achieve situations of maximum output and minimum cost simultaneously. Maximum output can be obtained only at a given cost or minimisation of cost situation will emerge at a given output level.

- **Maximisation of Output Subject to a Given Cost** : Suppose, a firm purchases two inputs—labour and capital—with a given expenditure to produce a commodity. Further, we also assume that input prices are given. A firm operates efficiently if it maximies output subject to input cost. To do this, it must select the proper input combination.

In Fig. 5.7, we have plotted an isoquant map labeled as IQ_1, IQ_2, etc. and an isocost line, AB. Given the cost constraint, the maximum amount of output that a firm can produce is IQ_2. Such choice of output level, given the cost constraint, is determined by the tangency point (E) of isoquant (IQ_2) and isocost line (AB). The

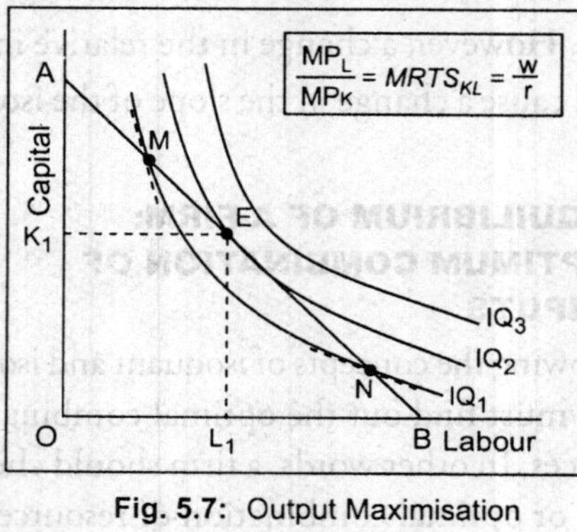

Fig. 5.7: Output Maximisation

optimum combination of inputs is, thus, OK_1 of capital and OL_1 of labour.

Let us see whether IQ_2 level of output is maximum or not. Note that though IQ_3 represents highest level of output and, hence, is desirable but that is unobtainable since available input combinations are limited to those lying on or below the isocost line AB. Given the cost constraint a firm cannot go beyond the line AB. Further, IQ_1 level of output though obtainable given the cost constraint, does not indicate higher level of output. A firm, even given the isocost line AB, can produce larger output if it stays on IQ_2. Thus, point E (on IQ_2 and isocost line AB) defines maximum producible amount of output given the cost constraint. In other words, a firm reaches equilibrium when the highest attainable isoquant becomes tangential to the given isocost line.

Alternatively, one can say that a firm reaches equilibrium when the slope of the isoquant becomes equal to the slope of the isocost line. In symbols,

$$MRTS_{KL} = \frac{MP_L}{MP_K} = \frac{w}{r}$$

This condition is known as the necessary condition or mathematically, first-order condition. This condition for equilibrium is fulfilled at the point of tangency (i.e., point E). But at point M, the slope of the isoquant is greater than the slope of the isocost line. To understand this, we have drawn a tangent at point M on IQ_1. The tangent at point M, i.e., $MRTS_{KL}$, is steeper than the tangent at point M on isocost line, AB. Thus $MRTS_{KL} > \frac{w}{r}$ at point M. Point M is not the equilibrium point.

In addition, there is another condition known as sufficient condition or mathematically, second-

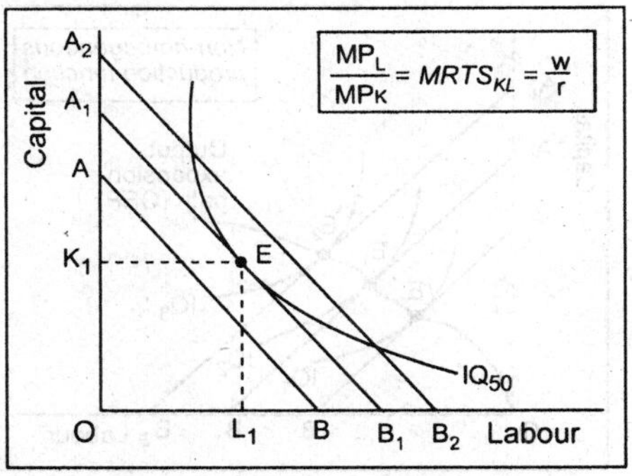

Fig. 5.8: Cost Minimisation

order condition. This condition requires that isoquant must be convex to the origin at the point of equilibrium. This condition is again fulfilled at point E.

- **Minimisation of Cost Subject to a Given Output:** An alternative to maximising output for a cost constraint is the minimisation of cost subject to a stipulated level of output. Under this least cost combination condition, a firm faces more than one isocost lines and only one isoquant to represent stipulated volume of output.

It is to be pointed out here that the conditions for equilibrium are the same. First-order condition states that MRTS equals input-price ratio. Second-order condition states that an isoquant must be convex to the origin. Because of the identical conditions for equilibrium of both the cases, these two yield identical results.

In Fig. 5.8, we have drawn three isocost lines represented by AB, A_1B_1 and A_2B_2. Higher isocost lines represent higher costs. The aim of the firm is cost minimisation. Here IQ_{50} represents the stipulated level of output. Our firm will not stay on isocost line AB since IQ_{50} output is not physically producible by an input combination available for this outlay. If the firm incurs an expenditure represented by the isocost line A_2B_2, it will experience a larger cost to produce IQ_{50} level of output. Since the same level of output can be produced on a lower isocost line A_1B_1, why should the firm choose A_2B_2 isocost line? Thus, a firm will select an input combination of OK_1 and OL_1 of capital and labour, respectively, to produce IQ_{50} level of output. Note that, at point E (i.e., where a given isoquant is tangent to lowest possible isocost line),

$$MRTS_{K \text{ for } L} = \frac{MP_L}{MP_K} = \frac{w}{r}$$

In addition to the fulfillment of this necessary condition or first-order condition for equilibrium (i.e., $MRTS_{KL} = \frac{w}{r}$), we need another condition, known as sufficient condition or second-order condition. This condition states that isoquant must be convex to the origin. This point E is the equilibrium point. Note that conditions for equilibrium are formally the same in both the cases.

This cost minimisation principle is usually observed in the construction industry.

5.12. OUTPUT EXPANSION PATH

To produce maximum output subject to a cost constraint or to produce a given output at a minimum cost, a firm will produce at that point where an isoquant is tangent to the isocost line, or where the slope of an isoquant is equal to the slope of the isocost line. Thus the point of tangency gives us the optimal input combination. While searching an optimal input usage, we assume that the costs of the firm, prices of inputs required to produce, etc., remain constant.

Now we relax some of these assumptions. Suppose monetary expenditure of the firm increases. Given prices of two inputs, now isocost line will shift up parallely. If the producer decides

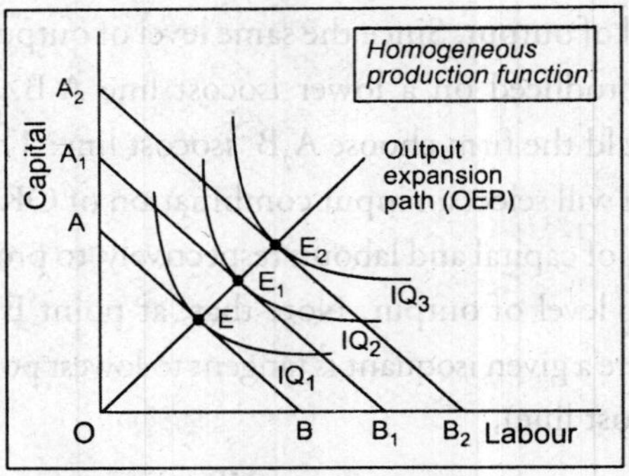

Fig. 5.9: Output Expansion Path

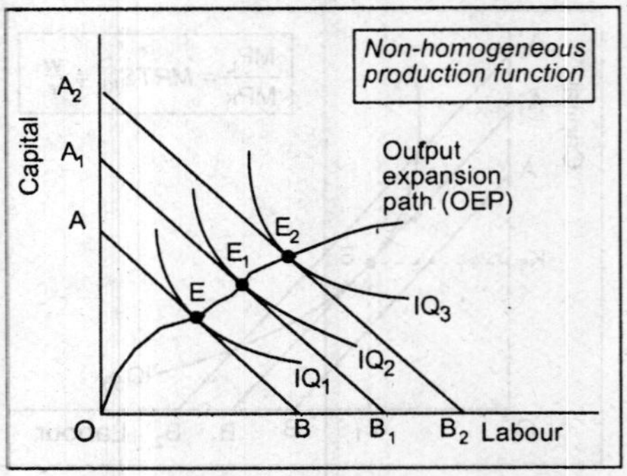

Fig. 5.10: Output Expansion Path

to increase output following an increase in outlay, isoquant will shift up. Now, new points of tangency between new isoquant and new isocost line will give us the minimum cost and optimal input combination for successive levels of output. By joining these points of tangency we obtain a line called output expansion path.

Fig. 5.9 illustrates output expansion path—which is similar to income consumption curve of the consumer.

In Figs 5.9, and 5.10, we have drawn three isoquants and three isocost lines. These two curves touch each other at points E, E_1 and E_2. Points E, E_1 and E_2 are the points of least-cost combination of resources. The line joining these points of tangency is called the output expansion path (OEP). In other words, the locus of tangencies of isocost lines to isoquants gives us long run output expansion path (OEP) of a firm. An OEP shows how the optimal input usage changes with the change in output, if input prices do not change. An OEP starts from the origin and becomes a straight line as drawn in Fig. 5.9. If OEP is a straight line, the production function is said to be linearly homogeneous (HGNS) or production function obeys constant returns to scale. A straight line OEP tells us that factor proportions depend only on input price ratio or factor proportions are independent of the level of output. This suggests that the rate of increase in physical output is the same as that of the rate of input proportions.

When production function is not a linearly homogeneous one, then OEP may take the shape of Fig. 5.10.

5.12.1. Output Expansion Path and Varying Returns to Scale

A short run production function gives us 'laws of returns to a variable input' while a long run production function gives us 'laws of returns to scale'. One of the important phases of law of returns to scale is the constant returns to scale. A firm can change its scale of operation when it increases all of its inputs in fixed proportion. Then why should output increase by the same proportion? In other words, in the production process, there is no guarantee that returns to scale will be unchanging. In fact, constant returns to scale is a temporary phenomenon that a firm might face. A firm in the production process may face actually varying returns to scale. As the scale of production expands by combining fixed doses of labour and capital, the production function will initially show increasing returns to scale, then, after a point, constant returns to scale and, finally, diminishing returns to scale.

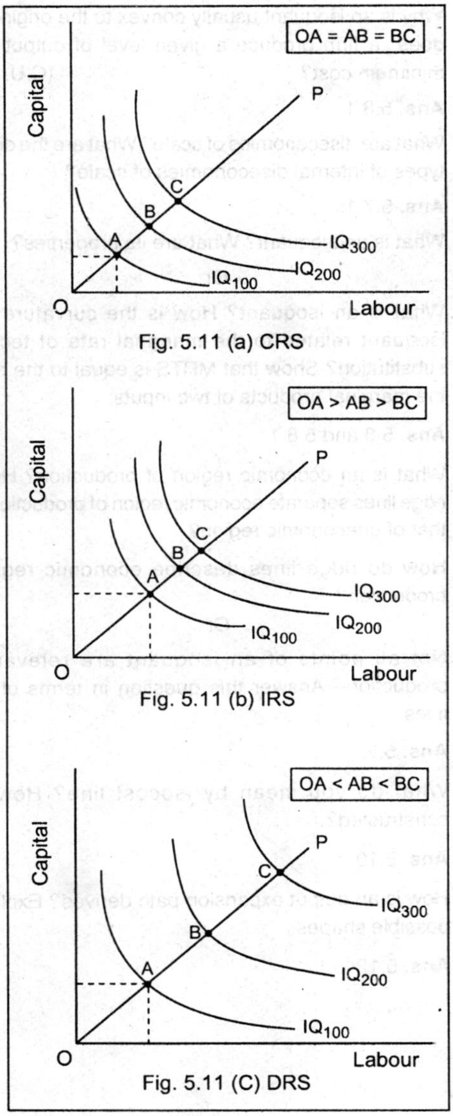

Fig. 5.11: Different Returns to Scale

The constant, increasing and diminishing returns to scale have been shown independently in each of the three figures in Fig. 5.11, respectively. In Fig. 5.11(a), isoquants labeled as IQ_{100}, IQ_{200}, IQ_{300} have been drawn equal-spaced. This means that the distance between isoquants along the ray OP is the same. This means that if we increase L and K by 1, output will be 100, described by IQ_{100}. Now if L and K increase by 2, output will rise to 200, represented by IQ_{200}. Thus, the distance OA = AB = BC along the ray OP. This means production function obeys constant returns to scale.

Fig. 5.11(b) explains increasing returns to scale. This means that if inputs are doubled, output will be more than doubled. In diagrammatic term, we can say that the distance between successive isoquants declines. (i.e, $OA<AB<BC$)This amounts to saying that proportionate increases in inputs are required less to obtain equal increments in output. In this case, obviously, production function is said to be HGNS of degree greater than one, provided the ray OP is a linear one.

Fig. 5.11(c) explains diminishing returns to scale. Returns to scale are said to be diminishing if equal proportionate increases in input causes output to expand less than that. Along the ray OP, the distance between successive isoqaunts rises (i.e, $OA < AB < BC$). This line suggests that larger proportionate increases in inputs are required to obtain an equal increase in output. Mathematically, such a production function is said to be homogeneous of degree less than one.

QUESTIONS (WITH ANSWER-HINTS)

Long Questions (16 marks)

1. Briefly explain the law of variable proportions. Explain why a profit-maximising firm will produce in stage II.

   Or

   What do you mean by return to a variable input? Discuss in this context the law of variable proportions.

   Or

   State the law of variable proportions with graphical illustration. How do you explain its different phases?

   Ans. 5.5 and 5.5.1.

2. What is meant by law of returns to scale? What are the different stages of returns to scale? How do you explain these stages?

   Ans. 5.6, 5.6.1, 5.6.2 and 5.6.3.

3. What do you mean by internal and external economies of large scale production? Analyse the different types of internal and external economies.

   Or

   What are the advantages of large scale production?

   Ans. 5.7.

4. How do you explain producer's equilibrium with the help of isoquant and isocost line?

   Or

   How does a firm select cost-minimising technique of production?

   Or

   Do you think that maximisation of output subject to a given cost constraint and minimisation of cost subject to a given output will give identical results?

   Ans. 5.11.

5. How do you define output expansion path? Can a firm have a production function that exhibits increasing returns to scale, constant returns to scale and diminishing returns to scale as output increases. Explain your answer in terms of output expansion path.

   Ans. 5.12 and 5.12.1.

Medium-sized Questions (8 marks)

1. What is production function? How does a long run production function differ from a short run production function?

   Ans. 5.3 and 5.4.

2. What do you understand by 'Returns to scale'? Discuss diagrammatically the different types of returns to scale

   Ans. 5.6. (C.U. 2008)

3. Why is an isoquant usually convex to the origin? How does a firm produce a given level of output at the minimum cost? (C.U. 2007)

   Ans. 5.8.1

4. What are diseconomies of scale? What are the different types of internal diseconomies of scale?

   Ans. 5.7.1.

5. What is an isoquant? What are its properties?

   Or

   What is an isoquant? How is the curvature of an isoquant related to the marginal rate of technical substitution? Show that MRTS is equal to the ratio of the marginal products of two inputs.

   Ans. 5.8 and 5.8.1.

6. What is an economic region of production? How do ridge lines separate economic region of production from that of uneconomic region?

   How do ridge lines describe economic region of production?

   Or

   Not all points of an isoquant are relevant for production—Answer this question in terms of ridge lines.

   Ans. 5.9.

7. What do you mean by isocost line? How is it constructed?

   Ans. 5.10.

8. How is an output expansion path derived? Explain its possible shapes.

   Ans. 5.12.

6

THE THEORY OF COST

6.1. INTRODUCTION

The study of business behaviour concentrates on the production process — the conversion of inputs into outputs—and the relationship between output and costs of production. In Chapter Five we have studied a firm's production technology and how inputs are combined to produce output. The production function is just a starting point for supply decisions of a firm. In this chapter we will show how cost is defined, determined and measured. For any business decision, cost considerations play a great role.

Cost function is a derived function. It is derived from the production function which captures the technology of a firm. The theory of cost is a concern of managerial economics. Cost analysis helps us allocation of resources among various alternatives. In fact, knowledge of cost theory is essential for making decisions relating to price and output. Whether production of a new product is a wiser one on the part of a firm greatly depends on the evaluation of costs associated with it and the possibility of earning revenue from it. Decisions on capital investment (e.g., new machines) are made by comparing the rate of return from such investment with the opportunity cost of the funds used.

The relevance of cost analysis in decision-making is usually couched in terms of short and long period of time by economists. In all market structures, short run costs are crucial in the determination of price and output. This is due to the fact that the basis for cost function is production and the prices of inputs that a firm employs.

On the other hand, long run cost analysis is used for planning the optimal scale of plant size. In other words, long run cost functions provide useful information for planning the growth as well as the investment policies of a firm. Growth of a firm largely depends on cost considerations. The position of the U-shaped long run AC of a firm suggests the direction of the growth of a firm. That is to say, a firm can take a decision whether to build up a new plant or to look for diversification in other markets by studying its existence on the long run AC curve. Further, it is the cost that decides the merger and takeover of a sick firm.

Non-profit sector or the government sector must also have a knowledge of cost function for decision making. Whether the Narmoda Dam is to be built or not, it should evaluate the costs and benefits 'flowing' from the dam.

6.2. COST FUNCTION

The relationship between output and costs is expressed in terms of cost function. By incorporating prices of inputs into the production function, one obtains cost function since cost function is derived from production function. However, the nature of cost function depends on the time horizon. In microeconomic theory, we deal with short run and long run time.

A cost function may be written as

$$C_q = f(q_f \cdot p_f)$$

where C_q is the total production cost, q_f is the quantities of inputs employed by the firm and p_f is the prices of relevant inputs. This cost equation says that cost of production depends on prices of inputs and quantities of inputs used by the firm.

6.2.1. Different Concepts of Cost

Cost often means different things to different people. The central fact is that accountants and economists measure cost of production in accordance with their own interests and purposes. The notion of cost as understood by accountants has little relevance to decision-making. Economists, however, consider not only accounting cost but also opportunity cost. It is, therefore, necessary to have an understanding of the different concepts of cost.

- *Accounting Cost*: The concept of accounting cost is used by accountants. Money expenses incurred for hiring different input services are calculated. These are then accounting costs or explicit costs or direct costs. These are in the nature of purchase of raw materials, equipment, wages, rent, interest, etc. Since actual payment has to be made to others by the firm, these costs are also called explicit costs. As these costs get reflected in accounting statements these are called accounting costs.

- *Opportunity Cost*: Cost is an important element in decision-making. That is why, economists evaluate cost in terms of the concept of opportunity cost or foregone alternatives.

Every action involves an opportunity cost. When an individual works in an office, he then sacrifices other alternative job opportunities. Suppose, a worker of a merchant office gives up a job fetching a salary of Rs. 5,000 per month and, instead, becomes a self-employed person. Thus, the accounting cost of this worker is zero while the opportunity cost is Rs. 5,000 per month—the earning he sacrifices by working for his own business. This is the opportunity cost. "The cost of using something in a particular use is the benefit foregone by (or opportunity cost) not using in its best alternative use." Thus, the opportunity cost is the forward-looking view of the firm over a range of choices. The firm compares the alternatives before selecting a particular one. The opportunity cost of any decision is the value that the next best alternative would give.

The opportunity cost may be greater or less than the accounting cost.

- *Imputed Cost or Implicit Cost*: Imputed cost is the cost attributed for using as factor of production which is owned by the user. Imputed cost is opportunity cost of not using an input or machine to its best alternative use. In other words, imputed cost (or implicit cost) represents the value of foregone opportunities but do not involve actual cash payments. Economists just impute or estimate a price for these owned resources equal to the return they would have received in their best use. This is called imputed cost or implicit cost not included in accounting cost.

  Thus, economic costs include both accounting costs and imputed costs to evaluate costs of production. To discover the profitable line of production economists evaluate costs both explicitly and implicitly. Economists count costs as

Economic cost = explicit costs + implicit costs

- *Sunk Cost*: A sunk cost is an expenditure of a firm incurred in the past which is not recoverable. Since it cannot be recovered it cannot influence production decision. In this sense, any fixed cost incurred in production is a sunk cost. Expenditure on specialised equipment of a firm much before production starts is a sunk cost since it has no alternative use. Its opportunity cost is, thus, zero. As sunk cost is not relevant to economic decisions even if it is seen as a mistake one should follow Jevons' famous economic maxim: "Bygones are for ever bygones."
- *Private and Social Costs*: Being a profit-maximiser, a firm simply estimates or calculates private costs of production that include both accounting cost and imputed cost or opportunity cost. These private costs do not include costs that are imposed on the society. A factory in the adjoining locality pollutes the environment, makes traffic congestion causing accidents and deaths. These are the costs that are borne by the society. Social cost is the sum of private cost plus any additional cost imposed on the society from any economic activity.

6.3. SHORT RUN COST ANALYSIS

A firm's cost of production will depend on the inputs it uses. Further, use or employment of an input depends on the length of time. In other words, cost of production will vary depending on the production period. Production may be conducted on a short run or on a long run basis. In view of this, inputs employed by a firm may be fixed and variable.

Short run is that period of time over which at least one input is held fixed. In the short run, a firm cannot change its fixed input to expand output. By varying variable inputs only, a firm can change its volume of output. Thus, in the short run, total cost (TC) is divided into two broad components: total fixed cost (TFC) and total variable cost (TVC).

Thus, TC = TFC + TVC

where $TFC = P_K.\bar{K} = r.\bar{K}$, and $TVC = P_L.L = w.L$. Here we have put bar sign over the head of K since K is assumed to be fixed (in the short run).

- **Total Fixed Costs:** A firm in the short run uses both fixed inputs and variable inputs. Costs that arise due to the use of fixed inputs are called fixed costs or overhead costs or unavoidable costs.

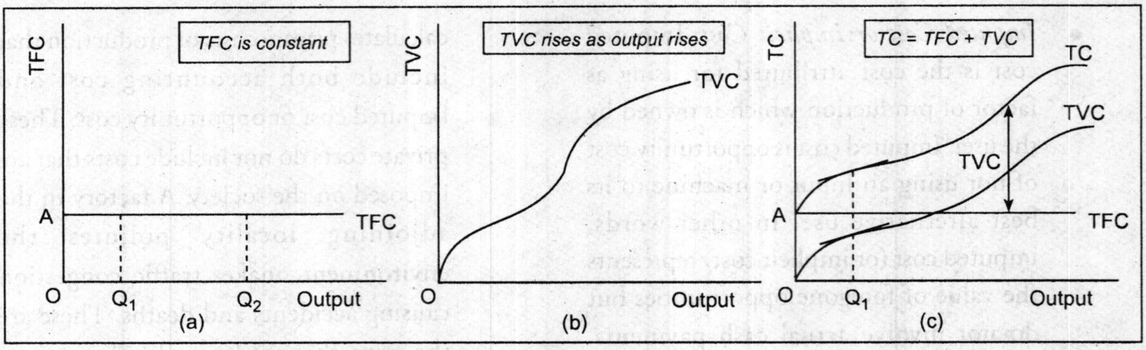

Fig. 6.1: TFC, TVC and TC Curves

It is the cost of all the firm's fixed inputs. Whether a firm produces or not it will have to incur fixed cost. Thus, fixed cost is independent of the level of output. Whatever be the level of output (even if it is zero), fixed costs do not change. This means, fixed costs are sunk costs. This is shown in Fig. 6.1(a) were TFC curve has been drawn parallel to the horizontal axis on which we measure output. It is clear from the figure that the firm incurs a total fixed cost of OA, whether it produces or not. Fixed costs or supplementary costs or overhead costs are : (i) expenses for municipal rent on land, (ii) salaries of top officers, (iii) interest on borrowed funds, (iv) depreciation of machine, etc.

- **Total Variable Cost:** Costs that arise due to the use of variable factors are called variable costs or direct costs. It is the cost of the firm's variable inputs. If the firm does not produce, it need not have to use variable inputs. Thus when no output is produced, variable cost is zero. But if the firm wants to produce it will have to increase the usage of variable inputs. Thus, more output means employment of more variable inputs and more variable cost. In other words, variable cost rises in response to an increase in output. Total variable cost curve has been drawn in Fig. 6.1(b) where the TVC curve starts from the origin showing that TVC is zero when no output is produced. As soon as output rises TVC starts rising. Thus, the TVC curve has broadly an inverse S-shape due to the operation of the law of variable proportions. That is why initially at a low level of output, TVC rises less than the rise in output. Later on TVC rises more than the rise in output.

Total variable costs include cost of raw materials, wages of daily wage-earners, transport cost, cost of packaging, electricity tariff etc.

- **Total Cost:** Total cost is the sum total of fixed and variable costs. TC curve has been drawn in Fig. 6.1(c). TC curve in the short run starts from that point where from TFC curve starts. This means that when output is zero total cost then includes only fixed cost. But as output rises TC rises since variable costs come into operation. That is why TC curve takes the shape of TVC curve. At any output level, the vertical distance between TC and TFC measures TVC. Alternatively, by adding TFC and TVC one obtains TC.

6.3.1. Cost Schedules

Total cost and its different variants are shown in the following hypothetical table. Consider a firm that uses both fixed and variable inputs to produce good X. Production is assumed to be subject to the law of diminishing returns. Table 6.1 illustrates various short run cost concepts for different levels of output of a commodity.

Table 6.1: A Hypothetical Short run Cost Data of Firm (n Rs.)

(1) Output (Q) (units)	(2) TVC	(3) TFC	(4) TC	(5) MC	(6) AVC	(7) AFC	(8) AC
			(2 + 3)	$\left(= \frac{\Delta TVC}{\Delta Q}\right)$	(= 2 ÷ 1)	(= 3 ÷ 1)	(= 6 + 7 or 4 ÷ 1)
0	0	4	4		0	∞	∞
1	10	4	14	10	10	4	14
2	16	4	20	6	8	2	10
3	24	4	28	8	8	1.33	9.33
4	34	4	38	10	8.5	1	9.5
5	46	4	50	12	9.2	0.8	10
6	60	4	64	14	10	0.67	10.67

Before explaining this table, we must know the meaning of different cost concepts. Table 6.1 suggests that as output rises, TVC continuously rises but TFC remains unchanged at all levels of output. Columns (2) and (3) show the behaviour of TVC and TFC. By adding columns (2) and (3), we obtain column of TC shown in column (4). Marginal cost is the additional cost resulting from the change in output. This is illustrated in column (5). This column (5) tells us that MC initially falls and then rises as output rises. AVC is the variable cost per unit of output. AVC, like MC, initially declines and thereafter rises as output rises. Column (6) describes the behaviour of AVC. Column (7) illustrates AFC—the fixed cost per unit of output. It gradually declines as output rises. AC schedule at different levels of output has been calculated in column (8). AC is the total cost per unit of output. It declines first and then rises.

6.4. SHAPES OF SHORT RUN COST CURVES

- **Average Fixed Cost (AFC)** : Average fixed cost is the fixed cost per unit of output. This is obtained by dividing the total fixed cost by the level of output:

$$AFC = \frac{TFC}{Q}, \text{ where } Q = \text{output}$$

As output increases and TFC remains fixed, AFC declines continuously. As the same volume of fixed cost is divided by the larger volume of output, AFC must decline. Further, AFC is a rectangular hyperbola in the sense that all rectangles formed by AFC are of equal sizes. AFC curve is asymptotic to both the axes. This means that it touches neither the horizontal axis nor the vertical axis.

Fig. 6.2 illustrates the derivation of AFC curve from TFC curve. In Fig. 6.2(a), we have drawn TFC curve parallel to the output axis. Here the outputs Oq_1, Oq_2 and Oq_3 have been measured in such a way that $Oq_1 = q_1q_2 = q_2q_3$. Since $AFC = \frac{TFC}{Q}$, AFC is given by the slope of a ray from the origin to a point on the TFC curve.

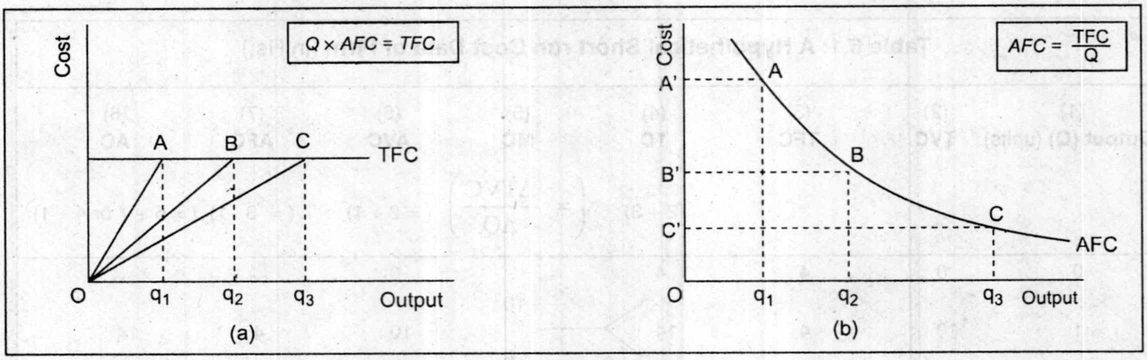

Fig. 6.2: Derivation of AFC Curve

We have chosen points A,B and C on the TFC curve and on all these points we have drawn rays OA, OB and OC. Consider output Oq_1. Corresponding to this output level, AFC is the slope of the ray OA, i.e., AFC = $\frac{q_1A}{Oq_1}$. Similarly for output Oq_2, AFC = $\frac{q_2B}{Oq_2}$ and for output Oq_3, AFC = $\frac{q_3C}{Oq_3}$. As fixed costs do not change, one can say that $q_1A = q_2B = q_3C$. TFC curve in panel (a) has been drawn in such a way that $Oq_2 = 2Oq_1$ and $Oq_3 = 3Oq_1$. Thus, AFC for Oq_2 output becomes $\frac{q_2C}{Oq_2} = \frac{q_1A}{2Oq_1} = \frac{1}{2}\left(\frac{q_1A}{Oq_1}\right) = \frac{1}{2}$ AFC for output Oq_1. This is shown in panel (b) by the difference in OA′ and OB′—more specifically OB′ = $\frac{1}{2}$ OA′. Likewise, AFC for Oq_3 output is

$$\frac{q_3C}{Oq_3} = \frac{q_1A}{3Oq_1} = \frac{1}{3}\left(\frac{q_1A}{Oq_1}\right) = \frac{1}{3} \text{ AFC for output } Oq_1.$$

OC′= $\frac{1}{3}$ OA′. In this way, AFC is obtained. Here all the rectangles are of equal sizes since fixed costs do not change. For instance, for Oq_1 output, AFC multiplied by output Oq_1 gives us TFC. Thus $OA'Aq_1$ rectangle is the TFC for output Oq_1. For output Oq_2 and Oq_3, though AFC declines, fixed cost remains constant because rectangle $OB'Bq_2$ = rectangle $OC'Cq_3$. In other words, AFC is a rectangular hyperbola.

- **Average Variable Cost (AVC):** AVC is the variable cost per unit of output. AVC is obtained by dividing TVC by the level of output :

$$AVC = \frac{TVC}{Q}$$

If AVC is plotted on a graph paper, one will find that, initially, AVC will decline, will reach a minimum, and, thereafter, it will rise. Thus, AVC curve is U-shaped. The reason is the law of variable proportions. In other words, there is a relationship between costs of production and input productivity. Let us assume that labour is the only variable input and, therefore, the only variable cost is labour cost—which is nothing but quantity of labour multiplied by wage rate, i.e.,

$$TVC = L.w$$

We know that

$$AVC = \frac{TVC}{Q} = w\left(\frac{L}{Q}\right)$$

But output divided by labour, i.e., $\frac{Q}{L}$, is the average product (AP). i.e., AP = $\left(\frac{Q}{L}\right)$

$$\text{Hence, AVC} = \text{w.}\left(\frac{1}{\frac{Q}{L}}\right)$$

$$\text{or AVC} = \text{w.}\left(\frac{1}{AP_L}\right)$$

Thus, AVC is the wage rate multiplied by the reciprocal of AP. Since, at the initial stage, AP rises, then reaches maximum and then declines, AVC must, therefore, fall, reach a minimum and rise thereafter. In other words, the movement of AP curve is just the reverse of the AVC curve. Or AVC is the mirror image of the AP.

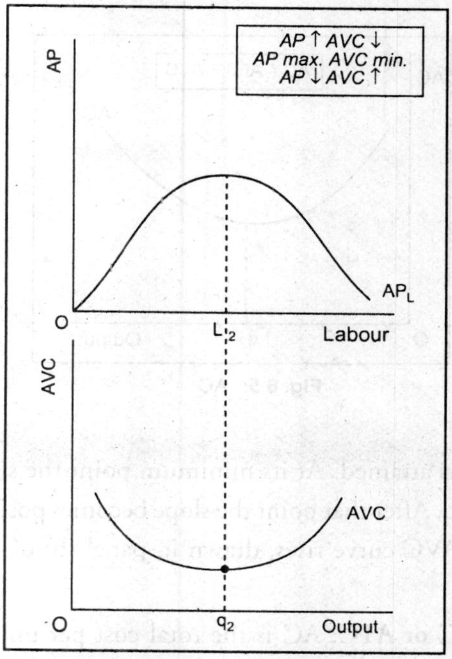

Fig. 6.3: AP and AVC Curves

Fig. 6.3 shows the inverse relationship between AP and AVC curves. The upper panel shows that as use of labour increases AP_L rises and, hence, AVC declines. At OL_2 level of employment since AP_L is maximum AVC at Oq_2 output must be minimum. Beyond OL_2 amount of labour, as AP_L declines AVC rises. Hence, AVC curve is U-shaped.

How is the AVC curve derived from TVC curve has been explained in Fig. 6.4. AVC at each level of output is given by the slope of a line drawn from the origin to the corresponding point on the TVC curve. For example, AVC at output Oq_1 is the slope of the ray OA from the origin. AVC at output Oq_2 is the slope of the line OB. The slope of the ray steadily diminishes until Oq_2 is produced. To the right of Oq_2, the slope rises. In other words, slope of TVC at output Oq_3 is larger than AVC at output Oq_2. That is why, the slope of AVC (drawn in panel b) is negative until output

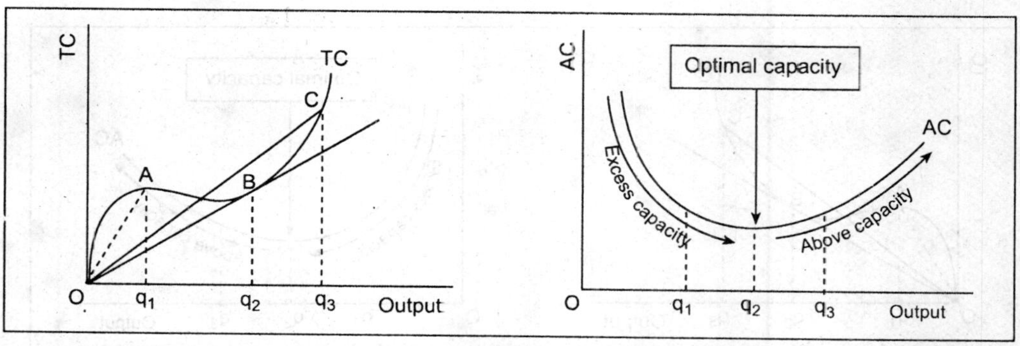

Fig. 6.6: Derivation of AC from TC

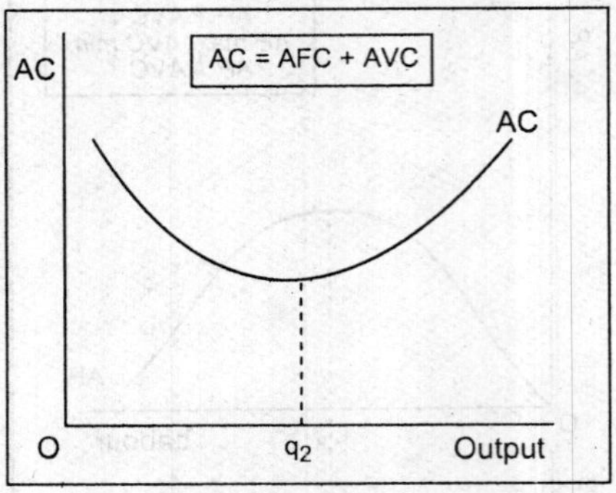

Fig. 6.5: AC

Oq_2 is attained. At its minimum point the slope is zero. After that point the slope becomes positive and AVC curve rises, drawn in panel (b) of Fig. 6.4.

- **AC or ATC**: AC is the total cost per unit of output. AC is obtained by dividing TC by output, i.e.,

$$AC = \frac{TC}{Q} = \frac{TFC + TVC}{Q} = \frac{TFC}{Q} + \frac{TVC}{Q}$$

$$= AFC + AVC$$

Thus, then AC is the sum of AFC and AVC. Obviously, the shape of the AC curve is governed by the shapes of AFC and AVC curves. Truly speaking, AVC curve is U-shaped. We know that as output increases both AFC and AVC decline, so AC must decline. Though AVC now rises, the significant decline in AFC causes AC to decline more. And that is why, AC's minimum point comes later than AVC's minimum point. Anyway, up to Oq_2 level of output AC declines. The level of output that corresponds to the lowest point of AC curve is called the 'optimal capacity' or 'efficient scale' of the firm. If a firm produces less than the minimum point of AC curve then it experiences 'excess capacity' and if a firm produces beyond the minimum point of AC curve it experiences 'above capacity'. Beyond Oq_2 output AC starts rising. This means that increase in output beyond Oq_2 will lead to an increase in AVC. In other words, the increase in AVC more than offsets the fall in AFC. That is to say, in this region of output, AVC becomes more strong than AFC and AC continues to rise. Thus, AC curve is U-shaped. It is U-shaped due to the operation of the law of variable proportions.

Graphically, AC curve is derived in the same way as AVC is derived from TVC. AC at each level is the slope of a line drawn from the origin to the corresponding point on the TC curve (see Fig. 6.6). The slope of the ray diminishes as one moves along TC until B is reached. This means AC must decline till Oq_2 is attained. Thereafter, the slope of line OC rises and AC takes a positive slope. So AC curve is U-shaped.

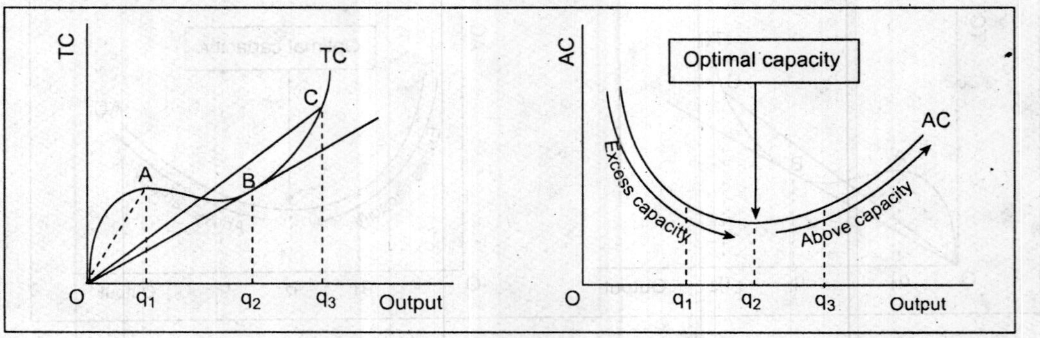

Fig. 6.6: Derivation of AC from TC

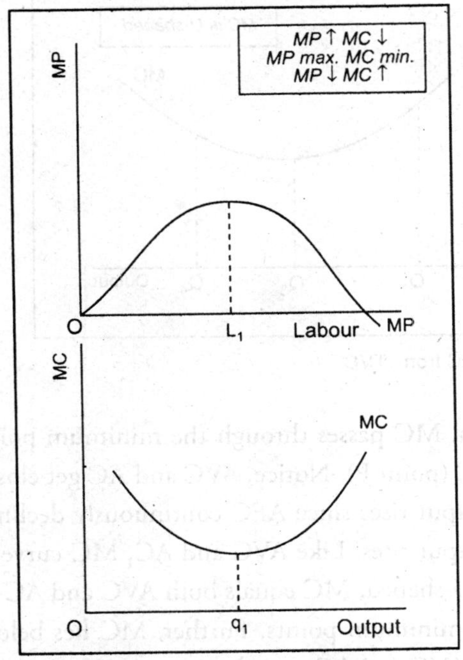

Fig. 6.7: MP and MC Curves

- **Marginal Cost (MC):** MC is the change in total cost attributable to a change in output. Thus, MC is an addition to the total cost. In symbols,

$$MC = \frac{\Delta TC}{\Delta Q}$$

$$MC = TC(Q) - TC(Q-1)$$

This means that MC is the difference between total cost for Q-th and Q-1th units of output. It is to be remembered here that, in the short run, fixed costs do not change. Here output changes due to change in the use of variable inputs. Thus, by change in total cost here we mean change in total variable costs only. Fixed costs do not have any bearing on MC. MC is independent of fixed cost. Thus,

$$MC = \frac{\Delta TVC}{\Delta Q}$$

MC refers to change in total variable cost which results from a change in output. We can prove this in the following way also :

$$MC = TC(Q) - TC(Q-1)$$

$$= (FC + VC_Q) - (FC + VC_{Q-1})$$

$$= FC + VC_Q - FC - VC_{Q-1}$$

$$MC = VC_Q - VC_{Q-1}$$

$$\therefore\ MC = \frac{\Delta TVC}{\Delta Q}$$

MC is also defined as the reciprocal of MP multiplied by the price of the variable input. Suppose, labour is the variable input whose cost (i.e., wage cost) is the variable cost. Thus,

$$\Delta TVC = w.\Delta L$$

Dividing this by ΔQ, we obtain

$$MC = \frac{\Delta TVC}{\Delta Q} = w.\frac{\Delta L}{\Delta Q}$$

But, $\frac{\Delta Q}{\Delta L} = MP$

$$\therefore\ MC = w.\left(\frac{1}{MP}\right) = \frac{w}{MP}$$

That is why it is said that the shape of the MC curve is governed by the shape of the MP curve. Since MP initially rises, reaches a maximum and then declines, MC initially falls, reaches minimum and thereafter rises. So MC curve is U-shaped due to the operation of the law of variable proportions. This has been shown in Fig. 6.7.

In this figure, as labour employment increases, MP initially rises and, consequently MC falls as output rises. MP reaches maximum when OL_1 units of labour are used. Corresponding output level is Oq_1. Here MC becomes minimum.

Thereafter, employment of labour causes MP to fall even to zero or to become negative while MC continuously rises. MC curve is, thus, the reciprocal of the MP curve.

How MC curve is derived from the TVC curve can be known from Fig. 6.8. Graphically, MC curve is the slope of the TVC curve. The slope of a curve at any one of its points is the slope of

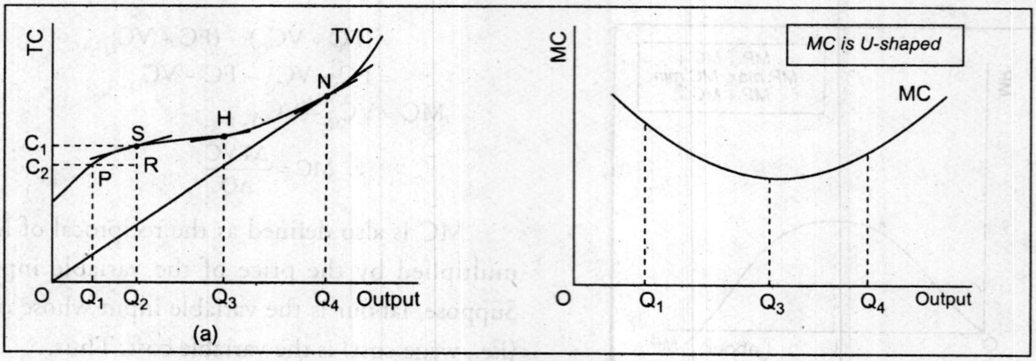

Fig. 6.8: Derivation of MC from TVC

the tangent at that point.

Suppose output increases from OQ_1 to OQ_2 and total cost increases from OC_1 to OC_2. We have drawn a tangent on the TVC curve at point S. MC at this point is equal to the slope of the tangent, i.e.,

$$MC = \frac{OC_2 - OC_1}{OQ_2 - OQ_1} = \frac{SR}{PR}$$

As one moves from P to S, the distance between these two points becomes smaller and smaller and the slope of the tangent gradually declines till point S is reached. At this point, the slope of the tangent corresponding to the output OQ_3 is smallest or even zero and MC is the lowest. This means that MC falls until OQ_3 is produced. The tangent at point N is also ray from the origin. However, as the slope of the tangent to the TVC curve rises after OQ_3 output, MC starts rising. Accordingly, MC curve is U-shaped.

Now, all the short run cost curves can be represented in a single diagram (Fig. 6.9). AFC curve has been drawn as a rectangular hyperbola. AFC curve is declining steadily. AVC curve is U-shaped. MC passes through its minimum point (N). AC being the sum of AFC and AVC, AC curve lies above both the AFC and AVC curves. Again, MC passes through the minimum point of AC (point P). Notice, AVC and AC get closer as output rises since AFC continuously declines as output rises. Like AVC and AC, MC curve is also U-shaped. MC equals both AVC and AC at their minimum points. Further, MC lies below both AVC and AC over the range in which these curves fall; and it lies above them when they are rising. It is to be kept in mind that all the cost curves—except AFC curve—are U-shaped.

6.4.1. Relationship between AC and AVC and between AC and MC

AC can be obtained in two ways :

First, $AC = AFC + AVC$

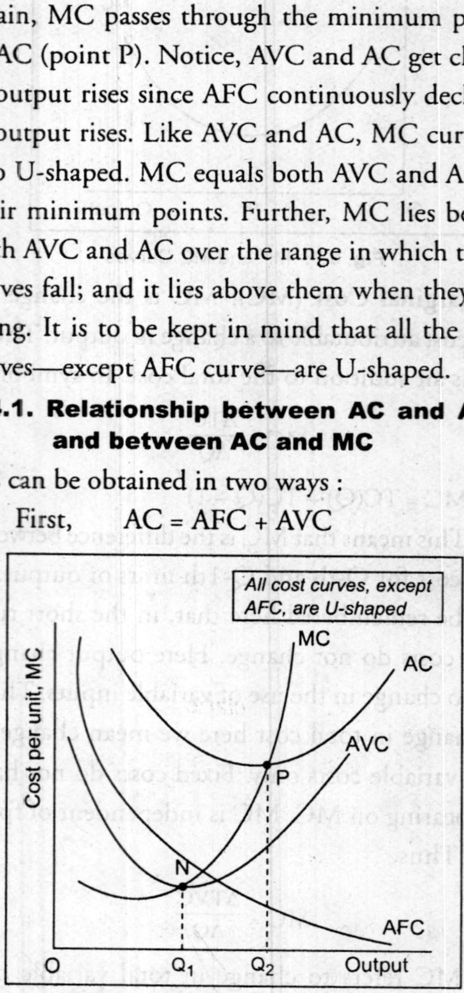

Fig. 6.9: AFC, AVC, AC and MC curves

Second, $AC = \frac{TC}{Q}$

AVC is obtained by dividing total variable cost by output, i.e. $AVC = \frac{TVC}{Q}$

Thus, AVC is a part of AC, given AC = AFC+ AVC. Furthermore, both AVC and AC are U-shaped due to the operation of the law of variable proportions. However, the minimum point of AC lies to the right of the minimum point of AVC. (See Fig. 6.9 where the point P, the minimum point of AC, lies to the right of the point N, the minimum point of AVC). This is because AC not only includes AVC but also AFC which falls continuously as output rises. Not only this, initially with increases in output AVC falls. So, AC must fall. AVC starts rising after OQ_1 output is being produced, its rise over a certain range is offset by a fall in AFC. That is why AC continues to fall over that range of output even if AVC rises. Further, AC's minimum point (point P) comes at a later range of output than AVC's minimum point. Once OQ_2 level of output is produced the influence of a rise in AVC becomes stronger than the fall in AFC, so AC starts rising.

Now we will establish a familiar relationship between MC and AC. We have said that MC is the change in total cost for a change in output. Three points about the relationship between MC and AC are:

1. If MC < AC, then AC must be falling.
2. If MC = AC, then AC is constant.
3. If MC > AC, then AC is rising.

This relationship can be proved in this way:

$$MC = \frac{\Delta TC}{\Delta Q}, \; AC = \frac{TC}{Q} \text{ and, therefore}$$

$$TC = AC.Q.$$

Thus one obtains by substitution

$$MC = \frac{\Delta(AC.Q)}{\Delta Q} = \frac{\Delta AC}{\Delta Q}.Q + AC.\left(\frac{\Delta Q}{\Delta Q}\right)$$

Since AC and Q are non-negative, MC > AC if, and only if $\frac{\Delta AC}{\Delta Q} > 0$. This means that AC increases with increase in output. Again, MC < AC, if and only if, $\frac{\Delta AC}{\Delta Q} > 0$. This means that AC declines as output increases.

This mathematical relationship can be established in terms of an example. Suppose, Sourav Ganguli scores 80 runs in the first innings of a Test Match and 90 runs in the second innings. His average score now becomes 85. If he scores 70 in the second match (let 80 be the marginal score), his average score will now decline from 85 to 80. This means, when marginal score is less than average score, average score must be falling. Notice that if MC < AC, then AC is falling. On the other hand, if he scores 85 in the second match then his marginal score (i.e., 85) will coincide with average score. In terms of cost, when MC = AC then AC is constant. Finally, if Ganguli scores 100

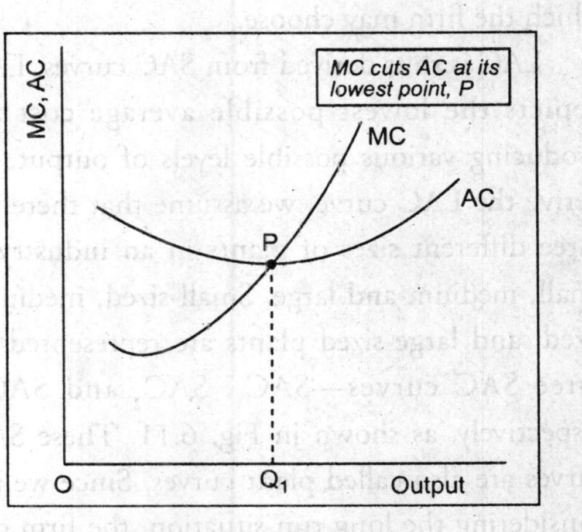

Fig. 6.10: MC and AC

runs in the next match (marginal score exceeds average score) his average score will now rise. Or whenever MC > AC, AC must be rising.

6.5. DERIVATION OF LONG RUN AVERAGE COST CURVE (LAC)

Long run is that time period when a firm can change all its inputs. In fact, there are no fixed inputs in the long run; all inputs are variable. Thus in the long run there is no fixed cost; all costs are variable. That is why, in the long run a firm can change its scale of production according to its needs. In the short run, size of a plant or scale remains fixed while, in the long run changes in plant size or in scale can be made. In the long run, a firm can move from one plant to another plant. If the situation demands, it can build up a large-sized plant or a smaller one. It is to be mentioned here that long run is a "planning horizon" in the sense that it acts as a guide to the firm relating to the future output decision. We know that production takes place in the short run. Every firm aims at production for a future date and chooses many aspects of the short run in which it operates in the future. Remember that long run consists of all short run situations among which the firm may choose.

LAC is thus derived from SAC curves. LAC depicts the lowest possible average cost for producing various possible levels of output. To derive the LAC curve, we assume that there are three different sizes of plants in an industry—small, medium and large. Small-sized, medium-sized, and large-sized plants are represented by three SAC curves—SAC_1, SAC_2 and SAC_3, respectively, as shown in Fig. 6.11. These SAC curves are also called plant curves. Since we are considering the long run situation, the firm can choose any plant size in which it will operate in the future to produce a given output level at the lowest possible cost.

If the firm decides to produce OQ_1, it will choose plant size denoted by SAC_1. A lower output (say) can also be produced on SAC_1 but at a higher cost. But the same plant size, i.e., SAC_1 will enable a firm to produce larger output at a lower cost. If OQ_2 is considered to be the most profitable level of output, the firm will select SAC_2 — the medium-sized plant. It will select the large-sized plant, SAC_3 to produce OQ_3 level of output. But taking such decision is not an easy job as it appears at first sight. Suppose, the firm operates at SAC_1 and demand for its product gradually rises. Of course, it can produce OQ_1 at the lowest cost even operating on SAC_1. Production beyond OQ_1 will entail a larger cost. If the firm expects to produce OQ_1(as in Figure 6.11), its choice of plant size becomes a difficult one since costs are the same for both the plant-sizes—SAC_1 and SAC_2. Now the choice of the optimal plant size depends on the firm's anticipation or expectation regarding its demand for product in the coming years. At this level of output, cost cannot be the determinant of the choice of a plant size. It is quite natural that the firm expects its demand for the product to

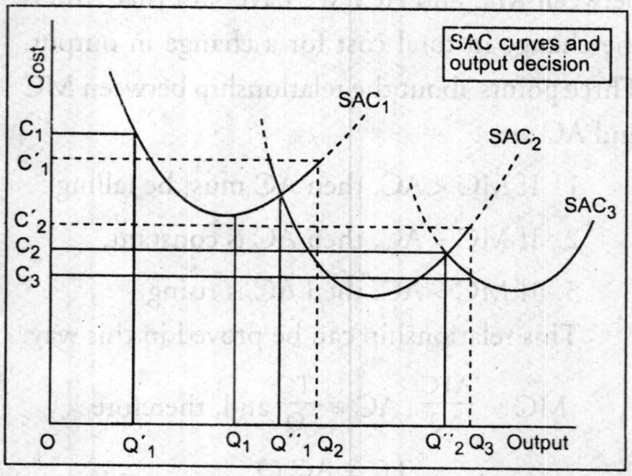

Fig. 6.11: SAC Curves for Three Plant Sizes

increase in future. So, the firm, quite likely, will install the plant number SAC_2 rather than SAC_1. Larger outputs can now be produced with lower cost. Similarly, though output OQ_2 can be produced by both the plant sizes, SAC_2 and SAC_3, it is better to use the plant size represented by SAC_3 since larger output (OQ_3) can be produced at a lower cost (OC_3).

However, let us assume that the industry faces a large number of plant sizes represented by, say, five SAC curves as shown in Fig. 6.12. These curves will generate a smooth and continuous curve called the planning curve or LAC curve. Each point on this curve shows the least possible cost for producing the corresponding level of output. The LAC curve is a planning curve because it is the curve which helps a firm to decide what plant is to be established in order to produce an output level consistent with the optimal cost. The firm selects that short run plant which yields the minimum cost of producing the anticipated output level. To produce a particular output in the long run, the firm must select a point on the LAC curve corresponding to that output, and it will then build a relevant short run plant and

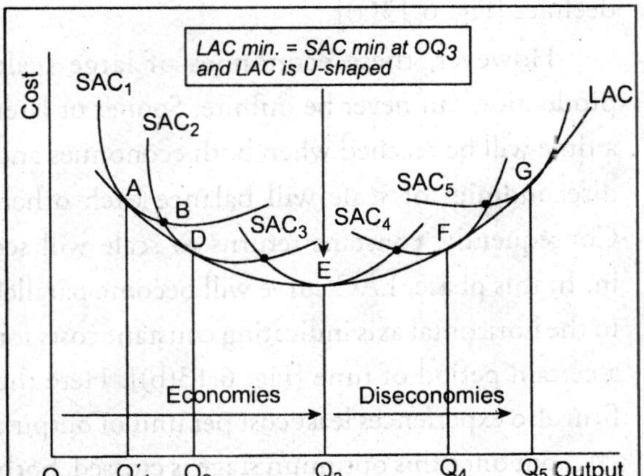

Fig. 6.12: LAC Curve

operate on the corresponding SAC curve.

Suppose, the firm thinks that for producing output OQ_1, point A on SAC_1 becomes the most profitable one. It will then build up a plant at the lower cost represented by SAC_1. [At point A, SAC_1 is tangent to the LAC curve]. However, the firm could reduce its cost by expanding output to the amount associated with point B, the minimum point on SAC_1. But the firm anticipates that demand for its product in future would be rising. So it would construct a new plant, represented by SAC_2 and will operate at point D on SAC_2, thereby lowering its unit cost and not on the lowest point of SAC_2. [Corresponding to the output level OQ_2, SAC_2 is tangent to LAC]. Similarly, for output OQ_3, the firm would construct SAC_3 and operate at E where unit costs become the lowest. [Again, SAC_3 is tangent to LAC]. Same would be the case for all other outputs in the long run. For output OQ_4, the firm would construct plant size SAC_4 and would operate at point F. However, the minimum point of SAC now lies to the left of the operational point, F. Similarly, OQ_5 output could be produced by the plant size SAC_5. The firm should operate at point G on SAC_5.

Each point of the LAC is, thus, the point of tangency with the corresponding SAC curves. LAC curve is the locus of all the tangency points. As a consequence of this, LAC curve is called the envelope curve as it envelops or supports a family of SAC curves.

It is to be remembered here that LAC, throughout its length, is not tangential to the minimum points of all SAC curves. When LAC is falling, it is tangential to the falling portion of SAC curves, not to the minimum point of SAC curves. For instance, the firm operates at point A on SAC_1, the falling portion, rather than B where

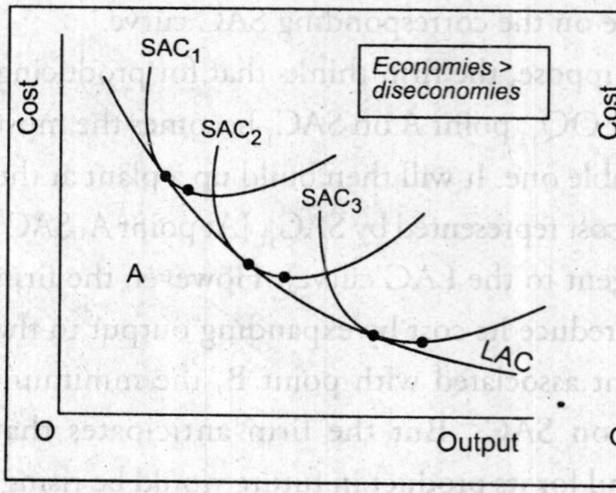

Fig. 6.13(a): LAC and IRS

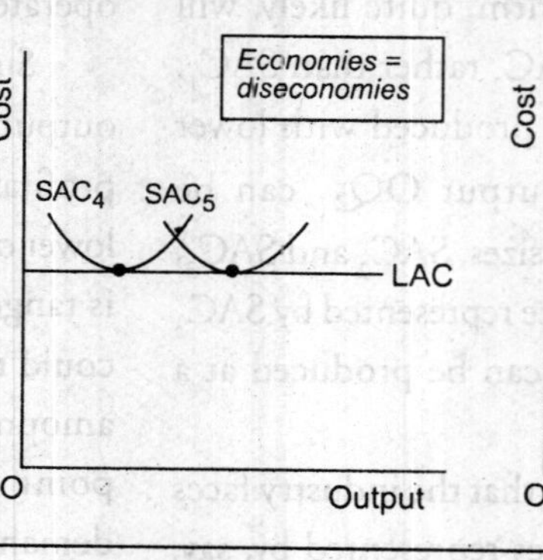

Fig. 6.13(b): LAC and CRS

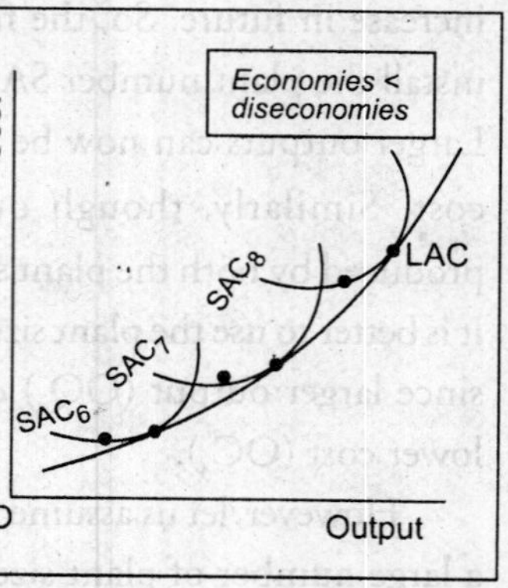

Fig. 6.13(c): LAC and DRS

costs are the lowest. In other words, since the slope of the LAC curve up to point E is negative, the slope of SAC curves must also be negative. This is because, at the tangency points, both SAC and LAC curves have the same slopes. Only at point E, minimum point of LAC is tangent to the minimum point of SAC. To the right of this point, as LAC is rising, it is tangent to the rising portion of SAC curves. Note that at the points of tangency, SAC = LAC, but to the right or left of the tangency point SAC > LAC. However, the minimum points of SAC curves below OQ_3 output lie to the right of the operational point. Beyond OQ_3 output, SAC's minimum points lie to the left of the operational point.

Thus, we can say that the LAC curve is U-shaped—it first falls, reaches minimum, and rises afterwards as output expands. But the U-shape of the LAC curve is less pronounced than the U-shape of the SAC curve.

6.5.1. Why is LAC U-Shaped ?

We have learnt that the SAC curve is U-shaped because of the operation of the law of variable proportions. The LAC curve is also U-shaped because in the long run what we find is the operation of the law of returns to scale. We also know that the law of returns to scale has three phases: increasing returns to scale (IRS), constant returns to scale (CRS), and diminishing returns to scale (DRS). In other words, as the scale of operation and the size of the plant become large, a firm experiences economies of scale which may be both internal and external. Because of the operation of both internal economies (such as, technological economies, managerial economies, risk-bearing economies, etc.) and external economies (such as, economies of specialisation, economies of research and development, etc.) of production, a firm initially experiences increasing returns to scale which bring down costs of production. That is why LAC curve initially declines [Fig. 6.13(a)].

However, these economies of large scale production can never be infinite. Sooner or later a time will be reached when both economies and diseconomies of scale will balance each other. Consequently, constant returns to scale will set in. In this phase, LAC curve will become parallel to the horizontal axis indicating constant costs for a certain period of time [Fig. 6.13(b)]. Here the firm also experiences least cost per unit of output.

But once this optimum stage is crossed, both internal and external diseconomies of scale will become operative. As a result, diminishing returns to scale or increasing cost will come into operation. And because of the increasing cost LAC curve is upward sloping as the scale of operation becomes larger [Fig. 6.13(c)].

Thus, these three phases of the law of returns to scale or the economies and diseconomies of large scale production explain the U-shaped behaviour of the LAC curve.

It is said that the analysis of long run cost behaviour depends on the principle of returns to scale. However, such assumption may not always hold good. Economists have shown that the LAC curve may show a declining trend over a long range of output in various manufacturing industries. Again, others have shown that theoretically the LAC curve need not be U-shaped; in practice, it may never be. It may be L-shaped [Fig. 6.14(a)].

Empirical evidence drawn from the industrial production of the American economy suggests that LAC may take any of the following shapes:

There may be L-shaped or saucer-shaped LAC curve — Fig. 6.14(a). Constant costs are the most dominant costs, where economies of scale are obtained for a small number of output, because for a little amount neither economies nor diseconomies of scale are evident. In Fig. 6.14(b) as economies of scale are prominent LAC may have a long falling portion and in Fig. 6.14(c) LAC may have a long rising portion. Diseconomies of scale are found to be stronger.

6.6 MODERN APPRCACH IN THE THEORY OF COSTS

The traditional approach towards the cost theory has been challenged by modern writers. Traditional economists assume U-shaped cost curves (except AFC curve) both in the short run and in the long run. However, recent empirical evidence indicates L-shaped long run AC curve rather than typical U-shaped curve.

Modern microeconomics distinguishes between short run and long run costs unlike the traditional theory. Modern theory says that AFC curve is not necessarily a rectangular hyperbola and AVC curve is saucer-shaped rather than a U-shaped one.

- AFC : In modern theory, AFC is the indirect cost that may include (a) salaries and other expenses of administrative staff, (b) salaries of workers involved direcly in production, but paid on a consolidated basis, (c) depreciation costs of machineries, (d) maintenance costs of factory building, land, etc.

Before the production starts, a firm decides the size of the fixed, indirect costs mentioned now,

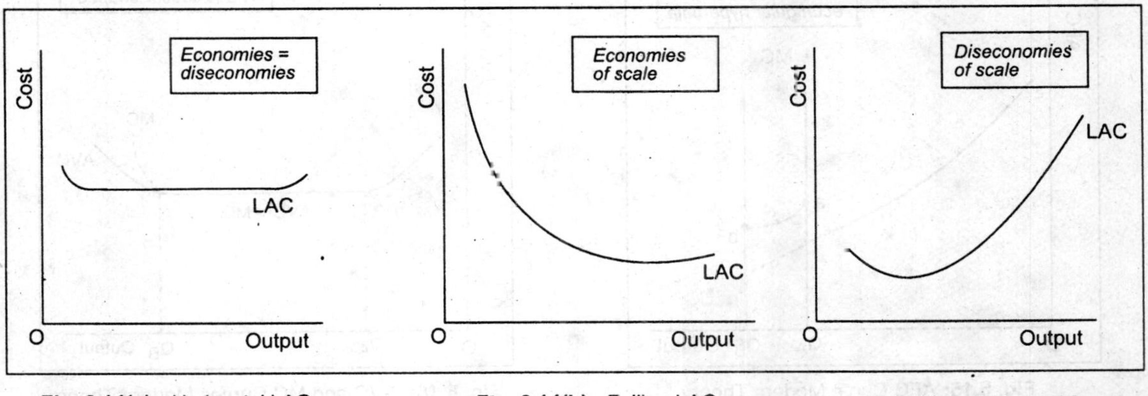

Fig. 6.14(a): Horizontal LAC   Fig. 6.14(b): Falling LAC   Fig. 6.14(c): Rising LAC

since the rate of utilisation of these fixed items determines the volume of profit. Obviously, a firm must set out its plan target for production in accordance with the demand or volume of expected sales. However, the size of the plant must not be strictly rigid so that increased demand for a firm's product can be met. In other words, a firm is expected to build up a capacity larger than the expected volume of demand or sales. This 'excess capacity' may be referred to as 'reserve capacity' in the plant, land and buildings. If reserve capacity is not maintained a firm will not be able to meet seasonal and cyclical fluctuations in demand.

Under these conditions, the AFC curve may look Fig. 6.15. Let us assume that a firm has two types of machinery — largest capacity machinery and small-unit machinery. Former machinery sets an absolute limit to the expansion of output (boundary B or Q_B in Fig. 6.15) and the latter machinery sets a limit to increase in output (boundary A or Q_A in Fig. 6.15). However, this is not an absolute boundary as it can increase output in the short-run up to absolute limit B either by paying more wages for using labour over the stipulated time or by buying additional small-unit machinery. In the first case, AFC is shown by the dotted line and in the latter case, AFC shifts up to 'a b' in-between boundaries A and B. Anyway, though AFC curve shifts up within the output levels Q_A and Q_B, AFC curve is a rectangular hyperbola.

- **AVC:** In the modern approach, AVC includes the cost of (a) direct labour which varies with output, (b) raw materials, and (c) running expenses of plant and machinery.

AVC curve in the modern theory is rather saucer-shaped. This means that it has long flat stretch over a range of output, that is, it is broadly U-shaped (Fig. 6.16). Between output Q_A and Q_B, AVC is parallel to the horizontal axis. This flat stretch of AVC corresponds to 'built-in-the plant reserve capacity.' At this output level since AVC is fixed, it coincides with MC. To the left of OQ_A output, as AVC > MC, MC curve lies below AVC curve and to the right of OQ_B output level, as MC > AVC, MC curve lies above the AVC curve. The explanation behind the rising and falling portions of AVC curve are the same as traditional theory.

- **AC:** AC is obtained by adding AFC and AVC at each level of output drawn in Fig. 6.17.

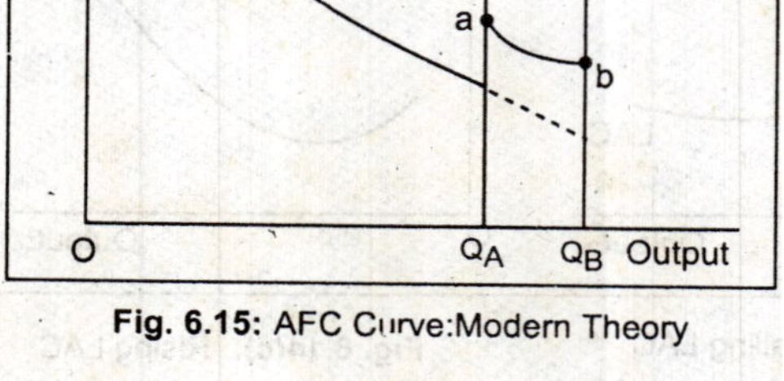

Fig. 6.15: AFC Curve:Modern Theory

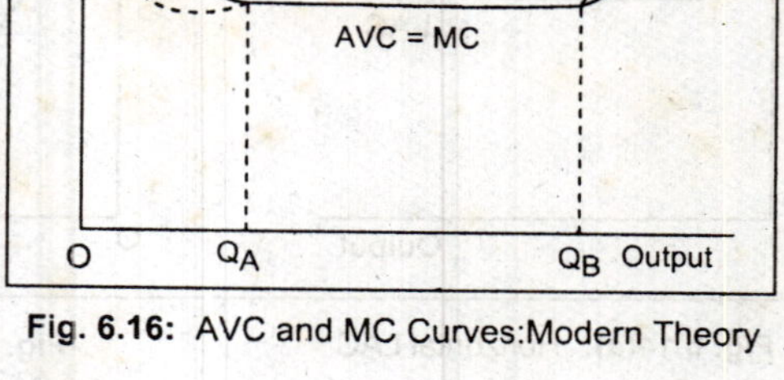

Fig. 6.16: AVC and MC Curves:Modern Theory

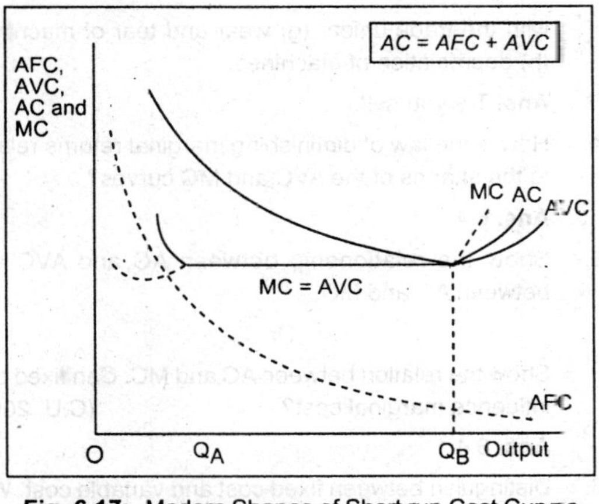

Fig. 6.17: Modern Shapes of Short run Cost Curves

AC continuously declines till OQ_B output is produced at which the reserve capacity is exhausted. Once this reserve capacity output is crossed, AC starts rising. As usual, MC will intersect AC at its minimum point.

6.2.1. Long Run Costs in Modern Approach

Empirical evidence suggests that LAC curve is U-shaped. This means that over a range of output, LAC exhibits a flat portion where costs remain unchanged. As output increases initially average costs decline. As a result, LAC starts falling. Here LMC curve lies below the LAC curve. Further increase in output may cause costs to remain fixed. This may correspond to minimum optimal scale of plant where all possible scale economies are reaped. LMC will lie below LAC till minimum optimal scale is reached. Consequently, LAC does not change and thus coincides with the LMC. This means that LAC becomes L-shaped. Beyond this output level, LAC starts rising and lies below LMC, i.e., LMC > LAC.

While explaining the shape of LAC curve, economists talk about production costs and managerial costs. Since these two types of costs are variable in the long run, LAC curve is U-shaped. However, it is to be kept in mind that

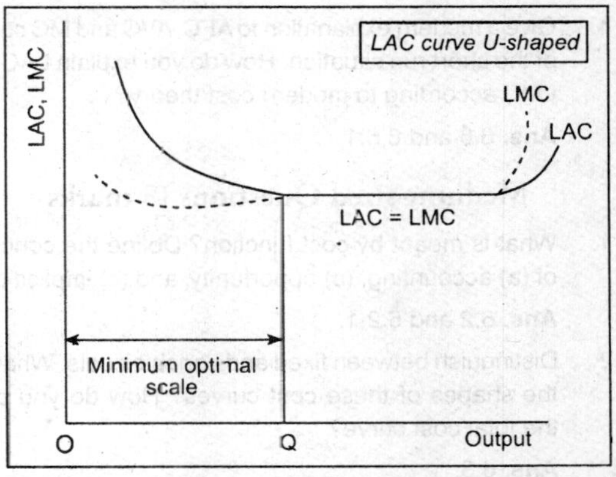

Fig. 6.18: Modern Shapes of Long run LAC and LMC

production costs may decline due to technological economies. In the initial stages as technical economies are substantial LAC declines. But after a certain level of output (or minimum optimal scale) is reached, economies are not attained. In other words, there are limits to technical economies of production. If the firm plans to have lower costs, it will have to invent newer techniques. Modern age innovates newer technologies resulting in reduced cost. Thus, in the long run, if only production costs alone are relevant, LAC will decline gradually. Now, if administrative costs are included and if managerial costs tend to rise, LAC will be upward rising.

QUESTIONS (WITH ANSWER-HINTS)

Long Questions (16 marks)

1. Explain the shapes of various short run cost curves? Why cost curves are U-shaped?

   Ans. 6.4.

2. Define AFC, AVC, AC and MC. Draw one graph showing all these curves. Explain their shapes.

   Ans. 6.4.

3. Define long run average cost (LAC). How is the LAC curve derived from a set of short run AC curves?

   Or

   How do you derive LAC curve of a firm? Show the relationship between short run and long run AC of a firm. (C.U. 2007)

   Ans. 6.5.

4. Give a modern explanation to AFC, AVC and MC curves of the short run situation. How do you explain LAC and LMC according to modern cost theory?

   Ans. 6.6 and 6.6.1.

Medium-sized Questions (8 marks)

1. What is meant by cost function? Define the concepts of (a) accounting, (b) opportunity, and (c) implicit cost.

   Ans. 6.2 and 6.2.1.

2. Distinguish between fixed and variable costs. What are the shapes of these cost curves? How do you draw the total cost curve?

   Ans. 6.3.

3. The following are some costs incurred by the Bata Shoe Company. Decide which one is fixed cost or variable cost or some combination of the two costs:

   (a) overtime pay before Puja, (b) electricity charges, (c) plant maintenance, (d) insurance, (e) wages paid to casual labour, (f) basic minimum wages agreed with the trade union, (g) wear and tear of machines, (h) depreciation of machines.

   Ans. Try yourself.

4. How is the law of diminishing marginal returns related to the shapes of the AVC and MC curves?

   Ans. 6.4.

5. Show the relationship between AC and AVC and between AC and MC.

   Or

   Show the relation between AC and MC. Can fixed cost influence marginal cost? (C.U. 2007)

   Ans. 6.4.1.

6. Distinguish between fixed cost and variable cost. Why is the short run AC curve of a firm U-shaped?

   Ans. 6.3 and 6.4. (C.U. 2008)

7. Why is LAC curve U-shaped? Can you think of any other shapes of LAC curve?

   Ans. 6.5.1.

7

MARKET STRUCTURE AND REVENUE CONCEPTS

7.1. INTRODUCTION

Microeconomics is concerned with the determination of price of a product. However, price determination depends greatly on the nature of the market. The favourite market structure to which economists pay greater attention is perfect competition; though it is unrealistic in character. Before 1920s, economists' only concern was perfect competition. It helps to analyse the business behaviour of a firm. It was believed to be an 'ideal' market. It is due to 'idealism', perfect competition could not be matched with the reality. Meanwhile, the two great publications in 1933 by two economists—The Economics of Imperfect Competition of Joan Robinson and The Theory of Monopolistic competition of E.H. Chamberlin caused greatest damage to the perfectly competitive market form. By 1933, imperfect competition was born under the initiative of Joan Robinson—a British Marxist economist—and E. H.Chamberlin—an American economist. The two important subdivisions of imperfect competition are: (i) monopolistic competition; and (ii) oligopoly.

In the following chapters, all these market forms will be discussed.

7.2. WHAT IS A MARKET?

In ordinary language, market means a place where goods are bought and sold. But, in economics, the term 'market' does not refer to a place. In economics, market refers to a group of buyers and sellers dealing in a particular commodity (e.g., gold market, oil market, car market, fruit market, etc.). A market is, thus, a trading zone where buyers and sellers are in such close contact that a single price for commodities of uniform quantity prevails. A market is created whenever sellers of a good or service are brought into contact with buyers and a means of exchange is available. The medium of exchange may be money or goods itself (i.e., barter). Whatever the medium of exchange, exchange agreements between buyers and sellers are reached through the operation of the forces of demand and supply. Market may, thus, be defined as any process of exchange between buyers and sellers. Thus, a market is an arrangement or institution that enables buyers and sellers to get information and to do business or arrange exchange of goods or with each other. Pindyick and Rubinfield say that "A market is a collection of buyers and sellers that interact, resulting in the possibility of exchange."

7.2.1. Morphology of Market

Broadly, a market is classified into product market where goods are transacted and a factor market where inputs are bought and sold. A goods market exists for both durable and non-durable and perishable good.

A: According to the extent of area covered, a market is classified into local, national and international. In a local market, perishable goods are transacted. A uniform price prevails over the local market. There are some goods bought and sold almost at the same price (barring taxes) all over the country, the markets for these commodities are national. Gold market is international in character in the sense that buyers and sellers all over the world come in contact with each other.

B: Marshall has classified market in accordance with the time period. He considers four kinds of markets : (i) the very short period market, (ii) the short period market, (iii) the long period market, and (iv) the very long-period market.

It is to be remembered that this is not a calender time. Above all, it depends on the nature of business and the nature of the commodity. A particular business may not have a long run view.

C: Perfect and Imperfect Markets: Market may be perfect and imperfect. In a perfect market quite a large number of firms compete in the supply of a single product. But in an imperfect competition, number of sellers may not necessarily be large. Markets can also be classified according to the nature of competition among buyers and sellers. We may have pure or perfect competition,

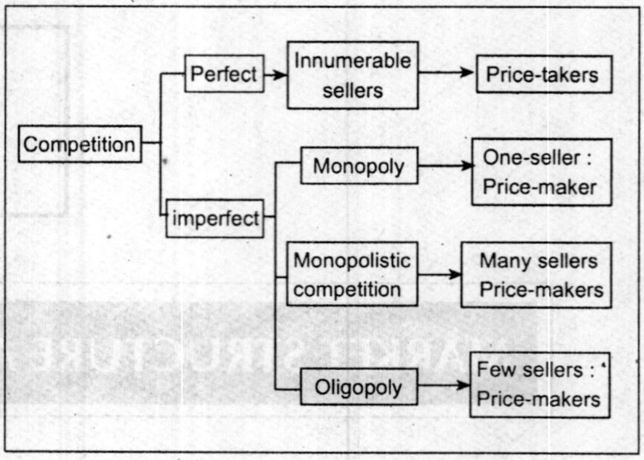

Fig. 7.1: Types of Competition

monopoly, monopolistic competition, oligopoly, etc.

Differences between these four markets classified on the basis of degree of competition can be presented in a tabular form (Fig. 7.1). Perfect competition is characterised by the following main features: (i) there is a large number of sellers. (ii) Sellers and buyers are price-takers. (iii) Goods produced are homogeneous. (iv) There is freedom of entry and exit.

Monopoly market exists when (i) there exists only one seller producing a commodity that has no close substitutes in the market; (ii) the monopolist behaves as a price-maker; and (iii) entry is completely blocked.

Monopolistic competition is an admixture of both perfect competition and monopoly. It combines the features of these markets. In this sense, monopolistic competition is a realistic market. Perfect competition and monopoly, in the true sense, are not found in reality. Monopolistic competition has the following characteristics: (i) there exists several or many sellers; (ii) sellers sell differentiated goods, that is, product of one seller is a fairly close substitute for that of other sellers; (iii) sellers have some influence over the price of their products; (iv) there is freedom of entry and exit.

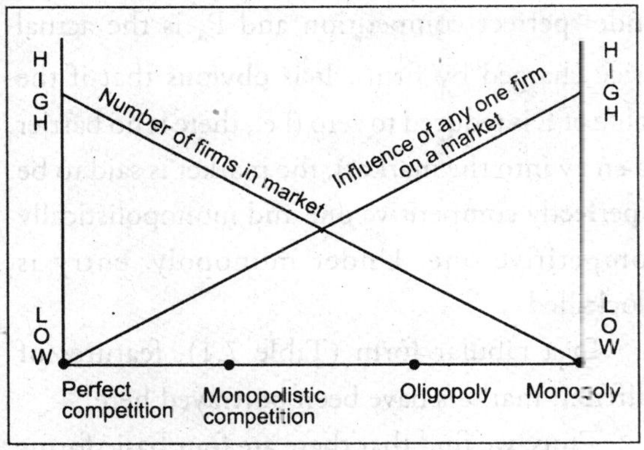

Fig. 7.2: Criteria for Classification of Markets

An oligopoly market has the following attributes: (i) there exists small number of sellers; (ii) sellers may sell homogeneous or differentiated goods; (iii) each oligopoly seller considers the effect of his action (namely, price) on other rival sellers (thus, sellers recognise their interdependence); and (iv) entry is restricted.

In other words, if any of the features of perfect competition are found to be absent then the market is to be called an imperfect one. There are several forms of imperfect competition : monopoly, monopolistic competition and oligopoly.

Market structures, thus, range from the theoretical extremes of perfect competition and monopoly. In practice, we focus on degree of market imperfection lying between these extremes (Fig. 7.2.). We have chosen two parameters—number of firms in a market and influence of any one firm in the market—to identify different types of market. If number of firms in any market is too high (too low) and if the influence of any one firm on the market is virtually nil (or too high), the market is said to be a perfectly competitive one (monopoly). Monopolistic competition and oligopoly lie between these two market forms.

7.2.2. Criteria for Classification of Markets

Three criteria for the classification of markets are often suggested. These are: (i) substitutability of product criterion; (ii) interdependence criterion; and (iii) ease of entry criterion.

The first criterion takes into account the existence and closeness of substitutes while the second criterion takes into account the reactions of competitive sellers. This criterion is closely related to the number of firms within the industry and the degree of product differentiation. The last criterion is the 'condition of entry' which takes into account the 'ease of entry' in various markets. Now, we will classify markets in accordance with the three criteria mentioned above.

- **Product Substitutability Criterion** : The first important criterion is the product substitutability criterion which is measured by the cross price elasticity of demand for the product. The cross price elasticity of demand measures the degree of responsiveness of quantity demanded for a product to a change in the prices of related goods. The coefficient of cross price elasticity of demand is positive for substitute goods and negative for complementary goods. Thus, greater the degree of substitution greater is the value of cross elasticity of demand. Under perfect competition, goods are perfect substitutes and, hence, the coefficient of cross price elasticity of demand is infinite. In monopoly, there is no rival good or substitute good So, the coefficient of price elasticity of demand is zero. As under monopolistic competition, sellers sel differentiated but closely related goods the coefficient of price elasticity of demand is greater than zero but less than infinite. On the other hand, if the value of cross price elasticity of demand is greater than zero but less than infinite, the market for the product becomes an oligopolistic one.

- **Interdependence Criterion:** The second criterion is the interdependence criterion which is closely related to the number of firms in the industry and the degree of product differentiation. Perfect competition is characterised by innumerable number of firms in the industry and homogeneous or identical products. Price-output decisions of a competitive firm are not in any way affected by the price-output decisions of another firm. Thus, there is no rivalry among producers. No question of interdependence arises in the monopoly market. Despite the existence of closely related goods in monopolistic competition, each firm sets its price-output decisions independently. Under oligopoly, each firm takes into account the actions and reactions of rival sellers.

- **Ease of Entry Criterion:** Let us now explain the condition of entry which is expressed by the following notations:

$$E = \frac{P_a - P_C}{P_C}$$

E stands for condition of entry, P_C is the price under perfect competition and P_a is the actual price charged by firms. It is obvious that if the value of E is reduced to zero (i.e., there is no barrier to entry into the market), the market is said to be a perfectly competitive one and monopolistically competitive one. Under monopoly, entry is blockaded.

In a tabular form (Table 7.1), features of different markets have been portrayed here.

Thus, we find that there are four basic forms of market: perfect competition, monopoly, monopolistic competition, and oligopoly.

In perfect competition, firms behave as price-takers while, in the last three market forms, firms act as price-makers. Anyway, one can show the differences among these market forms in terms of the underlying structural and behavioural assumptions (Table 7.2).

7.3. REVENUE CONCEPTS

The basic goal of a firm is the maximisation of profit which is nothing but the difference between total revenue and total cost. Here we are concerned with the concept of revenue. The term 'revenue' is the amount of money that a firm or a seller

Table 7.1 Features of Four Markets

Type of market	Number of firms	Ease of entry	Nature of the product	Example	Nature of the demand curve for a firm	Promotion strategy
Perfect competition	Innumerable	Unrestricted	Homogeneous	Potato, and other agricultural goods	Horizontal: Price-taker	None
Monopoly	One	Blocked	No substitutes	CESC supplies electricity in and around Kolkata	Downward sloping but more inelastic: price-maker	Little
Monopolistic competition	Many/ several	Free	Differentiated	Soap, tooth-brush of different varieties	Downward sloping but elastic: Price-maker	Large amount
Oligopoly	Few	Restricted	Homogeneous and/or differentiated	Car	Downward sloping and relatively inelastic: Interdependence in price setting	Little or large amount

Table 7.2 Differences among Market Forms

	Price-takers		Price-makers	
	Perfect competition	Monopoly	Monopolistic competition	Oligopoly
A. Structual assumptions				
1. Number of sellers:	Innumerable	One	Many	Few
	Underlying the number of sellers is an asssumption concerning to entry. The absence of barriers to entry and exit implies that there are large number of firms in the market. Because of barriers to entry oligopoly market is characterised by a few sellers. On the contrary, there is only seller in monopoly market because the entry of new firms in it is legally prohibited.			
2. Cost conditions:	In all the markets, one can expect increasing cost to operate in the sense that MC tends to rise. However, a monopoly or an oligopoly firm may even operate under constant or falling MC.			
3. Demand conditions:	Perfect substitutes	No substitutes	Very close subsitutes	Identical or close subsitutes
B. Behavioural assumptions				
4. Objective function :	All firms of all these market forms aim at short run profit maximisation. However, under oligopoly, short run profit maximisation may not be the goal. Oligopolistic firms may pursue goals other than profit maximisation.			
5. Strategic variables :	In all market forms, the firm adjusts price and output. Under perfect competition, given price, a firm adjusts output only. However, under oligopoly or monopolistic competition, quality of the product, sales promotional efforts seems to be other important strategic variables.			
6. Expectations of rivals' reactions:	None	None	Each firm expects his actions to go unnoticed by its rivals	Rival firms may ignore or match the firm's actions depending on what serves their objectives

earns by selling his product. Thus, what is expenditure on goods of the buyers is the revenue of the sellers. Revenue schedule, like cost and output schedules, is also of three types—total, average and marginal.

● **Total Revenue (TR) :** A firm's total revenue is the total receipt it gets from the sale of the product. Thus, TR depends on the volume of sale, As sales change TR changes, i.e.,

$$TR = f(Q)$$

where Q is the quantity of output sold.

However, TR resulting from the sale of a product depends on the price as well as the volume of goods sold, i.e.,

$$TR = P \times Q$$

So, TR is defined as equal to the price of the goods times the volume of goods sold.

● **Average Revenue (AR):** Average revenue is the revenue per unit of output sold. Dividing total revenue by the volume of output sold one obtains AR. It is expressed as :

$$AR = \frac{TR}{Q} = \frac{P \times Q}{Q} = P$$

Thus, AR equals price, irrespective of the nature of the market. In other words, price line is identical to the AR curve. AR curve is the firm's demand curve for a commodity since it expresses the relationship between price and quantity sold. Since the demand curve for the firm's product also shows the same relationship, these two curves must be identical.

• **Marginal Revenue (MR):** MR is the extra revenue obtained by a firm from the sale of one extra unit of output. Suppose, a firm obtains Rs. 1,000 as revenue from the sale of 100 units of output. If the volume of sale increases to 110 units, its total revenue will go up to, say, Rs. 1,100. Thus, MR is Rs. 100. So, MR of the Q-th unit can be written as the difference between TR of Q-th units of goods sold and TR of (Q-1)-th units of goods sold i.e.,

$$MR = TR(Q) - TR(Q-1)$$

It can also be defined as the change in total revenue consequent upon a change in goods sold, i.e.,

$$MR = \frac{\Delta TR}{\Delta Q}$$

The following two schedules help us in explaining the revenue concepts. The first schedule (Table 7.3) shows TR, AR and MR of a firm operating under perfectly competitive conditions.

Table 7.3: Revenue Schedules Under Perfect Competition (in Rs.)

Output (Q)	Sold price (P)	TR (=P×Q)	AR (=TR/Q)	MR (= ΔTR / ΔQ)
1	5	5	5	
				5
2	5	10	5	
				5
3	5	15	5	
				5
4	5	20	5	
				5
5	5	25	5	

As price of the goods remains constant under perfect competition, TR increases proportionately as volume of sales increases. Here ruling market price is determined by market forces of supply and demand. But, to an individual firm, price is fixed. That is why, price = AR = MR for all levels of output sold.

Table 7.4 shows TR, AR and MR of a firm under imperfect competition. A firm, under imperfect competition, can influence the price of the product that it wants to sell. Further, if it wants to sell more it will have to lower down price.

Table 7.4: Revenue Schedules Under Imperfect Competition (in Rs.)

Q	P	TR	AR	MR
5	2	10	2	
				0.54
13	1.10	14.30	1.10	
				0.52
23	.85	19.55	.85	
				0.42
38	.68	25.84	.68	
				–0.28
50	.45	22.50	.45	

This schedule shows that as sales increase, TR increases. But TR declines when 50 units of goods are sold at a price of Rs. 0.45. So long as TR rises, MR declines. But when TR declines MR becomes negative. Thus, MR can both be positive and negative at different levels of output. Note that as output increases AR declines. This means that if the seller wants to sell more he will have to reduce the price of his product. Further, Table 7.4 shows that AR exceeds MR at all levels of output.

7.3.1 Revenue Curves under Different Market Forms

A firm, under perfect competition, behaves as a 'priçe-taker' in the sense that no single firm can influence the price of the product. Under this situation, TR curve is a rising straight line from

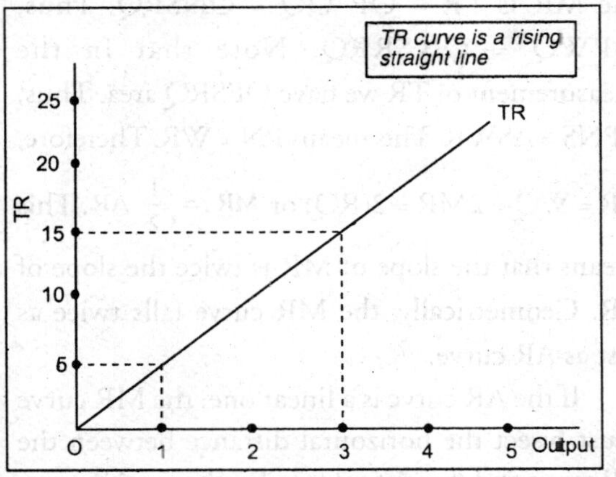

Fig. 7.3: TR: Perfect Competition

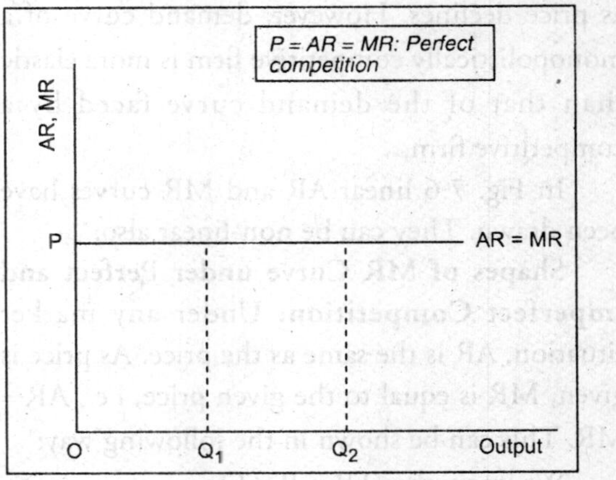

Fig. 7.5: AR = MR: Perfect Competition

the origin. TR rises in direct proportion to output. TR curve has been drawn in Fig. 7.3 whose slope is the given price in the market.

In any branch of imperfect competition (say, monopoly or monopolistic competition or oligopoly), a firm behaves as the 'price-maker' in the sense that it can influence the price of the product. A firm has to reduce the price of the product if it wants to sell more. So TR must rise. However, TR does not increase in proportion to the increase in the volume of sales. Under imperfect competition, TR initially rises, reaches maximum when OM units of output are sold and then starts declining as output sold increases over time. This shape of the TR curve has been shown in Fig. 7.4.

Shapes of AR Curve under Perfect and Imperfect Competition: As a competitive firm behaves as a price-taker, its AR remains the same even if volume of sales increases. That is why AR curve of Fig. 7.5 has been drawn parallel to the horizontal axis. The AR curve shows that at the price OP, any amount of the goods (OQ_1 or OQ_2) may be demanded. In other words, AR curve or the demand curve faced by a competitive firm becomes perfectly elastic.

Under imperfect competition, AR curve becomes negative sloping. It declines continuously

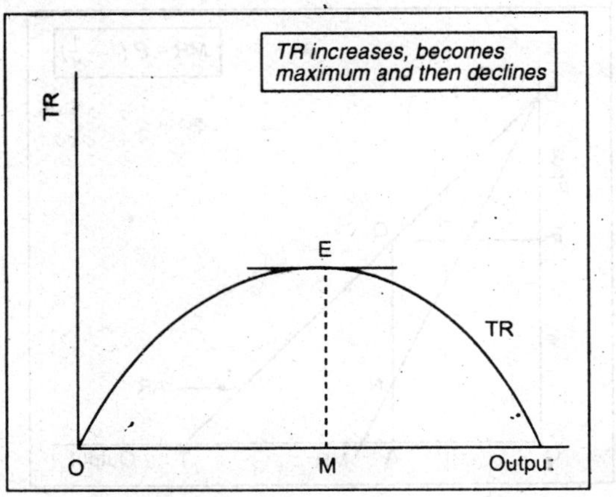

Fig. 7.4: TR under Imperfect Competition

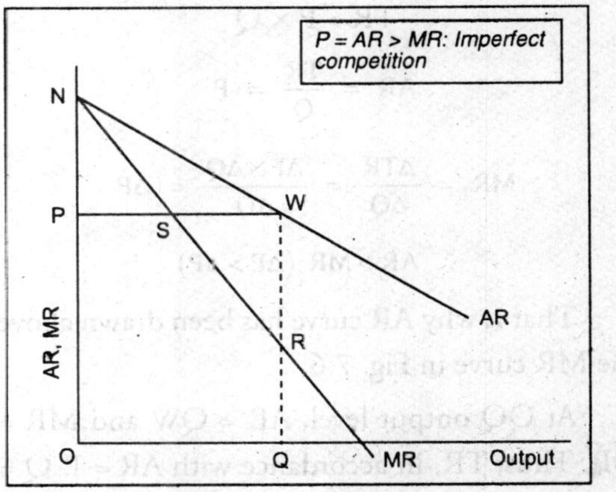

Fig. 7.6: AR > MR: Imperfect Competition

as price declines. However, demand curve of a monopolistically competitive firm is more elastic than that of the demand curve faced by a competitive firm.

In Fig. 7.6 linear AR and MR curves have been drawn. They can be non-linear also.

Shapes of MR Curve under Perfect and Imperfect Competition: Under any market situation, AR is the same as the price. As price is given, MR is equal to the given price, i.e., AR = MR. This can be shown in the following way:

We know that TR = P × Q

$$AR = \frac{TR}{Q} = \frac{P \times Q}{Q} = P$$

$$MR = \frac{\Delta TR}{\Delta Q}$$

Under perfect competition, as price does not change, TR changes only in proportion to the change in the volume of sales. Thus,

$$MR = \frac{P \times \Delta Q}{\Delta Q} = P$$

$$\therefore AR = MR$$

That is why AR curve is identical to MR curve under perfect competition, as shown in Fig. 7.4.

On the other hand, as a firm under imperfect competition can change the price of the product, AR no longer coincides with MR. Here

$$TR = P \times Q$$

$$AR = \frac{TR}{Q} = P$$

$$MR = \frac{\Delta TR}{\Delta Q} = \frac{\Delta P \times \Delta Q}{\Delta Q} = \Delta P$$

$$\therefore AR > MR \ (\Delta P > \Delta P)$$

That is why AR curve has been drawn above the MR curve in Fig. 7.6.

At OQ output level, AR = QW and MR = QR. Thus, TR, in accordance with AR = P. Q = OP. OQ = OPWQ and TR in accordance with the MR is TR = OP. OQ = ONSRQ. Thus, OPWQ = ONSRRQ. Note that in the measurement of TR we have OPSRQ area. Thus, ΔPNS = ΔSWR. This means PN = WR. Therefore, AR = WQ = 2MR = 2(RQ) or $MR = \frac{1}{2} AR$. This means that the slope of MR is twice the slope of AR. Geometrically, the MR curve falls twice as fast as AR curve.

If the AR curve is a linear one, the MR curve must bisect the horizontal distance between the AR curve and the vertical axis. Further, as AR curve is downward sloping, so is MR curve.

One thing should be remembered regarding TR and MR relationship. MR is the slope of TR. When TR rises as output rises, MR declines. When TR reaches maximum, MR becomes zero and when TR declines, MR becomes negative.

7.4. RELATIONSHIP AMONG AR, MR AND ELASTICITY OF DEMAND

Relationship among AR, MR and elasticity of demand (symbolied by 'e') can be established in terms of both geometry and algebra. First, we use geometrical method.

In Fig. 7.7, DT is the average revenue curve or demand curve of a firm operating under imperfect competition. We know that elasticity of demand on the demand the curve DT at point

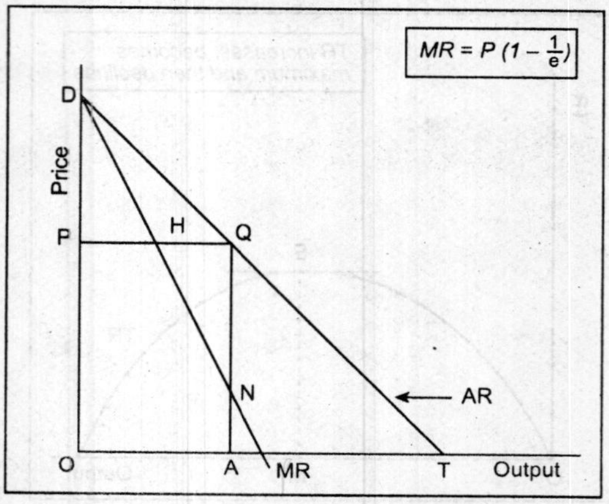

Fig. 7.7: Relationship among AR, MR and e

$Q = \frac{QT}{QD}$. A perpendicular QP is drawn to the vertical axis and another perpendicular QA has been drawn on the horizontal axis. MR curve bisects the perpendicular QP at point H.

Now, in triangles PDQ and AQT, we have

$\angle DPQ = \angle QAT$ (right angles)

$\angle DQP = \angle QTA$ (corresponding angles)

and, $\angle PDQ = \angle AQT$

Thus, triangles PDQ and AQT are equiangular. So, we can write

$$\frac{QT}{QD} = \frac{QA}{PD}$$

Again, in the triangles PDH and HQN, PH = HQ

$\angle PHD = \angle QHN$ (vertically opposite angles)

$\angle DHD = \angle HQN$ (right angles)

Therefore, triangles PDH and HQN are congruent (i.e., equal in all respects). Therefore, DP = QN.

Thus, elasticity of demand at point Q is

$$\frac{QT}{QD} = \frac{QA}{PD} = \frac{QA}{QN}$$

But, QN = QA – NA

$$\therefore \frac{QA}{QN} = \frac{QA}{QA - NA}$$

Hence, elasticity of demand at

$$Q = \frac{QA}{QA - NA}$$

It is clear from Fig. 7.7 that QA is the average revenue while NA is the marginal revenue for the output OA. Hence, elasticity at Q

$$e = \frac{AR}{AR - MR}$$

$$\text{or } e = \frac{A}{A - M}$$

where A stands for average revenue and M for marginal revenue.

By cross-multiplication one gets

$$eA - eM = A$$

$$\text{or} \quad eA - A = eM$$

$$\text{or} \quad A(e - 1) = eM$$

$$\therefore A = \frac{eM}{(e-1)}$$

Hence,

$$\text{price or AR} = M\left(\frac{e}{e-1}\right)$$

$$\text{and MR} = A\left(\frac{e-1}{e}\right)$$

$$\text{or MR} = A\left(1 - \frac{1}{e}\right)$$

This formula helps us to find MR at any output from AR at the same output. Suppose, price of a product is Rs. 10. If elasticity of demand is equal to 2, then

$$MR = AR\left(1 - \frac{1}{e}\right) = 10\left(1 - \frac{1}{2}\right) = \text{Rs. } 5.$$

If elasticity of demand equals one (1), then

$$MR = AR\left(1 - \frac{1}{e}\right) = 10\left(1 - \frac{1}{1}\right) = \text{Rs. } 0$$

If elasticity is equal to less than one, say $\frac{1}{2}$, then

$$MR = AR\left(1 - \frac{1}{e}\right) = 10\left(1 - \frac{1}{1/2}\right) = \text{Rs. } -10.$$

Thus, MR will be positive if the coefficient of elasticity of demand is elastic (i.e., e > 1). MR will be zero if elasticity is equal to one (i.e., e = 1), and MR will be negative if coefficient of elasticity is inelastic (i.e., e < 1).

Algebraic Method: A mathematical method is also employed to describe the relationship among AR, MR and e.

Suppose, initial price and quantity are P and Q respectively. Thus,

$$TR_0 = P \times Q$$

Now, let the price fall by ΔP and quantity rise by ΔQ. Now the total revenue will be

$$TR_1 = (P - \Delta P).\ (Q + \Delta Q)$$

$$\therefore \Delta TR = TR_1 - TR_0 = (P - \Delta P)\ (Q + \Delta Q) - P.Q$$

$$\text{or, } \Delta TR = PQ + P\Delta Q - Q\Delta P - \Delta P\Delta Q - PQ$$
$$= P\Delta Q - Q\Delta P - \Delta P\Delta Q$$

Ignoring $\Delta P\Delta Q$ as infinitesimally small,

$$\Delta TR = P\Delta Q - Q\Delta P$$

MR is defined as the change in total revenue consequent upon a change in output, i.e.,

$$MR = \frac{\Delta TR}{\Delta Q} = \frac{P\Delta Q - Q\Delta P}{\Delta Q} = P - \frac{Q\Delta P}{\Delta Q}$$

Now, we multiply this term by $\frac{P}{1}$, which does not change the equality. Thus,

$$MR = P - \left(\frac{\Delta P}{\Delta Q}\right)\left(\frac{Q}{P}\right)\left(\frac{P}{1}\right)$$

Factoring out P we obtain

$$\therefore MR = P\left(\frac{\Delta P}{\Delta Q}.\frac{Q}{P}\right) = P\left(1 - \frac{1}{e}\right)$$

$$\left[\because e = \frac{\Delta Q}{\Delta P}.\frac{P}{Q}\ \therefore \frac{1}{e} = \frac{\Delta P}{\Delta Q}.\frac{Q}{P}\right]$$

$$\therefore MR = P\left(1 - \frac{1}{e}\right)$$

Thus, we can say that (1) MR depends on: (i) the price of the product, and (ii) elasticity of demand for the product, and (2) as the value of e rises $\frac{1}{e}$ declines. If the value of e becomes infinite then

$$MP = 1\left(1 - \frac{1}{e}\right) = P\left(1 - \frac{1}{\alpha}\right) = p(1 - 0) = P$$

or MR coincides with AR (or P). This happens under perfect competition.

The formula $MR = P\left(1 - \frac{1}{e}\right)$ enables us to derive price, i.e., $P = MR \div \left(1 - \frac{1}{e}\right)$. If MR is 2 and e is also 2, then

$$P = 2 \div \left(1 - \frac{1}{2}\right) = 4$$

7.5. OBJECTIVES OF BUSINESS FIRM

A firm is a unit engaged in the production and / or distribution of goods and services. All firms (e.g., sole proprietorship, joint stock firm, cooperative, public sector firms, etc.) operating under perfectly competitive framework or monopoly framework or monopolistically competitive framework or oligopoly framework aim at profit maximisation, just as all students of all countries appearing at all kinds of examinations aim only at maximising marks. As all firms from perfect competition to oligopoly aim at profit maximisation, their marginal costs become equal to marginal revenues. In other words, price-output determination of this kind of marginal approach or standard approach suggests that when marginal cost equals marginal revenue, profit is maximised. Profit maximisation may be considered as a basic objective of a business firm.

But the attainment of such goal does not take into account the complexities of the real world and, hence, involves several obstacles. It is indeed true that a firm may not be able to maximise profit because of uncertainty in business conditions. Further, profit maximisation objective may change if the firm's behaviour changes. Our standard neo-classical approach may fit within the perfectly competitive model and monopoly model. But, modern business firms are mostly characterised by monopolistic competition and oligopoly. In this real business world, one finds mutual interdependence among firms. Profit maximisation then is not accepted as the primary goal. Again, in recent times one finds changing organisational structure of firms where we find different groups and sub-groups have different as well as conflicting goals.

In this complex world, no one aims maximising anything—everyone simply aims to 'satisfy' a range of objectives. For all these reasons, we today face supplement to the profit maximising goal. Alternatives to profit maximisation model are grouped into two: managerial theories and behavioural theories.

With the arrival of joint stock firms and the separation of ownership and control between shareholders and firm managers has led us to believe that managers are more interested in the maximisation of sales revenue rather than profit. This was stated by W. J. Baumol in 1959 who argues that some profit is necessary for survival. Managers can be seen to be operating with a profit constraint which would be required just to keep the shareholders happy. This model, alternative to profit maximisation, is concerned with the maximisation of sales value rather than volume, subject to a profit constraint.

Another model has been given by an Amercian economist Oliver Williamson in the 1960s who explains firm's behaviour in terms of managerial discretion. He argues that managers are not interested in profit maximisation. Rather, they want to maximise their own utility functions which include a number of personal goals and personal measures of well-being. The managerial utility function includes expenditure on staff (symbolised by S), managerial emoluments and perks (symbolised by M) and discretionary investment (represented by I_D). Thus, the managers utility function may be written as:

$$U = f(S, M, I_D)$$

subject to a minimum profit adequate to keep shareholders satisfied. Thus, like Baumol, maximisation as a goal is not ignored in this managerial approach.

Robbin Marris—a Cambridge economist—in the 1960s says that managers are interested in attaining a higher growth objective of the company and, hence, profits ploughed back into investment and their own personal goals (such as status, power, salary, etc.). However, in selecting the growth rate of the company, the management has to consider a lot of things. This is because of the fact that a high growth rate has two effects with opposite results on share prices—low dividend depresses the value of the shares and a high growth rate increases the value of shares. Thus, a higher growth may lead to takeover of the company. So the management may choose a growth rate somewhere between the rate that maximises market value of shares and the rate at which takeover would take place.

All these alternatives to profit maximisation goal suggest that these aim at maximising something. In real world, such maximising behaviour of firm is irrelevant. H. A. Simon in the 1950s says that firms are never guided by profit maximisation or sales revenue maximisation or utility maximisation or growth maximisation. According to Simon, firms intend to attain a 'satisficing profit'. Attainment of profit over this volume may be counterproductive.

Conclusion : Profit maximisation goal has not been rejected; within the alternative models presented here, profit exists as an important constraint. In view of this, some economists argue that time has come to reconcile all these goals.

QUESTIONS (WITH ANSWER-HINTS)

Long Questions (16 marks)

1. (a) Explain the shape of TR curve if price of a commodity is fixed. (b) Show the relationship between AR and MR. What is the relationship between these revenues and price elasticity of demand?
   Ans. 7.3, 7.3.1 and 7.4.
2. Profit maximisation is not always the aim of a business firm. Discuss.

   Or

   Define a business firm and discuss the main objectives of a business firm.
   Ans. 7.5.

Medium-sized Questions (8 marks)

1. What is meant by market in economics?
   Ans. 7.2.
2. What are the diferent market forms that are encountered in the world?
   Ans. 7.2.1.
3. Explain the criteria that are usually adopted for distinguishing between market forms.
   Ans. 7.2.2.
4. Define total, average and marginal revenues. Explain the shapes of these curves under different market situations.
   Ans. 7.3 and 7.3.1.

8

PRICE AND OUTPUT DETERMINATION UNDER PERFECT COMPETITION

8.1. INTRODUCTION

Price-output decision greatly depends on the organisation of the product market, that is, whether there are one, two or many firms, whether the product is homogeneous or not, and so on. Thus, we have to start with the classification of markets. In one of the earlier chapters, we did it particularly on the basis of three criteria—(i) the product substitutability criterion, (ii) interdependence criterion, and (iii) ease of entry criterion. On the basis of these criteria, some of the markets were labeled as perfect competition and some others imperfect competition. One of the extreme forms of imperfect competition is monopoly which is an anti-thesis of perfect competition. Most popular subdivisions of imperfect competition are: (i) monopolistic competition and (ii) oligopoly. In this chapter, the model of perfect competition will be presented.

The term 'perfect competition' in economics has a different as well as a diametrically opposite view of what a businessman holds. Competition always involves 'rivalry'. But as far as economics is concerned, rivalry is absent in perfect competition; competition here is entirely impersonal. So, perfect competition refers to a market situation where competition among economic agents is absent completely. Obviously, this sort of market situation is far from reality. Still, this model has usefulness since it provides a very useful analytical model. Above all, usefulness of any theory "lies in the predictions it can generate". That is why the model of perfect competition is the starting point of business decisions relating to output and price.

The concept of perfect competition is more than 230 years old. Adam Smith used this phrase in a casual way in his celebrated book *"Wealth of Nations"* (1776). Later, Edgeworth (1881) and Frank Knight (1921) gave a complete nature of the model of perfect competition.

8.2. FEATURES OF PERFECT COMPEQTITION

Perfect competition is a market structure characterised by the following four conditions :

- *Large number of sellers and buyers*: A perfectly competitive firm is characterised by the existence of innumerable number of sellers or firms and buyers so that every one in the market is so small that it cannot exert any influence on the price. Every firm in the market is so small relative to the market that it cannot affect market price by changing its output. Similarly, buyers aim at buying the product at a lower price. Such is ruled out since their numbers are so large that an individual cannot obtain special favour from the sellers. Thus, every economic unit behaves as a 'price-taker', or nobody possesses 'market power'. Price is or known to both buyers and sellers. Only market forces can bring about a change in the price of the product

- *Homogeneous product* : A closely related provision is that the goods sold by all firms are standardized or homogeneous or identical in quality. In other words, buyers could not differentiate the product as well as the services sold by one from those of another. That is to say, goods and services of each and every seller are perfect substitutes. It is due to the homogeneity of the product, price is uniform or same to all. Goods are not differentiated here by advertising, packaging or quality. Because of this, every participant in the market has "complete infomation" about prices ruling in the market. If goods were not differentiated, firms would have been able to influence the price, at least partially.

The assumptions of innumerable number of sellers and buyers and product homogeneity imply that the individual firm and consumer are price-takers and the demand curve (AR) faced by a competitive firm becomes perfectly elastic. Further, the demand curve or the AR curve coincides with the MR curve.

- *Free entry and exit*: Any firm is free to enter or leave the industry, if situation demands. If it wishes a new firm may join the industry; the existing firms will not put an obstacle. However, new firms become interested in joining an industry mostly when some or most of the existing firms enjoy something more than normal profit. Excess profit is, thus, an incentive on the part of a firm to join the industry. Similarly, if some of the firms incur losses chronically, they have the liberty to close down business. No existing firm will ask them to stay on. As a result, all firms in the long run enjoy only normal profit. Remember, this particular feature is valid only in the long run since entry or exit in the short run is not so easy. In other words, there are barriers to entry and exit in the short run, but not in the long run.
- *Perfect knowledge*: It is assumed that all the participants (consumers, producers, input suppliers) have perfect knowledge and information regarding the conditions of the market. If consumers have perfect knowledge of the market only, then a uniform price will prevail. If producers and buyers know costs, prices, product quality, etc. then there cannot be more than one price. Resource owners also supply their inputs at the going price. No one will charge price in accordance with his discretion. Further, everyone also has complete knowledge of the future.

- *Perfect mobility of resources*: Resources are completely free to move from one firm to another, not only geographically, but also among jobs. In other words, mobility of resources is costless.
- *Absence of externalities*: If consumption of one individual or production of one firm is not influenced by the actions of other individuals or firms, then we see absence of externalities either in consumption or in production. Under perfect competition, consumption and production decisions are not interdependent; rather, these are independent decisions. This means that there is no third-party effect.

Collectively, all these features define perfect competition. No industry, in actual practice, satisfies all these features. In this sense, this market form does not fit with the reality.

Anyway, with these assumptions in mind, we will now examine equilibrium of a firm—both in the short run and in the long run.

8.3. EQUILIBRIUM OF A COMPETITIVE FIRM IN THE SHORT RUN

The fundamental goal of a business firm is the maximisation of profit, irrespective of the time period under consideration. Profit becomes maximum only when a firm reaches equilibrium. A firm will reach equilibrium when the following two conditions are fulfilled simultaneously:

- MC = MR→ necessary condition or first-order condition (FOC) for equilibrium, and
- MC curve must cut MR curve from below, or the slope of MC > the slope of MR. This condition is known as sufficient condition or second-order condition (SOC).

Economists call MC= MR = P the 'golden rule of output determination' of a competitive firm.

Here, first we will examine short run equilibrium situation of a competitive firm. A competitive firm is characterised by: (i) large number of sellers, (ii) homogeneous product, and (iii) free entry and exit of firms. So far as the 'short run' is concerned, no new firms can enter the industry or the existing firms exit from the industry. However, in the long run, entry or exit is free.

We know that under perfect competition every firm/buyer behaves as a 'price-taker'. To all, price is given and known. However, this price is determined in the competitive industry in the short run by short run demand and supply curves for the industry. This price, once determined in this way, is accepted by all firms and buyers. No one has the power to influence the price. Against this backdrop of market price, a firm aims at maximising its profit by producing a certain level of output where P = MC.

The equilibrium output of a competitive firm operating in the short run has been shown in Fig. 8.1 where the revenue and cost curves have been drawn. It is to be kept in mind that a firm in the short run may enjoy abnormal profit if total revenue (TR) exceeds total cost (TC). Further, it may incur a loss in the short run if TC exceeds TR. Or it may earn only normal profit if TR equals TC. All these three possibilities have been shown in Fig. 8.1. Fig. 8.1(a) describes supernormal profit enjoyed by firm A. Fig. 8.1(b) shows normal profit enjoyed by firm B and Fig. 8.1(c) shows loss incurred by firm C. In all the figures, curves labeled as SAC and SMC are known as short run average cost and short run marginal cost curves.

Firm A is in equilibrium at point E_A since at this point both the conditions for equilibrium have been satisfied. Corresponding to this equilibrium point, profit-maximising volume of output becomes OQ_A. Firm A now earns revenue to the extent of $OP_AE_AQ_A$ from the sale of output of OQ_A. And, it incurs a cost of production to the extent of $OCDQ_A$. Since revenue exceeds cost, firm A earns supernormal profit by the amount P_AE_ADC.

For firm B, equilibrium output is Q_B corresponding to the equilibrium point E_B. Since revenue ($OP_BE_BQ_B$) for OQ_B output is the same as that of its cost of production ($OP_BE_BQ_B$), firm B enjoys only normal profit. Point E_B may be called break-even point since revenue equals cost.

Firm C incurs a loss though it remains in equilibrium at point E_C. In other words, a competitive firm may reach equilibrium even after incurring losses. Here, loss amounts to the area P_CE_CNM, since costs exceeds revenue.

Thus, a firm in the short run may

- earn supernormal profit if
  SMC = MR = AR > SAC,
- earn normal profit if
  SMC = MR = AR = SAC, and
- suffer a loss if
  SMC = MR = AR < SAC

Note that although the 'golden rule of output determination (P = MC)' is satisfied, the firm in the short run incurs loss.

Will a firm continue in business if it incurs a loss in the short run? In the short run, even after making negative profit (i.e., loss), a firm will stay in business if it can manage variable costs. A firm in the short run faces both fixed and variable costs. If no output is produced, the firm should bear fixed costs. So it must produce in the short run in such a way that it covers up at least variable costs. Then loss will be equivalent to fixed costs only. However, it will go out of business only if it fails to cover up variable costs from the sale of the goods. It will maximise profit only if it becomes an economic dropout by discontinuing production. Here 'dropout' is paying.

8.4. LONG RUN EQUILIBRIUM OF A COMPETITIVE FIRM

Long run is that time period when firms can adjust their fixed inputs. In other words, a firm in the

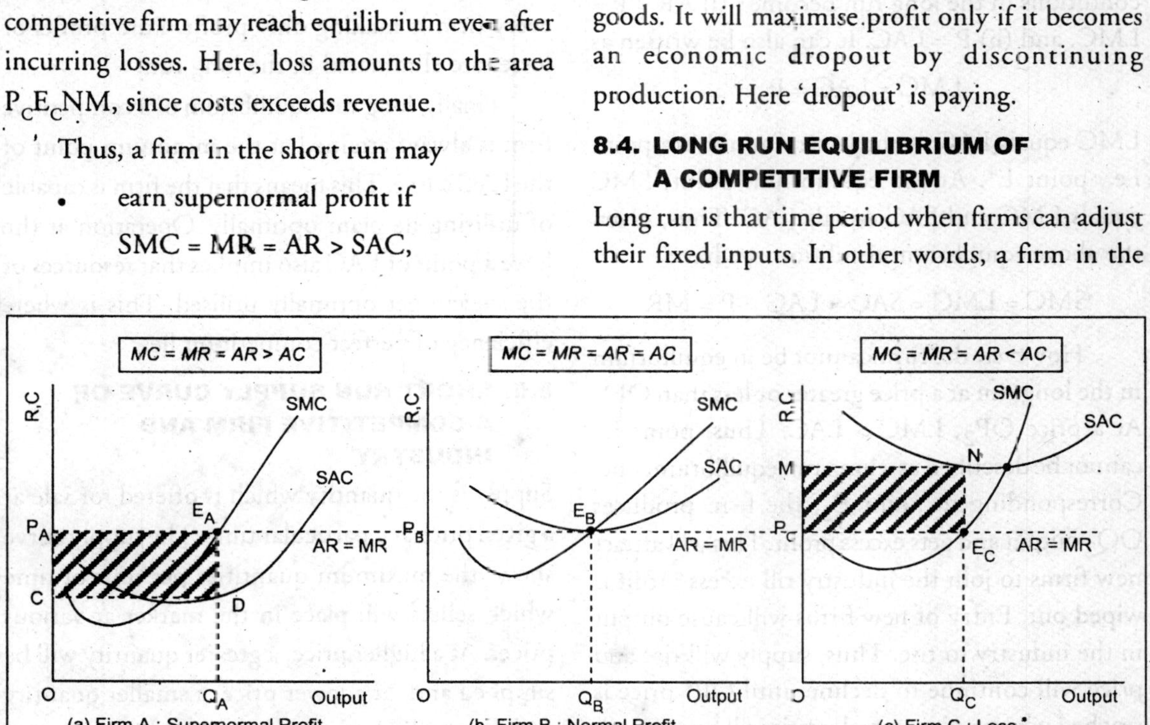

Fig. 8.1: Short run Equilibrium

long run can change its scale of production as well as output to achieve maximum profit. If some firms earn excess profit in the long run, new firms will be attracted to enter the industry. Similarly, whenever some firms incur losses for a long time, they will go out of business. This happens because in the long run under perfect competition, entry and exit are easy and free. As a result, all the firms in the industry enjoy only normal profit. In the long run, free entry and exit of firms ensure that abnormal profits or losses will be wiped out completely.

Fig. 8.2 explains long run adjustment of a competitive firm where LMC and LAC represent the long run marginal and average cost curves. Corresponding to the price OP*, the typical firm is in equilibrium at point E*. The equilibrium output, thus determined, is OQ* and the firm is making only normal profit. Thus, equilibrium conditions in the long run become : (i) AR = P = LMC, and (ii) P = LAC. It can also be written as

$$LMC = LAC = P$$

LMC equals LAC at the latter's minimum point i.e., point E*. At the equilibrium point, SMC equals LMC and SAC equals LAC. Thus, given the above equilibrium condition, we have

$$SMC = LMC = SAC = LAC = P = MR$$

However, the firm cannot be in equilibrium in the long run at a price greater or less than OP*. At a price OP_2, LMC > LAC. Thus, point E_2 cannot be described as a long run equilibrium one. Corresponding to point E_2, the firm produces OQ_2 output and gets excess profit. This will attract new firms to join the industry till excess profit is wiped out. Entry of new firms will cause output in the industry to rise. Thus, supply will rise and price will continue to decline until OP* price is reached where only normal profit will be enjoyed.

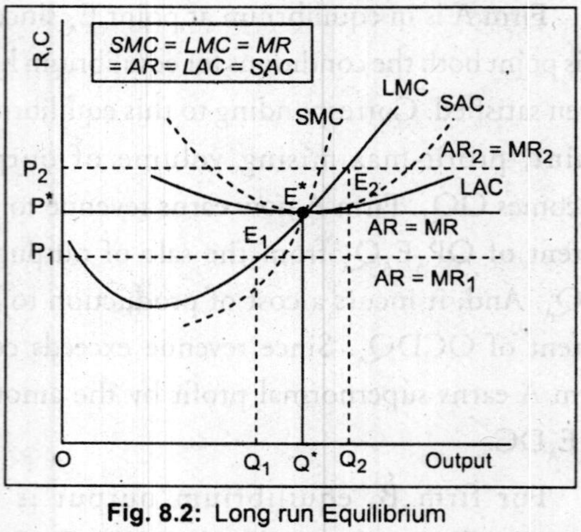

Fig. 8.2: Long run Equilibrium

Similarly, at the price OP_1, though the firm is in equilibrium at point E_1, it incurs a loss since LMC < LAC. Loss-making firms will, however, leave the industry. Consequently, output and supply in the industry will decline. This will cause price to rise to OP* where there is no incentive on the part of the firms to leave. At this price, every firm is making only profit. Pure profits or losses are eliminated in the long run.

Finally, long run equilibrium of a competitive firm is always attained at the minimum point of the LAC curve. This means that the firm is capable of utilising its plant optimally. Operation at the lowest point of LAC also implies that resources of the society get optimally utilised. This is where efficiency of perfect competition lies.

8.5. SHORT RUN SUPPLY CURVE OF A COMPETITIVE FIRM AND INDUSTRY

Supply is the quantity which is offered for sale at a given price at a particular time. The supply curve shows the maximum quantities per unit of time which sellers will place in the market at various prices. At a higher price, a greater quantity will be supplied and, at a lower price, a smaller quantity will be supplied.

Recall that supply of a commodity is a derived function. It is derived from the cost function. It is said that all supply curves are cost curves, but all cost curves (AFC, AVC, AC and MC) are not supply curves. Under perfect competition, in the short period, only MC curve is supply curve. As is known to all, MC curve is U-shaped having both negative and positive slopes while supply curve is positive sloping. So, we must not consider negative or downward sloping portion of MC curve. Only rising portion (i.e., upward sloping) of MC is the supply curve. To be more specific, rising portion of MC that lies above the AVC curve is the supply curve of a competitive firm in the short run.

Under perfect competition, a firm will produce that amount of output when P = MC. As price is given to a firm, the price line becomes parallel to the horizontal axis. This amounts to saying that demand curve or AR curve that coincides with the MR curve becomes perfectly elastic. In Fig. 8.3(a) AVC, SAC and SMC are the average variable cost curve, short run average cost curve and short run marginal cost curve, respectively. At a price OP, the firm is in equilibrium at point R since at this point all the conditions for equilibrium are satisfied. Corresponding to this equilibrium point, the firm produces OQ output. The total revenue that the firm expects to earn from the sale of OQ output is OPRQ. But costs are higher than revenue since AVC and SAC curves lie above the OP price line. At this output, the firm not only fails to cover up its fixed cost but also a part of the variable cost. As AVC exceeds price, the firm should go out of business. So, when price is below AVC (i.e., P < AVC), the short run equilibrium output is zero.

At a price OP_1, the firm reaches equilibrium at point M where P = MC. It produces OQ_1 output and earns revenue to the extent of OP_1MQ_1. At this output level, though cost exceeds revenue, the firm manages just its variable costs only. Here revenue equals variable costs only. It does not cover up its fixed costs. Even then the firm will continue production in the short run in view of producing larger output in the future. The firm expects to manage fixed costs in the future. At the price OP_1, however, MC = minimum AVC. The point at which MC = minimum AVC is known as 'shut-down point'. Note that the firm,

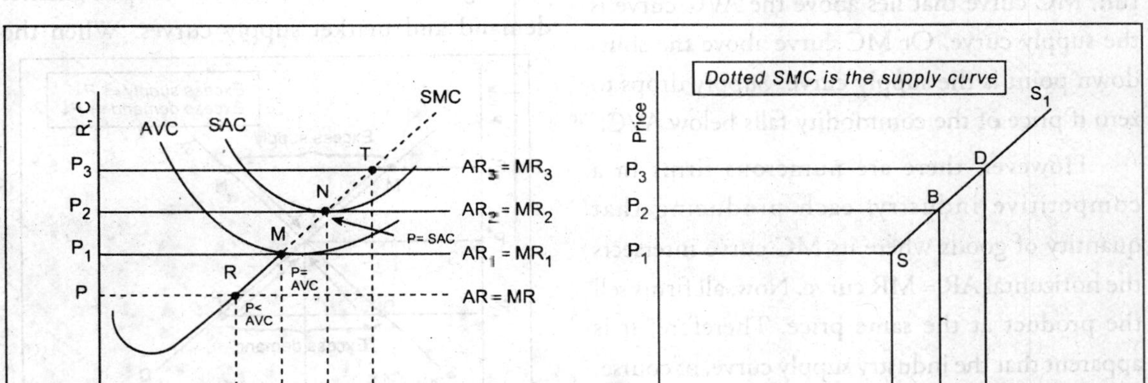

Fig. 8.3: Short run Supply Curve of a Competitive Firm

at the shut-down point, is indifferent between operating and shutting down. The firm has to apply its judgement whether it will stop production at this point in the short run or continue production with the hope of recovering some costs (fixed) in the short run. In view of this, shut-down point is also referred to as zero contribution margin. Below the shut-down point, the firm experiences negative contribution margin.

At a price OP_2, the firm covers up not only variable costs but also fixed costs since, at point N, MC = minimum SAC. Corresponding to the price OP_2, the equilibrium quantity of output is OQ_2, total revenue is OP_2NQ_2, total cost is OP_2NQ_2. As costs equal revenue, the firm must go on producing. At point N, MC = minimum SAC. This point is called 'break-even point'. Similarly, at price OP_3, the firm will produce and supply OQ_3 since it earns excess profit.

Points S, B and D of panel (b) are the points at the prices OP_1, OP_2 and OP_3, respectively. By joining these points, we get a curve known as supply curve SS_1. This curve corresponds to (dotted) SMC curve above the AVC curve of panel (a). Thus, under perfect competition in the short run, MC curve that lies above the AVC curve is the supply curve. Or MC curve above the shut-down point is the supply curve. Supply drops to zero if price of the commodity falls below AVC.

However, there are numerous firms in a competitive industry, each producing that quantity of goods where its MC curve intersects the horizontal AR = MR curve. Now, all firms sell the product at the same price. Therefore, it is apparent that the industry supply curve, of course, in the short run under perfect competition is equal to the horizontal summation of all firms' supply curves or MC curves above the minimum point of AVC. Thus, like the individual supply curve, short run industry supply curve is upward sloping. It is drawn in the same way as we draw the market demand curve from the demand curve of an individual.

In the words of Prof. R. G. Lipsey: "The supply curve for a competitive industry is the horizontal sum of the marginal cost curves of all the individual firms in the industry."

8.6. COMPETITIVE MARKET OR INDUSTRY EQUILIBRIUM

We have analysed the concepts of demand and supply in great detail. Now we are in a position to bring together these two concepts. Here we will see how the interaction of demand and supply forces determine equilibrium price in a perfectly competitive market or industry.

By equilibrium we mean a state of balance in which two opposing forces come into operation. An equilibrium is a state of rest from where there is no tendency to change the system. Market equilibrium occurs where demand and supply balance each other—there is no difference between these two opposing forces; and, hence, these are at rest.

Fig. 8.4 shows the normal-shaped market demand and market supply curves. When the

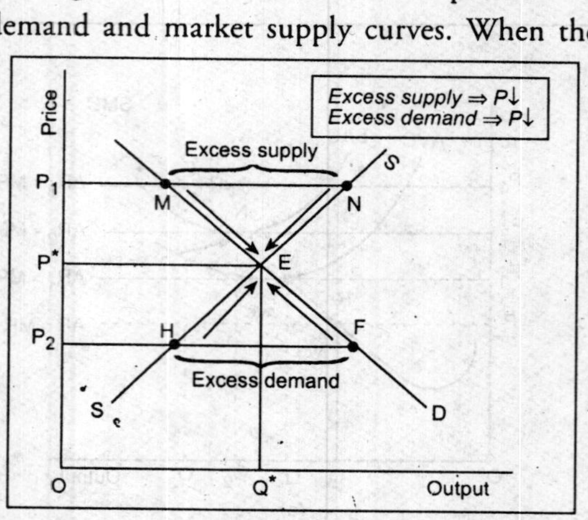

Fig. 8.4: Equilibrium in a Competitive Market

demand curve, DD, and supply curve, SS, intersect each other we obtain equilibrium price and equilibrium quantity. Equilibrium price is OP* and equilibrium quantity is OQ*. At this price, the amount that the sellers are willing to sell in the market is exactly matched by the amount that the buyers are willing to buy. At this price, both the parties are satisfied. Neither buyer nor seller is willing to disturb this situation.

The equilibrium price OP*—defined by the intersection of demand and supply curves—is also the "market clearing price" since at this price excess supply and excess demand are zero. We can explain this in the following way. If price is higher than OP*, say OP_1, buyers are willing to buy P_1M, while sellers are willing to sell a large quantity, P_1N. Thus, there is an excess supply to the tune of MN in the market. Sellers are dissatisfied. As a result, there will be a downward pressure on price (following competition among sellers). Price will continue to decline until OP* is reached. Similarly, at a price lower than OP*, say OP_2, there occurs an excess demand or shortage in the market to the extent of HF. Here buyers are dissatisfied. Now competition among buyers will lead to an upward pressure in price. It will rise till OP* is reached. Thus, OP* is equilibrium price or market-clearing price. Or all other prices except OP* are disequilibrium prices.

Under perfect competition, temporary disequilibrium (either a situation of excess supply or excess demand) gets removed automatically and equilibrium is restored. That does not mean that this equilibrium price will rule for all time. In fact, equilibrium situation will undergo a change if there is a change in demand or a change in supply or in both.

8.7. LONG RUN SUPPLY CURVE OF A COMPETITIVE INDUSTRY

The long run supply curve of a competitive industry is not obtained in the same way as the short run industry supply curve. In other words, simply by aggregating individual firms, long run MC curves, one cannot obtain long run industry supply curve. The procedure of deriving the long run industry supply curve is different since in the long run entry into and exit of firms from the industry come into action.

A competitive firm in the long run produces at that point where long run MC curve intersects the long run AC curve at the lowest point. (i.e., P = AR = MR = LMC = minimum point of LAC). Thus, in the long run, a competitive firm operates its plant size optimally and efficiently. In the long run, the supply of a commodity is determined by the minimum point of long run AC curve where optimum output is obtained. This results in a change not only in the size of the industry, but also in the supply of output. The change in scale of production in the long run brings about (external) economies and (external) diseconomies of production. Long run industry equilibrium depends on such economies and diseconomies. That is why variation in cost occurs in a competitive industry in the long run. In other words, as industry output expands in the long run, a perfectly competitive industry may experience constant cost or decreasing or increasing cost. How will the long run AC curve of an individual firm shift as industry output expands depends on whether the industry operates under constant cost condition or increasing cost condition or deceasing cost condition. Consequently, the shapes of the long run industry supply curves will be horizontal, increasing and decreasing—depending on the cost condition on which the industry operates.

A *constant cost industry* is one where cost structure of the individual firm remains stable as the industry expands its output. Prices of inputs employed by a constant cost industry do not change.

An *increasing cost industry* is one where cost of the individual firms rises as the industry expands its output. Here prices of inputs rise.

A *decreasing cost industry* is one where the expansion of output causes costs to decline. Under decreasing cost condition, prices of inputs decline.

8.7.1. Constant Cost Industry and Horizontal Supply Curve

A constant cost industry is one where expansion or contraction of the industry does not bring about a change in the prices of factors of production employed by it. Or a constant cost industry may be defined as one where external economies and external diseconomies balance each other. Expansion of a constant cost industry create neither external economies nor external diseconomies. Consequently, cost stays at the same level as industry expands. Under constant cost industry, no matter how many firms leave or join the industry, every firm will retain the same set of cost curves (LAC and LMC) with which it started.

Fig. 8.5 demonstrates long run equilibrium of an industry operating under constant cost condition. Panel (a) of Fig. 8.5 shows long run equilibrium of a competitive firm while panel (b) describes industry equilibrium determined by the intersection of demand curve and supply curve. Let us assume that DD and SS are the initial demand and supply curves. These two curves together (point 'm') determine equilibrium price at OP. Accepting this price, a typical firm would produce Oq output. Incidentally, all the firms are making zero economic profit since P = LMC = LAC. If we assume that there are 10,000 identical firms in the industry, then the industry output would be Oq × 10,000 firms = OQ (shown in panel b). Since these firms are making only normal profit at OP, the industry is in equilibrium with an output OQ.

Now, let us suppose that there is an increase in market demand to D_1D_1 following an increase in money income or a change in taste of buyers. As a result, market price rises from OP to OP_1

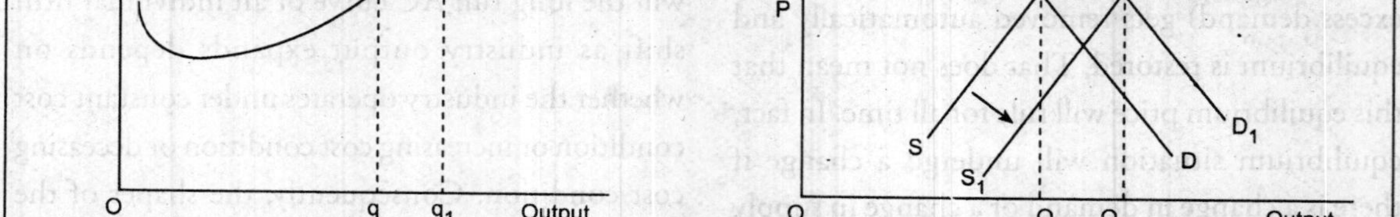

Fig. 8.5: Horizontal Supply Curve

and the firm's demand curve is now represented by $P_1=AR_1=MR_1$ line. The firm will now expand its output to Oq_1. It will earn supernormal profit equal to shaded area since $P = LMC = MR_1 = AR_1 > LAC$. Existence of this profit implies that the industry is out of equilibrium. This will then act as an incentive to new firms to join the industry.

Two things will now happen. *First,* demand for resources will go up. But, being a constant cost industry, input prices will remain unchanged. Thus, entry of firms will have no effect on cost curves. LAC and LMC curve will stay at the old level. However, firms will continue to enter until excess profit disappears. *Secondly,* entry of new firms in the industry will shift the supply curve rigthwad to S_1S_1. Industry equilibrium will now occur at point 'n' where the old price OP will be reestablished. At this OP price, each firm will be producing Oq output. Industry output is now larger since there are now more firms in the industry. At the price OP, OQ_1 output will be supplied in the industry. If we connect the various market equilibrium points—'m' and 'n'—we get the long run industry supply curve (LRS) drawn in panel (b). Thus, under constant cost industry, the LRS curve is a horizontal straight line or perfectly elastic even thóugh the short run supply has a positive slope.

8.7.2. Increasing Cost Industry and Rising Supply Curve

Sometimes, an expansion in industry output causes costs to rise in the long run. Thus, as industry expands, external diseconomies outweigh external economies leading to a net increase in costs. As industry expands, demand for inputs rise and costs rise since the industry operates under increasing cost condition. In other words, external diseconomies cause LAC curve to shift upwards as industry expands. Consequently, the long run industry supply curve becomes positive sloping.

Fig. 8.6 illustrates the long run adjustment process of a competitive industry operating under increasing cost condition. Panel (a) shows long run equilibrium of a competitive firm and panel (b) shows industry equilibrium. The industry is in equilibrium at the price OP and output OQ, as defined by the intersection of DD and SS curves at point 'm'. Corresponding to this price OP, each

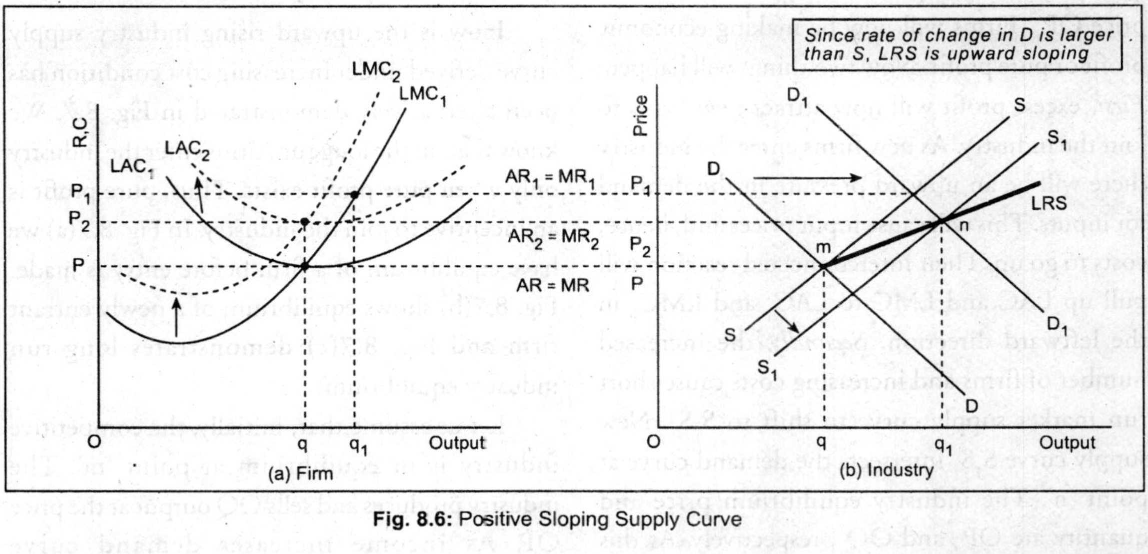

Fig. 8.6: Positive Sloping Supply Curve

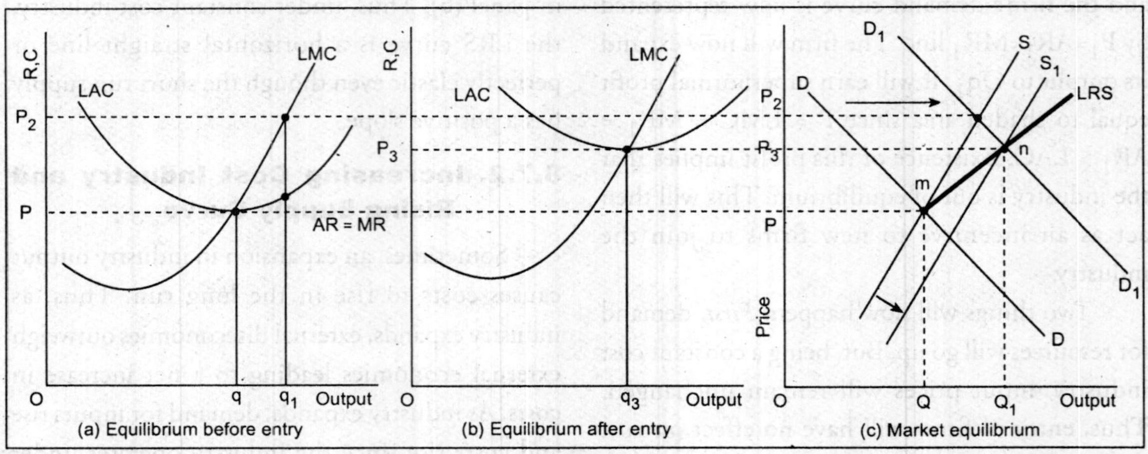

Fig. 8.7: Positive Sloping Supply Curve (Alternative Explanation)

firm produces Oq and is in long run equilibrium where P = AR = MR = LAC. Each firm is making only normal profit. Note that industry output OQ = Oq × number of firms.

Suppose demand curve now shifts to D_1D_1 following an increase in income of the buyers. The immediate impact of an increase in demand is the increase in price in the short run to OP_1. This new price will be accepted by all the firms. This is represented by the demand curve $P_1 = AR_1 = MR_1$. Each firm will now produce Oq_1 and sell it at the price OP_1. Firms will now be making economic profit or pure profit. Now two things will happen. *First,* excess profit will now attract new firms to join the industry. As new firms enter the industry there will be an upward pressure in the demand for inputs. This will cause input prices and, hence, costs to go up. Their interconnected reaction will pull up LAC and LMC to LAC_1 and LMC_1 in the leftward direction. *Secondly,* the increased number of firms and increasing costs cause short run market supply curve to shift to S_1S_1. New supply curve S_1S_1 intersects the demand curve at point 'n'. The industry equilibrium price and quantity are OP_2 and OQ_1, respectively. At this price, no firms are making excess profit. The typical firm at the price OP_2 now produces Oq—the old level of output. However, the output level that the firm now produces may be greater or less than the original one. Even then industry output is larger since more firms have joined the industry. Thus, industry output at the price OP_2 is Oq × number of firms = OQ_1. Now by joining points 'm' and 'n', we get a positive sloping LRS curve.

▲ Alternative Explanation

How is the upward rising industry supply curve derived under increasing cost condition has been alternatively demonstrated in Fig. 8.7. We know that, in the long run, firms enter the industry only when pure profit exists. Thus, pure profit is an incentive to join the industry. In Fig. 8.7(a) we have equilibrium of a firm before entry is made. Fig. 8.7(b) shows equilibrium of a newly entrant firm and Fig. 8.7(c) demonstrates long run industry equilibrium.

Let us assume that, initially, the competitive industry is in equilibrium at point 'm'. The industry produces and sells OQ output at the price OP. As income increases demand curve temporarily rises to D_1D_1 and short run equilibrium price rises to OP_2. Each firm now produces and sells Oq_1 output at the price OP_2 (panel a). Firms are now making abnormal profit. This attracts new firms to join. In an increasing cost industry, as firms enter, demand for input rises, price of input rises, cost rises. This leads to an upward shift in LMC and LAC curves as shown in panel (b). Costs will rise till excess profit vanishes. At the new price OP_3, the firm earns normal profit after producing Oq_3 output. Further, entry of new firms in the industry leads to a rightward shift in the supply curve to S_1S_1. Finally, equilibrium is achieved at point 'n'. The industry output is now OQ_3 and equilibrium price is OP_3. Now, by joining these equilibrium points ('m' and 'n') we get an upward rising long run industry supply curve, labelled as LRS.

8.7.3. Decreasing Cost Industry and Negative Sloping Supply Curve

It may happen that when a new industry is established in a locality it may enjoy a situation of decreasing cost. A decreasing cost industry is one when expansion in industry output causes input prices to fall, and, as a result, costs decline. Or in a decreasing cost industry, external economies outweigh external diseconomies. As a result, both new and old firms of the industry find their LAC and LMC curves to shift in the downward direction, indicating a decline in cost.

Fig. 8.8 explains this. As usual, panel (b) demonstrates industry equilibrium as defined by the intersection of the DD and SS curves. The industry is in equilibrium at point 'm'. Corresponding to this equilibrium point, equilibrium output is OQ and equilibrium price is OP. At this price, not only the competitive industry is in equilibrium but also all the firms within the industry are in equilibrium because P = AR = MR = LMC = LAC. The firm now produces and sells Oq output at the price OP and is enjoying only normal profit. Industry output is, thus, OQ = Oq × number of firms.

Suppose demand curve shifts to D_1D_1 because of the increase in income of the buyers or increase in the price of substitute goods. The immediate reaction is the rise in price to OP_1. At this ruling market price, each firm produces and

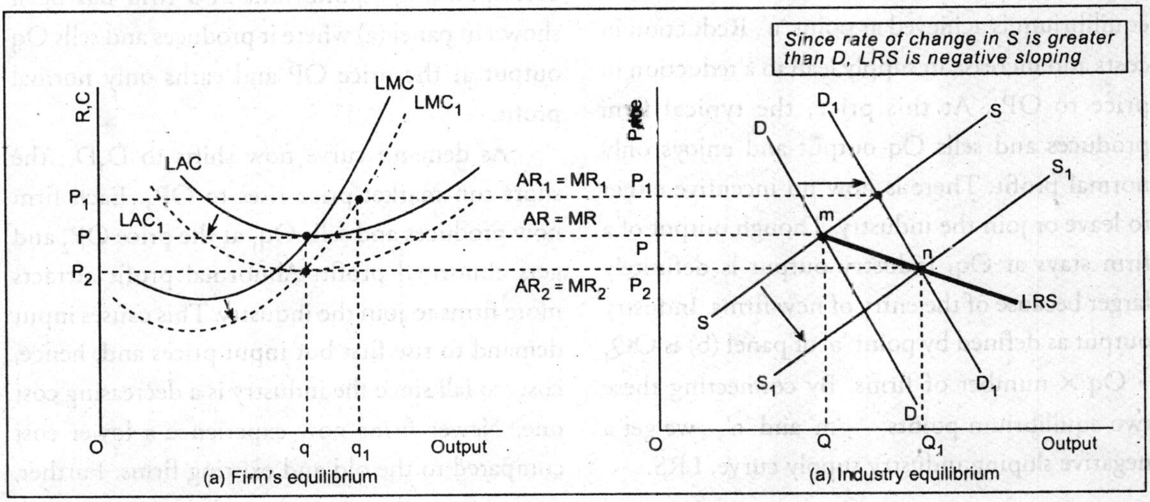

Fig. 8.8 : Negative Sloping Supply Curve

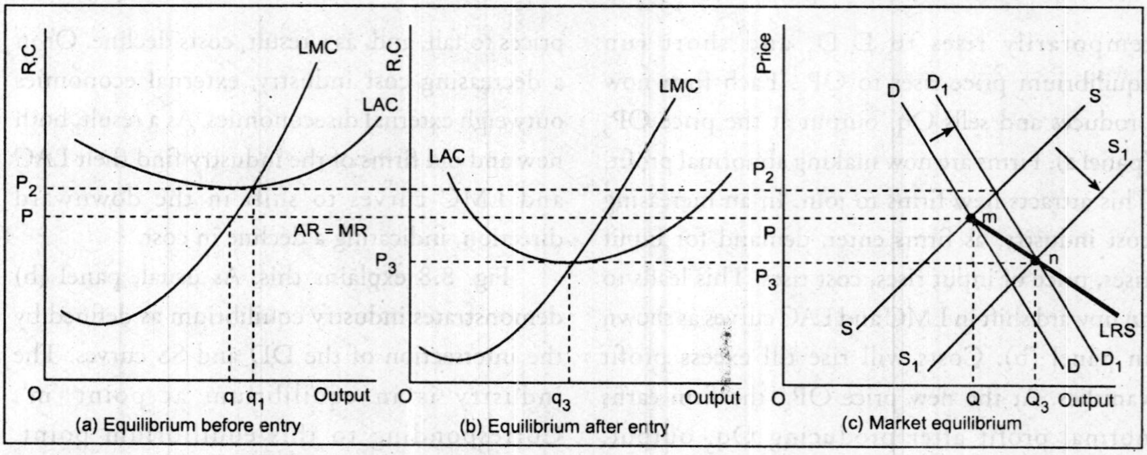

Fig. 8.9: Negative Sloping Supply Curve (Alternative Explanation)

sells Oq_1 at the price OP_1 and enjoys some supernormal profit. This encourages firms to join the industry.

Two things will now happen. *First,* because of the entry, demand for inputs will rise. But since the industry operates under diminishing cost, input price will decline and costs will decline. This is shown by the downward shift of LAC and LMC curves to LAC_1 and LMC_1 (here the dotted curves). *Secondly,* entry leads to an increase in the number of firms within the industry. This causes market supply curve to shift to S_1S_1. Final equilibrium is achieved at point 'n'. Reduction in costs and increase in supply lead to a reduction in price to OP_2. At this price, the typical firm produces and sells Oq output and enjoys only normal profit. There is now no incentive either to leave or join the industry. Though output of a firm stays at Oq, industry output is definitely larger because of the entry of new firms. Industry output as defined by point 'n' of panel (b) is OQ_1 = Oq × number of firms. By connecting these two equilibrium points — 'm' and 'n'—we get a negative sloping industry supply curve, LRS.

▲ Alternative Explanation

To derive a long run industry supply curve under decreasing cost, we use Fig. 8.9. Panel (a) shows equilibrium of a firm before entry, panel (b) explains equilibrium of a firm after entry takes place and panel (c) describes overall industry equilibrium.

Let us assume first that the competitive industry is in equilibrium at point 'm'. This means that the entire industry produces and sells OQ output at the price OP [panel (c)]. The corresponding equilibrium of a firm has been shown in panel (a) where it produces and sells Oq output at the price OP and earns only normal profit.

As demand curve now shifts to D_1D_1, the short run market price rises to OP_2. Each firm now produces and sells Oq_1 at the price OP_2 and gets abnormal profit. Abnormal profit attracts more firms to join the industry. This causes input demand to rise first but input prices and, hence, costs to fall since the industry is a decreasing cost one. Newer firms now experience a lower cost compared to the old and existing firms. Further, entry causes supply curve to shift to S_1S_1. New supply curve S_1S_1 intersects D_1D_1 curve at point 'n'. Corresponding to this equilibrium point, equilibrium price is OP_3. At this price, firm produces and sells Oq_3 but manages only normal profit, leaving no further scope for either entry or exit. Industry output is now larger at the price OP_3. OQ_3 (= Oq_3 × number of firms) is the industry output. Now by joining points 'm' and 'n' we get a supply curve which is negatively sloped, shown in panel (c).

Thus, an industry supply curve may be positive sloping in the short run but not in the long run. In the long run, the shape of an industry supply curve is governed by the cost condition in which an industry operates. It may be a horizontal one under constant cost industry, and negative sloping under decreasing cost industry. It is to be remembered always that the long run industry supply curve cannot be derived from the LMC curve. LAC curve determines the shape of long run industry curve. Finally, positively sloped supply curve is the most relevant and realistic one.

QUESTIONS (WITH ANSWER-HINTS)

Long Questions (16 marks)

1. When does competition become perfect in a commodity market? How are price and output determined in a competitive firm—both in the short run and in the long run?

   Ans. 8.2, 8.3 and 8.4.

2. Show the relationship among price, marginal cost and average cost under perfect competition in the short run.

   Ans. 8.3.

3. What is meant by perfect competition? In the long run, price equals average cost. Thus, no firm enjoys profit. Is it true? Answer graphically.

   Ans. : 8.2 and 8.4.

4. Explain the long run equilibrium of a firm and an industry operating under different cost conditions in perfect competition.

   Ans. 8.7, 8.7.1, 8.7.2 and 8.7.3.

5. Discuss the conditions that must exist for a long run supply curve of a competitive industry to be infinitely elastic. Can such supply curve be negative sloping?

   Ans. 8.7.1 and 8.7.3.

6. A long run industry supply curve may be negative sloping. Explain the statement graphically. Can there be a possibility of positive sloping supply curve of a competitive industry in the long run?

   Ans. 8.7.3 and 8.7.2.

Medium-sized Questions (8 marks)

1. How does a competitive firm determine equilibrium output? Will a firm continue production if it incurs loss in the short run?

   Ans : 8.3.

2. In the long run, all firms in a competitive industry earn zero economic profit. Why is this true?

   Or

   Why would the perfect competition model predict that if price remains above average cost, new firms would enter the industry and if price stays below AC, existing losing firms would leave the industry?

   Or

   Can a firm under perfectly competitive market earn super normal profit in the long run? Explain the long run equilibrium of a competitive firm. (C.U. 2007)

   Ans. 8.4.

3. How is the short run supply curve of a competitive firm determined?

   Or

   Explain with the help of a diagram the short run supply curve of a perfectly competitive firm. (C.U. 2008)

   Or

   MC curve above the shut-down point is the short run supply curve of a competitive firm. Explain.

   Ans. 8.5.

4. Will a firm under perfect competition in the short run continue to produce if price falls below AVC?

   Or

   Why would a competitive firm that incurs losses choose to produce rather than shut-down? Explain with a diagram.

   Ans. 8.5.

5. Graphically explain 'break-even point' and 'shut-down point' of a competitive firm.

   Ans. 8.5.

9

PRICE DETERMINATION IN IMPERFECT MARKET : MONOPOLY, MONOPOLISTIC COMPETITION AND OLIGOPOLY

9.1. INTRODUCTION

Prior to 1930s, economists were used to analyse the behaviour of two extreme forms of markets, viz., perfect competition and monopoly. Such markets are rarely found in the real world. It is virtually impossible to find a situation where all conditions necessary for perfect competition will be met. Nor is it likely that one can find an example of pure monopoly, i.e., there exists no competition at all. No competition means that there are no substitutes to which consumers can turn, and it is difficult to think of products of which there are no substitutes at all.

Most real life markets are a mixture of these two extreme forms, and contain elements of both competition and monopoly. Each firm has a monopoly of its own brand of product but it has to compete with firms producing different brands of that product. The implication is that products are said to be differentiated. For example, Tata produces Hamam soap, Godrej Cinthol and Hindustan Lever Lifebuoy. Each firm is a monopolist in the sense that it produces a differentiated product. But among the firms themselves there is some degree of competition. It is because the market for soaps in India is limited. Thus, if the market share of a particular firm increases, the share of other firms will fall. Although the actual products are very similar to one another—almost identical, even they are different in the eyes of the consumers. There are people who generally buy the same brand of the product, such as coffee, washing powder, shaving cream or toothpaste, because they believe that one product brand is better than any of the others. This type of attitude is encouraged by the competitive advertising that takes place. The advertisements often try to create the impression among the buyers that one particular brand is different (and superior) to any of the other brands.

Such markets, called imperfectly competitive markets, lie between the two extremes. For example, producer of most consumer goods like soaps, detergents, instant coffee, biscuits, toothpastes are monopolistic in the sense that they have the power to set their own prices; they are competitive in the sense that they actively compete with each other. In a broad sense, imperfect competition refers to markets in-between monopoly and pure competition.

Imperfect competition is said to exist when one of the assumptions of pure competition does not hold. Three major characteristics of imperfect competition are: (a) a relatively small number of firms, (b) differentiated products, and (c) restricted entry into the industry. Two most important varieties of imperfect competition are: (a) monopolistic competition, and (b) oligopoly. The former involves competition among a large number of firms, the latter involves competition among only a few (dominant) firms. Some economists even feel that monopoly is an extreme form of imperfect competition.

The term monopolistic competition was introduced by E. Chamberlin in 1933, reacting to the inapplicability of the theories of perfect competition and monopoly to a large sections of the economy. Monopolistic competition refers to competition among the monopolists. It has three important features: (a) the product of each firm is differentiated from those of other firms; (b) there is no barrier to entry of new firms into the industry; and (c) the industry contains many firms.

Oligopoly is the second important variety of imperfect competition. It refers to competition among a few dominant firms producing a homogeneous or a differentiated product. Thus, oligopoly is characterised by a few sellers' market.

9.2. MONOPOLY: ITS FEATURES

Monopoly, like perfect competition, is also an ideal market. These two market forms are polar opposites of each other. At the one end, there is perfect competition with substantially large number of sellers. At the other end, there is monopoly with just only one seller. The word monopoly is derived from the Greek words *monos polein*. *Monos* means 'single' and *polein* means 'to sell'. This single seller is called a monopolist. However, there may be a group of sellers who may be called monopolists. For instance, OPEC (Organisation of Petroleum Exporting Countries) — an association of 13 major producers of oil— enjoys monopoly power[1].

A monopoly market is said to exist when there is only one seller of a product which has no substitutes in the market. But this theoretical definition is not workable. To some extent, all goods are substitutes of one another. How much a seller enjoys monopoly power depends on the closeness of substitutes produced by rival firms. If goods produced by rival firms are found to be remote substitutes, the monopoly firm may exert enough power in the market. On the other hand, if one seller can eliminate rival sellers such that he controls the supply of his good in the market, then he is said to be a monopolist. In this sense, some close substitutes will enable a seller to wield monopoly power.

From the practical point of view, thus a monopoly market exists when only one seller sells a commodity that has no close substitutes in the market. The control over supply exercised by the monopolist may be either in the volume of output produced or volume of goods sold. It is because of this, a monopolist is one who can 'set' the price himself. Thus, a monopolist behaves as a 'price maker' or a 'price searcher'. Further, there are barriers to entry, thereby destroying the threat of potential (competition. In fact, barrier to entry

1. OPEC is a cartel of 13 countries made up of Algeria, Angola, Ecuador, Indonesia, Iran, Iraq, Kuwait, Libya, Nigeria, Qatar, Saudi Arabia, the United Arab Emirates, and Venezuela.

—that is, free environment—is the source of monopoly power. If firms are allowed legally to enter the business, there would be no monopoly. In addition buyers have very little or no knowledge or informtion about the cost, price, product quality, etc. A monopoly firm (or industry), thus, has the following characteristics :

- only one seller sells a commodity having no close substitutes in the market;
- a monopoly seller has complete influence over setting the price of goods;
- there are barriers to entry;
- imperfect dissemination of information.

9.3. WHY DOES MONOPOLY BUSINESS ARISE?

Many factors lead to the emergence of monopoly business.

First, the size of the market or the nature of production may be such that it does not permit the setting up of more than one firm in the industry. In particular, economies of scale are so important that only one firm can produce entire output. If this particular firm is capable of producing goods at lower average cost compared to two or more firms, the market creates 'natural monopoly'. For instance, a mini bus in a particular route carries 30 passengers per trip. Suppose there are 300 passengers in a day. Thus, 5 buses are required to be employed to transport 300 public daily. But all the 5 bus owners may find it unprofitable to serve the same route. In other words, it is the narrowness of the market that prevents all the buses to run profitably. If, instead, one bus owner is given the route permit, it could make profit. A monopoly firm with a very large minimum efficient scale can deliver services at lower average cost. This case is known as natural monopoly.

Usually, the government behaves as a natural monopolist who undertakes the production of public utilities, like electricity generation, railways, etc. Because of indivisibilities of inputs of public goods, government enjoys the power of a natural monopolist.

Secondly, control or ownership over crucial raw materials or knowledge of a low cost production technique may allow monopoly business to stay. Such control over the resources often discourages other firms to start new business, thereby shutting out competition. Or it may exhibit decreasing marginal costs over a wide range of output levels due to ownership of unique resources or the possession of unique managerial talent.

Thirdly, patents, copyrights and trademarks allow a monopolist to produce a specified commodity. This prevents other firms from producing the good without the permission of the patent holder or the copyright holder. In other words, the source of monopoly power is 'control over intellectual property, that is, property over inventions or expressions'. In view of this, patent right is given to the monopoly inventor that may guarantee an exclusive market power.

Finally, the government may protect the monopolist by creating tariff wall with the objective of eliminating foreign competition. A high tariff discourages new firms to start new business.

Anyway, for the existence of a monopoly firm or industry, there must be barriers to entry.

9.4. DEMAND AND REVENUE OF A MONOPOLY FIRM/INDUSTRY

Being a price-maker, a monopolist can select or set price of his own product. The demand curve faced by a monopoly firm is the industry (or market) demand curve as there is only one firm in the industry. Thus, the demand curve (AR) of a monopoly seller is a downward sloping curve. Its corresponding MR curve is also downward sloping and lies below AR curve (i.e., AR > MR).

As the monopolist desires to increase output, TR may increase and decrease after reaching a maximum. Whether TR will increase or decrease depends on whether MR is positive or zero or negative, which, in turn, depends on whether demand is elastic or unitary elastic or inelastic. In Fig. 9.1, we have shown such relationship between TR, AR, MR and elasticity of demand (e). We have already shown the following relationship among AR, MR :

$$MR = AR\left(1 - \frac{1}{e}\right)$$

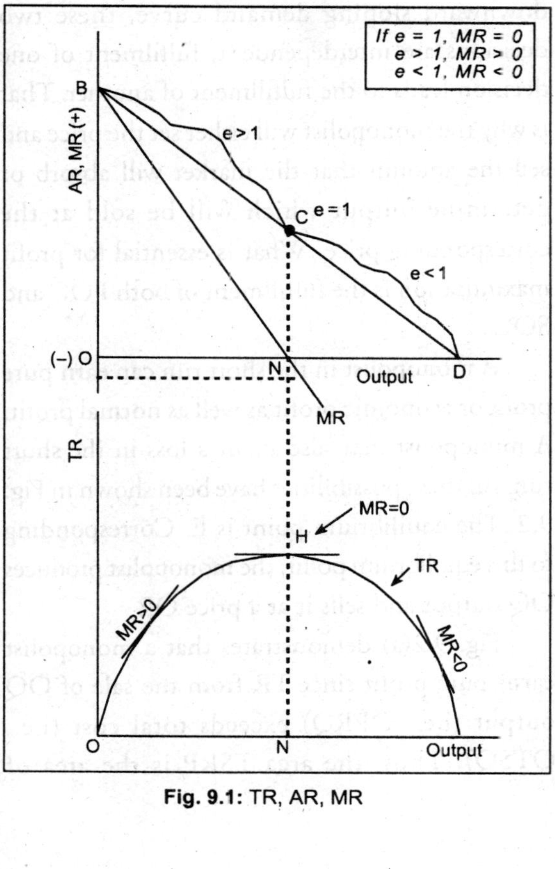

Fig. 9.1: TR, AR, MR

In this figure, TR curve has been drawn in the bottom part, while AR and MR curves have been drawn in the upper panel.

As monopolist expands output, TR rises, reaches maximum at point H corresponding to output ON, and, thereafter TR declines. AR curve or BD curve has been drawn as a negatively sloped straight line. Elasticity of demand varies from point to point on this demand curve. At the mid-point (point C) of BD or AR curve, coefficient of elasticity of demand is unity (e = 1). The corresponding MR is zero. Thus, a monopolist earns maximum TR by producing and selling ON units of output. In other words, at output ON, TR is maximum, MR is zero and elasticity of demand is unity.

Below ON output level, TR increases as output expands. Consider any point to the left of point C on the AR curve where e > 1. Note that at this output level MR is positive. Thus, when TR rises, MR > 0 and e > 1.

Beyond ON output, since TR declines as output expands, elasticity declines. Elasticity of demand becomes less than one to the right of point C on the AR curve. Consequently, MR becomes negative. Thus, when TR declines, MR < 0 and e < 1.

Obviously, a producer should produce in that region where MR is positive.

9.5. EQUILIBRIUM OF A MONOPOLIST

The goal of a monopolist is also profit-maximisation. In order to attain maximum profit or in order to be in equilibrium, the following two conditions are to be fulfilled. *First,* MC must be equal to MR. This condition is known as necessary condition or first-order condition (FOC) for equilibrium. *Secondly,* the slope of MC curve must be greater than the slope of MR curve.

This condition is called sufficient condition or second-order Condition (SOC) for equilibrium. Only when these conditions are satisfied simultaneously a monopoly firm reaches equilibrium irrespective of time period. Under monopoly, the golden rule of output determination is MC = MR.

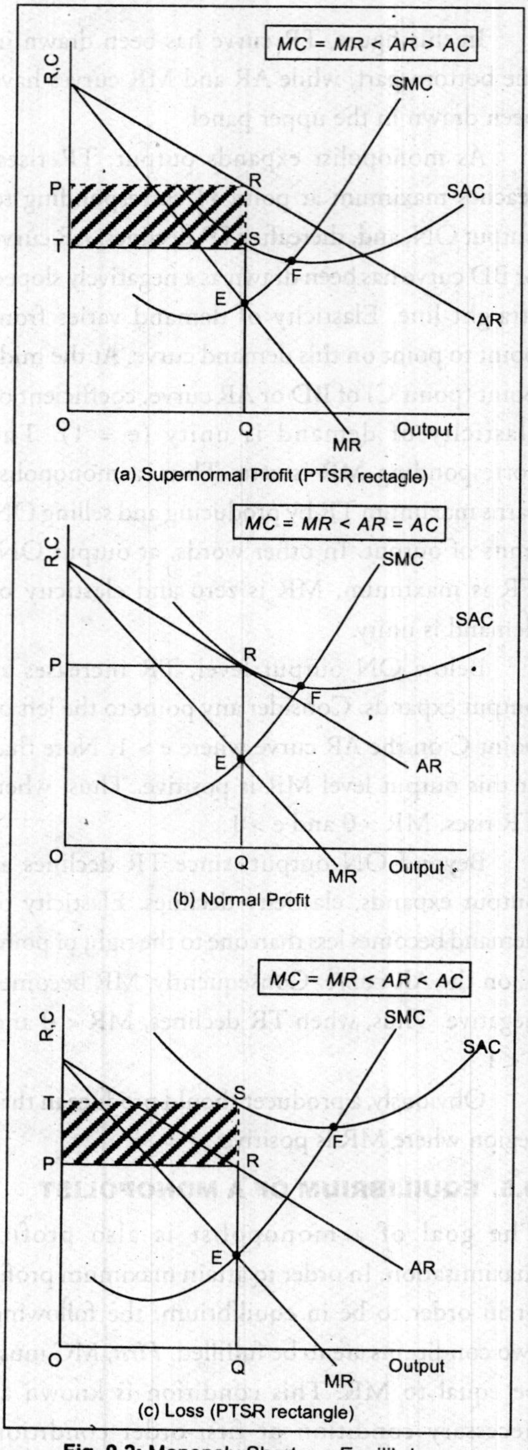

Fig. 9.2: Monopoly Short run Equilibrium

- **Short run Equilibrium:** A monopolist faces a negative sloping demand curve or AR curve. If he wants to sell more he must lower down the price of his product. The corresponding MR curve is also downward sloping and lies below the AR curve, i.e., AR > MR.

As a firm behaves as a price-taker under perfect competition, its concern is only output determination. Price is given to a firm. But since a monopolist is a price-setter he must take both price and output decisions. However, given the downward sloping demand curve, these two decisions are interdependent; fulfilment of one decision leads to the fulfillment of another. That is why the monopolist will either set the price and sell the amount that the market will absorb or determine output which will be sold at the corresponding price. What is essential for profit maximisation is the fulfillment of both FOC and SOC.

A monopolist in the short run can earn pure profit or economic profit as well as normal profit. A monopolist may also incur a loss in the short run. All these possibilities have been shown in Fig. 9.2. The equilibrium point is E. Corresponding to this equilibrium point, the monopolist produces OQ output and sells it at a price OP.

Fig. 9.2(a) demonstrates that a monopolist earns pure profit since TR from the sale of OQ output (i.e., OPRQ) exceeds total cost (i.e., OTSQ). Thus, the area TSRP is the area of

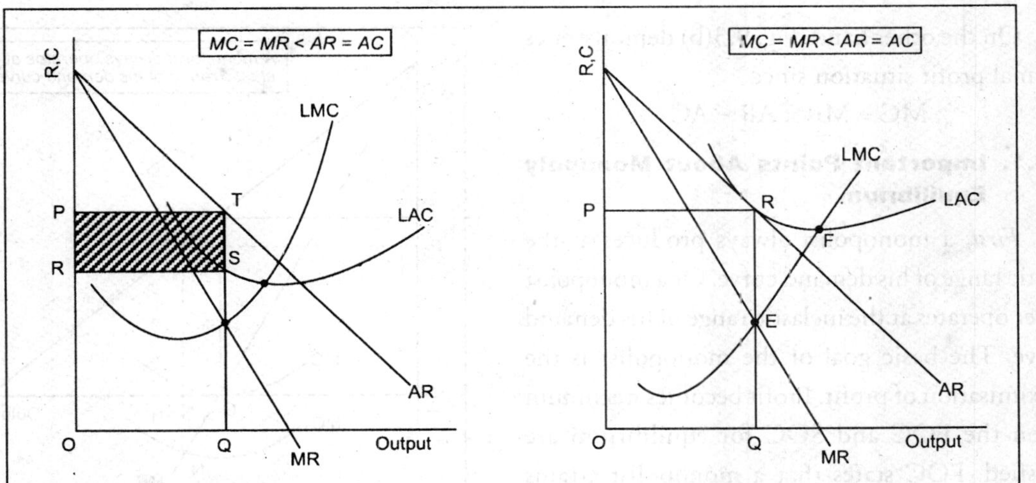

(a) Supernormal profit (RSTP rectangle) (b) Normal profit

Fig. 9.3: Long run Equilibrium of a Monopolist

supernormal profit. A monopolist earns supernormal profit when

$$MC = MR < AR > AC$$

That is to say, if AC curve lies below the demand curve the monopolist will enjoy supernormal profit.

Fig. 9.2(b) shows normal profit since TR (i.e., OPRQ) equals TC (i.e., OPRQ). The condition for normal profit is, thus,

$$MC = MR < AR = AC$$

That is to say, normal profit is enjoyed by the monopolist when AC curve at a particular point coincides with the AR curve.

There is a misconception that a monopolist always earns supernormal profit and does not suffer from loss. A monopolist may also incur a loss, of course, in the short run. Fig. 9.2(c) shows that the monopolist suffers a loss of PRST amount since TC (i.e., OTSQ) exceeds TR (i.e., OPRQ). A situation of loss will arise when

$$MC = MR < AR < AC$$

In other words, if AC curve lies above the AR curve at the corresponding level of output, the firm will suffer a loss. However, a monopolist will continue production in the short run (i.e., minimising losses) if he covers up only AVC. In other words, if the loss of the monopolist is equivalent to fixed cost he will stay in business. Loss then amounts to only fixed cost. But if the monopolist fails to cover up variable cost, i.e., if P < AVC, only then he will suspend production. He will 'drop out'. Of course, there cannot be loss in the long run.

- **Long run Equilibrium:** In the long run, the monopolist can change his scale of production so that profit becomes the greatest. Since entry is blocked, excess profit will be enjoyed by the monopolist. A monopolist also earns normal profit in the long run but does not incur a loss. Fig. 9.3 demonstrates these two possibilities.

In Fig. 9.3, LAC and LMC are long run average cost and long run marginal cost curves. Corresponding to the equilibrium point E, our monopolist produces and sells OQ output at the price OP. Fig. 9.3(a) shows a situation of supernormal profit to the extent of RSTP since costs are lower than revenue, i.e.,

$$MC = MR < AR > AC$$

On the other hand, Fig. 9.3(b) demonstrates normal profit situation since

$$MC = MR < AR = AC$$

9.5.1. Important Points About Monopoly Equilibrium

First, a monopolist always produces at the elastic range of his demand curve. Or a monopolist never operates at the inelastic range of his demand curve. The basic goal of the monopolist is the maximisation of profit. Profit becomes maximum when the FOC and SOC for equilibrium are satisfied. FOC states that a monopolist attains equilibrium when MC equals MR. We know that $MR = AR\left(1-\frac{1}{e}\right)$. If the coefficient of elasticity of demand becomes greater than one (i.e., $e > 1$) at a particular point of a straight line demand curve, MR becomes positive. Costs are always positive. Equilibrium must occur when positive MC equals positive MR. But, if the coefficient of elasticity of demand is less than one (i.e., $e < 1$), MR will be negative. Negative MR can never be equated with positive MC. Thus, in this range of demand curve, a monopolist cannot reach equilibrium. *Finally,* when the coefficient of elasticity of demand is unity (i.e., $e = 1$), MR will be zero. Equilibrium cannot be attained even in this case since positive MC cannot be matched with the zero MR. So, a monopolist will not also produce in this range of demand curve. In other words, a monopolist always operates at the elastic range (i.e., $e > 1$) of his demand curve to obtain maximum profit.

Let us explain these two situations in terms of Fig. 9.4. If coefficient of elasticity of demand is one, MR becomes zero. Therefore, to reach equilibrium MC must be zero. This happens at OQ output where MC equals MR. The monopolist sells the output at price OP. But zero

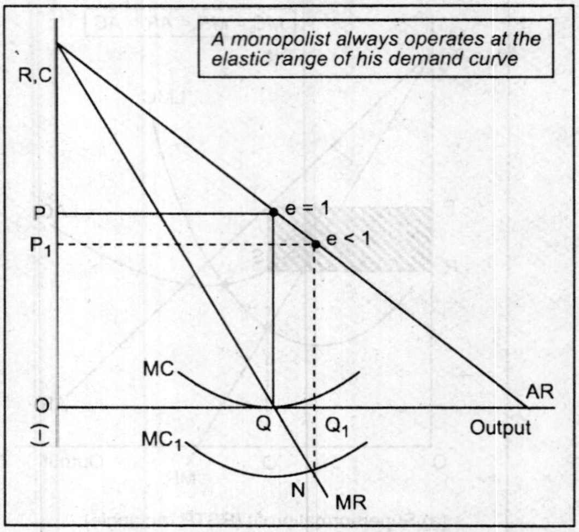

Fig. 9.4: Monopoly Equilibrium

marginal cost is hardly conceivable. Again, if $e < 1$, MR will be negative. Equilibrium requires MR-MC equality. Since MR is negative, MC must be negative. It is clear from Fig. 9.4 that the monopoly firm reaches equilibrium at point N(i.e., the negative quadrant) and it produces OQ_1 output and sells it at a price OP_1. But negative MC is hard to imagine. Therefore, the monopolist will always operate at the elastic range of his demand curve where both MC and MR become positive.

Secondly, a monopolist never operates at the lowest point of his AC curve where cost becomes the least. Actually, he operates somewhere to the left of the minimum point of his AC curve, be it in the short run or in the long run. In Figs. 9.2 and 9.3, the lowest point of AC curve has been represented by point F. Consider Fig. 9.3(b) where the monopoly firm operates at point R—a point to the left of point F, the lowest point of LAC curve. This happens due to the nature of the demand curve. As demand curve is downward sloping it must be tangential to the falling portion of the AC curve. Operation at this point implies that the monopoly firm cannot utilise its plant optimally. Or it implies underutilisation of resource. As entry is closed, there is no urgency of a monopoly firm to operate at the lowest point of AC curve. However, a competitive firm always operates at the lowest point of its AC curve since demand curve is perfectly elastic.

However, some economists have suggested that in the long run, a monopoly firm may not only operate to the left of the minimum point of AC curve (i.e., sub-optimal scale), but may also operate at the lowest point of AC curve (i.e., optimal scale) and may also operate to the right of the minimum point of AC curve (i.e., over-optimal scale) depending on the extent of market or demand for the monopoly product. This means that demand for the monopoly product is such that it is profitable on the part of the monopolist in the long run to operate at the minimum point of AC curve or to the right of the minimum point of the AC curve.

9.6. MONOPOLY SUPPLY CURVE

A monopoly firm has no well-defined supply curve. In other words, there is no unique supply curve for the monopolist derived from his MC curve. Under perfect competition, short run MC curve above the shut-down point is the supply curve which shows a unique relationship between price and quantity. At a particular price, particular amount of the commodity will be supplied. Under monopoly, there is no such one-to-one correspondence between price and quantity supplied. This is because of the fact that output decision of a monopolist not only depends on marginal cost but also on the shape of the demand curve. "As a result, shifts in demand do not trace out a series of prices and quantities as happens with a competitive supply curve."

It may happen that a monopolist, given his

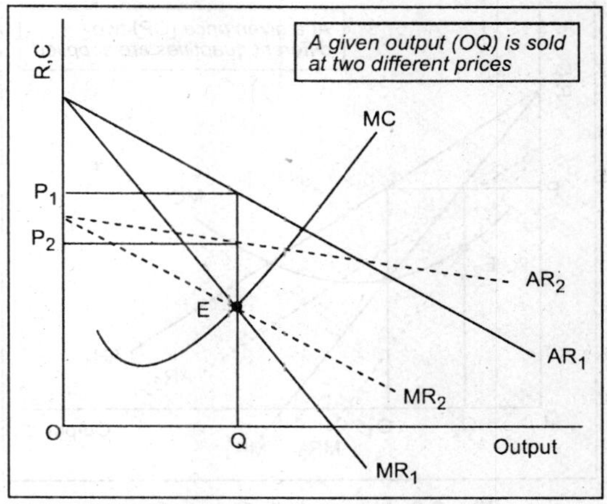

Fig. 9.5: Monopolist's Supply Curve

MC curve, may supply a particular quantity at different prices depending on the elasticity of demand. Thus, the construction of supply curve from the MC curve is impossible under monopoly or under any branch of imperfect competition.

Fig. 9.5 shows that the monopolist produces and sells output OQ but at two different prices depending on the price elasticity of demand. AR_1 and MR_1 are the initial average and marginal revenue curves of the monopolist. If the demand curve is AR_2 then the corresponding MR curve becomes MR_2. MC curve cuts MR_1 and MR_2 at point E. Corresponding to this equilibrium point, our monopolist produces and sells output OQ at the price OP_1 if the demand curve is AR_1, or he will sell the same amount at the price OP_2 if the demand curve is AR_2. Thus, due to differences in elasticity of demand for the monopoly product, same quantity is offered for sale at two different prices. Thus, there is no unique relationship between price and quantity.

Fig. 9.6 shows that two different quantities may be sold at a particular price depending on the elasticity of demand for the monopoly product. Here MC curve cuts MR_1 and MR_2 at points E_1 and E_2 corresponding to the demand

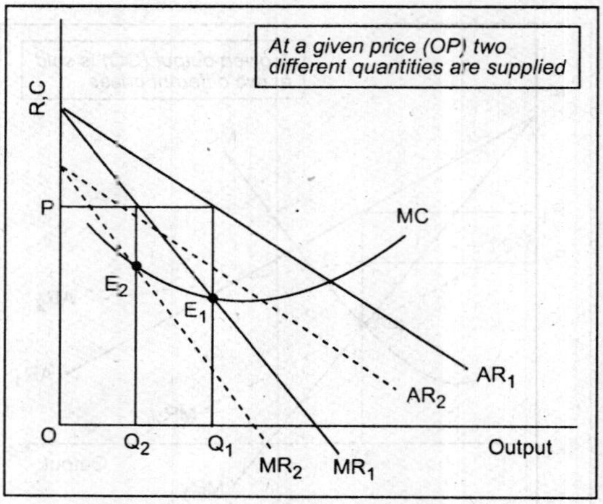

Fig. 9.6: Monopolist's Supply Curve

curves AR_1 and AR_2, respectively. The firm may produce and sell OQ_1 (as determined by point E_1) at the price OP or may produce and sell OQ_2 (as determined by E_2) at the same price OP. Thus, two different quantities can be sold at the same price, given the MC of the monopolist. There is no unique relationship between price and quantity offered for sale.

9.7. PERFECT COMPETITION VS. MONOPOLY

Neither perfect competition nor monopoly corresponds to reality. In this sense, both the market forms are 'ideal'. But perfect competition is the polar opposite of monopoly. That is why dissimilarities rather than similarities between the two are many. As far as the goal is concerned, both competitive firms and monopoly firms are profit-maximisers. In order to attain maximum profit both of them rely on marginalistic principle—the principle of equality between MC and MR. Anyway, following differences are noted below :

- *Differences in market conditions*: In perfect competition there are innumerable number of sellers who cannot change the market price and supply of the commodity. They behave as 'price-takers'. On the other hand, a monopoly firm—a firm or an industry of a single seller—can alter the price of the product. Under perfect competition, product is homogeneous. Monopoly product may or may not be homogeneous. Entry (and exit) is free under perfect competition, while entry is blocked under monopoly.
- *P = MR and P > MR* : Due to product homogeneity the demand curve (P = AR) faced by a competitive firm is perfectly elastic. Further, AR curve coincides with MR (i.e., AR = MR) since every firm behaves as a 'price-taker'. In monopoly, demand curve or AR curve is downward sloping. MR curve is also downward sloping and lies below AR curve, i.e., AR > MR.
- *P = AR = MR = MC and P = AR > MR = MC*: A competitive firm reaches equilibrium when MC is equal to MR. Since AR = MR, the equilibrium condition of a competitive firm can be written as MC = MR = AR = P. But in monopoly, since AR > MR, the equilibrium condition becomes MC = MR < AR = P.
- *Equilibrium and cost conditions*: Only when MC is rising equilibrium is possible under perfect competition. A competitive firm fails to reach equilibrium if MC is falling or MC is constant because of the non-fulfilment of SOC for equilibrium. Monopoly equilibrium is consistent with rising, falling and constant MC provided the slope of MC is greater than the slope of MR.

- *Optimal capacity vs excess capacity*: A competitive firm always operates at the lowest point of AC curve. This means that the firm produces at an optimum cost. In the long run, as a competitive firm earns only normal profit (because of free entry and exit), P = minimum AC. That is to say, in the long run, competitive equilibrium occurs when P = AR = MR = MC = minimum AC. This means optimal utilisation of resources.

  A monopoly firm, on the other hand, does not operate at the lowest point of its AC curve. Because of the nature of the demand curve, a monopoly firm operates somewhere to the left of the minimum point of long run AC curve. This means underutilisation of monopoly plant or wastage of resources. That is why price charged by a monopolist is higher than the price charged by a competitive firm and output is smaller under monopoly than under perfect competition. Further, in the long run, a monopoly firm may earn abnormal profit. Fig. 9.7 demonstrates this difference.

Demand curve of a competitive firm is represented by the horizontal AR = MR curve. A monopolist's demand curve and the corresponding marginal revenue curve are downward sloping represented by AR and MR curves, respectively. As far as perfect competition is concerned, equilibrium occurs at point F where AR = MR = LMC = minimum point of LAC. Corresponding to this equilibrium point, equilibrium output of a competitive firm is OQ_P. Equilibrium price is OP_P.

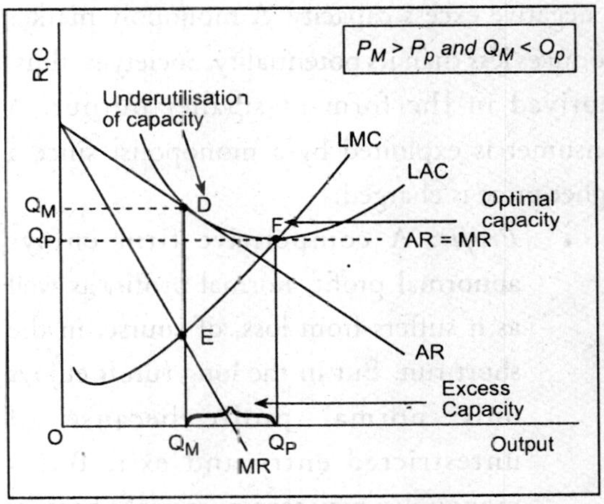

Fig. 9.7: Optimal Capacity vs Excess Capacity

On the other hand, monopoly equilibrium is defined by point E where LMC = MR < AR = LAC. The monopolist now produces OQ_M and sells it at the price OP_M. It is quite clear that the monopoly price (OP_M) is higher than competitive price (OP_P) while monopoly output (OQ_M) is lower than the competitive output (OQ_P). Since the monopolist does not produce at the minimum point of his AC curve, output is less compared to perfect competition. Here, our monopolist operates at point D rather than F on the LAC curve. This suggests that the monopolist operates at the sub-optimal scale (i.e., falling part of LAC). Had resources been fully utilised the firm would have operated at point F on the LAC curve. Such fuller or optimum utilisation of resources is possible only under perfect competition. So, an ideal allocation of resources results in a larger output. The distance Q_MQ_P measures negative excess capacity of a monopoly business.

Perfect competition is, thus, an ideal market in the sense that resources are optimally utilised. This results in larger output and lower price of the product. Social welfare is, thus, maximised under perfect competition. There occurs a misallocation of resources in monopoly resulting in negative excess capacity. A monopoly market produces less than its potentiality. Society is, thus, deprived in the form of smaller output. A consumer is exploited by a monopolist since a higher price is charged.

- *Profit*: A competitive firm enjoys abnormal profit, normal profit, as well as it suffers from loss, of course, in the short run. But in the long run it enjoys only normal profit because of unrestricted entry and exit. But a monopolist may earn pure profit both in the short run and in the long run, and may also earn normal profit. Like a competitive firm, a monopolist may suffer from losses in the short run.
- *Supply curve* : Under perfect competition, MC curve above the AVC curve is short run supply curve which shows a particular relationship between price and quantity supplied. But, in monopoly, the concept of supply curve is irrelevant. In other words, MC curve is not the supply curve.
- *Discrimination*: A monopolist can practice price discrimination in the sense that he can charge different prices for his product to different buyers. Because of homogeneity of the product, price discrimination under perfect competition is ruled out.

Thus, these two market forms are poles apart.

9.8. PRICE DISCRIMINATING MONOPOLIST

A monopolist often charges different prices for his product to different buyers. This practice of charging different prices for the same product is known as third degree price discrimination. Under perfect competition, sellers cannot charge different prices to different buyers since market conditions do not permit them to do so. All buyers are treated equally. Under price discrimination, a monopolist treats different customers differently. In this case, the monopolist is called the discriminating monopolist.

- **Forms of Price Discrimination**: There are mainly two types of price discrimination:
  - **Personal**: Personal discrimination is usually found in the realm of services. For instance, a doctor charges for his services higher fees for rich patients and lower fees for the poor ones.
  - **Use of Trade**: Sometimes a particular commodity of a monopolist is used by different buyers in different ways. For instance, electricity is used for domestic or commercial or industrial purposes. The Calcutta Electric Supply Corporation (CESC) charges higher electricity rate to the commercial establishments than to domestic consumers.

9.8.1. Conditions for Price Discrimination or When is Price Discrimination Possible?

Under price discrimination, different buyers pay different prices. So, price in one market must be higher and lower in another market. Electricity rates charged by the CESC for domestic and commercial buyers are different. [Knowing fully well the high electricity rate for commercial establishments businessmen cannot buy the product from the low-priced market.] Knowing the differences in prices they should buy at a low price. But such is ruled out. Thus, the following two necessary conditions must be fulfilled for the system of price discrimination to function:

- To make price discrimination possible, goods must not be transferred from one market to another. So, price discrimination must preclude resale of the goods. In other words, price discrimination will break down if buyers purchase the monopoly product from the low-priced market and sell it in the high-priced market. For instance, electricity rate of commercial establishment is high compared to domestic consumers. Now, if domestic consumers resale the electricity to commercial customers then the CESC would be forced to charge the same price. However, legally such is not possible on the part of any consumer. That is why the CESC charges two different electricity rates for two different types of customers. So, what is required is that there must not exist any possibility of resale of the monopoly product.
- Second condition is that demand must not be shifted from the dearer market to the cheaper market. Price discrimination will not be possible if buyers of the product transfer themselves from one market to another market. For instance, in a locality, a doctor having monopoly practice charges higher fees to the rich people and lower fees to the poor patients. Now, if rich patients disguise themselves and pose as poor patients then the doctor would be forced to charge uniform fees for all. So, price discrimination is possible if unit of demand is not transferred from one market to another.

There are other conditions too. For instance, it may happen that buyers do not know prices that the monopolist charges are prevailing in different markets. Such ignorance may cause price discrimination to exist. Again, laziness of consumers may lead to differences in prices of the monopoly product. Customers may care little for the differences in prices though they know the difference in prices. Nature of the product may demand price discrimination to stay. Personal services of say, doctors and lawyers are such that price discrimination is supposed to exist. Finally, there may be legal sanction for price discrimination. For example, the railway authority charges different fares to different passengers. First-class passengers pay more than the second-class passengers for the same distance, though there are differences in services. Again, electricity rates are different for different customers as permitted by law.

9.8.2. When is Price Discrimination Profitable: Price-Output Determination under Price Discrimination

Even if price discrimination is possible, it may not be profitable for the monopolist to discriminate price. Charging two different prices to different buyers may not necessarily result in higher profit.

To make price discrimination profitable, two conditions must be fulfilled:

- **Different elasticities :**
  - Elasticity of demand for the monopoly product in different markets must be different. Market which is insensitive to price changes or relatively less elastic (but not inelastic) must have a price greater than the market in which demand is relatively more elastic. If elasticities of demand for the monopoly product in two markets are same (i.e., iso-elastic) then uniform price would be charged. Thus, for profitability of a discriminating

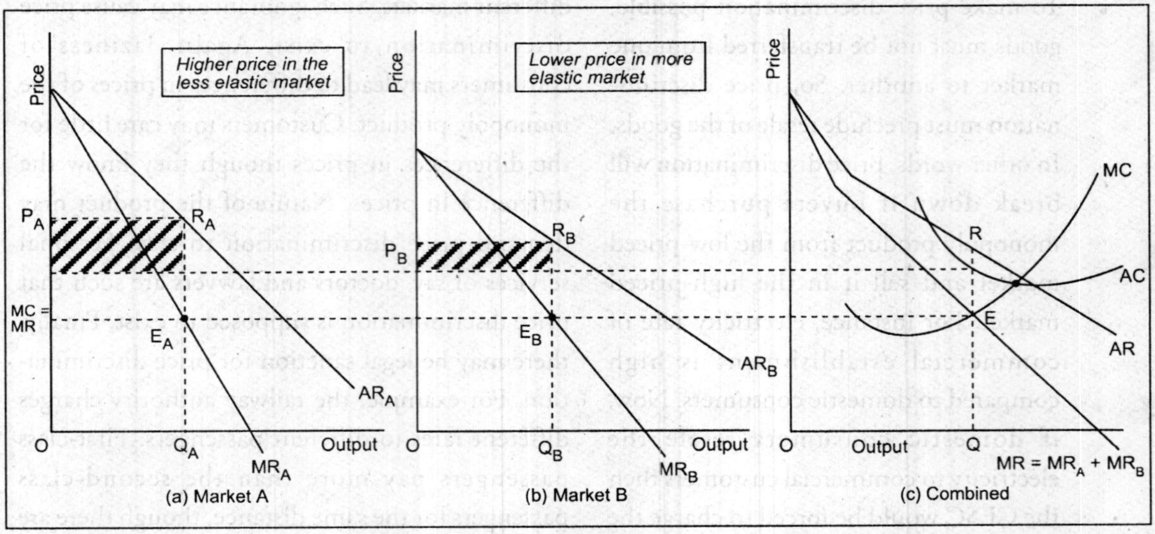

Fig. 9.8: Equilibrium of Discriminating Monopolist

monopolist, what is required is the difference in elasticities of demand.

- **Same MR_S :**
  - Price discrimination will be profitable only when marginal revenues in different markets are the same. It is true that as these two markets have different demand curves implying different values of elasticities of demand, marginal revenues may not be the same. However, the monopolist can increase his total revenue by transferring his product from the market that has lower marginal revenue to the market that has higher marginal revenue. When the process of transfer of a commodity from one market to another market brings about an equality in marginal revenues in two markets, price discrimination becomes profitable.

Let us assume that our monopolist sells his product in two markets—A and B. The above-noted conditions for profitability can be expressed in the following notational form:

- $e_A \neq e_B$, and
- $MR_A = MR_B$

where e_A and e_B are the elasticities of demand for the monopoly product in markets A and B and MR_A and MR_B are the marginal revenues in markets A and B.

Now a discriminating monopolist has to take two decisions in order to attain maximum profit : (i) how much should he produce, and (ii) how should the output be allocated in two markets and what price he should charge.

Like an ordinary monopolist, a discriminating monopolist reaches equilibrium when MC = MR. Here equilibrium condition should be MC = MR_A and MC = MR_B and MC = MR_A + MR_B. In panel (a) of Fig. 9.8, we have drawn the demand curve and marginal revenue curves of market A as AR_A and MR_A. Panel (b) shows the same for market B as AR_B and MR_B. By combining these AR_A and AR_B curves, we obtain 'combined AR curve', represented by AR shown in panel (c) of Fig. 9.8. Corresponding 'combined MR curve', has been represented by MR = MR_A + MR_B in panel (c). For equilibrium of the discriminating monopolist, MR must be equal to MC. This occurs at point E in panel (c). In the aggregate market, monopolist produces OQ output. If there were no price discrimination, monopolist would have charged a uniform price, QR, for all buyers. But, price discrimination is more profitable.

Now the task of the monopolist is to allocate the total product OQ in markets A and B in such a way that marginal revenue in all markets are the same (i.e., $EQ = E_AQ_A = E_BQ_B$). So, OQ_A must be sold in market A and OQ_B in market B (since $OQ = OQ_A + OQ_B$). Now the monopolist will charge price OP_A in A market for the output OQ_A and OP_B in market B for the output OQ_B. Total revenue that the monopolist will earn from the sale of OQ_A in market A, is $OP_AR_AQ_A$ and from market B total revenue is $OP_BR_BQ_B$. If these two revenues are added together (i.e., $OP_AR_AQ_A + OP_BR_BQ_B$), it would exceed the total revenue of the monopolist ($OQ \times RQ$). The shaded portions in panels A and B describe profit enjoyed by the discriminating monopolist in markets A and B. Thus, price discrimination is profitable. Further, it is to be remembered here that in the market in which elasticity is comparatively low, price would be higher and the market in which elasticity is comparatively high, price would be lower. As market A is less sensitive to price changes compared to market B, price in the former market is higher than the latter (i.e., $OP_A > OP_B$).

The relationship between elasticity of demand and the policy of price discrimination can be established with the help of the following formula. We know that

$$MR = AR\left(1-\frac{1}{e}\right)$$

Therefore, $MR_A = AR_B\left(1-\frac{1}{e_A}\right)$ and

$$MR_B = AR_B\left(1-\frac{1}{e_B}\right)$$

and $MR_A = MR_B = MC$

Thus, $AR_A\left(1-\frac{1}{e_A}\right) = AR_B\left(1-\frac{1}{e_B}\right)$

$$\text{or } \frac{AR_A}{AR_B} = \frac{P_A}{P_B} = \frac{\left(1-\frac{1}{e_B}\right)}{\left(1-\frac{1}{e_A}\right)}$$

If then $e_A = e_B$ then $\frac{P_A}{P_B} = 1$, or $P_A = P_B$

This means that if elasticities of demand are uniform in all markets then it will not be possible and profitable to discriminate between buyers. The monopolist, in this case, will charge the same price to all buyers.

On the other hand,

If $e_A > e_B$, then $\left(\frac{1}{e_B}\right) > \left(\frac{1}{e_A}\right)$

or $\left(1-\frac{1}{e_A}\right) > \left(1-\frac{1}{e_B}\right)$

or $\frac{\left(1-\frac{1}{e_B}\right)}{\left(1-\frac{1}{e_A}\right)} < 1$ or $\frac{P_A}{P_B} < 1$ or $P_B > P_A$

or if $e_A < e_B$ then $P_A > P_B$

Thus, the monopolist will charge a higher (lower) price in the market in which demand is less (more) elastic.

However, the coefficient of elasticities of demand for the product in all the markets must have a value greater than one since the monopolist always operates at the elastic range ($e > 1$) of his demand curve. If elasticity of demand in market A is 0.9 (i.e., inelastic) but in market B it is 1.1

(i.e., elastic), price discrimination will be unprofitable since MR in market A will be negative and in market B, positive. Equilibrium solution does not exist.

9.9. MONOPOLY IN HOME MARKET BUT PERFECT COMPETITION IN FOREIGN MARKET: ANOTHER EXAMPLE OF PRICE DISCRIMINATION

Price discrimination is said to occur when goods are sold at a higher price in the home market but at a lower price in the foreign market. This sort of international price discrimination is often referred to as 'dumping'.

We are considering a situation in which a producer exercises monopoly power in the domestic market. Because of this monopoly position, AR curve lies above the MR curve. These curves have been labeled AR_H and MR_H. Again, this producer faces keen competition in the foreign market. As a result, average revenue coincides with marginal revenue. These curves have been labeled $AR_F = MR_F$. Equilibrium of the firm is established at that point where MC equals MR. MR curve in these two separate markets have different slopes —downward sloping for the home market and horizontal for the foreign market. Combined MR

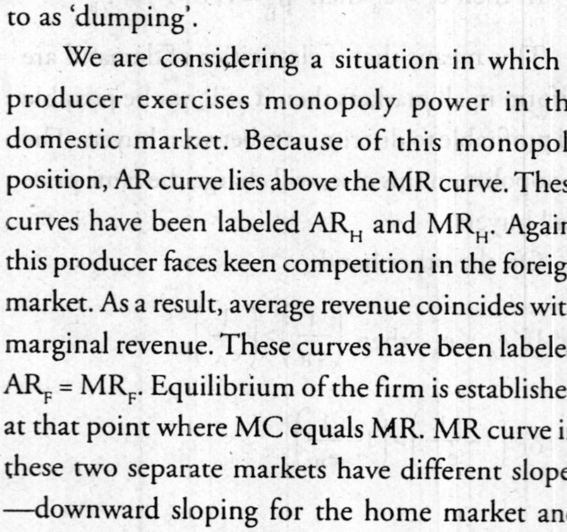

Fig. 9.9: Dumping and Price Discrimination

is the sum of MR_S of these two markets. It is given by LKP_1D curve. Since equilibrium occurs at P_1 (where $MC = MR_F$), total output produced is OM_1. This output has to be distributed in both domestic market and foreign market in such a way that MR of these two markets must be equal and equal to MC. Since the firm enjoys monopoly power in the domestic market, it will supply OM output and sell it at a price OP. This is because at this output level MR_S (i.e., MK) equals MC (i.e., M_1P_1). On the other hand, MM_1 output will be sold at the price M_1P_1 in the foreign market where the monopoly firm faces competition. Note that goods are sold in the foreign market at a price below that charged in the home market, (ON < OP). This practice is called dumping which is regarded as an unfair practice and countries often take action against this sort of price discrimination.

9.10. MULTI-PLANT MONOPOLIST

A monopoly firm maximises profit by selling output where MR equals MC. To find profit-maximising output we assume that the monopolist operates only one plant. But in reality, the monopolist may produce his profit-maximising output in two or more plants. We assume that our monopolist produces output in two plants. If so, the multi-plant monopolist has to decide how much output should be produced and how much of that total output should be produced by each plant.

Profit-maximising output of the multi-plant monopolist is determined by the MR-MC equality. Each plant has its MC. Let us assume that the MC of plant 1 is represented by MC_1 curve and of plant 2 by MC_2. Marginal cost for the monopolist is the horizontal sum of each plant's MC curves and it is represented by MC.

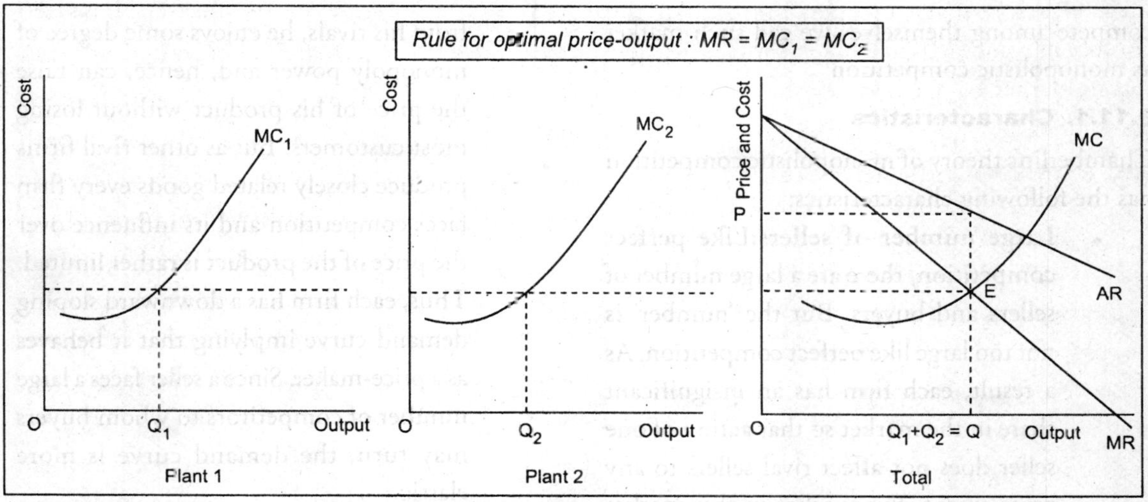

Fig. 9.10: Multi-plant Monopolist

Optimal output of the multi-plant monopolist is OQ and price charged is OP. This optimal output and price are determined by the intersection of MR and MC curves of each plant. That is to say, $MR = MC_1 = MC_2$.

Now we will determine how much of output will be produced in each plant. Plant 1 will produce OQ_1 and plant 2 will produce OQ_2 units of output. To determine each firm's output, we have drawn a horizontal line from point E. This line can be thought of as each firm's MR. The intersection of MR line with MC_1 and MC_2 give the optimal output of each firm. We have drawn MC curve in such a way that $OQ_1 + OQ_2 = OQ$. These output levels satisfy the condition that $MR = MC_1 = MC_2$.

9.11. MONOPOLISTIC COMPETITION: MEANING

Perfect competition and monopoly were the two favourite analytical models of the economists before 1920s. However, these two extreme market forms are far from reality. What we find in reality is some sort of middle-ground between these two extreme forms. Most of the producing firms are not monopolists since they face competition against each other. On the other hand, these firms are not price-takers since they do not operate under perfectly competitive conditions. This sort of intermediate market structure was built up independently by Joan Robinson of England in 1933 and E. H. Chamberlin of the U.S.A. in the same year. Robinson called this newly built but realistic market form as 'Imperfect Competition', while Chamberlin called his market as 'Monopolistic Competition'. Here we are interested in developing Chamberlin's, model of monopolistic competition.

Meaning: The two important subdivisions of imperfect competition are monopolistic competition and oligopoly. Most of the economic situations "are composites of both perfect competition and monopoly." Chamberlin's monopolistic competition is an amalgam or an admixture of perfect competition and monopoly. Thus, monopolistic competition has elements of both perfect competition and monopoly. That is why it is said that this market form, in some sense, is akin to perfect competition and, in some other sense, is akin to monopoly. Since monopolists compete among themselves we call such market as monopolistic competition.

9.11.1. Characteristics

Chamberlin's theory of monopolistic competition has the following characteristics:

- **Large number of sellers:**Like perfect competition, there are a large number of sellers and buyers. But the 'number' is not too large like perfect competition. As a result, each firm has an insignificant share in the market so that action of one seller does not affect rival sellers to any great extent. Every seller in this market form believes that his actions will go unnoticed by his rivals in the market. Thus, each seller behaves independently in the market.
- **Differentiated products:** Sellers sell differentiated products, but they are close, but not perfect, substitutes. Buyers may not mind if they do not get Lux soap rather than Rexona. Different varieties of soap that are available in the Indian market are slightly differentiated goods and, hence, close substitutes. It is the degree of differentiation that creates both monopoly and competitive elements. Every product is unique to the buyers. So, every seller enjoys some degree of monopoly of his own product over other sellers. But since these goods are close substitutes, sellers face competition. Because of brand loyalty of buyers, sellers exercise some monopoly power. And sales of closely related goods create a competitive atmosphere. Thus, monopolists compete among themselves.
- **Negative sloping demand curve :** Since product of each seller is slightly different from his rivals, he enjoys some degree of monopoly power and, hence, can raise the price of his product without losing most customers. But as other rival firms produce closely related goods every firm faces competition and its influence over the price of the product is rather limited. Thus, each firm has a downward sloping demand curve implying that it behaves as a price-maker. Since a seller faces a large number of competitors to whom buyers may turn, the demand curve is more elastic.
- **Non-price competition and selling cost:** Besides price competition, Chamberlin suggested cases of non-price competition that arises due to product variation and selling activities. A seller always tries to establish the fact that his product is superior to others by improving the quality of his product. And in doing so, he incurs selling costs or makes advertisement to attract more customers in his fold. It is the product differentiation that causes selling costs to emerge, in addition to production costs.

In Chamberlin's model, demand for any commodity is not only affected by the price of a commodity but also by non-price competition (i.e., product variation and selling activities). Selling costs or advertising outlays are peculiar to this market.

- **Free entry and exit:** Like perfect competition, there is complete freedom of entry and exit.
- **Product group:** Chamberlin used the term 'group' rather than industry. An industry is a set of firms that produces homogeneous goods. But under

monopolistic competition goods are heterogeneous or slightly differentiated. Thus, the term 'industry' cannot be applied here. That is why, Chamberlin used 'product group' which is defined as a collection of firms producing almost similar goods, but not identical goods.

9.11.2. Concepts of Proportional Demand Curve and Perceived Demand Curve

We have said that monopolistic competition is an amalgam of perfect competition and monopoly. A monopolistically competitive firm does not face a horizontal demand curve. On the other hand, a competitive firm experiences horizontal demand curve since goods produced by all firms are homogeneous goods. Product differentiation, however, is one of the chief assumptions of monopolistic competition. In this market, goods are not perfect substitutes like perfect competition. Goods produced by large number of monopolistic competitors are closely related to each other. Each product is a very close substitute of the product of others. It is due to this product differentiation that every firm enjoys some sort of monopoly power. Each product is unique. Then the demand curve faced by a monopolistically competitive firm is negative sloping.

For building up his model of monopolistic competition, Chamberlin considers two demand curves—proportional demand curve or actual-sales curve and perceived demand curve or anticipated demand curve. The former is drawn by assuming that all the monopolistically competitive firms charge the same price. On the other hand, a perceived demand curve is drawn on the assumption that the competitor sellers will not change the original price. The curve D_P is the proportional demand curve. This is the demand curve faced by a particular firm when all the sellers charge the same price. D_A is the anticipated or perceived demand curve facing the firm if all sellers maintain the original price.

Let us start with a price of OP_1 and output sold OQ_1. Now if a typical firm wishes a cut in price from OP_1 he will expect his sales to go up. This is because Chamberlin assumes that all other firms will keep their prices at OP_1. Similarly, if the particular seller plans to raise the price of the product, he can expect a drastic drop in sales since all other sellers will keep their price at OP_1. Thus, the individual firm perceives a demand curve D_A at price OP_1 since every seller 'expects his action to go unnoticed by his rivals'.

D_A curve is more elastic than D_P because each firm in this model believes that no other firms will react or respond to changes in its price change.

Anticipating elastic demand, each firm has an incentive to lower the price of its product in order to capture a larger share of the market. In other words, if a particular firm reduces price of its product from OP_1 to OP_2, it can expect its sales to increase to OQ_3. Since every firm hopes

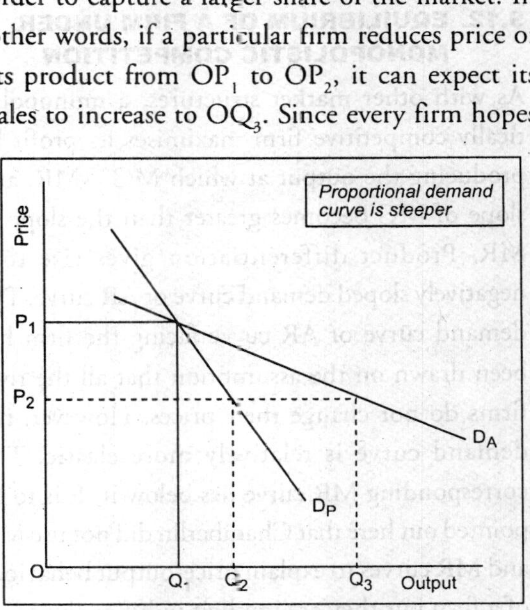

Fig. 9.11: Two Demand Curves

that no other firms will cut price, the gain in the ultimate analysis will be smaller. If all firms reduce price to OP_2, the actual sales will be OQ_2 instead of OQ_3. In view of this, D_P curve is more steep or less elastic than D_A curve.

D_P curve shows the actual sales since it takes into account the effects of the actions of competitor sellers to the price changes. On the other-hand, D_A curve shows anticipated changes in quantity sold when it contemplates a price change. Under this market form, every seller believes that his actions will go unnoticed. Thus, every firm ignores the reaction of rival sellers and, hence, behaves independently. All firms acting independently actually sell less than what they anticipate.

However, to make it simple, we have not used anticipated or perceived demand curve to describe equilibrium situation of a firm under monopolistic competition both in the short run and in the long run.

9.12. EQUILIBRIUM OF A FIRM UNDER MONOPOLISTIC COMPETITION

As with other market structures, a monopolistically competitive firm maximises its profit by producing the output at which MC = MR, and slope of MC becomes greater than the slope of MR. Product differentiation gives rise to a negatively sloped demand curve or AR curve. The demand curve or AR curve facing the firm has been drawn on the assumption that all the rival firms do not change their prices. However, the demand curve is relatively more elastic. The corresponding MR curve lies below it. It is to be pointed out here that Chamberlin did not use MC and MR curves to explain price-output behaviour of a firm but they are implicit in his analysis.

9.12.1. Short Run Equilibrium

Equilibrium of a firm under monopolistic competition is often couched in terms of short period and long period. In the short run, Chamberlin's model of monopolistic competition comes closer to monopoly. That is to say, there is virtually no difference between monopolistic competition and monopoly in the short run. Thus, Chamberlin's firm may earn super normal profit, normal profit or incur loss in the short run since entry and exit are not allowed during this time period.

In Fig. 9.12, short run marginal cost curve, SMC, is equal to MR at point E. Thus, E is the equilibrium point. Corresponding to this equilibrium point, the firm produces OQ output and sells it at a price OP. Thus, the firm earns pure profit to the extent of PARB since total revenue (OPAQ) exceeds total cost of production (OBRQ).

A firm, in the short run, may earn only normal profit if MC = MR < AR = AC occurs. A loss may result in the short run if MC = MR < AR < AC happens.

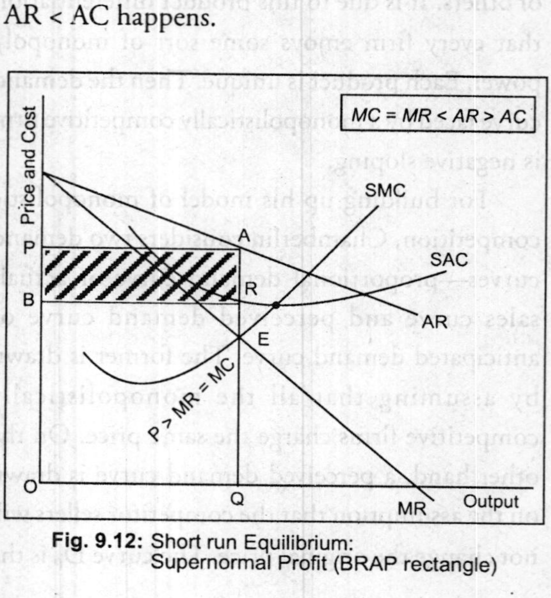

Fig. 9.12: Short run Equilibrium: Supernormal Profit (BRAP rectangle)

9.12.2. Long Run Equilibrium

In the long run, monopolistic competition comes closer to perfect competition because the freedom of entry and exit allows firms to enjoy only normal profit. Whenever some firms earn pure profit in the long run some other firms may be attracted to join this product group—thereby driving excess profit to zero. Seeing losses for a long time, losing firms may be induced to leave the product group—thereby eliminating losses. Thus, all firms in the long run earn only normal profit.

Long run equilibrium is achieved at point E where LMC equals MR (Fig. 9.13). The equilibrium output thus determined is OQ_M. At this output, AR equals AC. The firm gets normal profit by selling OQ_M output at the price OP_M. Note that a monopolistically competitive firm always operates somewhere to the left of the minimum point of its AC curve. In other words, as the demand curve is not perfectly elastic or as the demand curve is negative sloping the AR curve becomes tangent to the left of the lowest point of AC curve (say, point N). Each firm thus produces at a cost higher than the minimum and gets only normal profit.

Under perfect competition, long run equilibrium is achieved at that point where MC = MR = AR = AC. Because of the perfectly elastic AR curve, a tangency occurs between AR and AC at the latter's lowest point. In Fig. 9.13 the dotted AR = MR curve is the demand curve faced by a competitive firm. Equilibrium is attained at point R where LMC = MR = AR = lowest point of LAC. The competitive output thus determined is OQ_P which will be sold at the price OP_P. So we can conclude that monopolistically competitive output (OQ_M) is less than the perfectly competitive output (OQ_P) and monopolistically

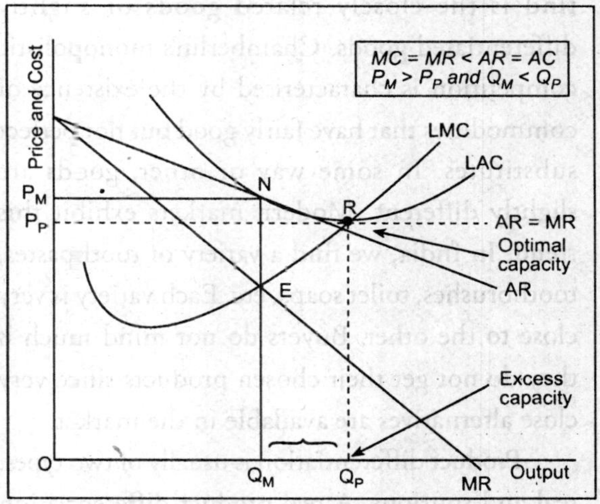

Fig. 9.13: Long run Equilibrium : Normal Profit

competitive price (OP_M) is larger than competitive price (OP_P). Thus, the difference in output—Q_MQ_P—measures excess capacity or unused capacity faced by monopolistically competitive firm Production at a higher cost implies wastage of resources or underutilisation of resources.

Since production takes place at the lowest point of AC curve under perfect competition, there does not occur any wastage of resources. Society gets larger output and consumers get output at a lower price. Thus, as perfect competition maximises social welfare, it is an ideal market. But social welfare is not maximised under monopolistic competition since society gets lower output compared to perfectly competitive output and buyers buy the differentiated products at a high price.

However, Chamberlin's notion of excess capacity does not tally with the arguments advanced here.

9.13. PRODUCT DIFFERENTIATION AND NON-PRICE COMPETITION

We see that goods are not homogeneous or identical in quality in modern business. What we find is the closely related goods or slightly differentiated goods. Chamberlin's monopolistic competition is characterised by the existence of commodities that have fairly good but not perfect substitutes. In some way or other, goods are slightly different. Modern markets exhibit this trend. In India, we find a variety of toothpastes, toothbrushes, toilet soaps, etc. Each variety is very close to the other. Buyers do not mind much if they do not get their chosen products since very close alternatives are available in the market.

Product differentiation is usually of two types: real and spurious. A real product differentiation arises when the inherent characteristics of products (e.g., chemical composition of, say, Neem soap, is different from that of Dettol soap) are different. Product differentiation may be fancied or spurious. Under this, product is basically the same but differences are established through advertisements or packaging, e.g., hard-bound or paper-bound book.

It is due to product differentiation sellers enjoy some degree of monopoly power. Buyers are usually fascinated to purchase a particular brand of a product. It is the brand loyalty that creates some sort of monopoly. Thus, product differentiation causes negative sloping demand curve. However, the monopoly power is limited since rival firms' products are in the market to which customers may move. In other words, monopoly sellers face competition. So, demand curve faced by a monopolistically competitive seller must be relatively elastic.

It is often observed that sellers often engage themselves in price war to promote their sales. Chamberlin, in addition to price competition, stressed emphasis on non-price competition. Product differentiation justifies the importance of selling expenses. Chamberlin argues that product differentiation and selling costs are two forms of non-price competition. Even without price-cutting, more buyers can be induced to purchase the product of a seller by spending on attractive advertisement expenditure. This means that selling expenses influence demand for a product greatly. Thus, in Chamberlin's model, demand is influenced not only by the price of the product, "but also by the style of the product, the services associated with it, and the selling activities of the firm." In order to attract more customers in their fold, sellers often compete with each other that influences demand for the product. Such demand-influencing variables (other than price of the product) are the elements of non-price competition.

- **Product differentiation and short run equilibrium**: While discussing product differentiation and equilibrium, we assume that price of the product remains unchanged while product adjustment takes place rather regularly. Such changes in the product are made to differentiate one's product from others and to make it a unique one in the mind of the consumers.

A firm has to make a choice from amongst the many varieties of the product so that profit is maximised. Of course, volume of profit depends on the degree of product differences. As product differences are made, the possibilities of sales rise. Costs also change as product quality is changed. With given price of the product (hence non-price competition), a firm chooses that variety of the product which yields greatest profit.

For simplicity's sake, we assume that a firm has to select one product out of two. Costs of both these varieties are represented by the curves C_A

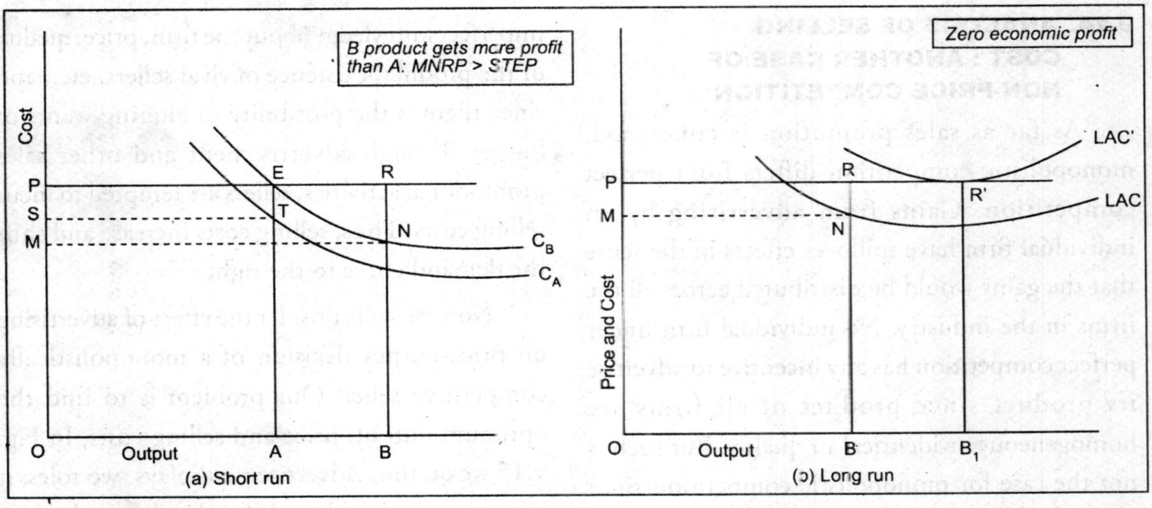

Fig. 9.14: Product Differentiation

and C_B—product B being more expensive. As price is assumed to be fixed, it is represented by the horizontal line OP. This is not to be confused with the horizontal demand curve. If the firm sells OB amount of B good at a price OP, its total profit will be MNRP rectangle. But if it chooses A variety, and decides to sell OA amount, then its profit will be STEP rectangle—a lower volume of profit compared to B-variety. In this way, a firm can adopt trial and error method and choose a particular variety that gives largest profit.

- **Product differentiation and group equilibrium** : Long run or group equilibrium will be achieved at that point where AC curve touches the fixed price line. To start with long run equilibrium, we assume that some firms in the product group enjoy super normal profit. This induces some firms to join the product group. As a result, volume of sales of many firms will decline and, hence, profit. To prevent losses or to prevent fall in profit, some firms will introduce newer variety of products with better quality. Introduction of quality products means increase in costs. This will cause cost curve to shift up until it touches the price line. If a firm sells OB amount of good, it will enjoy a profit to the extent of MNRP. This will attract more firms to join the product group. As a result, LAC will continue to shift up until it touches price line at R′ where all the firms within the product group enjoy only normal profit. There is now no incentive on the part of any firms either to leave or join the group and hence no scope for increasing profit by making an improvement of the product.

However, this Chamberlinian discussion on product differentiation does not fit in reality because it is difficult to determine price of the product, quality of the product and the selection of a particular product to be produced independently. These variables, in fact, are interdependent. Here we assumed non-price competition and then determined an optimum product variety. On the contrary, a firm takes into account all these variables simultaneously : assuming one variable constant, we can't determine other variables. In other words, introduction of newer product is always associated with price changes.

9.14. ANALYSIS OF SELLING COST : ANOTHER CASE OF NON-PRICE COMPETITION

As far as sales promotion is concerned, monopolistic competition differs from perfect competition. Gains from advertising by an individual firm have spillover effects in the sense that the gains would be distributed across all the firms in the industry. No individual firm under perfect competition has any incentive to advertise its product since product of all firms are homogeneous or identical in quality. But such is not the case for monopolistic competition since different sellers produce slightly different goods. It is the product differentiation that enables a monopolistically competitive seller to exercise some sort of monopoly power. Under the circumstance, sales promotional activities are undertaken by sellers to persuade more buyers to buy their products. Sales promotion, thus, involves selling cost which is to be distinguished from production cost. As far as monopolistic competition is concerned, total cost of producing a product is the sum of total production cost and total selling cost.

It was Chamberlin who first introduced the concept of selling cost. Through various sales promotion activities and advertising, a firm claims that its product is better than its rivals' product. Thus, selling costs are those costs which are incurred by a firm to influence or persuade buyers to buy its product instead of others' products. According to Chamberlin, selling costs are defined as those costs which are incurred by a monopolistically competitive firm 'to alter the position or shape of the demand curve for a product'. The purpose of selling cost is, thus, to capture the saleable markets so as to increase total revenue and, ultimately, profit. Since buyers have imperfect knowledge about the firm, price, quality of the product, existence of rival sellers, etc., and since there is the possibility of altering wants of buyers through advertisement and other sales promotional activities, sellers are tempted to incur selling costs. Thus, selling costs increase and shift the demand curve to the right.

Now we will consider the effect of advertising on price-output decision of a monopolistically competitive seller. Our problem is to find the optimum output, price and selling costs. In Fig. 9.15 we do this. Advertisement plays two roles: it increases costs and it shifts the demand curve upwards. AR curve is the average revenue of the firm prior to incurring any selling expense. AC is the average production cost that do not take into account selling costs or advertising cost. For the neatness of the diagram, we have not used MR and MC curves. However, the profit-maximising output that has been described here is determined by the intersection of MR and MC curves. Our firm maximises profit by producing OQ output where price OP is determined, since at this output MC and MR curves (not drawn) are equal to each other. Total profit is represented by the shaded area. Profit is earned before any advertisement is made because AC curve lies below AR curve.

Let us assume that our firm spends a amount of selling cost. This selling expense raises both the demand curve to AR_α and average cost curve (inclusive of advertisement cost) to AC_α. Consequently, equilibrium output becomes OQ_α and optimum price, thus, determined becomes OP_α. At this level of output volume of profit has gone up. Since profits have increased following advertising expenditure, our firm will be tempted to spend more on advertisement (β amount). As a result, AR curve will shift to AR_β. AC curve will now shift to AC_β. Now the equilibrium output is OQ_β and equilibrium price is OP_β. This time, our firm earns some profit but the volume of profit is comparatively less than when a amount was spent. It is to be noted here that the firm does not get maximum profit by spending β amount of money. Therefore, it should choose to produce OQ_α amount and sell it at price OP_α with the selling expenditure represented by AC_α as an optimal advertising expenditure for the firm.

So, we can conclude that it will be profitable on the part of the firm to increase additional selling cost so long as each increment of selling expenditure adds more to revenue than to its costs. Only when the additional revenue net of production costs generated equals the additional or marginal amount spent in order to generate such net revenue, profit will be the largest.

Sales promotion, thus, may not necessarily cause profits to rise. There is an optimal level of selling cost. However, if advertising campaign does not cause demand curve to shift to the right,

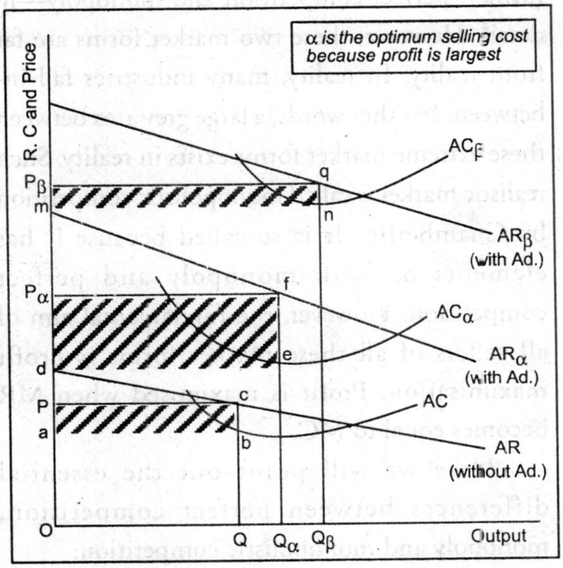

Fig. 9.15 : Selling Cost and Equilibrium

profits are then likely to decline. Particularly, when all firms in the monopolistically competitive market go for sales promotion, excess profit will be eliminated eventually because of free entry and free exit.

9.15. ELEMENTS OF PERFECT COMPETITION AND MONOPOLY IN MONOPOLISTIC COMPETITION

The market that has the qualities of both perfect competition and pure monopoly has been characterised as monopolistic competition by Edward Chamberlin. The important characteristics of this market form are :

First, there is quite a large member of firms in this market form. However, the number of firms is not 'too large', as in perfect competition. Anyway, each firm in the market has rather an insignificant share of the market. Therefore, actions of one seller do not exert enough influence on rivals. This means that each firm, in making its decisions, does not consider how its rivals will react. It assumes that each seller expects his actions to go unnoticed by his rivals. This assumption is called the assumption of independence.

Secondly, there is the freedom of entry of new firms into the industry, or, to be more specific, the product group, and the exit of old firms from the product group. When firms in a product group make profits, new firms will be interested in joining this product group and drive down pure profit to zero. Similarly, some firms may go out of business if they incur a loss for a long time. Thus, in the long run, abnormal profits and loss cannot emerge in this market form.

Remember that these two characteristics of monopolistic competition are very similar to those of perfect competition. That is why it is said that so far as the long period is concerned, there appears to be very little monopoly in monopolistic competition.

Thirdly, each firm produces slightly differentiated products. In other words, products are homogeneous rather than heterogeneous. It is due to the product differentiation each firm exercises some degree of monopoly power (i.e., ability to raise price of its product above MC), but, since goods are close substitutes, some sort of competition takes place among sellers of differentiated products.

So far as 'short run' is concerned, there is virtually no difference between monopolistic competition and monopoly. In other words, competitive elements are missing in monopolistic competition in the short run. Each seller aims at maximising profit and minimising loss in the short run. A monopolistically competitive firm, like a monopolist, reaches equilibrium when MC = MR < AR. A situation of abnormal profit may emerge if

$$MC = MR < AR > AC.$$

A firm incurs a loss when

$$MC = MR < AR < AC.$$

But, in the long run, monopoly element—blockaded entry—is missing in monopolistic competition. In the long run, because of freedom of entry and exit, P = AC. Thus, only normal profit is earned by monopolistically competitive sellers. So, in the long run, this market largely corresponds to perfect competition.

But, unlike perfect competition, no firm in this market form does operate at the lowest point of its AC curve leading to the emergence of excess capacity. Since firms operate somewhere to the left of the minimum of AC curve, price charged by monopolistically competitive firms is higher than perfectly competitive price and output is smaller than under perfect competition.

In brief, monopoly and competitive elements of monopolistic competition are of the following nature :

- *Monopoly elements*: (i) AR and MR curves are negatively sloped; (ii) equilibrium price is determined when MC = MR < AR; (iii) sellers enjoy some sort of monopoly power due to product differentiation; and (iv) smaller output and higher price and, hence, underutilisation of resources occurs.

- *Competitive elements*: (i) there is large number of sellers; (ii) there is freedom of entry and exit in the long run; (iii) in the long run P = AC and, hence, optimum utilisation of resources; and (iv) only normal profit is enjoyed in the long run.

9.16. COMPARISON AMONG PERFECT COMPETITION, MONOPOLY AND MONOPOLISTIC COMPETITION

We have examined the two extreme market forms—perfect competition and monopoly—in detail. However, these two market forms are far from reality. In reality, many industries fall in-between. In other words, a large grey area between these extreme market forms exists in reality. Such realistic market is called monopolistic competition by Chamberlin. It is so-called because it has elements of both monopoly and perfect competition. However, the fundamental aim of all sellers of all these market forms is profit maximisation. Profit is maximised when MR becomes equal to MC.

Here we will point out the essential differences between perfect competition, monopoly and monopolistic competition:

- **Structural differences**: Under perfect competition, there are innumerable number of firms who produce homogeneous goods. Each firm in the market is so small that it cannot exert any influence on price and output. Each firm, thus, behaves as a price taker. Under monopolistic competition, there is quite a large number of sellers who sell slightly different products. Product differentiation enables a firm to exercise some power over price and output. This means that sellers behave as 'price-makers'. However, a monopoly seller has full control over its price-output decision.

There is complete freedom of entry and exit of firms—both in perfect competition and in monopolistic competition. This condition is true during the long period only. In the short run, entry or exit is ruled out in both these market forms. But, a monopoly business is characterised by the absence of a rival seller. Entry of new firms is legally prohibited in monopoly.

- **Behavioural differences**: A firm behaves as a price-taker under perfect competition, and the demand curve faced by it is a horizontal one. Since price is fixed, AR curve coincides with the MR curve. A monopoly firm, however, faces a negatively sloped demand curve because it can have perceptible influence over price and output. Consequently MR curve is also negative sloping and lies below AR curve. This is also true under monopolistic competition. The only difference between monopoly and monopolistic competition is that the demand curve faced by a monopolistically competitive seller is relatively more elastic.

Since price is fixed to a competitive firm, it has only to undertake output decisions. Further, goods sold by competitive firms are perfect substitutes. Because of complete product homogeneity, no firm finds any incentive to spend money on any kind of sales promotional activity. A monopoly firm also does not find any urgency to spend money on advertisement since there is no rival seller. But, a monopolistically competitive seller has to incur some sort of "selling costs" just to provide information about its product or rivals' products. In fact, in order to attract more and more customers in its pocket, additional expenditure on selling cost is a necessity.

In every market, sellers adopt independent price-output policy. But all sellers of all market forms follow a basic principle. The basic behavioural rule is the equality between MC and MR. Under perfect competition, since AR = MR, MC = MR = AR = P. But, in monopoly and in monopolistic competition this behavioural rule is slightly altered to MC = MR < AR = P, since in these two markets AR > MR.

A monopoly firm or a monopolistically competitive firm produces in that region of its demand curve where the coefficient of elasticity of demand must be greater than one. But, under perfect competition, coefficient of elasticity of demand is infinite.

- **Optimum capacity and sub-optimal capacity of production**: A competitive firm always produces at the minimum point of its AC curve. This means that a firm utilises its plant optimally. Since AR curve is a horizontal one, a competitive firm will always produce at the lowest point of its AC curve. But, under monopoly or under monopolistic competition, the demand curve is negative sloping. It is due to the nature of this demand curve, a firm fails to operate at the minimum point of its AC curve. It operates somewhere to the left of the lowest point of the AC curve. The implication of this is that resources are not utilised optimally. As a result, a higher price for the product is charged and a lower output is produced. In this sense, perfect competition is an ideal market where social welfare gets maximised. But social welfare gets reduced in monopoly or in monopolistic competition.

- **Supply curve**: Under perfect competition, MC curve above the shut-down point is the short run supply curve. But under monopoly or monopolistic competition, the supply curve remains indeterminate. In other words, in these market forms, MC curve is not the supply curve.

9.17. OLIGOPOLY MARKET: ITS NATURE

At a first sight, many of the markets resemble monopolistic competition where sellers behave independently, i.e., actions of one seller go unnoticed by his rival sellers. In contrast, many of the markets, in reality, are dominated by a few sellers where interdependence among sellers is the main element. Each seller takes into account the actions of other sellers while taking price-output decision. Such a market form is popularly known as oligopoly. This term is derived from *oligos* meaning few and *polis* meaning sellers. Thus, oligopoly is said to exist when there are few sellers. Some define that when the number of sellers vary between 2 and 20, the market is said to be an oligopolistic one. The extreme form of oligopoly is duopoly when number of sellers is exactly two. Truly speaking, there is no such precise 'number limit'. In other words, the key issue is not numbers but rather the interdependence among sellers.

While in real world economies oligopoly market is found, it has not been so far possible to build up a satisfactory integrated general theory of oligopoly behaviour. The failure to build up a general theory of oligopoly is due to the differences in the structure of this market form as well as in the behaviour of firms. Because of the differences in structure of oligopoly market, economists often prescribe different models explaining different behaviour of the oligopolists. This market differs from the market forms of perfect competition, monopoly and monopolistic competition. Firms in perfect competition or in monopolistic competition engage in 'non-strategic behaviour' implying that cost and demand curves of one seller are drawn without considering the actions of a large number of rivals. In contrast, an oligopolist's behaviour is strategic. This means that each seller is affected by the actions of his rival sellers. Likewise, decision of a seller will affect his rivals. In view of these, oligopolistic industries are of many types. The industries exhibiting oligopoly business differ widely in their institutional set-up. In practice, there may be as many varieties of arrangement as the number of industries. Empirical investigation suggests that each oligopolistic industry is to some extent unique. That is why quite a large number of theoretical models have been built up by economists to describe the oligopoly form of market. In fact, difficulty of building a general theory of oligopoly is due to the peculiar characteristics of the oligopoly market.

The most distinctive feature of an oligopolistic industry is the interdependence among sellers. In its own decision-making, every firm takes into account the behaviour or actions of its rival firms. That is to say, actions and reactions of each firm are studied seriously by rival firms. However, there may be different reaction patterns to actions of the first firm. A rival seller may ignore the actions of the competitors. In some cases, some firms may engage in price competition. They may also engage in non-price competition. No specific or predictable behavioural pattern is discernible since a great deal of uncertainty is involved as far as actions and reactions are concerned. That is why there is no satisfactory and comprehensive model of oligopoly.

Above all, the complexities and diversity of oligopoly business makes analysis of price and output determination difficult. A broad theory—with assumptions so general that they cover all the possible oligopoly situations stated above—offers no guidance to analyse particular oligopoly situation, while developing separate theories based on all possible assumptions is virtually an impossible task.

9.17.1. Classification of Oligopoly

An oligopoly market is beset with the problem of price determination since the actions and reactions of rival firms vary from industry to industry. So, before determining the price of a product, it is better to classify oligopoly market on the basis of: (i) specific assumptions about the actions and reactions between firms, (ii) nature of the product, etc.

Oligopoly may be classified according to the nature of the product. It may be homogeneous or differentiated:

- **Homogeneous oligopoly**: If the products of different firms are homogeneous then we have a case of homogeneous oligopoly or pure oligopoly. When oligopoly sellers sell homogeneous goods, price differences between the products will be rather insignificant. In other words, greater the homogeneity of the product, greater will be interdependence among sellers. Whenever a seller changes the price of his product, the sales of the rival sellers will be affected. Consequently, rival sellers will change their pricing policy.
- **Differentiated oligopoly**: In this market, sellers sell slightly different products. Price change of one seller will now have less direct effect upon his rival sellers. In other words, under differentiated oligopoly the assumption of interdependence among few sellers becomes less significant. This fact, i.e., insignificant rival consciousness, greatly complicates the price-output determination model of oligopoly. Most of our oligopoly models are differentiated oligopoly models.

  Oligopoly market is characterised by 'competition' and 'collusion'. Interdependence of firm may encourage firms to compete with their rivals or may cause sellers to collude with each other. Former oligopoly market is known as non-collusive oligopoly and the latter is known as collusive oligopoly.
- **Non-collusive oligopoly** : Under non-collusive oligopoly market, firms behave independently even though they are interdependent in the market. The behaviour of a seller under non-collusive oligopoly will depend on how he thinks

his rivals will react to his decision-making. Here the seller just guesses the reaction of the competing firms' selling homogeneous goods. Thus, an autonomous or conjectural behaviour is studied by firms of all rival firms. While setting the price of his product, the firm believes that rival firms won't make any countermove when he changes price of his product. This behaviour is known as autonomous behaviour. But as far as oligopoly market is concerned, this sort of autonomous behaviour is self-contradictory. That is why, the 'classical' non-collusive models of oligopoly—the Cournot model, Bertrand's model and Edgeworth's model—fail to determine equilibrium of a firm and industry. However, in the absence of collusion, some economists have succeeded in explaining equilibrium of a firm. Most important of these non-collusive oligopoly models are : (a) Cournot's duopoly model, (b) Sweezy's kinked demand curve model, (c) Stackleberg's leadership model, and (d) game theory.

- **Collusive Oligopoly**: If firms collude then we have a case of collusive oligopoly. Non-collusive oligopoly may often lead to cut-throat competition among sellers, ultimately leading towards monopoly business. Influential sellers may retaliate. To prevent this competitive price-cutting or retaliation, sellers may make a collusive agreement. Such agreement may be open or tacit. One form of open collusive agreement is the formation of cartel. A tacit form of collusion is price leadership, rule of thumb or average cost pricing.
- Non-price competition : Again, one finds a situation of non-price competition in oligopoly. Product differentiation and advertisement are two important sources of non-price competition. Sellers want to induce buyers to buy their products by some means, e.g., introduction of a newer variety of product (may be a deluxe variety or a 'Janata' variety), advertisement, etc. One of the most popular (non-price competition) oligopoly model is of W. J. Baumol's sales maximisation model.

The upshot of the above discussion is that, like other markets, there is no single oligopoly model that can explain the behaviour of a seller. "In fact, there are just about as many different results as there are oligopolies."

9.17.2. Non-Collusive Oligopoly: Cournot Model

Oligopoly is a few sellers' market. Duopoly—a two firm model—is an extreme form of oligopoly. Duopoly model was first popularised by the French economist Augustin Cournot in 1838. Cournot assumes that there are two firms—1 and 2—that produce homogeneous goods, say X, and know the market demand curve. Both firms have the same cost functions. It is also assumed that each firm takes its rivals/competitors into account and assumes that its competitor is doing likewise.

The basic element of the Cournot model is that each firm treats its rival's output as constant at the existing level and then decides its own output level so as to maximise profit. Thus, the output decision of one firm will depend on how much the rival is expected to produce.

Let us first consider the output decision of firm 1. Firm 1 thinks that firm 2 will produce nothing. Then firm 1's effective perceived demand

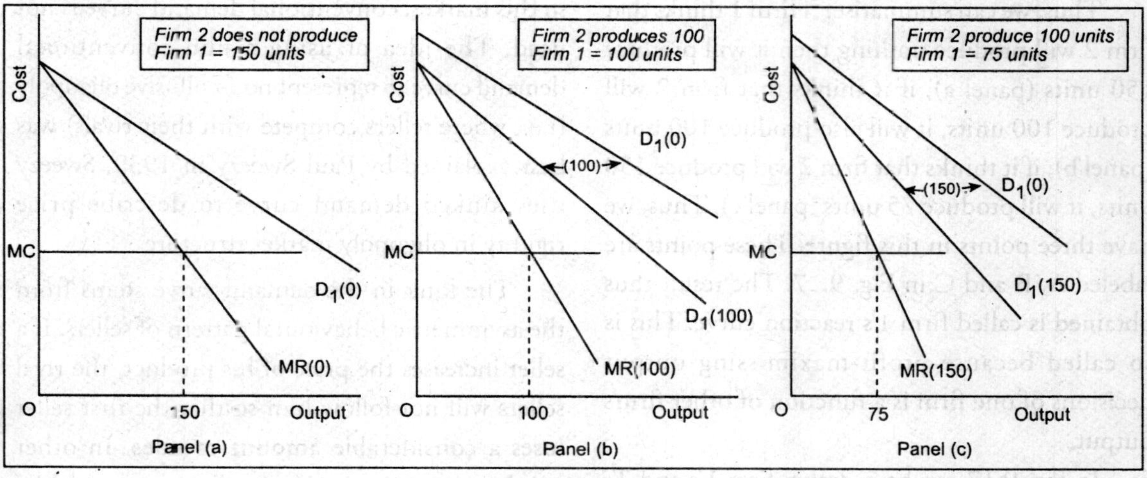

Fig. 9.16: Ccurnot Duopoly Model

curve can be thought of as the market demand curve. This is shown by the curve $D_1(0)$ in panel (a) of Fig. 9.16. Thus, its profit-maximising output is 150, determined by MR(0) and constant MC curves. If firm 1 thinks that firm 2 will produce 100 units, then its demand curve would be the market demand curve shifted to the left by 100 units. Thus to maximise profit, firm 1 would now produce 100 un ts—determined by the intersection of MC and MR(100) curves (shown in panel b). Now suppose firm 1 thinks that firm 2 will produce 150 units. Then firm 1's demand curve is the market demand curve shifted to the left by 150 units. It is labeled $D_1(150)$ and the corresponding MR curve is MR(150). Profit-maximizing output of firm 1 would now be 75 units, the point where MC = MR(150) (shown in panel c).

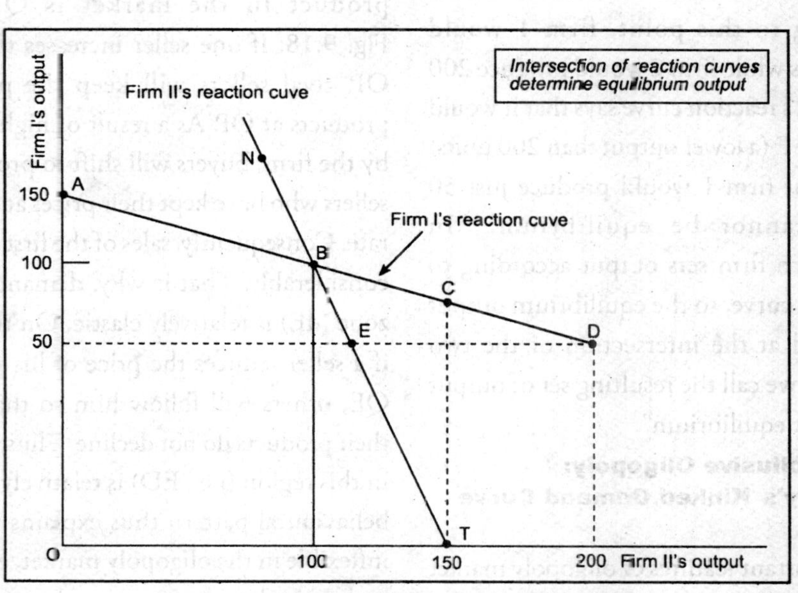

Fig. 9.17: Reaction Curve and Cournot Equilibrium

Thus, we can summarise: If firm 1 thinks that firm 2 will produce nothing then it will produce 150 units (panel a); if it thinks that firm 2 will produce 100 units, it will also produce 100 units (panel b); if it thinks that firm 2 will produce 150 units, it will produce 75 units (panel c). Thus, we have three points in this figure. These points are labeled A, B and C in Fig. 9.17. The result thus obtained is called firm 1's reaction curve. This is so called because profit-maximissing output decisions of one firm is a function of other firm's output.

In Fig. 9.17, we have drawn firm 1's and 2's reaction curves. Firm 1's reaction curve ABCD shows how much it will produce as a function of how much it thinks firm 2 will produce. Likewise, firm 2's reaction curve NBET shows its output as a function of how much it thinks firm 1 will produce. Equilibrium occurs at point B where the the two reaction curves intersect each other. Both firms would now produce 100 units of output. To see why B is the equilibrium point, let us consider point D on firm's 1's reaction curve. Corresponding to this point, firm 1 would produce 50 units while firm 2 would produce 200 units. But firm 2's reaction curve says that it would produce at point E (a lower output than 200 units) if it believes that firm 1 would produce just 50 units. This cannot be equilibrium. "In equilibrium, each firm sets output according to its own reaction curve, so the equilibrium output levels are found at the intersection of the two reaction curves; we call the resulting set of output levels a Cournot equilibrium"

9.17.3. Non-Collusive Oligopoly: Sweezy's Kinked Demand Curve Model

One of the important features of oligopoly market is price rigidity. And, to explain the price rigidity in this market, conventional demand curve is not used. The idea of using a non-conventional demand curve to represent non-collusive oligopoly (i.e., where sellers compete with their rivals) was best explained by Paul Sweezy in 1939. Sweezy uses kinked demand curve to describe price rigidity in oligopoly market structure.

The kink in the demand curve stems from the asymmetric behavioural pattern of sellers. If a seller increases the price of his product, the rival sellers will not follow him so that the first seller loses a considerable amount of sales. In other words, every price increase will go unnoticed by rivals. On the other hand, if one firm reduces the price of its product the other firms will follow the first firm so that they must not lose customers. In other words, every price will be matched by an equivalent price cut. As a result, the benefit of price cut by the first firm will be inconsiderable. As a result of this behavioural pattern, the demand curve will be kinked at the ruling market price.

Suppose the prevailing price of an oligopoly product in the market is QE or OP of Fig. 9.18. If one seller increases the price above OP, rival sellers will keep the prices of their products at OP. As a result of high price charged by the firm, buyers will shift to products of other sellers who have kept their prices at the old market rate. Consequently, sales of the first seller will drop considerably. That is why, demand curve in this zone (dE) is relatively elastic. On the other hand, if a seller reduces the price of his product below QE, others will follow him so that demand for their products do not decline. Thus, demand curve in this region (i.e., ED) is relatively inelastic. This behavioural pattern thus explains why prices are inflexible in the oligopoly market, even if demand and costs change.

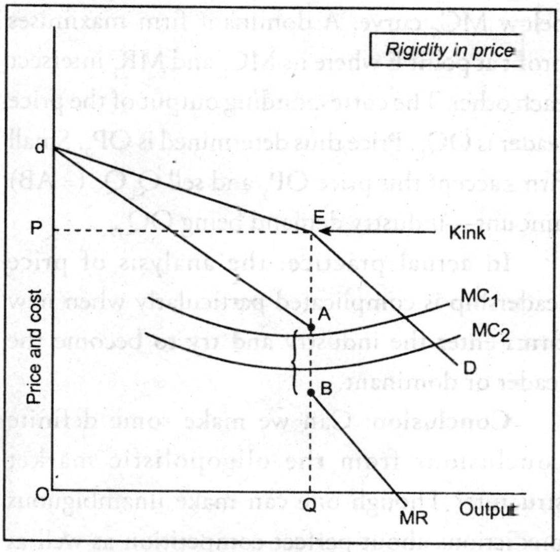

Fig. 9.18: Kinked Demand Curve and Oligopoly Equilibrium

The kink in the demand curve at point E results in a discontinuous MR curve. The MR curve has two segments: at output less than OQ, the MR curve, (i.e., dA) will correspond to dE portion of AR curve and for output larger than OQ, the MR curve (i.e., BMR) will correspond to the demand curve ED. Thus, discontinuity in MR curve occurs between points A and B. In other words, between these two points, MR curve is vertical.

Equilibrium is achieved when MC curve passes through the discontinuous portion of the MR curve. Thus, the equilibrium output is OQ to be sold at a price OP. Suppose, costs rise. As a result, MC curve will shift from MC_1 to MC_2. The resulting price and output remain unchanged at OP and OQ, respectively. This fact explains stickiness of prices. This model suggests that in oligopoly price is more stable than costs.

At the first sight, the model seems to be attractive since it explains the behaviour of firms realistically. But the model has certain limitations. *First,* it does not explain how the ruling price is determined. It explains that the demand curve has a kink at the ruling price. In this sense, it is not a theory of pricing. *Secondly,* price rigidity conclusion is not always tenable. Empirical evidence suggests that higher costs force a further price rise above the kink. Despite these limitations, the model is popular.

9.17.4. Collusive Oligopoly: Price Leadership Model

Non-collusive oligopoly models presented in the earlier section is based on the assumption that firms act independently even though they are interdependent in the market. A vigorous price competition may result in uncertainty. How do oligopoly firms remove uncertainty? Firms enter into pricing agreements with each other instead of competing with each other. Such agreements, either explicit of implicit, may be called collusion. Always, every firm has the tendency to become more powerful than its competitors. In an oligopolistic industry, one finds quite a few powerful competitors. Not all powerful competitors can be eliminated by a powerful firm. Under the circumstances, some of the firms within the oligopolistic industry act together or collude with each other to reap the maximum advantage. In fact, in oligopolistic industry, there is a natural tendency for collusion. The most important forms of collusion are cartel and price leadership.

When a formal collusive agreement becomes difficult to launch, oligopolists sometimes operate on informal tacit collusive agreements. One of the most common form of informal collusion is price leadership. Price leadership arises when one firm —may be a large as well as a dominant firm— initiates price changes while other firms follow.

An example of dominant firm price

leadership is shown in Fig. 9.19 where D_T is the industry demand curve. Since small firms follow the leader—dominant firm—they behave as "price-takers". MC_S is the horizontal summation of the MC curves of all small firms. Suppose the dominant firm sets the price at OP_1 (where D_T and MC_S intersect each other at point C). The small firms meet the entire demand P_1C at the price OP_1. Thus, the dominant firm has nothing to sell in the market. At a price of OP_3, the small firm will supply nothing. It is obvious that price will be set in between OP_1 and OP_3 by the leader. The demand curve faced by the leader firm of the oligopoly industry is determined for any price—it is the horizontal distance between industry demand curve, D_T, and the marginal cost curves of all small firms, MC_S. In Fig. 9.19, D_L is the leader's demand curve and the corresponding MR curve is MR_L.

Being a leader in the industry, the dominant firm's supply curve is represented by MC_L curve. Since it enjoys a cost advantage, its MC curve lies

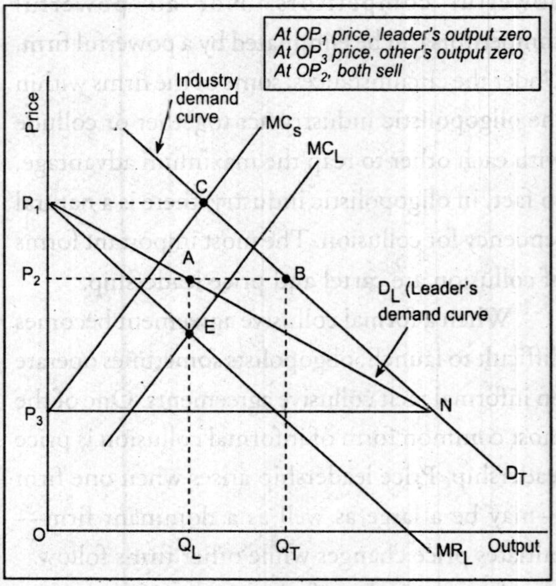

Fig. 9.19: Price Leadership Model

below MC_S curve. A dominant firm maximises profit at point E where its MC_L and MR_L intersect each other. The corresponding output of the price leader is OQ_L. Price thus determined is OP_2. Small firms accept this price OP_2 and sell Q_LQ_T (= AB) amount—industry demand being OQ_T.

In actual practice, the analysis of price leadership is complicated particularly when new firms enter the industry and try to become the leader or dominant.

Conclusion: Can we make some definite conclusions from the oligopolistic market structure? Though one can make unambiguous predictions about perfect competition as well as monopoly, no such predictive element of an oligopolistic competition exists. It is, thus, a perplexing market structure. One important characteristic of an oligopoly market is interdependence among sellers. Each seller's price-output decision is influenced by the perceptions of countermoves of rival sellers. Given the large number of possible reactions, we come up with different models based on different assumptions about the behaviour of the rival sellers, the extent and form of exit and entry, the likelihood of collusion between firms. 'Unfortunately, economic theory does not suggest which assumptions to use. In any event, each of these theories must ultimately stand or fall on its predictive powers'.[1]

1. Miller R. L. and Meiners R. E.(1986)—*Intermediate Microeconomics;* McGraw Hill International Edition.

QUESTIONS (WITH ANSWER-HINTS)

Long Questions (16 marks)

1. How does a monopolist determine price and output both in the short run and in the long run?

   Or

   Explain how a non-price discriminating moncpolist determines his profit-maximising output, the price to charge and the resultant economic profit, if any, both in the short run and in the long run.

   Ans. 9.5.

2. Contrast the long run equilibrium of a monopolist with that of a perfectly competitive firm.

   Or

   Show that monopoly price is higher than competitive price and monopoly output is smaller than competitive output. What is its economic significance?

   Or

   Why is the price changed by a monopolist greater than marginal cost? In what way can this be seen as inefficient?

   Ans. 9.7.

3. Compare perfect competition with monopoly.

   Ans. 9.7.

4. What is meant by price discrimination under monopoly? Under what conditions it is possible? Is price discrimination always profitable?

   Ans. 9.8, 9.8.1 and 9.8.2.

5. What is price discrimination? How does a profit-maximissing discriminating monopolist determine the prices that he charges in different markets?

   Or

   Under what conditions can a monopolist discriminate among different buyers in fixing the price of a commodity? When is price discrimination profitable? Explain the attainment of equilibrium diagrammatically. (C.U. 2007)

   Ans. 9.8 and 9.8.2.

6. What are the main characteristics of a monopolistically competitive market? How is the short run price-output determined in this market form? Explain how, in the long run, any economic profits will be competed away in a monopolistically competitive market.

   Ans. 9.11.1, 9.12, 9.12.1 and 9.12.2.

7. What is meant by product differentiation? Describe short run and long run equilibrium in case of non-price competition of product differentiation.

   Ans. 9.13.

8. What are selling costs? Why does advertising play a very important role in a market characterised by monopolistic competition? How will an advertising firm decide how much it should spend on advertisment?

   Or

   Distinguish between selling cost and production cost. Discuss the effect of advertisement on the price-output decision of a monopolistically competitive seller.

   Ans. 9.14.

9. Point out the essential differences between perfect competition, monopoly and monopolistic competition.

   Ans. 9.16.

10. What is oligopoly? How many types of oligopoly firms are found in businesses?

    Ans. 9.17 and 9.17.1.

Medium-sized Questions (8 marks)

1. What is imperfect competition? What are its different varieties?

   Ans. 9.1.

2. What is meant by moncpoly? What are the factors that give rise to monopoly?

   Ans. 9.2 and 9.3.

3. Explain the shapes of total revenue, average revenue and marginal revenue under monopoly. Summarise the relation between price elasticity of demand, average revenue and marginal revenue.

   Ans. 9.4.

4. Show that a monopolist will never set a price and produce corresponding output at which the demand is price inelastic.

   Or

   A monopolist will always produce at the elastic range of his demand curve. Explain the statement.

   Ans. 9.5 and 9.5.1.

5. Why is it impossible tc construct supply curve under monopoly?

   Ans. 9.6.

6. What is meant by dumping? How does price discrimination take place under dumping?

   Ans. 9.9.

7. Suppose a monopolist produces output in two plants. How does he decide how much output is to be produced in two plants?

   Ans. 9.10.

8. What is monopolistic competition? What are the characteristics of a monopolistically competitive market?

   Ans. 9.11 and 9.11.1.

9. **Show the relationship between the perceived demand curve and proportional demand curve. Which curve determines the firm's choice of output and price?**

   Ans. 9.11.2.

10. **A monopolistically competitive firm operates somewhere to the left of the minimum point of his AC curve. Explain. Is this output level efficient?**

    Or

    A monopolistically competitive output is smaller than perfectly competitive output. What is its economic implication?

    Or

    Analyse the long run equilibium of a firm under monopolistic competition (C.U. 2008)

    Ans. 9.12, and 9.12.2.

11. **What are the monopolistic and competitive elements of monopolistic competition?**

    Ans. 9.15.

12. **Define oligopoly. Point out its main features.**

    Ans. 9.17.

13. **What is duopoly? Describe Cournot equilibrium in terms of reaction curves.**

    Ans. 9.17.2.

14. **The kinked demand curve model explains price rigidity. Explain how the model works. How useful is the model in explaining pricing under oligopoly?**

    Or

    Explain the significance of the kinked demand curve model under oligopoly. (C.U. 2008)

    Ans. 9.17.3.

15. **What is meant by collusive oligopoly? How does a price leader determine profit-maximising price?**

    Ans. 9.17.4.

10

FACTOR PRICING—RENT, WAGES, INTEREST AND PROFIT

10.1. INTRODUCTION

Till now we were concerned with the modern *theory of value* that is used to explain the origin of demand, supply and, finally, the price of a commodity under different market conditions. However, for production, inputs are required. A business firm must know the cost of factors of production. For the sake of analysis, we assumed cost or the prices of inputs as constant and given. But, in this chapter, we intend to determine the prices of inputs. An understanding of input markets is necessary for a complete understanding of the market economy. Theory may be employed to determine the price of inputs. The theory of factor pricing is popularly known as the *theory of distribution*. Theories of value and distribution comprise modern microeconomics. Anyway, the theory of distribution deals with the determination of prices of productive resources. It, thus, studies how the rates of interest, wages, rent, etc., are determined.

Earlier economists dichotomized commodity pricing from input pricing. Today, no such dichotomy is recognised. Rather, it is said that the theory of input pricing does not differ from product pricing. The principles that are employed to determine product price are also applied in the case of input pricing. Like prices of product, input prices are determined by the demand for and supply of inputs.

The theory of input pricing has evolved around the marginal productivity (MP) theory of distribution. In other words, it is the marginal productivity theory of distribution that determines the price of a resource. Such view was popularised by J. B. Clark in the late 1890s. However, A. Marshall and J. R. Hicks argue that the marginal productivity is not a theory of input pricing. On the other hand, marginal productivity principle determines the demand for input. The Marshall-Hicks interpretation of the marginal productivity theory is outside the scope of this book. Here, the Clarkian version of the marginal productivity theory of distribution will be presented. To do so, one requires the understanding of the following concepts of marginal product.

10.2. CONCEPTS OF MARGINAL PRODUCT

Before presenting the marginal productivity (MP) theory of distribution, we must define 'marginal physical product' (MPP), 'value of the marginal physical product' (VMP) and 'marginal revenue product' (MRP) of the productive input.

• **MPP**: MPP is the change in total product consequent upon a change in the use of an input. For the sake of analysis, we assume that our firm uses labour as a variable input and all other inputs are held constant. Thus, MPP of labour or symbolically MPP_L, is the change in total product (TP) due to a change in the use of labour, i.e.,

$$MPP_L = \frac{\text{change in total product}}{\text{change in number of labourer}}$$

$$\text{Or } MPP_L = \frac{\Delta TP}{\Delta L}$$

• **VMP**: When MPP is expressed in monetary terms we obtain VMP. If we multiply MPP by the price of the good, say X (P_X), we obtain money value of MPP:

$$VMP = MPP \times P_X$$

Assuming labour as the variable input,

$$VMP_L = MPP_L \times P_X$$

• **MRP**: MRP is the change in total revenue resulting from the employment of additional unit of a variable input in question. In other words, MRP of labour is the change in total revenue attributable to a change in the employment of labour, i.e.,

$$MPP_L = \frac{\text{change in total revenue}}{\text{change in number of labourer}}$$

$$\text{or } MPP_L = \frac{\Delta TP}{\Delta L}$$

MRP may also be defined as MPP of the variable input multiplied by marginal revenue (MR). In terms of labour,

$$MRP_L = MPP_L \times MR$$

10.2.1. An Illustration of the Concepts

To have a clear understanding of these concepts, we have constructed two tables—one for perfect competition and another for imperfect competition. In these tables we assume labour as the variable input while other inputs are held constant. We also assume that labour along with other fixed inputs produces good X. If we assume

Table 10.1: MPP, VMP and MRP under Perfect Competition

(1)	(2)	(3)	(4)	(5 = 2×4)	(6 = 3×4)	(7 = 3×4)	(8)
L *(Labour)*	TP *(Kg.)*	MPP_L *(Kg.)*	P_X *(Rs.)*	TR *(Rs.)*	VMP_L *(Rs.)*	MRP_L *(Rs.)*	W (Wage) *(Rs.)*
0	0	—	5	0	—	—	20
1	10	10	5	50	50	50	20
2	19	9	5	95	45	45	20
3	27	8	5	135	40	40	20
4	34	7	5	170	35	35	20
5	40	6	5	200	30	30	20
6	45	5	5	225	25	25	20
7	49	4	5	245	20	20	20
8	52	3	5	260	15	15	20
9	54	2	5	270	10	10	20

Table 10.2: MPP, VMP and MRP under Imperfect Competition

(1)	(2)	(3)	(4)	(5 = 2 × 4)	(6)	(7)
Labour	TP	MPP	P_X	TR	VMP	MRP
	(Kg.)	*(Kg.)*	*(Rs.)*	*(Rs.)*	*(Rs.)*	*(Rs.)*
0	0	—	—	—	—	—
1	10	10	10	100	100	100
2	19	9	9.05	172	85.50	72
3	27	8	8.45	228	67.60	56
4	34	7	7.94	270	55.58	42
5	40	6	7.50	300	45.00	30
6	45	5	7.11	320	35.55	20
7	49	4	6.78	332	27.12	12
8	52	3	6.44	335	19.32	3
9	54	2	6.20	335	12.40	0

that the market for good X resembles perfect competition, then price of the product X remains invariant. It is also assumed that labour market is characterised by perfect competition. This means that at a given wage rate any amount of labour may be supplied. Let the price of the product X be Rs. 5 and the wage rate be Rs. 20.

According to Table 10.1, for all units of labour employed, $VMP_L = MRP_L$. If perfect competition exists in the product market, VMP_L must coincide with MRP_L (since AR = MR).

However, if perfect competition does not exist, we reach a different conclusion. Under imperfect competition a seller can influence the price of the product that he sells in the market. In other words, as a monopoly seller or a monopolistically competitive seller behaves as a price-maker, price of the commodity does not remain constant. Under the circumstance, as AR>MR, VMP_L must exceed MRP_L. This is shown in Table 10.2.

In this table, price of X is not fixed. Since under imperfect competition P = AR > MR. VMP diverges from MRP for all units of labour. To be more specific, $VMP_L > MRP_L$. Above all, MRP_L can be zero and negative.

In this connection, it may be referred that under perfect competition, $VMP_L = MRP_L$ is the firm's demand curve for labour. This curve is drawn negatively sloped. This means that at a high wage less labour and at a low wage more labour is demanded.

On the other hand, under imperfect competition as VMP exceeds MRP, the VMP curve must lie above the MRP curve. Further, MRP_L curve—not VMP_L curve—is the firm's demand curve for labour.

10.3. A COMPETITIVE FIRM'S DEMAND CURVE FOR AN INPUT

A profit-maximising firm hires variable input till that point at which MC of input equals the (VMP or MRP). Here by MC of input we mean price of the input. Since we consider labour as the variable input, its MC is nothing but wage rate. If labour market is characterised by perfect competition, wages will remain fixed. Since wage rate is fixed, average cost (AC_L) and marginal cost (MC_L) coincides. At a given wage rate, the supply of

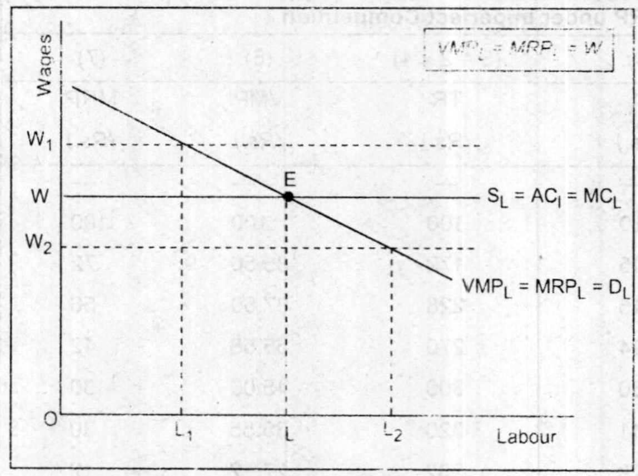

Fig. 10.1: Labour Demand Curve under Perfect Competition

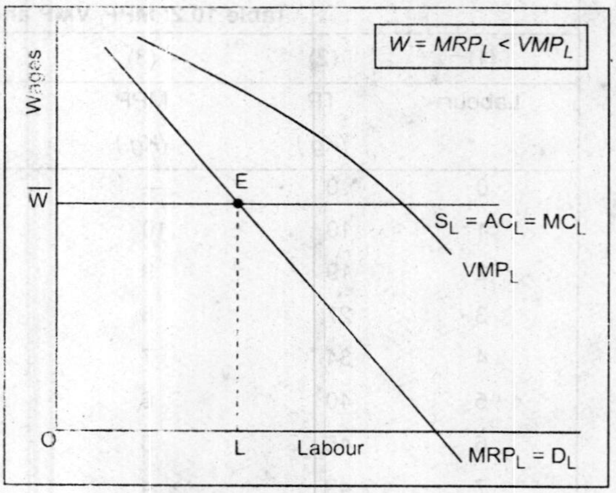

Fig. 10.2: Labour Demand Curve under Monopoly

labour, S_L, (i.e., $AC_L = MC_L$) becomes horizontal. Assuming perfect competition in both product market and labour market, a profit-maximising firm reaches equilibrium when VMP(=MRP) equals the price of labour, i.e., wage rate. Thus,

$$VMP_L = MRP_L = AC_L = MC_L = W$$

In Fig. 10.1, we have drawn a horizontal supply curve of labour. We have also drawn $VMP_L = MRP_L$ curve as the downward sloping curve. Equilibrium occurs at point E, where $VMP_L = MRP_L = W$. Corresponding to this equilibrium point, OL amount of labour is demanded. If the firm decides to employ OL_1 units of labour then $VMP_L > OW$. It would be wise if the firm hires more labour. It will continue to employ labour until wage equals VMP_L. Similarly, the firm will not be maximising profit if it employs OL_2 units of labour where wage exceeds VMP_L. Therefore, to have more profit, it must reduce employment of labour until OL is reached where $W = VMP_L$. Thus, at OW wage rate, OL amount of labour is demanded by the firm. If wage rate is OW_1, the firm will hire OL_1 units of labour and it will demand OL_2 units of labour if wage rate is reduced to OW_2. Thus, $VMP_L = MRP_L$ curve can be thought of as the demand curve for labour under perfect competition. In Fig. 10.1, $VMP_L = MRP_L = D_L$ curve is drawn as a negatively sloped labour demand curve.

10.4. DEMAND CURVE FOR LABOUR UNDER IMPERFECT COMPETITION

Under imperfect competition, VMP curve is not the demand curve for a variable input. In this branch of market, labour demand is governed by MRP, and not by VMP. Let us further assume that labour market is perfectly competitive. Therefore, supply curve, MC_L, would be horizontal.

A profit-maximising non-competitive firm which purchases labour input from the competitive labour market will employ labour up to that point at which MC = W equals MRP i.e.; $VMP_L > MRP_L = MC_L = W$.

At a given wage rate OW, a monopoly firm reaches equilibrium at point E. At this wage rate, the firm hires OL units of labour since $W = MRP_L$. If wage rate is increased, less labour will be demanded. More labour will be demanded if wage rate is lowered down. Thus, under imperfect competition, $MRP_L = D_L$ curve is the firm's demand curve for labour (Fig. 10.2).

10.5. AN INPUT DEMAND IS A DERIVED DEMAND

Product demand is a direct demand because it satisfies our wants directly. As a commodity satisfies want, we demand it straight-forward. But an input demand is a derived demand in the sense that inputs are not directly demanded. We, in fact, demand final consumer goods, rather than inputs, like land or labour. To meet the consumer demand, firms demand inputs. In other words, with the help of inputs, a firm produces a commodity. Thus, first comes consumer demand, then comes input demand. As an input demand is derived from consumption demand, demand for any input is a derived demand. This idea links product market with the input market.

10.6. MARGINAL PRODUCTIVITY THEORY OF DISTRIBUTION

MP theory of distribution is used to determine the price of an input. For simplicity's sake, we want to determine the price of labour i.e., wage rate. Anyway, this theory can be applied in the determination of any input.

The origin of the MP theory is rather obscure. However, J. B. Clark, an American economist, is greatly responsible for the popularisation of this theory in the late 1890s and early twentieth century. Jevons, Walras, Wicksteed, Marshall, Hicks, etc., have also given their own marginal productivity theories of distribution. In certain respects, each version is somewhat different. Seeing different versions of the MP theory of distribution, Joseph Schumpeter, also an American economist, remarked that there are as many marginal productivity theories as there are economists. Anyway, here we are concerned with the Clarkian presentation of the theory.

- **Clark's Version**: J. B. Clark's MP theory of distribution states that price of any input is determined according to the marginal product of that input. Thus, the price of labour—the wage rate—is determined by the volume of marginal product, or, to be more specific, the value of marginal physical product (VMP). Assuming a perfectly elastic supply of labour, wage of labour is determined in accordance with the VMP_L. Since product market is characterised by perfect competition, VMP_L becomes equal to MRP_L. Thus, wage of labour tends to become equal to $VMP_L = MRP_L$. A competitive profit-maximising firm will go on employing labour until wage equals $VMP_L = MRP_L$ i.e., $W = VMP_L = MRP_L$. This is the essence of the Clarkian version of the MP theory of distribution.

Assumptions: Before presenting his theory, Clark made some simplifying assumptions abstracting from the real world. He assumed a completely static society where population, stock of capital, and techniques of production are constant. Following are the important assumptions of this theory:

- Perfect competition exists both in product market and in input market. As a result, price of the product and price of the input are given.
- Every unit of input is homogeneous and easily substitutable.
- Inputs are perfectly mobile.
- There exists full employment of resources.
- Employer can measure the marginal product of an input in advance.
- Law of variable proportions operates.
- Firm hires input with the objective of profit-maximisation.

- If all inputs are paid according to their marginal products total product would be exhausted—there would be neither surplus nor deficit.

Perfect competition in input market implies that neither input seller nor input buyer can influence the price of an input. At a given price, any amount of the input may be supplied. As a result, price of any input becomes equal to its average cost and marginal cost i.e., P = AC = MC. This means that the input supply curve must be perfectly elastic.

For the sake of analysis, we assume labour as the variable input. So, $VMP_L=MRP_L$ curve is the labour demand curve. $S_L = AC_L = MC_L$ curve is the supply curve of labour.

Diagrammatic Representation of the Theory: In Fig. 10.3 units of labour are measured on the horizontal axis and the price of labour i.e., wage rate or marginal product is measured on the vertical axis. Negative sloping labour demand curve ($VMP_L=MRP_L= D_L$) intersects the perfectly elastic labour supply curve ($AC_L=MC_L=S_L$) at point E. Point E is the equilibrium point because, at the going wage rate OW, the firm employs labour till wage rate equals $VMP_L=MRP_L$. In other words, the firm maximises profit by employing OL amount of labour at the wage rate OW. In fact, OW(= LE) is the marginal product of labour. Thus, wage of labour is determined by $VMP_L= MRP_L$.

OL is the profit-maximising level of employment because, at the ruling wage rate OW, the firm will not be able to maximise profit if it employs more than OL or it stops employment short of OL. If the firm hires less than OL units of labour at the wage rate OW, it means $VMP_L= MRP_L>$ OW. So, it will be wise on the part of the firm to go on employing more labour until $VMP_L=MRP_L= AC_L=MC_L$. Further, if the firm employs more than OL units of labour at the wage rate OW, $VMP_L=MRP_L$ falls short of OW. This means that the marginal cost of labour is higher. So the firm will cut short of employment until $VMP_L=MRP_L=AC_L=MC_L$ is reached. So, the profit-maximising firm should employ OL units of labour at the wage rate OW.

Labour, in this case, is the variable input while other cooperating inputs—say, land, capital and organisation, are the fixed inputs. Total output is, thus, the area under the $VMP_L=MRP_L$ curve. Thus, the total production is the area OAEL. Out of this total output, the firm pays OWEL as wages and the rest (i.e., WAE) is being paid as the rewards of the other inputs in the form of rent, interest and profit. Thus, payment made in accordance with the marginal product exhausts the total product—there is neither surplus nor deficit.

However, this interpretation of the MP theory fails to determine the price of an input because input price is given or pre-determined. At a given wage rate OW, for an individual firm or industry, how many units of labour are employed can be known from this MP theory. In fact, what we have determined is the level of employment, given the wage rate. Thus, from the micro point of view, Clark's theory is a theory of employment, rather than a theory of input price determination.

From a society's point of view, what is pre-determined is the level of employment rather than the reward of an input. This is shown in Fig. 10.4 where we have drawn a perfectly inelastic supply curve of labour. This means that in the economy OL amount of labour is available. The supply of labour intersects the $VMP_L = MRP_L = D_L$ curve at point E. Thus, E is the equilibrium point.

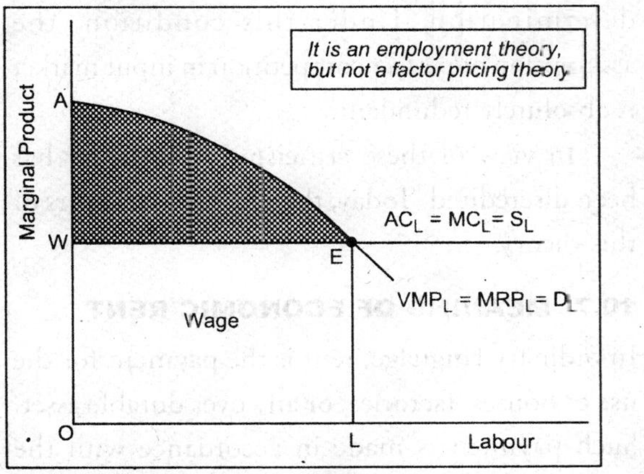

Fig. 10.3: MP Theory : A Micro View

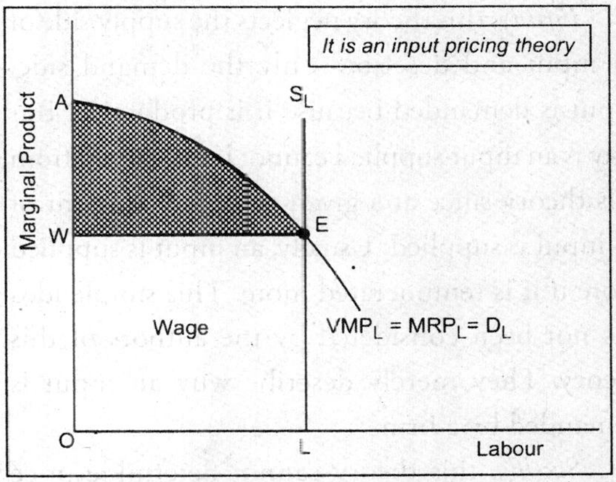

Fig. 10.4: MP Theory : A Macro View

Equilibrium wage rate thus determined is OW —the marginal product of OL units of labour. Out of the total product OAEL, OWEL will be paid as wages and WAE will be paid as rent, interest and profit. Thus, total product gets exhausted. Given the labour supply, now we have determined the reward of labour i.e., wage. Thus, from the macro point of view, MP theory is a theory of input price determination.

Thus, the Clarkian presentation of the MP theory of distribution has two versions : from the micro point of view (i.e., from the viewpoint of a firm or an industry), Clark's theory is an employment theory rather than a wage theory and from the macro point of view (i.e., from the viewpoint of an economy), this theory is a wage theory, rather than a theory of employment.

Criticisms: Several criticisms have been levelled against this theory since most of the assumptions are unrealistic. Following are the main criticisms against this theory :

In the *first* place, the MP theory of distribution becomes operative only when perfect competition exists. But, in reality, perfect competition does not exist either in the product market or in the input market. What we find in reality is the imperfect competition in both the product and input markets. This theory is inapplicable in the real world. In this sense, this is an unrealistic theory.

However, J. Robinson and E. Chamberlin have shown that Clark's theory can be applied even in the imperfect market. In an imperfect market, inputs are rewarded less than their value of the marginal products. Thus, inputs are exploited. Inputs always get their 'just' shares provided perfect competition exists.

Secondly, inputs can never be homogeneous. Some inputs must be more efficient than others. Further, inputs are not easily substitutable. For instance, there are some inputs which are used in fixed proportions. In such a situation, no degree of substitution exists.

Thirdly, full employment of resources is another unrealistic assumption.

Fourthly, this theory assumes that the employer can measure the marginal product of an input in advance. Truly speaking, no employer measures marginal product either consciously or unconsciously. Further, if inputs are jointly demanded then calculation of marginal product of an input is virtually impossible.

Fifthly, this theory neglects the supply side of an input and describes only the demand side. Input is demanded because it is productive. But why is an input supplied cannot be answered from this theory since at a given price any amount of an input is supplied. Usually, an input is supplied more if it is remunerated more. This simple idea has not been considered by the authors of this theory. They merely describe why an input is demanded by a firm.

Sixthly, this theory cannot determine price of each and every input. Each input has certain peculiarities not found in others. Thus, the price of every input is not influenced solely by the marginal product. For instance, rent is greatly influenced by the inelasticity in the supply of land rather than its marginal product. Collective bargaining strength of a trade union has an important bearing on the wage rate. Profit is the result of risk and uncertainty borne by the entrepreneur rather than his marginal product.

Seventhly, total product gets exhausted if inputs are rewarded according to their marginal products. This is known as product exhaustion problem of the marginal productivity theory. Such product exhaustion takes place only when constant returns to scale operates. But constant returns to scale and perfect competition are incompatible. Further, under increasing returns to scale or diminishing returns to scale, total product does not get exhausted—there occurs either deficit or surplus.

Finally, micro-presentation of the Clarkian version fails to determine the price of an input, since, from the micro point of view, it is an employment theory rather than a theory of input price determination. However, from the macro point of view, it is a theory of input price determination. Under this condition, the assumption of perfect competition in input market is absolutely redundant.

In view of these criticisms, this theory has been discredited. Today, there are few believers of this theory.

10.7. MEANING OF ECONOMIC RENT

In ordinary language, rent is the payment for the use of houses, factories, or any over durable asset. Such payment is made in accordance with the contract made between the parties concerned. This is called contractual rent. In economics, the term 'rent' is used in a specific sense. Here, by rent we mean economic rent. Economic rent is defined in two senses. First, Ricardo's economic rent is the payment made to the landowners to lease their land. Today, modern economists define it in the following way:

Economic rent refers to the payment made for the use of factors of production over and above their transfer earnings—the earnings of an input which are just sufficient or minimum necessary to keep in its present employment. Thus, economic rent is a 'surplus'—a producer's surplus beyond the full cost of production.

Ricardo applied the concept of rent to the use of agricultural land only whose supply is completely inelastic. It is the surplus income that is enjoyed by the landlords without making any effort. Such surplus income has been named as 'unearned income' by Ricardo. Ricardo, therefore, suggested a tax on land rent. Modern economists have demonstrated that rent is not specific to land. It can be applied to any input if its supply is inelastic. Further, economic rent is the payment made to any input in excess of minimum supply price or transfer income.

10.8. RICARDO'S THEORY OF RENT

According to Ricardo, economic rent is enjoyed by land only. Rent arises due to the niggardliness of nature. According to Ricardo, rent is producer's surplus. Rent is paid for the use of land whose supply is completely inelastic.

Ricordo's theory is based on the following assumptions :

- From the standpoint of the society, the supply of land is fixed. Thus, the supply of labour tends to become completely inelastic—its minimum supply price is zero in the sense that it supplies its working hours whether any payment is made or not.
- Law of diminishing marginal product operates.
- Malthus' theory of population is operative. In brief, this theory states that a country's population has the tendency to become double within 30 - 35 years.
- Land, being a gift of nature, has no cost of production. In view of this, rent does not enter into cost of production or price. Ricardo believed that price influences rent and not the other way.

  Ricardo gave us a two-fold reason for the emergence of rent: (1) scarcity rent and (2) differential rent. Former type of rent arises due to the limited supply of land and the latter type of rent arises due to the differences in the productivity of land.

10.8.1. Scarcity Rent

Let us assume that land available for cultivation is fixed and is therefore completely inelastic. Labour is the variable input. Let us also assume that marginal product of the variable input, labour, diminishes. As population tends to rise demand for land rises. So, according to Ricardo, rent must arise since supply of land is fixed in relation to demand. Consequently, prices of corn rise and surplus from land emerges. Such a surplus is Ricardo's scarcity rent.

Land is fixed and homogeneous in quality. Land is used for the production of a single crop, corn. To explain Ricardos concept of scarcity rent, we use the following diagram. Panel (a) of Fig. 10.5 shows the equilibrium of an agricultural farm, while panel (b) shows the same for the market. SS is the market supply curve. DD is the initial demand curve for the agricultural product that intersects the SS curve at point H. The market output, thus, determined is OQ and the corresponding price is OP. The corresponding equilibrium at the farm level occurs at point E where MC = MR = AC. A farm thus produces Oq and sells it at the price OP. Since P = AC, there is no surplus and, hence, no rent.

Let us assume that there is an increase in population following Malthusian logic. Thus, a rise in population results in an increase in the demand for corn. Market demand curve now shifts to D_1D_1 and it intersects the SS curve of point H_1. A higher price of corn (OP_1) thus results in and to feed more mouths now a pressure to increase production develops. Since land is fixed in supply, farms are now forced to increase production by making more intensive use of land. At a higher price OP_1, the farm now produces Oq_1, where MC and $AR_1 = MR_1$ are equal. Since, revenues earned by the farm (OP_1Tq_1) exceeds cost ($ONRq_1$), the land, which was initially a free good, now has an economic value. Thus, the area $NRTP_1$ represents economic rent or surplus. Further, increase in the demand for corn following a rise

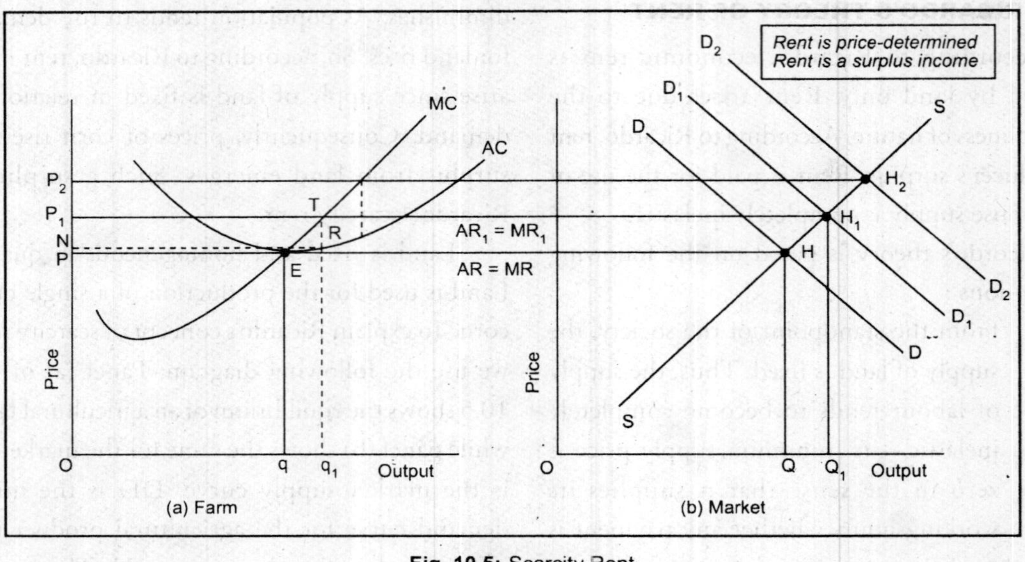

Fig. 10.5: Scarcity Rent

in population will lead to an increase in the price of corn (OP_2—determined by the intersection of D_2D_2 and SS curves at point H_2) and, hence, increase in surplus or rent.

The volume of rent is, thus, determined by the price of the product. Thus, rent is a price-determined cost but not price-determining cost. This sort of rent has emerged due to the inelasticity in the supply of land.

10.8.2. Differential Rent

It is quite likely that all lands are not of uniform quality. Truly speaking, lands are not homogeneous in quality, some lands are more fertile than others. Such differences in fertility or productivity of land result in the emergence of economic rent. This sort of economic rent has been described by Ricardo as differential rent.

For the sake of simplicity, we assume that in our society, there are three grades or categories of land where X is the superior and Z is the inferior land and Y grade of land lies between X and Z. In panel (d), market equilibrium has been shown. Product price is OP. The farm accepts this OP price. Ricardo assumed that a cultivator would produce first in the superior quality of land. As its supply is limited, the cultivator would then use next-best land whenever demand for corn rises consequent upon a rise in population.

Panel (a) of Fig. 10.6 shows that a farmer produces and sells Oq_1 output produced in superior-most land and enjoys a surplus or economic rent (the shaded area). As population rises, demand for corn rises. Since the supply of X-grade of land is fixed, people would then use Y-category of land—a less-superior land. Panel (b) shows that at a price OP the farmer sells Oq_2 output and enjoys a smaller volume of surplus (the shaded area). Again, because of the population increase, farmer would now use inferior category of land where production becomes Oq_3. However, at the price OP, this output fails to yield any surplus and hence economic rent is zero (in panel c) since P=AC. Ricardo called this inferior or category-Z land as the marginal land. Marginal land does not yield any rent. Rent, thus, arises only in superior land (here X- category) and intra-

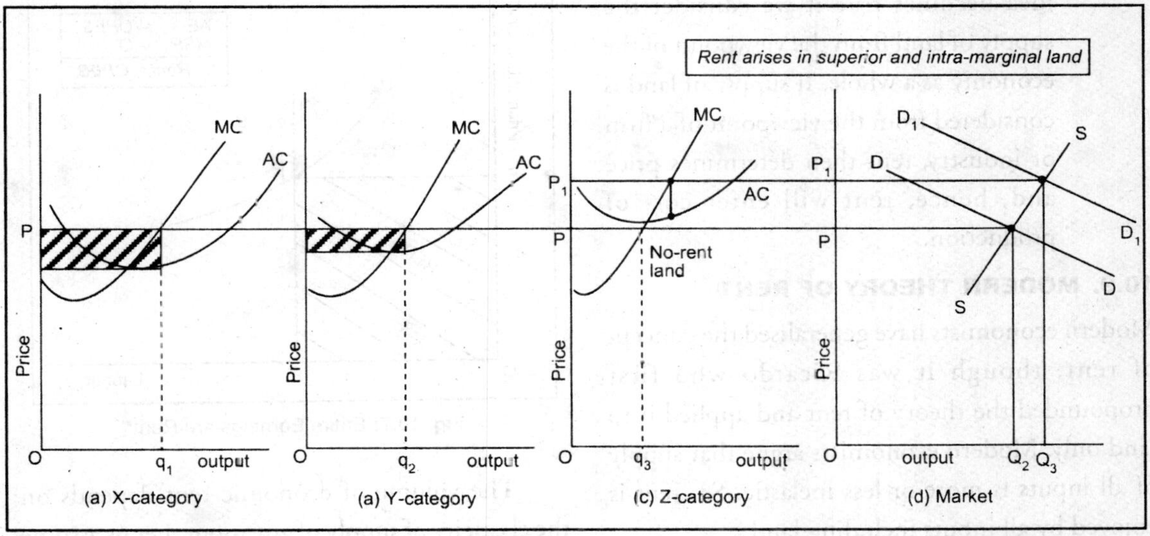

Fig. 10.6: Scarcity Rent

marginal land (here Y-category) — land that lies between superior and marginal land.

Now, if demand for corn rises, price will rise. Consequently, rent will rise. Note that, as demand curve shifts to D_1D_1, price of corn rises to OP_1. Consequently, surplus or economic rent increases in all grades of land. Now the marginal land or no-rent land yields economic rent and this land becomes intra-marginal land. Thus, rent is a price-determined cost, but not a price-determining cost. As price of corn rises, rent rises.

Further, economic rent is an 'unearned surplus' since rent is governed by the price of corn.

Limitations: Ricardo's theory of rent is subject to criticisms. They are :

- First, it may be objected that land does not have any original and indestructible powers. Such power of land can be changed through scientific way.
- It is unrealistic to assume that land has only one use. Instead, land has alternative uses. It can be used for variety of purposes. As Ricardo assumed that land has only one use its supply is completely inelastic. A particular plot of land may be used for the production of either wheat or jute. As land has alternative uses, the supply of land to a particular use cannot be addressed as perfectly inelastic.
- Lands are never cultivated in descending order of fertility as was assumed by Ricardo. Actually, cultivation is pursued in accordance with the location of land and other reasons.
- The concept of marginal or no-rent land is not found in reality.
- According to Ricardo, rent is specific to land. In other words, rent arises only in the case of land. But modern economists have demonstrated that rent arises not only in the case of land but also in the case of other factors of production.
- Finally, Ricardo has shown that rent is determined by the rice of corn. That is to say, in Ricardo's theory rent does enter into cost of production. This Ricardian

idea becomes true if we consider the supply of land from the viewpoint of the economy as a whole. If supply of land is considered from the viewpoint of a firm or industry, rent then determines price and, hence, rent will enter cost of production.

10.9. MODERN THEORY OF RENT

Modern economists have generalised the concept of rent, though it was Ricardo who first propounded the theory of rent and applied it to land only. Modern economists argue that supply of all inputs is more or less inelastic. So, rent is enjoyed by all inputs including land.

An alternative definition of rent has been given by modern economists. Economic rent is defined as the difference between actual earnings and transfer earnings or minimum supply price of any input. Actual earnings are the earnings what an input actually earns after rendering services for a given period of time. Transfer earnings are the payment that must have to be paid to keep an input in its present use. Transfer earning or the minimum supply price is the price that must have to be paid to an input in order to retain its job. Thus, economic rent is a payment to any input over and above what is required to keep the input in its current employment. In other words, economic rent is any payment in excess of transfer earnings or minimum supply price or opportunity cost. Transfer earnings are regarded as opportinity cost of keeping a factor of production in its present use or it is regarded as the input's supply price in its present occupation. Whenever an input does not have an alternative use, its opportunity cost becomes zero. Thus, the entire earnings of that input become rent.

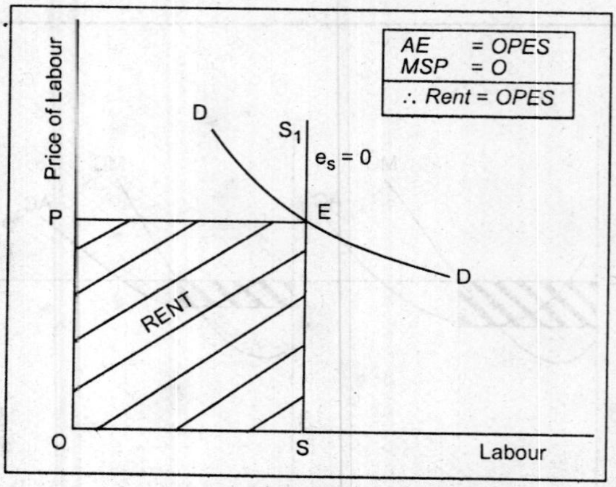

Fig. 10.7: Entire Earnings are Rent

The volume of economic rent depends on the elasticity of supply of any input. Let us assume that the supply of labour is perfectly inelastic as drawn in Fig. 10.7. In the short run, the supply of labour may be completely inelastic. Here SS_1 is the supply curve whose coefficient of elasticity of supply is zero. This means that whatever the price, its supply is always OS. Even if the input is not rewarded its supply would be fixed at OS. That is why, the supply curve of this input is completely inelastic ($e_S = 0$). Actual earnings (AE) of an input are determined by the intersection of the demand curve for an input and the supply curve of that input. Thus, the actual earning of the input becomes equal to OPES. Since opportunity cost or minimum supply price (MSP) is zero, the entire earnings of the input are economic rent (i.e., OPES).

In Fig. 10.8, we have drawn a perfectly elastic supply curve of labour, PS. This means that at a given price OP, any amount of labour will be supplied. Thus, the minimum supply price of that input is OP. Actual earnings are determined by the intersection of DD curve and PS curve at point E. Actual earnings now equal to OPEA. Since

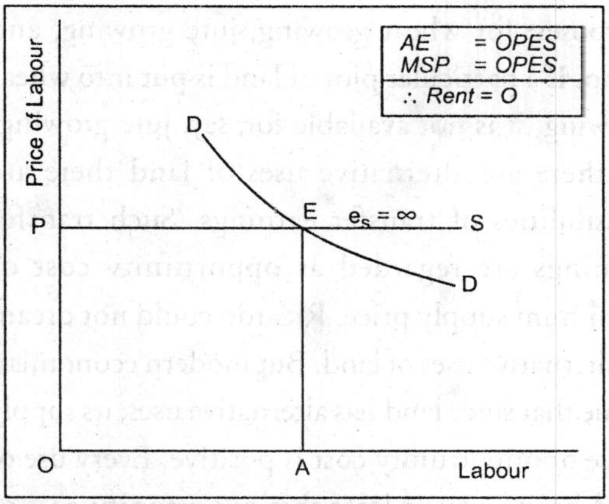

Fig. 10.8: Zero Rent

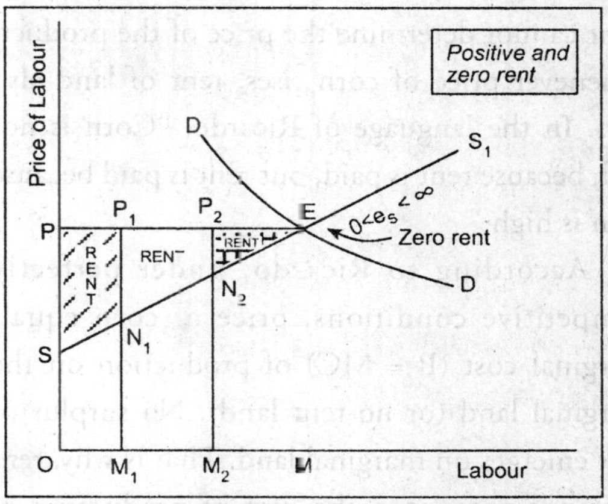

Fig. 10.9: Mix of the Two

actual earnings and opportunity cost are the same, labour does not enjoy any amount of economic rent.

In case of an upward rising supply curve of an input, part of its earnings become rent. In Fig. 10.9, we have drawn a positively sloped supply curve of labour, SS_1. Its slope indicates that as price of labour increases, its supply increases. Demand curve DD intersects the supply curve SS_1 at point E. Actual earnings are, therefore, OPEM. Now these actual earnings can be split into two parts: opportunity cost and the economic rent. Suppose, OM_1-th unit of labour is supplied whose opportunity cost is the area under the supply curve, i.e., M_1N_1. Its actual earnings are M_1P_1 (= OP). Thus, the OM_1-th unit of labour earns rent to the tune of P_1N_1 or SN_1P_1P area. Similarly, OM_2-th unit of labour enjoys rent of P_2N_2 amount since actual earnings (M_2P_2) exceed opportunity cost (M_2N_2). For the OM-th unit of labour since actual earnings and opportunity cost are equal, no economic rent accrues. In other words, OM-th unit of labour does not receive any surplus or economic rent. But, for OM units of labour, opportunity cost or minimum supply price equals OSEM area, while actual earnings are OPEM. Thus, OM units of labour get rent to the extent of PSE.

Thus, we can conclude that the volume of economic rent depends on the elasticity of supply of any input. Greater the elasticity of supply, lower is the economic rent, and lower the elasticity of supply, greater is the economic rent.

Finally, modern economists challenged Ricardion contention—rent is price-determined but not price-determining. This Ricardo's view is correct only when the supply of land is viewed from the society's angle. In this situation, opportunity cost is zero, since land has no alternative use. In such a situation, rent is price-determined. But, from a firm's or industry's point of view, opportunity cost is positive. So, rent will then determine price and not the other way, as Ricardo argued.

10.10. RELATIONSHIP BETWEEN RENT AND PRICE

One of the important conclusions, of course a controversial one, of the Ricardian theory is that whether rent enters into the price of the product or in the cost of production. According to Ricardo, rent of land does not enter into price since rent is determined by the price of the product or corn.

Rent cannot determine the price of the product. Whenever price of corn rises, rent of land also rises. In the language of Ricardo, "Corn is not high because rent is paid, but rent is paid because corn is high."

According to Ricardo, under perfectly competitive conditions, price of corn equals marginal cost (P = MC) of production on the marginal land (or no-rent land). No surplus or rent emerges on marginal land. That is why, rent does not enter into the cost of production of marginal land. Thus, rent cannot influence the price of the product. Rather, rent is determined by the price of corn. This is because of the fact that, as population of a country rises, demand for corn rises. Rising demand for corn causes its price to shoot up. Farmers then go on cultivating more and more less fertile or marginal land to feed newer mouths. Now the marginal land or no-rent land will yield a surplus or rent, and intra-marginal as well as superior-most lands will yield greater surplus. As price of corn rises, rent on intra-marginal land rises. Thus, price of corn and its demand determines the volume of rent. So, rent does not enter into price or cost of production. In Ricardo's view: Rent is price-determined but not price-determining.

This Ricardian view is based on two fundamental assumptions. *First,* the supply of land from the society's point of view is fixed or limited in relation to demand. *Secondly,* land has no alternative use and hence its opportunity cost is zero. Since opportunity cost or the minimum supply price of land is zero, the entire earning of land is rent. In this situation, as price of corn rises rent rises. So rent is determined by price.

But modern economists argue that land has alternative uses. It can be used for a variety of purposes: for wheat growing, jute growing, and so on. If a particular plot of land is put into wheat growing, it is not available for, say, jute growing. As there are alternative uses of land there are possibilities of transfer earnings. Such transfer earnings are regarded as opportunity cost or minimum supply price. Ricardo could not dream of alternative uses of land. But modern economists argue that since land has alternative uses, its supply price or opportunity cost is positive. Every use of land has to pay at least this opportunity cost or transfer earnings, or minimum supply price, if it is to be used for specific purposes. Any earnings over the transfer earnings constitute rent. From the viewpoint of a firm or an industry, land rent enters into cost of production. Whenever price for the use of land equals opportunity cost then such opportunity cost enters into cost of production. Further, if it exceeds opportunity cost then the excess is to be included into the cost of production. Thus, rent can influence cost of production or the price of the product.

Thus, the modern theory of rent teaches us that whether rent influences price or price influences rent depends on the viewpoint from which we look. In Samuelson's words: "Whether rent is or is not a price-determining cost depends upon the viewpoint from which we look: firm or industry or the whole economy."

10.11. DIFFERENCES BETWEEN THE RICARDIAN THEORY AND THE MODERN THEORY OF RENT

There are two theories at our disposal relating to the emergence of economic rent. They are: (i) Ricardo's theory, and (ii) modern theory. These two theories have striking dissimilarities, rather than similarities.

First, according to Ricardo, rent is a

producer's surplus beyond the full cost of production. Rent is enjoyed only by the gift of nature i.e., land. But modern economists have shown that rent is not to be tied to land only. Rent is an income that may be enjoyed by all the inputs. In other words, rent is not a specific income. Labour, capital and organisation may also earn income. Every input has the minimum supply price below which no services will be available. Earning above the minimum supply price is rent. There is a rent element in wages, interest, and profit.

Secondly, Ricardo considered scarcity rent and differential rent. However, he emphasised more on differential rent. Land may differ qualitatively due to two reasons: One is the difference in productivity, and the other is the difference in location of land. But modern economists have demonstrated that rent arises due to the inelasticity in the supply of any input. Greater the inelasticity in supply, higher is the rent.

Thirdly, and most importantly, the difference between Ricardian and modern theory centres around the relationship between rent and price. According to Ricardo, rent is price-determined but not price-determining. This implies that rent depends on the price of corn. As price of corn rises, rent rises. This Ricardian view holds when land is viewed from the society's point of view. As land is fixed in quantity its elasticity of supply is zero. Further, land, being a gift of nature, has no alternative use; thus, its opportunity cost is zero. So, rent does not enter into price or cost of production.

But modern economists argue that land is not limited in supply. When it is considered from the point of view of a firm or an industry, supply of land is elastic. Further, land has alternative uses. A particular land may be used for either paddy production or wheat production. If that land is used for paddy production it earns a surplus of Rs. 100 and if it is used for wheat production it earns a surplus of Rs. 80. This suggests that alternative to paddy production is wheat cultivation. Now, if this land is to be used for paddy production it must be paid at least Rs. 80, otherwise it will go for wheat production—the next best alternative. As it is used for paddy production, land earns a surplus or rent of Rs. 20. Now, if income from wheat production rises, minimum supply price of land for paddy production will rise. Consequently, the supply curve of land for paddy production will shift upwards. This will cause price of paddy to rise. Thus, it is the rent that governs the price of the product, not the other way round—if the supply of land is considered from the viewpoint of a firm or industry.

10.12. RENT ELEMENT IN OTHER FACTOR INCOMES

Rent is a surplus beyond the full cost of production. Economic rent, as explained by classical economist Ricardo, is restricted to land alone. Rent is due to the original and indestructible powers of the soil paid to the landlord.

But modern economists have given a new orientation to the concept of rent. Rent is not restricted to land alone; other inputs may also earn rent. According to them, rent is a surplus payment over and above what is necessary to put an input in its present use. Thus, any input can enjoy rent. In other words, there is a rent element in the earnings of labour, capital and entrepreneur.

How does rent element appear in the earnings of all inputs?

• **Labour**: As rent of land arises due to the inelasticity in the supply of land, so labour may earn rental income. A labour enjoys rent when actual earnings exceed opportunity cost, or minimum supply price or transfer earnings.

Let us assume that the transfer earning of a labour per month is Rs. 1,000. This is the price that must be paid to retain the job of this labour. If it is not paid, he will move to the next best available employment. If the actual earning of this worker becomes Rs. 1,100 then he will enjoy an economic rent of Rs. 100. Thus, economic rent is the difference between actual earnings and transfer earnings. Earnings above opportunity cost are economic rent.

Further, let us assume that the opportunity cost of a labour is zero. This means that this labour is willing to work even if no payment is made. Apparently, this seems to be an unrealistic proposition. But, in reality, such a situation can never be conceivable at a particular point of time. Sometimes a worker in order to accumulate experience or to receive some sort of practical training for conducting his service in a near future date—may be willing to work at a zero price. But if he is paid something for the job rendered, his entire earnings become rent.

Again, in the earnings of talented people, say, a football player like Maradona, filmstar like Amitabah Bachchan, etc., one finds huge rental income. These people are very much in short supply in relation to demand. Because of the specific quality possessed by these individuals they receive huge payments in excess of what is needed to keep them from transferring to other occupations. This sort of rent is, thus, attributed to ability of labour. This is called 'rent of ability'. The economics of superstars then has the 'superstar effect'—a phenomenon where people with small differences in ability or productivity earn more than the average persons endowed with average quality.

• **Capital**: There is a rent element in interest also. Suppose, an individual expects at least 15 p.c. p.a. interest income from an investment project. Let it be the minimum supply price. Now, if that project yields a rate of interest of 17 p.c. p.a. then an interest income of 2 p.c. is nothing but a rental income.

This is also true for a machine or any capital goods which enjoys surplus over and above the opportunity cost.

• **Entrepreneur**: Like land, labour and capital, the supply of entrepreneur is more or less inelastic. In fact, profit is the rent of ability. Not all organisers are equally efficient. Efficient ones earn more than the normal profit earned by a less efficient organiser. Inefficient organisers do not enjoy any rent—just like Ricardo's no-rent land or marginal land. As rent arises due to the differences in ability of organiser, this rent is called 'rent of ability'.

Thus, each and every input earns economic rent which is an excess over minimum supply price. However, one point should be added here. Land is more or less fixed—both in the short run and in the long run. But labour, capital, etc. may be inelastic or fixed in the short run and not in the long run. In the long run, all these inputs are to some extent, elastic. That is why, in the long run, rent element in incomes of other factors like labour, capital, etc. disappears or becomes less. But land rent always arises due to its high inelasticity even in the long run. That is why Marshall had to say: "The rent of land is the leading species of a large genus."

10.13. QUASI-RENT

The term quasi-rent was coined by Alfred Marshall. Economic rent, as defined by Ricardo and modern economists, is a long run reward to any input, including land. In the short run, some inputs are fixed and some are variable. But, in the long run, all inputs are variable. Economic rent persists in the long run while quasi-rent arises in the short run. Fixed inputs in the short period receive a quasi-rent. It evaporates in the long run because, in the long period there are no fixed inputs. Marshall argued that quasi-rent arises in the case of man-made inputs (like machines, buildings, etc.,) whose supplies are inelastic. Since the supplies of these inputs are variable or elastic in the long run, quasi-rent disappears. Thus, quasi-rent is an ephemeral reward; it is of a temporary nature. As it is not a true rent it is called quasi-rent. True rent or long run rent refers only to factors which are fixed in supply.

Quasi-rent may be defined as the difference between total revenue and total variable cost, i.e.,

$$\text{Quasi-rent (QR)} = TR - TVC$$

Since, in the long run, all costs are variable

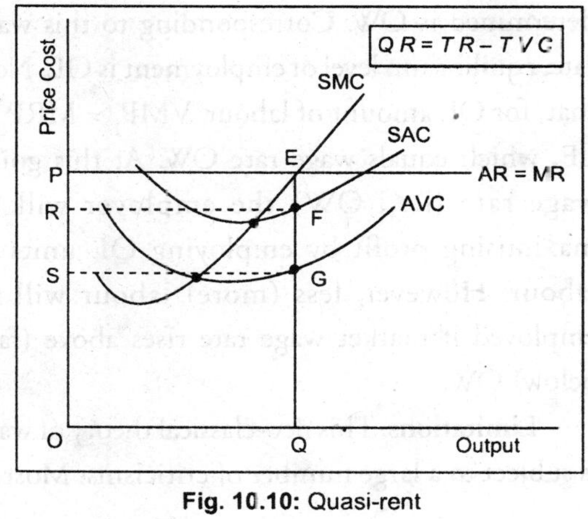

Fig. 10.10: Quasi-rent

and total revenue equals total variable costs, quasi-rent vanishes in the long run. Thus, quasi-rent is the reward of man-made inputs whose supplies are fixed in the short run. We can explain quasi-rent in terms of Fig. 10.10.

At a price OP, the firm is in equilibrium at point E. It produces thus OQ units of output. Total revenue is OPEQ, while return to the variable input is OSGQ. Thus, quasi-rent is OPEQ – OSGQ = SGEP. At output OQ, since the firm incurs a fixed cost of RFGS, it enjoys profit of RFEP amount. This excess profit is the difference between quasi-rent and total fixed cost i.e.,

$$QR = TFC + \text{excess profit}$$

$$\text{or} \quad QR = SGFR + RFEP$$

In the long run, the firm earns only normal profit and quasi-rent then becomes zero.

10.14. WAGE DETERMINATION

How is the wage rate determined? Economists have travelled a long way in this direction. Classical economists put forward theories free from any validity in the real world. These are: (i) *subsistence theory of wage,* (ii) *standard of living theory of wage,* (iii) *wage-fund theory,* and (iv) *residual claimant theory.* With the discovery of the neo-classical marginal productivity theory of distribution in the late 1890s, all the classical theories went into disrepute.

10.14.1 Marginal Productivity Theory of Wage

The marginal productivity theory of wage states that price of labour i.e., wage rate is determined according to the marginal product of labour. This was stated by neo-classical economist, especially J. B. Clark, in the late 1890s. The term marginal product of labour is interpreted here in three ways: marginal physical product of labour (symbolised by MPP_L), value of the marginal product of labour (symbolised by VMP_L) and marginal revenue product of labour (symbolised by MRP_L). When marginal product of labour is expressed in money terms we obtain VMP_L. MRP_L is the change in total revenue following a change in the employment of labour. Marginal productivity theory of wage states that wage of labour equals VMP_L (= MRP_L). Employer will employ labour up to the point until market wage equals labour's value of the marginal product and marginal revenue product.

Assumptions: Following are the important assumptions of this theory:

- Perfect competition prevails in goods market and in labour market. Perfect competition in goods market implies that goods produced are homogeneous and the price of the goods is given for all firms in the market. Perfect competition in labour market also implies that labour as well as firms behave as 'wage-taker's. No one can influence the wage rate. Consequently, labour supply curve, S_L, becomes perfectly elastic. Since wage rate does not change, labour supply curve incidentally becomes the average cost curve of labour (AC_L), and it coincides with the marginal cost curve of labour (MC_L).
- Law of variable proportions operates.
- The firm aims at profit maximisation.
- All labourers are homogeneous and are divisible.
- Labour is mobile and is substitutable to capital.
- Resources are fully employed.

Wage rate will be determined by the interaction of demand and supply curves of labour in the market. Labour demand curve is explained by the VMP_L curve. Since perfect competition exists in the product market, VMP_L curve coincides with the MRP_L curve. VMP_L = MRP_L curve is the firm's demand curve for labour. This curve slopes downwards because of diminishing marginal returns. In Fig. 10.11, $VMP_L = MRP_L = D_L$ represents a firm's demand curve for labour.

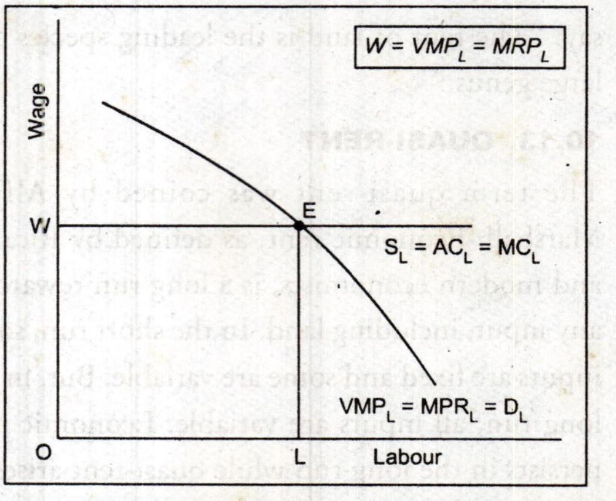

Fig. 10.11: MP Theory of Wage Determination

Further, as perfect competition exists in the labour market, the labour supply, $S_L = AC_L = MC_L$, curve has been drawn perfectly elastic.

In Fig. 10.11, E is the equilibrium point since, at this point, labour demand equals labour supply. The equilibrium wage rate thus determined is OW. Corresponding to this wage rate, equilibrium level of employment is OL. Note that, for OL amount of labour, $VMP_L = MRP_L$ is LE, which equals wage rate OW. At this going wage rate (i.e., OW) the employer will be maximising profit by employing OL units of labour. However, less (more) labour will be employed if market wage rate rises above (falls below) OW.

Limitations: This neo-classical theory of wage is subject to a large number of criticisms. Most of the criticisms of this theory are directed against the assumptions. Most of the assumptions are unrealistic. The main criticisms are explained below :

- In the real world, perfect competition does not exist both in product market and in labour market. Imperfect competition is found in all the markets. This theory, therefore, has the limited applicability in the real world. If it is applied to the imperfectly competitive market, worker will be subject to exploitation.
- Labour can never be homogeneous—some may be skilled and some may be unskilled. Wage rate of a worker is greatly influenced by the quality of labour. A higher wage rate is enjoyed by the skilled labour compared to the unskilled labour. This simple logic has been totally ignored by the authors of this theory.
- Perfect mobility of labour is another unrealistic assumption. Mobility of labour may be restricted due to socio-political reasons.
- The marginal productivity theory of wage ignores supply side of labour and concentrates only on the demand for labour. It is said that labour is demanded because labour is productive. But why labour is supplied cannot be answered in terms of this theory. This is because of the fact that, at a given wage rate, any amount of labour is supplied. But, we know that higher the wage rate higher is the supply of labour. This positive wage-labour supply relationship has been ignored by the makers of this theory.
- Full employment of resources is another unrealistic assumption.
- This theory, in fact, is not a wage theory but a theory of employment. Wage rate is pre-determined. At the given wage rate OW, how many units of labour are supplied can be known from this theory. In this sense, it is a theory of employment and not a theory of wages.
- Finally, this theory ignores the usefulness of trade union in wage determination. Trade union through its collective bargaining power, also influences wage rate in favour of the members of the organisation.

In view of all these criticisms, the marginal productivity theory of wages has become useless.

10.15. MEANING OF INTEREST

Capital is a produced factor of production. Interest is the rate of return over capital. Just as the price of land is rent, so interest is the price of capital. To calculate the return on capital or income going to capital, one must remember that interest represents the cost of capital. Usually, money is borrowed for purchasing capital. Interest can, therefore, be defined as the price of purchased capital. Again, a firm may finance its investment project from its own sources of funds. Economists consider opportunity cost of capital. Again, a firm may finance its investment project from its own sources of funds. Economists consider opportunity cost of capital. The interest that the firm could have obtained by lending his money to someone else is called the opportunity cost. Capital will leave firms if the rate of return on capital falls below the opportunity cost. Anyway, we consider now interest as the rate earned on capital invested. Before discussing how interest is determined we must clarify the concepts of gross interest and net interest.

10.15.1. Gross Interest and Net Interest

Interest paid on borrowed funds includes (i) risk of non-repayment of loan, (ii) administrative charges (i.e., cost of maintaining accounts), (iii) the opportunity cost for not using own money. The interest charged by the lender includes all these elements. Such interest payment is called gross interest. If these elements are deducted from gross interest, we obtain net or pure interest. Net interest is, thus, the price of capital or the rate of return earned on capital invested.

A lender is always supposed to demand a high rate of interest to cover the risk of non payment or default—the whole of the interest rate cannot be the price of loans. In other words, gross interest includes the reward for risktaking. Similarly, a lender always maintains accounts of borrowers. He may even have to maintain an office for that purpose. Since this administrative function is performed by the lender, he should include such administrative expenses for management while determining gross interest rate. Further, there is an opportunity cost for not using money. Whenever an individual gives loan to someone else he scarifies his present consumption or undergoes the inconveniences for not spending money for himself. This is the opportunity cost for not using own money. Interest is the price of such inconveniences. Sometimes, gross interest may include a monopoly element. A moneylender in a locality may enjoy some sort of monopoly element. A moneylender in a locality may enjoy some sort of monoploy power and, hence, may demand a high rate of interest (e.g., village moneylenders, mahajans, seths etc.).

Pure or net interest is the price for the use of capital only. Lender charges more than pure interest. When 'more' is added to pure interest, we get gross interest. Thus, gross interest =

reward for risk of non-payment + reward for administrative function + opportunity cost + monopoly element + pure interest.

10.16. THEORIES OF INTEREST RATE DETERMINATION

Economists are not unanimous regarding the determination of interest rate. In the classical tradition, rate of interest is determined by the demand for and supply of capital. To the classical economists, it is the real factors that determine the rate of return on capital invested. In contrast to the classical ideas, neo-classical economists hold that the rate of interest is determined by the demand for, and supply of, loanable funds. Neo-classical theory concentrates on both real and monetary forces in the interest rate determination. Keynes viewed interest from the monetary side alone. According to him, rate of interest is determined purely by demand for, and supply of money, rather than other forms of wealth. His theory is known as liquidity preference theory. Now we will discuss all these theories.

10.16.1. Classical Theory or Real Interest Rate Determination

Regarding the nature of interest, classicists were not unanimous. They regarded the nature and the determinants of the rate of interest in terms of a more complex pattern. Some classical economists like A. Marshall, N. W. Senior, Bohm-Bawerk, I. Fisher, etc., viewed interest from the supply side of capital i.e., saving. On the other hand, economists like J. B. Clark explained the nature of interest from the viewpoint of the demand for capital i.e., investment. Since demand for and supply of capital are composed of real factors, classical theory is regarded as the real interest rate theory.

• **Supply of Capital or Saving**: According to N. W. Senior, saving involves a sacrifice. People abstain from consumption. Since abstinence involves a sacrifice, savers must be rewarded in the form of interest. This is called abstinence theory of interest. Because of criticism made by Karl Marx against the concept of abstinence, Marshall substituted the term 'waiting' for abstinence. Marshall's theory is regarded as the 'waiting theory or interest. According to this theory, whenever money is lent by an individual he has to wait to get back his money. As he 'waits' for future he has to be given interest. Thus, interest is the price for waiting. Higher the interest, higher is the period of waiting. In other words, people will save more if they are rewarded more. Thus, supply of capital comes from saving.

Bohm-Bawerk, Fisher, etc., provided another theory that also governs the supply of capital. Their theories are popularly known as 'time preference theory of interest.' According to them, as people prefer current consumption over future consumption, they become impatient to spend

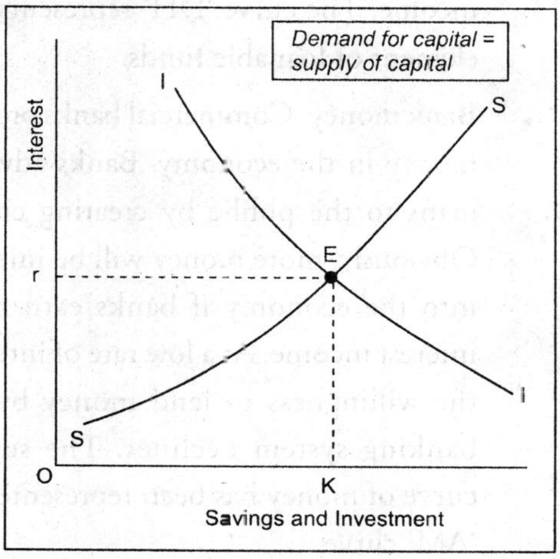

Fig. 10.12: Classical Theory

money now. To make future consumption more profitable, an individual must be given inducement in the form of interest income.

Thus, supply of capital is dependent on real or psychological factors like (i) abstinence, (ii) waiting, and (iii) time preference. Obviously, higher the rate of interest greater is the volume of savings. In other words, saving or supply of capital is directly related to the rate of interest. Thus, the saving function becomes

$$S = f(r)$$

• **Demand for Capital or Investment**: The principle of marginal productivity can be employed in determining the volume of investment. Like other inputs, capital has marginal productivity. According to the marginal productivity theory of capital, which is a part of marginal productivity theory of distribution, price of capital is determined in accordance with the marginal revenue product. Marginal revenue product of capital or demand for capital or investment will rise if the rate of interest declines. Investment demand is inversely related to the rate of interest. Thus, investment function becomes

$$I = f(r)$$

Since supply of capital or saving function is positively related to the interest, the saving curve SS has been drawn upward sloping in Fig. 10.12. Investment curve II has been drawn downward sloping. Equilibrium rate of interest is determined at point E — the point at which investment and saving curve intersect each other. Or is the equilibrium rate of interest which brings savings (OK) into balance with investment (OK).

Criticisms: Classical theory of interest rate determination has come in for sharp criticisms:

• This theory is based on full employment assumption. But, what we find in reality is the unemployment or under-employment of resources. Classical theory does not work below full employment.

- Keynes charged the classical theory as an indeterminate one. According to Keynes, saving depends on income level. There will be different saving schedules at different income levels. As income rises saving curve shifts upward. Thus, we cannot know the position of the saving curve unless we know the level of income and, if we do not know the volume of savings, we cannot determine interest rate. Thus, interest rate remains indeterminate if the level of income is not known. But we do not know the level of income without knowing the interest rate because it is the rate of interest that brings about a change in investment and income level. Hence the indeterminacy in the interest rate.
- Finally, according to Keynes, rate of interest is determined by the monetary factors rather than by real factors.

10.16.2. Neo-classical Theory or Loanable Funds Theory

An improved version of classical interest rate theory was provided by neo-classical economists like K. Wicksell, D. H. Robertson. This theory has come to be known as the loanable funds theory. This theory holds that the rate of interest, like any other price is determined by the demand for and the supply of loanable funds. This theory further holds that the rate of interest is not determined alone either by real factors as assumed by the classicists or by monetary factors as assumed by Keynes. In fact, both real and monetary factors determine interest rate.

Now we consider sources of supply of and demand for loanable funds.

- **Supply of Loanable Funds** : By loanable funds we mean money available for lending in financial markets. There are three sources of supply of loanable funds : (a) savings, (b) dishoarding of money from past savings, and (c) bank created money.
  - **Savings:** Households and firms supply loanable funds in the capital market out of their savings. Savings are the surplus over consumption. This theory assumes that given the level of income, savings vary directly with the rate of interest. In Fig. 10.13, savings have been represented by the 'S' curve which is interest-elastic.
  - **Dishoarding from past savings:** Individuals hoard cash from their previous incomes. If now these hoarded wealth are dishoarded, idle money (i.e. hoarded money) now becomes active money and, therefore, supply of loanable funds rises. If more interest is given people will be induced to dishoard their wealth in order to earn more interest income. The curve 'DH' represents this element of loanable funds.
  - **Bank money**: Commercial banks provide money in the economy. Banks advance loans to the public by creating credit. Obviously, more money will be injected into the economy if banks earn more interest income. At a low rate of interest, the willingness to lend money by the banking system declines. The supply curve of money has been represented by 'ΔM' curve.

By lateral summation of all these sources of loanable funds, we obtain total supply of loanable funds in the financial markets :

$$S_{Lf} = S + DH + \Delta M$$

where S_{Lf} represents supply of loanable funds. The curve S_{Lf} is the supply curve of loanable funds. This curve has an upward slope indicating that its volume rises as interest rate rises.

- **Demand for Loanable Funds**: Like supply of loanable funds, demand for loanable funds arises from three sources. They are: (a) investment, (b) dis-saving, and (c) hoarding.
  - **Investment**: In the loanable funds theory, investment demand is governed by the marginal revenue productivity of capital. Since the productivity curve has a negative slope, investment demand is inversely related to the rate of interest. The 'I' curve represents this element of demand for money.
  - **Dis-saving**: Demand for loanable funds arises from consumption. People take loans to finance their consumption activities. Dis-saving or consumption is inversely related to the rate of interest. 'DS' curve represents this element of demand for loanable funds.
  - **Hoarding**: Hoarding is another source of demand for loanable funds. Demand for hoarding money arises from preference for liquidity or in short, liquidity preference. As liquid cash is attractive, people hoard money. Demand for hoarding money also depends on the interest rate. At a higher rate of interest, willingness to hoard money on the part of individuals, business firms, etc. declines while willingness to lend money rises. Such relationship between hoarding of money and interest is depicted by the curve 'H' in the Fig. 10.13.

By summing up all these sources of demand for loanable funds we obtain total demand for loanable funds. Thus,

$$D_{Lf} = I + DS + H$$

where D_{Lf} represents total demand for loanable funds. The curve D_{Lf} represents this.

In Fig. 10.13, DH, ΔM and S curves are upward sloping curves showing a positive relationship between them and interest rate. When all these elements are added together we get positive sloping S_{Lf} curve. Similarly, negative sloping D_{Lf} curve has been drawn on the basis of summation of DS, H and I curves. These two curves intersect each other at point E and the equilibrium rate of interest, thus, determined is 'Or'. The interest rate brings demand for and supply of loanable funds in balance.

Limitations: One of the chief merits of this neo-classical loanable funds theory is that it is an improvement over the classical theory of interest rate determination. Unlike the classical theory, it does not include only savings as the source of loanable funds. Further, it considers monetary factors like bank money and dishoarding as the two major sources of loanable supply of funds. Keynesian interest rate theory is purely a monetary theory. Neo-classical loanable funds theory again scores marks over the Keynesian theory as this theory emphasises on real factors, such as savings, marginal productivity of capital or investment to determine interest rate. But this does not mean that this theory is fault-free. It has too certain strongest limitations. These are the following :

- Like the classical theory, this theory assumes a fixed money income. Given

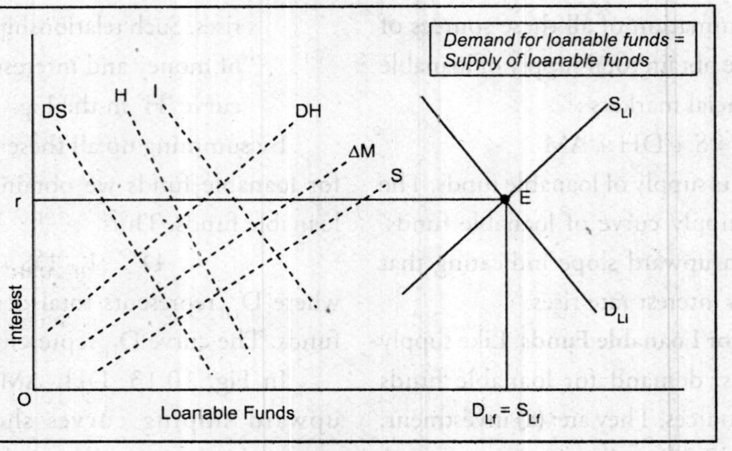

Fig. 10.13: Neo-classical Theory

income, a change in interest rate brings about a change in the savings and investment. As interest rate rises, saving rises. But, Keynes argued that an increase in interest rate means a fall in investment. Fall in investment leads to a fall in income and hence ultimately fall in savings.

- Keynes charged this theory on the ground that, like the classical theory, it cannot provide a determinate solution to the interest rate determination. Without knowing the income level the supply of loanable funds remains unknown, and without knowing the supply of loanable funds rate of interest remains indeterminate. In other words, we cannot determine the rate of interest unless we know the level of income. Hence indeterminacy.
- The theory is based on unrealistic assumption of full employment of resources.
- Saving in modern days is often influenced by habit and custom as well as security, irrespective of the rate of interest. However, this theory assumes a direct relationship between saving and interest.

In view of these reasons, the loanable funds theory has little to say in policy formulation.

10.16.3. Keynes' Liquidity Preference Theory

The determinants of the equilibrium interest rate in the classical model are the "real" factors or the supply of saving and the demand for investment. On the other hand, in the Keynesian analysis, determinants of the interest rate are the "monetary" factors. Keynes' analysis concentrates on the demand for, and supply of, money as the determinants of interest rate. According to Keynes, the rate of interest is purely "a monetary phenomenon." Interest is the price paid for borrowed funds. People like to keep cash with them rather than investing cash in assets. Thus, there is a preference for liquid cash. People, out of their income, intend to save a part. How much of their resources will be held in the form of cash and how much will be spent depend upon what Keynes calls 'liquidity preference'. Cash being the most liquid asset, people prefer cash. And interest is the reward for parting with liquidity. However, the rate of interest in the Keynesian theory is determined by the demand for money and supply of money.

• **Demand for Money**: By demand for money, we mean demand to hold an asset. The desire for liquidity or demand for money arises because of three motives : (a) transaction motive, (b) precautionary motive, and (c) speculative motive.

• **Transaction demand for money**: Money is needed for day-to-day transactions. As there is a gap between the receipt of income and spending money is demanded. Since payments or spending are made throughout a period and receipts or incomes are received after a period of time, an individual needs 'active balance' in the form of cost to finance his/her transactions. This is known as transaction demand for money which directly depends on the level of income of an individual and businesses. Symbolically,

$$T_{dm} = f(Y),$$

where T_{dm} stands for transaction demand for money and Y stands for income.

• **Precautionary demand for money**: Future is uncertain. That is why people hold cash balances to meet unforeseen contingencies, like death, accidents, danger of unemployment etc., The amount of money held under this motive called 'idle balances'—also depends on the level of income of an individual. The relationship between precautionary demand for money (P_{dm}) and the volume of income is normally direct. Thus,

$$P_{dm} = f(Y)$$

• **Speculative demand for money**: This sort of demand for money is really Keynes' contribution. The speculative motive refers to the desire to hold one's assets in liquid form to take advantages of market movements regarding the uncertainty and expectation of future changes in the rate of interest. The cash held under this motive is used to make speculative gains by dealing in bonds and securities whose prices and rate of interest fluctuate inversely. If bond prices are

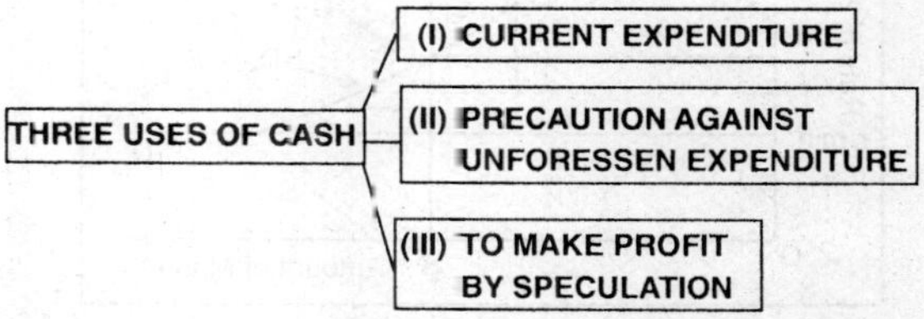

expected to rise (or the rate of interest is expected to fall) people will now buy bonds and sell when their prices rise to have a capital gain. In such a situation, bond is more attractive than cash. Contrarily, if bond prices are expected to fall (or the rate of interest is expected to rise) in future people will now sell bonds to avoid capital loss. In such a situation, cash is more attractive than bond. Thus, at a low rate of interest liquidity preference is high and at a high rate of interest securities are attractive. Now, it is clear that the speculative demand for money (S_{dm}) varies inversely with the rate of interest. Thus,

$$S_{dm} = f(r)$$

where 'r' is the rate of interest.

• **Total demand for money** : The total demand for money (D_M) is the sum of all three types of demand for money. That is, $D_M = T_{dm} + P_{dm} + S_{dm}$. The demand for money has a negative slope because of the inverse relationship between the speculative demand for money and the rate of interest. However, the negative sloping liquidity preference curve becomes perfectly elastic at a low rate of interest. According to Keynes, there is a floor interest rate below which rate of interest

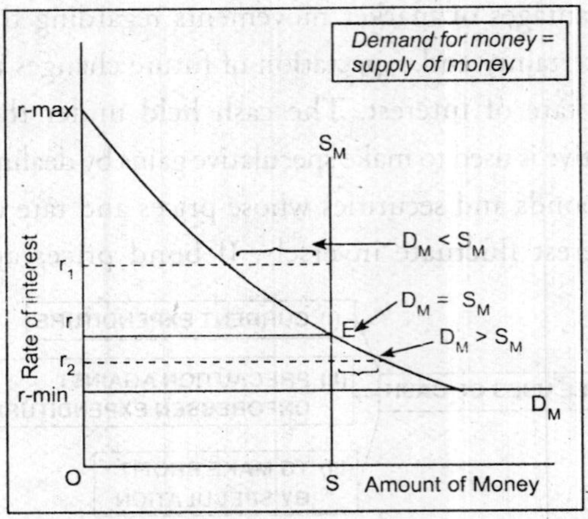

Fig. 10.19: Keynesian Theory

cannot fall. This minimum rate of interest indicates absolute liquidity preference of the people. This is what Keynes called 'liquidity trap'. In Fig. 10.14, D_M is the liquidity preference curve. At minimum rate of interest, *r-min,* the curve is perfectly elastic. However, there is a ceiling of interest rate, say *r-max,* above which it cannot rise. Thus, interest rate fluctuates between *r-max* and *r-min.*

- **Money Supply**: The supply of money in a particular period depends upon the policy of the central bank of a country. Money supply curve, S_M, has been drawn perfectly inelastic.

- **Determination of the Rate of Interest**: According to Keynes, rate of interest is determined by the demand for money and supply of money. OS is the total amount of money supplied by the central bank. At point E, demand for money becomes equal to the supply of money. Thus, the equilibrium interest rate is determined at 'Or'. Now, suppose rate of interest is greater than 'Or'. In such a situation supply of money will exceed the demand for money. People will purchase more securities. Consequently, its price will rise and interest rate will fall until demand for money becomes equal to the supply of money.

On the other hand, if the rate of interest becomes less than 'Or', demand for money will exceed the supply of money, people will sell their securities. Price of securities will tumble and the rate of interest will rise until we reach point E.

Thus, the rate of interest is determined by the monetary variables only.

Limitations: Keynes' liquidity preference theory is also not free from criticisms.

First like the classical and neo-classical theories, Keynes' theory is an indeterminate one. Keynes charged the classical theory on the ground that it assumed the level of employment fixed. Same criticism applies to Keynes since he assumes a given level of income. Keynes' theory suggests that D_M and S_M determine the rate of interest. Without knowing the level of income we cannot know the transaction demand for money as well as speculative demand for money. Obviously, as income changes, liquidity preference schedule changes, leading to a change in the interest rate. Therefore, one cannot determine the rate of interest until the level of income is known, and the level of income cannot be determined until the rate of interest is known. Hence indeterminacy. Hicks and Hansen solved this problem in their IS-LM analysis by determining simultaneously the rate of interest and the level of income.

Secondly, Keynes committed an error in rejecting real factors as the determinants of interest rate determination.

Thirdly, Keynes' theory gives a choice between holding risky bonds and riskless cash. An individual holds either bond or cash, and never both. In the real world, it is the uncertainty or risk that induces an individual to hold both. This gap in Keynes' theory has been filled up by James Tobin. In fact, today people make a choice between a variety of assets.

Conclusion: Despite these criticisms, Keynes' liquidity preference theory tells a lot on income, output and employment of a country. His basic purpose was to demonstrate that a capitalist economy can never reach full employment due to the existence of the liquidity trap. Though the liquidity trap has been over-emphasised by Keynes, yet he demolished the classical conclusion —the goal of full employment. Further, his theory has an important policy implication. A central bank is incapable of reviving a capitalistic economy during depression because of the liquidity trap. In other words, monetary policy is useless during depressionary phase of an economy.

10.17. DEFINITION OF PROFIT

It is the profit that motivates an enprepreneur to undertake business. In a market economy, this profit motive serves as an incentive in allocating resources in the production of a commodity in accordance with the needs and tastes of the buyers as well as the society as a whole. Profit is the reward that goes to the entrepreneur. Since the entrepreneur is in charge of an enterprise he must get profit as his income.

Profit is generally understood as the difference between total revenue received after the sale of the product and total expenses incurred for producing the product. Profit, thus obtained, is called gross profit. Gross profit is a mixed income. It includes certain elements which are not really profit at all. When these certain elements are deducted we obtain profit or pure profit. In economics, by profit we mean net or pure profit.

Gross profit includes: (i) rent on land, (ii) interest on capital. (iii) wages of management, (iv) other things like depreciation charges, insurance charges.

Gross profit includes rent on land supplied by the organiser himself. The rent—which entrepreneur's own land would have earned had it been leased to someone else—cannot form pure profit. Similarly, interest on own capital rather than borrowed capital is not to be taken into account while estimating net profit. Likewise, remuneration of reward as a manager of one's own business enterprise must not form a part of net profit. In other words, expenses incurred for all these owned resources of an entrepreneur form implicit costs. In addition, the firm hires land, labour, capital, etc., from different resources. The costs for hiring these resources are called explicit costs. Total cost is the sum-total of both explicit and implicit costs. Now, gross profit is the difference between total revenue and only explicit costs. Net or pure profit is measured by the difference between total revenue and both explicit and implicit costs.

Pure or net profit, therefore, includes (i) the reward for undertaking risk, (ii) the monopoly gain, (iii) the fortuitous or chance gain, (iv) income from exploiting consumers and labour, (v) the reward of innovation, etc.

10.18. DISTINGUISHING FEATURES OF PROFIT

Profit differs from other factor earnings (i.e., rent, wage and interest) in the following ways:

- Rent, wage and interest are all contractual incomes since these are paid in accordance with the agreement or contracts made between the parties. Profit, on the other hand, is a residual income. After the payment made for contractual income, if there is any surplus, the entrepreneur will receive that. An entrepreneur—being the boss of any organisation—must become the residual claimant. There is no guarantee that an ordinary shareholder will receive dividend income arising out of profit of a business firm. As such, there is no contractual obligation on the part of a company to pay dividend to an ordinary shareholder.

- Being contractual income, rent, wage and interest can never be zero or negative. But, profit may be zero or negative.
- Profit fluctuates rather more widely than the income of other factors of production. Rent, interest and wages fluctuate rather steadily. But, profit may change violently whenever economic conditions change.
- Rent, interest and wage form a part of cost of production. A firm has to meet this cost if it wants to stay in business. If it fails to meet this cost or cannot pay dividend to its shareholders, it will have to go out of business in the long run. Since (net) profit is a surplus income it does not form cost of production.

10.19. HOW PROFITS ARE DETERMINED?

Profit income is something peculiar income since it is a mixed income or a hotchpotch income. In view of this, we find many theories regarding the emergence of profit. Various theories have been propounded because economists are not unanimous regarding the nature of profit. Some of the theories that have become obsolete over time are (i) *Walker's Rent Theory of Profit,* (ii) *Taussig's Wage Fund Theory of Profit,* (iii) *J. B. Clark's Dynamic Theory of Profit,* and (iv) *Marginal Productivity Theory of Profit.* In addition, Schumpeter has given us an *Innovation Theory of Profit.* We will discuss, in brief, all these theories.

10.19.1. Rent Theory of Profit

Rent theory of profit—as developed by Francis L. Walker—says that pure or net profit is the rent of ability. Just as land is heterogeneous in quality, entrepreneurs are also of different qualities. Rent arises due to differences in productivity of lands. Rent arises in the case of superior or intra-superior land. Rent does not arise in the case of marginal land. According to Walker, this is also true of entrepreneurs. Some entrepreneurs, say superior ones, earn profit while inferior or marginal entrepreneurs do not earn any profit. Thus, profit is attributed to the differences in ability. Like rent, profit is a differential surplus which accrues to the superior or intra-superior entrepreneurs.

Criticisms

- Profit may arise due to differences in ability. But profit may arise due to monopoly, innovation, risk, etc. Walker ignores all these elements.
- Walker's logic is not convincing when he says that the marginal entrepreneurs are non-profit earners and therefore profit does not enter into price. In economics, normal profit is included in the cost of production and therefore enters into price.
- The concept of no-profit entrepreneurs as envisaged by Walker is rather an unrealistic one. Profit is the best guide for an entrepreneur to stay in business. If marginal entrepreneurs do not get profit, what is their incentive to stay in business. They should shut down their businesses. This does not happen in real world.

- In modern business, there has been a separation of ownership from management. Owners or the shareholders earn dividends—whether they are superior or not. So, profit is not the result of rent of ability even if the sleeping shareholders get profit in the form of dividends.
- *Finally,* profit is the result of managerial function. An organiser is supposed to manage, coordinate various functions. But, at the same time, the organiser undertakes risk. Profit arises because organiser undertakes risk. This important function has been ignored by Walker.

In view of all these criticisms, there is not a single believer of this theory.

10.19.2. Wages Fund Theory

Davenport and Taussig's name are associated with the wage funds theory. According to Taussig, profits are regarded as simply a form of wages. They accrue to the entrepreneur on account of his special ability. Therefore, profit is not a chance income; it arises due to special skill possessed by the entrepreneur. As skill is the characteristic of labour, profits of the entrepreneurs should be regarded as wages. Since an entrepreneur is a special class of factor of production, he must receive profit.

Criticisims

- This theory finds an equivalence between wages and profit. But, we know that wages are earned income—the result of toil and work; while profit is the result of a variety of things, including a 'chance'.
- Workers get wages so long as they work. But profit is an uncertain income. It may be zero or even negative.
- Shareholders, without performing any economic function, earn profit. This theory cannot explain this phenomenon.
- Profit may arise due to (i) imperfection, (ii) innovation, (iii) risk taking, etc. Walker did not appreciate these elements.

In view of these criticisms, one can label this theory as a highly unsatisfactory theory.

10.19.3. Dynamic Theory of Profit

J. B. Clark propounded that profit arises in a dynamic society. In other words, profit does not arise in a static economy. A stationary economy is characterised by unchanged size of population, supply of capital, the methods of production, the organisation of business, etc. Thus, a static economy is a changeless economy. According to Clark, five generic changes go on, everyone of which reacts on the structure of society. In a dynamic state, population increases, capital increases, methods of production change or improve, forms of business organisation change, quantity and quality of human wants change. We know that profit is a surplus beyond full cost of production. It is defined as the difference between selling price and, hence, total revenue and total cost. In a changeless economy, there does not occur any difference between revenue and cost; price tends to equal cost. Consequently, profit disappears. Profit is, thus, the result of five dynamic changes.

Criticisms

- There is no guarantee that a dynamic society always earns profit. We live in a changing world where variety of changes take place. Under the circumstances, one finds lot of loosing firms. So, profits are not to be attributed to changes alone.

- Clark emphasises too much on changes and neglects managerial function of an entrepreneur. An efficient manager may earn profit if he performs his functions efficiently. So, profit is the result of entrepreneurial function.
- No economy is a static one. An efficient innovative entrepreneur always brings about a change. Obviously, profit will arise. It is to be remembered that all changes may not give rise to profit. Only those changes which are unpredictable may give rise to profit.
- Profit may arise due to risk-taking. Clark did not find any relation between risk-taking and profit.

10.19.4. Marginal Productivity Theory of Profit

Marginal productivity theory of distribution can be applied to any input, including entrepreneur. In other words, it is the marginal productivity that determines the reward of an entrepreneur. Profit is determined in accordance with the marginal revenue product of an entrepreneur. Greater the marginal revenue product, greater will be the profit.

Criticisms

- This theory is based on unrealistic assumptions of perfect competition, homogenuity of entrepreneurs, etc. If these assumptions are removed, marginal productivity theory of profit will break down. For instance, entrepreneurs differ in quality. For each entrepreneur there must be separate marginal revenue product. Profit thus determined involves inaccuracies.
- The theory fails to explain why does windfall profit or monopoly profit arise.
- This theory is a one-sided theory as it neglects the supply side of an entrepreneur.

Thus, marginal revenue product cannot determine the price of an entrepreneur. No entrepreneur can—consciously or unconsciously measure the marginal revenue product. In view of all these reasons, no one believes the theory.

10.19.5. Risk and Uncertainty Theory of Profit

- **Hawley's Risk Theory:** People go into business with the hope of getting profit. But the future is uncertain. In this uncertain world, nothing works out in accordance with the plans and targets the business makes. Business decisions are made and actions are taken. Because of uncertainty, such actions may be right and so profits may arise. If such actions prove to be worng, losses arise. Thus, profit is the consequence of uncertainty.

According to F. B. Hawley, the main function of an entrepreneur is to bear risk. Profit is the reward for undertaking risk. An entrepreneur produces goods in anticipation. If his anticipation goes alright then his currently produced goods could be sold in future. Otherwise, if his anticipation turns out to be false, he will have to suffer losses. This, in fact, is the risk in business. Obviously, an entrepreneur must be rewarded in the form of profit. Otherwise, he won't undertake any business. Risks vary from business to business. Greater the risks involved in any business undertaking, greater will be the profit.

However, this theory has been criticised on the following grounds. *Firstly,* some people think that the whole amount of profit is not due to risk. Occasionally, organiser reaps windfall gain not connected with risk. *Secondly,* risky business may not always ensure greater profit. It is the plastic surgeon who gets larger profit despite a minimum risk compared to an abdominal surgeon who is susceptible to larger risk. Ironically, it is the latter who gets smaller remuneration. *Thirdly*, an entrepreneur always tries to minimise his risk. In fact, minimisation of risk involves greater profit. *Fourthly*, all risks do not generate profit. Only non-insured risk generates profit. Non-insured risk arises due to uncertainty. Profit is the reward of uncertainty. Knight suggested this.

- **Knight's Uncertainty Theory**: F. H. Knight extended and modified Hawley's risk theory and finally provided uncertainty theory of profit. According to him, there are two types of risk. One is certain risk and another is uncertain risk. Risks which can be known beforehand are known as certain risks or foreseeable risks, such as the possibility of catching fire in a godown. This sort of risk can be avoided by insurance policy. Insurance companies are willing to bear this type of risk against premium. These risks do not cause the emergence of profit. On the other hand, there are certain risks which cannot be known earlier and, therefore, non-insurable. These risks are called uncertain risks e.g., change in fashion, innovation of new product, etc. Businessmen can never insure these risks since insurance companies do not come forward to undertake these risks even if a fantastic amount of premium is paid. These non-insured risks arise due to uncertainty. In other words, it is the uncertainty that causes the emergence of profit. Profit is the reward for bearing uncertainty. Knight also suggested that producers may experience negative profit. It is to be borne in mind that the 'market economy is a profit and loss economy'—such profit and loss can arise only in an uncertain world.

Criticisms: In the *first* place an entrepreneur's only function is not to bear uncertainty, though this theory claims so. Profit may arise due to organisational ability, innovation, etc. Knight did not consider these. *Secondly*, it is absolutely difficult to make a monetary measure of uncertainty. Naturally, amount of profit must remain indeterminate. *Thirdly*, profit may also arise due to imperfections of the market. This theory is silent in this respect. *Finally*, uncertainty is not only borne by organisers. Almost all factors of production face some sort of uncertainty.

10.19.6. Innovation Theory of Profit

J. Schumpeter is of the opinion that the main function of an entrepreneur is innovation. Profit is the result of innovation. A free enterprise capitalistic economy is characterised by perfect competition. In the long run perfectly competitive situation, economic profits tend to become zero. There cannot be pure profits. But, Schumpeter argues that even in the long run, source of competition never dries up. In addition to routine job, entrepreneurs always innovate. An innovation may consist of the introduction of a new product, a new method of production, the opening up of a new market, the discovery of a new source of raw materials, the introduction of a new method of production, and the carrying out of the new organisation of any industry like the creation of monopoly position, etc. As a result of these innovations, some entrepreneurs enjoy pure profit because of reduced cost of production. But, in the long run, other entrepreneurs imitate the innovations of earlier entrepreneurs or innovators, thereby reducing profit. Ultimately, profits tend to zero. But again, a newer innovation will appear and consequently, pure profit.

Criticisms : In the *first* place, Schumpeter emphasises on innovating function of an entrepreneur. But there are other functions of an entrepreneur for which profit may arise. Schumpeter ignores these factors. It provides only an incomplete explanation. *Secondly,* profit is due to risk-taking and uncertainty as has been emphasised by Hawley and Knight. Schumpeter does not regard risk-taking as the function of an entrepreneur.

Conclusion: So far, no satisfactory theory regarding the emergence of profit has come out. All the theories described above give an inadequate explanation of profit. Possibly, such differences in argument may be due to the peculiar nature of profit. It is said that profit is a mixed and vexed income. It is a hotch-potch income in the sense that profit is due to the interplay of various factors.

However, of all the theories given here, the risk-and-uncertainty bearing theory of profit seems to be the most popular.

QUESTIONS (WITH ANSWER-HINTS)

Long Questions (16 marks)

1. Critically discuss the marginal productivity theory of distribution.

   Or

   From the micro point of view, marginal productivity theory is a theory of employment, and from the macro point of view, it is a theory of input pricing. Explain the statement.

   Or

   Discuss the major features of the marginal productivity theory of distribution under conditions of perfect competition in the output market and input market.

   Ans. 10.6.

2. Price of any input is determined in accordance with the marginal product of that input. Critically examine the statement.

   Ans. 10.6.

3. Critically discuss Ricardo's rent theory.

   Ans. 10.8, 10.8.1 and Limitations.

4. Point out the essential differences between Ricardo's and the modern theory of rent.

   Ans. 10.11.

5. How does rent element enter in other factor incomes other than land income.?

   Ans. 10.12.

6. Critically examine the marginal productivity theory of wage determination.

   Ans. 10.14.1.

7. How is wage rate determined under imperfect competition? (C.U. 2007)

   Ans. 10.14.2.

8. Loanable funds theory of interest rate determination combines both the classical and Keynesian theory. Explain.

   Or

   How is the interest rate determined in the neo-classical theory?

   Ans. 10.17.2.

9. Critically examine the risk-and-uncertainty bearing theory of profit.

   Ans. 10.20.5.

Medium-sized Questions (8 marks)

1. Define MPP, VMP and MRP of a variable input with illustrations drawn from both perfect competition and imperfect competition.

   Ans. 10.2, 10.2.1.

2. (a) Under what conditions VMP = MRP and VMP > MRP? (b) An input demand is a derived demand. Explain.

   Ans. (a) 10.2.1, (b) 10.5.

3. How do you derive the demand for labour—both under perfect competition and monopoly when the firm uses only one variable input?

   Ans. 10.3 and 10.4.

4. Define economic rent as understood by Ricardo. How do you attribute economic rent to the scarcity of land?

   Ans. 10.7, 10.8 and 10.8.1.

5. Economic rent may arise due to differences in the fertility of land. Critically examine the statement.

   Ans. 10.8.2.

6. How is rent defined by modern economists? How do you explain that economic rent depends on the elasticity of supply of an input?

   Ans. 10.9.

   Or

   Explain the modern theory of rent. (C.U. 2007)

7. Define rent in the modern sense. Show that economic rent is due to the inelasticity of supply of any input.

   Ans. 10.9.

8. Rent is not peculiar to land; it can arise due to any input whose supply is (i) perfectly inelastic, (ii) less than infinity. Explain.

   Ans. 10.9.

9. Discuss the relationship between economic rent and price.

   Or

   Analyse that rent is price-determined but not price-determining.

   Ans. 10.10.

10. What is quasi-rent? How does quasi-rent arise?

    Or

    Show that quasi-rent is a temporary earning that arises due to the inelasticity in the supply of an input.

    Ans. 10.13.

11. What is interest? Distinguish between gross and net interest.

    Ans. 10.16 and 10.16.1.

12. Briefly discuss the classical theory of interest rate determination.

    Ans. 10.17.1.

13. Write a note on the monetary theory of interest rate determination.

    Or

    Discuss the statement that the rate of interest is determined by the demand for and supply of money.

    Or

    Critically examine Keynes' liquidity preference theory of interest rate determination.

    Ans. 10.17.3.

14. Distinguish between gross profit and net profit. How do you distinguish between profit and other factor incomes? (C.U. 2008)

    Ans. 10.18 and 10.19.

15. Write notes on (i) rent theory of rent, and (ii) wages fund theory of profit.

    Ans. (i) 10.20.1, (ii) 10.20.2.

16. Critically discuss (i) dynamic theory of profit, (ii) innovation theory of profit, and (iii) marginal productivity theory of profit.

    Ans. (i) 10.20.3, (ii) 10.20.6 and (iii) 10.20.4.

INDIAN BUSINESS ENVIRONMENT

11

INDIAN BUSINESS ENVIRONMENT

11.1. MICROECONOMIC AND MACRO-ECONOMIC ENVIRONMENT OF BUSINESS

Ours is a changing world where economic, political and social environments are changing faster than ever before, particularly with the onset of the 'information revolution' that occurred in the last quarter of the 20th century. Indeed, it has revolutionised the entire capitalist world. Anyway, business success or failure depends on how these changes are accommodated by the business decision-makers. Only by taking right decision, a business firm—a microeconomic unit—may achieve necessary goals and targets. Usually such decisions are made against the backdrop of competitive environment. In other words, this microeconomic decision-making is made in a microeconomic environment that involves the determination of prices, costs, revenues, and so on.

In this connection, one may note that micro-economic environment of business is a complex one. This is because of the fact that the environment of a business firm is largely influenced by the general, social, political and economic conditions of the larger system in which business firms operate. A country's socio-political arrangements, economic relation of the business firms with the government, capital market, etc., influence strongly on the business sector. This wider environment of business firm may be called 'macroeconomic environment.' In a macro-economy—a single firm is 'a minute part of the larger system'. But the macroeconomic environment, such as general inflation and unemployment, is beyond the control of the business firm. A business firm must take decisions in the light of macroeconomic environment. These external economic as well as non-economic factors are extremely complex and dynamic.

Business success, therefore, depends on how a business firm adapts to a changing, dynamic macroeconomy. Business managers can never overlook this macroeconomy environment. If firms pay attention to these wider external factors (i.e., wider domestic and international economies) and if all firms on average strike a better growth rate, national economy will ultimately grow. The ever-changing environment forces businesses regularly to review their operations and their business strategies so as to achieve their pre-determined as well as well-defined goals and objectives. If businesses remain ignorant about the changing envirronment of business then they will be left behind by their rivals and competitors. In earlier chapter, we were concerned with the microeconomic environment of business. The present and the rest of the chapters of this book are concerned with macroeconomic—i.e., Indian business environment—rather than economic environment of a business firm.

11.2. ELEMENTS OR COMPONENTS OF MACROECONOMIC ENVIRONMENT

Macroeconomic environment of business is complex as well as fast changing. Therefore, it is rather difficult to identify various aspects of macroeconomic environment. Indeed, all elements of macroeconomic environment are important. Here we want to identify those elements that affect the economy as a whole. In other words, we want to scan the essential components of macroeconomic environment of business and limit our focus on some of them. These components, however, are to be studied not in isolation since they are interrelated. Further, some of these elements are directly controlled by the government and/or indirectly affected by the economic policies of the government. In addition to this non-market institution like government, market forces also constitute an important element of macroeconomic environment of business. Political institutions like ideology of the political party in power, legal framework, etc., also have an important bearing on the environment of business in a macroeconomic setting. An appraisal of business environment thus demands discussion of economic, social, political, technological, legal, environmental, and ethical issues. All these parameters affect business environment. Business environment should also address the global nature of modern business. In brief, macroeconomic environment of business has reference to the broad characteristics of the economic system in which firms attempt to carry out their activities.

Thus, the basic component of macro-economic environment of business is the economic system or the institutional framework of the environment in which fundamental economic problems are solved. But, economic system alone cannot constitute macroeconomic environment of business since it encompasses a variety of things that assume great importance in decision-making in a wider plane. Global economic trends and developments in international economy arising out of WTO provisions, rules and regulations cannot be bypassed while viewing the macroeconomy. This is because of the fact that cross-border developments provide both opportunities and challenges to individuals, businesses and governments. All attempt to adjust to the dynamic global economy. In the process, some countries exert influence over other countries and assume international power. This, inevitably, however, results in strains and conflicts between nations which put a drag on the overall economic performance of a nation.

Since macroeconomic environment is a multi-faceted concept, its components are very wide and large. For analysis' sake, we group them into two: domestic environment of business, and international environment of business. With the huge growth of international business following deregulation, privatisation and globalisation, macroeconomic environment of a country has assumed greater significance. Domestic economy is now being married successfully to the global economy. Therefore, macroeconomic environment of an economy cannot help to ignore developments in global plane. The crucial components or building blocks of macroeconomic environment are summarised here under the general headings of

- Economic system,
- Anatomy of the economy,
- National economic planning,
- Economic policy instruments (such as fiscal policy, monetary policy, supply-side or demand-side policy, employment policy, external trade policy, rules and regulations governing business and trade, etc.).

It is, thus, clear that macroeconomic environment of a nation is studied under both physical and institutional framework of an economic environment. It is to be kept in mind that these components are not always mutually exclusive; rather, these elements overlap at different stages of development of an economy.

11.3. ANALYSING COMPONENTS OF INDIAN BUSINESS ENVIRONMENT

Now we intend to describe and analyse the above-said components of business environment in the light of India's macroeconomy.

11.3.1. Economic System

Economic activities are not uniform all over the world. Each economy has its own institutions, laws, rules and regulations that influence what is produced, how it is produced and who gets it. This is what is actually called economic system. Economic system, thus, is not uniform; it varies from country to country. Economic system ranges from free market capitalism to planned socialism and their variants.

Capitalism is the product of the Industrial Revolution of the mid-18th century. It is called a market economy or a *laissez-faire* economy as the institution of 'market' or 'price system' functions. Socialism as an economic system gained its strength in the first quarter of the last century (1917) when the erstwhile USSR embraced it. Socialist economy may be called a planned economy as it relies on planning mechanism—instead of market principles—to solve the basic economic problems. Meanwhile, under the impact of the Great Depression of the1930s, free market capitalism received the severest blow. To salvage the capitalist world, J. M. Keynes recommended the retention of capitalism with governmental interference. Such economic system is called mixed economy—a halfway house between capitalism and socialism. With the breakdown of the Soviet style socialism in the late 1980s, market principles with little public investment or governmental interference, mainly in social sectors, gained currency all over the world. Planning mechanism has received a backseat while market principles are put on the driver's seat. Anyway, even in this latest variant of mixed economic system, we find both planning and market mechanism to operate. The difference is only on the degree of use of planning mechanism.

Economic system that we find today in India can be designated as 'mixed economy'. When India got her political independence from foreign power on 15 August 1947, she accepted the socialist path of development with the state playing the major role. She adopted planning in 1951 and plans were implemented in the framework of a mixed economy under a strong interventionist state. Since economists at that time argued that 'market failure' was the rule, government had an important and bigger role. But, market mechanism had not been altogether given up as private sector was the biggest sector in terms of its contribution towards the national output. In fact, private sector was given adequate space to operate in keeping with the concept of mixed economy. However, the growth of India's private sector was subject to controls and regulations. India's mixed economy is, thus, characterised by a mixture of planning and market-determined price mechanism. It is an admixture of plan stimulus and control and market efficiency.

Mixed economy of the Indian variety is a planned economy in which public sector has to have an economic plan. In this planning process, the State allocates resources for the development of industry, agriculture, infrastructure, etc. Indian planning strategy of the early years (1951-1990) came to be known as Nehru-Mahalanobis strategy that continued up to 1980s. This planning strategy received a big jolt in the early 1990s when (P.V. Narsimha) Rao-(Monmohan) Singh model of planning strategy was introduced against the backdrop of unprecedented crises—an IMF-World Bank model based on the free market economy.

Now we will spell out some of the policy instruments that were designed and adopted in the initial years of the planned regime. The most important policy instrument is the Industrial Policy clearly indicating the areas of operation of the state and of the private sector. The first Industrial Policy Resolution of 1948 made it clear that India was going to have a mixed economy. The principal instruments of 1948 Industrial Policy and subsequent industrial policies announced from time to time are: Industries (Development and Regulation) Act 1951, the Monopolies and Restrictive Trade Practices Act, 1969 (MRTP), the Foreign Exchange Regulation Act (FERA) of 1973, and various other legislative and regulative controls and regulations. Since 'market failure' argument prevailed at that time, the expanding role of the state was the hallmark of India's mixed economy principle. Participation of the state in various economic activities demanded nationalisation. As a result, the size of the public sector became enormous—its tentacles could be felt everywhere.

But, there occurred a dilution in the mixed economy philosophy in mid-1991 when the reversal of this policy took place. From a controlled regime, India switched over to an uncontrolled regime. Through privatisation, the state has been withdrawing from various direct production of goods and services except in the areas of basic and social infrastructures, 'leaving the rest of the production economy to the animal spirits of the private entrepreneurs'.

11.3.2. Anatomy and Functioning of the Economy

So far, we concentrated on institutional framework of India's macroeconomic environment which focusses on the role and status of public and private sectors, small and large business houses cooperatives and multinational/transnational corporations, etc. We are now in a position to discuss the structural features of the Indian business environment.

By structure of Indian economic environment we mean an interrelationship between different sectors of the economy i.e., primary, secondary and tertiary sectois. These three sectors constitute the structure of the Indian economy. As economic growth takes place, structural changes occur. For a complete understanding of the anatomy and the functioning of the Indian economy, we consider the primary, secondary, and tertiary sectors. As economic growth occurs, interrelationship among these sectors undergo changes. Such changes are called structural changes.

Economic development brings about a change in the structure of national output and occupations. For instance, at the time of independence, India was basically an agrarian economy as it contributed more than 55 p.c. of its GDP. Now, its contribution has declined to one-fifth (19.4 p.c. in 2007-08) of GDP. This is a sign of structural change. There has also been a change in India's industrial structure where we find the predominance of consumption goods—mainly durable goods—sector. Economic development, however, necessiates the growth of the capital goods sector.

Employment pattern has, however, not changed significantly over the last 60 years or so. Today (as per 2001 census), slightly more than 56 p.c. of the total population are engaged in the primary sector. One hundred years ago in 1900, it was 72 p.c. or so. This indicates stationary occupational pattern.

These structural changes are accompanied with the change in the structure of productivity. In the industrial sector, labour productivity is higher than the agricultural sector.

India's structural changes are also associated with changes in the structure of foreign trade. One easily finds that the structure of Indian exports has undergone a remarkable change. There has been a steady decline in the share of agricultural raw materials and allied products in the total exports and, in its place, exports of non-traditional items are on the rise. Pattern of imports has also changed a lot. Such structural change takes place with the change in the strategy of growth. The share of capital goods in total imports rose from 20.2. p.c. in 1950-51 to 45.5 p.c. in 1956-66. After then with a change in policy shift, the share of capital goods declined to 15.8 p.c. in 2005-06. Between 1950-51 and 2005-06, the share of raw materials and intermediate goods in the total imports rose from 54 p.c. to nearly 60 p.c. Anyway, the country exports manufactured goods, while imports raw materials, intermediate goods and capital goods.

In describing the anatomy and the functioning of the Indian economy we must not ignore two other sectors—the infrastructure sector and the social sector. As far as India is concerned, these two sectors, upon which the edifice of the economy stands, are rather the neglected sectors. With the introduction of new economic policy measures in mid-1991, deliberate and conscious efforts are being made to upgrade infrastructure sectors to tone up economic efficiency. To make economic efficiency a meaningful one, social equity and justice have to be ensured. Because of the existence of private ownership over the means of production, one finds wide inequalities in the distribution of income and wealth. More than one-fourth of the Indian population now live below the poverty line (27.5 p.c. in 2004-05). Economic development demands an improvement in the lot of vulnerable sections of the population. This requires huge investment in social sectors like health, education, sanitation and hygienic conditions, etc. The last decade of the 20th century saw an increased expenditure on social sectors and poverty alleviation schemes. The infrastructure and social sectors are not to be addressed seriously here since these two sectors remain outside our syllabus. But, one must not debunk the importance of these two sectors.

11.3.3. National Economic Planning

Economic planning is often regarded as a technique of managing an economy. When the structure of an economy becomes complex and subject to rapid change and transformation, some sort of advance thinking becomes necessary to resolve that complexity and to prepare the economy for those changes. Such preparation is nothing but economic planning.

The First Five Year Plan was launched in April 1951 to realise the aspirations and hopes of the newly independent Indian people. The dominant economic philosophy at the time was 'market failure' and 'state intervention'. While the idea of a mixed economy was accepted, democratic planning became an integral part of action to create an environment for a richer and more varied life. During the first four decades (1951-1990) of planning, she registered a satisfactory overall growth rate, but that too fell short of our expectations. Economic planning—coupled with bureaucratic controls, licence and permit restrictions—had created such a mess that the net effect of various economic policies and economic legislations was not indeed a happier one.

Meanwhile, 'government failure' in economic functioning became a great source of anxiety. The days of classical capitalism and classical socialism have come to an end. The situation was then crying for a change in the nature of state intervention, nature of the mixed economy of Indian variety. The Eighth Plan (1992-1997) in this sense was unique as it attempted to manage the transition from the so-called centrally planned economy to the market-oriented economy.

Globalisation-liberalisation-decontrol of the Indian economy brought changes in the nature of Indian planning. As market forces are believed to be the catalysts for economic activities, role and relevance of the planning is being diluted. Today, an integrated approach that considers both planning and market mechanism has been adopted. It is because of this change in thought—that India's Eighth Plan may be described as an indicative planning rather than conventional central planning variety. Under indicative planning, markets function—but the state has been assigned certain special responsibilities. Areas of government action or planning have been earmarked. For instance, human resource development urgently calls for government initiative. It is argued that the most important function of planning is to 'lobby for the poor in economic policy marking'. Although planning, as understood in 1950-1980s, in India is dead. In its place, indicative planning has been incorporated in our plans. Development planning continues; only the content of planning has changed. The Eighth Plan is a pace-setter in this direction. We are now in the midst of Eleventh Plan (2007-2012) of indicative variety.

11.3.4. Economic Policy Instruments

Macroeconomic management calls for adjustment of existing economic policies of the government in the light of changing environment—both in the domestic and international plane. Earlier, we have talked about policy parameters like industrial policy, trade policy, fiscal policy, monetary policy, etc. It is to be remembered that these policy parameters can never be uniform throughout; rather, these are required to be adjusted with the changing situation. It is true that some policies are more effective as well as more appealing than others when the macroeconomic environment of business changes. For instance, economic policies designed in 1958 by Nehru-Mahalanobis have been reoriented to promote greater efficiency and higher growth in the economy in 1991 as the current economic philosophy all over the globe demands more space for liberalisation, competition, privatisation, globalisation, etc. Today, the climate is quite different than what it was in the Nehru-Gandhi days. All the Governments have accepted the changes—a change of development policy from import substituting industrialisation (ISI) strategy to market-oriented import liberalisation strategy.

• **Import Substituting Industrialisation (ISI) vs Export-led Industrialisation:** Indian policy- makers placed great emphasis on the policy of import substitution in the early years of planning. The policy of ISI aims at reducing dependence on imports through the supplies of local needs by domestic manufacturing. The policy of export promotion coupled with the ISI was the foundation stone of Indian planning. Now this is history—since changes in the world economy in the 1970s and 1980s have brought in other policies. The ISI has been given a goodbye and, in its place, a new economic policy based on market principles called import liberalisation along with export-led industrialisation (ELI) strategies has been introduced in 1991.

Against these two divergent broad policy measures introduced first in the 1950s (pre-reform era) and latter changed in the 1990s (reform era), Indian policy makers charted out the following sub-set of policies from time to time. Most important among them are industrial policy, agricultural policy, national population policy, fiscal policy, monetary policy, trade policy or export-import (EXIM) policy, employment policy, etc.

• **Industrial Policy**: The first Industrial Policy based on the mixed economy principle was announced in 1948 which demarcated clearly the areas of operation of the public and private sectors. This policy was revised in 1956 which laid greater emphasis on the expanding role of the public sector. This was in keeping with the Mahalanobis strategy of industrialisation embodied in the Second Five Year Plan (1956-1961). Trade-related ISI strategy of industrialisation demanded control and regulation of the industrial sector. The basic instrument of control was given by the Industries (Development and Regulation) Act, 1951, which provided the legislative framework for licensing of industrial investment in the country. The MRTP Act, 1970—another regulatory mechanism—aimed at controlling the concentration of economic power in the hands of a few big monopoly business houses. The FERA, 1973, was designed to control foreign investment in India. All these controls and regulations were consistent with the broad ISI policy.

India reached the crossroads in 1991 when unprecedented economic crises called for unprecedented changes in economic policies. Making a sharp departure from the 1956 Industrial Policy, the Government of India announced liberalised Industrial Policy on July 24, 1991. Instead of state-sponsored development, the new policy put emphasis on market-led development.

Indeed, this new policy takes a bolder step towards the process of deregulating the economy so that Indian industry becomes more competitive—domestically and internationally. This policy marks a great leap towards privatisation and liberalisation. It envisages disinvestment of government equity. The new policy has laid a red carpet for foreign direct investment. It is in line with the current economic philosophy of the government to liberalise the existing industrial and commercial policies with the objective of increasing efficiency, gaining competitive advantage and achieving modernisation of the economy.

• **Trade Policy**: Trade policy involves measures taken by the government to influence the magnitude and direction of trade. India adopted an 'inward looking' strategy or ISI strategy of industrialisation. An elaborate system of government trade controls—such as quotas and tariff restrictions, import licences with a complex system of export incentives—was instituted in 1950s and continued with little changes up to mid-1991. In fact, trade policy became highly restrictive and complex. However, the then Prime Minister Rajiv Gandhi made an attempt at liberalisation, but in a hesitant manner. Such measures could be termed window-dressing. For genuine reforms based on 'outward looking strategy', we had to wait till mid-1991 when Rao-Singh brought in markets and price mechanism in trade policies. The chief elements of the EXIM policies announced at different times since 1991 are—devaluation of the Indian rupee, convertibility of rupee in current account, abolition of import licensing, reduction in export subsidies, and so on, so forth. Instead of import substitution, current trade policies are mainly governed by globalisation and international competitiveness of Indian goods.

• **Monetary Policy**: Monetary policy or credit policy concerns itself with the cost (i.e., the rate of interest) and the availability of credit to affect the overall supply of money. The hallmark of the RBI's monetary policy in the 1950s was that of controlled monetary expansion. To supplement the process of macro stabilisation and structural adjustment programmes launched in mid-1991, monetary policy has been redesigned. Market-oriented reforms (such as interest rate liberalisation, entry of private Indian and foreign banks, development of alternative system of monetary controls, etc.), are being constantly made since monetary policy measures are continuous.

• **Fiscal Policy**: Another arm of economic policy is the fiscal policy which is concerned with the policy of taxation, expenditure and borrowing. Fiscal policy as evolved over time has resulted in a tax structure with its great reliance on indirect taxation. As it has failed to contain non-plan expenditures, reinvestible surpluses could not be generated. The government then relied on deficit financing and public borrowing. All these widened fiscal deficit. However, the situation worsened in the early 1990s when fiscal imbalances rose to an unprecedented height. Necessary fiscal policy measures were made, first in mid-1991. Since then fiscal policy has been aiming at promoting a market-led development of the economy. For instance, a continuous effort is being made even today to simplify both the tax structure and tax laws. In its new fiscal policy, the Government has taken initiative to strengthen methods of expenditure control. Above all, the new fiscal policy aims at improving allocation of resources in terms of market principles. It aims at giving demand stimulus on the one hand, and restraining supply on the other hand by calibrating tax rates.

One finds a large degree of overlap between these various economic policies and their impact upon the macroeconomic variables. Economic policy measures announced by the Government have been presented in a tabular form so as to form a quick idea about macroeconomic management of the country.

Economic Policy Instruments: 1951-2008	
Pre-reform era (1951-1991)	**Reform era (1991-2008)**
• Import-substituting industrialisation, Dominance of control in the form of licenses, permit, quotas, etc.	• Export-led industrialisation Removal of controls and hence delicensing, deregulation, debureaucratisation, etc.
• State-sponsored development	• Market-driven and technology-dominated development
• Inward-looking trade policy (closed economy)	• Outward-looking trade policy (open economy, globalisation), competition and knowledge-driven society.
• Restrictions on foreign direct investment	• Removal of restrictions on foreign investment for the entry of multinational corporations (MNCs)
• Controls on interest rates	• Deregulation of interest rates, sale of shares of public sector enterprises, and gradual removal of subsidies, entry of private banks, movement towards capital account convertibility
• High as well as complex tax rates and dominance of indirect taxes	• Simplification of tax structure and laws and control of expenditure
• Buyer-oriented agricultural price policy, running of PDS for achieving food security	• Decontrol over internal movement of foodgrains, abolition of subsidies and introduction of contract farming

Days of Nehruvian socialism characterised by state-sponsored development in an environment of rigid controls, bureaucracy and inward-looking development of the Indian economy are over. The concept of highly centralised planning was the dominant economic philosophy of the Indian economy since 1951 to 1991 (with minor reform measures taken in 1980s). However, as the development experience of the late 1980s and early 1990s was hardly satisfactory, it called for changes in the economic policy. However, crises and changes in economic policy were not peculiar to India at that time. Even in the Republic of China, erstwhile Soviet Union and the East European countries—where centralised planning was practiced we heard changes in economic policy. India brought changes in her economic policies in mid-1991 as a part of overall global process. Marketisation, liberalisation, privatisation, deccentralisation and outward orientation of the economy are the essential ingredients of the new economic policy measures introduced by Rao-Singh in July 1991.

Conclusion: Demise of the Soviet planning system in 1989 and increasing globalisation and marketisation of the Chinese economy launched in 1978 accompanied by remarkable growth performance and above all India's homemade domestic crises created over the years have brought a change in macroeconomic environment from a controlled or often called over-controlled economy to a liberalised free market-oriented economy. The early 1990s saw protests: globalisation would cause more harm than benefits. But now it is accepted that globalisation is an irreversible process and India has to be integrated more and more with the world economy. Prosperity lies in it. The cycle of reforms is yet to stop and thus its full benefits are yet to accrue. At the same time, its costs are not too low. The following chapters will unfold costs and benefits of both pre-reform economic policy measures and reform policy measures and will assess overall economic performance made over these years.

QUESTIONS (WITH ANSWER-HINTS)

Long Questions (16 marks)

1. Analyse the different components of India's macroeconomic business environment.

   Ans. 11.3,.11.3.1 - 11.3.4.

Medium-sized Questions (8 marks)

1. What do you mean by microeconomic and macroeconomic environment?

   Ans. 11.1.

2. Explain the main elements or components of macroeconomic environment.

   Ans. 11.2.

3. Discuss briefly the basic components of India's business environment. (C.U. 2008)

   Ans. 11.3.1-11.3.4. (To be addressed in brief)

12

ECONOMIC GROWTH TRENDS IN INDIA

12.1. INTRODUCTION

In a broad sense, the entire world can be divided into two categories: developed and under-developed. Underdeveloped countries are alternatively called 'less developed countries', 'developing countries,' 'Third World countries' (LDCs), 'backward countries', etc. The United Nations and the World Bank classified economies according to their GNP per capita, measured in US dollars : low-income, middle income, low-and-middle income and high-income countries. Low-income countries are also known as developing countries.

This practice of classifying economies has now been given up and, in its place, countries are placed lexicographically. Following statistics collected from the World Development Report, 2008 will help in understanding the crucial differences between developed countries and the less developed countries (LDCs) or the under-developed countries (UDCs) :

Table 12.1: Selected Indicators of Development

	Population (Millions) 2006	GNP per Capita 2006
Low Income	**2,403**	**650**
Middle Income	**3,086**	**9,415.4**
(Lower middle income)	2,276	4,835.2
(Upper middle income)	810	4,789.7
Low and Middle Income	**5,489**	**10,977.7**
East Asia & Pacific	1,900	3,539.1
Europe & Central Asia	460	2,205.8
Latin America & Caribbean	556	2,650.3
Middle East & N. Africa	311	771.2
South Aisa	1,493	1,142.7
Sub-Saharan Africa	770	848.3
High Income	**1,029**	**37,528.9**

Source: World Development Report, 2008

However, no economy ever remains static; they grow over time. Industrialised countries of Europe first got their tastes of economic development. These countries of the North or the so-called capitalist countries are called 'First World' countries. Part of Western and Eastern European countries belong to the 'Second World' countries as their levels of development rose to a great height in-between the two World Wars. Poor, backward countries are called 'Third World' countries that aimed at higher economic development after most of them became politically independent in the late 1940s and 1950s. Again, some of these countries have, meanwhile, made some remarkable progress and, as a result, moved out from the circle of developing countries to the ranks of middle-income countries. These are the newly industrialising countries of South East Asia, mainly Hongkong, Singapore, Taiwan and South Korea. These countries are called 'Asian Tigers'.

On the other hand, developed countries comprise mainly those in Western Europe, Australia, Canada, New Zealand, the United States, and Japan. The contrast between these categories is indeed great. It is indeed amazing that more than 100 billion people, roughly one-sixth of the world's population that live in the Third World countries, live on less than one dollar a day. Developed countries or North had such living standards at least two centuries ago.

The economic distance between these two categories needs to be narrowed down as soon as possible to have a prosperous, healthy, and, a competitive global economy. Otherwise, the North (First World countries) will politically and economically exploit the South (Third World countries) as it is used to do at the present time.

12.2. COMMON CHARACTERISTICS OF UDCs/LDCs

Just as there are large differences between developed and developing countries, so too there are great differences among the developing countries. Their differences may be observed in resource endowment, size and income of the country, political environment, dependence on external sources, levels of human development, etc. Some developing countries are better endowed with natural resources while some of them can boast of huge human resource. In this sense, every country is unique and that is why the structure of all developing countries is divergent. Thus, LDCs are a diverse group—their cultures, politics, and even their geography vary enormously. It is neither proper to treat them as belonging to a homogeneous group nor suggest the same strategy of development for each country. In fact, depending upon the nature and extent of underdevelopment, the development potential of these countries differ significantly.

But a close look reveals that in spite of their diversity, different LDCs of Asia, Africa and Latin America have some common characteristics. These common characteristics have been nicely summed up by M. P. Todaro. He says that most of the Third World nations have a set of common and well-defined goals. These are the reduction of poverty, inequality, and unemployment; the provision of minimum levels of education, health, housing and food for every citizen, and so on. Common problems that these countries face, of course in varying degrees, are : widespread poverty, gross income inequality, massive unemployment, low level of agricultural and industrial output growth, absence of housing and sanitation facilities, high infant mortality rate and low expectancy of life, prevalence of child labour, etc.

We now describe the most common characteristics of LDCs :

- *Low per capita income and widespread poverty*. The most important indicator of economic backwardness is per capita income. Per capita GNP of LDCs is very low. That is why most people in such countries live under severe hardships. They do not get sufficient food to eat, adequate medical care and minimum educational opportunities. About 40-50 p.c. people in such countries live below the poverty line. In terms of per capita income and living standards not only the gap between the developed and underdeveloped countries is large, but the gap is widening over the years. For example, in 2006, India's per capita GNP (in U.S. dollars) was a modest $ 820 compared to $ 44,970 of the USA, $ 66,530 of Norway, and $ 57,230 of Switzerland, Norway. The average GNP per capita of low income countries in 2006 stood at $ 650 compared to $ 37,529 for high-income countries. (Data Source: World Development Report 2008, Table 1)

- *Shortage of capital*: In LDCs like India, there is a shortage of capital of all varieties. There is shortage of not only private capital like structure, factories, steel mills, etc., but also shortage of social overhead capital such as roads, highways, railroads, hospitals, schools, etc. This is largely due to low per capita income and widespread poverty. Since most people are poor they cannot save much. In fact, poor people have a high propensity to consume (or a low propensity to save). Ragnar Nurkse has pointed out that most LDCs are caught in a vicious circle of poverty: A country is poor because it is poor. Low per capita income leads to low saving. Low saving leads to low growth and low growth, in turn, leads to low per capita income. In fact, low per capita income is both the cause and the consequence of poverty.
- *Population explosion and high dependency*: Another major characteristic of LDCs is the high rate of growth of population. The population bomb has exploded in most such countries, as has been predicted by T. R. Malthus in 1798. This is due to a two-fold reason: (a) a sudden fall in the death rate, and (b) almost unchanged or constant birth rate. As a result, population has virtually exploded. Population in these countries is increasing annually at the rate of almost 2 p.c. On the contrary, supply of inputs is inelastic. Consequently, land-labour ratio has become unfavourable leading to a growth of an army of surplus labour. These labourers are unproductive in the sense that they depend on productive labourers. In fact, due to lack of adequate employment opportunities, the dependency burden is very high.
- *Massive unemployment*: Another important characteristic of LDCs is the existence of a considerable amount of unemployment, underemployment, and disguised unemployment. Traditional agricultural sector cannot cope with the rising population. As a result, the magnitude of disguised unemployment is mounting in these countries. Finding no alternative employment opportunities, rural people flock to the urban areas in order to survive. But, the rate of

industrial growth is not encouraging to absorb rural masses. In addition to this, a large number of educated youth do not find employment in these countries.

- *Predominance of agriculture*: An underdeveloped economy is predominantly an agrarian economy. Predominance of agriculture is viewed from two angles—*first* is the contribution of this sector towards national income. In LDCs, agriculture contributes roughly 30-50 p.c. towards national income. On the other hand, in the developed countries, agriculture occupies a secondary position since 2 p.c. to 8 p.c. of national income comes from this sector. *Secondly,* LDCs mainly depend upon agriculture and extractive industries like mining, fisheries and forests. This means that the bulk of the population is engaged in agriculture and allied pursuits. About 55-75 p.c. of the people are engaged in agriculture. Only 10 p.c. are employed in the secondary sector, and the rest in the tertiary sector. In advanced countries, agriculture provides employment to a small fraction of the people (2 p.c. to 5 p.c.). All these explain the predominance of agriculture in LDCs.

  Though agriculture occupies a predominant position in LDCs, it is always in a backward condition leading to low productivity.
- *Unproductive investment*: It is anybody's knowledge that due to massive poverty people have very little power to save in LDCs. These countries are not capable of saving of more than 15 p.c. of GDP as compared to more than 35 p.c. of GDP saved by people of advanced countries. The small amount, which is saved in LDCs is not invested properly. Some of it is used in hoarding, black marketing and other unsocial activities. like decorating 'gods' in temples by gold ornaments. A large part is used to buy unproductive assets like gold and jewellery. This sort of unproductive investments cannot promote economic growth.
- *Low levels of productivity*: Another feature of an LDC is low productivity of land, labour and capital. The productivity of land is low for various reasons—institutional, technological, and natural.

Productivity of labour is also low for various reasons. Most workers are poor and do not get either sufficient food or adequate medical care. So they cannot work hard. They are most illiterate, unskilled and lack technical training. They do not have sufficient complementary resources such as land and capital to work with.

In short, low productivity of labour is both a cause and an effect of the low levels of overall productivity and living in these countries. Low levels of living and low productivity go hand in hand. It is really difficult, in practice, to identify the cause and the effect.

12.3. FEATURES OF THE INDIAN ECONOMY

India got her independence in 1947. At that time she exhibited features of underdevelopment. Her economy during about 200 years British rule (1757-1947) was a stagnant one. She has been, however, making sincere efforts to come out from the low level equilibrium trap. Her success in this respect cannot be belittled. She advanced in many areas. No longer is Indian economy a stagnating economy. But, Indian economy can be safely characterised as a typical LDC/UDC. At the best, we can call it a developing economy. Most of the common characteristics of LDCs are present in the Indian economy even after 58 years of economic planning

Here we will point out some of the distinctive features of the Indian economy:

- *Low level of national income and per capita income*: Economic growth of any country can be viewed from its level of national income and per capita income. It is said that higher the level of national income, higher is the rate of economic growth. India's net national product (NNP) at factor cost in 2007-08 at 1999-2000 prices stood at Rs 27,60,325 crore. Population during the time stood at 1124 million. This amounts to saying that per capita NNP came to Rs 24,256 or Rs 2,021 per month. Standards of living of masses are miserably low. Even the basic necessities are beyond the means of the majority of population. Comparing India's per capita income with the other countries of the world, one comes to the conclusion that India is one of the poorest nations of the world.
- *Vast inequalities in income and wealth*: Not only per capita income is low, but Indian economy is also marked by great inequalities in the distribution of income and wealth. In India, as years roll on, inequalities are on the rise. The logical corollary of this inequality is mass poverty. Nearly 60 p.c. of the total population share one-third of India's national income while only rich 5 p.c. of the total population enjoy the same amount of national income. This inequality widens the problem of poverty. Even in 1972-73, more than 50 p.c. of the total population lived below the poverty line. Thanks to some economic progress it has come down from 36 p.c. in 1993-94 to about 27.5 p.c. in 2004-05, poverty estimate based on Uniform Recall Period. In short, Indian economy still reels under the vicious circle of poverty.
- *Predominance of agriculture*: Less developed countries live mainly upon agriculture and extractive industries, like mining, fisheries and forests. Predominance of agriculture is explained from the viewpoint of sectoral composition of national income and occupational pattern. In India, in 1950-51, more than 55 p.c. of our GDP came from the agricultural sector or the so-called primary sector. In 2007-08, however, the contribution of this sector toward GDP came down to 19.4 p.c. The contributions of the secondary and tertiary sectors were 24.9 p.c. and 55.7 p.c., respectively. Thus, even after 58 years of planning, agriculture alone contributes less than one-fifth of our national income. Occupational structure also tells a story of predominance of the agricultural sector and the backwardness of the industrial sector. In India, 52 p.c. of the total population was engaged in agriculture in 2004-05.

  Though agriculture occupies a predominant position in India, it is still backward.

- *Tremendous population pressure*: In LDCs, the rate of growth of population is very high. So far as the size of population is concerned, India ranks second next only to China (1312 million in 2006). India's population is now 1110 million in 2006-07. During the decade of 1991, the growth rate of population in India was 1.61 p.c. per annum, as compared to 0.7 p.c. growth rate of population of developed countries. High birth rate (23.5 per 1000) coupled with low death rate (7.5 per 1000 in 2005-06) is the genuine cause for population explosion in India. In the 20th century, India's population went up by 5 p.c. as against 3 p.c. increase in the world's population as a whole.
- *Massive unemployment*: In LDCs, not only natural resources are underutilised but also a massive wastage occurs in the case of manpower resources. Slow economic growth rate on the one hand, and rapid growth of population on the other hand, has accentuated the problem of unemployment in India. Between 1971 and 1999, the number of unemployed in India increased by 10 times though the number of job-seekers increased by 2.5 p.c. annually; but the employment possibilities increased by a modest rate of 1.8 p.c. Number of registered job-seekers in 2006-07 stood at 40.7 million. Unemployment rate has been rising persistently since the days of economic reforms began. It rose from 1.96 p.c. in 1993-94 to 2.39 p.c. in 2004-05.

  However, employment growth in 2004-05 that stood at 2.89 compared to 0.98 p.c. in 1999-2000 is an encouraging development. But employment growth in recent decades is not comenusurate with the labour force growth rate. What we experience now is the 'jobless growth'. The rate of growth of employment in the organised sector came to a negative of 0.31 p.c. during 1994-2005 as compared to 1.20 p.c. in 1983-1994. Some people call it 'job loss growth'.

  Not only this, Indian agriculture exhibits a considerable amount of under-employment and disguised unemployment. In the urban areas also, we find disguised unemployment. It is somewhat tragic as well as paradoxical that, despite massive investment made during the plan period, unemployment problem has assumed a gigantic proportion. This amounts to huge wastage of human capital.
- *Scarcity of capital and low rate of capital formation*: As people in LDCs are poor, their capacity to save is low. This results in a low rate of capital formation. That is why development economists suggest that to break the vicious circle of poverty it is necessary to push up the rate of investment. Since India is a capital-poor country, capital per head is low. This scarcity of capital causes overall backwardness of the Indian economy. In 1950-51, net savings and net investments stood at slightly more than 6 p.c. and these two increased to 14.8 p.c. and 16 p.c., respectively in 2001-02. The

position, however, in recent times has improved a lot. These two figures increased to 27.1 p.c. and 28.4 p.c. of NDP in 2006-067 This is an encouraging development for the Indian economy.

Along with the low volume of physical capital, human capital formation is also low. As per 2001 Census, 34.62 p.c. of the total population at that time was illiterate. The literacy rate has gone up to about 64.8 p.c. by 2001—of course, by mathematical jugglery. Mass illiteracy acts as an impediment to India's economic development.

India has the dubious distinction of having largest number of illiterate poulation (304 million) in the world. (Source : Eleventh Five Plan, Vol. 1) India has an adverse sex ratio with only 933 women per 1,000 men in 2001.

- *Underdeveloped infrastructure*: Being an LDC, India's infrastructural facilities or economic and social overheads of capital are inadequate. It consists of (a) transport and communications, (b) energy, (c) finance, housing and insurance, (d) science and technology, and (e) health, education, etc. Availability of these infrastructures creates the conditions for favourable growth. The superstructure of an economy largely depends on the availability of infrastructural facilities.

  As far as social and economic overheads are concerned, India is poor. It is indeed true that her railway and road networks are comparable to the developed nations. But her demand for infrastructural facilities and services outpace their supplies. Per capita energy use (oil equivalent) of an Indian in 2004 was 531 kg vis-a-vis USA's 7,921 kg. Even China's per capita energy use was higher (1,242 kg.) than India's. Compared to other countries, India is poor in information technology. In 2005, the use of personal computers per 1,000 Indians was as low as 16 as against 762 per 1,000 US people. India's health expenditure as a percentage of GDP was 1.39 p.c. in 2007-8 over the USA's 15 p.c. of GDP. Thus, India's social infrastructural facilities are not only inadequate compared to the needs, but also awfully low compared to different countries of the world.

- *Low level of technology*: Due to illiteracy, use of advanced or sophisticated technology is rather an exception in India. Because of the limited growth of technological institution, we are forced to use primitive methods of technology whose productivity is low. Though modern industrial sectors employ advanced technology, village industries still employ old and hackneyed methods even in the age of modern science and globalised world. This is nothing but technological dualism that persists in LDCs like India. Truly speaking, low productivity of Indian labour is explained in terms of low level of technology.

From the above discussion, we can conclude that all the characteristics of LDCs are found in India. No doubt, during the planning era, she has made progress in different directions. Still, considering the needs of the country, it is inadequate. Indian economy is characterised by low per capita income, widespread poverty, massive unemployment, gigantic rise in population, and so on. So, India is an underdeveloped country. India is one of the poorest nations of the world. Her position is worse compared to even some African countries!

12.4. IS INDIAN ECONOMY A DEVELOPING ECONOMY?

There is hardly any doubt that the present Indian economy is still a less developed economy because it exhibits all the characteristics of an LDC. But it is not a stagnant economy. It has achieved modest growth. It is also achieving some degree of modernisation. Moreover, some important structural changes have occurred in the economy in the post-independence period. All these made it clear that the Indian economy is gradually marching towards a distant but clearly visible goal, viz., the goal of a developed economy—after being locked in the vicious circle of undevelopement and suffering from secular stagnation.

With the launching of the Five Year Plans in 1951, a growth momentum appeared in the Indian economy. Over the passage of time, far-reaching changes have taken place in the economy. Here we group these changes into two broad categories — quantitative and qualitative. We find quantitative expansion in national and per capita income with an expansion in agricultural and industrial output. By qualitative change we mean structural change. Apparently, these changes seem to be permanent. Undoubtedly, these changes symbolise economic development. Here, first of all, we will describe quantitative changes and, finally, qualitative changes.

▲ Quantitative Changes

- *Rising trend of national income and per capita income*: Economic growth of any country is measured by the increase in national and per capita output. During the plan period, national income of the country has certainly gone up. In 1950-51, net national product at factor cost or national income (at 1999-2000 prices) stood at Rs. 2,06,493 crore. It rose to Rs. 27,60,325 crore in 2007-08 (at 1999-2000 prices). This means that between 1950-51 and 2007-08 national income grew at the compound rate of 4.7 percent per annum. Compared to the pre-independence figure, this is really remarkable. However, the performance of the Indian economy in this direction in the 1980s, 1990s was certainly praiseworthy since it recorded a growth rate of more than 6 p.c. p.a. GDP growth rate in the 2000s is unprecedented. It rose from 5.8 p.c. in 2001-02 to 9.2 p.c. in 2006-07. If the present trend contunues, the country will be able to achieve a double digit growth rate within one or two years.

However, the better measure of economic development is the per capita income. Per capita NNP rose to Rs 24,256 in 2007-08 (at 1999-2000 prices) as against Rs 6,122 of 1950-51 at 1999-2000 prices. This means that during this period, compound annual growth rate of net per capita income rose by 2.5 p.c. p.a. Historically, it exhibits a better growth rate. Yet, it is inadequate compared to the needs of the country. The only encouraging aspect is that it shows a rising trend.

- *Increase in agricultural and industrial output*: Over the plan period, Indian economy experienced a higher growth rate in agriculture as well as in industry. Pre-plan period recorded an agricultural growth rate of 0.3 p.c. while the plan period showed a growth rate of 2.66 p.a. Performance of the industrial sector is certainly a better one. During the plan period, 1950-2007, the overall achievement in this sector is more than 4.8 p.c. Trend growth of India's exports shows Indian agricultural and industry on the move.

▲ **Qualitative Changes or Structural Changes:** During the plan period, not only economic growth picked up, but also economic development i.e., 'growth plus change' occurred in India. This amounts to saying that the Indian economy witnessed structural changes. By economic structure we mean interrelationship among the different productive sectors i.e., agriculture and allied activities (known as the primary sector), manufacturing and industries (called the secondary sector), and trade and services (or the tertiary sector). At a low level of economic development, one finds predominance of the primary sector. The predominance of any sector can be viewed from the sectoral composition of national income and occupational structure. When, in an economy, primary sector is considered as the predominant one then it means that the contribution of this sector towards national income is the largest. Not only this, the bulk of the population derives their livelihood from this sector. On the other hand, in the sectoral composition of national income as well as in the occupational pattern, the importance of the secondary and tertiary sectors gets reduced. As economic development proceeds, the interrelationships among these sectors undergo a change. As economic development takes place, the primary sector (from the standpoint of sectoral composition of national income and occupational pattern) looses its importance and secondary as well as tertiary sectors gain in importance.

Thus, structural changes indicate economic development. This is what Colin Clark hypothesised. We will see whether structural changes have taken place in India during the Plan Period :

- *Sectoral composition of national income:* In 1950-51, the contribution of the primary sector towards India's gross domestic product or GDP was nearly 55.9 p.c., while it was 14.9 p.c. for the secondary sector-Since then there has been a steady decline in the share of the primary sector in GDP and it declined to 19.4 p.c. in 2007-08. On the other hand, over the plan period, as the industrial sector expanded, its contribution to GDP has been on the rise and it rose to 25 p.c. in 2007-08. Along with the growth of the secondary sector, the services sector also registered a higher growth rate. In 2007-08, its contribution was 55.7 p.c. Thus, it is clear that as economic development took place during the last five decades of planning, the primary sector lost its preeminence, as against 29.2 p.c. in 1950. This, of course, is a sign of economic development.

Table 12.2 : GDP and its Sectoral Share (1999-2000 prices)

	Agriculture and allied	Industry	Services
1950-51	55.9	14.9	29.2
1970-71	45.2	21.7	33.1
1980-81	38.1	25.9	36.0
1990-91	33.2	25.2	41.6
2006-07	20.5	24.7	54.8
2007-08	19.4	24.9	55.7

Source: Statistical Outline of India: 2007-08

One can make a better analysis of structural changes if the entire period is divided in the following sub-periods, as shown in Table 12.3 :

Table 12.3 : Sectoral Growth Rates (in percentage)

Year	Primary	Secondary	Tertiary	GDP
1950-51 to 59-60	2.3	5.7	4.1	
1960-61 to 69-70	2.5	6.5	4.9	3.5
1970-71 to 79-80	1.3	3,7	4.5	
1980-81 to 91-92	3.9	6.3	6.4	5.4
1992-93 to 2001-02	3.3	6.3	7.8	6.1
2001-02	6.2	2.7	7.1	5.8
2003-04	10.0	7.6	8.2	8.5
2005-06	6.0	9.6	9.8	9.0
2006-07	2.7	10.0	11.2	9.2

Source : (i) C.S.O., (ii) Economic Survey

The GDP growth rate between 1950-51 and 1979-80 came to be known as 'Hindu rate of Growth' of 3.5 p.c. p.a. But this long-term trend has been broken and in 2006-07 GDP growth rate went past 9 p.c. p.a. along with the rising growth trend of especially service sector and then industry sector. But primary sector's performance is rather unsatisfactory in the current year.

It is clear that despite the green revolution in agriculture, the share of the primary sector to GDP has been continuously declining. However, between 1980-81 and 1991-92, primary sector displayed a better growth rate. Variation in the performance of agriculture is always worth noticing.In the last three or four years, because of good monsoon, agricultural growth rate was remarkable, but in the year 2007-08, its performance has slackened in a larger degree. Further, the secondary and tertiary sectors are continuously growing at a double rate than that of the primary sector during the first decades. In the subsequent periods, the tertiary sector outstripped the growth of the secondary sector. Unfortunately, between 1990-91 and 2007-08, there has been a fall in the growth of the secondary sector from 25.2 p.c. to 24.9 p.c. Thus, the pattern of structural changes that has taken place in India has deviated from developed economies.

Present growth trend is dominated by the services sector. Very aptly, it is called service-led growth. But what we see in India is the 'excess growth of the service sector'. Possibly, India may display a new paradigm of development.

Another important aspect of sectoral composition of national income is the contribution of the public sector towards GDP. As time progresses, the contribution of this sector rises. In 1970-71, the public sector contributed 14.9 p.c. towards GDP, but it rose to 24 p.c. in 2001-02. However, following the introduction of new economic policy in 1991, the contribution of public sector enterprises towards GDP is on the decline. Their share in GDP at market prices declined from 11.68 p.c. in 2004-05 to 11.12 p.c. in 2005-06.

Finally, one can notice a structural change by studying the contribution of the commodity sector and non-commodity or service sector in net national product. Between 1950-51 and 1976-77, the rate of growth of the services sector (4.90 p.c.) was satisfactory as compared to the growth of the commodity sector (2.90 p.c.). Furthermore, between 1980-81 and 1995-96, growth rate of the commodity sector came to 5.30 p.c., while that of the services sector rose to 6.50 p.c. Same story has been repeated for the period 1991-2008.

Expansion of the tertiary sector is tantamount to modernisation. Yet, we must say that the growth of the services sector at the expense of the commodity sector is undesirable. Though sectoral composition of national income itself indicates economic development, the growth of the service sector at the cost of the commodity sector reflects some sort of 'structural retrogression'.

• *Occupational Pattern*: In the light of structural change, one finds India's occupational structure as a static one. But we know that as economic development takes place, occupational structure also undergoes a change. The Clark-Fisher thesis says that, in an expanding economy, employment situation shifts more and more in favour of secondary and tertiary sectors. That is to say, the number of people engaged in the primary sector tend to decline while it tends to rise in the other two sectors. This sort of change in the occupational structure indicates economic development.

But, considering the development of the Indian economy in the last six decades, recently one finds some favourable change in the occupational structure of India. Throughout the 20th century, the percentage of people engaged in agriculture has not fallen appreciably. Even in 2001, 57 p.c. of the total population were engaged in the primary sector, compared to 72.1 p.c. in 1951. On the other hand, between 1951 and 1981, percentage of population engaged in the secondary sector increased marginally from 10.6 p.c. to 13.5 p.c. but it declined to 12.7 p.c. in 1991 and then rose to 17.5 p.c. in 2001. The only sector that showed a steady rise in employment is the tertiary sector. It rose from 17.3 p.c. in 1951 to 25.8 p.c. in 2000. This is shown in Table 12.4.

Table 12.4: Distribution of Working Population

(in percentage)

Sector	1951	1981	1991	2000
Primary	72.1	68.7	66.8	56.7
Secondary	10.6	13.5	12.7	17.5
Tertiary	17.3	17.8	20.5	25.8

Thus, it is clear that the occupational pattern is not only a static one but also an unbalanced one. In view of this, V. K. R. V. Rao commented that India's occupational structure exhibits 'structural retrogression.' This, of course, is not a healthy sign and it explains underdevelopment. The reasons behind such static occupational structure are: (i) massive rise in population, and (ii) inadequate growth of both industries and services sector. Only in recent year (2004-05), there has been a drop in the number of people dependent on agriculture. It is around 52 p.c.

• *Development of basic and heavy industries*: Immediately after independence, India's industrial structure was devoid of any heavy and basic industries. In other words, India's industrial structure at that time tilted heavily in favour of consumer goods industries. But under the impact of planning, especially the Second Five Year Plan (1956-1961), industrial structure had been diversified and newer and newer types of industries had been set up. This symbolises economic development.

• *Economic and social capital formation*: By social capital we mean transport, irrigation, power, education, health, etc. Building up of social capital is one of the prerequisites of economic development. Infrastructural development helps quicker economic development. So, social capital formation is equivalent to economic development.

During the plan period, we have made rapid strides in respect of construction of railway lines, irrigation, power, health and sanitation, education, etc.

Conclusion: If all these are considered as criteria for development, then we must say that the Indian economy has witnessed enormous changes which are not only synonymous with development but also help the process of development. Despite these, black spots of under-development are still prominent. At the same time, it is true that we have been able to come out of the 'low level equilibrium trap' engineered by the British Raj. Signs of development are positive in nature. Thus, we find both the pictures of development and underdevelopment. It exhibits thus pictures of contrast. The British economist Joan Robinson once remarked about India that whatever could be said about it, so could the opposite. Anyway, Indian economy can be lablled as an 'underdeveloped-developing economy.'

12.5. CONCEPT OF NATIONAL INCOME

Economic growth of any country is measured by its growth of national and per capita incomes. In other words, national income is the yardstick of measuring the growth performance of any economy. Increase in national income is tantamount to economic growth. In view of this, every country prepares statistics on national income as well as its various facets. The method through which national income statistics is prepared and compiled is called national income accounting. Thus, national income accounts can be defined as a set of systematic statements which reflect the aggregate money value of all goods and services produced in the different sectors of the economy (e.g., primary, secondary, and tertiary sectors) together with the records of distribution of factor incomes among different groups and final expenditures (either gross or net) of the economy. In national income accounts, all types of transactions conducted, say, in a year, are recorded. These are systematically classified and entered into national income accounts by the statisticians. Thus, national income accounts reflect how millions of transactions that are conducted are interrelated. Above all, by reading these accounts one gains knowledge about the working of the economy.

12.6. MEASUREMENT OF NATIONAL INCOME

The national product or national income measures the overall economic performance of a nation. To measure the national product, we add up the value of all final goods and services produced in a country in a year. Thus, we focus on firms or sellers which receive payments for the production. This is the product method of seeing national income.

National product can also be seen from the income side. Production by firms generates incomes for households who supply input services. If all the incomes received by households are added then we obtain national product from the income side. Thus, national income is the sumtotal of all incomes earned by input owners.

National product can also be viewed from the expenditure side. The circular flow of income and expenditure illustrates that whatever is produced is sold. The value of what is sold must be the value of what is currently produced. This is the expenditure side of national product.

Thus, there are three ways of measuring the national product or income of a country. These are: (i) production census method or output received method or value-added method; (ii) income census method or income method or income received method; and (iii) expenditure method. These three methods of measuring national product yield the same result. Thus,

National Product ≡ National income ≡ National Expenditure.

[≡ These three-pronged lines indicate identity]

- **Production Method or Value-added Method:** To obtain national product figure of a country, we aggregate the *money value* of all *final* goods and services produced in a country in a year. The figure that we obtain is called GNP or GDP. [For the moment, we won't make any distinction between these two concepts. We will use them interchangeably.] The italicised words 'money value' and 'final' require little elaboration. We cannot really add up the physical quantities of all goods and services produced in a year. It is meaningless to compute the sum of 10 Indica cars + 70 litres kerosene oil + 50 metres cloth + ... Thus, we have to transform these physical quantities into money values by multiplying the quantity of goods produced multiplied by price per unit of each good. That is :

price per car × 10 cars + price per litre × 70 litres of kerosene + ...

When this is done we get the money value of all goods. The word 'final' deserves elaboration. Only final goods are to be taken into account. Intermediate goods are not to be used to compute national product to avoid the problem of multiple counting.

- **Some Precautions**

While computing GNP or GDP, one has to take certain safeguards.

- *Intermediate goods not to be recorded : Firstly* only final goods—not intermediate goods—are to be taken into account. Note that final goods (such as, consumer goods and capital goods) are purchased or consumed by the final users (i.e., both consumers and firms). As intermediate goods are partly final goods which form inputs to another firm's production process, these are not included in national income accounting.

- *Current year's production only: Secondly,* value of goods and services produced in the current year is to be reported. If the value of goods and services produced in the earlier years are taken into account, we would then either overestimate or underestimate the value of the country's total output.

- *Self-produced goods to be included : Thirdly,* there are some goods and services that do not come to the market for transactions. Should these non-marketed products be excluded from the GNP estimate? In poor agriculture dominated countries, a large portion of the agricultural output is consumed by the farmers themselves. In fact, there does not arise any surplus left after consumption. In other words, production virtually equals consumption. This is called subsistence agriculture. Thus, agricultural commodities are not exchanged for money. The commodities which do not have market valuations must be imputed at current prices. Such is true in the case of services received from owner-occupied housing (i.e., unmarketed services). In this case what is required is the imputation of rent — the amount which the houseowners would have had to pay if they were in rented houses, even though no such rents are actually paid. Likewise, free lunch coupon issued to workers is to be valued at current market prices to estimate GNP.

However, the value of a housewife's performance in preparing meals and other household activities as well as house husband services—though an important economic activity—are not considered here because of the practical difficulty of valuing such activity. But, public goods and services, such as park, police, defence do not have market place since these are not bought and sold in the market. However, we cannot exclude these commodities from the GNP estimate. To tackle this problem, values are imputed for these services. GNP includes these services by valuing them at their cost.

- **Income Census Method:** National income is the sum of the values earned by each factors of production, land, labour, capital, and entrepreneurship. The measures derived are comparable to those obtained from the product side of the accounts. Since GNP is the sum of all values added, it must also be the aggregate of all incomes subdivided into rent, wages, interest, and profit.

- **Some Precautions:**

• *Transfer payments to be excluded : Firstly,* national income accountants consider only those incomes that arise from the current production of final goods and services. Thus, some incomes are excluded. The principal exclusion is transfer payments that include unemployment allowance, retirement pensions, flood or drought relief, etc. Transfer payments are the payments for which no direct service is rendered by the beneficiaries. As these payments involve no exchange of goods and services and only incomes are redistributed from one pocket to another, these transfer payments are not included in GNP.

• *Capital gains and windfall gains not to be included: Secondly,* capital gains arising out of asset transactions are excluded from GNP. If the sale price of a house exceeds its purchase price, a situation of capital gains emerges. Such gains are coincidental. Any such gain may lead to a rise in personal incomes but not national income since there is no economic production. Similarly, any windfall incomes (i.e., incomes from lottery, word puzzle) are not included in GNP.

• *Self-owned inputs ought to be included: Thirdly,* owner's own capital and labour required to produce goods may create problem while estimating national income. Even if no money is paid for these owned-input services, an imputed value is assigned to each of all these and included in national income. Likewise, undistributed corporate profits are included in national income estimation.

• *Illegal income not to be included : Fourthly,* though illegal activities, like gambling, may provide a great deal of income to the gamblers, they are excluded from the accounts even though a market price is charged for these activities.

- **Expenditure Method:** The third or final approach is to add up all expenditures on final goods and services. In a two-sector economy consisting of consuming sector and producing sector, total expenditure is divided into consumption spending (symbolised by C) and investment spending (symbolised by I). 'C' includes expenditure on all types of goods (both durable and non-durable) and services produced and sold. 'I' is defined as the expenditure on newly produced capital goods acquired for the purpose of providing services in the future. It includes investment in fixed capital formation, stock building and residential housing. Again, investment may be gross or net. Net investment is obtained by subtracting depreciation expenditure or capital consumption allowance from gross investments. Thus,

$$GNP = C + I$$

If we now consider a three-sector economy (i.e., closed economy) that includes governmental sector then GNP from the expenditure side becomes

$$GNP = C + I + G$$

'G' consists of expenditure on goods and services provided by the government. However, not all government expenditures are included in GNP accounts. Expenditure on government transfer payments (e.g., unemployment benefit, welfare grants, interest on national debt, etc.) are excluded.

The fourth category of expenditure in a four-sector economy, i.e., open economy, arises from international trade. Here we will now include export (symbolised by X) and exclude imports (symbolised by M). Market value of all exportable goods should be included in national income. But, market value of all imported final goods and services are to be subtracted from the GNP figure. This is because that national income figures of any country must not reflect the contribution of foreign nationals. Thus, in an open economy

$$GNP = C + I + G + (X - M)$$

If X = M, we deal with a closed economy.

12.7. CONCEPTS OF GDP, GNP AND NNP

• *GDP:* GDP measures the aggregate money value of output produced by an economy over a year. In other words, GDP is obtained by valuing all final goods and services produced in a year at market prices. GDP is also calculated by adding all the incomes generated by the act of production. Since only domestically produced goods and services produced is estimated or since only the incomes earned by nationals are aggregated, we use the word 'domestic' to distinguish it from the gross national product. The word gross means that no deduction for depreciation is allowed.

GNP includes GDP plus net property income from abroad. Thus, GNP includes income that nationals earn abroad, but it does not include the income earned by foreign nationals. On the other hand, GDP is concerned with incomes generated domestically even by the foreigners.

An example will help our understanding. Suppose, an Indian doctor goes to the USA temporarily to work there. The income he earns by rendering his service in the USA is included in the US GDP and not in India's GDP because it is earned in the USA. But this income is not part of the US GDP because the Indian doctor is a foreign national there. Similarly, the income of a US Ambassador in New Delhi is included in the US GNP, but it is a part of India's GDP.

Thus, GNP =

GDP + net property income from abroad.

Thus, GDP measures the aggregate money value of all goods and services produced by factors of production located and paid for in the domestic economy, even if these factors are owned abroad.

• *GDP at market prices*: When national product is measured, it is measured initially at current market prices. Market prices always reflect taxes and subsidies on the commodities produced. Once indirect taxes are imposed on commodities, market prices of the commodities go up. A 10 p.c. tax on a book on Economics will raise its price. Tax is included in the price of a commodity and tax is not a production. Similarly, subsidies are provided on some commodities, as a result of which prices decline. If we do not make any adjustment for such taxes and subsidies, we obtain GDP at market prices.

• *GDP at factor cost*: GDP at market prices do not reflect true incomes of factors of production. It includes tax and subsidies but such are not production and, hence, they cannot enter into incomes of productive inputs.

So; taxes and subsidies are to be excluded to obtain the true figure of production. Value of output can never be equal to the value of incomes paid to all productive inputs. By adjusting taxes and subsidies, we obtain GDP at factor cost i.e.,

GDP at factor cost =

GDP at market prices – taxes + subsidies.

An example may be enough here. Suppose, an excise duty on Indica car goes up to Rs 2.75 lakh (Rs 5 lakh being the excise duty). Value of car output, is, in fact, Rs. 2.70 lakh. This means different factor inputs have earned incomes in the form of rent, wages, etc. to the extent of Rs. 2.70 lakh. Value of output must equal value of incomes generated. Thus, indirect taxes are to be excluded.

Subsidies have the opposite effect of taxes. A subsidy per unit on coarse cotton cloth has the effect of reducing its market price. As a result of, say, one rupee subsidy per metre, consumers get cotton cloth at Rs 20 per metre. But incomes received by input owners in this cloth mill are Rs. 21 per meter. Value of output must equal the value of all income. So subsidies are to be added. Thus, by subtracting taxes and adding subsidies from GDP at market prices, one obtains GDP at factor cost.

GNP at market prices and GNP at factor cost are calculated in the same way as described above.

• *NNP*: If we deduct depreciation from gross product we obtain net product. GDP minus depreciation is called NNP. NNP is sometimes called national income.

12.8. GROWTH OF INDIA'S NATIONAL INCOME

The Central Statistical Organisation (C.S.O.) publishes National Accounts Statistics (NAS) annually which provides information on various aspects of the country's national income. Up to 1980-81, the national income estimates were made at 1980-81 price level. In 1999, the government took a decision of change in base year. Now, national income data are available at 1999-2000 prices.

• *National Income Trends*: The rate of growth of national income since the First Plan has been around 3.5 to 4 p.c. substantially below the targeted rates of 5 to 5.5 p.c. Above all, there are ups and downs in the growth rates achieved during the plan period. The First Plan (1951-56) experienced an annual growth rate of 3.7 p.c. while it marginally increased to 4.1 p.c. in the Second Plan. But there was a downturn in the growth rate during the Third Plan because of two wars and severe drought. The growth rate achieved during the Third Plan period stood at 2.8 p.c. Though the three Annual Plans registered a somewhat better growth rate (3.9 p.c.), the Fourth Plan witnessed a growth rate of 3.4. p.c. per annum due to sharp price rise, power crisis and underutilisation of capacity of the industrial sector. Seen against this, in the Sixth Plan the growth rate was more than 5.5 p.c. The Seventh Plan contemplated a rise in the growth rate of national income by 5 p.c. annually. The actual growth rate has been of the order of 5.5 p.c. for the entire plan. The Eighth Plan recorded a growth rate of 5.5 p.c. The growth rate slipped to 5.5 p.c. in the

Ninth Plan. However, a record breaking growth rate of national income was struck (7.8 p.c.) in the Tenth plan (2002-07) (See Table 12.5).

Table 12.5: Growth Rates (NNP at factor Cost) Achieved in Successive Plan Period

	Period	Growth rate (per cent)
First Plan	(1951-56)	3.7
Second Plan	(1956-61)	4.0
Third Plan	(1961-66)	2.8
Three Annual Plans	(1966-69)	3.9
Fourth Plan	(1969-74)	3.4
Fifth Plan	(1974-79)	5.0
Annual Plans	(1979-80)	–5.0
Sixth Plan	(1980-85)	5.4
Seventh Plan	(1985-90)	5.5
Eighth Plan	(1992-97)	6.6
Ninth Plan	(1997-02)	5.5
Tenth Plan	(2002-07)	7.8

In absolute terms, the net national product at factor cost, i.e., national income at 1999-2000 prices was Rs 2,06,493 crore in 1950-51. National income has risen from Rs 5,66,931 crore in 1980-81 to Rs 27,60,325 crore in 2007-08. Between 1950-51 and 2007-08, the Indian economy registered rate of growth of 4.8 p.c. per annum. However, in the 1980s and 1990s, we have been able to grow at the rate of about 6 p.c. It is a welcome development. The growth rate of GDP achieved in the 2000s (i.e., 2000-01—2007-08) came to more than 8 p.c. This higher growth path seems sustainable on a long-term basis.

We see an encouraging spot, i.e., higher growth rate in national income in the growth profile of the country. However, the better measure of economic development is the per capita income which is obtained by dividing national income by the population of the country. Remember that per capita national income is equivalent to per capita net national product at factor cost.

The growth rate of per capita income since the First Plan has been of the order of around 1.3 to 1.5 p.c. Actually, in the First Plan, it was 2.6 per cent. But we achieved a higher growth rate of per capita income above the trend rate during the the Fifth (2.7 p.c.), Sixth (3.1 p.c.), Seventh (3.3 p.c.), Eighth (4.5 p.c.), Ninth (3.5 p.c.), and the Tenth Plan (6.1 p.c.)

In absolute terms, India's per capita income at 1999-2000 prices was Rs. 6,122 in 1950-51. It rose to Rs. 8,590 in 1980-81. It increased to Rs. 24,256 in 2007-08. Per capita income growth per month is thus assumed to be Rs. 896.

Features of Growth in the Planning Era: From the above description, one can point out several features of growth during the planning period.

First, the growth rates of national income and per capita income over the last 58 years have been encouraging, particularly in the light of the growth rates achieved during the British period. But, at the same time it is to be noted that the actual performance has been below the targets set. Barring the First, Seventh, Eighth, Ninth and Tenth Plan, actual growth rate remained below the target growth rate. In the First Plan, actual growth rate (3.6 p.c.) exceeded the targeted (2.5 p.c.) rate. In all the plans, targeted growth rate was kept at 5 p.c. or 5.5 p.c. The actual growth rate achieved in various plans has been shown in the Table 12.5. As is expected, the economy must grow at a higher rate as plan period rolls on. The annual growth rate for the period 1981-91 works out to be 5.75 p.c. and for the period 1993-07 it is 7.5 p.c. Obviously, if these growth rates are explained in real terms (i.e., at constant prices) the annual growth would be much below the targeted rates of 6.0 and 6.5 p.c.

Secondly, per capita income is also very small by current standards though it is rising. Unimpressive growth rate of national income over the plan period has resulted in a marginal increase in per capita income. It is observed that, out of 58 years of economic planning, the rate of increase in NNP was lower than the population growth rate for more than 22 years. As a result, per capita income registered a decline in all these years. Even there are some years when the country has suffered economic retrogression. Consequently, levels of living of the poor have gone down to a low level. This can be evidenced from the fact that in 2004-05 27.5 p.c. of total population lived below the poverty line compared to 36 p.c. in 1993-94. This poverty estimate has been made on consumption distribution using a 30-day recall—called Uniform Recall Period (URP). However, poverty eastimates based on Mixed Recall Period (MRP) has declined from 26.1 p.c. in 1999-2000 to 21.8 p.c. in 2004-05.

Thirdly, India's national income, even after 58 years of planning, is largely dependent on agriculture. Good harvests result in higher growth rates in income and bad harvests cause a fall or even negative growth rate. So India's growth rate of national income is very much linked with the agricultural growth rate. In recent years, tertiary sector has been contributing largely.

Fourthly, compared to the growth rates of different countries between 1950-1980, India's performance is rather disappointing. At the moment, world's highest per capita income country is Norway whose per capita income was equivalent of $ 66,530 in 2006. India's per capita income was of the order of $ 820 . Burundi ranked lowest among the 133 members of the World Bank with a 2006 annual per capita income of just $100. Hence the necessity of raising the growth rate arises to close the increasing gap between developed countries and India and even between India and other underdeveloped nations of the world whose growth rates are higher than India.

Again, as far as per capita income trends are concerned, one notices favourable change also. There was a break in the Sixth Plan when per capita income rose by 3.1 p.c. p.a. In the Seventh Plan, it rose further to 3.3 p.c. p.a., in the Eighth Plan, to 4.5 p.c. p.a., and to a high of 6.1 p.c. p.a. in the Tenth Plan. This is not a mean achievement against the background of population growth rate of approximately 2 p.c. Between 1990-01, per capita income grew at the rate of 3.14 p.c. p.a. This amounts to saying that in the 1990s and early 2000s number of people living below the poverty line is on the decline. Even then roughly after 58 years of planning nearly 260 million population live below the poverty line by any measure.

Sectoral composition of national income between 1950 and 1980-81 clearly showed predominance of the primary sector in terms of its contribution towards GDP. Its share was 38.1 p.c. as contrasted to 36 p.c. of the tertiary sector in 1981. In 2007-08, the relative share of primary sector declined to 19.4 p.c. of GDP, while the share of the tertiary sector rose to 55.7 p.c. This suggests a progressive development of the Indian economy.

Finally, India's performance is not altogether discouraging if she is compared with other nations though India's per capita income is one of the lowest in the world. India's average annual GNP per capita between 1985 and 2006 grew at the rate of 7.4 p.c. as contrasted to the U.S.A's and U.K's 1.3 p.c. However, China performed much better than India. Its GDP per capita during the same period grew at the rate of 9.8 p.c. In recent years, growth rates in all the economies have slumped down due to global recession.

Now, we may sum up the main points. We have registered a higher growth rate in national income and per capita income—an improvement over the Hindu rate of growth of 3.5 p.c. during the previous three decades. The query is whether such high growth can be sustained or not. Sustainability of higher growth rate for a long period is of utmost importance.

However, after the initiation of economic reforms process in 1991, the country is poisd for higher economic growth. Between 1992-93 and 2001-02, GDP grew at an average annual rate of 6.1 p.c. Although, the GDP growth rate declined to 5.3 p.c. in 2002-03, it increased to around 8.5 p.c. in 2003-04 and 9.2 p.c. in 2006-07. Thus, an air of optimisim prevails. It is hoped that sustainable growth on a long-term basis has been achieved against some unexpected shocks like the East Asian crisis, global recession, unprecedented rise in international oil prices, Indo-Pak border tension, severe natural calamities, the Iraq war, etc. Above all, there is some sort of macroeconomic stability (like low rate of inflation, reasonable stable exchange rate, high foreign exchange reserves, adequate stocks of foodgrains even in the midst of drought). It may not be out of place to point out here that the primary objective of the New Economic Policy was to put the Indian Economy on a sustainable high growth path.

We may conclude this section with a quotation from *'Oxford Companion to Economics in India'* edited by Kaushik Basu: "It has now become the latest poster child for how economic growth can be unleashed with a turn towards free markets and open trade. India has yet to catch up with China's growth rates (or China's level of income), but thanks to its solid democratic institutions and impressive performance in information technology, the country is increasingly vying with China as the country of the future."

12.9. SECTORAL DISTRIBUTION OF NATIONAL INCOME OF INDIA

By economic structure we mean interrelationship among different productive sectors—agriculture and allied activities, manufacturing and mining and trade and commerce. The relationships among these sectors change gradually as economic development proceeds. In other words, structural changes indicate economic development. In the course of economic growth, the high rates of increase in population and output have been associated with noticeable changes in the relative shares of various sectors in total output and in total resources used.

Colin Clark viewed economic development through a triad of structural changes. Nations beginning as initial primary goods producers (agriculture and fishing) move to a higher level of development with the production of manufactured goods. The secondary stage comes through advancement in knowledge and skill. With the concomitant material accumulation, nations then seek greater welfare through higher forms of culture and labour moves from a goods-orientation to a service-orientation. Contribution of this sector toward national product rises. Representative of the tertiary stage is the growth in the transport, distribution and public administration sector. The highest levels of income are attained through non-material output.

The process of economic development as experienced by the developed nations is marked by three distinct phases : an early initial phase of the dominance of the primary sector, an intermediate phase dominated by industry and manufacturing, and, a final phase dominated by the services sector. At its peak, the secondary sector's contribution stood at around 50 p.c. of the total output in many of the developed countries. Later period showed its decline in contribution to one-fourth of the total output. Tertiary sector in these countries now contribute 70-75 p.c.

In the course of economic growth, the high rates of increase in population and output have been associated with noticeable changes in the relative shares of various sectors in total output and in total resources used. Here we distinguish three major sectors: *primary* (agriculture, forestry, fisheries, hunting, mining and quarrying), *secondary* (manufacturing, construction, electricity, gas and water supply), and *tertiary* (trade, transportation, communication, finance, tourism, insurance and real estate). The sumtotal of net value added of these three sectors constitute the Net Domestic Production (NDP) of an economy.

With the launching of the Five Year Plans, far-reaching changes in India's economic structure involving more and more direct participation of the State have taken place. This is described below.

First, as the pace of economic development quickens, the importance of primary sector towards its contribution to national income declines while secondary and tertiary sectors attain more prominence in terms of its contribution to national income. This sort of change in the sectoral distribution of national income has taken place in India during the planning period, thereby indicating economic development.

In 1950-51, the share of the primary sector in GDP was as high as 55 p.c., while it was 16.1 per cent for the secondary sector. There has been a steady decline in the share of primary sector in GDP and it declined to 19.4 p.c. in 2007-08. On the other hand, over the planning period, as the industrial sector expanded, its contribution towards GDP had been on the increase and it rose to 24.9 p.c. in 2007-08. Along with the growth of the secondary sector, the service sector has also registered a higher growth during the last 58 years of planning. Table 12.2 (p.245) shows that, compared to the secondary sector, the share of the tertiary sector (comprising mainly the service sector) improved much, from 29.2 p.c. in 1950-51 to 55.7 p.c. in 2007-08. The increase in contribution has been shared equally by the sub-sectors like transport, communication and trade, finance and real estate, community and personal services. The tertiary sector, whose present contribution is more than one-half of the GDP, grew at the rate of 6.8 p.c. p.a. in the 1990s and about 9 p.c. in 2000s. Table 12.2 indicates the sectoral distribution of GDP during the period between 1950-51 and 2007-08.

The changing structure of national income, therefore, indicates industrialisation, albeit at a slow pace. Further, one also notices structural changes within the industrial sector. During the planning period, India's industrial structure has undergone a change. Till the mid-1960s, India's industrial structure tilted heavily in favour of capital goods industries. This, of course, is a sign of industrialisation. But, since then, industrial structure is heavily biased in favour of consumer goods industries which mainly cater to the needs of the rich urban population. Again, among the industries, it is the organised manufacturing and mining industries that have fared well as compared with unorganised small enterprises. Still then, unregistered small and tiny sectors occupy a dominant position in the Indian economy as necessary supports to these industries are given by the Government.

The tertiary sector is not a homogeneous category. It indicates trade, transport and communications, banking and insurance, real estate and dwellings, public administration, community and persoanl services. The share of these heterogeneous activities rose from 29.2 p.c. in 1950-51 to 55.7 p.c. in 2007-08 at 1999-2000 prices. As a result of a better growth recorded in the tertiary sector, one sees a significant change, a "change from a subsistence to a market-oriented economy." This suggests modernisation of the economy.

Thus, over the period under discussion, the Indian economy today is now less geared to the primary sector and more attuned to the secondary and tertiary sectors. And between the last two sectors, the growth of the tertiary sector is remarkable. Such growth rate has become possible due to the employment of modern technology-intensive computers, automation, telecommunica-tions. Coupled with this, one notices massive growth of informal sector both in rural and urban areas. Informal sector includes casual building labour, domestic servants, cottage industries not subject to licence, taxation, etc. This may be regarded from the development point of view as a progressive change in the structure of the Indian economy during this period.

However, these is a caveat. During the last 20 years or so, we see a steady decline of the agricultural sector while the share of industry remains somehow constant at around 24-25 p.c. But the share of tertiary sector is more than 55 p.c. "Such a large share for services in the total output at a relatively early stage of development is untypical—a trend that has prompted some economists to wonder if India has defied the conventional paradigm of economic development by 'leapfrogging' over the manufacturing sector by shifting directly from agriculture to services."

Secondly, as regards structural change in the distribution of GDP between commodity and service sector, one finds a faster growth of the latter. Such a shift in favour of the service sector indicates modernisation. But the growth of the non-commodity sectors at the expense of the commodity sector does not augur well as far as structural changes are concerned.

Finally, another aspect of India's national income growth is the rise in contribution of the public sector in GDP. The contribution of the public sector in GDP rose from 10.7 p.c. in 1960-61 to 20.8 p.c. in 1981-82 and to 24 p.c. in 2000-01. This increase is attributed to the massive extension of government activities and their diversification. However, in 2005-06 the contribution declined to 11.12 p.c. of GDP.

On the basis of these national income trends and structural changes, we can conclude that the Indian economy can no longer be described as a typical underdeveloped country. Definitely some developments have taken place.

Most importantly, she is one of the great economic powers of the world. The growth model that the country has been pushing since 1991 is, thus, an examplary one. Over the last four or five years her steady economic growth rate is only comparable with the neighbouring country–China. However, this quantitative growth is not the only yardstick of development. Indicators of human development—such as literacy and education, and maternal and infant mortality rates show steady improvement, but they also suggest that the progress is slow and we continue to lag behind many neighbouring Asian countries.

12.10. CAUSES OF SLOW AND FLUCTUATING GROWTH OF NATIONAL INCOME IN INDIA

Raising of national and per capita incomes has been one of the basic objectives of Indian planning. This is known as "growth objective." Despite some gains in this direction, freakish and erratic growth trends continue. Above all, the growth rates are low and are less than those of some African countries. Table 12.6 highlights the slow and fluctuating growth trends of national and per capita incomes.

Table 12.6: Annual Growth Rates of National and Per Capita Incomes (at 1999-2000 prices) [annual percentage]

	GNP at Factor cost		Per Capita NNP
	Target	Actual	Actual
First Plan	2.1	3.6	2.6
Second Plan	4.5	4.0	1.7
Third Plan	5.6	2.8	0.4
Fourth Plan	5.7	3.9	0.8
Fifth Plan	4.4	5.0	2.6
Sixth Plan	5.2	5.4	3.1
Seventh Plan	5.0	5.5	3.3
Eighth Plan	5.6	6.6	4.5
Ninth Plan	6.5	5.5	3.3
Tenth Plan	8.0	7.8	6.1

Source: Economic Survey, 2006-07, 2007-08

Growth of national income in the First Plan was well ahead of the target. Between Second and Fifth Plans, growth rate of national income fell below the targeted rate. The growth rate picked up marginally in later plans. Ninth and the Tenth Plan also exhibited an actual growth rate that remained below the target rate. However, not only actual growth rate was low but it also exhibited ups and downs. For instance, both national income and per capita income dropped very sharply in the Third and Fourth Plans as compared to that in the Second Plan. Though both national and per capita incomes rose in the Fifth Plan, they again showed accelerating trends in the Sixth Plan. Tempo of higher growth rate has been maintained all along during the 1980s and 1990s. From 1975 onwards, one finds a steady growth rate of national income at a rate of roughly 5.70 p.c. Year to year there may be fluctuations, but trend growth suggests a growth rate of more than 5 p.c. Thus, the growth of national and per capita income has never been uniform during the entire plan period. Now we will explain and analyse the reasons of slow and fluctuating trends of national income.

In the *first* place, the performance of the Indian economy is very much linked with the performance of the agricultural sector. When agricultural production suffers due to some accidental factors like flood or drought, India's national income is bound to decline. This is happening even after 58 years of planning! If normal weather conditions prevail, a relatively higher growth rate could be struck. Thus, the dependence of the economy on agriculture does not only cause wide fluctuations in growth rate but also results in a slow growth. This dependence on agriculture must be liquidated, so that stability in the growth rate could be maintained.

Secondly, population growth in India at a rate of slightly less than 2 p.c. per annum has resulted in a low per capita income. Resources for investment in productive sectors are now being diverted to feed extra mouths that are appearing in the economy every year. Consequently, standards of living have fallen and the number of people below the poverty line is on the rise.

Thirdly, the high capital-output ratio is also contributing towards slow growth of income. Capital-output ratio (K/O) is defined as the ratio of investment to change in output. If 5 rupees worth of capital or investment results in an addition of one rupee, then capital-output ratio (K/O) becomes 5 : 1. In India, capital-output ratio has been rising at a faster rate which appears to be non-plausible and undesirable in the present context. This ratio has been doubled to above 6.0 in the Sixth and Seventh Plans from 3.0 in earlier plans. This ratio hovered between 4 and 4 in the last three plans. This higher K/O has failed to result in an increase in income. Underutilisation of capacity is one of the contributing causes of high K/O in India, though it is expected that the ratio would increase as economy advances and modernises. Lack of demand, slowdown of public investment, inefficiency of management, industrial recession, etc., have all contributed towards low level of capacity utilisation.

Fourthly, slowdown of public investment is another cause. Thus, the phenomenon of under-investment has resulted in a small output growth of investment goods. Further, this has created various types of infrastructural bottlenecks, resulting in a low growth of various sectors. Above all, following the slowdown of public investment, investment in the private sector has been crowded out. That is to say, all these have led to the slow expansion of output in all the sectors of the economy.

Fifthly, power generation has an important bearing on economic activity. Terrific power shortage that has gripped the Indian economy has had a disastrous effect on agricultural and industrial output. Power supply has been deteriorating in most states and power shortages are becoming endemic and acute. The consequence of all these is the low growth rate as well as unstable growth rate of the Indian economy.

Finally, fluctuations in the international market as well as global recession have had an important bearing on the nation's output.

What is clear from this discussion is that an unstable (virtually inherent) growth rate affects the average level of performance not just in terms of the volume of production but also in terms of quality of production in the sense that instability affects (i) income distribution, and (ii) price expectations.

12.11. DIFFICULTIES IN ESTIMATING INDIA'S NATIONAL INCOME

National income of a country is computed or estimated by three methods: (i) national expenditure method, (ii) national income method, and (iii) national product method. Though these methods yield more or less the same figure of national income, we combine all these methods to arrive at the national income figure.

In India, the national income statistics are regularly published and prepared by the Central Statistical Organisation (CSO) in its annual publication—National Accounts Statistics. It is also known as the "White Paper." The CSO estimates national income by the product method in the commodity sectors. These are: agriculture, forestry and logging, fishing, mining and quarrying and large scale manufacturing, electricity, gas and water supply, transport, storage and communication, trade, hotels and restaurants, housing and insurance real estate and ownership of dwellings and business services, public administration and defence. Both commodity flow and expenditure methods are adopted for this construction industry. Former is used in urban construction and the latter is used in rural construction. The expenditure method is employed in *kutcha* construction while the commodity flow method is employed in *pucca* construction.

Thus the sumtotal of net value added at factor cost of all the sectors gives us the net domestic product (NDP) at factor cost. By adding net factor income from abroad to NDP at factor cost, we obtain the figure for NNP at factor cost or the national income of India.

- **Difficulties of Measuring National Income in India**: However, the calculation of national income in any country is beset with many problems. Problems are more acute in underdeveloped countries like India than any advanced country. These problems are grouped into two : (i) conceptual or theoretical problems, and (ii) practical or statistical problems. However, as there is no escape route to avoid all the conceptual problems related to the estimation of national income in our country, we set aside these problems and consider practical problems. Of course, over the planning period, we have been able to overcome some of the statistical problems following an improvement in the methodology of national income estimation.

Following are the practical problems:

- *Lack of reliable data*: The reliability of data relating to national income is often questioned in India. National income estimate is made on the basis of primary data relating to incomes and values of goods produced. In India, this is because of the fact that many producers, particularly small-scale producers, do not maintain any accounts relating to their incomes or goods produced in a financial year. Obviously, the primary data collected from this sector is supposed to be vague. The reason behind this is illiteracy. Further, people are reluctant to cooperate with the data collectors. Above all, data collectors often 'fabricate' data even without approaching the door of producing sectors or economic units. If this information is considered as the basis of the judgement, then the judgement will suffer from inaccuracy.
- *Existence of non-monetised sector*: In India, the soundness of national income estimate is affected badly since there exists a large non-monetised sector. This, consequently leads to valuation problem. One witnesses the existence of an unorganised barter economy in rural India where money is not used. In each situation, the problem of valuation of goods produced crops up. Further, our farmers retain a large chunk of their production for self-consumption. Naturally, a large amount of output does not come to the market at all and is not subject to the valuation process. By imputing values to these goods, the problem of valuation can be partially removed. But considering the vastness of the country, such imputation is really a stupendous task. Even if imputation is possible, its reliability may also be doubted.
- *Difficulties in the classification of working population*: In India, 'working population' is not very clearly defined. Agriculturists in India are not engaged

in agriculture round the year. Obviously, in the off-season, they engage themselves in alternative occupations. Thus, the data relating to the people engaged in different occupations is bound to be unsatisfactory. Consequently, different sources of income become undefined.

In view of these problems and limitations, estimation of national income of India is not an easy task. However, conscious efforts are being made constantly to improve their methodology of estimation.

12.12. SAVINGS AND CAPITAL FORMATION TREND

Capital formation or investment is the kingpin of economic development. Or one can also say that an important element in the growth process of developing countries like India is the rate of saving or the saving-income ratio. It is because the accumulation of capital—perhaps the most important source of growth in such countries—depends on the rate of savings. Savings and investment are, thus, crucial to capital formation.

One of the basic goals of Indian planning is the step-up of the rate of capital formation. In fact, the rate of capital formation or investment has risen substantially during nearly six decades (1951-2007) of planning. However, the 70s and early 80s can rightly be called the *golden era* in Indian savings and investment rate. Gross domestic savings increased from 8.9 p.c. of GDP in 1950-51 to 24.8 p.c. of GDP in 2006-07. Net domestic capital formation increased from 5.2 p.c. to 28.4 p.c. during this time. Table 12.7 shows growth of domestic savings and capital formation in the period 1950-2007.

Table 12.7: Rates of Saving and Capital Formation (%)

	Gross Domestic Savings (as % of GDP)	Net Domestic Savings (as % NDP)	Net Domestic Capital Formation
1950-51	8.9	5.5	5.2
1970-71	14.6	8.6	9.5
1980-81	18.9	11.3	12.9
1990-91	23.1	15.1	18.7
2000-01	23.7	15.6	16.3
2005-06	34.3	26.5	27.9
2006-07	34.8	27.1	28.4

Source: SOI : 2006 -07, 2007-08

In the 1980s, the performance of the Indian economy in relation to saving-investment rate was respectable by international standards and was certainly high for a market economy and in an unregimented society like India. At present, gross domestic savings stands out around 35 p.c., though less than the level attained in the late 70s. However, what was paradoxical in the Indian context is that although the rate of savings and capital formation increased particularly in the late 70s, the rate of growth of the Indian economy—as measured by national and per capita incomes—was low. Between 1970-71 and 1979-80, national income grew by 3.3. p.c. while per capita income rose by 1.1 p.c. National income growth rate was in the vicinity of Raj Krishna's "Hindu rate of growth"—3.5 p.c. This peculiar phenomenon has been dubbed by economists as 'saving-investment puzzle'.

On the other hand, investment rate in the 1970s increased considerably. For instance, gross capital formation went up from 16.9 p.c. in 1972-73 to 23.7 p.c. in 1978-79. Net capital formation as percentage of NDP also registered phenomenal increase from 11.9 p.c. to 19.0 per cent during the said time period. The most striking aspect of saving-investment rate of this period was that domestic saving exceeded domestic investment rate between 1975-76 and 1978-79, thus resulting in an outflow of foreign resources. During this time, the country also experienced an unprecedented growth of precious foreign exchange reserves but the government could not utilise them in a meaningful way. As a result of all these, domestic savings could not be channelised for genuine investment, though buoyancy in investment rate was clearly visible. In fact, the high investment rate achieved so far could not be utilised in building up the capital stock of the country.

Meanwhile, capital-output ratio of 2.6 in the 1950s rose to almost 6.21 in the late 1970s. This high capital-output ratio indicates declining productivity of investment (largely due to an inefficient pattern of investment and underutilisation of production capacity), which largely explains India's unimpressive growth performance.

Thus, saving-investment problem of the country in the 1970s, on a closer scrutiny, appears to be unsatisfactory. Obviously, the country could not register a higher growth rate.

- **Saving-investment rate in the 1980s, 1990s and 2000s**: In Table 12.7, we have shown the growth rates of savings and investment in the 1980s, 90s and 2000s. In the 80s, their growth rates were also impressive, though there had been some stagnation in the level of savings in relation to GDP for some years. Gross capital formation also showed a similar trend. Stagnation in the level of saving in the 80s was due to the fact that net savings of the public sector was negative and low as far as private corporate sector was concerned. Household sector's savings is still the mainstay of the nation's saving.

In fact, it continues to grow. Further, one may deserve that the household sector today saves more through financial assets rather than physical assets. However, in recent times because of the rising popularity of housing loans, investment in physical assets is also on the rise. Also, a variety of consumer loans through banks help people to acquire assets. All these also indicate growing consumerism in the reform decades. Explosive consumerism has its toll on the growth forces. Liberalisation-globalisation mode is yet to develop satisfactory results. Low rates of growth and high rates of savings go ill together with national integration.

Still then, gross and net saving rates standing around 35 p.c. and 27 p.c. in 2007 were definitely on the high side and comparable to the advanced nations of the world.

Needles to say, adequate domestic saving is not an end in itself. What is required is how this increased saving is invested.

It is said that high rates of investment are critical for rapid growth. Investment rate in the Eighth Plan averaged 24.4 p.c. and it remained almost unchanged in the Ninth Plan. After then it rose and in the Tenth Plan (2002-07), it accelerated to nearly 36 p.c. It is hoped by the planners that such high ratio of investment would be helpful to attain the growth rate of 9 p.c. during the Eleventh Plan (2007-2012).

QUESTIONS (WITH ANSWER-HINTS)

Long Question (16 marks)

1. What is meant by a developing economy? What are the common characteristics of underdeveloped countries/developing a country?

   Ans. 12.2.

2. The Indian economy possesses the major characteristics of underdevelopment. Comment on the statement.

   Or

   What are the general features of underdevelopment? According to them, do you think that India is an underdeveloped economy?

   Or

   What are the basic characteristics of the Indian economy? State whether the Indian economy can be regarded as an underdeveloped economy because of those features.

   Ans. 12.3.

3. Discuss the nature of economic underdevelopment of India.

   Ans. 12.3.

4. "Indian economy is a developing economy". Discuss this statement in the light of the changes that have occurred in the Indian economy in the last 58 years or so.

   Or

   What type of structural changes do you expect in the course of economic development? Has India experienced such changes?

   Or

   Explain the main features of the Indian economy. Do you agree that it is a developing economy?

   Ans. 12.4 and 12.9.

5. Comment on the trends in the occupational distribution of workforce and the sectoral composition of national income of India. Do these trends indicate any significant change in the structure of the Indian economy?

   Ans. 12.4.

6. How do you estimate national income or national product of a country?

   Or

   Discuss the various methods of measuring national income of a country.

   Ans. 12.6.

7. Discuss the salient features revealed by an analysis of the growth pattern of India's national income since 1951.

   Ans. 12.8.

8. Discuss the trends in India's national income during the plan period. What are the causes of slow and fluctuating growth of national income in India?

   Ans. 12.8 and 12.10.

9. Analyse the change in the structure of Indian economy as seen in the national income data.

   Or

   Comment on the changes in the sectoral composition of India's national income.

   Ans. 12.4 and 12.9.

Medium-sized Questions (8 marks)

1. What do you mean by national income accounts?

   Ans. 12.5.

2. Distinguish between GDP and GNP. Define GDP at market prices, GDP at factor cost and NNP.

   Ans. 12.7.

3. What are the difficulties generally faced in carrying out national income computations?

   Ans. 12.11.

4. Make a brief review of growth rates of savings and capital formation during the plan period.

   Ans. 12.12.

13

INDIAN AGRICULTURE—PROBLEMS, PERFORMANCE AND POLICIES

13.1. ROLE OF AGRICULTURE IN THE INDIAN ECONOMY

Most people in less developed countries (LDCs) like India depend upon agriculture— directly and indirectly. Thus, agricultural growth and conditions governing the distribution of agricultural produce are of direct relevance to such countries. So, it is necessary to know at the outset the place of agriculture in India's economy.

Even after about six decades (1951-2008) of planning, agriculture continues to remain the most dominant sector of the Indian economy. The majority (52 p.c.) population of India depend on agriculture as a means of livelihood. In fact, agriculture is more a way of life than a mode of business although its contribution to GDP has been declining persistently to one-fifth. Also the forward and backward linkage effects of agricultural growth have the potentiality of raising incomes and employment in the non-agricultual sector. This suuggests that agriculture not only helps in pushing the overall growth of the economy but also helps in reducing (rural) poverty by providing employment and food security to the Indian masses.

The important place of agriculture in the Indian economy can be assessed by considering different roles of agriculture. These are reviewed below :

- *Contribution to Gross Domestic Product (or National Income)*: In 1950-51 agriculture contributed about 55 p.c. of India's national income (GDP). However, the percentage gradually dropped down to 19.4 p.c. in 2007-08. In other countries, the percentage contribution of agriculture in national income is much lower. In most developed countries of the world—like the UK, and the USA, Canada, Japan and Australia— it is below 5 p.c. In fact, the sectoral composition of GDP indicates the level of development of a country. The greater the contribution of agriculture and allied activities in GDP, the more economically backward a country is supposed to be. Thus, the preponderance of agriculture in India's national production is a symptom of backwardness.

- *Employment generation*: Most people in India derive their livelihood from agriculture. Agriculture is still the most dominant sector in as much a high proportion of working population continues to depend on agriculture. In India, the percentage of working population depending on agriculture was 69.7 as per 1961 and 1971 censuses. The percentage has remained more or less unchanged since then. In 2001, it dropped down to 57 p.c. In 2006-07 it was 52 p.c. of the workforce. In most industrially advanced countries the percentage varies between 1 and 7. By contrast, it varies between 40 and 70 in most developing countries. In China, the percentage is probably the highest (72), followed by India (52.7), Indonesia (52), Myanmar (50) and Egypt (42).
- *Contribution to industrial development*: Agriculture is also important for another reason. If it fails to develop at a suitable pace, it could prove to be a major constraint on the growth of industrial and other sectors. It is not only the supplier of an essential wage good, viz. food, but also of raw materials to industry. Moreover, agriculture could provide the motive for industrial expansion by being a major market for industrial goods.

In India, agriculture has all along been the major supplier of raw materials to the basic industries like jute and cotton textiles, sugar, vanaspati, and plantations. Additionally, some industries depend on agriculture indirectly such as small-scale and cottage industries like handloom weaving, oil crushing, rice husking, and so on. Such agro-based industries—which depend on agriculture for their raw materials—together account for half of the income generated in India's secondary (manufacturing) sector.

Over the last 58 years of planning, interdependence between agriculture and industry has been strengthened by various linkages. These are: (i) production linkages, (ii) demand linkages, and (iii) savings-investment linkages. Production linkages occur through the use of inputs—agriculture draws some raw materials from the industry and industry too draws from agriculture. Further, because of green revolution in agriculture, demand for some industrial goods has increased in rural areas. Industrialisation, urbanisation and the consequent rising incomes have increased the demand for agricultural product. In addition, there is a savings-investment linkage between these two sectors.

However, in recent years, the importance of agriculture has declined mainly due to industrial diversification. Some important industries set up during the plan period—iron and steel, petrochemicals, machine tools, light and heavy engineering, aircraft, etc.,—do not depend on agriculture at all.

- *Contribution to foreign trade*: Agriculture has all along played a very important role in India's external trade. Three major items of India's traditional exports viz. tea, jute and cotton textiles, are agro-based. Other items include sugar, oilseeds, tobacco, and spices. According to an estimate, farm exports constituted about 50 p.c. of India's total exports in 1960-61. In addition, manufactures with high agricultural output (such as jute goods, clothing and sugar) accounted for another 20 p.c. This export contribution of agriculture is of considerable significance in as much as agricultural exports enable the country to pay for its maintenance and development, imports of raw materials and capital goods (such as machinery and transport equipment). In 2000-01, its contribution declined to as low as 13.5 p.c. Weak export infrastructure, problem of gradation of agricultural export goods, defective packaging seem to be the reasons for declining volume of exports of agricultural goods over the period of time. However, net exports of foodgrains exceed net import of foodgrains. In recent times, exports of non-traditional items like vegetables, flowers milk products, animal meat, marine products, food processing goods have seen a amountum increase. This diversification of exportsaugurs well.
- *Role in planning*: The importance of agriculture can be discovered in other spheres also. For example, the success of planning in India depends on adequate resource mobilisation. This, in its turn, is largely conditioned by the progress made on the agricultural front. For instance, bumper crop implies prosperity all-round i.e., large purchasing power with the farmers and greater demand for industrial goods and, therefore, satisfactory prices. Thus, industrial prosperity largely depends on the prosperity of the farmers. On the other hand, a setback on the agricultural front, i.e., crop failure in one or two consecutive years, implies famine or near-famine conditions, and widespread poverty and starvation. This, in its turn, leads to a fall in the demand for manufactures and causes recession. In fact, a fall in revenue of the farmers leads to a fall in demand for clothing, radio sets, T.V. sets, etc. Thus, the success of planning in India largely depends on the performance of agriculture.
- *Revenue*: In fact, finances of the Government, especially State Governments, largely depend on agricultural prosperity. Agriculture is a State subject and agricultural taxation is a source of revenue of the State Governments.
- *Internal trade and transport*: Moreover, agriculture seems to provide the main support to the country's transport system. Railways and roads secure the major portion of their business from the movement of agricultural commodities from producing to distant consuming centers. In fact, India's internal trade largely consists of purchase and sale of agricultural commodities.

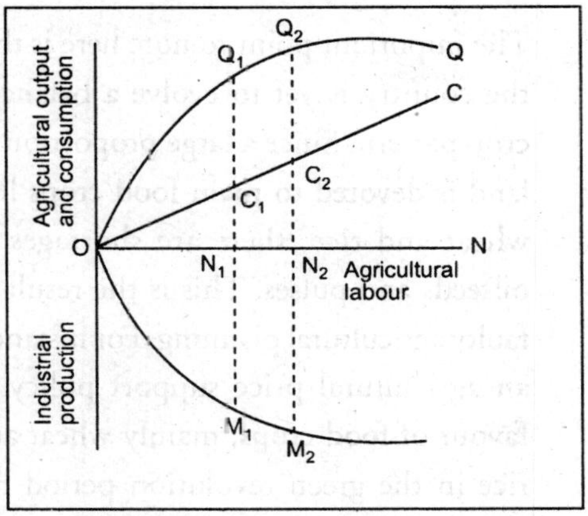

Fig. 13.1: Interdependent Development

How does increased agricultural productivity contribute towards greater economic development can be explained in terms of Fig. 13.1. Here we consider two sectors—agriculture and industry. Argicultural production and consumption are measured on the vertical axis above the origin while industrial output is measured on the vertical axis below the origin. Horizontal axis (ON axis) measures agricultural labour. Agricultural output is indicated by OQ curve. Its shape is governed by the law of variable proportions. OC curve measures consumption of agricultural output. The difference between OQ and OC curve measures the value of surplus generated by the agricultural sector. At ON_1 level of employment made in the agricultural sector, C_1Q_1 surplus agricultural output is available. Investment of such surplus generates N_1M_1 output in the industrial sector. As employment increases to ON_2 in the primary sector, industrial output rises to N_2M_2. Technological change will generate more surplus and, hence, more output in the industrial sector.

Thus, there is no denying the fact that agriculture is the backbone of the Indian economy. At the same time, agriculture itself is characterised by low land and labour productivity. In fact, there is a feeling among most contemporary economists that the over-dependence on agriculture continues to remain the root cause of India's economic backwardness even after 58 years of planning. Thus, unless the dependence on agriculture is considerably reduced, India's per capita income growth will never be satisfactory.

13.2. MAJOR FEATURES OR PROBLEMS OF INDIAN AGRICULTURE

Although agriculture is the dominant sector of the Indian economy, it is characterised by low productivity. This, in turn, is attributable to a number of factors. Truly speaking, even at the beginning of the 21st century, Indian agriculture is beset with a multitude of problems. Some of these problems have the origin in the pre-independent India. These are discussed below:

- *Instability*: It is said that Indian agriculture is a 'gamble of monsoon'. It is at the mercy of the weather god. Being of rain-fed, Indian agriculture exhibits instability in production, leading to fluctuations in national income as well as general price level. This is what we experienced in 2002-03 when agriculture made a disastrous start. An all-time record in foodgrains production was achieved in 2001-02. In 2002-03, the first ever deficient monsoon in 15 years was declared. The rainfall deficiency for the country as a whole amounted to more than 20 p.c. in 2003-04. As a result, the production of foodgrains fell by about 14 p.c. and non-foodgrains by 9 p.c. Reports of starvation death from two drought-hit states of Rajasthan and Madhya Pradesh indicate the dismal performance of the agricultural sector over the last 58 years or so. Thus, the fortune of the Indian economy is very much tied to rain-dependent agriculture. This element of instability makes it a precarious occupation.

Besides weather-induced fluctuations, one also finds that output of this sector is also affected due to reduced capital investment and plateauing of yield levels in major crops. Further, with uncertainties in global markets, and hardening of the prices of food, fuels and edible oils all over the world, domestic price stability and food security critically depend on the growth of this sector.

- *Cropping pattern*: The crops that are grown in India are divided into two broad categories: food crops and non-food crops. An unhealthy competition exists between these two crops. Of the total cropped area, nearly three-fourths are occupied by food crops. The ratio of foodgrains to non-foodgrains was 80:20 in 1980-81 vis-a-vis 77:23 in 1950-51. By 2000-01, the area under non-foodgrains increased to roughly 35 p.c. Within foodgrains, largest increase in area has been recorded by wheat, followed by rice. Within commercial crops, largest increase has occurred in the case of sugarcane, followed by oilseeds and cotton. The horticulture sector contributed about 28 p.c. of GDP in agriculture in 2005-06. Such diversification of farming towards horticulture crops may be related to (i) demand-driven, (ii) supply-driven, and (iii) policy-driven forces.

  The important point to note here is that the country is yet to evolve a balanced crop pattern. Since a large proportion of land is devoted to main food crops like wheat and rice, there are shortages of oilseeds and pulses. This is the result of faulty agricultural planning. For instance, an agricultural price support policy in favour of food crops, mainly wheat and rice in the green revolution period has distroted the cropping pattern. Very little attention has been given to agricultural diversification. Floriculture and horticulture are two profitable agro-busineses that require special attention.
- *Land ownership*: Vast inequality exists in the distribution of land in India. A great chunk of land is owned by a relatively small section of the rich farmers, landlords and money lenders, while a very little amount of land is owned by the majority farmers. Nearly 76 p.c. of small and marginal farmers own less than 2 hectares of land (2000-01). Total cultivable land belonging to these people covers as much as 35 p.c. On the other hand, big farmers owning more than 10 hectares land hold as much as 14 p.c. of the cultivable lands.
- *Average size of holding*: Another peculiarity as well as an important problem is the smallness in average size of holding. The average size of holding declined from 2.28 hectares in 1970-71 to 1.41 hectanes in 1995-96 and 1.32 hectares in 2002-01. This makes the efficient use of land virtually impossible and add to the difficulties of increasing capital equipment on the farms.

Table 13.1: Output and Yield of Selected Crops of Selected Countries, 2003

	Rice		Wheat		Cotton (Lint)		Groundnut (in shell)	
	Output	Yield (100 kg per hectare)	Output	Yield (100 kg per hectare)	Output	Yield	Output	Yield
India	22.4	30.0	11.7	26.2	11.2	7.5	21.0	9.4
China	28.2	60.7	15.5	39.1	27.8	34.7	37.7	26.2
USA	1.5	74.5	11.4	29.7	17.9	20.6	5.3	35.4

Source: Statistical Outline of India, 2006-07

- *Land tenure*: The land tenure system of India is also far from perfect. Tenants do not enjoy security of tenure. They are evicted by landlords on any pretext.
- *Production technique*: The technique of production in India's agriculture is old and outmoded. Still, Indian farmers are using cow-plough method of cultivation on a large-scale. Use of chemical fertilisers, high-yielding varieties of seeds, tractors, machines are used on an insignificant scale. However, in recent times because of the introduction of the green revolution in the 1960s, some improvements have taken place. Still then, their uses are not significant and uniform throughout India.
- *Excessive pressure on land*: Another problem from which Indian agriculture suffers is that the pressure on land as compared to the availability of land is too high. Finding a bleak employment prospects, people take up agriculture as an important occupation. But they ultimately reduce themselves to part time jobs. As a result, Indian agriculture exhibits the existence of a large bogey of unemployeds and disguisedly un-employeds. They remain unemployed in part of the seasons. This causes backwardness in Indian agriculture.

Further, marketing of agricultural products is far from satisfactory. Because of low productivity, the quantum of surplus generated in the agricultural sector is low. Moreover, the collection of these surpluses for the purpose of marketing presents a serious problem.

Again, the typical Indian farmer who has to work on an 'uneconomic holding', using traditional methods of cultivation and being exposed to the risks of poor agricultural season, is always in debt. The Indian farmer is a perennial debtor. NSSO in its 59th Round of surveys observed that 48.6 p.c. of rural households were indebted and, of the total number of indebted farmers, 61 p.c. had operational holding below 1 hectare.

Because of the said problems plaguing Indian agriculture, another vital problem that emerges from this analysis is the low productivity per unit of land and labour, though India is an agricultural country. Technological, economic and social factors are responsible for the sorry productivity performance. However, in recent years, several measures have been adopted by the government to improve productivities. Some achievements have been recorded, but still inadequate compared to the country's needs.

13.3. LOW PRODUCTIVITY OF INDIAN AGRICULTURE

Agricultural productivity can be analysed from two different angles—from the point of view of productivity per acre (i.e., land productivity), and from the point of view of each worker employed (i.e., labour productivity). At the outset, it may be stated that Indian agriculture is characterised by miserably low land and labour productivity. Let us see, in greater detail, trends in agricultural productivity.

An unfortunate dichotomy is that while in terms of total output India compares favourably, but in terms of yield per hectare her position is hopeless. This can be gauged from (Table 13.1).

Causes of Low Productivity: The causes of low productivity may be grouped into three broad categories: (a) general factors, (b) institutional factors, and (c) technological factors.

▲ General Factors

- *Overcrowding in agriculture*: The real problem of Indian agriculture seems to be that there are too many people who depend on agriculture. The natural increase in population—from about 35 crore in 1947 to 113 crore in 2007—over 3 times could not be absorbed in industries. Moreover, dependence on agriculture increased due to the decline of handicrafts. Over-crowding and the consequent pressure of population on land have led to subdivision and fragmentation of holdings, decline in the area of land per capita, disguised unemployment and almost zero marginal productivity of labour.
  The area of cultivated land per hectare between 1901 and 1991 declined from 0.43 hectare to 0.22 hectare.
- *Unhealthy rural atmosphere*: The Indian farmers, generally speaking, are illiterate, ignorant, superstitious, conservative and bound by old customs and institutions such as the caste system, and the joint family system. Superstition and belief in fate are the curse which keep the farmers totally satisfied with their primitive system of cultivation. They are just happy if they manage to get two square meals a day. They have non-experimental outlook and are hardly motivated by considerations of economic progress.
- *Inadequate non-farm services*: Indian agriculture has suffered because of the inadequacy of such non-farm services as provision of irrigation, seed, finance, marketing, etc. Irrigation facilities in India are inadequate. Even after 60 years of planning, gross irrigated area as percentage of cropped area stands at 40.3 p.c. in 2003-04. This means 60 p.c. of the cropped area are rain-dependent. If the current trends in irrigation expansion by less than 1 million hectare per annum persist, we are afraid that more than half of the cultivated land would remain unirrigated even by 2012. Indian farmers are yet to learn intensively the use of improved seed-fertilisers. Agricultural credit arrangments are inadequate. Institutional sources of credit are mostly directed to the rich farmers. Problems get multiplied once the question of marketing of agricutural produce becomes dominant. Marketing facilities are extremely inadequate.

▲ Institutional Factors

- *Size of holdings*: The average size of holding in India is very low, less than 2 hectares or 5 acres. Not only agricultural holdings are small but they are fragmented too. So no scientific cultivation with improved implements, seeds, etc., is possible.
- *Insecurity of land tenure* : A potent force behind low agricultural productivity has been the absence of proper incentives. The cultivator does not often own the land; he has no security of tenancy; and he may be turned out of his land at any time the landowner desires. So the landless worker has little, if any, desire to increase productivity.

It is true that through various land reform measures semi-feudal agrarian structure had been broken to provide a greater fillip to agricultural productivity. The land reform measures are yet to break the semi-feudal rural structure. Landlordism in a different garb still prevails; eviction of tenants from land is still continuing. Rack-renting is not uncommon; ceiling laws have been violated. Thus, land reform measures not only failed to ensure social justice but also productivity of land could not be raised.

- *Investment inadequacy*: Low productivity in Indian agriculture may be attributed to low volume of governmental investment compared to the industrial sector. In the First Plan (1951-1956), investment in the agricultural sector stood at 31 p.c. It declined gradually to 19 p.c. by the Ninth Plan Period (1997-2002). Further, the possibility of resource mobilisation in the agricultural sector is rather bleak. Income generation in the form of land revenue and income tax is rather low. On the contrary, agricultural sector is largely subsidised. All these result in low volume of investment in the agricultural sector. In recent years, investment has declined to 1.3 p.c. of GDP. This is attributed to stagnation in public investment in the reform years.

▲ Technological Factors

- *Poor techniques of production*: The Indian farmers have been using old and inefficient methods and techniques of production generation after generation. Increase in production is possible only if proper and adequate manures are used. But, in India, the use of both farmyard manure and chemical fertilisers is mostly inadequate compared to our needs. The importance of good quality seeds to increase agricultural productivity hardly requires any emphasis. But, Indian farmers have been using seeds of very poor quality for decades.

With the launching of the New Agricultural Strategy in the mid-60s, the agricultural sector has witnessed a remarkable increase in production and productivity during the last three decades. Still then, it is inadequate compared to the country's needs. For instance, modern agricultural technology has had little spread effect among Indian farmers due to a variety of reasons. And, because of slower diffusion of knowledge of improved technology, its applicability is limited and, therefore, productivity differs from region to region. Some regions exhibit higher productivity compared to other states where new agricultural technology is used selectively.

- *Inadequate irrigation facilities*: One of the proximate causes of the weaknesses of Indian agriculture has been that most of the farmers throughout the country have to depend upon rainfall and very few of them can enjoy the facilities of artificial irrigation. It is the inadequate spread of irrigation facilities that acts as the main barrier for the adoption of HYV seeds. It is to be noted here that irrigated area in India generally tends to be used for rice and wheat cultivation while the other crops are grown mostly in rain-fed and unirrigated condition. This demands spreading of irrigation facilities to all crops.

Even after about 60 years of planning, Indian agriculture is highly monsoon-dependent. Roughly 40 p.c. of the total agricultural land is irrigated. This amounts to saying that the Indian agriculture is deficient of investment, though agriculture is the backbone of the nation. Such a step-motherly attitude towards agriculture, of course in a covert manner, has a deleterious effect on productivity and profitability. During the decade of reforms, the agricultural profitability has fallen by 14.2 p.c. Investment in this sector must be stepped up.

All these suggest that a proper long-term strategy for agricultural development had not been undertaken by the government. Truly speaking, a national agricultural policy had never been drawn up by the government. A national agricultural policy has just now been checked out, say after 58 years of planning. In addition, another distrubing factor is the neglect of capital formation in agriculture. All these have an impact on agricultural production in the future years.

National Agricultural Policy (2000) and Tenth Plan have given higher priority on raising agricultural productivity to promote faster growth of the agricultural sector as well on promoting the growth of the rural non-farm sector.

A centrally sponsored scheme on National Food Security Mission set up in 2007 aims at increasing foodgrains production through area expansion and productivity enhancement; restoring soil fertility and productivity; etc.

Suggested remedies: After identifying the causes of low productivity, we may now suggest some remedies for the same. *Prima facie*, attempts are being made to find alternative employments for rural population and to change the occupational structure in such a way that less than 45 p.c. of people continue to depend on agriculture. On the institutional front, the Government is trying to solve the problems of agriculture through land reforms. On the technological front, a modest beginning has been made in converting farmers to the use of improved implements, seeds, chemicals, manures, etc. Green revolution illustrates the point. Irrigation facilities are being increasingly made available. Double cropping, better rotation of crops, fighting plant diseases and pests, etc. are given due emphasis. However, it may be noted that "productivity enhancing investment in agriculture, however, depends not only on the state of knowledge but also on conditions governing the adoption of technology; it depends on the land tenure system which determines how the agricultural produce is divided between owners of land and agricultural labour; on the terms of trade between agriculture and industry, which determine the relative cheapness of industrial inputs vis-a-vis agricultural produce; and on the level of demand of agricultural produce."

It is only through an integrated measure of a policy/programme that the challenges facing Indian agriculture can be squarely met. The objectives of government policy should be to develop effective system and provide similar benefits to agriculture as does industry experience. Unfortunately, one finds a declining trend of investment in the agricultural sector. In view of this, prognosis for the future will be of dubious nature.

13.4. PROGRESS OF AGRICULTURE DURING THE PLAN PERIOD

- **The First Plan (1951-56)**: Immediately after independence, the country was faced with two major problems: food crisis, and shortage of industrial raw materials such as raw jute and raw cotton. The major objectives of the First Plan in the field of agriculture were to correct the imbalances caused by partition in the supply of foodgrains and commercial crops and improve infrastructural facilities. Agriculture, including irrigation and power, was, therefore, accorded the highest priority. That is why the First Plan assigned the maximum priority to the agricultural sector. This is clear from the fact that 31 p.c. of the total plan outlay was devoted to agriculture. But the First Plan set very modest targets for the production of most crops. The results achieved during the First Plan were quite satisfactory for two-fold reason—favourable weather conditions and effective implementation of plan programmes. Consequently, the target for foodgrains production was exceeded. As against the target of 62 million tonnes, actual production of foodgrains was nearly 66 million tonnes.

Efforts to improve agriculture were spread throughout the country and to involve every village in it through the Community Development Programme. A new land policy was also adopted with a view to eliminating exploitation and extending security of tenure.

- **The Second Plan (1956-61)**: However, there was a sudden reversal of strategy during the Second Plan. The emphasis shifted from agriculture to industry for three different reasons: (a) the smooth performance of agriculture during the First Plan period, (b) the possibility of financing economic development through foreign aid, particularly food aid, and (c) the consideration that heavy industry was the leading sector of economic development. The Government adopted the strategy of developing heavy industries following the then Soviet model of industrialisation. Consequently, the outlay on agriculture was reduced to 20 p.c from 31 p.c. made in the First Plan. But, as far as production of major crops was concerned, quite ambitious targets were set. However, due to the adoption of a wrong strategy, miscalculation and poor implementation of most of the programmes, the performance of the agriculture was quite dismal.

- **The Third Plan (1961-66)**: The planners subsequently realised that the strategy of development adopted during the Second Plan was wrong. It was felt that, in an agrarian economy, any setback on the agricultural front would spell disaster for the whole economy. Thus, during the Third Plan the Government made greater allocation for agriculture i.e., Rs 1,745 crore compared to Rs 950 crore in the Second Plan. However, the percentage share of agriculture in total plan outlay remained unchanged at 20.

The main objectives of the Plan were to achieve self-sufficiency in foodgrains and increase in agricultural production to meet the requirements of industry and export. A number of institutions were set up to extend support to development activities in different fields. The performance of the Plan was more or less satisfactory—at least in the first four years. A record output of 89 million tonnes had been achieved in case of foodgrains. However, the performance in the last year was dismal due to the disastrous drought of 1965-66 and two wars (one with China in 1962 and another with Pakistan in 1965).

However, in 1966-67, a new strategy of agricultural development was adopted. Its main planks were: (a) High Yielding Varieties Programme (HYVP), and (b) the Multiple Cropping Programme — both based on the exotic, high-yielding, short duration crop varieties. The other elements of the strategy were the new concepts of irrigation and water management, adaptive research and price guarantee to producers. However, due to failure on the agricultural front, the whole planning process received a severe jolt and formulation of the Fourth Plan was delayed by no less than three years.

- **The Fourth Plan (1969-74)**: While most of the programmes adopted under the new strategy were continued in the Fourth Plan, a new orientation was imparted to agricultural policy. In order to achieve growth with social justice, the agricultural policy laid stress on helping the weaker and vulnerable sections of the population and backward areas. High priority was accorded to technology as a major input. Besides attainment of self-sufficiency, the Plan envisaged building up of a sizable buffer stock and stoppage of concessional imports of foodgrains.

Modest targets were fixed for agricultural production and realistic allocations were made for agriculture and irrigation. The Plan started with a happy note. The production of foodgrains reached an all-time high of 108 million tonnes in 1970-71. However, poor monsoons in the next two years led to crop failure and this created the problem of price inflation.

- **The Fifth Plan (1974-79)**: Renewed emphasis was placed on agriculture in the Fifth Plan. The growth target in the agricultural and allied sectors had been fixed at 3.94 p.c. Necessary allocation was made for important programmes like minor irrigation, high-yielding varieties of seed and distribution of fertilisers.

As in the Fourth Plan, outlay on agriculture was 21 p.c. of total Fifth Plan outlay.

Ambitious targets were fixed for the agricultural sector. However, the performance was not satisfactory in the first year due to fall in production. Due to setback on the agricultural front, the rate of growth of the economy (as measured by per capita income) reached a vanishing point. The performance of the agricultural sector, however, started improving from the second year as output reached a new record. In spite of this, the Fifth Plan was cut short by one year by the erstwhile ruling party, the Janata Government.

- **The Sixth Plan (1980-85)**: The agricultural growth pattern during the Sixth Plan period took into account the immediate as well as long-term needs of agricultural commodities—both for domestic consumption and for export. The highest priority was assigned to bridging the gap prevailing between actual and potential farm yields even at current levels of technology through the removal of existing constraints. Agriculture and allied activities received adequate attention through the development of appropriate packages of technology, services and public policies.

- **The Seventh Plan (1985-90)**: Total outlay on agriculture, irrigation and rural development was Rs. 48,100 crore or 22 p.c. of the total plan outlay. The Seventh Plan aimed at an agricultural growth rate of 4 p.c. p.a. and the target for foodgrains output was kept at 3.7 p.c. p.a. The major programme thrusts in the Seventh Plan were (i) special rice production programmes in the Eastern region, (ii) National Oilseeds Development Projects, (iii) National Watershed Development Programme for rainfed agriculture, and (iv) social forestry. This sector withnessed a growth rate of 3.2 p.c. p.a.

During the Seventh Plan, the area under irrigation was proposed to be increased at the rate of 2.5 million hectares p.a.

- **The Eighth Plan (1992-97)**: The Eighth Plan gave priority to the "growth and diversification of agriculture to achieve self-sufficiency in food and generate a surplus for exports." Investment in agriculture, irrigation and allied sectors showed a sharp rise over the previous plans. The share of public and private sectors investments in the Eighth Plan in agriculture and rural development stood at 22 p.c. of the total investment as compared to 11.23 p.c. in the Seventh Plan. The Eighth Plan aimed at achieving an agricultural growth rate of 4 p.c. during the Plan period. A major effort was given during the Eighth Plan period to increase the output of rice, pulses and oilseeds.

During the plan period, there has been a shortfall in investment in all the sectors, including agriculture where, actual investment was just 59 p.c. of planned investment. Despite this, agriculture recorded a growth rate of 4.7 p.c. At the end year of that Plan, foodgrains output, however, touched a record level of 199.3 million tonnes against the target of 210 million tonnes.

- **The Ninth Plan (1997-2002)**: The thrust of the Ninth Plan was to achieve agriculture-led growth. For the first time since 1960s, the Planning Commission had focussed on agriculture, instead of industry, in the Ninth Plan.

It was targeted to grow at 4.5 p.c. p.a. during the Ninth Plan period. It envisaged a food production of 230 million tonnes against the 1990 million tonnes attained in 1996-97. Actual production of foodgrains fell far short of the targeted production. Actual production was 212 million—a shortfall of 18 million tonnes. In case of production of oilseeds, performance was disappointing. Anyway, food crisis did not emerge because of building up of huge buffer stock of foodgrains.

To achieve this growth rate, the Planning Commission recommended a four-pronged strategy including a viable minimum support price and input subsidy policy.

The public sector had been allocated Rs 8,75,000 crore. Agriculture got a whopping 19.4 p.c. of the total on outlay. The actual growth rate in agriculture and allied activities fell short even of the revised targets of 3.9 p.c. Realised growth rate for 1997-2002 came to 2.1 p.c. The reform process had failed to stimulate our agricultural sector.

- **The Tenth Plan (2002-07)**: The Ninth Plan experienced a slowdown in the growth potential of the economy that needed to be reversed in the Tenth Plan. As for as the sectoral allocation of public resources is concerned, agriculture did not receive high priority in the Tenth Plan. Tenth Plan allocation for agriculture, irrigation, etc., amounted to Rs 3,05,055 crore—an increase of 51.4 p.c. over the Ninth Plan. It aimed at pushing up the growth rate of agriculture 2.1 p.c. on the average attained during the Ninth Plan to 4 p.c. during the entire Plan period of the Tenth Plan.

Tenth Plan recorded a growth rate of 2.3 p.c. (because of poor monsoon. Deficient rainfall in 2002, 2004 and 2006 has led to (i) poor agricultural growth, (ii) reduction in the share of agriculture in GDP from 23.8 p.c. in 2002-03 to 20.5 p.c. in 2006-07. Economic Survey, 2006-07 says, "The structural weaknesses of the agriculture sector reflected in low level of public investment, exhaustion of the yield potential of new high yielding varieties of wheat and rice, unbalanced fertiliser use, low seeds replacement rate, inadquate incentive system and post-harvest value addition were manifest in the lacklustre growth during the new millenium."

• **The Eleventh Plan (2007-12) and Second Green Revolution:** Against the backdrop of miserable performance of Indian agriculture during the Tenth Plan, a higher annual growth rate of 4 p.c. p.a. to achieve the targeted GDP growth rate of 10 p.c. over this plan period is urgently needed in the current plan. To attain such growth rate, what is needed is an improvement in the scale of operations and quality of agricultural refoms introduced by State Governments and various agencies. These reforms must aim at efficient use of various agricultural resources and conservation of soil, water and energy on a sustainable basis and in a holistic framework.

However, this plan places emphasis on corporate investment to boost agricultural growth. The approach paper envisages contract farming as a method of attracting corporate investment in Indian agriculture.

The Approach Paper of the Eleventh Plan has highlighted this holistic framework and mapped out this following strategies to be adopted during the Eleventh Plan period: (i) doubling the rate of growth of irrigated areas; (ii) improving water management, water harvesting and watershed development; (ii) diversification of crops into high value outputs (fruits, vegetables, flowers, herbs and spices) without disturbing food security; (iv) providing easy access to credit at affordable rates, (v) refocussing on land reform issues.

Thrust areas of the Eleventh Plan relating to agriculture and irrigation cover: (i) ensuring food security; (ii) supportive State-specific agriculture strategy and programmes; (iii) better seed production, (iv) development of modern markets, etc. The Approach Paper of the Eleventh Plan supports the recommendations of the National Commission on Farmers relating to soil health care and enhancement, water harvesting, credit and insurance reform, technology delivery, assured and remunerative marketing, etc. Finally, this Approach paper calls for a 'Second' green revolution that involves improvement in farm productivity on a sustainable basis—without injuring ecology.

13.5. INDIAN AGRICULTURAL POLICY: AN OVERVIEW

Immediately after independence, the country was faced with two major problems: food crisis and shortage of industrial raw materials. The major objectives of the First Plan in the field of agriculture were to correct the imbalances caused by Partition in the supply of foodgrains and commercial crops and improve infrastructural facilities. Agriculture, including irrigational power, was, therefore, accorded the highest priority. However, Indian agriculture is characterised by low productivity and backwardness. This demanded agrarian reforms. In fact, there are two ways of improving productivity in agriculture: institutional and technological.

At the time of launching of the First Five Year Plan (1951), socialists believed that institutional factors were responsible for low productivity. Another school of thought pointed to the technological backwardness as the prime factor in holding back agricultural production. Ultimately, institutional measures dominated the government's agricultural policy up to mid-1960s. In the mid-60s, technological measures were introduced. High priority was accorded to technology as a major input. Focus now shifted to broadening base of agricultural growth and modernisation through infrastructure development: irrigation, drainage, roads, markets and credit institutions, extension of new technology, appropriate price and procurement policies, etc.

However, in the 1990s, the Indian economy introduced structural programmes and new economic policies. In response to these changes, some important policy changes were announced in the agricultural sector. The creation of the World Trade Organisation (WTO) has brought a new era for agricultural economies. It has created avenues to export farm products. To exploit such global opportunities, National Agricultural Policy was announced in 2000. The current policy will be described in detail. Before that, we mention briefly the important policy measures introduced in the agricultural sector during 1951-1990.

During the first three Five Year Plans (1950-65) the institutional reforms and public investment packages were the most dominant policies. Both Central and State governments formulated and enacted various laws relating to land reforms.

- *Land reforms*: Land reforms not only contribute to higher productivity but also brings social justice. It entails a redistribution of the rights of ownership and/or use of land away from big cultivators or jotedars and in favour of small cultivators with limited or no landholdings.

  The following land reform measures have been taken in India after independence: (a) abolition of the intermediary system, (b) tenancy reforms comprising rent regulation, security of tenure and conferment of ownership rights to tenants, (c) ceiling on landholdings and redistribution of acquired landholdings by the state among the landless workers and small farmers. The twin objectives of land reform policy were higher agricultural growth rate and social justice so as to abolish exploitation of the tenants.

  During 1950-65, Indian agriculture had been shaped by public investment in agriculture with the objective of achieving self-sufficiency in foodgrains. Such public investment concentrated in the construction of irrigation reservoirs. distribution systems.

- *New agricultural strategy encompassing new technology* : In spite of the land reform measures undertaken in the early decades of planning, the country faced severe food crisis resulting in huge import of foodgrains. Necessity was felt to introduce technological measures to raise agricultural production and productivity in the quickest possible time. During mid-60s to 1990, Government strategy in agriculture evolved around incentive policies for the adoption of modern technology in agriculture coupled with public investment policy. In the mid-1960s, the Government of India adopted a new agrarian strategy which goes by different names—seed-fertiliser-water technology, modern agricultural technology, green revolution, etc. It refers to the breeding of high-yielding varieties of wheat and rice and the introduction of modern technologies so as to achieve a sustained breakthrough in agricultural production.

Satisfactory results have been achieved. There has been a considerable increase in production and productivity of major foodcrops. No longer the country is import-dependent; rather, she is now exporting some foodcrops. Virtual self-sufficiency in foodgrains has been achieved. This achievement relating to productivity of Indian agriculture is described as 'forest or land-saving agriculture'. Truly speaking without the green revolution it would not have been possible to achieve the state of self-sufficiency in agriculture.

- *Institutional credit*: Indian farmers are too poor to make arrangements for self-financing their agricultural operations. In view of this, they rely greatly on non-institutional private sources of credit which are exploitative in nature. In view of this, the Government of India decided to provide institutional credit to farmers to replace the widely prevalent usurious money-lending. Barring the creation of cooperative credit societies, commercial banks were nationalised in 1969 with the object of ensuring a smooth flow of credit to agriculturists. Regional rural banks have also been set up to meet the credit needs. An apex credit organisation, called National Bank for Agriculture and Rural Development (NABARD), was set up in 1982. In view of the creation of financial institutions, the monopoly position of the village moneylender in the provisioning of agricultural finance has been broken.
- *Agricultural price policy*: Price policy measures relating to the prices of foodgrains not only aim at increasing production but also aim at acquiring marketable surplus, building up buffer stock of foodgrains to protect the interests of both farmers and consumers. There are two distinct phases of India's agricultural price policy—one covering the period up to 1965 since independence, and other covering the period from 1965 till date. Every season, minimum support prices, procurement prices, etc., are announced in a bid to provide incentive to the farmers to increase production as well as marketable surplus.

- *Food security—Public Distribution System PDS*: In order to ensure adequate supplies of essential foodgrains and consumer goods such as rice, wheat, edible oils, sugar, kerosene, etc. to consumers, especially weaker sections of the community at cheap and subsidised prices, an elaborate food security system, popularly known as Public Distribution System (PDS) has been built up. This is an essential element of the government's safety net for the poor. The PDS seeks to control prices, reduce fluctuations in them and achieve an equitable distribution of certain essential consumer goods. It is also an important element of anti-poverty programmes of the government. Thus, the PDS provides food subsidy.

- *Input subsidies*: In addition to food subsidy given to consumers, input subsidies are provided to farmers on a massive scale with the aim of increasing both production and productivity. Subsidies are mostly given to inputs like irrigation, power and fertilisers. Provisioning of such inputs at prices below the market rate not only enables improved use of inputs but also avoids food and raw materials to go up. As a result of input subsidisation and various cross-subsidies of an astronomical height, the state exchequer has become dry. There has now been a strong demand for cut in food subsidies and input subsidies as these have already reached fiscally unstainable level.

- *Provisioning of non-farm services*: We have already said about the policy developments in respect of agricultural institutional credit. An important component of agricultural policy is the provisioning of non-farm services like marketing including credit. Agricultural development becomes self-sustaining when additional output can be sold in the market at a remunerative price. Policy measures relating to agricultural marketing may be grouped into (a) setting up of marketing organisation, (b) establishment of regulated markets, (c) provision of storage and warehousing facilities, and (d) crop insurance scheme.

- *Trade Policy:* Because of highly state interventionist and discriminating treatment against agricultural trade before 1991, Indian agriculture had little exposure to international trade. Trade liberalisation since 1991, however, bypassed Indian agriculture. But, towards the end of 1990s, trade liberalisation has been faster in tune with the WTO agreements.

  In recent years (since 2000), several policy measures have been taken to promote exports of agricultural products. For instance, quantitative restrictions on agricultural trade flow have been dismantled; Export Oriented Units (EOU) in the floriculture sector have been set up; import of capital goods, plant and machinery for establishing food processing units have been made more flexible and liberal, etc.

13.5.1. National Agricultural Policy, 2000

In view of the problems associated with the agricultural sector during the 1990s, the National Agricultural Policy was announced on July 2000. The policy document aims to attain objectives :

- an annual growth rate of over 4 p.c. in the agricultural sector;
- growth that is based on efficient use of resources and conserves our soil, water and biodiversity;
- growth with equity i.e., growth which is widespread across regions and farmers;
- growth that is demand-driven and caters to domestic markets and maximises benefits from exports of agricultural products;
- growth that is sustainable technologically, environmentally and economically.

In order to attain these objectives, the NAP-2000 envisages measures in the following areas: sustainable agriculture; food and nutritional security; generation and transfer of technology; incentives for agriculture; investment in agriculture, institutional structures, and risk management.

In the section on sustainable development, specific measures have been suggested. There are measures (a) to contain biotic pressures on land and to control indiscriminate diversion of agricultural lands for non-agricultural purposes; (b) to use unutilised wastelands for agriculture and afforestation; (c) to increase cropping intensity through multiple-cropping and inter-cropping. Agro-forestry and social forestry will receive a major thrust.

Special efforts will be made to increase production and productivity of crops to meet the growing demand for food generated by unabated population pressures and raw materials required for agro-based industries. A major thrust will be put on irrigation, horticulture, floriculture, animal husbandry, fisheries, etc.

The government will emphasise on the generation and dissemination of appropriate technologies in the field of animal production as also health care priority will be given to improve the processing, marketing and transport facilities. Besides this, cooperatives and private sector will be encouraged—more particularly in areas like agricultural research, human resource development, post-harvest management, marketing, etc.

Above all, the NAP-2000 does not ignore the importance of institutional reforms. Land reform measures now embrace (a) consolidation of small and fragmented holdings, (b) redistribution of ceiling surplus lands, (c) tenancy reforms, (d) updating of land records, (e) development of land-lease markets, and (f) recognition of women's rights in land.

This policy envisages National Agriculture Insurance Scheme to provide a package of insurance policy to all farmers and all crops so as to insulate them from natural disasters.

Comments : The NAP 2000 seeks to harness the vast untapped potential of Indian agriculture and to strengthen rural infrastructure that is necessary for faster agricultural development. Therefore, this policy seeks to promote technically sound, economically viable, environmentally non-degrading, and socially acceptable use of country's natural resources—land, water and genetic endowment—to promote sustainable development of agriculture, to raise and to serve as a vehicle for building a resurgent national economy.

The new policy promises a lot. It hopes to achieve green revolution, white revolution (pertaining to milk) and blue revolution (pertaining to pisciculture). In other words, it promises 'rainbow revolution'. But most of the intentions of the policy are indeed tall and lofty. In view of the current state of problems prevailing in the agricultural sector, one can simply say that achievement of an annual growth rate of more than 4 p.c. in agriculture is a distant dream.

The policy aims at removing controls and restrictions and subsidies to inputs. But subsidies continue unabated. We are afraid that this will reduce the competitiveness of agricultural products in the global market.

The policy also lays emphasis on private sector (i.e., corporatisation of agriculture) through contract farming by land-leasing arrangements. This contract or capitalist farming will reduce employment potentialities of the agricultural sector. Further, private investment may not flow in agricultural sector as it is hoped by the policy makers. Private capitalist farmers may not adhere to environmentally non-degrading socially acceptable norms.

The NAP 2000 paths and measures are mere intentions. Very little has been said about how these intentions are going to be converted into reality. In other words, the policy has not outlined any machinery for its implementation. Its success largely depends on the cooperation between the Center and the states. But no blueprint for action or implementation has been spelt out in the NAP2000. Thus, there are huge gaps in the policy.

It has been estimated that a 10 p.c. increase in government expenditures on agricultural research and development, irrigation and rural roads contributes to increases of 2.6 p.c., 0.4 p.c., 0.6 p.c. total factor productivity and reductions of 0.6 p.c., 0.1 p.c., and 0.5 p.c. in the rural poverty rate.

13.5.2. National Policy on Farmers, 2007

In recent years, the impacts of green revolution have been fading away as the shadow of food insecurity is being lengthened. 'Food for all' by 2010 seems to be a distant reality against the backdrop of rising population. We have to increase our foodgrains production to 420 million tonnes within 2015. This demands restructuring of the farm sector. The National Commission on Farmers headed by eminent agricultural scientist M.S. Swaminathan has recommended a comprehensive national policy for farmers to give an all-round boost to the agricultural sector. The Commission has forcefully argued that land and hence average firm size has not only been shrinking because of growth in human numbers but also cost-risk-return structure of farming has become adverse. It calls for completing the "unfinished agenda" in land reforms and to initiate comprehensive and agrarian reforms in rural India i.e., a holistic approach to development of the farm sector.

Government of India has approved the recommendation of the National Commission on Farmers. The broad areas of its coverage comprise: (i) economic well-being of the farmers in addition to production and productivity; (ii) asset reforms; (iii) water use efficiency; (iv) encouragements of use of new technologies; (v) seeds and soil enhancement; (vi) irrigation water supply augmentation; (vii) better provisioning of credit and insurance; (viii) use of appropriate social security systems; (ix) implementation of minimum support system mechanism; (x) enlargement of food security basket, etc.

13.6. LAND REFORM

Land reform is a broad term. It refers to an institutional measure directed towards altering the existing pattern of ownership, tenancy and management of land. It entails "a redistribution of the rights of ownership and/or use of land away from large landowners and in favour of cultivators with very limited or no landholdings." Thus, in a broad sense, land reform refers to an improvement in agro-economic institutions. It includes measures and policies relating to redistribution of land, regulation of rent, improving the conditions of tenancy, cooperative organisation, agricultural education, and so on.

Objectives: Land reform is a part of heritage of the country's freedom movement since the agrarian structure that we inherited from the British at the time of independence was of the feudalistic exploitative character. Zamindars-intermediaries-moneylenders played a big role in exploiting the masses. It is in this background that we have to examine the objectives of land reform policy in India.

Land reform measures aim not only at raising agricultural productivity. It is also viewed as a tool for social uplift.

The major objectives of land reform package, as identified in the Eighth Plan, are:

- restructuring of agrarian relations to achieve an egalitarian structure;
- elimination of exploitation in land relations;
- actualisation of the goal of "land to the tiller";
- improvement of socio-economic conditions of the rural poor by widening their land base;
- increasing agricultural production and productivity;
- facilitating land-based development of rural poor; and
- infusion of a great measure of equality in local institutions.

In fine, growth and social justice are the basic objectives of land reform measures.

▲ Land Reform Measures

The comprehen-sive land reform policy that evolved so far after independence consisted of:

- abolition of intermediaries between the State and tenants;
- tenancy reforms that provide (a) security to tenants, (b) rationalisation and regulation of rent, and (c) conferment of ownership rights on tenants;
- fixation of ceiling on landholdings;
- consolidation of holdings; and
- choice of appropriate farm organisation.

▲ Abolition of intermediaries

Abolition of zamindari and similar intermediary tenures during 1950-55 essentially involved removal of intermediary levels or layers of various amorphous and parasitic groups in land between the State and the actual cultivators. However, such abolition of intermediaries involved compensation to the owners of land.

As a result of this measure, about 2.5 crore farmers were brought into direct relationship with the State. This facilitated distribution of 61 lakh hectares of land to landless farmers. Large areas of privately-owned forests and wasteland now vested in the State.

Despite abolition of intermediary rights, poor peasantry continued to be exploited in various ways. It led to large-scale ejectment of poor tenants from land. While landlordism has been abolished, absentee landlordism now continues to flourish. The legislation conferred ownership rights not upon the actual cultivator, but on the statutory tenant, who himself was an intermediary with a chain of sub-tenants under him. All this happened because (i) the law permitted the intermediaries to retain their home farms, (ii) no limit was put on the area of land they could retain, (iii) the term 'personal cultivation' was ill-defined, and (iv) no protection was given to sharecroppers and other tenants-at-will.

Thus, the abolition of intermediary rights on land has not been an unmixed blessing. "Not every 't' was crossed and every 'i' was dotted, but the job was done." Undoubtedly, this zamindari abolition has paved the way for a remarkable shift in the balance of power. But the goal of "land to the tiller" is yet to be achieved.

▲ **Tenancy Reforms**

Tenancy legislations have taken three forms: (i) regulation of rent, (ii) providing security of tenure, and (iii) conferring rights of ownership for tenants.

Rent payable to the landowners should not exceed one-fifth to one-fourth of the gross produce of land. In the light of this guideline, all the states have enacted laws for fixation of rent. However, large inter-state variations exist in the fixation of land rent rates. Further, one notices inter-state differences in land rents. Even the tenancy reforms have failed to regulate rent. Owing to the weak position of tenants, demand for fair and just rent from landowners occasionally lead to ejectment from land.

Tenancy legislations have made it clear that in no case the tenants can be evicted except only in the situation where landlords themselves want to resume cultivation. Even in the event of resumption of cultivation by the owners, tenancy legislations have made it obligatory to leave a minimum area for the tenant.

A very important aspect of land reform is the conferment of ownership rights to tenants in respect of non-resumable land. As a result of this measure, by 2000, only around 124.2 lakh tenants operating no more than 4 p.c. of the cultivated area have been benefited from this ownership rights or their rights have been protected on 63.2 lakh hectares of land. On the eve of tenancy reforms, the area under tenancy was around 50 p.c. As a result of this action, this area has been reduced to 15 p.c. of the operated area by 2000.

Overall impact of tenancy reforms has been rather limited. *Firstly*, tenancy laws have been violated. For instance, in Bihar, the maximum limit of rent was kept at 25 p.c. of the gross produce. But tenants are required to pay even more than 50 p.c. as their social standing is abominably low. *Secondly*, as regards the security of tenant-cultivator, escape clauses have been misused against the interest of tenants. Tenancy laws that have been framed in different states contained a provision for the resumption of land by the landowners for 'personal cultivation' with the object of protecting the interests of landowners, rather than tenants. Due to a loose definition of the term personal cultivation, landowners continued to resume land for self-cultivation. The law also permitted the voluntary surrender of tenancies. Informal or concealed and oral tenancies are still prevalent. Thus, the right of resumption of land for self-cultivation has rendered all tenancies insecure. *Finally*, there is no legal provision for conferring ownership rights in the tenancy laws of some states. In reality, legislation for conferment of ownership rights could not yield good results because many tenants are incapable of buying land from the landowners and many of them are unwilling to do so.

▲ **Ceiling on Landholdings**

To reduce the existing disparities in the pattern of land-ownership and make some land available for distribution to landless agricultural workers, the Second Plan (1956-1961) recommended the imposition of ceilings on agricultural holdings. It was envisaged that land above a certain limit would be acquired by the State and redistributed among the landless workers and small farmers so as to meet their hunger for land and, thus, to enable them to create economic holdings.

Land ceiling laws were passed in two phases. In the first phase—which lasted up to the end of 1972— 'landholder' was treated as the unit of the cultivation. This ceiling unit was changed to 'family' after 1972. The ceiling limits have also been lowered in the second phase with differences varying as between irrigated land with two crops, irrigated land with one crop, and dry land. But exemption for orchards, grazing land, cattle-breeding farms, religious/charitable/educational trusts, sugarcane plantations, tank, fisheries have made the ceiling laws virtually redundant. Up to end September 2001, the total amount of land declared surplus was 73.67 lakh acres, 64.95 lakh acres of land have been taken over by the states. A total of 53.79 lakh acres of land have been distributed among 54.84 lakh tenants. This amounts to saying that about 12 lakh acres of land could not be distributed because of variety of reasons, of which litigation is considered to be the most inhibiting factor.

The operations of the ceiling law made virtually no impact on the agrarian structure. The enforcement of the ceiling law was preceded by a public debate spread over several years. This enabled landowners to manipulate land records leading to fictitious *(benami)* and fraudulent partitions of lands among their relations, friends, fictitious trusts, etc. We have seen that the extent of area declared surplus is much less than the estimated surplus, mainly due to a wide range of exemptions provided in the ceiling laws, shortcomings and loopholes in the laws and inefficient implementation of the laws. As a result, only the small landowners were caught in the net and most of the big landowners or jotedars circumvented it and, even if the land was taken from them, it was not redistributed among the landless peasants. Lack of political will is considered to be the greatest stumbling block for its speedy implementation.

▲ **Consolidation of landholdings**

Fragmented and subdivided landholdings as well as small-sized holdings have made Indian agriculture unremunerative. So consolidation of these lands is necessary to boost efficiency and economy in India's agriculture. It has been completed in the states of Punjab, Haryana and Uttar Pradesh. Till December 2001, nearly, 163.3 lakh acres of land or 1/3rd of the total cultivated area have been consolidated. Thus, the success story in this regard is rather disappointing. One of the reasons for the tardy progress of this aspect of land reforms is that small farmers have a strong fear that consolidation favours large farmers. That is why the threat of eviction of tenants from land out of consolidation is the greatest.

An overall appraisal: After more than 60 years of independence, one notices some achievements in the sphere of land reforms. At the same time, our efforts in this direction have not yielded desired results. Most of the planks of land reform measures are ambivalent and there are large gaps between policy and legislation and between legislation and implementation. And "land reform measures were conceived boldly but were implemented badly"—observed an expert.

The laws for the abolition of intermediaries had been implemented fairly well. As a result, 20 million cultivators were brought into direct relationship with the State. But this reform led to large-scale ejectment of tenants from land which they had been cultivating for generations as the laws failed to offer any protection to these masses. Thus, the slogan "land to the tiller" virtually remained unfulfilled. A class of neo-zamindars or absentee landlords has sprung up in rural India who grab the produce of the earth as well as the land!

It was hoped that tenancy reforms would ensure better results as far as the lot of tenants and sharecroppers were concerned. Tenancy reforms devised so far have not brought to an end of the system of absentee ownership of land nor have led to disappearance of tenancies. Everywhere the immediate consequence was the ejectment of tenants on a massive scale. The consequence of the tenancy policy was to push tenancies underground. Most of the tenancies that still exist take the form of informal or concealed crop-sharing arrangements.

Again, there are reports of large-scale evasion of ceiling laws because of non-implementation of the laws. For instance, in the district of Purnea of Bihar "there are several landowners who own, and effectively control, at least 1,000 acres each, a few of them owning as many as 5,000 acres..... But land records show them to be owning not more than 15 acres—the upper limit according to the ceiling laws—the rest of land being transferred to mostly *benamis* (fake owners)." [C. H. H. Rao]

To sum up, land reform programmes implemented since 1948 have not led to any radical distribution of land or removal of some of the obstacles to raising agricultural productivity. Nevertheless, it should not be written off as a 'non-event'. It brought great changes. It did away with the numerous layers of parasitic intermediaries in almost all the states. All the measures listed above, however, have left untouched the bottom layer of the agrarian structure consisting of agricultural labourers, sharecroppers, except in the states of West Bengal and Kerala where left-wing political parties changed the destiny of the poor peasantry *vis-a-vis* the jotedars, are poor customers.

13.6.1. Impact of the Land Reform Policy

Land reforms are being attempted for two-fold reason: to improve production and productivity and the distribution of income/asset. Land reform measures are costless methods of increasing production in the agricultural sector. It serves the purpose of social justice too. Let us see how far land reform measures have improved productive efficiency of the agricultural sector and ensured social justice.

- *On productive efficiency*: So far as productive efficiency is concerned, the land reform measures adopted in recent years have not made any significant impact. The probable reason is that the reforms have not been effectively implemented. The ownership of land has not yet been fully transferred to the tillers. The actual rents still rule high. The consolidation of holdings has not been completed. Cooperative farming has not made much headway. In the absence of economical holding being in actual possession of the tiller, in which he has a permanent interest, the modern techniques cannot be applied to land. Naturally, productivity continues to be low.

• *On Social Justice* : The objective of social justice has, however, been achieved to a considerable degree. The intermediary rights have been abolished. India no longer presents a picture of feudalism at the top and serfdom at the bottom. The tenancy laws have given the tillers protection from exploitation by providing them security of tenure and fixing maximum chargeable rents.

It is true that the pace of implementation of land reform measures has been slow. Moreover, there is a marked unevenness in respect of progress in various states. This does not, however, mean that there has been no achievement at all in the sphere of land reform since independence. But the progress has been slow and it needs to be accelerated. The manifold problems of our land are to be solved through the introduction of a suitable land policy.

13.7. GREEN REVOLUTION

By revolution we mean sudden catastrophic changes. It may be social or political. All revolutions bring about certain fundamental changes which are not only distinct and well-marked but also the impact of the change is felt over a long period of time. However, as far as green revolution (henceforth GR) is concerned, it aims at bringing about fundamental changes whose impact can be sustained over a fairly long period of time. The only point to note here is that the word "green" is symbolic of the colour of agricultural crops. The GR involves the development of certain new seeds, use of fertiliser, pesticides, pump-sets, tractors, etc., that generate very large increase in crop yields. The application of these joint inputs leads to a larger increase in the volume of foodgrains by raising yield per acre. Technology and productivity movement is the driving force of Indian agriculture in the green revolution areas.

In the mid-60s, the Government of India adopted a new agrarian strategy which goes by different names—seed-fertiliser-water technology, modern technology, or more popularly GR. It may also be called a yield per acre take-off in agriculture in as much as it seeks to raise productivity per acre by cultivating the same plot of land more intensively. The impact of the GR should be studied in terms of the effects of the new technology on production, cropping pattern, employment, regional and interpersonal distribution of gain, etc. We may first consider the effects of GR on output.

13.7.1. Effects of Green Revolution

• *Effect on production*: The successful application and gradual spread of modern technology has a favourable effect on both production and productivity. Yield per acre has increased substantially because of the use of miracle seeds, chemical fertiliser, tractors, etc. Moreover, production has increased due to extensive cultivation i.e., bringing new land under the plough. Foodgrains output increased from 81 million tonnes in the Third Plan (1961-1966) to 209.8 million tonnes in 1999-2000. As a result of favourable monsoon, foodgrains production reached 216.1 million tonnes in 2006-07. In that year, the production of wheat was 76.4 million tonnes from 75 millon tonnes in 1970-71. It fell 69.7 million tonnes in 2001-02 and rose to 74.9 million tonnes in 2006-07. This increase in production is due to the application of HYV

Mexican wheat seed and imported rice seed from the Philipines and Taiwan, irrigation and chemical fertilisers, pesticides in large doses. In spite of occassional drop in output, GR has enabled India to stop import of foodgrains from the USA under PL 480.

It is to be pointed out that the new agricultural strategy was confined mainly to five foodgrains—wheat, rice, maize, jawar and bajra. As for commercial crops like oilseeds, sugarcane, cotton and jute, the progress had been definitely slow. Again, within the foodgrains, wheat registered a phenomenal growth. Wheat production increased from 11.1 million tonnes in the Third Plan to 41.2 million tonnes in the Sixth Plan (1980-1985). A record production of wheat was achieved in 1999-2000 when output of wheat rose to 76.4 million tonnes and it declined 74.9 million tonnes in 2006-07. The production of rice, which received a setback in the early year of the GR, has started picking up of late. In 2001-02, a record production level of 93.3 million tonnes was achieved and declined to 92.7 million tonnes in 2006–07. Performance of other cereals like jawar, bajra and maize is not remarkable though they increased between 1990-91 and 2001-02 and Jawar output remained stationary at 6.5-7.5 million tonnes between 2001-02 and 2006-07.

As a result of the GR, the average yield per hectare of all foodgrains increased from 710 kg in 1960-61 to 1734 kg in 2001-02 while wheat production rose from 851 kg to 2,762 kg by the same period and declined to 2,671 kg in 2006-07. On the other hand, productivity of rice was low even up to the end of Sixth Plan. It went up to 2093 kg per hectare in 2005-06 as against, 1,336 kg. in 1980-81. It increased further to 2127 kg in 2006-07. On the contrary, productivity of coarser varieties of foodgrains remained almost stationary during this period. Definitely, production and yield per hectare have gone up under the impact of the GR. But, there is another side of the picture which tells a shocking story. For instance, per capita availability of foodgrains has declined from 510.1 gm. (1991) per day to 422.4 gm. (2005) per day. However, it marginally increased to 444.5 gm. per day in 2006.

Furthermore, in the case of commercial crops, the progress has been slow and that is why the country has been importing edible oils every year. It is worth noting here that among the foodgrains, wheat is the greatest beneficiary of GR. GR technology, in other words, had been applied extensively in the case of wheat. That is why the largest increase in wheat output took place during the period under consideration. In view of this, economists call green revolution the 'wheat revolution'.

• *Increase in regional imbalances*: GR has failed to ensure balanced regional development. Rather, it has led to an unbalanced growth. GR did not touch all the states of India uniformly. Those states which were originally rich derived the benefits of GR, e.g., Punjab, Haryana and Western U.P. As the benefits of new technology concentrated mainly in these areas, other Indian states could not match them. For instance, the share of the Punjab and Haryana in total foodgrains production was 75 p.c. in 1964-65 compared to 15.6 p.c. in 1988-89. On the contrary, the rate of growth of output of foodgrains in the eastern states of India, Rajasthan, Kerala, etc. turned out to be about 3 p.c. to 4 p.c. per annum. Thus, we can say that the GR has led to an increase in regional imbalances. Some of the reasons behind this different rates of growth are: (i) differences in the availability of water supply; (ii) differences in the nature and attitude of agriculturists relating to risk and uncertainty.

• *Increase in inter-personal inequalities*: The new agricultural strategy necessitated the use of costly seeds, fertilisers and agricultural implements (such as, capital goods and machinery). These were beyond the reach of small farmers in India. Only about 5-6 p.c. of the rich farmers consisting of only 5-6 p.c. of the total rural households (numbering about 82 million), possessing about 40-42 p.c. of the total cultivable land, could afford the use of modern technology. Consequently, the new technology has promoted capitalistic farming in India. In other words, it has accentuated the problem of inequality. It has conferred hardly any benefit to the poor farmers.

It has been observed by researchers that even in the Punjab, where GR has been totally successful, nearly one-third marginal farmers and 24 p.c. small farmers live below the poverty line. Thus, GR has increased inter-personal inequalities undoubtedly.

• *Impact on employment*: We have already noted that GR is biological-cum-technological in character. Biological innovations are based on labour-saving technology, while technological innovations are capital-augmenting or labour-saving in nature. C. H. Hanumantha Rao's study relating to the Punjab has found that: "If the green revolution is regarded as a package consisting of HYV and fertilisers, its contribution to employment has been substantial. Also, tubewells seem to have contributed significantly to the employment of labour...." "The net employment of tractor-use may turn out to be negative when tractorisation of farm is complete. A harvest combine would displace labour on a large scale while its land-augmenting effect would be negligible." Billings and Singh, in their studies based on the Punjab, have found that the use of irrigation tends to increase the demand for labour while the use of tractors or wheat reapers tend to reduce the demand for labour. However, due to inadequate data, it is difficult to assess the impact of biological-technological innovations on farm labour.

Conclusion: Thus, from the above discussion, it is clear that the GR has made limited coverage at least in India. In other words, so far GR has been concentrated to (a) a few crops, (b) a few areas, and (c) a few classes. Cropwise, its effect can be mostly felt in wheat production. That is why, critics call it 'wheat revolution' instead of green revolution. Area-wise, GR has been successful in Punjab, Haryana and western UP. These three states benefited most as wheat is the principal crop. So it cannot be called GR in the full sense of the term. Finally, class-wise, GR is meant for capitalist farmers.

However, the peformance on the food front is not altogether satisfactory since we have been experiencing a decline in crop productivity and production. The target for foodgrains output for 2005-06 and 2006-07 fell far short of actual output. The present food production is not sufficient enough to feed more than 1,130 million population, if the entire half-fed people are fully fed. Latest estimates of poverty suggest that one third of the country's population is half-fed due to poverty and lack of purchasing power. Another disgraceful development is the starvation deaths of more than 9,000 farmers over the last 7 or 8 years (since 2000) in seven states.

It is often suggested that India attained food self-sufficiency around early 1970s (i.e, 35 years ago). But today 35. p.c. of its population remains food insecure, despite green revolution. A recent estimate says that about 32 crore Indians go to bed daily without having their two ends' meal! This is a sad commentary on our agriculturlal planing.

We are sorry to say that the era of GR has reached a dead end, as there has been no breakthrough in seeds of, say, coarse grains and pulses, or yield since then. On the contrary, problems arising out of the GR are now emerging. There has been both a quantitative, and qualitative degradation of land, water and bio-resources; fertile lands have been facing soil health problems in respect of waterlogging and salinity; post-harvest losses have been substantial. The dwindling natural resources, depleting under-ground water resources, growing indebtdness of farmers and shifting to profitable cash crops there by threatening the country's food security are the new challenges in the farm sector.

13.8. ECONOMIC REFORMS AND INDIAN AGRICULTURE

Before 1991, markets and price mechanism were not the policymakers' tool. On the other hand, governments, both at the Centre and at the States, were serious in intervening markets for agricultural commodities and inputs. In the early years of planning, agricultural development strategy centered around land reform programmes and in the late 1960s and 1970s, green revolution technology became the dominant policy. Progress, as a result, became impressive. In fact, planning for agriculture has been an outstanding example of indicative planning in this country since output decisions as well as investment decisions are independently taken by millions of farmers who aim at achieving the public goal of self-sufficiency in foodgrains. Despite remarkable achievement in this area, there is no room for complacency. She imports some foodgrains occasionally. Though the 'ship-to-mouth' situation on imported wheat from the USA in the late 1950s and early 1960s is still away from that point now, the shadow of food insecurity looms large in the skies of India. Prospects of hunger-free India seem to be grim at the moment.

Meanwhile, structural adjustment programmes and economic reforms were launched in July 1991 in all the sectors, except agriculture. Reforms affected agriculture indirectly. One of the reasons is that unlike industry, Indian agriculture had never been controlled and regulated. As it is the privately dominated sector, the scope for reforms in this agricultural sector is limited. Still then, reforms in all sectors including agricultural sector are needed as government intervenes in agriculture in various forms. Above all, export market of Indian agricultural commodities had not been explored before 1991. At this present juncture, Indian agriculture cannot remain insulated from the international market in the midst of growing globalisation and integration of the Indian economy with the global economy. Here we will present the types of economic reforms that have been introduced in Indian agriculture.

Agricultural reform policies may be related to foreign trade as industrial and trade policies hurt the agricultural sector. Restrictions and controls were in the form of (i) protection of industry leading to unfavourable terms of trade against agriculture, (ii) export restrictions on agricultural products, (iii) massive subsidies for food, fertiliser, irrigation, power, credit, etc.

Recognising the crucial role of agriculture in the Indian economy, a Draft Agricultural Policy Resolution was placed in December 1992. It seeks to dovetail agricultural development and research programmes to meet the challenges in Indian agriculture and seeks to arrest the declining trends in capital formation in agriculture and step-up public investment. This policy attaches great importance to the problems of unemployment and poverty by employment generating activities through diversification of agriculture and promotion of agro-based industries.

Further, growth of Indian agriculture is hampered due to both domestic and export market restrictions. One often observes restrictions on the movement of commodities not only across states but also even within the states. Externally, Indian agriculture is not integrated with the world markets. Some domestic restrictions and regulations in the reform era have been removed, while some of them still remain. However, there has been significant trade liberalisation. Again, excessive protection earlier given to the manufacturing sector has been greatly reduced. Another policy change is the adoption of market-oriented policies. Subsidies on various agricultural inputs have been cut. An epoch-making agricultural reform process has been set in motion in February 2002 to remove licensing and stocking requirements and movement restrictions of agricultural crops, enabling free movement and unrestricted stocking and trading in wheat, rice, coarse grains, edible oils, oilseeds and sugar. It is hoped that this would enable farmers to view the entire country as one single market.

Over the years, globalisation process for agriculture has been strengthened through both domestic and foreign trade deregulation and market orientation. In this connection, we intend to consider some provisions relating to agriculture in the WTO agreements. These are reduction and removal of various trade barriers, increased market access and reduction in aggregate measure of support (AMS). These are the direct provisions relating to agriculture. Indirect provisions relates intellectual property rights and particularly patenting of seeds.

The impact of economic reform on agriculture is a mixed one. She has attained near self-sufficiency in foodgrains. Both green revolution and liberalisation of India's agriculture have favourable effects on overall as well as agricultural GDP. But the structural adjustment programme for agriculture has increased the vulnerability of agriculture. Despite good monsoons for the entire decade of 1990s, the rate of growth of foodgrains is unsatisfactory in the reform era, *vis-a-vis* the green revolution era. This growth performance, shown in Table 13.2, is a matter of great concern.

Table 13.2 : Compound Growth Rates : Production and Yield of Agricultural Crops

	1981-82 — 1989-90		1990—91 2006-07	
	Production	Yield	Production	Yield
Foodgrains	2.85	2.74	1.19	1.74
Non-foodgrains	3.77	2.31	4.62	3.66
All	3.19	2.56	2.61	3.07

Source: Ministry of Agriculture, GOI
Agricultural Statistics at a Glance, 2006-07

Growth rates of foodgrains and non-foodgrains production over the period 1991-92 to 1999-2000 and 2000-01 to 2006-07 have declined significantly. Average growth rales of area of foodgrains and non-foodgrains between

1994-95 and 2006-07 stood at 0.14 p.c. and 0.86 p.c. respectively. This may be attributed to growing slackness in agricultural public investment. Plan outlay on agriculture, rural development, special area programme and irrigation and flood control as a proportion of total plan outlay in 1990s has been less than in 1990-91. In the name of reducing fiscal deficit, plan outlay in agriculture as a proportion of total outlay declined from 20.4 p.c. in 1991-92 to 9.9 p.c. in 1997-98. Such fall in investment in agriculture affects capital formation adversely. It may be pointed out here that trade liberalisation policies and the fast growing middle class families seem to be the two great causes of diversion of cultivated area from foodgrains to non-foodgrains and especially high-value horticulture. This, thus, raises the issue of food security.

The attempt to globalise and marketise agriculture has been a serious setback to the food security of the poor and vulnerable people. These people are now being squeezed by rising costs of inputs (e.g., credit, power, etc.), reduction of subsidies, etc. Per capita availability of foodgrains has deteriorated in recent years. In the midst of plenty, food crisis has reappeared. A paradoxical situation has emerged—stocked foodgrains are rotting in godowns while starvation deaths take place. This is 'a pointer to continued mismanagement that is now reaching criminal proportions'.

India is now an important player in external trade after joining the WTO. Despite high hopes raised in the early years of 1990s, the evidence is not altogether happy. Here one finds declining growth rates in major agri-business exports from India. Despite level-playing field given to all players, few countries control most of the world markets. WTO is indeed silent in this respect. This has reduced the competitive edge in the prices of India's agri-exports. An author thus remarks that the external sector—instead of giving strong push in demand for Indian agriculture—seems to have posed further challenges to its existence and growth.

However, one must remember that external liberalisation is not a sufficient condition for the growth of India's agricultural sector; at best it can be a necessary condition. Thus, what is required is that reform has to be made in domestic Indian agriculture. 'The world cannot marginalise India but India can marginalise itself'.

A minimum commitment to WTO provisions has to be maintained so that the opportunities of improved trade in agriculture can be exploited. India has to do much more than what the WTO requires. Mismanagement of domestic economy will ultimately spell disaster.

QUESTIONS (WITH ANSWER-HINTS)

Long Question (16 marks)

1. Discuss the role of agriculture in India's economic development.

   Or

   "Agricultural development holds the key to rapid economic development in India." Explain the statement.

   Ans. 13.1.

2. Discuss the main features of Indian agriculture.

   Or

   Discuss the major problems of Indian agriculture.

   Ans. 13.2.

3. Examine the causes of low agricultural productivity in India. Suggest measures to increase agricultural productivity in India.

   Or

   Dicuss the causes of low productivity in Indian agriculture. What measures have been adopted to solve these problems? (C.U. 2008)

   Ans. 13.3.

4. Give an outline of the progress of Indian agriculture during the plan period.

   Ans. 13.4.

5. Make a review of Indian agricultural policy pursued before 1990s.

   Ans. 13.5.

6. Critically analyse National Agricultural Policy, 2000.

   Ans. 13.5.1.

7. Examine the main features of the land reform policy instituted in India since independence.

   Ans. 13.6.

8. What is meant by land reforms? What are its objectives? Briefly discuss the land reform measures undertaken in India since 1951.

   Or

   What is meant by land reforms? What are the major objectives of land reforms in India? Evaluate achievements in India in this respect. (C.U. 2007)

   Ans. 13.6.

9. What are the objectives of land reform policy in India? What has been the impact of this policy on (i) the improvement of productive efficiency, and (ii) social justice?

   Ans. 13.6 and 13.6.1.

10. Discuss the nature and effects of the new agricultural technology adopted in India.

    Or

    Give an account of the effects of green revolution on the Indian economy.

    Ans. 13.7 and 13.7.1.

11. What sort of economic reforms have been introduced in Indian agriculture in the 1990s? Discuss their overall impacts.

    Ans. 13.8.

Medium-sized Questions (8 marks)

1. What is green revolution? Discuss briefly its consequences on the Indian Economy. (C.U. 2007)

   Ans. 13.7 and 13.7.1.

2. Mention the essentials of National Policy on Farmers, 2007.

   Ans. 13.5.2.

14

INDUSTRIAL DEVELOPMENT IN INDIA

14.1. ROLE OF INDUSTRIALISATION IN INDIA'S ECONOMIC DEVELOPMENT

Economic development of any country is associated with industrialisation. Western capitalist countries amply demonstrate this thesis. Their high rates of growth are attributed to industrialisation. Therefore, there is a strong case for industrialisation of countries like India where the level of development is still low compared to that of capitalist countries. Along with agricultural development, industrialisation is a must for these countries since there is a strong interdependence between agricultural and industrial sectors.

Through a concerted programme of industrialisation, a country can provide a basis for a rapid rate of growth of national income and per capita income. The empirical evidence suggests that there is a strong relationship between industrialisation and high income. The high rate of growth of income of industrially advanced countries is due to the fact that these countries are industrially advanced. And, that is why in these countries the contribution of the industrial sector towards national income is the highest. Therefore, countries like India should give positive encouragement to rapid industrialisation. In 2007-08, India's industrial—or the so-called secondary sector's share in GDP stood at 24.9 p.c.

Secondly, industrialisation brings about a favourable change in the country's occupational pattern. Employment opportunities in the agricultural sector in the underdeveloped countries are rather slim. On the contrary, agriculture is highly overcrowded. Industrialisation offers the only way to the creation of employment. Even by reorganising agriculture, one cannot expect to absorb a large number of labourers in the agricultural sector. In this circumstance, i.e., in the light of employment creation, planners must give correct emphasis on industrial development.

Thirdly, no one denies the interrelationship between agriculture and industry. Agricultural development is largely conditioned by industrial development. As industrialisation proceeds demand for wage goods, like foodgrains, rises. This causes the market for agricultural products as well as the demand for cash crops to rise. Ultimately, agro-based industries expand. Not only that, as the pace of industrialisation gathers momentum, demand for agricultural raw materials rises and industry expands. Thus, industrialisation creates a climate conducive to agricultural development.

Fourthly, there are some people who want to put more emphasis on the agricultural sector. These thinkers believe that a country can earn huge foreign exchange by exporting agricultural produce. Moreover, foreign exchange can be spent for importing goods required for industrialisation. This is possible if agricultural sector is allowed to grow. However, one can make some counter-arguments against this. They argue that even in countries like India, demand for agricultural goods is not so high. On the other hand, in the industrially advanced countries, as demand for agricultural goods is not so high, the possibility of earning foreign exchange by exporting agricultural products is limited. Thus, industrialisation seems to be a better route. In fact, such industries should be set up which are by nature import-substituting. This strategy will not only reduce the import demand for industrial goods but will also increase the export demand for the same.

Finally, for security consideration, no one denies the role of industrialisation in an economy. Dependence on foreign countries for defence goods is a dangerous and risky proposition. Thus, to protect one's country against any type of contingency, all sorts of military goods must be produced domestically. Self-sufficiency in defence materials can be achieved only through industrial development.

Thus, it is quite clear that industrial development is of urgent necessity in a country like India. Of course, industrial development in these countries is often handicapped by certain problems which are varied in nature. Problems may be economic or administrative or international. But these problems are not insurmountable. Furthermore, our plea for rapid industrialisation does not prevent us from making any programme for agricultural development. By excluding agricultural development, the path of industrialisation alone in a country like India is a suicidal one.

14.2. TRENDS OF INDIA'S INDUSTRIAL GROWTH DURING THE PLAN PERIOD

At the time of independence, India was basically an agrarian country. In terms of its contribution to national income and employment generation, India was industrially backward. Still, India is an agrarian economy. Development of industry in India is a must. Realising this, the planners placed emphasis on the development of industries during different plans. And, in fact, India has recorded a massive industrial growth over the years. Here we will make a brief review of the industrial development during the planning period.

- **The First Plan (1951-1956)**: The First Five Year Plan was basically an agrarian plan since a greater investment was made in this sector. A sum of Rs 293 crore was envisaged in the First Plan for industries. However, a major reliance was placed on investment in the private sector when its share in total investment was as high as Rs 233 crores. Several new industries in the public sector were set up. However, despite low priority to industrialisation, the average annual rate of growth of industries stood at 6.5 p.c. However, capital goods industries registered a better performance.

• **The Second Plan (1956-1961):** The Second Plan was, undoubtedly, biased towards industrialisation. Following the Mahalanobis Strategy of development, topmost priority was given to the development of basic and capital goods industries to lay a firm foundation of industrial development of the country in the future. A total outlay of Rs 1,094 crore was provided for industrial development in this Plan. But the actual figure was Rs 1,570 crore—an excess of 30 p.c. over the original figure. Several heavy industries and consumer goods industries were set up whose output increased substantially. Expansion programmes were undertaken for the industries set up in the First Plan. As a result, industrial structure underwent a change. Along with this structural change in the industrial front, we also notice diversification of the industries. The rate of industrial growth during the Second Plan was 14.7 p.c. p.a. The massive growth took place in capital goods industries (21.3 p.c. p.a.). Next in importance was the intermediate goods industries as it recorded an annual growth rate of 15.6 p.c.

• **The Third Plan (1961-1966):** A great deal of emphasis was placed on the basic, capital and producer goods industries in the Third Plan. The public sector was deemed to be an agent in this respect. Out of the total investment of Rs 2,750 crore in the Third Plan, a sum of Rs 1,520 crore was invested in the public sector—a greater allocation in favour of the public sector as against private sector for the first time. But industrial progress was markedly uneven during this Plan and most of the targets of industrial production remained unfulfilled.

• **The Fourth Plan (1969-1974):** The Fourth Plan was postponed for full three years because of the emergence of some extraordinary situations in the economy in the mid-1960s. Instead, three Annual Plans were made for 1966-69 when output of several industries dropped significantly. However, the better performance of the agricultural sector in 1968 resulted in a better growth of the industrial sector during 1968-69.

Against this backdrop the, Fourth Plan was launched when a total investment of Rs 5,338 crore was earmarked for the organised industry and mining. Of this, Rs 3,338 crore was envisaged for the public sector. However, the actual investment turned out to be Rs 4,046 crore. Target of industrial growth of 8-10 p.c. was kept for the Fourth Plan. But the performance of the industrial sector fell short of expectations not only in terms of investment, but also in terms of production. The annual rate of growth of industries came to even less than 4 p.c. (actually 3.9 p.c.) during the Fourth Plan. The capital goods industries registered a growth rate of 5.9 p.c. p.a. against 17.1 p.c. p.a.—a miserable performance indeed. Basic industries also grew at a rate much less than the target rate.

• **The Fifth Plan (1974-79):** The Fifth Plan laid emphasis on (i) rapid growth of core sector industries, (ii) increase in the production of export-oriented goods and articles of mass consumption, (iii) restraint on the production of non-essential goods, and (iv) development of small industries. Of the revised public sector outlay of Rs 38,303 crore for the entire Fifth Plan, the share of industries and minerals amounted to Rs 10,201 crore—or 25.9 per cent of the total outlay.

Like the Fourth Plan, the Fifth Plan was also marked by unsatisfactory industrial performance.

In the Revised Plan, the average rate of growth of industries was estimated at 7 p.c. But the actual rate of growth was 5.2 p.c. p.a.

• **The Sixth Plan (1980-1985)**: The Sixth Plan provided for an investment of Rs 20,407 crore in the public sector including coal and petroleum. It laid down a target of 8 p.c. p.a. for industrial growth during the Sixth Plan period. The average achieved growth rate was 5 p.c. p.a. The growth rate recorded by different industries during this Plan showed uneven performance. However, in electronic industry, which had been identified as the "sunrise industry" in the Seventh Plan, a growth rate higher than the targeted rate was achieved in the Sixth Plan. The overall sluggish performance of the industrial sector in this Plan was due to the interplay of various factors like shortage of power, shortage of coking coal for steel and shortage of raw materials for jute, labour trouble, inadequate demand, etc.

• **The Seventh Plan (1985-1990)**: So far as allocation of investment of resources is concerned, the Seventh Plan heavily tilted towards power and agricultural and rural development. Energy sector got nearly one-third of the total outlay. Of the total public sector outlay of Rs 1,80,000 crore, the Seventh Plan envisaged an outlay of Rs 22,650.83 crore for industry and minerals. This works out to be 12.48 p.c. of the total outlay. This Plan envisaged a growth rate of 8 p.c. p.a. for the industrial sector. The actual growth rate was 0.5 p.c. higher than the targeted rate. The manufacturing sector witnessed an average growth rate of 8.8 p.c.—well above the targeted growth rate of 8 p.c. Thus, the satisfactory performance of the manufacturing sector during the Seventh Plan pulled up the average industrial growth rate. However, electricity, mining and quarrying lagged behind the Plan target.

• **The Eighth Plan (1992-1997)**: The Eighth Plan is an aftermath of the New Economic Policies. In the midst of deregulation and less target setting, the course of industrialisation was mapped out in the Eighth Plan. As the Eighth Plan places greater reliance on the market, private sector is supposed to play a greater role. The total public sector outlay for industry and minerals envisaged in the Eighth Plan is Rs. 40,623 crore. The proportion of public investment has been put to 23.61 p.c. for the Eighth Plan compared to 26 p.c. for the Seventh Plan. The Eighth Plan envisaged a growth of 7.4 p.c. p.a. in the manufacturing sector.

In the first two years of the NEP, the industrial sector fared badly both in real and financial terms. Fortunately, the industrial sector witnessed a more than modest recovery "and it appeared as if industry had finally taken off on the road to self-sustained growth."

One finds a turnaround in the performance of the capital goods sector which is considered as a positive signal of high potential growth in future production, since new capital goods expand the productive capacity of the economy.

• **The Ninth Plan (1997-02)**: The Ninth Plan gave greater emphasis to the private sector and market-based decision-making. At the same time, government intervention was encouraged. Against this backdrop, the Ninth Plan envisaged a growth rate of 8.2 p.c. To achieve this, priority had been given for augmenting the availability of infrastructural facilities. However, this Plan assumed a declining share of public investment. Plan size suggests that 25.1 p.c. of total public sector outlay had been earmarked for the energy sector. The share of industry and minerals had been declining since the Sixth Plan. It had been reduced to 8.1 p.c. in the Ninth Plan.

During the Ninth Plan period, the actual economic growth rate was 4.5 p.c. while a compound annual growth rate of 5 p.c. in industrial production was recorded. The compound annual growth rate in manufacturing, mining and electricity generation stood at 5.3 p.c., 2.5 p.c. and 5.5 p.c., respectively. This industrial slowdown is attributed to slowdown in domestic and global demand, decline in mainly private investment, infrastructure bottlenecks in power and transport, etc. In brief, there has been a failure of the industrial sector in achieving the growth rate compared to the Eighth Plan.

• **Tenth Plan (2007-12):** The target growth of industry during this Plan was kept at 10 p.c. consistent with an ovrall GDP growth of 8 p.c. The four objectives of industry's during the Tenth plan were (i) raising industry's share in GDP, (ii) raising share in the world exports of manufactured goods, (iii) balanced industrial development, and (iv) creation of jobs. The average growth rate of the industrial sector is expected to exceed 8 p.c. in the Tenth Plan. This optimistic rate follows from higher allocation for the industrial sector—an increase of 32 p.c. over the Ninth Plan. The total allocation for the sector had been ear-marked Rs 58,939 crore.

The Tenth Plan target of 10 p.c. industrial growth could not be met. The compound annual growth rate rose from 4.5 p.c. in the Ninth plan to 8 p.c. in the Tenth Plan. Within the industrial sector, manufacturing recorded a better gowth rate of 8.7 p.c. in this Plan compared to 3.8 p.c. achieved in the Ninth Plan. Further, during this plan the sectoral share of industry in GDP started rising from 25 p.c. in 2001-02 to 26.6 p.c. in 2006-07. The performance of capital goods industries was another positive feature of the Tenth Plan but that of mining and quary was not rosy. A remarkable increase in the export share of manufacturing was achieved—19.9 p.c. as against 6.3 p.c. in the Ninth Plan. But in terms of employment creation, performance is indeed pathetic.

• **Eleventh Plan (2007-12):** The Eleventh Plan aims at achieving an average growth rate of 9 p.c. p.a. in GDP, while industrial sector aims at growing at a double-digit growth. This accelerated growth is expected to provide higher growth in organised sector employment, which is a matter of great concern.

14.3. ACHIEVEMENTS AND LIMITATIONS OF INDUSTRIAL DEVELOPMENT DURING THE PLAN PERIOD

▲ *Positive Features of Industrial Growth during the Plan Period*

The trend in industrial growth over about 60 years appears to be impressive. During this period, both the pattern and the structure of Indian industries have undergone a significant change.

• **Significant growth rate:** The trend in industrial production in India shows a compound growth rate of 6 p.c. The growth rate for the period 1951-55 was 5.7 p.c., 7.2 p.c. in 1955-56 and 9 p.c. in 1960-65. Thus, from the 50s to the mid-60s, there was a significant acceleration in the industrial growth. It declined to a very low level around 3.7 p.c. in 1966-70. This period was marked by recession in Indian industries. However, industrial production started picking up after the mid-70s. Still then, the recovery was not high enough. The growth rate of industrial production was around 5.2 p.c. during 1975-83. The decade of 1980s, however, showed a remarkable growth of the industrial sector following liberalisation measures introduced in the mid-1980s. But the decade of 1990s did not augur well.

The early years of reform yielded unsatisfactory dividends as far as growth of the industrial sector was concerned. After responding to economic reforms with vigour and registering a robust growth rate of 12.8 p.c. in 1995-96, there had been a slowdown in industrial expansion since 1996-97 when growth rate decelerated to 5.6 p.c. against a growth rate of 13 p.c. in 1995-96. Declining trend continued in 1998-99 with overall industrial production registering 4.1 p.c. growth during 1998-99. Minor recovery took place in 1999-2000 when overall growth rate increased to 6.7 p.c. The position deteriorated again in the next year when trends in industrial growth and by sectors also suggested an allround slowdown in industrial activity in 2000-01 (2.7 p.c.) and 2001-02 (2.8 p.c.). Industrial growth rate, however, picked up in the Tenth Plan when the growth rate rose to 8 p.c. against the target industrial growth rate of 10 p.c.

• *Increase in the share of industrial sector in national income*: The contribution of the industrial sector towards national income is rising continuously. Its share was 16.1 p.c. in GDP in 1950-51. It rose to 25.2 p.c. in 1990-91. This indicates industrialisation. Since then it is on the declining trend. It has come down to 24.9 p.c. in 2007-08.

• **Expansion of public sector**: Over the planning period, public sector has registered a phenomenal growth. The idea for giving emphasis to the public sector was to provide a firm base for setting up core industries like power, coal, steel, fertilisers, atomic energy and machine building in the public and to leave the rest for the private sector. The Seventh Plan has, however, shown preference to the private sector. The Eighth, Ninth and the Tenth Plans, of course, have placed great emphasis on this private sector.

• *Strengthening of industrial base*: Besides these quantitative aspects of industrial growth, we also find large progress in strengthening the base of future industrial growth. From the very beginning of the planning period, basic and capital goods industries received utmost attention. Consequently, its performance in total industrial output and gross value added become remarkable as compared to consumer goods industries. These industries are the base of industrialisation. Because of the strengthened industrial base including adequate building up of infrastructural facilities, other industries registered a better growth, particularly intermediate goods industries. This, of course, is not a mean achievement.

• *Modernisation*: India has now a large variety of industries producing goods of varied nature which shows the degree of modernisation. Some modern industries have really come up and they are competing effectively with the outside world. Modernisation is also evident in the field of technological and managerial skills. This has reduced our dependence greatly on foreign experts and technologists. On the contrary, India is exporting trained personnel in relatively less developed countries.

• *Self-reliance*: Another positive aspect of industrial growth is the attainment of the goal of self-reliance. We have achieved self-reliance in machinery, plant and other equipment. Today, the bulk of the equipment required for industrial and infrastructural development is produced within the country.

▲ *Negative Aspects of Industrial Growth*

Industrial growth in India has been exposed to certain undesired lines. These suggest the failure of industrial planning. The most significant failure of industrial planning of India are: (i) the structural retrogression in the industrial structure; (ii) expansion of large industrial houses and concentration of economic power; (iii) miserable performance of the public sector; (iv) underutilisation of capacity; and (v) industrial sickness. These negative aspects of India's industrial growth are presented below one by one.

• *Structural retrogression in the industrial sector*: By industrial structure we mean interrelationship among different industry groups like consumer goods, intermediate goods and capital goods industries. At the initial stages of industrialisation, consumer goods industries predominated in the Indian economy. As the pace of industrialisation quickened, consumer goods industries lost importance and capital and intermediate goods industries got prominence. This sort of structural change reflects industrialisation of a country. India was on the road to industrialisation at the early stages of planning till 1965 when there was a remarkable expansion of basic and capital goods industries as compared to consumer goods industries. And the period after 1965 witnessed deceleration in industrial output for all types of industries, excepting consumer goods industries. Within the consumer goods industries, durable consumer goods industries registered a high growth. Thus, Indian industries after 1965 showed not only poor growth but also reflected phenomenon of structural retrogression.

The situation continues to be almost similar in the 1990s and 2000s. Basic industries fared badly in 2005-06 when it struck a growth rate of 6.7 p.c. as against 10.8 p.c. in 1995-96. However, the year 2006-07 showed more than 10 p.c. growth of basic goods industries. Intermediate goods industries showed a remarakable decline. However, growth of capital goods industries in 2005-06 was remarkable. And, this upbeat continued in 2006-07 when capital goods industries recorded a growth rate of 18.2 p.c. Along with this pattern of industrial development, one finds an increase in import-intensity of domestic manufacturing industry as a consequence of liberalisation. Hence, a process of liberalisation-induced import substitution in the manufacturing sector has emerged.

• *Expansion of large industrial houses and concentration of economic power*: It is the large industrial houses which have flourished over the planning period. There were two monopoly houses worth the name in 1953-54. They were Tata and Birla. Over time, these two houses have not only grown in size enormously, but also 18 other indutrial houses have come up very much with a menacing speed, despite legislative measures (say, the MRTP Act). Growth of these industrial houses is definitely an impediment towards the establishment of a socialistic pattern of society. Another allied evil of the growth of large industrial houses in India is the concentration of economic and political power in their hands.

However, the objective of establishing a socialist pattern of society in India has been buried underground in the 1990s. No longer private monopolists are required to be controlled and regulated. They are given enough latitude to produce any commodity even with multinational corporations (MNCs). Reduction of concentration of economic power in the hands of a few private industrialists is no longer the objective of Indian Five Year Plans since de-statisation policy has assumed a great proportion after 1991. The

MRTP Act has been replaced by the Competition Act, 2002.

• *Miserable performance of the public sector*: It is the public sector that must flourish to fulfil the avowed objective of the government being purshed since the launching of the First Plan. Its growth is phenomenal over the years. Still then, its performance has come in for sharp criticisms. It has failed to generate adequate resources for development. Following the introduction of New Economic Policy in 1991, the importance of the public sector in India's industrial planning has been pushed behind. On the contrary, what one finds is the privatisation of the public sector enterprises through a policy of disinvestment. However in recent years the performance of the public enterprises is not altogether bad.

• *Underutilisation of capacity*: A large number of Indian industries suffer from underutilisation of capacity. However, the degree of utilisation of capacity differs from industry to industry and from year to year.

• *Industrial sickness*: Along with under-utilisation of capacity, another phenomenon that marked the industrial scene in recent years is the growing sickness of Indian industries. In 1990, the number of sick industrial units was 2,21,097 The number rose to 2.50 lakhs in March 2001. Of these, slightly less than 2.50 lakh units were in the small-scale sector. The growing sickness of industrial units is a major growth constraint. Since then, this trend has been arrested. In March 2003 the number of total sick units declined to 1.71 lakhs. It declined further to 1.31 lakh in March 2006. Of these, the number of small units stood at 1.26 lakh in 2006 and it declined further to 1.14 lakh in March 2007.

To sum up, India's industrial expansion over the plan period presents a mixed picture. Compared to the pre-independence level, industrial growth in the planning period is phenomenal. But, in the process, some undesirable elements have come out in recent years which have vitiated the industrial climate. Policy implication is, thus, equally apparent.

14.4. ROLE OF GOVERNMENT IN INDIA'S INDUSTRIALISATION PROCESS

Modern governments have a big role to play in removing the basic impediments to development. On the whole, it may be said that the State has a two-fold motivation in intervening in the economic activities of the individual: to maximise welfare and to render economic development possible. The latter is, of course, ancillary to the former. In a mixed economy like India, where private and public sectors go hand in hand, the government assumes a special role. In pursuing its economic policies of state policy, the government adopts carrot-and-stick measures. That is to say, the government gives encouragement to private sectors to produce more. But, as we have adopted the socialistic principles of state policy the government does not allow private sectors to run uninterruptedly. In fact, if the private sector is allowed to do whatever it likes, the objective of attaining a socialistic pattern of society is bound to be frustrated.

In view of this, the government controls and regulates the activities of the private sector. One such form of control and regulation of private industrialists is industrial licensing. The licensing policy is in operation since 1951. However, before the adoption of the industrial licensing policy—a key instrument of industrial policy—the Government of India declared its industrial policy in April 1948, clearly indicating the sphere of the private and public sectors. To implement the 1948 Industrial Policy Resolution, the Government of India announced its Industries (Development and Regulation) Act in 1951 which provided the legislative framework for the licensing of industrial investment in the country.

14.4.1. Meaning of Industrial Policy

Any government action aimed at affecting industry may be considered to be part of industrial policy, which makes it a limitless field. It usually means government action to influence the ownership and structure of industry and its performance and it takes the form of paying subsidies or providing finance in other ways, or of regulation. It excludes macroeconomic policies affecting industry, but it may be viewed as supporting macroeconomic policy by improving the performance of an important part of the supply side of the economy as a whole. The concept is, thus, a comprehensive one. It includes procedures, principles (i.e., the philosophy of a given economy), policies, rules and regulations, incentives and punishments, the tariff policy, the labour policy, government's attitude towards foreign capital, etc. A country must formulate industrial policy as an instrument of industrialisation. The public sector may be invited to implement industrial policy. In a country like India, where private sector is allowed to coexist in business, its control and regulation is necessary. Industrial policy is a necessary step in this direction.

In the immediate post-independence period, inflation appeared, production declined and economic security dwindled. Labour leaders demanded total nationalisation while the industrialists wanted free enterprise. "In view of the various cross-currents that confused the industrial climate, a statement of industrial policy was necessary to clear the foggy atmosphere."

In the following few pages, an attempt is made to describe and analyse the various policy statements and proposals which have relevance for the current economic environment of the country.

14.4.2. Industrial Policy Resolution of 1948

In a mixed economy of our sort, the government should declare its industrial policy clearly indicating what should be the sphere of the State and of the private enterprise. A mixed economy means coexistence of the two sectors —public and private. This the Government of India did by a policy resolution on 30 April 1948 called the First Industrial Policy Resolution or Industrial Policy Resolution of 1948, which made it clear that India was going to have a mixed economy.

The Industrial Policy Resolution 1948, drawn in the context of our objectives of Democratic Socialism through mixed economic structure, divided the industrial structure into four groups :

- Basic and strategic industries such as arms and ammunition, atomic energy, railways, etc. shall be the exclusive monopoly of the State.
- The second group consisted of key industries like coal, iron and steel, ship-building, manufacture of telegraph, telephone, wireless apparatus, mineral oils, etc. In such cases the State took over the exclusive responsibility of all future development and the existing industries were allowed to function for ten years after which the State shall review the situation and explore the necessity of nationalisation.

• In the third group, 18 industries including automobiles, tractors, machine tools, etc. were allowed to be in the private sector subject to government regulation and supervision.

• All other industries were left open to the private sector. However, the State may participate and or intervene if circumstances so demand.

To ensure the supply of capital goods and modern technology, the IPR, 1948 encouraged the free flow of foreign capital. The government ensured that there shall be no discrimination between Indian and foreign undertakings; facilities shall be given for remittance of profit and due compensation shall be paid in case a foreign undertaking is nationalised. The IPR also emphasised the importance of small-scale and cottage industries in the Indian economy.

The Industries (Development and Regulation) Act was passed in 1951 to implement the Industrial Policy Resolution, 1948.

14.4.3. Industrial Policy Statement of 1956

On 30 April 1956, the Government revised its first Industrial Policy (i.e., the policy of 1948), and announced the Industrial Policy of 1956. The reasons for the revision were: (i) introduction of the Constitution of India, (ii) adoption of planned economy, and (iii) declaration by the Parliament that India was going to have a socialist pattern of society. All these principles were incorporated in the revised industrial policy as its most avowed objectives. And the revised policy still provides the basic framework for the government's policy in regard to industries. The 1956 Policy emphasises, *inter alia,* the need to expand the public sector, to build up a large and growing cooperative sector and to encourage the separation of ownership and management in private industries and, above all, prevent the rise of private monopolies. "The IPR, 1956, has been known as the Economic Constitution of India" or "The Bible of State Capitalism."

The Resolution classified industries into three categories having regard to the role which the State would play in each of them:

- Schedule A consisting of 17 industries shall be the exclusive responsibility of the State.

  Out of these 17 industries, four industries—arms and ammunition, atomic energy, railways, air transport—could be Central Government monopolies; new units in the remaining industries shall be developed by the state Governments.
- Schedule B, consisting of 12 industries, shall be open to both the private and public sectors; however, such industries shall be progressively State-owned.
- All the other industries not included in these two Schedules constitute the third category which is left open to the private sector. However, the State reserves the right to undertake any type of industrial production.

The classification of industries into three categories did not mean that they were being placed in watertight compartments. In appropriate cases, the private sector might be allowed to produce an item falling within Schedule A for meeting its own requirements. Further, heavy industries in the public sector might obtain their requirements from the private sector while the private sector, in turn, would rely on the public sector for many of its requirements.

The IPR, 1956, stressed the importance of

cottage and small scale industries for expanding employment opportunities and for wider decentralisation of economic power and activity. The Resolution also called for all efforts to maintain industrial peace; a fair share of the proceeds of production should be given to the toiling mass in keeping with the avowed objectives of democratic socialism. Regional disparities in industrialisation should be reduced. The government's attitude to foreign capital would remain unchanged.

The features of the new policy that distinguish it from the previous one are:

- *Expansion of the role of the State*—This was in keeping with the Mahalanobis Strategy of large-scale industrialisation embodied in the Second Five Year Plan.
- *Reduced threat of nationalisation*—The apprehensions of nationalisation contained in the previous policy were reduced to the bare minimum.
- *More meaningful approach to our concept of a 'mixed economy'*—Various complementaries of the public and private sectors were made clear.

Criticisms: The 1956 IPR came in for sharp criticisms from the private sector since this Resolution reduced the scope for the expansion of the private sector significantly. Private sector apprehended that the expansion of public sector meant swallowing of the private sector. But this criticism is unfounded. No doubt, public sector had been given an adequate role to play, but, in a mixed economy, public sector must assume the role of a senior partner in the acceleration of economic development. In fact, the Resolution gave ample scope for expansion of the private sector. Even in Schedule A, private sector had been allowed to operate in appropriate cases, though the development of industries mentioned in Schedule A was the exclusive responsibility of the State.

14.4.4. Industrial Policy of 1991

The long-awaited liberalised industrial policy was announced by the Government of India on 24 July 1991. There are several important departures in the latest policy. The New Industrial Policy has scrapped the asset limit for MRTP companies and abolished industrial licensing of all projects, except for 18 (now 5) specific groups. It has raised the limit for foreign equity holdings, thereby demanding a greater participation of foreign capital in the country's industrial landscape. The new policy has dismantled all needless, irksome bureaucratic controls on industrial growth. The new policy has re-defined the role of the public sector and has asked the private sector to operate even in those areas which were hitherto reserved for the public sector. Thus, the new policy considers that no longer big and monopoly business houses and foreign capital and multinational corporations (MNCs) are "fearsome" and, in fact, they are benign to the country's industrial growth. Anyway, the new policy has decided to take a series of initiatives in respect of the policies relating to the following areas: (a) industrial licensing, (b) MRTP Act, (c) public sector policy, (d) foreign investment, and (e) foreign technology agreements.

The highlights of the new policy are:

- Industrial licensing will be abolished for all projects except for a short list of industries (18 select sectors mentioned in Annexure II). The exemption from licensing will apply to all substantial expansion of existing units. The existing and new industrial units will be provided with a broad banding facility to enable them to produce any article so long as no additional investment in plant and machinery is involved. However, the small-scale industries taking up manufacture of those products reserved for small sector will not be subjected to compulsory licensing procedures. As a result, all existing registration schemes (like de-licensed registration, exempted industries registration, DGTD registration) will be abolished. Now, entrepreneurs are required to fill an information memorandum on new projects and substantial expansion.

- The policy provides for automatic clearance for import of capital goods in cases where the foreign exchange availability is ensured through foreign equity.

  As for the MRTP Act, the policy states that the pre-entry scrutiny of investment decisions by the so-called MRTP companies will no longer be required.
- The policy intends to scrap the asset limit of the MRTP companies.
- The policy envisages disinvestment of government equity in public sector to mutual funds, financial institutions, general public and workers. For the first time, sick public units will come under the purview of the Board of Industrial and Financial Reconstruction (BIFR) for their revival. A social security mechanism to protect workers' interests in such affected public sectors has been proposed in this policy. Pre-eminent place of public sector in two core areas production of atomic energy, and rail transport will, however, continue.

  Reservation for the public sector, as on 2008, is very limited—covering only manufacturing involving certain substances relevant for atomic energy and provision of railway transport.
- In order to invite foreign investment in high priority industries, requiring large investments and advanced technology, it has been decided to provide approval for direct foreign investment up to 51 p.c. foreign equity in such industries.
- In a departure from the present locational policy for industries, the policy provides that in locations other than cities of population of more than one million, there will be no requirement for obtaining industrial approvals except for industries subject to compulsory licensing.

Comments: The new industrial policy radically differs from the fundamental industrial policy of 1956. It is said that these policy decisions of the government are "a series of measures to unshackle the Indian industrial economy from the cobwebs of unnecessary bureaucratic controls." The new policy is a bolder step towards the process of deregulating the economy so that Indian industry becomes more competitive—internally and internationally. The delicensing of a large number of industries—scrapping the asset limit of MRTP companies and the abolition of registration schemes—will free Indian entrepreneurs from needless government controls.

This new policy has been hailed as a 'landmark' in the opening up of the Indian economy. This policy is a great leap towards privatisation. Under this new policy, like foreign capital and multinational corporations, large industrial houses have been respected by the Government. However, in earlier policies, in the name of building up a socialistic pattern of society, the Government controlled and regulated private industrial houses through several important controlling devices. Thus, the Centre's new industrial policy package will definitely strengthen the control of monopoly industrial houses in the country's landscape, thereby overthrowing the cherished goals of building a socialistic pattern of society.

The current industrial policy says that the private sector, rather than the public sector, should be viewed as an 'ideal' institution for industrialisation. That is why the policy has scrapped the asset limit for the MRTP companies and abolished industrial licensing for all projects except for 18 (now 2) specific groups. But in India, private industrial houses are not 'ideal'. These houses don't have the minimum sense of social responsibility. Not only this, some of the private industrial houses, unlike the public sector, also suffer from losses. So, these are not "ideal". Again, by building up large industrial houses under the umbrella of the current policy, it is feared that the interests of the consumers are unlikely to be served.

The other area in which the Government has taken a giant leap is with respect to foreign participation in Indian companies and allowing access to foreign technology. But it is apprehended that most of the foreign investment would be channelised in the direction of non-priority sectors rather than priority sectors. It is a strange phenomenon that despite curbs on the coming of foreign capital in the past, a huge amount of foreign investment was made in such industries as cars, soft drinks, potato chips, etc. Thus, there is a serious distortion of our industrial structure through the current industrial policy. It tilts more in favour of industries producing luxury goods.

Finally, seeing the ills of the public sector for a couple of years, the Government, in its new industrial policy, went for privatisation of the public sector. Privatisation—or the so-called part-privatisation—is not the solution to the ills of the public sector. Without diagnosing the problems and curing those, the policy envisages disinvestment of government equity in the public sector.

Thus, the Government's statement of industrial policy has overnight altered the industrial scenario in India. The new policy is definitely a step towards privatisation of Indian industries. It is now up to industry to show that it has the will and the ability to respond. But, if past experience is any guide then we can say that private industrialists will not rise to the occasion since our industrialists, over time, have fallen under the complacent habit of growing under the protected environment. However, it is feared that foreign investment will trickle down to this country despite liberalisation. In any case, the government thinks that no longer the big bourgeoisie or private capital and foreign capital are deadly in the Indian business world. The somersault in Government's policy merely speaks that "bad policy drives out good policy."

Anyway, competition among firms is the essence of new industrial policy. In order to improve competition, and thus contain the distortions caused by monopoly power, the Competition Act, 2002, was passed in December

2002. The Act aims at promoting competition through prevention of anti-competitive practices, and abuse of dominance. This Act replaces the MRTP Act.

14.4.5. Differences Between 1956 and 1991 Industrial Policies

The new industrial policy has brought about a revolutionary change in the structure of the Indian economy. For roughly 35 years, Indian industries were subject to undue control and regulation. The new Industrial Policy announced in July 1991 was in line with the current economic philosophy of the Government to liberalise the existing industrial and commercial policies with the objective of increasing efficiency, gaining competitive advantage, and achieving modernisation of the economy. The current policy makes an attempt to integrate the Indian economy with global capitalism. 3Ds, i.e., delicensing, deregulation and debureaucratisation are the main items of agenda of the 1991 industrial policy. On the contrary, the Industrial Policy of 1956 was designed to control and regulate the industrial policy to move on socialist lines.

The current policy differs from the basic Industrial Policy of 1956 in many respects. *First,* the 1956 Resolution classified industries into three categories having regard to the role which the State would play in each of them. Schedule A consisted of 17 industries whose future development would be the exclusive responsibility of the State. The 1991 Policy Resolution aimed at restricting the role of public sector in only two industries where security and strategic sectors (that is, production of atomic energy and railway transport) predominate. Core industries like iron and steel, generation and distribution of electricity, etc. are now free from the reserved list. The development of these industries would now be left into the hands of the private sector. This amounts to saying that the current Industrial Policy is a step towards privatisation in critical areas.

Secondly, prior to 1980s, industrial development was governed by licence and other regulatory mechanisms. The new policy intends to remove the 'licence-permit-quota raj' of the earlier period. The Government has ultimately admitted that control and regulation of the older days crippled India's industrial development. Hence the need for liberalisation measures. The current policy aims at liberalisation of the industrial economy. In view of this, it has abolished the industrial licensing requirements for all industries except 18 (now 5 such as, alcholoic drinks, tobacco manufacturing, electronic aerospace and defence equipment, industrial explosives and hazardous chemicals) industries. This means that nearly 95 p.c. of the industries have been delicensed, thereby making a smooth sailing of the private sector in the industrialisation programme of the country.

Thirdly, the new policy has scrapped the MRTP asset limit. Previously, under the MRTP Act, MRTP companies were not allowed to enter selected industries without any prior approval of the Government. The objective of the Government was to build up a socialistic pattern of society by restricting the growth of the large industrial houses. Such an objective has been watered down by scrapping the asset limit of the MRTP companies.

Finally, the 1956 Industrial Policy and the subsequent policies required foreign investment normally limited to 40 p.c. equity participation. In this respect, the current policy marks a great departure from the past ones. Under this, a specified list of industries has been prepared wherein automatic permission would be given for direct foreign investment up to 51p.c. foreign equity. The new policy also provides for automatic approval to foreign technology agreements in the case of 34 priority industries. Thus, the current policy recognises 'outward-looking development strategy' instead of the old 'inward-looking strategy.'

14.5. RATIONALE FOR PRIVATISATION OF THE PUBLIC SECTOR IN INDIA

Over the last 58 years or so, the performance of India's public sector enterprises has been severely criticised. Truly speaking, the public sector enterprises have been set up not merely out of ideological considerations of building a socialistic pattern of society. In truth, the necessity for creating adequate infrastructural facilities was the most important consideration leading to the expansion of the public sector. This is in view of the fact that the private sector is not only hesitant, but also incapable, of building social overhead capital. In a mixed economy framework, the two sectors are expected to play a complementary role.

But what happened in India during the planning period was that the public sector acted as a feeder to the private sector, in spite of inefficiencies of the former. Furthermore, loss of public sector helps private sector to accumulate profits. That is why, in the early 1990s, a question cropped up in the minds of our national leaders: How long public sector industries should bear losses by merely playing the complementary role? An argument often advanced by them is that, over time, private sector industries in India have attained a fair degree of maturity. Investment potentiality, as well as managerial efficiency, of these industries are no less inferior to those of public sector industries. Hence, the necessity for expansion of the private sector.

In the light of failure of the public sector and success of the private sector industries, demand for privatisation of the public sector came to the forefront when the Cong.(I) Government under the leadership of P.V. Narasimha Rao came to power in 1991. This was the time when the then socialist country U.S.S.R. embarked upon economic reforms under the banner 'Perestroika' (meaning 'reconstruction' or 'restrcturing' of the economic system) aimed at dismantling socialist stance and introducing privatisation. This wave of privatisation swept all over India. International financial institutions also preached the gospel of privatisation. The World Bank, in its 1991 report, clamoured for the introduction of 'market-freiendly' approach and advised us to deregulate and decontrol the public sector. It is argued by these institutions that the market will take care of all problems. The market mechanism is the 'open sesame' for all sorts of economic ills. Is it really so? To answer this question, we must first know the meaning of privatisation.

The term 'privatisation' is used in different ways, ranging from 'transition to private legal forms' to 'partial or complete denationalisation of assets.' In India, privatisation is sought to be achieved through two measures: (i) the disinvestment of the government's equity in public sector undertakings, and (ii) the opening up of hitherto closed areas to private participation. The issue of privatisation has come to the forefront due to the poor performance of several public sector enterprises and the consequent huge fiscal deficits faced by the government. Since the government has to give fiscal support to losing public concerns, the fiscal deficit of the government kept on mounting year after year. One specific step that has been taken to reduce the deficit was privatisation, through an act of disinvestment, i.e., selling of public sector equity to mutual funds, financial institutions and the private sector.

The privatisation process began in 1991-92 with the sale of minority stakes in some PSUs. From 1999-2000 onwards, the focus has been shifted to strategic sales. As a part of strategic sales, the government plans to ensure that at least for a period of one year after privatisation there would be no retrenchment of employees.

Another major shift in disinvestment policy was made in 2004-05 when it was decided that the government may "dilute its equity and raise resources to meet the social needs of the people"—a distinct departure from strategic sales.

The Government has been able to realise nearly Rs 51,573 crore by way of disinvestment of PSEs over the period 1991-92—March 2007-08. Till 1990-2000, disinvestment was primarily through the sale of minority shares in small lots. Between 1999-2000 and 2003-04, the emphasis on disinvestment changed in favour of strategic sale. At present, the policy is to list large, profitable CPSEs on domestic stock exchanges.

One can conclude from this move of the Government that the private sector industries in India are not inefficient as public sector industries. Administrative and managerial inefficiency are the hallmarks of public sector industries. Government is unable to run these high cost public sector industries. Unable to correct this situation, the Government went for privatisation. So, it was a forced privatisation.

The current direction of privatisation policy has been spelt out in December 2002. Government has announced in the Parliament its policy that the main objective of disinvestment is to put national resources and assets to optimal use and in particular to unleash the productive potential in our public sector enterprises. The policy of disinvestment now aims at (i) modernisation and upgradation of PSEs; (ii) creation of new assets; (iii) generation of employment; (iv) retiring of public debt.

Criticisms: Mishra and Puri have rightly commented : "In fact, there seems to be no clarity regarding the objectives of such privatisation. Instead of revamping the public sector enterprises, the entire way in which disinvestment has been undertaken gives the impression that it is an exercise to bridge the budgetary deficit." Critics have argued that privatisation does not necessarily lead to better economic performance. In fact, there is hardly any correlation between ownership and operational efficiency (performance). No doubt competitive markets are necessary to achieve an efficient and vigorous economy, but full-scale private ownership is not necessary for the successful operation of competitive markets (i.e., for keeping competition alive and markets free).

The fact is not that all public sector enterprises are models of inefficiency or loss-making concerns and that all units in private sector are efficient in their operation. There are both efficient and inefficient enterprises in both the sectors—private and public. Thus, it appears, on balance, that in order to improve the performance of inefficient units the creation of a competitive market environment is absolutely essential. The crux of the matter is that it is a competitive environment, rather than ownership, which ensures an efficient allocation of society's productive wealth i.e., its capital.

Critics also point out that if shares of public sector enterprises are offered for sale to the private sector, the latter will naturally be interested only in the shares of profit-making concerns. This would virtually amount to transferring public profit to the private pockets. This cannot be justified by any rational economic canon.

It may be reminded that the disinvestment policy has wide fiscal ramifications. It is observed that disinvestment plans did not run as it was derived; it led to low resource mobilisation in most of the years. Further, it has not been successful in addressing fiscal difficulties.

Finally, one may note that the sale of real assets of large enterprises like the SAIL or Coal India Ltd. is likely to weaken the very base of the economy by creating infrastructural deficiency. If the new owners of these companies (the replacement values of the assets of which are in the neighbourhood of Rs 25,000 crore each) enjoy the discretion of using the resources as they deem fit, this will virtually amount to giving control over the vast resources at throwaway prices.

Ours is a mixed economy. In the name of liberalisation, private sector is being pampered. Market principles are being allowed to play freely. What is needed at this juncture is the debureaucratisation of the public sector, instead of privatisation. Public sector industries in India are plagued with inefficiencies due to excessive bureaucratisation. Instead of removing the ills of the public sector industries, the Government went for privatisation. To achieve the goals of social justice public sector investment has to be stepped up.

A logical question that will arise is the question of financing public sector industries. Resources must be garnered to step up investment in the public sector. However, to this problem we have an answer. The Government should have disinvested its share of luxury hotels and restaurants, bakery, etc. By disinvesting shares of these luxury goods producing public sector industries, the Government could have raised a great deal of financial resources. Furthermore, loss-making public sector industries should not be allowed to function unless they improve their performance. However, the Government thought it proper to disinvest shares of profit-making public sector enterprises. But, experts firmly believe that privatisation is not the solution to the problems from which our economy is suffering.

14.6. REFORMS INTRODUCED IN PUBLIC SECTOR ENTERPRISES IN THE 1990S AND AFTERWARDS

India has seen changes in domestic policies in July 1991 that have fundamentally altered its development strategy. The Government headed by Sri Narasimha Rao undertook the major task of stabilising and liberalising the Indian economy which had hitherto been a unnecessarily controlled, regulated economy. It also saw an over-extended public sector. A series of reforms were introduced in the public sector to tone up its efficiency. But, so far as the reforms are concerned, reform in PSEs seems to be the "weakest element."

Reforms were made in the following areas: *First,* from the original list of 17 reserved sector, now only two areas (namely, production of atomic energy and railway transport) remain reserved for PSEs. Moreover, most of the manufacturing industries earlier reserved for the public sector have now been exempted from the purview of industrial licensing and control. Thus, PSEs are now subject to competition from new private, domestic and foreign industries. Obviously, the performance of

PSEs is likely to depend on how they respond to these competitive challenges. As a result, the power and the telecom sectors have been identified by the Government where private investments should flow. Till today, such privatisation effort, carried out with much fanfare, has brought very little. Despite providing a number of incentives and concessions to build up the private sector hitherto reserved for the public sector, managers of PSEs have not been given the authority to introduce measures essential for restructuring—such as large-scale retrenchment, closure or selling of units or joint ventures with private investors.

Second, many PSEs are chronically sick. Thus, what is required is the revival/rehabilitation of such sick PSEs. In order to establish a system of rehabilitation and restructuring of PSEs without having the Government to bear the whole financial burden, the Sick Industrial Companies Act, 1985, was amended in 1991 to bring these enterprises under the purview of the Board for Industrial and Financial Reconstruction (BIFR), for rationalisation.

It is to be pointed out here that the BIFR—a quasi-judicial body—can only order a wind-up. This, of course, has to be implemented by the respective High Courts subject to State government's clearances of winding-up, retrenchment, and sale of land. State Governments, because of financial and political compulsions, are reluctant to grant clearances. As a result, the results have been less than satisfactory.

To help the PSEs to turnaround financially, the Government set up the Board for Reconstruction of Public Sector Enterprises (BRPSE) in 2004 to recommend measures for restructuring/reviving sick and loss-making PSEs refrrred to them. The BRPSE also rcommends cases where disinvestment or closure or sale are justified.

Thirdly, since efficiency of PSEs in their functioning needs to be boosted, the Government has taken steps to processionalise the Boards of PSEs. To tone up the spirit of competition, an attempt has been made to evaluate the performance of PSEs on the basis of sales and growth of sales, net profit and growth in net profit, etc.

Fourthly, a National Renewal Fund (NRF) was set up in 1992 to shed the load of excess employment in PSEs and provide a safety net for employees affected by restructuring or closure of industrial units. An important aspect of NRF is the financing of the Voluntary Retirement Scheme (VRS) or 'golden handshake' for workers in PSEs. An estimated number of 5.33 lakh workers have opted for voluntary retirement so far. Since 1998 till March 2004, a major portion of NRF has been utilised in the textile sector. But this is far below the target set in the business plan of NRF.

Fifthly, another important aspect of structural reforms is the reduction of budgetary support to PSEs. Loans to PSEs have declined from 0.7 p.c. of GDP in 1990-91 to 0.4 p.c. of GDP in 1992-93, but again rose to 0.6 p.c. in 1993-94.

Sixthly, a major aspect of reform involves disinvestment of shares of PSEs to raise resources and encourage wider participation of general public and workers in the ownership of PSEs. The Industrial Policy Statement of July 1991 envisaged disinvestment of a part of government holdings in the share capital of selected PSEs in order to provide market discipline and to improve the performance of PSEs as well as to increase their public accountability by broadbasing their management and ownership. Till March 2008, a total amount of Rs 51,573 crore has been disinvested to the public sector financial institutions, mutual funds and general public. In August 1996, a Disinvestment Commission was established for working out the terms and conditions as well as modalities pertaining to disinvestment of public utilities. The Commission has suggested dismantling of the administered price mechanism for petroleum products in a phased manner as necessary precondition to disinvestment of petroleum companies.

The stated objective of disinvestment is to ensure market discipline and to improve the performance of PSEs. But the experience of disinvestment shows that neither market discipline nor performance of PSEs is linked to disinvestment. It is also entirely unclear as to how disinvestment can ensure viability and sustainability of PSEs.

In 1997, the Government granted autonomy to 9 profit-making PSEs, popularly known as *'Navaratnas.'* These enterprises now have greater freedom in incurring capital expenditure, in raising capital resources from domestic and international markets in opening up subsidiaries/offices abroad. In addition, 97 profit-making enterprises labelled as *'Mini-ratnas'* have been given greater financial and managerial autonomy.

Lastly, efforts are being constantly made for easier access of FDI. FDI has been permitted through the automatic route for all industries except a small negative list. Government's present Industrial Policy addresses removal of caps on FDI. 100 p.c. FDI has been permitted in oil refining, telecom sector, business to business, e-commerce, etc. Easier conditions for royalty payments have been made.

In 2006, wide-ranging policy changes e.g., extending automatic routes, increasing equity caps, removing restrictions, simplifying procedures extending the horizon of FDI, etc., were notified. At the end of the Tenth plan period, FDI up to 100 p.c. was permitted in all manufacturing activities except where the foreign investor had an existing joint venture/technical callaboration/trademark agreement in the same field of activity.

Thus, reform measures are not so satisfactory till to date. It is to be remembered here that the objective of the PSE reforms should not be tied to the apron strings of the financial compulsions of the State, but should subserve the special purpose and national priorities which PSEs are supposed to serve. Increased disinvestment cannot be seen as the panacea for all the ills of PSEs. Starving of all sick PSEs by denying the budgetary support and autonomy, referring them to the BIFR on the basis of financial performance, cannot form part of the guidelines for PSE reforms. Since most of the PSEs are products of special considerations, the reform should be designed to meet specific situations.

One finds a change in policy shift in 2004-05 when the Government, while expressing a commitment towards a strong and effective public sector, decided that 'generally profit-making companies will not be privatised'. In addition, the other two major elements of the policy of the Government of India are (i) full managerial and commercial autonomy to profit-making PSEs, and (ii) modernisation and restructuring of sick PSEs as well as a sell-off or closure of sick of PSEs.

14.7. INDUSTRIAL SICKNESS

One of the disquieting trends observable in the corporate sector of India is the growing incidence of sickness. It is causing concern to planners and policymakers. It is also putting a severe strain on the economic institutions, particularly the banks.

• **Criteria of Sickness**: There are various criteria of sickness. According to the criteria accepted by the Reserve Bank of India: "A sick unit is one which has reported cash loss for the last year of its operation and in the judgement of the financing bank is likely to incur cash loss for the current year as also in the following year." A major symptom of sickness is a steady fall in debt-equity ratio and an imbalance in the financial position of the unit. Simply put, a sick unit is one which is unable to support itself through the operation of internal resources (that is, earnings from plough back). As a general rule, the sick units continue to operate below the break-even point and are, thus, forced to depend on external sources of funds for their long-term survival.

In order to examine the bottlenecks in industrial and corporate restructuring and to suggest suitable measures for the early closure of unviable units and quick revival of viable ones, the Government appointed a Committee on Industrial Sickness and Corporate Restructuring in May 1993 under the chairmanship of Onkar Goswami. It submitted its report in July 1993. The Committee suggested a change in the definition of sickness:

(i) default of 180 days or more on repayment to term-lending institutions, and (ii) irregularities in cash-credits or working capital for 180 days or more.

• **External and Internal Causes**: Industrial sickness has become a major problem of the Indian corporate industrial sector. Of late, it has assumed serious proportions. A close look reveals that there are, at least, five major causes of industrial sickness, viz., promotional, managerial, technical, financial, and political.

The causes of industrial sickness may be divided into two broad categories: (i) external, and (ii) internal.

External causes are those which are beyond the control of its management, and seem to be relatively more important than internal causes. The external causes which have been identified so far include: (a) delay in land acquisition and building construction; (b) delay in obtaining financial assistance from public financial institutions; (c) delayed supply of machinery by the manufacturers; (d) problems related to recruitment of technical and managerial staff; (e) dilatoriness on the part of the government in sanctioning licences, permits, etc.; (f) shortages of basic inputs like power. Other causes include: (f) cost overruns due to factors beyond the control of management; (h) lack of demand for products or shift of demand to products of rival firms due to delays in project implementation; (i) unsatisfactory performance by collaborators—financial and technical; and, last but not the least, (j) changes in the policy of the Government relating to movement of goods from one place to another within the country, or the Government's export-import policy.

Internal causes are many. The primary one seems to be (i) "lack of experience of the promoters in the line of activity." The other causes are: (ii) differences among various persons associated with the promotion and management of the enterprise; (iii) mechanical defects and breakdown; (iv) inability to purchase raw materials at an economic price and at the right time; (v) failure to make controls effective in time in case of deficiencies in workings; (vi) deteriorating labour management relations and the consequent fall in capacity utilisation, and, above all; (vii) faulty financial planning and lack of balance in the financial (capital) structure.

It is often observed that many projects are started without making any proper feasibility study. Hardly any long-term view of the future is taken. Often industrial projects are started on an *ad hoc* basis without gathering much about the expertise and competence needed for the purpose.

Internal causes for sickness are summarised as: (i) project appraisal deficiencies, (ii) project management deficiencies, and several external factors like, (iii) shortage of raw materials, (iv) power crisis, (v) changes in government policy, (vi) transport and financial bottlenecks, (vii) increase in overhead costs, etc. Marketing problems in the form of market saturation, product obsolescence and demand recession are considered to be other factors responsible for industrial sickness.

Incidence : As at the end of March 2006, the total number of sick units stood at 1,31,553 units involving an outstanding bank credit of about Rs. 38,819 crore. 1,26,824 units (i.e., 99 p.c.) were in the small scale sector. Of these, their share in the aggregate locked in bank credit was only 17.5 p.c. The three major industries affected by industrial sickness are jute, engineering goods, and textiles.

Government Policy: The policy framework in respect of measures to deal with the problem of industrial sickness has been laid down in the guidelines issued in October 1981 (which were subsequently modified in February 1982) for guidance of administrative ministries of the Central Government, State Governments, and financial institutions.

The Central Government has set up a Board for Industrial and Financial Reconstruction (BIFR) with effect from January 12, 1987 in pursuance of enactment of the SICA—Sick Industrial Companies (Special Provisions) Act, 1985. This is a major step for intervening at an early stage and detecting, preventing as well as taking ameliorative, remedial, and such other measures which need to be taken with respect to sick and potentially viable companies.

A number of measures have been taken to tackle the problem of industrial sickness. The importance of detection of sickness at the incipient stage has been emphasised by the RBI. Since its inception (1987) up to the end of March 1998, BIFR received 7,7,158 applications. It is to be remarked here that the number of cases being registered with the BIFR has been decreasing gradually. Till October 2002, the Board has sanctioned rehabilitation schemes of 748 central and state PSUs. It has so far recommended winding up of 1,303. A small set of 485 companies have been declared no longer 'sick' and have been discharged from the purview of SICA, since net worth of these public and private companies turned positive after the implementation of rehabilitation schemes.

The Industrial Reconstruction Bank of India (IRBI) set up in 1985 has initiated various steps for checking the growth of industrial sickness and helping in industrial revival. Out of 393 units assisted by the IRBI till the end of June 1986, 136 units have been revived. By March 1997, cumulative financial assistance sanctioned and disbursed stood at Rs 4,312 crore and Rs 2,954 crore, respectively.

The IRBI was taken over by the Industrial Investment Bank of India in 1997. It functions as the principal credit and reconstruction agency for industrial revival.

A significant measure taken during 1986 was the setting up of Small Industries Development Fund (SIDF) in the IDBI. This is meant to provide special financial assistance to the small-scale sector.

The Government has set up two funds, the Textile Modernisation Fund and the Jute Modernisation Fund—for modernisation in the textiles and jute sector. Under these two funds, assistance is provided not only to the healthy units for modernisation at 11.5 p.c. rate of interest, but also to sick but potentially viable units. Special loans are given to the weak units for meeting a part of the promoters' contribution. These special loans carry 6 p.c. rate of interest with a repayment period of 12 years and an initial moratorium period of 6 years.

Meanwhile, the Government appointed a 'Committee on Industrial Sickness and Corporate Restructuring' in 1993 under the chairmanship of Onkar Goswami. The Committee recommends liquidation of sick concerns instead of their rehabilitation. Government is now considering the repeal of SICA and winding up of the BIFR. It is feared that in view of the 2008 recession, in the immediate future large number of sick units would be closed down thereby raising the bogey of unemployed workers.

14.8. FOREIGN CAPITAL

Need: Most of the LDCs are characterised by shortage of resources required for economic development. Resources may be domestic and foreign. By the shortage of domestic resources we mean scarcity of savings. Economists call such shortage of domestic resources the 'savings gap'. On the other hand, shortage of foreign resources refer to the scarcity of foreign exchange. We call such scarcity of foreign exchange the 'trade gap'. Foreign capital can bridge these two gaps. It permits a country to invest more than it is able to save domestically. In summary, the resource constraint that stands in the way of development of LDCs can be greatly removed if foreign capital is invited. Furthermore, foreign capital also bridges 'technological gap' of the developing countries. Technological assistance given by the developed countries to the poor countries has brought more rapid progress to these countries. Hence the necessity of foreign capital in LDCs.

Foreign capital increases competition in markets, brings new technology and faster skill acquistion amongst domestic labour. It serves as a platform for global production chains, which would pave the way for strong exports growth.

In brief, the FDI benefits domestic Indian industries as well as Indian public by providing opportunities for technological upgradation, access to global managerial skills and practices optimal utilisation of both human natural and physical resources, making Indian industry internationally competitive, opening up export markets in different countries, providing backward and forward linkages and access to international quality goods and services.

Types: Important forms of private foreign investment are: portfolio investment (PI) and foreign direct investment (FDI). Portfolio investment may take the form of equity participation by foreigners' and creditors' capital. Participation can either be in the form of an enterprise completely owned by it or purchase of shares of a domestic concern or it can take the form of collaboration. PI is a form of foreign capital which is used to purchase the shares of companies to claim share of profits and to exercise some sort of control over production. In this sense, PI is a floating capital. It is, thus, volatile in nature and it reflects speculative behaviour of foreign investors.

FDI, on the other, takes the form of equity capital that refers to investment in shares of a company in a foreign country. In India, it comes as direct investments via foreign branches of the parent companies and controlled by Indian companies. This sort of investment is considered as 'sunk capital' and, hence, preferred as it directly increases capital formation of the recipient country. Portfolio investment implies only transfer of resources. As this sort of capital is volatile in nature, its impact on capital formation is 'one step removed'. Unfortunately, the bulk of foreign capital that is coming to India particularly after the mid-1991 is in the form of PI, rather than FDI.

In addition, foreign capital may take the form of inter-governmental loans, loans from international financial institutions, and grants.

14.8.1. Government Policy towards Foreign Capital (1948-1991 June)

At the time of independence, the Government of India's attitude towards foreign capital was one of fear and suspicion, of course, quite expectedly. Apathy towards foreign capital was even marked in the Government's Industrial Policy of 1948. In this policy, the Government insisted upon the gradual Indianisation of foreign companies. This scared the foreign firms from investing more in India. As a result, the Government had to assure the foreign capitalists in 1949 in the following three directions:

- There shall be no discrimination between Indian and foreign undertakings.
- Facilities shall be given to foreign investors for remittance of profit and repatriation of capital.
- Due compensation shall be paid in case a foreign undertaking is nationalised.

The attitude towards foreign capital remained unchanged in the 1956 Industrial Policy Resolution. In view of all these announcements and assurances on the part of the Government, private foreign capital entered India rather happily since the beginning (1956) of the Second Plan. Since then, more and more liberal policies had been announced at different times.

For instance, in 1972, the Government permitted entry of wholly-owned subsidiaries of foreign companies provided they undertake to export 100 p.c. or more of their output. In 1977, the Janata Party showed its reservations against foreign collaboration when Coca-Cola and IBM were asked to close their businesses in India.

14.8.2. Policy Towards Foreign Capital since 1991

However, the 1990s saw a U-turn in the policy of the Government towards foreign capital. Earlier, Government regulated its foreign capital investments and collaborations in such a way that these fit into the overall framework of the national economic plans. It now allows huge concessions and relaxations rather than its selected stand taken earlier when foreign capital was permitted only in certain areas which were of basic and/or strategic importance to this country. The 1991 Industrial Policy announced several concessions and relaxations as far as foreign capital is concerned. It has opened up doors of several industries even of minor importance for foreign investment.

The policies and procedures pertaining to FDI and PI have been progressively liberalised over the years.

With increased liberalisation, Goverment has permitted FDI up to 100 p.c. under automatic route in most sectors, Equity caps on FDI now exist in limited sectors. These are:

- Insurance, defence production, petroleum refining in the PSUs, print and electronic media up to 26 p.c.
- Air transport services, cable network, etc. up to 49 p.c.
- Atomic reactors, private sector banking, telecom services up to 74 p.c.
- FDI prohibited in retail trading, except for single brand product retailing, gambling and betting, lottery and atomic energy
- FDI up to 100 p.c. allowed under automatic route in most sectors activities.

A comprehensive review of the FDI policy was made in 2006 to consolidate the liberalisation already effected and further rationalise the FDI up to 100 p.c. now permitted in tea plantation with some conditions. FDI up to 100 p.c. is permitted under the automatic route in floriculture, horticulture, development of seeds, animal husbandry, pisciculture, aquaculture and services related to agro and allied sector.

At the end of the Tenth Plan period, FDI up to 100 p.c. was permitted in all manufacturing activities except where foreign investor had an existing joint venture.

These measures have so far been taken to make India a most favourable destination for FDI. In 2006-07, electrical equipment including computer software and electronics to attract the largest volume of FDI is channelled into services sector (both financial and non-financial), Telecomunications stand at the third (10.39 p.c.).

Extent of Foreign Investment Inflows: It is clear that private foreign investment and foreign capital are now entering India in a significant scale as a substitute for declining foreign aid. FDI that stood at a low of $ 97 in 1990-91 rose to $ 3,358, in 2005. Portfolio investment during the same period rose from $ 6 to $ 2,760. Gross foreign investment inflows thus rose from $ 103 to $ 5099 during 1990-91 and 2000-01. However, these are mere approval figures. The actual or realised foreign investments are considerably low. Roughly 65 p.c. of FDI approved is not realised—and they are on paper.

As a proportion of GDP, foreign investment remained at 0.2 p.c. fell in 1992-93. It picked up with reforms and has remained almost stationary at 2 p.c. since 2003-04.

A country-wise FDI inflows during 2000-07 reveal that the largest source of FDI in India is Mauritius (44 p.c.), followed by the USA (9 p.c.). The third position is occupied by UK (8 p.c.). It may be added here that Mauritius-based investments are nothing but US investments since these are routed through Mauritius to avoid the problem of complex tax laws. Many MNCs send their investments to India via Mauritius since here tax rates are rather lowest in the world.

Comment: Foreign investments in India pose some serious problems. *First,* the jump in foreign investment is not so big as is assumed by many. The Government set a target of attracting $ 10 billion of such inflows; the actual figure is just a third of the targeted goal. Between 1991 and 2006, actual inflow of FDI came to Rs. 1,81,566 crore vis-a-vis the approved amount of Rs. 2,84,812 crore. Further, foreign investment inflows into India are less than a tenth of that flowing into China. This indicates that India has failed to exploit the benefits of FDI even in this liberalised era.

Secondly, the gap between approved and actual inflows of investment is widening over time. Approximately 35 p.c of FDI is actually realised and, thus, 65 p.c. remain on paper. This gap may be attributed to the existence of hurdles in the way of implementing foreign investment plans.

Thirdly, so far foreign investors have chosen sectors like power generation and oil extraction. In addition, the most important sectors are telecom, electrical equipment including computer software, energy, and the transportation industry. These four sectors now account for roughly 50 p.c. of FDI inflows. Such preference is due to the wide possibility of profit margin. By contrast, they are neither going into green-field projects, nor aimed at production for the world as opposed to domestic markets. Foreign firms are showing a great deal of preference for joint ventures in India with the aim of increasing their share in equity held in these companies. So far, FDI, in areas like equipment manufacturing or export-oriented production, has not come to notice.

Actual FDI now concentrates on domestic appliances, finance, services, food products, etc. There is nothing high-technology about the bulk of FDI inflows and that they are aimed at capturing the market of middle class and upper class. The aspiration of this neo-rich classes is an incentive to foreign investors. It is said that "300 million strong" Indian middle class's "appetite for consumption... will not be satiated for the next 50 to 100 years." "No (other) country could aspire for such a large market, as India, for investment, where an ever-increasing middle class is hungry for quality goods and services." What is more important is that the balance of payments impacts of such foreign investment inflows are likely to be clearly against long-term interests of the country, without any corresponding gain in productive capacities of the country.

Finally, the strengthening of foreign investment through mergers, acquisitions and takeovers is posing a great threat to Indian monopolists and big businesses as some of them have lost ground to MNCs. A study of the Indian Institute of Management, Calcutta, observed that "not only has there been an accumulation in mergers and acquisitions since liberalisation, but also a dramatic increase, amounting almost to 50 p.c., in the share of such mergers and acquisitions accounted for by TNCs." The policy has also failed in creating additional job opportunities for Indian people.

QUESTIONS (WITH ANSWER-HINTS)

Long Questions (16 marks)

1. Give a brief account of the industrial development during the plan period.

   Ans. 14.2.

2. Point out the brighter as well as negative aspects of industrial growth during the plan period.

   Or

   What are the achievements and limitations of India's industrial development during the plan period?

   Ans. 14.3.

3. What is meant by industrial policy? What are the distinguishing features of the first Industrial Policy Resolution of the Government of India.

   Ans. 14.4.1 and 14.4.2.

4. What were the reasons behind changes in the Industrial Policy in 1956? What are its main features?

   Ans. 14.4.3.

5. Discuss critically the current Industrial Policy of the Government of India announced in 1991.

   Ans. 14.4.4.

6. Discuss the nature of changes that have been proposed

in the Industrial Policy of 1991 over the 1956 policy. In what respects does the current policy differ from the 1956 policy?

Ans. 14.4.4 and 14.4.5.

7. Point out the rationale for privatisation of India's public sector industries.

Or

Do you think that the public sector has lost its importance under the changing economic scenario in India? In this context, give your arguments for and against privatisation. (C.U. 2008)

Ans. 14.5.

8. What is industrial sickness? What are its causes? What measures have been taken to minimise the incidence of industrial sickness?

Ans. 14.7.

9. Write a critical note on the Government of India's policies towards foreign capital/investment.

Ans. 14.8, 14.8.1 and 14.8.2.

Medium-sized Questions (8 marks)

1. Discuss the role of industrialisation in the economic development of a country like India.

Ans. 14.1.

2. Evaluate the various structural reforms introduced in public sector enterprises in the decade of 1990s.

Ans. 14.6.

3. What is industrial sickness? Discuss the reasons behind industrial sickness In India. (C.U. 2008)

Ans. 14.7.

4. Explain the rationale behind encouraging the inflow of foreign capital for industrial development in India.

Ans. 14.8. (C.U. 2007)

15

INDIA'S FIVE YEAR PLANS

15.1. INTRODUCTION

Economic planning is often regarded as a technique of managing an economy. When the structure of an economy becomes complex and subject to rapid change and transformation (due to population growth, discovery of resources, industrialisation, etc.,) some sort of advance thinking becomes necessary to resolve that complexity and to prepare the economy for those changes. Such preparation is nothing but planning.

Most often than not, an economic plan is regarded as a programme of action. It may also be taken to mean an instrument for regulating a free private enterprise economy.

It should be remembered that as plan is just a programme of action; it is not a guarantee for action. In short, a good plan is one which makes adequate provision for and ensures that its targets are properly fulfilled. With the gradual collapse of the then Soviet or socialist economy in the late 1980s, there developed a 'plan weariness'. Both rightist and leftist economists came to a conclusion that the so-called socialist planning has failed to deliver the goods. In view of this development in thinking, many of the countries, including China and the erstwhile USSR, introduced various economic reforms. These economic reforms were incompatible with planning. In other words, economic reforms introduced in the regime of a planned economy were absolutely 'misfit'. These countries came out of the straight-jacket of economic planning and introduced liberalisation in their economies. They now came to believe that a deregulated, decontrolled and a much more open and liberalised economy would usher in quicker economic growth. Instead of planned economy, thus, what we have now is a market economy. The 1980s saw the revival of the debate between plan and market. The debate has not been settled. It continues even in the early years of the 21st century.

Indian economy has seen some dramatic changes in the 1990s. Planning, however, has not been shelved. But the Indian economy has been made now more free and uncontrolled. Liberalisation and globalisation of the Indian economy now seem to be uppermost in the minds of our leaders.

15.2. A BRIEF HISTORY OF INDIAN PLANNING

Although officially the plan era started from 1 April 1951 with the launching of the First Five Year Plan, the idea of economic planning in India may be traced back to earlier years. "The idea of economic planning gained currency in India during and after the years of the Great Agricultural Depression (1929-33). The then Government of India was by and large guided by a policy of leaving economic matters to individual industrialists and traders." The Congress organisation essayed on it as early as in 1938 and Sri M. Visvesvarya still earlier. Then there were the blueprints of the then Bombay industrialists, popularly called the Bombay Plan (1943), M. N. Roy's People's Plan, and M. N. Agarwala's Gandhian Plan.

All these were before independence and basically unofficial exercises. However, some official thought was given to it after the Second World War. In 1946, an Advisory Planning Board was appointed which published its report in 1947. The Board recommended the formation of a Planning Commission at the centre as also a statistical department. The Industrial Policy Resolution of 1948 also suggested the setting up of a National Planning Commission and framing the policy of a mixed economic system.

Ultimately, the Planning Commission was set up by the Government of India in 1950. The Commission was instructed to (a) make an assessment of the material capital and human resources of the country, and formulate a plan for the most effective and balanced utilisation of them; (b) determining priorities, define the stages for carrying the plan and propose the allocation of resources for the due completion of each stage; (c) identify the factors which are tending to retard economic development; and (d) determine the conditions which (in view of the current socio-political conditions) should be established for the execution of the plan.

The planning process was initiated in April 1951 when the First Five Year Plan was launched. Since then Ten five-year plans have been completed and the Eleventh Plan is on the card. The timing of these plans are given here in a tabular form :

Table 15.1: Timing of Plans

Plan	Period
First Plan	1951-56
Second Plan	1956-61
Third Plan	1961-66
Three Annual Plans	1966-69
Fourth Plan	1969-74
Fifth Plan	1974-78
Sixth Plan	1980-85
Seventh Plan	1985-90
Eighth Plan	1992-97
Ninth Plan	1997-02
Tenth Plan	2002-07
Eleventh Plan	2007-12

15.3. THE FIRST FIVE YEAR PLAN TO THE SEVENTH FIVE YEAR PLAN

The First Plan (1951-52 to 1955-56), had two main objectives: (i) to meet certain urgent problems that had arisen out of the World War II and the 1947 Partition of the country, and (ii) to raise standard of living of the people by a rapid and balanced economic development.

The Second Plan (1956-57 to 1960-61) sought to rebuild rural India, to lay the foundations of industrial development and to secure to the poorer sections of our people opportunities for better living. Consequently, the Second Plan laid emphasis on: (i) a quicker pace of economic development, (ii) a wider industrial base, (iii) larger employment opportunities, and (iv) socialist bias.

The Third Plan had the following objectives: (a) to secure a rise in national income of over 5 p.c. per annum; (b) to achieve self-sufficiency in foodgrains; (c) to expand basic industries, so that the requirements of further industrialisation can be met from within the country within a period of ten years or so; (d) to utilise to the fullest possible extent the manpower resources of the country and to ensure a substantial expansion of employment opportunities; and (e) to reduce inequality in income and wealth of the people.

The two main objectives of the Fourth Plan were: (i) growth with stability, and (ii) progressive achievement of self-reliance. The Planning Commission had also envisaged a growth rate of over 5 p.c. annum.

The two basic aims of the Fifth Plan were (a) removal of poverty, and (b) achieving economic self-sufficiency. It may be remembered that the Fifth Plan aimed also to 'move toward self-reliance' and that was the most important of the three basic objectives. However, the objective of removal of poverty overshadowed all others in the Fifth Plan.

The main objectives of the Sixth Plan were :

- a significant step-up in the rate of growth of the economy;
- strengthening the impulses of modernisation for the achievement of economic and technical self-reliance;
- progressive reduction in the incidence of poverty and unemployment;
- a progressive reduction in regional inequalities;
- controlling the growth of population through voluntary acceptance of small family norm;
- promoting the protection and improvement of ecological and environmental assets.

The Seventh Five Year Plan came into operation in April 1985. Seventh Plan started its career rather in somewhat favourable conditions in contrast to the unfavourable conditions on the eve of the Sixth Plan.

The Seventh Plan, unlike earlier Plans, had the following basic objectives : high rate of economic growth, modernisation, self-reliance and social justice. Besides these basic objectives, the Seventh Plan laid down certain specific objectives. These were, increase in the output of agricultural commodities, creation of employment opportunities and acceleration in the productivity of the economy.

15.4. THE EIGHTH FIVE YEAR PLAN (1992-97)

The Eighth Plan was delayed by 2 years because of uncertain political situation and unprecedented economic crises of the late 1980s and early 1990s. The Eighth Plan began on 1 April 1992 and treated years 1990-91 and 1991-92, as years of Annual Plan.

The nature and content of the Eighth Plan was different from earlier plans since this Plan had been influenced by the latest economic policies of the Government and the changing world situation. From a highly centralised planning system, we moved gradually towards indicative planning. Further, this was an integrative plan in the sense that our development efforts had to be integrated. Again, this Plan recognised human development as the core of all developmental efforts. The provision of the basic elements like education, health, population control, etc.,—which help the development of human capital remained the primary responsibility of the Government.

The Eighth Plan assigned a special role and responsibility to planning as well as market mechanism. These two had been dovetailed in such a manner that both act as complementary to each other.

The Eighth Plan gave priority to the following objectives :

- generation of adequate employment to achieve near full employment level by the turn of the century,
- containment of population growth through people's active cooperation and effective scheme of incentives and disincentives,
- universalisation of elementary education and complete eradication of illiteracy among the people in the age group of 15 to 36 years,
- provision of safe drinking water and primary health care facilities accessible to all the villages and the entire population,
- growth and diversification of agriculture to achieve self-sufficiency in food and to generate exportable surplus, and
- strengthening the infrastructure (energy, transport, irrigation, communication, etc.,) in order to support the growth process on a sustainable basis.

Targets: The Eighth Plan envisaged a growth rate of 5.6 p.c. per annum of GDP. This growth was supported by a domestic savings rate of 21.6 p.c. and foreign savings of 1.6 p.c. of GDP. Thus, the expected investment rate was 23.6 p.c. of GDP. With an incremental capital-output ratio of 4 :1, this would enable the economy to achieve the target growth rate of 5.6 p.c.

Comments: The success of any plan rests on the attainment of its target. Objectives are laudable, considering the objectives of generation of near full employment by the turn of the century. Thus, the Eighth Plan scored good marks in certain fronts. For instance, the average growth rate during the Eighth Plan was better (6.8 p.c.) than the Seventh Plan (6 p.c.). Agricultural sector grew at the rate of 3.7 p.c. The BOP position did not cause serious anxiety. However, all these positive trends could not be maintained in the year 1997-98 when GDP decelerated to 5.7 p.c. from 7.5 p.c. in 1996-97. Such a drop could be attributed mainly to a sharp fall in the growth rate of agriculture and a deceleration in the growth of industry. The most disturbing feature of the Eighth Plan in the realm of infrastructural sectors was that it had fallen short not only of its targets, but also of the realised performance of the Seventh Plan. Reduction of expenditure in social sector, in the ultimate analysis, has had a damaging effect on the economy.

15.5. THE NINTH FIVE YEAR PLAN (1997-02)

The Ninth Plan officially commenced on April 1997. Ninth Five Year Plan Document was released on March 1999—nearly two years after its launching.

Objectives: The focus of the Ninth Plan was on 'growth with social justice and equality'. The ultimate objective of planning were to improve the living conditions of the poor and the various disadvantaged sections of the society. The specific objectives of the Ninth Plan were the following:

- priority to agriculture and rural development with a view to generating adequate productive employment and eradication of poverty;
- accelerating the growth rate of the economy with stable prices;
- ensuring food and nutritional security for all, particularly the vulnerable sections of the society;

- providing the basic minimum services of safe drinking water, primary health care facilities, universal primary education, shelter and connectivity to all in a time-bound manner;
- containing the growth rate of population;
- ensuring environmental sustainability of the development process through social mobilisation and participation of people at all levels;
- empowerment of women and socially disadvantaged groups such as Scheduled Castes, Scheduled Tribes and Backward Classes and minorities as agents of socio-economic change and development;
- promoting and developing people's participatory institutions like Panchayati Raj Institutions (PRIs), cooperatives and self-help groups; and
- strengthening efforts to build self-reliance.

Targets: A growth rate of 7 p.c. p.a. in GDP had been targeted for the Ninth Plan period. In its major policy prescriptions for achieving a GDP growth rate of 7 p.c., the Draft Document made the following recommendations:

- reduction of non-plan expenditure from 10.3 p.c. to 8.7 p.c.;
- hastening of the pace of financial reforms with the objectives of encouraging more private and foreign direct investment;
- broadening of the base of direct tax to garner resources;
- encouraging the expansion of public sector utilities along commercial lines; and
- increasing public sector investment, mainly in the core sector.

The Planning Commission had focused on agriculture, instead of industry, for the first time since 1960s. The thrust of the Ninth Plan was to achieve agriculture-led growth. An agricultural growth target of 4.5 p.c. had been fixed.

The Ninth Plan aimed at increasing the industrial growth rate of 8.2 p.c.

An 11.8 p.c. growth in exports and a 10.8 p.c. growth in imports were envisaged.

Table 15.2 : Macro-Parameters for the Ninth Plan

	VIII Plan	IX Plan
1. Domestic savings rate	23.8	26.1
2. Current account deficit (% of GDP at market price)	1.1	2.1
3. Investment rate (% of GDP at market price)	24.9	28.2
4. Incremental capital-output ratio (ICOR)	3.7	4.0
5. GDP growth rate (per cent per annum)	6.8	6.5
6. Export growth rate (per cent per annum	11.9	11.8
7. Import growth rate (per cent per annum	11.7	10.8

Source: Planning Commission, Ninth Five Year Plan (1991-02), Vol. I, Table 2-4(a), P. 54

The Ninth Plan intended to create 50 million jobs. This meant a reduction in the unemployment rate from 1.87 p.c. in 1996-97 to 1.66 p.c. at the end of the Ninth Plan.

The Ninth Plan predicted that poverty would come down from 29.10 p.c. to 17.96 p.c.

Resources and Allocation: To achieve a growth rate of 6 5 p.c. p.a. the public sector outlay for the Ninth Plan had been fixed at Rs 8,59,200 crore at 1996-97 prices—an increase of 33 p.c. over the approved Eighth Plan outlay. Central support to the plan is proposed at Rs 4,89,361 crore.

Agriculture including irrigation and rural development in the Ninth Plan had been allocated 19.4 per cent of the total plan outlay. In all, 21.2 per cent would be spent on social services, 25.1 per cent on the energy sector and 14.1 per cent on transport.

Financing of the Plan: The financing pattern of the Ninth Plan was significantly different from the earlier pattern in as much as deficit financing had been kept at zero level.

The Ninth Plan visualised great efforts for mobilisation of additional resources through budgetary measures. Out of the aggregate resources of the Center of the order of Rs 6,59,379 crore, the Internal and Extra Budgetary Resources (IEBR) of Central Public Sector Enterprises were expected to contribute Rs 2,85,379 crore (i.e., 43.28 p.c.) The balance amount constituted budgetary resources. The Ninth Plan fund channelled through external grants of Rs. 10,062 crore.

Comments: The Ninth Plan had emphasised on the importance of the people and talked about cooperative federalism. Elaborating on the distinctive features of the Ninth Plan, it was said that while the government would have to play a major role in promoting such development, there would have to be an increasing reliance on people's initiatives through institutionalised structures at the grassroots level on the basis of cooperative federalism.

The Plan called for a 6.5 p.c. average annual growth rate in GDP during the Ninth Plan. Sectoral composition of growth (Table 15.3) reveals that the reform process had failed to push a high growth rate in agriculture. Annual average growth of agricultural sector for the Ninth Five Year Plan came to 2.1 p.c. as against a target growth rate of 3.9 p.c.

Table 15.3: Sectoral Real Growth Rates in GDP in Ninth plan (1997-2002) (%)

Sectors	Target	Actual
Agriculture and allied	3.9	2.1
Industry	7.1	4.5
Services	8.5	7.8
Total	6.5	5.4

Source: Economic Survey 2001-02, Table 1.3, p.5.

Since there was a wide gap between target and actual sectoral growth rates, overall GDP growth rate had come down to 5.4 p.c. against the targeted growth rate of 6.5 p.c. This unsatisfactory growth scenario could be attributed to declining both public and private investment. For instance, against the targeted public sector investment of 33.5 p.c. of the total, public investment fell below 28 p.c. p.a. on average. This had led to a rise in government borrowing over the entire Plan Period.

In 1993-94, the data released by the Planning Commission showed that 36 p.c. of the total population lived below the poverty line. The Ninth Plan predicted a fall in poverty rate to 17.96 p.c. by 2002. Even if a 7 p.c. GDP growth rate is achieved, the reduction of people living below the poverty line from 36 p.c. to 18 p.c. is merely a dream. Poverty ratio declined from 26.2 p.c. in 1999-00 to 24.4 p.c. in 2000-01.

The Ninth Plan had assumed an unrealistic export target, if the then trend was any guide.

Thus, the basic aim of the Ninth Plan—'growth with social justice and equality'—remained unfulfilled. As usual, the poor suffered the most.

15.6. THE TENTH FIVE YEAR PLAN (2002-07)

Tenth Five Year Plan was indeed a milestone in India's history of planning as it coincided with the first plan of the 21st century—thereby linking one era to another. An Approach Paper to the Tenth Five Year Plan was released by the National Development Council in September 2002 and the final document was approved by the Union Cabinet on October 2002. It was thus eight months behind schedule. Anyway, the Tenth Plan has some distinctive features.

First, it aimed at achieving a higher growth rate through realising improvements in efficiency, including a greater integration of the domestic economy with the world. The twin processes of globalisation and liberalisation had been highlighted. The Tenth Plan underline, the importance of 'external sector dimensions' in the development strategy.

Secondly, the Tenth Plan Document in three volumes was a unique one. For the first time, a new chapter 'State Plans—Concerns and Strategies' had been added in Volume III. If growth rates were to be realised, state-level performances had to be taken into account. A state-wise growth target had been fixed in consultation with the States. This was an innovative exercise. Further, the Tenth Plan for the first time had emphasised plans and regional development against the backdrop of growing regional imbalances that engenders stability of the country.

Thirdly, the Tenth Plan has added a chapter on governance, not talked in the earlier nine plans. Governance aimed at achieving various plan goals.

Goals and Targets: The Tenth Plan aimed at achieving a higher growth rate, employment rate and significant reduction in poverty rate. This Plan, which outlined a strategy to achieve a GDP growth rate of 8 p.c., had a specific focus on human development. Aiming at enhancement of human life and quality of life, this Plan stated that not only an adequate supplies of food and other basic consumer goods were required but also access to basic services (e.g., education, health, drinking water and basic sanitation) were required to be ensured.

The Tenth Plan aimed at doubling the per capita income in the next 10 years. For this to happen, GDP should grow at a rate of 8 p.c. during the 10th Plan period. This higher growth rate is necessary for accomplishing a menu of social and economic targets. The Tenth Plan did not attach much importance to trickle down effects i.e., growth-induced percolation of benefits.

It has set monitorable targets for the Tenth Plan and beyond for raising human well-being and better quality of life.

- reduction of poverty ratio by 5 percentage points by 2007 from 26 p.c. to 21 p.c. and by 15 percentage points by 2012;
- providing gainful high-quality employment to the addition to the labour force;
- reduction of gender gaps in literacy and wage rates by 50 p.c.;
- reduction in the decadal population growth rate between 2001 and 2011 to 16.2 p.c.;
- reduction in infant mortality rate to 45 per 1,000 live births by 2007 and to 28 by 2012;
- all children in school by 2003; and all children to complete 5 years of schooling by 2007;
- provisioning of potable drinking water in all villages;
- increase in forest/tree cover from 19 p.c. to 25.5 p.c. by 2007 and 33 p.c. by 2012.

Sectoral growth rates and incremental capital-output ratios (ICORs) for the Tenth Plan may be

Table 15.4: SECTORAL STRUCTURE OF GROWTH

SECTORS	NINTH PLAN		TENTH PLAN	
	Growth rate (%)	ICOR	Growth rate (%)	ICOR
1. Agriculture and allied activities	2.06	4.05	3.97	1.99
2. Mining and Quarrying	3.81	5.44	4.30	7.99
3. Manufacturing	3.68	18.37	9.82	7.77
4. Electricity, Gas and Water supply	6.46	15.43	7.99	14.97
5. Construction	6.82	1.00	8.34	0.99
6. Trade	5.86	1.01	9.44	0.91
7. Rail Transport	4.70	9.87	5.40	14.66
8. Other Transport	5.63	6.09	7.54	5.37
9. Communication	17.14	5.28	15.00	8.38
10. Financial Services	8.93	1.35	11.69	1.56
11. Public Administration	9.21	4.09	6.43	5.45
12. Other Services	8.19	3.70	9.26	3.53
Total GDP	**5.35**	**5.27**	**7.93**	**4.22**
ICOR		4.53		3.58

Source: Planning Commission; Tenth Five Year Plan

noted here. Agriculture and allied activities were expected to grow at almost 4 p.c. during 2002-07. Greatest focus had been given on communication (15 p.c.). Next in importance came financial services (11.69 p.c.).

Sectoral ICORs assumed for the Tenth Plan were lower except in mining and quarrying, rail transport, communication, other transport, etc. As a result, the aggregate ICOR for the Tenth Plan (3.58) was lower than the Ninth Plan (4.53). This decline was to be obtained through better utilisation of productive capacity, suitable sectoral allocation of capital and efficient utilisation of capital.

Sectoral investment-saving profile for the Tenth Plan also showed a big jump in the light of 8 p.c. growth rate. On the investment side, the Tenth Plan projected an investment rate of 28.4 p.c. of GDP. A large proportion of this capital formation is expected to come from the private sector (roughly 20 p.c.). Gross domestic savings and external savings were projected to go up to 26.84 p.c. and 1.7 p.c. of GDP during the Tenth Plan (Table 15.5).

Table 15.5 : Macroeconomic Aggregates for the Tenth Plan

	(per cent of GDP)
1. **Gross domestic savings**	**26.84**
of which:	
Private	26.40
Public	0.44
2. Total consumption	75.06
3. **Gross capital formation**	**28.41**
of which:	
Private	19.97
Public	8.44
4. Public borrowings	8.00
5. Current account deficit	1.57
6. Exports (% p.a.)	12.38
7. Imports (% p.a.)	17.13

Resources and Allocation: To achieve a growth rate of 8 p.c. during the Tenth Plan period, the public sector outlay had been kept at Rs 15,92,300 crore at 2001-02 prices. Out of this total outlay, Central Plan outlay had been earnmarred at Rs. 9,21,291 crore and Rs. 6,71,009 crore for the States and Union Territories. The Central budgetary support to this Plan had been fixed at Rs. 7,06,000 crore.

Mobilisation of such huge budgetary support was contingent upon (i) the attainment of projected tax-GDP ratios to 9.9 p.c., (ii) realisation of disinvestment proceeds of Rs. 78,000 crore, (iii) decline in non-plan expenditure to 9.9 p.c., and (iv) attainment of GDP growth targets.

Strategy: In the Tenth Plan, agricultural sector had been assigned a centerstage of all development efforts. The Plan aimed at bringing wasteland and degraded lands under cultivation or forest cover. Infrastructure had been given a greater role as it supports both agriculture and all rural economic activities. The Tenth Plan envisaged a comprehensive and coherent strategy for attaining rapid industrial growth through the creation of a positive investment climate. This necessitates deepening and widening of economic reforms. This new Plan had assigned a special role to States in realising national objectives. In view of this, this new Plan included a State-wise breakdown of the broad development targets consistent with the national targets. However, these are in the nature of indicative guidelines for facilitating planning in States. The Tenth Plan had also built up a comprehensive programme of district level development as districts with the states were required to be integrated with overall growth process.

The Tenth Plan marks a significant departure from the past in the evolution of planning and in terms of development strategy. Attainment of the growth rate of 8 p.c. in the Tenth Plan and 9.3 p.c. in the Eleventh Plan essentially implies a greater and faster process of liberalisation and globalisation. It is a challenge for our policy-makers to achieve the projected growth targets in the midst of adverse fall out arising out of liberalisation and globalisation process. If these are tackled efficiently in the Tenth Plan, Eleventh Plan would pave the way for more ambitious growth rate.

15.6.1. Mid-Term Appraisal (MTA) of the Tenth Plan

This MTA is necessary to take stock of the progress in plan implementation, review ,the feabisibility of targets and to provide corrective action if necessary.

- *Growth performance:* The Tenth Plan had targeted an average annual growth rate of GDP of 8 p.c. for the entire period of 2002-07 to be achieved by a steady acceleration. However, we are afraid that the growth rate at the end of this Plan Period would not be achieved, if the mid-term appraisal is any guide. For the first two years of the Plan, growth rate averaged at 6.4 p.c. If the country could achieve 11 p.c. growth rate in the next years only then Plan target could be achieved.

Sectorally, agriculture's targeted contribution toward GDP should be 4 p.c. per year. This is nowhere to be achieved as for as the trend in agricultural growth is concerned. For the first two years of the Plan, agricultural growth rate came to 1.8 p.c. Industrial growth also fell short of expectations. In the first two years, it averaged 6.7 p.c. as against the Plan targets of 10 p.c.

Recent years have seen the remarkable performance of the knowledge-based industries. Against the backdrop of decelerating trend in production in agriculture and industry, the position relating to employment is disturbing. The economy has not been generating sufficient productive jobs to absorb the addition of the country's labour force. It is inteed true that growth of employment and reduction in poverty are intimately linked to growth performance, especially in agriculture.

The Approach Paper has expressed anxiety over the erosion of resources as a result of the National Common Minimum Programmes (NCMPs) commitments. The resources constraint will be especially difficult because the NCMP has established new priorities, which required a substantial increase in allocation in critical areas, such as health, education, irrigation and employment programmes. This Paper has recognised that implementation of the National Rural Employment Guarantee Scheme (NREGS) requires huge resources hovering between Rs. 27,000 crore and Rs. 40,000 crore.

The Approach Paper also talks about the non-fulfilment in the targets relating to basic education. Targets of 100 p.c. education in primary schools to be achieved is unlikely to be achieved by 2007.

We conclude this MTA in the words of Dr. Manmohan Singh—the Prime Minister: "It appears that even with optimistic projections about the next two years, the average growth rate in the Tenth Plan period is not likely to cross the 7 p.c. mark, well below the target of 8.1 p.c. p.a. Employment generation is also unsatisfactory so far. The cornerstone of the Plan had been a reversal of the declining trend in the growth rate of agriculture eventually to take it above 4 p.c. The actual performance of agriculture appears to have deteriorated even further and will possibly not exceed 1.5 p.c. during the first three years of the Plan."

15.7. THE ELEVENTH FIVE YEAR PLAN (2007-12)

India is now in the midst of the Eleventh Plan period with an impressive record of growth, though the Ninth plan recorded a lacklustre performance when GDP grew at only 5.5 p.c. p.a. but the Tenth plan may exceed the GDP growth rate of 8 p.c. It is hoped that India would become one of the fastest growing economies in the world in the coming years. Like earlier plans, the 11th Plan provides an opportunity to act decisively to consolidate the gains achieved and also correct the deficiencies of the previous plan.

The 11th Plan has set a target of 9 p.c. GDP growth over this plan period. If such GDP growth rate is achieved by the end of the Plan, per capita GDP is expected to grow at 7.6 p.c. p.a. to double in less than 10 years. However, the Planning Commission while setting the target growth rates has expressed categorically a growth that must be inclusive in the sense that a growth process must yield broad-based benefits and ensure equality of opportunity for all.

The major macroeconomic parameters for achieving a GDP growth rate of 9 p.c. are given in Table 15.6. This growth rate of 9 p.c. is premised upon the investment rate of 36.7 p.c. of GDP and ICOR of 4.1.

Table 15.6 : Macroeconomic parameters (at 2006-07 prices)

	Tenth Plan	Eleventh Plan
1. Investment rate (% of GDP)	32.4	36.7
2. Domestic saving rate (% of GDP)	30.9	34.8
3. Current account deficit (% of DGP)	1.5	1.9
4. ICOR	4.3	4.1
5. GDP growth rate (% of GDP)	7.5	9.0

Table 15.7 : Sectoral Growth Rates (% per annum)

Sector	Eighth Plan	Ninth Plan	Tenth Plan	Eleventh Plan
1. Agriculture	4.72	2.44	2.30	4.00
2. Industry	7.29	4.29	9.17	10-11
3. Services	7.28	7.87	9.30	9-11
4. **Total**	**6.54**	**5.52**	**7.74**	**9.0**

A broad picture of sectoral growth rates realised in the Eighth, Ninth and Tenth Plans (2002-06) and targeted growth rates for the Eleventh plan have been presented in Table 15.7. This Plan has set a sectoral target of doubling agricultural growth to 4 p.c. p.a. and a double digit growth rates for both industry and services. All these are expected to provide better opportunities for employment.

High levels of investment are critical for rapid growth. Eleventh Plan aims at an increase in the investment rate to reach 36.7 p.c. of GDP and domestic savings rate to increase to 34.8 p.c. of the GDP by the end of the Plan.

The total public sector outlay for the Eleventh Plan stands at Rs. 36,44,718 crore at 2006-07 prices. Major share of outlay goes to education (19.39 p.c. of the total), then rural development, land resources and Panchayeti Raj (13.39 p.c.). About 74 p.c. of the total Central allocation for this Plan has been put aside for the priority sectors.

Comments: Eleventh Plan talks about inclusive growth i.e., growth that is braod-based. It, thus, admits that so far economic growth has not been inclusive because nearly 27 p.c.–28 p.c. of the population now live below the proverty line.

Further, the present trend of achievement in the first year of this Plan is not so rosy. Global situation is also gloomy against the backrop of rising global food prices, the unprecedented rise in the price of oil and most importantly current global economic meltdown. If this trend persists, we are afraid that the GDP growth rate to be achieved at the end of the Eleventh Plan will remain unfulfilled as usual. That is to say, history will repeat.

Even this idea of inclusive growth deserves special mention. But the growing private expenditure on health and education will make poor people poorer thereby leading to a situation of 'exclusive growth'.

15.8. OBJECTIVES OF PLANNING IN INDIA

In LDCs like India, the paramount objective of an economic plan is to bring into new forms of productive capital, which will raise the overall productivity of the economy and, thus, raise people's income by providing them adequate employment opportunity and, thereby, remove the twin problems of destitution and mass poverty. In an underdeveloped country like India, these objectives may be broadly grouped under:

(a) a higher rate of growth than was being realised in the absence of the plan;
(b) a greater degree of economic equality than was possible under free enterprise;
(c) full employment opportunities for the growing labour force of a country;
(d) economic self-reliance; and
(e) modernisation.

It is to be remembered that the above said objectives are long-term objectives of India's Five Year Plans. Now these objectives will be explained here :

- **Economic Growth:** Of all the objectives, the objective of economic growth has received the strongest priority in all the plans. Economic planning in India aims at bringing about a rapid economic development in all sectors. The key sectors are agriculture, power, industry and transport. Through development of the economy, the country aims at increasing national and per capita incomes. Thus, poverty will be removed and the standard of living improved. National income in the First Plan increased by 18 p.c. against the targeted growth rate of 11 p.c.

National income during the Second Plan period increased by 20 p.c. against the target of 2.5 p.c. p.a. On the other hand, per capita income grew at a rate of 1.8 p.c. p.a. as against the contemplated rate of growth of 3.3 p.c. The Third Plan sought to increase national income by 5.6 p.c. p.a. But the progress card of the Third Plan showed that national income increased by only 2.6 p.c. p.a. Per capita income during this time failed to rise (just 0.4 p.c. p.a.)

The Fourth Plan aimed at achieving the growth rate of national income and per capita income by 5.7 p.c. p.a., and 3 p.c. p.a. respectively. In reality, the actual achievement of national income was merely 3.4 p.c., while per capita income rose by only 1.1. p.c. The Fifth Plan proposed a growth rate of 3.5 p.c. p.a., but later revised to 4.37 p.c. However, the economy now fared well and attained a growth rate of 4.9 p.c. p.a. The Sixth Plan aimed at an annual growth rate of 5.2 p.c. Actually, this growth rate was achieved. The Seventh Plan (1985-90) achieved an annual growth rate of 5.5 p.c. The average growth rate during the Eighth Plan was much better (6.7 p.c.) than the Seventh Plan. This growth rate slipped down to 5.3 p.c. in the Ninth Plan against a contemplated growth rate of 6.5 p.c. An ambitious target of 8 p.c. GDP growth rate had been set in the Tenth Five Year Plan.

Actual growth rate achieved in the Tenth Plan (2002-06) stands at 7.8 p.c. against the targeted growth rate of 8 p.c.

- **Economic Equality and Social Justice:** The twin aspects of social justice involves, on the one hand, the reduction in economic inequalities and, on the other, the reduction of poverty.

A rise in national income with concentration of economic power in the hands of a few people is not desirable. In India's socio-political set-up, vast inequalities exist. Indian plans aim at reducing such inequalities, so that the benefits of economic development percolate down to the lower strata of the society.

The objective of removal of poverty got its clear-cut enunciation only in the Fifth Plan for the first time. Due to the defective planning approach, income inequality widened and poverty became rampant. The incidence of poverty was on the rise. In view of this paradoxical development, the slogan of 'Garibi Hatao' was raised in the Fifth Plan for the first time. It was estimated that approximately 30 p.c. of the total population was below the poverty line in 1974. In 1983-84, 44.5 p.c. of the total population were below the poverty line. Recently, the Planning Commission has given a new estimate of poverty-stricken people. In 2004-05, it has been estimated that 27.5 p.c. of the population lived below the poverty line as against 36 p.c. in 1993-94.

Though the poverty ratio declined over time, the number of poor people remained at around 260 million in 1999-00.

- **Full Employment**: Removal of unemployment is considered another important objective of India's Five Year Plans. But, unfortunately, it never received the priority it deserved. In the Sixth Plan (1978-83) of the Janata Government, employment was accorded a pride of place for the first time. However, the Seventh Plan treated employment as a direct focal point of policy. As a result, the employment generation programme in India has received a rude shock and the problem of unemployment is mounting up plan after plan. Although unemployment rate has fallen from 9.22 p.c. in 1983 to 8.28 p.c. in 2004-05, the absolute number of unemployeds has increased from 24.34 million to 34.74 million during the period 1983—2004-05.

• **Economic Self-reliance**: Self-reliance, or for that matter self-sufficiency, refers to the elimination of external assistance. In other words, it means zero foreign aid. India is typically a dependent economy. She is used to import huge foodgrains, fertilisers, raw materials and industrial machinery and equipments. But this objective could not be concertised before the launching of the Fourth Plan. The basic aim of the Fifth Plan was the attainment of self-reliance. To achieve this goal, the Fifth Plan aimed at increasing production of foodgrains, necessary consumption goods and raw materials and the level of exports. While emphasising the increase in exports, the Plan emphasised the need for establishing import substitute industries as an important facet of economic self-reliance. In the new era dating from July 1991, the objective of self-reliance has lost its present interpretation. No longer it refers to self-sufficiency in the present globalised environment. Still then, it is an important component of India's development policy.

• **Modernisation**: This objective is a newer one. This objective was categorically mentioned for the first time in the Sixth Plan. Modernisation means such variety of structural and institutional changes in the economic activities that can change the feudal and colonial economy into a progressive and modern economy. The important component of modernisation is the development of a diversified economy that produces a variety of goods. This requires the setting up of variety of industries. It also refers to an advancement of technology. No doubt, certain technological advances have taken place in agriculture, energy, etc. But there is a real danger of this objective in the present context. The country faces an alarming unemployment problem and, hence, poverty. But modernisation will definitely arrest the employment generation activities. Hence emergerd the conflict between the objective of modernisation and the objectives of unemployment and poverty eradication.

Besides these long-term objectives, each five Year Plan in India had some short-term objectives. For instance, the First Plan stressed agricultural development, control of inflation and rehabilitation of refugees. The Second Plan aimed at rapid industrial growth, specially basic and heavy industries. The Third Plan emphasised an expansion of basic industries, but shifted to defence development.

Evaluation of Objectives: The objectives of Indian planning are quite comprehensive and its scope is wide. But it has various short-comings.

First, Indian plans are ambitious. Most of the plan objectives remain unfulfilled. Again, some of the objectives are not quantifiable. Furthermore, desired objectives never match with the actual results. Actual results lag behind targets.

Secondly, Indian plans suffer from inconsistency of the objectives that are set. For instance, the objective of accumulation of capital is inconsistent with the objective of reduction of income disparities.

Finally, there are conflicts between objectives. Higher economic growth objective may not commensurate with the employment generation objective. Rapid economic growth requires the use of capital-intensive technology which is by nature labour-displacing. Thus, any attempt to improve

GDP growth rate is most likely to frustrate the objective of removal of unemployment.

Despite these shortcomings of Indian planning, we must say that the objective of higher economic growth is the most fundamental of all. Plan objectives must be spelt out as to make them consistent with the country's needs.

15.9. ACHIEVEMENTS AND FAILURES OF INDIA'S FIVE YEAR PLANS

India is a pioneer in initiating economic planning among developing countries. In India, the planning process was initiated in 1950-51. By this time, she has completed ten Five Year Plans. Roughly, within the span of 60 years, the Indian economy has travelled a long way. She has attained a fair degree of maturity as compared to the pre-independent India, but, at the same time, India's development experience does not augur well. Indian plans have failed to fulfill the hopes of the general people. Thus, it would be of great interest to have a general appraisal of the achievements and failures of the Indian Plans.

- **Major Accomplishments of the Process of Planning**
  - *A higher growth rate*: Economic planning in India aims at bringing about a rapid economic development in all sectors. That is to say, it aims at a higher growth rate.

    India's macroeconomic performance has been only moderately good in terms of GDP growth rates. The overall rate of growth stands at 4.8 per cent for the whole planning period (1950-2007) Compared with India's own past (1900-1920) when she was caught in a low level equilibrium trap, growth acceleration during the last 60 years has been impressive indeed.
  - *Growth of economic infrastructure*: India's performance in building up the necessary economic infrastructure is really praiseworthy. At the inception of economic planning, road kilometer was 4 lakh kms. India has now more than 3 million km of road network, making it one of the largest in the world. Railway route length increased from 53,596 kms in 1951 to nearly 63,500 kms in 2005-06. Today, the Indian railway system is the largest in Asia and the fourth largest in the world. Similarly, other modes of transport like shipping, civil aviation, etc., have also expanded phenomenally.
  - *Development of basic and capital goods industries*: Another major area of success of Indian planning is the growth of basic and capital goods industries. With the adoption of the Mahalanobis Strategy of development during the Second Plan period, some basic and capital goods industries like iron and steel witnessed spectacular growth.
  - *Higher growth of agriculture*: The most significant aspect of India's Five Year Plans is that the overall rate of growth of food production has now exceeded the rate of growth of population. Though in the early years of planning, agricultural performance was miserable resulting in the emergence of food crisis. But now, due to the impact of bio-chemical revolution in Indian agriculture, food crisis seems to be a thing of the past. She has attained self-sufficiency in foodgrains.
  - *Savings and investment*: The rise in the domestic savings rate from 10 p.c. of GDP at the initial stages of planning to

around 19 p.c. in 1980-81 is definitely impressive. However, this rate increased to 34.8 p.c. by the end of March 2007. Similarly, India's record in gross domestic capital formation rose from 20.3 p.c. in 1980-81 to 22.8 p.c. of GDP in 2001-02. But it rose to 36 p.c. in 2006-07.

- **Major Failures of Planning**

Indian planning is yet to score good marks. The major areas of failure of planning in India are:

- *Inadequate growth rate*: In quantitative terms, the growth rate of the Indian economy may be good but not satisfactory by any standards.

  Except the First and Sixth Five Year Plans, the actual growth rate remained below the targeted growth rates of GNP and per capita income. Only in recent plans (both Ninth and Tenth plan), actual growth rate has exceeded the plan targets. In terms of per capita income, India is one of the poorest nations of the world even after more than 58 years of democratic planning.

- *Whither India's socialistic society*: Indian planning aims at building up a 'socialistic pattern of society', in an otherwise capitalistic framework, through various socialistic measures.

  We have not yet made any significant progress towards the goal of attaining a socialistic pattern of society even after nearly 58 years of planning. The concept of socialistic pattern of building a society has been altogether discarded when we introduced new economic policy measures in mid-1991. Instead, Indian economy very much moves on the capitalistic path.

- *Economic inequality and social injustice* : The twin aspects of social justice involves on the one hand, the reduction in economic inequalities, and, on the other, the reduction of poverty.

  A rise in national income with concentration of economic power in the hands of a few people is not desirable. In an otherwise capitalist framework, inequality in the distribution of income and wealth is inevitable. In India's socio-political set-up, vast inequalities exist. Indian plans aim at reducing such inequalities, so that the benefits of economic development percolate down to the lower group of the society.

  The objective of removal of poverty got its clear-cut enunciation only in the Fifth Plan for the first time. Due to the defective planning approach, income inequality widened and poverty became rampant. The incidence of poverty was on the rise. It is now nearly 28 p.c. (2004-05)

- *Unemployment* : Removal of unemployment is considered to be another important objective of India's Five Year Plans. But, unfortunately, it never received the priority it deserved. In the Sixth Plan (1978-83) of the Janata Government, employment was accorded a pride of place for the first time. However, the Seventh Plan treated employment as a direct focal point or policy. As a result, the employment generation programme in India has received a rude shock and the problem of unemployment is mounting up plan after plan. The number of job-seekers increased from 363 lakh as on December 1991 to 406 lakhs as on June 2006. In the recent years, the trend is on the rise. In view of this, it is jokingly said that "how many plans the country needs to make the whole country unemployed?"

In view of these failures, Sukhamoy Chakraborty remarks that Indian plans may be good on paper, but are rarely good in implementation. So, the need of the hour is to formulate a correct economic policy as well as its implementation.

QUESTIONS (WITH ANSWER–HINTS)

Long Questions (16 marks)

1. Critically analyse the objectives, targets and overall performance of the Indian economy during the Ninth Plan period.
   Ans. 15.5.
2. Write a note on the Tenth Five Year Plan.
   Ans. 15.6.
3. Make an appraisal of the Tenth Five Year Plan.
   Ans. 15.6. and 15.6.1.
4. Write a note on the Eleventh Five Year Plan.
   Ans. 15.7.
5. What are the objectives of India's Five Year Plans? Comment on these objectives.
   Ans. 15.8.
6. Discuss the achievements and failures of the Indian economy under the five year plan period.
   Ans. 15.9.

Medium-sized Questions (8 marks)

1. What do you mean by economic planning? State the objectives of economic planning in India. (C.U. 2008)
   Ans. 15.1 and 15.8.
2. Comment on 'growth with social justice' objective of India's five year plans.
   Ans. 15.8.
3. Point out major areas of failures of Indian planning.
   Ans. 15.9.

16

INTERNATIONAL ECONOMIC ENVIRONMENT

16.1. INTRODUCTION

The distinctive feature of today's international economy is that national economies are being steadily integrated since trade, investment and financial capital now do not have any border or demarcation line. Today, no country can afford to remain isolated and stand to remain immuned from the developments in the international arena. The two forces for increased flow of goods and finances from one country to another country are technology associated with information revolution and liberalisation leading to the entry of foreign capital rather freely. This is what is called globalisation.

Globalisation is a process of increasing integration and growing economic interdependence of countries worldwide. It refers to "the expansion of economic activities across political boundaries of nation states." Its important attribute is its increasing degree of openness of domestic economies. It is associated not only with the increasing cross-border movement of goods and services, capital and technology, information and people, but also with an organisation of economic activities which straddles national boundaries. Its four broad dimensions are, international trade, international investment, international finance and multi-country production network of multinational corporations (MNCs).

16.2. GLOBAL SITUATION

Globalisation is the most talked about word today all over the globe. But it is not a new concept or a new phenomenon. It can be traced in the 16th century when the different countries participated in the global economy, *albeit* insignificantly. The process gathered momentum during the days of industrial revolution (1760 onwards). Globalisation today represents a resumption of the 18th century trend. However, the process of globalisation came to a halt abruptly during the First World War. Since then, countries one after another indulged themselves in tariff wars. In those days of protectionism, volume of world trade squeezed and international capital flows virtually dried up. Capital controls were imposed by all the governments.

To boost world trade it was realised that controls were to be lifted. Removal of trade barriers would ensure recovery. Some leading nations set up the General Agreement of Tariffs and Trade (GATT) in 1947 with the objective of reducing trade barriers gradually.

In 1995, the GATT was replaced by the World Trade Organisation (WTO). Barring these policy changes and setting up of institutions, disintegration of European and the then USSR economies (i.e., the so-called socialist countries) gave a strong incentive toward globalisation and liberalisation.

Today's globalisation frame includes liberalisation of trade, liberalisation of capital flows from outside the country, and decontrol of domestic financial markets, etc. All these elements have significant impact on the balance of payments situation of a country. Ultimately, this has an important bearing upon the domestic economic activity.

Further, international trading or macro-economic environment is largely shaped by the exchange rate policy. What exchange rate will be chosen is determined by the nature of economic stance taken by the national governments and the problems faced by them.

16.3. ELEMENTS OF INTERNATIONAL TRADING ENVIRONMENT

In Chapter 11, we have said about components and features of Indian business environment. Since various aspects of macroeconomic environment are not mutually exclusive, these have impacts on both domestic and international economies. Likewise, international business environment also produces significant impacts on the domestic economy. In this sense, various economic variables are interrelated. For instance, a change in international trade policy not only brings about a change in the magnitude and direction of foreign trade, balance of payments situation, but also influences industrial growth and hence, economic growth. In addition, international trading economy is largely shaped by international power and influence. Social, technological, economic and—more importantly political factors determine a country's power and influence in the international field. Finally, international trading environment is also conditioned by the policies of international institutions, like the IMF, the World Bank, the WTO, etc. These institutions aim at establishing an international monetary order to promote trade and development and to prevent financial crises.

Thus, the crucial elements of international business environment are (i) international trade policy, (ii) prevailing politico-economic situation i.e., international power and influence, (iii) managers or institutions of the global economy i.e., international trading institutions and trade agreements. All these elements are, however, overlapping.

16.3.1. International Trade Policy

Whether external trade should be allowed to prosper uninterruptedly or be regulated by various means is a matter of great controversy. A country's position on this issue is commonly known as commercial policy or trade policy. A country's trade policy, thus, centres around free trade vs protection.

The policy prescription of Ricardo's comparative cost theory of trade is free trade. By free trade we mean no restrictions on trade. In other words, it refers to the absence of tariffs, quotas, exchange restrictions, taxes and subsidies on production, factor use and consumption.

On the other hand, by protection we mean restricted trade. Free trade eliminates tariff while protective trade imposes tariff or duty. If tariffs, duties and quotas are imposed to restrict the inflow of imports then we have protected trade. This means that government intervenes in trading activities. Intervention in trade by the government is called protection.

In the middle decades of the 19th century, virtually all governments of the world pursued free trade policy. However, Great Britain was the champion of free trade policy at that time. But this tide could not be maintained in the early years of the 20th century. Protectionist tide reached a peak in the depression years of the 1930s. Virtually free trade policy had been abandoned by all the countries of the world. But, as restrictive trade policy failed to deliver the right amount of goods, industrially advanced nations after the Second World War switched over to free trade policy under the auspices of the International Monetary Fund (IMF).

As far as commercial policy was concerned, the entire world became divided into two camps : developed world and developing world. Throughout 1950s and 1960s, developed countries gradually moved towards free trade policy and currency convertibility. International institutions like the IMF, GATT (General Agreement on Tariffs and Trade) advocated free trade policy. But developing countries did not oblige these institutions. The prevailing view for the developing countries was of the United Nations Conference on Trade and Development (UNCTAD) which recommended import substituting industrialisation strategy or inward-looking strategy in which goods are produced mainly for the domestic market. It is to be mentioned here that India followed the import substituting industrialisation (ISI) strategy since the beginning (1951) of the Five Year Plans. As a means of development, substantial protection to domestic industries was granted in India. This was the time when it was believed that "government" or the "state" is better.

Protection or ISI strategy may be seen as one of the manifestations of the government. Protectionist policy received a big jolt in the developing countries in the 1980s when these countries experienced poor economic performance. It was said by the IMF and the World Bank at that time that dramatic economic success could be achieved in developing countries if these countries 'open up' or become 'outward', instead of being 'inward'. Outward looking trade policy emphasises on export-oriented pattern of industrialisation. The basic stimulus for this kind of trade reform came from the experiences of the four high-performing East Asian countries—Taiwan, South Korea, Singapore and Hong Kong. This means industries are not to be 'protected' by state intervention but to be 'promoted' by market mechanism.

India followed a restrictive or protective trade policy upto June 1991 when liberal free trade environment was ushered in. India now moved from 'inward' to 'outward' looking trade policies. She then gradually removed various kinds of trade restrictions.

16.3.2. International Trading Institutions and Agreements

Since the second element of international business environment—i.e., international power and influence—is beyond the scope of this book, we intend to discuss the third element, i.e., international institutions and agreements that govern global trade. In addition, international trading environment is greatly governed by exchange rate policy.

Exchange rate connects the price system of trading countries since this (special) price shows the relationship between all domestic prices and all foreign prices. Exchange rate management policy has great implications for macroeconomic environment. For instance, unstable exchange rates affect costs of production by influencing the prices of raw materials and various components. Further, downward (or upward) pressure on the exchange rate will help in generating inflation (or deflation) which has obvious and important implications for exports and imports, employment, investment, etc. There are many types of exchange rate policy options. The choice of 'right' exchange rate is essential given the degree of globalisation which has evolved in recent years.

The international monetary system before the World War I comprised the gold standard system. Under this system, government does not intervene the foreign exchange market and follows a policy of keeping the exchange rate of its currency at a fixed rate. Fixed exchange rate under the gold standard system, however, did not end in 1914; rather there was a brief return to the gold standard system as well as a period of floating exchange rate system (1914-45). From then, the international monetary system moved into the Bretton Woods pegged exchange rate system (1945-71) under the auspices of the International Monetary fund (IMF) set up in July 1944.

The IMF was established with the objective of promoting international monetary cooperation to tackle recession and protectionism. The main function of the IMF is to provide temporary financial support to its members so as to correct fundamental balance of payments (BOP) disequilibrium. The Fund is a strong believer of the principles of market economy. It aims at opening up of the economies by removing various kinds of trade barriers for the free movement of trade. To achieve these objectives, it closely supervises the exchange rate policies of the member countries. There was, however, a breakdown of the IMF's pegged exchange rate system in 1971 and in its place 'managed' floating exchange rate was introduced in 1973.

Today, exchange rates[1] are market-determined rates. Currency of one country can be converted to another currency, without any restrictions and control, at the market-determined exchange rates. Hence the name convertibility of currency. By convertibility of rupee, we mean that the Indian rupee can be converted into dollar and other currencies of the world without any restriction. Conversion, however, is determined by market forces of demand for and supply of foreign exchange. The rate of exchange between rupee and other foreign currencies is, thus, not 'administered'. So far, India has made her rupee convertible on current account. Capital account convertibility of rupee is yet to be introduced. By full convertibility we mean abolition of all exchange controls including those on capital account. Under this full convertibility, an Indian is free to sell his property in India and transfer the money to any foreign country.

1 Every independent country has its own currency. For example, India has rupee, the USA the dollar, the European Monetary Union the Euro. If trade takes place between countries currencies are required to be mutually exchanged. If an Indian buys a US computer Indian rupee has to be exchanged for US dollar. In the foreign exchange market, trading of currency takes place. Transactions made in the foreign exchange market determine exchange rates at which currencies are exchanged.

In addition to the IMF, there are various institutional arrangements that encourage free trade policy. These are, WTO, UNCTAD, etc. Further, international trade agreements, normally bilateral agreements, have also great implications for international trading environment. One finds multilateral trade agreements among nations to develop free trade by removing barriers to trade. For instance, single European Market of the European Union, Association of South East Asian Nations (ASEAN), North American Free Trade Area (NAFTA) and, above all, WTO, are some of the agreements and institutions that function for propagating the principles of free trade all over the globe and for creating common policies with respect to trade with the rest of the world.

16.4. TRENDS IN WORLD TRADE AND DEVELOPING COUNTRIES

Mid-18th century saw industrial revolution and the last quarter of the 20th century saw information revolution. As transport costs declined under the impact of industrial revolution, international trade flourished. Globalisation of this period was also driven by reduction in various trade barriers and controls. However, globalisation came to a halt and several trade restrictions were imposed in the first half of the 20th century. Further, advanced capitalist countries believed that reduction of trade barriers or the promotion of unrestricted trade was vital to recovery. GATT was one of such form that gradually reduced import tariffs. In 1995, GATT was replaced by the WTO. Trade has now flourished, national economies have now been greatly integrated. Such integration of the world economy may be attributed to (i) technology, and (ii) liberalisation. Information technology has revolutionised the entire world. Information or digital product has brought down the costs of communication. The natural barriers of time and space that separate national markets have fallen. As a result, consumers are buying more foreign goods than ever before. Some firms or multinational corporations (MNCs) are now operating across national borders. People invest their surplus funds outside the domestic border. These are the trends towards globalisation and the closer integration of the national economies.

Growing economic interdependence between countries is reflected in the rising volume of trade, mainly exports than the volume of world commodity output. Between 1963 and 1983, volume of world exports rose three-fold while the volume of world output rose slightly more than double. Another measure of integration of the world economy is the ratio of imports to gross national product of different countries. In the 1990s, economic interdependence has assumed a significant proportion, particularly in developing economies. These countries have become increasingly integrated into global goods and financial markets. From 2 p.c. during the 1980s, these economies have seen a jump in export volume by 9 p.c. in the 1990s. Net long-term capital flows remained almost three times the 1990-level.

It may be added that since the early 1950s to 2006, the volume of trade in manufactures grew at an annual rate of 7.5 p.c., while agricultural products grew by 3.5 p.c. p.a. and mining product by 4 p.c. Asia has the highest share of manufactures in total exports, with more than 80 p.c. of the region's exports coming from this product group. Asia's merchandise exports remained buoyant of all regions.

Between 2000 and 2006, world merchandise exports rose by 5.5 p.c. p.a., in which contribution of the manufactures was the highest (6 p.c.) and that of agricultural products was the second (4 p.c.). World exports and imports grew by the same percentages (11 p.c. p.a.) during 2000-06. Asia's imports grew by 12 p.c., while India and China's imports rose by 23 p.c. each. as against their export growth of 19 p.c. and 25 p.c. respectively, during the same time period.

But there is also a gloomier part of economic interdependence. It has brought more economic costs than benefits. European currency crises of 1992 and 1993 are often attributed to the forces of globalisation. South-East Asian crisis that erupted in 1997 was a challenge to the present form of free trade and export-led growth strategy, although these SE Asian countries showed an impressive performance in the 1970s and 1980s. It is because of closer integration of the world economies, most of the countries including India, of this region have been adversely affected.

Despite the current trend of globalisation, some countries (e.g., China, Hong Kong, Singapore, Taiwan, etc.,) have so far managed the currency crisis that erupted in major SE Asian economies in 1997. But what is important is that some sort of financial instability has been created. Possibly for this reason, the world economy since 1999 has been caught into the grip of recession. It is because of growing globalisation it is indeed true that the East Asian crisis had produced adverse effects on global trade volumes.

16.5 TRADE AND DEVELOPMENT

In today's global economy, international trade is at the heart of development. Nations—developed or underdeveloped— trade with each other because trade is mutually benefical. In other words, the basic motivation of trade is the gain or benefit that accrues to nations. In the case of autarky or isolation, benefits of international division of labour do not flow between nations. It is advantageous for all the countries of the world to engage in international trade. However, the gains from trade can never be the same for all the trading nations. Thus, benefits or gains from trade may be inequitable; but what is true is that "same trade is better than no trade".

There is, however, a strong debate around the role of trade in the development of mainly less developed countries. Historically, there was a consenous amongst many people that trade acts as an 'engine of growth' (in the 19th century and early 20th century). But in the 1950s, evidence showed that benefits of trade did not accrue to the LDCs; trade was beneficial to the developed countries only. Here this debate will be focused.

- **Benefits of Trade :** Virtually, every nation finds it advantageous to trade with other nations. They are linked to one another, in varying degrees, by trade flows and financial networks that surround the globe. Benefits of trade are summarised here :

Gains from trade accrue from specialisation, i.e., division of labour. Division of labour and specialisation within a country make necessary a greater amount of exchange, so greater division of labour necessiates an extension of trade. Specialisation is the logical offshoot of exchange among nations Thus, a greater variety of products in larger quantities may be available. Thus, we have both production gain and consumption gain. Every country produces goods maximum on the basis of comparatie advantage. By exchanging these goods, nations can consume more than before trade. It was Adam Smith who first pointed out the advantages of trade in reaping the advantages of specialisation and the economic benefits flowing from it, viz; imporvement in production and productivity and hence national wealth/income of every participating country.

Secondly, a similar gain from trade, called 'vent for surplus', has bean illustrated by Adam Smith. International trade increases the level of productive activity by stimulating efficient utilisation of resources. Countries may then experience surplus produce. Smith then argued that trade was a means of disposing of surplus produce for exports. Thus, trade, 'vents' a surplus productive activity that would otherwise go unsold in the absence of trade.

Thirdly, there are other three kinds of gains from trade : (i) those that remove the narrowness of domestic market, induce innovations, achieve the full advantages of economies of large scale production and increase productivity; (ii) those that make savings and capital accumulation easier; and (iii) those that acquire new knowledge, new ideas and cultures, new skills and entrepreneurship and disseminate technical knowledge.

Fourthly, empirical evidence suggests that trade can boost productivity which, in turn, raises the incomes and standards of living even of poor developing countries. The link between trade and productivity, being a potential one, can be identified with exports and imports. Through imports, countries stand to gain by importing machinaries and various capital goods embodying new, modern technologies as well as by importing ideas that help rise in productivity. Mastering and adaptability of new technologies require a learning process. It is through learning, benefits of technological improvement can be reaped. On the export side, we must say that market access supports the learning process. It is said that trade helps to promote specialisation and sustain production tempos of goods in which 'learning effects' are embodied. Thus, by opening up channels to the export and import markets, a country 'can support technological upgrading via learning'. Trade-induced learning processes help all countries to improve incomes and, thus, economic welfare over the long run. This is what makes trade a powerful 'engine of growth'.

Finally, trade is not considered as an important 'engine of growth', but also it can contribute to poverty alleviation by expanding markets, making larger investments in various fields, creating jobs, raising productivity which, in turn, raise incomes of the poor people. However, the link between trade and poverty reduction is a 'potential' one, rather than an automatic one.

For all these reasons, it is said that 'trade is an engine of growth'. There is no reason for any country to remain in isolation.

- **Disadvantages of Trade:** The 'trade engine' theory lost its 'fuel' in the developing countries after the World War II. Some economists suggested that gains from trade can never be unambiguous for all the trading countries—both developed and developing. Thus, the message runs—free international trade is harmful for the poor developing countries.

Raul Prebisch, Hans Singer, Gunnar Myrdal argued in the 1950s that the gains from trade are biased—rich countries gain at the expense of the poor countries. Their arguments are as follows : Poor LDCs are, by nature, primary goods producing countries while rich countries are producers of manufacturer articles. Former buys manufactured goods from the latter countries by exporting their primary goods. at a low prices or at unfavourable terms of trade. Thus, these countries pay more to the developed countries for their imports while developed countries pay less to the developing countries for their imports. In other words, gains from trade largely accrue to the developed countries. Benefits of lower prices of exportables of LDCs are transferred to the overseas consumers rather than producers of developing countries. It is, thus, clear that LDCs cannot gain much from the export of primary commodities.

Secondly, some left economists argue that trade results in 'dependent development'. In other words, trade between rich and poor nations is exploitative in nature. These economists argue that underdevelopment of poor countries is to be explained in terms of external factors, rather than internal factors. Hitorically, colonial countries of the past say, Asia, Africa and Latin America, did not have economic independence where European capitalist imperialist powers ruled. From these colonies, capitlist countries drew their economic resources and filled their coffers simply by exploiting them. For the existence of the capitalist order, existence and generation of surplus and then transferring them to their countries, was indispensable. Thus, without assisting the poor developing countries, capitalist imperialist countries flourished. This is called 'development of underdevelopment' as a deliberate consequence of free international trade.

Danger of dependence in often explained in the following way. A country may face economic depression if its international trading partner suffers from it and then it spreads from one country to another. The Great Depression that emanated during 1929-30 in the US economy swept all over the world and all counties suffered badly even if their economies were not caught in the grip of Depression. Such overdependence becomes catastrophic during war.

Further, commercial rivalries resulting from trade may lead to war.

Conclusion: Against this backdrop, one must not jump to a conclusion that poor LDCs must not trade with anyone, particularly developed nations. This is highty unrealistic since no country, whatever the size and whatever the level of development, is self-sufficient. Thus for surival, trade is essential. All countries trade. To reap the maximum advantages of trade right trade policies need to be adopted. In addition, cooperation among all countries can promote more benefits from growth. Sometimes, some form of trade and economic cooperation among equals may be suggested so as to get larger benefits from trade.

16.6. INTERNATIONAL ECONOMIC GROUPINGS

Trade expansion, economic cooperation and integration is an important element of international trade strategy. Regional economic groupings, integration or other forms of economic cooperation should be promoted among countries as a means of promoting intra-regional and extra-regional trade. By economic integration we mean such type of arrangement that removes artificial trade barriers between the integrating economies. Economic cooperation, on the other hand, includes actions aimed at abolishing discrimination within an area.

Important integration schemes of developed countries are, North American Free Trade Agreement (NAFTA), European Free Trade Area (EFTA), etc. Important integration schemes operating in developing countries are, Latin American Free Trade Association (LAFTA), Association of South East Asian Nations (ASEAN), etc.

The poor South is heavily dependent on the developed North for its development. However, backward countries of the South are subject to exploitation and low level of economic development. Against this unequal world, developing countries among themselves should strengthen and diversify South-South cooperation. The main objectives of such cooperation are (i) the protection of interests of South vis-a-vis the North; and (ii) the reduction of dependence of the South on the North. Economic cooperation may centre around finance, trade, industry and business, services, science and technology, environment and development, food security etc.

While strengthening inter-regional trade within the South, trade preferences are often given. The most important step in this direction was the launching of the programme of Global System of Trade Preferences (GSTP) in 1987. For promoting trade preferences among major industrialised countries, Generalised System of Preferences (GSP) was introduced. To improve prospects for developing countries' trade and to prevent the emergence of balance of payments problem, the United Nations Conference on Trade and Development (UNCTAD) was set up in 1965.

However, one of the most important institutions that was established in 1944 to encourage international cooperation in the monetary field and to facilitate multilateral payments system between countries is the International Monetary Fund. A sister institution of the IMF — called the World Bank was set up in 1944 with the aim of providing economic aid to member countries, mainly developing countries. General Agreement on Tariffs and Trade (GATT) was established in 1947 to promote the expansion of trade through the removal of tariffs and other barriers on trade. In 1995, GATT was replaced by the WTO.

One should say something above countertrade—an unconventional form of international trade practices in which import of goods are paid for by export of goods. This kind of trade dispenses with currency transactions. Thus, countertrade is a kind of barter trade. Here we will present the workings of the IMF, World Bank, GATT and WTO— international economic institutions.

16.7. THE INTERNATIONAL MONETARY FUND

At Bretton Woods, New Hampshire of the USA, there were proposals for setting up three institutions to deal with different aspects of international cooperation in monetary affairs. In the event, only the International Monetary Fund (IMF) and the International Bank for Reconstruction and Development (IBRD)—more commonly the World Bank—were created in July 1944. Together, they came to be known as the 'Bretton Woods twin sisters'.

Objectives : The origin of the IMF goes back to the days of international chaos of 1930s. During the Second World War, plans for the construction of an international institution for the establishment of monetary order were taken up. At the Bretton Woods Conference in July 1944, delegates from 45 countries negotiated an agreement on the structure and operation of the international monetary system. The Articles of Agreement of the IMF provided the basis of the international monetary system. The IMF commenced financial operations in 1 March, 1947, though it came into official existence on 27 December 1945, when 29 countries signed its Articles of Agreement (its charter). Today (July 2008), the IMF has 185 member countries. Virtually the entire world belongs to the IMF.

Article 1 of the Articles of Agreement spell out 6 purposes for which the IMF was set up. They are as under :

- To promote international monetary cooperation through a permanent institution.
- To facilitate the expansion and balanced growth of international trade, and to contribute thereby to the promotion and maintenance of high levels of employment and real income and to the development of the productive resources of all members as primary objectives of economic policy.
- To promote exchange stability, to maintain orderly exchange arrangements among members and to avoid competitive exchange depreciation.
- To assist in the establishment of a multilateral system of payments in respect of current transactions between members and in the elimination of foreign exchange restrictions which hamper the growth of world trade.
- To give confidence to members by making the general resources of the Fund temporarily available to them under adequate safeguards, thus providing them with the opportunity to correct maladjustments in their balance of payments.
- In accordance with the above, to shorten the duration and lessen the degree of disequilibrium in the international balance of payments of members.

All these objectives of the IMF may be summarised now. To promote international cooperation; to facilitate the expansion and balanced growth of international trade; to promote exchange stability; to assist in the establishment of a multilateral system of payments; to make its general resources available to its members experiencing balance of payments difficulties under adequate safeguards; and to shorten the duration and lessen the degree of disequilibrium in the international balance of payments of members.

Functions : The principal function of the IMF is to supervise the international monetary system. Several functions are derived from this. These are granting of credit to member countries in the midst of temporary balance of payments deficits, surveillance over the monetary and exchange rate policy of member countries, issuing policy recommendations.

The main function of the IMF is to provide temporary financial support to its members so that 'fundamental' BOP disequilibrium can be corrected. However, such granting of credit is subject to strict conditionality. The conditionality is a direct consequence of the IMF's surveillance function over the exchange rate policies or adjustment process of members. Surveillance is the process by which the IMF appraises its members' exchange rate policies within the framework of a comprehensive analysis of the general economic situation and the policy strategy of each member. Surveillance is based on the conviction that strong and consistent domestic economic policies will lead to stable exchange rates and a growing and prosperous world economy.

The Fund provides financial assistance. It includes credits and loans to member countries with balance of payments problems to support policies of adjustment and reform. It makes its financial resources available to member countries through a variety of financial facilities. It also provides concessional assistance under its poverty reduction and growth facility and debt relief initiative. It has decided to provide fund to combat money-laundering and terrorism in view of the attack on the World Trade Centre of the USA in 11 September 2001.

In addition, technical assistance is also given by the Fund. Technical assistance consists of expertise and support provided by the IMF to its members in several broad areas : the design and implementation of fiscal and monetary policy; institution-building, the handling and accounting of transactions with the IMF; the collection and retirement of statistical data and training of officials.

Maintenance of stable exchange rate is another important function of the IMF. It prohibits multiple exchange rates.

It is to be remembered that unlike the World Bank, the IMF is not a development agency. Instead of providing development aid, it provides financial support to tide over BOP difficulties to its members.

16.7.1. Organisation and Management of the IMF

Like many international organisations, the IMF is run by the Board of Governors, an Executive Board and an international staff. Every member country delegates a representative (usually heads of central banks or ministers of finance) to the Board of Governors — the top link of the chain of command. It meets once a year and takes decision on fundamental matters such as electing new members or changing quotas.

The Executive Board is entrusted to the management of day-to-day policy decisions. The Board comprises 24 executive directors who supervise the implementation of policies set by member governments through the Board of Governors.

The IMF is headed by the Managing Director who is elected by the Executive Board for a 5-year term of office.

Rights and obligations i.e., the balance of powers in the Fund is determined by a system of quotas. Quotas are decided by vote of the Board of Governors. Quotas or subscriptions roughly reflect the importance of members in the world economy. It is the quota on which payment obligations, credit facilities and voting rights of members are determined.

16.7.2. Financial Structure of the IMF

The capital or the resources of the Fund come from two sources, viz., (i) subscription or quota of the member nations, and (ii) borrowings.

Each member country is required to subscribe an amount equivalent to its quota. As soon as a country joins the Fund, it is assigned a quota. At the time of formation of the IMF, the quota of each member was made up of 25 p.c. in gold or 10 p.c. of its net official holdings of gold and US dollars (whichever was less). Now this has been revised. The capital subscriptions or quota is now made up of 25 p.c. in Special Drawing Rights (SDRs) or widely accepted currencies, (such as the US dollar, euro, the yen or the pound steling) instead of gold and 75 p.c. in country's own currency. The size of the Fund equals the sum of the subscriptions of members. Total quotas at the end-August 2008 were SDR 217.4 billion (about $341 billion)

The Fund is authorised to borrow in special circumstances if its own resources prove to be insufficient. It sells gold to member countries to replenish currency holdings. It is entitled to borrow even from international capital market. Though the Articles of Agreement permit the

Fund to borrow from private capital market, till today no such use has been made by the Fund.

16.7.3. Working of the IMF

There are two phases in the working of the IMF over the last 64 years. The first phase covers the period late 1940s to 1973. This phase is popularly known as "Bretton Woods System". The IMF system or the Bretton Woods System provides for exchange rate stability in the short run but allows for the possibility of exchange rate adjustment when a country experiences fundamental disequilibrium in its BOP accounts. Thus, the pegged exchange rate is adjusted in accordance with the IMF. Hence the name 'adjustable peg system'. As the system was the source of some major problems, it was abandoned in 1971 and more flexibility was introduced in the monetary system. In other words, the demise of the Bretton Woods System made room for the floating exchange rate regime, requiring changes in the role of the IMF. After prolonged negotiation (1973-78), the IMF started its second-leg journey in 1978.

The decade of 1970s saw massive borrowings by developing countries. It rose to $600 billion by 1982. Meanwhile, the rise in interest rates in the USA from 1979 and the appreciation of dollar caused tremendous difficulties to the developing countries in servicing their debts. On the other hand, the switch to the floating exchange rate system coincided with the deteriorating economic conditions in the industrialised countries. Debt crisis that emerged in many developing countries had a dramatic effect. Mexico—a Latin American country—announced its failure to honour debt obligations. The IMF now played a crucial role to put the international financial system in order. It came in for mobilisation of additional financial resources so as to reduce the debt burden. As a result of this and other related measures, many countries regained access to the international banks and creditors and the severity of the debt problem moderated considerably in Latin America in the early 1990s.

With the break up of the Soviet Union in 1991, a new category of countries, especially communist countries, joined the IMF. The IMF now came forward to assist countries undergoing transition from a centrally planned economy to a market-oriented economy. Privatisation is indeed a crucial element of the transition process. That is why, the IMF is providing financial assistance and technical support for the development of sound economic management and the privatisation of state enterprises.

In 1997, East Asian financial crisis began when currencies of 'tiger' economies plummeted, and stock market crashed. Rescue packages were launched by the IMF.

- **Achievements** : From this balance sheet of the working of the IMF, we are now in a position to evaluate its performance over the last 64 years or so. Firstly, we state the achievements of the Fund.

The IMF acts as both a financing and an adjustment-oriented international institution for the benefit of its members. It has been providing financial assistance to the deficit countries to meet their temporary disequilibrium in BOP.

The Fund aims at promoting exchange rate stability. In its early phase, the Fund made arrangements of avoidance of competitive exchange depreciation.

It has made an attempt to solve the problem of international liquidity. To create international liquidity, Special Drawing Rights (SDRs)—an artificial currency—were created in 1969 as foreign exchange reserves to benefit the developing countries in particular. SDR allocations are made to member countries to finance the BOP deficits.

It is an institution through which consultation in monetary affairs takes place in an on-going way. It acts as a forum for discussions of the economic, fiscal and financial policies of member countries keeping the BOP problems in mind.

Previously, the poorest developing countries did not receive adequate treatment from the Fund. But during the 1980s and 1990s—when debt crisis broke out in poor countries—the Fund decided to divert its financial resources to these countries.

In 1980s, centrally planned economies were not hitherto members of the Fund. With the collapse of the Soviet Union in 1991, ex-Communist countries became members of the Fund and the Fund is providing assistance to these countries so as to instil the principles of market economy. It has decided to finance resources to combat terrorism and money-laundering.

Finally, the IMF has assisted its members in the formulation of appropriate monetary, fiscal and trade policies.

- **Failures :** Despite these achievements, its failures are glaring. In other words, its success is, on the whole, limited. There are some serious charges against this institution that cannot escape attention. These are :

The Fund provides short term finance to its members to tackle BOP disequilibrium. For this purpose, it adopted an adjustable peg system in the first phase of its life. But it failed to establish a stable exchange rate Its role in controlling the competitive exchange depreciation policies adopted by the members was subject to serious scrutiny, although it was created to avoid devaluation as a BOP measure as much as possible. Truly speaking, the IMF is incapable of taking independent policy decisions. It complies with the 'ordes' of the superpowers. Further, it has minimal influence over the policy decisions of the major industrial powers. In these cases, its mandate to exercise 'firm surveillance' over some influential members or superpowers is virtually meaningless —it has no influence over the US deficits or European interest rates.

Secondly, the Fund imposes conditions on the poor countries while sanctioning loans. Now, it is ignoring its central concern—exchange rate management and BOP problems. It is now championing the issue of 'market principle'. It suggests poor developing countries to cut expenditure-borrowing-subsidy, raise prices of state enterprises, privatisation of state-owned enterprises, etc. If such measures, most popularly known as structural adjustment programmes, are adopted only then IMF credit would follow. Most of these measures are anti-people in character. It is said that third world debt crisis is due to the Fund policies and working.

Thirdly, the Fund has failed to eliminate foreign exchange restrictions imposed by its members that hamper the growth of trade.

We now conclude this discussion in the words of Richard Roberts : "It also has little moderating influence on the swollen international financial markets. The vast expansion in the scale of international financial flows in the 1980s and 1990s, floating exchange rates, liberalised and integrated capital markets, and the ability of the industrial countries to formulate coordinated policies have together put the international financial markets beyond the IMF's exhortations, let alone its discipline. Prevention is better than cure, but there is no point in blaming the doctor if the patient does his own thing and medical help is only called in when matters are already out of hand."

16.7.4. IMF vis-a-vis India

India is one of the founder members of the Bretton Woods institutions. The IMF provides short-term financial assistance to the members so as to enable them tide over critical balance of payments situation. To ease the problem of international liquidity, Special Drawing Rights (SDRs) were created in 1969. The SDRs are allocated to the members in proportion to their quotas. India borrowed both financial and other assistance from the IMF quite a number of times under several lending provisions of the Fund.

Although India borrowed from the Fund immediately after independence, her dependence on it for financial assistance became critical during the Second Five Year Plan (1955-56 to 1960-61) when she witnessed a sharp fall in foreign exchange reserves. She borrowed $200 million to meet the crisis. As the BOP crisis remained precarious she again borrowed $250 million in 1961. As there was no sign of improvement in BOP position, India devalued her currency in 1966 to the extent of 36.5 p.c., allegedly on the advice of the IMF.

India again made a huge borrowing from the IMF in 1981 to tide over the BOP difficulties following the second oil price rise made by the OPEC and the large volume of trade deficit. Under the borrowing arrangement with the IMF, India agreed to draw SDR 5 billion, over a three-year period. As BOP situation as well as economic conditions improved, actual drawing from the Fund was only SDR 3.9 billion, rather than SDR 5 billion.

The situation deteriorated in the late 1980s and early 1990s when foreign exchange reserves position were satisfactory for two weeks' imports as against the generally accepted 'safe minimum reserves' of three months' equivalent. Several face-saving measures were taken by the Government, but with little or no achievements. The Government headed by Narasimha Rao entered an agreement with the IMF to borrow from it. In August 1991, the Government applied for stand-by loan of $2.3 million for a 20-month period. For this, a letter of intent was issued. In this letter, India promised to launch several structural reforms in the coming years. In other words, conditionality clause was incorporated by the IMF against loans. The recent economic reforms of 1990s in India are said to have been introduced at the instance of the IMF-World Bank.

India has been receiving benefits from the Fund from time to time. Quite a large number of time, India got financial accommodation from the Fund to cover deficits in BOP. As the IMF and the World Bank are inseparable twins, membership in the former is a prerequisite for membership in the latter. That is why, India receives various kinds of help for various development projects from the World Bank. The Fund provides technical expertise and support to India in various broad areas particularly fiscal and monetary policy. Its staff frequently exchange views on India's balance of payments situation, fiscal situation, exchange rate problems, etc., and suggest appropriate remedies to the problems. Thus, India gains from the Fund.

However, conditionality clause of the IMF loan in recent years is subject to serious debate. Measures suggested by the Fund in the early years of 1990s involved serious stress and strains. The IMF medicine — devaluation of Indian currency, reduction in budgetary and fiscal deficit, cut in government expenditure and subsidy, import liberalisation, industrial policy reforms, trade policy reforms, banking reforms, etc.,— involves some costs that are mostly unwarranted. Instead, higher economic growth rate following structural adjustment policies, India has been facing recession in industries. Unemployment problem is on the rise. Public sector enterprises are facing extinct. Number of people living below the poverty line is on the rise. It is true that the BOP problem is not so serious today than what it was 10 years ago, but debt burden is not showing any sign of abatement. Deb-service payment rose from $ 8.2 billion in 1992 to $ 11.9 billion in 2007. However debt-service during the period 1992-2007 declined from 30.1 p.c. to 4.8 p.c.

Anyway, the IMF prescriptions on India as well as on other countries present a mixed picture of failures and successes. Some of the measures adopted were urgently called for. One such measure is the creation of a free, competitive economy. The IMF has to be created for the creation of competitive economy. Still more has to be done. But in the process, it has generated enough problems. We must not brush aside these as transitional problems. These problems are to be tackled promptly.

16.8. THE WORLD BANK

The World Bank (WB) was originally created as the International Bank for Reconstruction and Development (IBRD) in 1944 along with its twin, the IMF. Together they came to be known as the 'Bretton Woods twin sisters'. When it was set up it was decided that this international bank would assist in the economic reconstruction of the World War II-damaged European economies. In early 1949, this international bank launched its career as the multilateral development bank and since then the IBRD came to be known as the World Bank. Its headquarters is located in Washington, opposite the IMF building and it lies as the next door neighbour of the White House.

Functions : Being twin sisters, membership in the IMF is a prerequisite for membership in WB (185 countries in July, 2008).

The Bank performs the following functions:

- To assist in the construction and development of the territories of its members by facilitating the investment of capital for productive purposes, including the 'restoration of economies destroyed or disrupted by war', and the encouragement of the 'development' of productive facilities and resources in less developed countries.
- To promote private investment and long run balanced growth of international trade and BOP equilibrium by means of guarantees or participations in international loans and investments.
- To arrange loans made or guaranteed by it, so that more useful and urgent projects receive preference.
- To provide finance to projects from its own capital, funds raised by it and by participating with other members.

Objectives : The purposes and objectives are constantly changing. For instance, the WB decided to put emphasis on the alleviation of poverty in less developed countries in the late

1960s and 1970s. It also introduced structural adjustment programmes (SAPs) in developing countries so that not only macroeconomic stability can be attained but also structural reforms aimed at accelerating growth can be undertaken. It has shifted its emphasis from the financing of specific projects towards non-project linked programmes. It works in developing economies with the focus of helping the poorest people and the poorest countries. For all its clients, the Bank emphasises the need for

- investing in people, particularly through basic health and education;
- focussing on social development, governance and institution-building as the major elements of poverty alleviation;
- strengthening the ability of the governments to deliver quality services with greater efficiency and transparency;
- protecting the environment;
- supporting and encouraging private business development; and
- promoting reforms to create a stable macroeconomic environment conducive to investment and long-term planning.

Through its loans, policy advice and technical assistance, the WB supports a broad range of programmes aimed at reducing poverty and improving living standards in the developing world including the achievement of the Millenium Development Goals (MDGs) by helping countries develop an environment for investment, jobs and sustainable growth. The WB works with government agencies, non-governmental organisations (NGOs), and the private sector to formulate various assistance strategies.

Activities : The WB offers two basic types of loans—investment loans for the support of economic and social development projects and development policy loans to support countries' policy and institutional reforms. The WB grants loans only to the developing countries (and not all 185 members) annually at nearly $20 billion a year usually for a period of 15 to 20 years for the purpose of building roads, dams and other physical capital that contribute to their economic development. Its lending rate is bit low and is fixed every six months. The Bank offers hard currency loans. It accepts hard currency at the time of repayment. The Bank functions as an agent on the international capital markets for countries which are unable to obtain sufficient loans on concessional terms. Its loan provisions are (i) project loans, (ii) sectoral loans, and (iii) structural adjustment loans (SALs). The Bank provided $24.7 billion loans in the fiscal year 2008, with Africa receiving 23 p.c. of the total; Latin America and the Caribbean 19 p.c.; East Asia and Pacific 18 p.c.; South Asia 17 p.c.; Europe and Central Asia 17 p.c.; and Middle East and North Africa 6 p.c. With Bank support — both lending and advice — governments are reforming their economies and strengthening the entire financial and banking systems.

It has made remarkable success in achieving its basic objectives over the last 64 years or so. Its concern for developing countries deserve special attention. It has taken up various poverty-reduction strategies and poverty-focused lending. Bank programmes give high priority to sustainable, social and human development and strengthened economic management. Still then, the modus operandi of the Bank has come in for sharp criticisms.

One of the serious charges against the WB loan is its structural adjustment lending (SAL) or policy-based lending. The essence of SAL is loans disbursed in exchange for policy reforms like trade liberalisation, privatisation, financial sector reforms, tax reforms, etc. But various studies have shown that SALs have failed miserably in establishing a basis for healthy economic and social development in debtor country. In most of the developing countries average incomes, investment, import, etc., have fallen drastically. Unemployment and inflation have become major problems. Number of people living below the poverty line does not show any declining trend in these countries. On the contrary, global poverty has increased and its activities are alleged to be detrimental to the environment, public health, and cultural diversity. It is also said that their Bank is an instrument that serves the interests of the USA as well as Western countries. Its functioning lacks transparency.

Thus, the World Bank has not come up to the expectations of many of the developing countries. At the same time, one must not ignore the useful role the Bank has been playing all these years.

16.9. GENERAL AGREEMENT ON TARIFFS AND TRADE (GATT)

Recongnising both the temptation of short-sighted trade policy and the gains from trade since World War II, nations—both large and small—have engaged themselves in a variety of efforts to reduce trade barriers. At the global level, the prominent effort is known as the GATT and on a small scale, regional trading blocs have also been developed.

After World War II, the countries of the world realised that there was much to be gained from establishing an international economic order in which barriers to trade were to be reduced. They established the GATT in 1947 and it came into operation in January 1948. The GATT is the multilateral treaty that provides and monitors a global system of rights and obligations accepted by its member countries. The fundamental purpose of the GATT is to foster free and fair trade among its members, on the basis of reciprocity, transperancy and non-discrimination.

GATT was, thus, founded on three guiding principles—reciprocity, transperancy and non-discrimination. *Reciprocity* principle says that if one country lowers its tariffs it could expect other countries in the GATT umbrella to lower their tariffs. *Transperancy* principle says that import quotas and other non-tariff barriers to trade should be converted into tariffs so that their effective impacts could be ascertained. The final principle is *nondiscrimination*. No member of the GATT could offer a special trade deal that favours only one or a few other member countries.

GATT has proceeded in a number of stages, called Rounds (the Kennedy Round, 1962-67; the Tokyo Round, 1973-79; and the most recently, the Uruguay Round, 1988-93, etc.). Collectively, these Rounds have reduced tariffs on industrial goods markedly. The average tariff on manufactured goods was 40 p.c. in 1947. By 1992, they had been reduced to 5 p.c. and the Uruguay Round reduced them still further. The Eighth Round of multilateral treaty negotiations was launched in Uruguay and is generally referred to as the Uruguay Round, named after the host country. The Dunkel Draft is the outcome of the Eighth Round and the man who submitted this document after prolonged negotiations was Mr. Arthur Dunkel, the then Director General of GATT. The Eighth Round is considered as a global package of treaties to cover all the sectors of an economy — agriculture, industry and services. In the Uruguay Round, not only were negotiations confined with regard to traditional GATT aspects like tariff and non-tariff matters, but they were also extended to new areas such as, Trade Related Intellectual Property Rights (TRIPS), Trade Related Investments Measures (TRIMs), and General Agreement on Trade in Services (GATS).

The Dunkel proposals have been the subject of lively debate in India as well as in other participating countries. The agreement was finally reached in Geneva and had been signed in Marrakesh on 14 April1994 and came into effect in 1995. Following the Uruguay Round agreement, GATT was converted into a formal international organisation called the World Trade Organisation (WTO) in January 1,1995. GATT as an organisation is now dead, but GATT agreement continues to exist, however, in an amended form.

16.10. THE WORLD TRADE ORGANISATION (WTO)

Recognising both the temptation of shortsighted trade policy and the gains from trade, nations—both large and small—have, since World War II, engaged in a variety of efforts to reduce trade barriers. After the termination of the War (1945), the countries of the world realised that there was much to be gained in establishing an international economic order in which barriers to trade were to be reduced. As a result, the General Agreement on Tariffs and Trade (GATT) was launched in 1947. GATT, since 1947, proceeded in a number of stages, called rounds (the Kennedy Round completed in 1967, the Tokyo Round completed in 1979, and the last round the Uruguay Round completed in 1993). As a result of the Uruguay Round, the World Trade Organisation (WTO) was created on 1 January 1995. GATT was, thus, replaced by the WTO. One should note that WTO is the successor of GATT and not an extension of the GATT. The WTO is the only global international organisation dealing with the rules of trade between nations. At present (July, 2008), it has 153 members. The goal of the WTO is to improve the welfare of the peoples of the member countries.

Structure : The WTO secretariat (numbering 625 of many nationalities) is headed by Director General.

However, the WTO is headed by the Ministerial Conference who enjoys absolute authority over the institution. It not only carries out functions of the WTO but also takes appropriate measures to administer the new global trade rules. In addition to these, the structure of the WTO consists of a General Council to oversee the WTO agreement and ministerial decisions on a regular basis. The Council sits in its headquarters Geneva, Switzerland usually once a month. Besides General Council, there is the Council for Trade in Goods, the Council for Trade in Services, the Council for Trade Related Intellectual Property Rights (TRIPS). These Councils and their respective subsidiary bodies perform their respective functions.

Decision-making is made by consensus. If consensus is not reached then majority voting plays the crucial rate.

The significant task facing the WTO is that of making the new multilateral trading system truly global. Implementation of WTO agreements and ministerial decisions are crucial to credibility of the multilateral trading system and indispensable for expanding global trade, creating additional jobs and improving the standard of living.

Functions : At the heart of the Organisation are the WTO agreements, negotiated and signed by the bulk of the world's trading nations. The goal is to help producers of goods and services, exporters, and importers conduct their business. The WTO's overriding objective is to help trade flow smoothly, freets. fairly, and predictably. With these objectives in mind, we can state the following six specific functions :

- It shall facilitate the implementation, administration and operation of the WTO trade agreements, such as multilateral trade agreements, plurilateral trade agreements.
- It shall provide forum for negotiations among its members concerning their multilateral trade relations.
- It shall administer the 'Understanding on Rules and Procedures' so as to handle trade disputes.
- It shall monitor national trade policies.
- It shall provide technical assistance and training for members of the developing countries.
- It shall cooperate with various international organisations like the IMF and the WB with the aim of achieving greater coherence in global economic policy-making.

The WTO was founded on certain guiding principles—non-discrimination, free trade, open, fair and undistorted competition, etc. In addition, it has special concern for developing countries.

16.10.1. WTO Agreements

General Agreement on Tariffs and Trade was established in 1947. In 1995, GATT was replaced by the World Trade Organisation (WTO). As far as the old system or GATT was concerned, there were two GATTS : (i) GATT the organisation, and (ii) GATT the agreement. The second one refers to the agreement between different governments setting out the rules for trade. GATT, the organisation, has been replaced by the establishment of the WTO. GATT, the agreement, however, exists along with the additional WTO new agreements, viz. (i) General Agreement on Trade in Services (GATS), and (ii) General Agreements on the Trade Related Aspects of Intellectual Property Rights (TRIPS).

It is, thus, clear that the WTO Agreements cover goods, services and intellectual property. The three agreements establishing the WTO are :

(i) GATT,
(ii) GATS, and
(iii) TRIPS.

- **GATT** : GATT is related to increasing market access by reducing various trade barriers operating in different countries. Dismantling of trade restrictions was to be achieved by the reduction in tariff rates, reductions in non-tariff support in agriculture, abolition of voluntary export restraints or phasing out the Multifibre Arrangement (MFA), cut in subsidies, etc.

To improve market access, industrialised countries will have to reduce tariffs by 36 p.c. over six years and 24 p c. for developing nations over 10 years. World trade in textiles and clothings is governed by the MFA which requires to be phased out within 10 years (1993-2002). On 1 January 2003, textiles and clothing sector will stand integrated into GATT, with the elimination of MFA restrictions. GATT aims at elimination of farm support and export support in developed countries. The agreement says that all countries will have to reduce agregate support levies if it is in excess of 5 p.c. of the total value of agricultural produce, but for developing countries it is more than 10 p.c. The value and the volume of direct export subsidies will have to be cut by 36 p.c. and 21 p.c., respectively, over six years for developed countries.

- GATS : Multilaterally agreed and legally enforceable rules and disciplines relating to trade in services are covered by General Agreement on Trade in Services. It envisages free trade in services, like banking, insurance, hotels, construction, etc., so as to promote growth in the developed countries by providing larger markets and in the developing countries through transfer of technologies from the developed countries. As a result of this agreement, access of service personnel into markets of member countries will henceforth be possible on a non-discriminatory basis under transparent and rule-based system. Under the agreement, service sector would be placed under most favoured nation (MFN) obligations that prevents countries from discriminating among different nations in respect of services.

- TRIPS : The TRIPS Agreement covers seven specific areas, viz. copyrights, trademarks, industrial designs, integrated circuits, geographical indications, trade records and patent. Of these seven areas, the most important as well as debatable aspect is the patents right. The basic principle of the patent system is that an inventor, who makes a full disclosure of what he has invented, is granted a statutory monopoly to exploit his invention. Patents should be available for any invention, whether products or processes, in all fields of technology provided they are new, involve an inventive step and capable of industrial application. Patents should be available and patent rights enjoyable without discrimination. TRIPS also say that members must provide for the protection of plant varieties either by patents or by an effective *sui generis* system. The *sui generis* system commonly refers to the system of Plant Breeders' Rights (PBRs)—the exclusive right to produce seed of the protected variety for the seed trade and control of its marketing.

In addition, WTO members have set procedures for setling disputes arising out of the violation of trade rules. Thus, there exists a multilateral system of settlement of disputes.

The WTO agreement also allows governments to take appropriate action against dumping.

Criticisms : Free trade policy pursued by the WTO over the years has widened the income gap between rich and poor nations, instead of minimising the gap. *Secondly,* WTO functions in a discriminatory way as it is more biased to the rich countries and MNCs. In fact, this strategy of the WTO has not benefited the developing countries. One can see that the market access of these countries in industry has not improved, non-tariff barriers like anti-dumping measures have increased and domestic support and export subsidies for agricultural products in the rich countries still remain high. *Thirdly,* it is criticised that labour relations and environmental issues have been sidelined or ignored by the WTO. *Finally,* decision-making process in the WTO is rather non-transparent, ineffective and non-inclusive since "the vast majority of developing countries have very little real say in the WTO system."

16.11. GATT VS WTO

We have said that there are many international organisation that govern trade.

The General Agreement on Tariffs and Trade (GATT) came into operation in 1948 with the aim of liberalising trade. The international trading system since then was guided by the rules and precedures of the GATT till 1994. The GATT was transformed into the World Trade Organisation on January 1995. In fact, prior to 1994 there was as such no international or multilateral trade organisation that addresses all the tissues relating to trade.

GATT, the organisation is now dead and the WTO is now functioning with the adjective of promoting the liberalisation of world trade. It formulates rules of trade in such a way that the process of globalisation becomes easier—the idea is to create a 'global village'. Like the IMF or the World Bank, GATT did not have any international status. As an international organisation, WTO differs from its predecessor, the GATT, in many respects. These are :

First, the number of member cerentries of the WTO is larger. At present (July 2008), it has 153 members.

Secondly, GATT was *ad hoc* and provisional. The WTO is a permanent organisation having sound legal basiss.

Thirdly, the area of business of the WTO is more widespread than the GATT. The WTO facilitates the implementation, administration and operation of multilateral and plurilateral trade agreements especially concerning services, protection of intellectual property rights, etc.

Fourthly, the WTO is a more powerful body than the GATT as the former operates with better rules and enlarged functions than the latter.

Fifthly, the dispute settlement under the WTO is faster than the GATT.

Sixthly, although GATT recommended protection in smaller doses for very few sensitive commodities, the WTO is totally committed to the removal of any kind of protection and subsidy. It also aims at trading reforms of agricultural commodities.

On the whole, one can say that the 'WTO is GATT plus a lot more'. The WTO acts as a watchdog of trade expansion. If any dispute or conflict arises between nations concerning trade, the WTO intervenes. It performs advisory role. It aims at preventing protective policy at any cost.

16.12. GLOBALISATION

Globalisation is the most talked about word today all over the globe. But it is not a new concept or a new phenomenon. It can be traced in the 16th century when the different countries participated marginally in the global economy. The process gathered momentum during the days of industrial revolution. A new international economy emerged in the 1940s when the global economic system emerged. Globalisation today represents a resumption of the 19th century trend, but, of course, with a more closer economic integration among nations. Barring policy changes, massive technological advances of the last quarter of the 20th century are attributed to the emergence of globalisation in a vigorous form. The process received a great boost from the disintegration of the East German (1989) and the USSR (1991) economies. Technological advances of the current period have brought out continuing revolutions in the technology of global communication. It is said that communication revolution is the most important cause of globalisation.

Meaning : Globalisation is a process of increasing integration and growing economic 'interdependence' of countries worldwide. It refers to "the expansion of economic activities across political boundaries of nation states." Its important attribute is its increasing degree of openness of domestic economies. It is associated not only with the increasing cross-border movement of goods and services, capital and technology, information and people but also with an organisation of economic activities which straddles national boundaries. Its three broad dimensions are international trade, international investment, and international finance.

Thus, globalisation brings about changes through these three channels that impart dynamism in the economy. *First* is the export earning. Through liberalisation of tariff and trade, export-oriented industries are required to be developed. *Second* is the foreign capital flow, mainly via multinational corporations (MNCs) that bring technology. *Third* is the deregulation of financial sector so that cross border mobility of resources gets momentum. In addition, trade policy, exchange rate policy, industrial policy, etc. are all relaxed. As the process of globalisation strengthens, all producers depend on global networks which establish links from the stage of raw materials to the final stage of delivery and marketing.

Globalisation also refers to the adoption of market-friendly approach, thereby making the economy more open and competitive. It is to be kept in mind that globalisation does not remove planning or state authority in regulation and control of the economy.

- **Case of Globalisation** : At the outset, one must say that globalisation is a controversial issue because it impinges both gains and pains. We will first put forward the arguments favouring globalisation.

- Globalisation is expected to promote efficiency, productivity and, hence, higher economic growth rate. In a controlled and regulated economy, there is no inducement to the industries to become efficient and self-reliant as these are protected from foreign competition through import restrictions and from domestic competition through industrial licensing. Globalisation has one pillar of liberalisation. Liberalisation and the market principles improve the allocative efficiency of resources. This will increase export earnings, allow the inflow of foreign capital and technology. Industries and farm sector, banking and financial sectors are then exposed to international competition. Competition enhances efficiency, productivity and ultimately a better economic growth rate is likely to be achieved.
- As far as consumers are concerned, quality goods at the right price will be delivered. This helps to bring down prices. Quality improvement and price reduction will then be enjoyed.
- Foreign capital is attracted. It augurs the advent of multinational entrerprises (MNEs) who bring modern up-to-date technology in less developed countries. Not only MNCs bring with them modern technology but also it brings investment funds, organisational structure, managerial culture, distribution network, etc. All these create income and employment in the country.

Case Against Globalisation : Critics argue that globalisation cannot make any dent on poverty reduction, employment generation, export promotion, foreign direct investment and growth rates of the economy. Critics perceive threat of the global market manifested in terms of falling rate of growth, industrial recession especially in America and some major industrial countries and poor rate of growth of export.

- It is feared that globalisation will promote fierce and unhealthy competition. Instead of competition and cooperation, one may argue that MNCs will swallow the domestic producers of poor backward countries overtime. Ultimately, this will cause concentration of economic and political power into the hands of the foreign business enterprises.
- Merely opening up the domestic economy without reaching out to foreign markets or helping industries to meet the global challenges has limited the benefits of globalisation without reducing its costs.
- The apparent increase in export earnings of the less developed countries as a consequence of globalisation is not expected to provide great benefits, particularly those in the lower income brackets. Further, modern technologies used by the MNCs have the potentiality of making the unemployment situation worse. This widens inequalities in the distribution of income and wealth. In India, food, employment and health scenarios have been adversely affected for the poor people as a consequence of new economic policy reforms introduced in the 1990s. Above all, integration of the domestic economy into the world economy provides larger benefits to the developed countries than to the LDCs.
- Foreign capital is not interested in producing goods that an underdeveloped country requires. Globalisation then distorts production structure of an economy.

Thus, the policy of globalisation should be pursued with caution since there is no escape from globalisation in today's interconnected and interdependent world. It is necessary that economies must open up much more. But, this should be done much more critically. Globalisation is not the panacea for all the ills from which an economy suffers. There are other measures too that can hardly be bypassed to achieve a higher growth rate.

16.12.1. Ingredients of Globalisation of the Indian Economy

Globalisation refers to the closer integration of the world economy resulting from the channels of increased international trade, investment, finance and multicountry production networks of MNCs. In 1991, a new era of Indian economic history began. She started her journey in 1951 with a mixed economy model characterised by the coexistence of both public and private sectors with government controls and regulation directed to various economic activities. The means chosen to energise India's economy was planning. Performance during these first forty years of planning is not altogether happy. The country witnessed an unprecedented balance of payments crisis leading to a classic debt trap. Finding no other alternative, she had to pledge gold in foreign banks in lieu of loans. In order to rescue the economy, the IMF asked 'shock therapy' strategy of wholesale reform. India then, following the IMF's advice, adopted a market-based regime by initiating a macroeconomic stabilisation and adjustment programme. These are called New Economic Policies.

The essential ingredients of globalisation or the so-called India's New Economic Policies are (i) privatisation of the public sector, (ii) dismantling of bureaucratic controls and regulations, (iii) opening up and the closer integration of the Indian economy with the world economy through deregulation of trade and finance, etc.

- **Privatisation of the public sector :** Most public sector undertakings (PSUs) in India are reported to be running at a huge loss. How long public sector industries in India should bear losses and stand as a liability? Against the backdrop of the failure of public sector enterprises (PSEs) and success of the private sector industries, the Indian reform strategy envisaged privatisation of these public sector industries in 1991.

The term 'privatisation' is used in different senses. In India, privatisation is sought to be achieved through two measures : (i) the disinvestment of the government's equity (ownership) in PSEs, and (ii) the opening up of hitherto closed areas to private participation. The issue of privatisation has come to the forefront because of poor performance of PSUs, and the consequent huge fiscal deficit. One specific step that has been taken to reduce the deficit was privatisation, through an act of disinvestment, i.e., selling of public sector equity to mutual funds, financial institutions and the private sector including foreign firms (up to 49 p.c.) equity.

- **Dismantling of controls and regulations:** Before 1991, our industrial and trade policies were mostly controlled and regulated by the government. The system witnessed plethora of bureaucratic controls and rigidities. The area of industrial policy reform was characterised by the virtual dismantling of the industrial licensing. Portfolio investment has now been opened to foreign institutional investors. The limit of foreign equity holding has been raised from 40 p.c. to 51 p.c. Today, FERA (Foreign Exchange Regulation Act) companies are now treated at par with domestic investors. In fact, some great hurdles relating to direct foreign investment have been greatly simplified. The result is the emergence of the MNCs in India and a significant flow of investment funds and technology and management practices from abroad.

India's trade regime is now characterised by lesser controls and regulations. For most cases, import restrictions have been dismantled. Tariff levels have been reduced substantially. Removal of quantitative controls and reduction in customs tariffs are the hallmarks of import liberalisation. The process of external economic liberalisation, especially with respect to finance, has provided the domestic private sector with the opportunity to access credit abroad directly. The essence of these policy measures suggests that India has entered a global portfolio regime.

The Government of India devalued currency in 1991 to make exports more competitive and imports more expensive. The most significant change that was made was the floatation of exchange rate to a market-determined rate. In the Union Budget for 1992-93, a revolutionary provision of partial convertibility of rupee was made under which 60 p.c. of the foreign exchange earnings were to be surrendered at a market-determined rate. The 1993-94 Budget went a step forward and introduced full convertibility of rupee on trade account (i.e., with respect to import and export of merchandise). The Union Budget for 1994-95 made rupee fully convertible on current account. Instead of 'administered rate of exchange', an element of market has been injected in the exchange rate determination.

- **Deregulation of trade and finance:** Reform in the financial sector aimed at strengthening banks and at deregulating capital markets with the objective of financing investment in the private sector and at attracting foreign portfolio capital. As far as the reform packages are concerned, foreign institutional investors are allowed to invest in the capital market. Interest rates in the domestic capital market have been deregulated. In addition, the government has done away with the quantitative restrictions on a wide range of imports. The process of import liberalisation which began in 1991 is now complete as far as quantitative restrictions (QRs) are concerned. The removal of QRs on 715 items in 2001-02 EXIM policy has opened the gates for free flow of imports. The peak rate of customs duty has been reduced to 10 p.c.

All these reform measures have brought intense public debate in this country. However, reform measures have not been coming with great speed. Further, market principles that are operating in India are neither free nor perfect. In addition, the space vacated by the 'state' cannot be taken by the 'market'. On the other hand, one cannot back out from this ongoing reform process; it is unstoppable and irreversible. Reform measures must take all these elements into account so that the goal of social justice is not bypassed.

16.12.2. Impact of Globalisation on the Indian Economy

No country can afford to remain isolated. Before 1990s, India followed an inward-looking strategy or import substitution of growth rather than outward growth strategy. The economic reforms were introduced in 1991 in the wake of macroeconomic crises. These reform measures sought to improve the efficiency of resource allocation and expand the productive capacity of the economy, included trade and exchange rate liberalisation, a more market-oriented industrial policy, and taxation reform. These measures were supplemented by reforms of the financial and capital markets. The process of globalisation is one such element of our outward-looking growth strategy. Almost two decades of these new economic policy measures have passed. Now we will review these performance of the Indian economy in the light of globalisation.

India is a small player in international trade. As time passes, her share of world trade declines. India's share of world trade at the time of independence was roughly 2 p.c. and by 2006-07 it went down to 1 p.c. Anyway, the economy of the country is globalising at a faster rate. This is evidenced from the following facts :

The ratio of international trade to India's GDP has gone up from 15.6 p.c. in 1990-91 to 20.8 p.c. in 1999-2000. Imports and exports together currently (2004-05) account for 23 p.c. of GDP as against 15 p.c. in 1990-91.

India's engineering goods like automobiles and motorbikes are now competing with the industrilised countries of the world both in terms of quality and price. Currently, the world economy and in particular Asian countries are expanding rapidly. This is expected to give a spur to India's growth prospect.

Current account balance for the last two years (i.e., 2002-03, 2003-04) has turned surplus (0.7 p.c. in 2002-2003) compared to a deficit of 3.1 p.c. of GDP in 1990-91. All these suggest that current external receipts pay for current external liabilities. In adddition, there has been an unprecedented accumulation of foreign exchange reserves.

There has been a spectacular jump in the ratio of foreign investment to exports from just 0.6 p.c. in 1990-91 to 13.4 p.c. in 1999-2000. Although direct investment showed a significant decline, the portfolio investment showed a substantial increase. In this connection, Prof. R. S. Bawa's remarks deserve mention : "The stock market indices in the country are moving in line with those of other parts of the world. The corporate sector of the country are getting aligned with those in other countries. The exchange rate adjusts to the pressure from the international market. The financial market of the country is much more integrated with global finance today than a decade back. The volatile nature of private capital flows and development elsewhere in the world have started impinging more on the economy of the country. The behaviour of the producers and consumers is changing fast. The strong winds of globalisation have made the Indian corporate sector feel shy of manufacturing sector and they are now attracted more towards the service sector."

Annual growth rates of national income rose from 5.7 p.c. during 1985-90 to 7.9 p.c. during 2002-07. This rise in GDP is attributed mainly to the remarkable growth of the service sector at the expense of both primary and secondary sectors. As a result, occupation pattern has tilted more in favour of the service sector. It is argued by the reformists that the reduction in inequalities in income distribution and poverty in recent years may be attributed to a shift of employment in favour of the tertiary sector and construction as well as informal/unorganised sector. The rate of inflation fell to a record level of 1.5 p.c. in February, 2002. But, it rose to 3.9 p.c. in January 2008. However the later months saw inflation rate to rise to as high as almost 13 p.c. in September, 2008. It has come down to less than 3.5 p.c. in 12 February, 2009. Foodgrains production reached a record level of 212 million tonnes in 2001-02. Though foodgrains production fell in 2004-05 and 2005-06, it again rose to a record level of 217 million tonnes in 2007-08. As a result, despite global food crisis prevailing in mid-2008, India did not experience such food crisis. Thanks to good performance of the agricultural sector!

As far as external sector is concerned, balance of trade position has shown some improvement and the country's foreign exchange reserves have risen to all-time high of Rs. 10,85,056 crore in November 2007. Although, export growth is not steady, it grew at the rate of 15 p.c. in 2003-04. It cimbed up to 28 p.c. in the next year, but grew at the rate of 25.3 p.c. in 2006-07.

It is true that although exports now finance roughly 70 p.c. of imports, growth is inadequate. Number of foreign collaborations increased from 289 involving foreign investment of Rs. 534 crore in 1991 to 2,270 involving foreign investments of Rs. 26,875 crore in 2001. The quality of business is changing rapidly showing greater profitability, competitiveness, efficiency and technology upgradation.

There are some glaring dark sides of globalisation. There has been a steady widening of trade deficit as well as current account deficit. The commodity composition of exports has remained almost the same. Direction of exports is also unchanged. What is worrisome is that there has been an increase in the import intensity of exports. Despite massive rise in foreign investments, export sector is lagging far behind. India's outstanding external debt rose from $ 85,285 million in 1992 to $ 155,033 million in March, 2007. Debt service payment in terms of US $ billion rose from 8.2 to 11.9 during the same time period. However, debt-service ratio that rose as high as 30.1 p.c. in 1992, has been showing a great decelerating trend since the late 1990s. In March 2007, this ratio fell as low as 4.8 p.c.

India is yet to gain from integrating the domestic economy with the world economy. She is facing stiff competition with the MNCs. In the midst of competition, Indian firms are being driven out. In the process, imports to turnover ratio 'have been increasing' resulting in a great strain on external payments for India. Indian firms are yet to máke any significant dent outside the country. As it is a competition among unequals, poor developing countries like India are definitely at a disadvantageous position. In addition, there are pressures from the IMF, World Bank—as well as the USA—to go for more globalisation and removal of all sorts of rigidities, controls and restrictions.

Conclusion : Thus, our performances during the reform years are a mixed bag. The country over the last 17-18 years has seen both quantitative and qualitative changes. Economic growth rate in a market-led economy is surely worth emulating. India is considered as one of the great economic powers of the world. It is hoped that she would sooner be a prospective interntional power. In spite of this development, the economy has not been able to adjust with a human face. We see some adverse, inadequate and cunterproductive results which may be attributed to economic reforms/ globalization, etc.

During this period, there has been a decline in social expenditure from 28.26 p.c. in 2001-02 to 27.19 p.c. in 2006-07. The country spends much below the required amount on education, health, etc. Injustices are meted out to a vast number of people. Number of people living below the poverty line in 2004-03 stood at 27.5 p.c. Per capita availability of cereals and pulses per day for an Indian has declined from 510.1 gms in 1991 to 422.4 gms in 2005. It however, rose to 444.5 gms per days in 2006. During the reform period, nearly 15,000 farmers all over the country committed sucides because of debt, malnutrition, etc. On the other hand, there are at least three Indians who belong to top 10 richest men of the world. They are : Lakshmi Mittal (4th), Mukesh Ambani (5th) and Anil Ambani (6th). Further, child manutrition in India is unparalled in the world. More than 304 million people lack what is called 'entitlement to basic education', as there are as many as 35 p.c. of the total population are illiterate.

So we can conclude that a large section of the Indian population is feeling insecure. Development that has taken place is called 'exclusive development. Reforms have not made people 'inclusive' in the sense that its benefits did not reach ordinary people who constitute the bulk of the country. This is not called economic reforms with a human face. We want 'inclusive growth' so that the needs of the people are not ignored.

QUESTIONS (WITH ANSWER-HINTS)

Long Questions (16 marks)

1. "Foreign trade is an engine of growth".—Explain (C.U. 2008)

   Ans. 16.5.

2. Discuss the objectives and functions of the International Monetary Fund.

   Ans. 16.7.

3. Discuss the achievements and failures of the IMF.

   Ans. 17.7.3.

4. Describe the functions and activities of the World Bank. How far has it been successful in achieving its objectives?

   Ans. 16.8.

5. Distinguish between GATT and WTO. Explain briefly the main functions of the World Bank. (C.U. 2007)

   Ans. 16.11 and 16.8.

6. What do you mean by globalisation? Give arguments for and against globalisation.

   Ans. 16.12.

7. What are the essential ingredients of globlisation of the Indian economy?

   Ans. 16.12.1.

Medium-sized Questions (8 marks)

1. What are the essential elements of international trading environment? Point out the main aspects of international trade policy.

   Ans. 16.3 and 16.3.1.

2. Give a brief review of the trends in world trade in relation to developing countries.

   Ans. 16.4.

3. Write a note on the structure and management of the IMF.

   Ans. 16.7.1 and 16.7.2.

4. Discuss the functions of the IMF. (C.U. 2008)

   Ans. 16.7.1 and 16.7.2.

5. Discuss the role of the IMF vis-a-vis the Indian economy.

   Ans. 16.7.4.

6. Write a note on GATT.

   Ans. 16.9.

7. Give an account of the structure and functions of the World Trade Organisation.

   Ans. 16.10.

8. What do you know about the WTO agreements?

   Ans. 16.10.1.

9. Discuss the overall impact of globalisation on the Indian economy.

   Ans. 16.12.2.

17

SHORT QUESTIONS AND ANSWERS

BASIC PROBLEMS OF AN ECONOMY AND PRICE MECHANISM

Q.1. Why do economic problems arise?

Ans. : Human wants are unlimited and are insatiable. But the resources needed to satisfy wants are really scarce. Thus, the scarcity of resources gives rise to fundamental economic problems of a nation.

Q.2. What are the central economic problems of an economy? (C.U. 2007)

Ans. : Every economic system, regardless of its type, faces three fundamental economic problems. These are (i) What goods and services are to be produced and in what quantities? (ii) How are these goods to be produced? (iii) For whom are these goods to be produced?

Q.3. What do you mean by the problem of 'resource allocation'?

Ans. : Scarcity and choice are intimately related to each other. As resources are scarce, choice is inevitable. One of the major economic problems faced by any economy is what goods and services are to be produced. Obviously, limited resources are to be allocated among alternative uses in such a manner that all wants can be met. This is the problem of picking and choosing from the unlimited wants.

Q.4. What is a production-possibility curve?

Ans. : With given resources and technology, a production-possibility curve depicts the maximum obtainable combinations of two commodities that an economy can produce at the full employment level.

Q.5. Explain the shape of a production-possibility curve.

Ans. : A production-possibility curve is concave form below or a bowed-out curve because of the operation of the law of diminishing returns to a variable input or law of increasing costs.

Q.6. How does price mechanism operate in a capitalist economy?

Ans. : In a free enterprise capitalist economy, the price mechanism, i.e., the free market forces of demand and supply, help to solve the fundamental economic problems of an economy. Price system indicates what goods and services should be produced. *Secondly,* how goods are to be produced can be learnt from the price system.

Thirdly, prices play a role in the distribution of goods and services among the members of the society.

Q.7. In the following figure, we measure gun on the horizontal axis and butter on the vertical axis. Answer the following questions with the help of the production-possibility frontier AB.

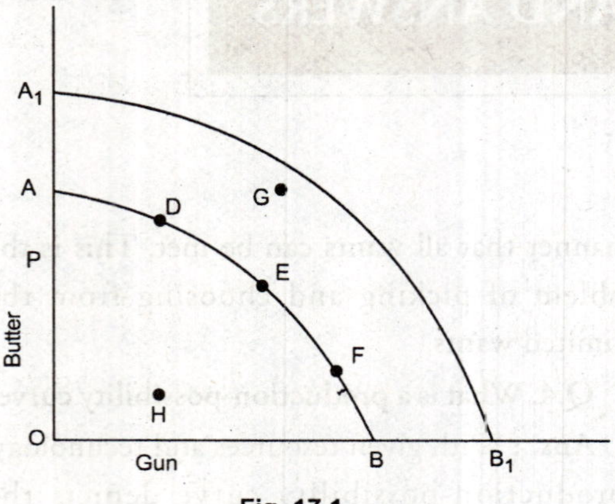

Fig. 17.1

(i) At which point on the curve AB a country will operate if it decides to produce only gun or only butter?

(ii) What is the economic significance if a nation stays at point H and at point G?

(iii) What sort of effect an economy might experience if it contemplates to move from point D to E and from E to F along the curve AB?

(iv) How will the curve AB shift if economic development takes place?

Ans. :

(i) If a nation decides to produce only gun, it will operate at point B on the curve AB. Oppositely, if only butter is manufactured, the country will stay at point A on the AB curve.

(ii) Operation inside the production possibility frontier, such as point H, implies that the available resources are not being fully employed and/or inefficiently utilised. On the other hand, operation outside the AB curve such as point G, merely suggests that the economy is incapable of producing more of both the commodities with its given resources.

(iii) If a nation moves from point D to E and to F along the curve AB, it will sacrifice butter for gun production. Gun output will increase since resources are now being constantly transferred from butter industry to gun industry. Hence, the reallocation of resources.

(iv) A production-possibility curve will shift rightward if economic development occurs. The curve A_1B_1 is the result of economic development indicating larger quantities of both commodities.

Q.8. What is microeconomics?

Ans. : Microeconomics or price theory studies and analyses the economic activities of individual economic units, such as a consumer, a producer and an input owner. Primarily, this branch of economics is concerned with the determination of prices of a product and an input.

Q.9. What is meant by price mechanism ? (C.U. 2007)

Ans. : Price mechanism is one in which all economic decisions are taken through the medium of prices which are, by nature, self-adjusting and self-correcting. Decisions of production, consumption and distribution are taken by invisible hand or the price system. Prices act as communicating or interacting devices.

THE BASICS OF DEMAND AND SUPPLY

Q.1. Why is a product demand curve negative sloping?

Ans. : For a normal, non-Giffen goods, demand curve slopes downwards from left to right because of three reasons. *First* is the law of diminishing marginal utility. *Second* is the substitution effect, while the *third* reason is the income effect of price change.

Q.2. Draw an unusual demand curve and explain why you consider it an unusual.

Ans. : In some unusual cases, demand curve becomes upward rising indicating a direct

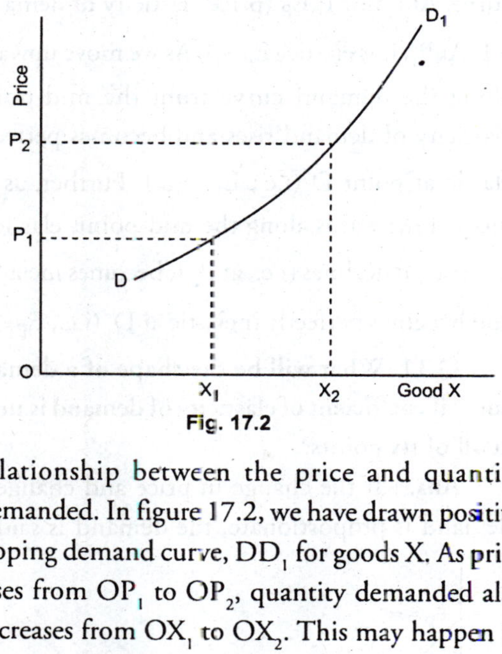

Fig. 17.2

relationship between the price and quantity demanded. In figure 17.2, we have drawn positive sloping demand curve, DD_1 for goods X. As price rises from OP_1 to OP_2, quantity demanded also increases from OX_1 to OX_2. This may happen in cases of (i) Giffen goods, (ii) conspicuous consumption goods, etc.

Q.3. Give reasons why demand curve slopes upwards.

Ans. : The demand curve slopes upwards in the case of conspicuous consumption goods, Giffen goods, etc. People buy conspicuous consumption goods, particularly when their price rises, merely to display their riches. Further, Sir Robert Giffen found that the Irish people during the 19th century famine in Ireland, consumed more of potatoes when its price was higher than meat. Here, potato is a Giffen good. Again, in the share market, people buy share more (or less) when its price rises (or falls).

Q.4. Demand for a commodity depends on the price of that commodity. Are there any factors that affect the demand for a commodity?

Or

What is the demand function?

Ans. : The law of demand establishes the functional relationship between the quantity demanded of a goods and its price. However, demand for any commodity depends not only on the price of that commodity, but also on other factors. So, the demand function can written as.

$$D_X = f(P_X, P_a \ldots P_C, Y, T, E, N)$$

D_X = demand for goods X; f = functional relationship;

P_X = price of goods X;

Q.5. Make a distinction between a change in demand and a change in quantity demanded.

Ans. : Change in demand refers to an increase or a decrease in demand following a change in one of the determinants of demand other than the own price. Consequently, the demand curve will shift (upward or downward). On the other hand, a change in quantity demanded refers to a rise or fall in demand following a change in own price, assuming other things constant. So, a change in quantity demanded refers to a movement along the same demand curve.

Q.6. Point out the factors leading to a change in demand.

Or

How does the position of a demand curve change?

Ans. : Causes of change in demand are numerous. They are : (i) change in income and wealth of the consumer, (ii) change in tastes and preferences of the consumer, (iii) change in the prices of substitute and complementary goods, (iv) change in the number of buyers, (v) anticipation of consumers about a future change in prices, (vi) change in the pattern of income distribution, (vii) advertisement, (viii) governmental taxation policy, (ix) change in climatic condition (e.g., increase in demand for woollen garments during winter weather), etc.

Q.7. Define price elasticity of demand.

Ans. : Price elasticity of demand is defined as the ratio of the proportionate change in quantity demanded to the proportionate change in own price. Thus,

$$E_P = \frac{\%\text{ change in quantity demanded } (\Delta Q / Q)}{\%\text{ change in price } (\Delta P / P)}$$

Q.8. Define income ealsticity of demand.

Ans. : Income elasticity of demand is defined as the ratio of the proportionate change in quantity demanded to a proportionate change in income. Thus,

$$E_M = \frac{\%\text{ change in quantity demanded } (\Delta Q / Q)}{\%\text{ change in price } (\Delta M / M)}$$

$$\text{Or } E_M = \frac{\Delta Q}{Q} \div \frac{\Delta M}{M} = \frac{\Delta Q}{M} \cdot \frac{M}{Q}$$

Q.9. Mention the different types of elasticity of demand.

Ans. : As the rate of change in price and consequently the rate of change in quantity demanded is not the same for all types of goods, we find different degrees of price elasticity of demand. These are (i) elastic demand, (ii) inelastic demand, (iii) unitary elasticity of demand, (iv) perfectly elastic demand, and (v) perfectly inelastic demand.

Q.10. Would the elasticity of demand be the same at all the points of a linear demand curve?

Or

At which point on a downward sloping straight line demand curve the absolute value of the price elasticity is unity? (C.U. 2007)

Ans. : Elasticity of demand is not the same at all points of a straight line demand curve. At the middle point of the curve, elasticity of demand is equal to unity. In Figure 17.3, DD_1 is the demand curve. At point P, E_P (price elasticity of demand) = 1. At P_1, it is elastic $(E_P >_1)$. As we move upwards along the demand curve from the mid-point, elasticity of demand rises and becomes perfectly elastic at point D (i.e., $E_P = \infty$). Further, as we move downwards along the mid-point, elasticity of demand declines (i.e., at P_2 it becomes inelastic) and becomes perfectly inelastic at D_1 (i.e., $E_P = 0$).

Q.11. What will be the shape of a demand curve if coefficient of elasticity of demand is unity at all of its points?

Ans. : If the change in price and change in demand is proportionate, the demand is said to

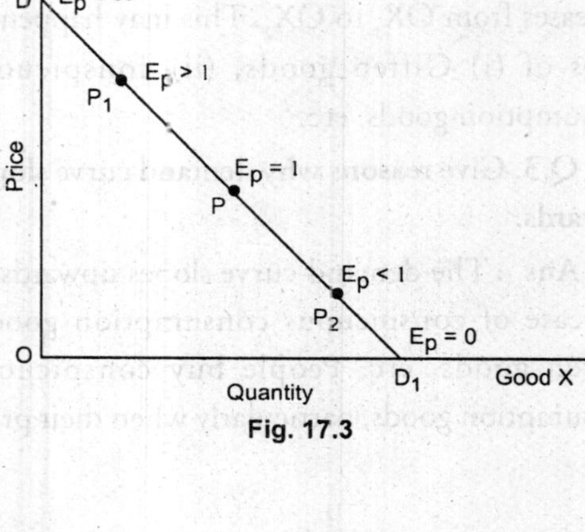

Fig. 17.3

be unitary elastic. The coefficient of elasticity of demand is one. The demand curve becomes a rectangular hyperbola (Fig. 17.4) The curve in

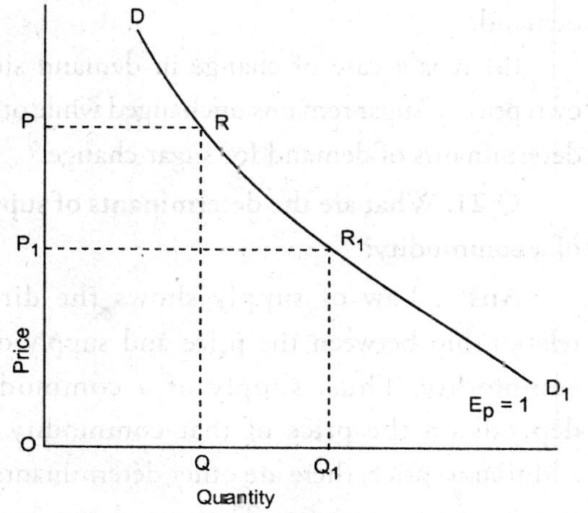

Fig. 17.4

which every rectangle is equal to every other (rectangle OPRQ = rectangle $OP_1R_1Q_1$) is known as a rectangular hyperbola.

Q.12. What will be the coefficient of elasticity of demand when a fall in price leads to an increase, decrease and no change in total outlay?

Ans. : If the fall in price of a commodity cause consumer's outlay to increase, the demand becomes elastic. *Secondly,* if the fall in price leads to a fall in consumer's expenditure, demand becomes inelastic. *Finally,* the coefficient of elasticity of demand becomes zero when changes in price do not cause any change in total consumer's outlay.

Q.13. The elasticity of demand for a commodity is unity. If the price of a commodity is Rs. 4, the demand for it is 300 units. If the price drops down to Rs. 3 how will the demand react?

Ans. : If the change in price does not lead to any change in consumer's total expenditure, elasticity of demand is everywhere equal to unity. Before change in price, total outlay is Rs. 4 × 300 units = Rs. 1,200. As price drops from Rs. 4 to Rs. 3. total demand increases to 400 units. So, the total expenditure after the fall in price becomes Rs. 3 × 400 units = Rs. 1,200. Hence, no change in total expenditure.

Q.14. If the price of tea falls, how will the demand for sugar be affected? How will the demand for coffee be affected?

Ans. : Normally, tea and sugar are complementary to each other and tea and coffee are considered as substitutes. As price of tea falls, its demand will increase and, hence, demand for its complementary good, sugar, will also increase. Oppositely, as price of tea falls, tea becomes cheaper and coffee becomes expensive. Naturally, demand for coffee will go down.

Q.15. Explain three important factors on which elasticity of demand for a product depends.

Ans. : Whether the elasticity of demand for a product is elastic or inelastic depends on the (i) nature of commodities, (ii) range of substitutes, and (iii) product consumed out of habits. *Firstly,* in the case of necessary goods, elasticity of demand is inelastic while in the case of luxury commodity it is elastic. *Secondly,* a commodity having a large number of substitutes will be relatively elastic. *Finally,* the demand for some goods (cigarette) becomes inelastic as these goods are consumed by people out of habit.

Q.16. Define cross elasticity of demand.

Or

If cross price elasticity of two related goods is positive, what is the relationship between the aforesaid goods? (C.U. 2008)

Ans. : The cross elasticity of demand measures the relative responsiveness of quantity demanded of a given commodity to a change in the price of a related commodity, i.e., substitute and complementary goods. Formula for the cross elasticity of demand is

$$E_{XY} = \frac{\%\ \text{change in the demand for X}}{\%\ \text{change in the price for Y}}$$

Here, X and Y are related commodities. If these two are substitute goods, cross elasticity of demand will be positive. Oppositely, in the case of complementary goods, cross elasticity of demand will be negative.

Q.17. What will be the coefficient of income elasticity of demand in the case of (i) necessary goods, (ii) luxury goods, and (iii) inferior goods?

Ans. : The coefficient of income elasticity of demand is less than one (i.e., inelastic) in the case of necessary goods, greater than one (i.e., elastic) in the case of luxury goods, and negative in the case of inferior goods.

Q.18. What is the significance of negative income elasticity of demand?

Ans. : If the income elasticity of demand for a goods is negative then such commodity is described as "inferior goods."

Q.19. If demand is elastic how will total revenue change if price falls?

Ans. : If the fall in the price of a commodity causes consumer's total outlay to increase then demand is said to be elastic.

Q.20. (a) Suppose the price of sugar comes down from Rs. 5 per kilogram to Rs. 4 and the demand for sugar increases from 1,000 quintals to 1,500 quintals. Is it a case of elasticity of demand or a change in demand?

(b) Suppose the price of sugar does not change but the quantity demanded increases from 1,000 quintals to 1,500 quintals. Is it a case of elasticity of demand or a change in demand?

Ans. : (a) It is a case of own price elasticity of demand.

(b) It is a case of change in demand since own price of sugar remains unchanged while other determinants of demand for sugar change.

Q.21. What are the determinants of supply of a commodity?

Ans. : Law of supply shows the direct relationship between the price and supply of a commodity. Thus, supply of a commodity depends on the price of that commodity. In addition to price, there are other determinants of supply of a commodity. They are shown in the form of a supply function equation :

$$S_X = f(P_X, P_a \ldots P_C, P_L \ldots P_O, T, G, S_T)$$

where, S_X = supply of X,

P_X = price of X,

$P_a \ldots P_C$ = prices of the other goods related to X,

$P_L \ldots P_O$ = prices of inputs,

T = time

G = nature of the commodity, and

S_T = technology.

Q.22. What does a normal-shaped supply curve indicate?

Ans. : The relationship between price and supply of a commodity is a direct one—higher the price, greater the supply; and, lower the price, the smaller the supply. Thus, the supply curve is upward rising.

Q.23. Mention why supply curve is upward rising.

Ans. : The two forces behind the upward sloping supply curve are (i) the law of diminishing marginal returns, and (ii) the profit maximisation motive of the producer.

Normally, if output is increased by employing more variable inputs, beyond a certain limit, the return from these inputs diminishes or the cost of production for using these resources increases. So, unless the price of a commodity is high, it will not be produced or supplied in greater quantity. If price increases, profit per unit increases. Naturally, larger quantities will be produced and supplied at the higher price.

Q.24. Draw an abnormal supply curve and explain why it is not normal-shaped.

Ans. : Supply curve for goods which cannot be produced (e.g., paintings of a dead painter)

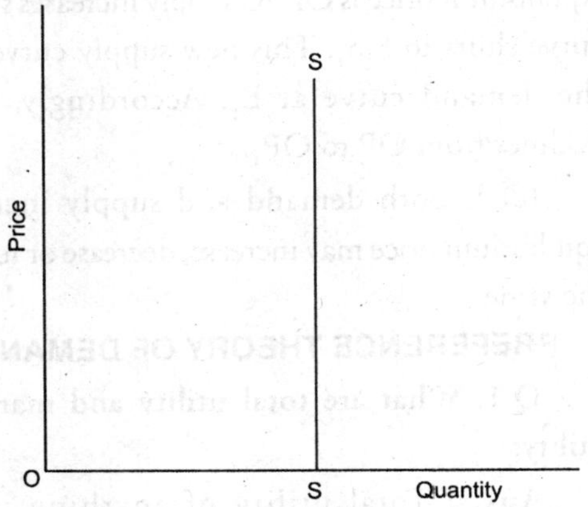

Fig. 17.5

becomes a vertical straight line. Supply curve for perishable commodities also takes this shape.

Here SS curve, drawn in Fig. 17.5, is the supply curve for such commodity whose quantity remains unchanged at all prices.

Q.25. Make a distinction between a change in supply and a change in quantity supplied.

Ans. : Change in supply refers to an increase or decrease in supply following a change in one of the determinants of supply, other than own price. Such a change involves a shifting of the supply curve in the rightward or in the backward direction. On the other hand, a change in quantity supplied means that the supply will expand at higher price and contract at lower prices, assuming other things remaining constant. Here, such a change involves a movement along the same supply curve.

Q.26. What are the causes of change in supply?

Ans. : A change in supply occurs when (i) prices of related goods change, (ii) prices of inputs change, (iii) production technique changes, (iv) mode of transportation of goods changes, (v) taxation policies of the government change, (vi) climatic condition (especially for agricultural products) changes, etc.

Q.27. Define elasticity of supply.

Ans. : Elasticity of supply is defined as the percentage change in quantity supplied by the percentage change in price. Symbolically, elasticity of supply (E_S) is

$$E_S = \frac{\%\ \text{change in quantity supplied}\ (\Delta Q / Q)}{\%\ \text{change in price}\ (\Delta P / P)}$$

$$E_S = \frac{\Delta Q}{Q} \div \frac{\Delta P}{P} = \frac{\Delta Q}{\Delta P} . \frac{P}{Q}$$

Q.28. Show that price does not change if demand increases and supply is perfectly elastic, and that quantity does not change if demand increases and supply is perfectly inelastic.

Ans. : In Figure 17.6, PS is the perfectly elastic supply curve. Intersection point between demand curve, DD, and supply curve, PS, determines equilibrium price OP Now if demand increases to D_1D_1 quantity will rise to OQ_1, but the price remains the same (OP). On the other hand, if supply curve is perfectly inelastic, QS, then

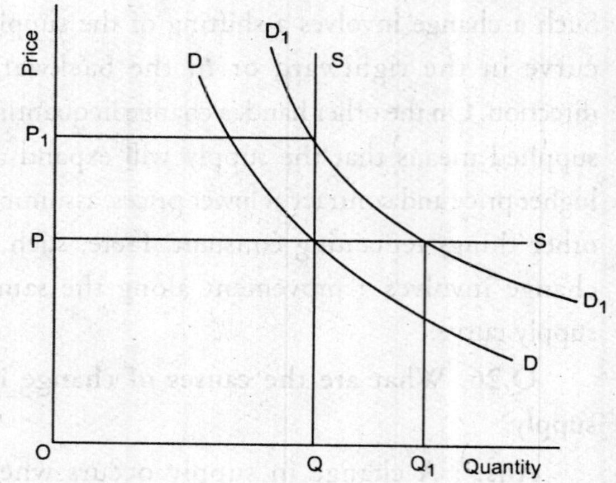

Fig. 17.6

increase in demand from DD to D_1D_1 causes price to increase to OP_1, but the equilibrium quantity remains the same (OQ).

Q.29. Determine equilibrium price by drawing demand and supply curves. What will happen to equilibrium price if (a) only demand increases, (b) only supply increases, and (c) both demand and supply?

Ans. : (a) Suppose DD is the original demand curve and SS is the supply curve (Fig. 17.7). Point E is the equilibrium point. So, equilibrium price becomes OP. Now if demand increases to D_1D_1, new equilibrium point will be E_1. Thus,

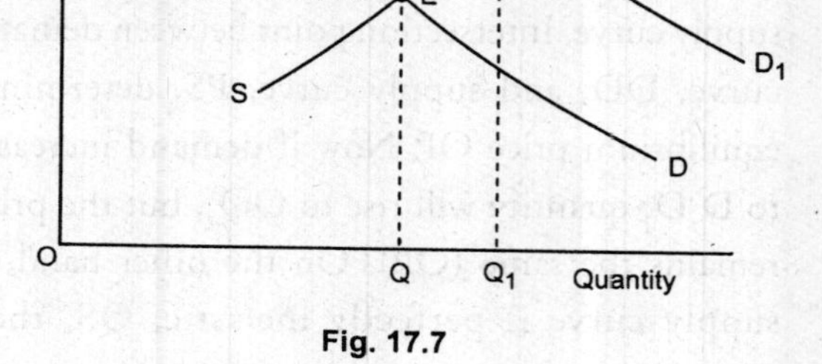

Fig. 17.7

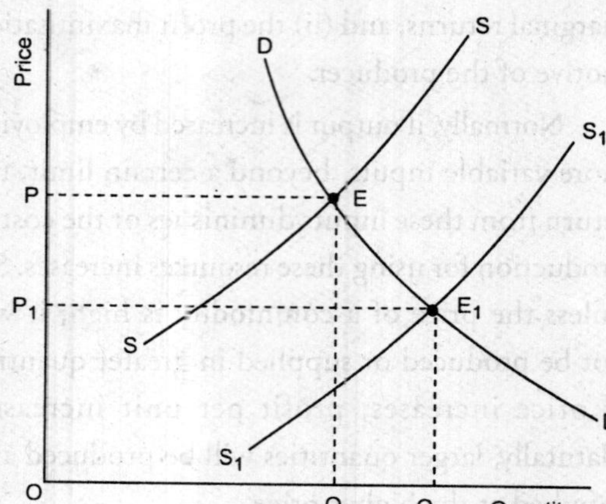

Fig. 17.8

equilibrium price rises from OP to OP_1.

(b) SS is the initial supply curve intersecting demand curve DD at point E (Fig. 17.8). Thus, equilibrium price is OP. As supply increases supply curve shifts to S_1S_1. This new supply curve cuts the demand curve at E_1. Accordingly, price declines from OP to OP_1.

(c) If both demand and supply increase, equilibrium price may increase, decrease or remain the same.

PREFERENCE THEORY OF DEMAND

Q.1. What are total utility and marginal utility?

Ans. : Total utility of anything to an individual is the total pleasure or benefit it yields at a given period of time. Marginal utility is the change in total utility resulting from a change in the consumption of that commodity i.e., MU = $TU_n - TU_{n-1}$. This means that MU is the difference between total utility obtained from the n-th unit and n–1th unit of the commodity.

Q.2. What is the relation between marginal utility curve and the demand curve?

Ans. : Demand curve for a commodity is related to the marginal utility (MU) curve. MU curve is a downward sloping curve. A consumer reaches equilibrium when MU of a commodity equals its price. MU curve is a diminishing one which leads to a negative sloping demand curve.

Q.3. Define income effect, substitution effect and price effect.

Ans. : If the price of a commodity, tastes and preferences of a consumer, etc., remain unchanged, change in income of the consumer involves a change in satisfaction. A consumer will then be able to enjoy more (less) satisfaction as his income rises (falls). The result of this type of change is known as *income effect.*

Given a constant money income, a change in relative prices involves a change in the purchase pattern of the consumer. He substitutes the relatively cheaper goods for the relatively dearer ones. The change is known as the *substitution effect.*

A consumer's purchase plan undergoes a change with the change in the price of one of commodities, money income remaining constant. Change in relative prices alone yields a greater or a smaller satisfaction than before because real income has changed. This change is called the *price effect.*

Q.4. Are Giffen goods and inferior goods the same commodity?

Or

What is the difference between Giffen good and inferior good? (C.U. 2008)

Ans. : Giffen goods and inferior goods are not the same commodity. There are some commodities whose demand fall as income of the consumer rises. These commodities are called inferior goods. So, inferior goods are those goods whose income effect is negative.

On the other hand, in case of some commodities when price rises (falls) consumers buy more (less). These commodities are called Giffen goods, after the name of Sir Robert Giffen.

Thus, inferior goods is an income phenomenon and Giffen goods is a price phenomenon.

Q.5. State the condition of consumer's equilibrium in terms of utility approach.

Ans. : A consumer will reach equilibrium when marginal utility from commodity X (MU_X) is equal to its price (P_X) i.e., $MU_X = P_X$. However, in the case of two commodities, say, X and Y, a consumer will reach equilibrium when the ratio of marginal utilities for X and Y, i.e., $\frac{MU_X}{MU_Y}$ is equal to the price ratio, $\left(\text{i.e., } \frac{P_X}{P_Y}\right)$

$$\text{or } \frac{MU_X}{MU_Y} = \frac{P_X}{P_Y}.$$

Q.6. What is an indifference curve?

Ans. : An indifference curve represents different combinations of two goods that yield the same level of satisfaction to a consumer. He cannot say which combination gives him the best satisfaction. As all combinations give him same satisfaction level, a consumer remains indifferent on the curve.

Q.7. Why is an indifference curve convex to the origin?

Ans. : An indifference curve is convex to the origin because of diminishing marginal rate of substitution (MRS) between two goods.

Q.8. What is marginal rate of substitution? (C.U. 2007)

Ans. : The marginal rate of substitution (MRS) is the rate at which one good, say Y, can be substituted for another good, say X, so that the satisfaction of the consumer remains unchanged. The slope of an indifference curve is the MRS between two goods.

Q.9. What is price line?

Ans. : Price line shows different purchasable combination of two goods that a consumer can buy with his limited money income and given prices of two goods. The slope of the budget line is the price ratio of two goods, i.e.,

$$\frac{P_X}{P_Y}$$

Q.10. What is an indifference map?

Ans. : A family or a set of indifference curves is called an indifference map. A consumer is indifferent between different points on an indifference curve. On the other hand, a consumer expresses his preference in an indifference map.

Q.11. How do you explain consumer's equilibrium in terms of ordinal approach?

Ans. : A consumer reaches equilibrium when the following two conditions for equilibrium are satisfied simultaneously. *First* is the equality between the slopes of indifference curve and the budget line, i.e., $MRS_{XY} = \frac{P_X}{P_Y}$. This condition is called necessary condition for equilibrium. Sufficient condition requires that an indifference curve must be convex to the origin.

Q.12. What is an income consumption curve?

Ans. : An income consumption curve shows the various optimum levels of consumption of two goods that a consumer purchases at various levels of income, holding prices of two goods constant. Income consumption curve may be positive sloping as well as negative sloping.

Q.13. What is price consumption curve?

Ans. : Price consumption curve shows various optimum consumption combinations of two goods that a consumer purchases at various prices, holding price of another commodity and money income constant.

Q.14. Draw an indifference curve for which MRS is constant.

Ans. : MRS remains constant when indifference curve becomes a straight line. An

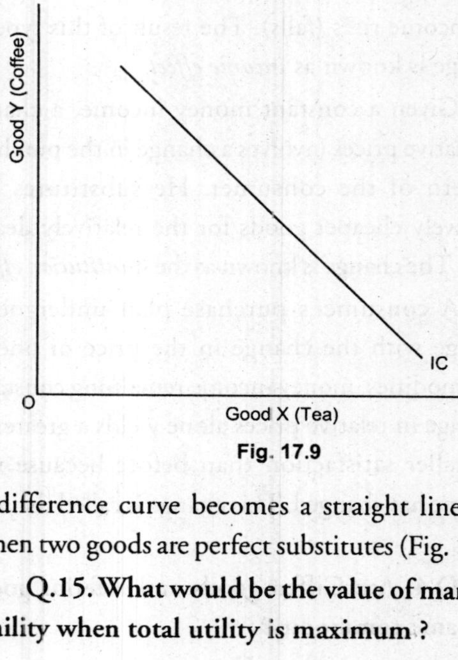

Fig. 17.9

indifference curve becomes a straight line only when two goods are perfect substitutes (Fig. 17.9).

Q.15. What would be the value of marginal unility when total utility is maximum? (C.U. 2008)

Ans. : Marginal utility becomes zero when total utility is maximum.

Q.16. What are the characteristics of an indifference curve? (C.U. 2007)

Ans. : An indifference curve has three properties : (i) It has a negative slope. (ii) It is convex to the origin. (iii) No two indifference curves intersect or touch each other.

THEORY OF PRODUCTION

Q.1. Define average product (AP) and marginal product (MP).

Ans. : AP is the total product per unit of a variable input. MP is the change in total product consequent upon a change in variable input.

Q.2. What is meant by 'short run' and 'long run' in the analysis of a firm.

Or

Distinguish between 'shor trun' and 'long run' in the context of production (C.U. 2007)

Ans. : Short run is that time period when a firm cannot change all its inputs; some are held fixed. Output can, therefore, be increased by changing only variable inputs. Long period is that time period when the firm can change all its inputs including fixed inputs. In the long run, all inputs are, therefore, variable.

Q.3. How do total product, average product and marginal product change due to a change in the use of one input, keeping other inputs constant?

Ans. : For simplicity, we are assuming that labour is the only variable input while other inputs are constant. Now, if number of labourers are increased with fixed inputs, initially total product (TP), average product (AP) and marginal product (MP) will increase as TP increases at an increasing rate. Further employment of labour will cause TP to increase at a diminishing rate. Consequently, AP and MP will decline. When TP becomes maximum, MP becomes zero. Now, more employment of labour will lead to a fall in TP and MP will be negative.

Q.4. What is meant by production function? (C.U. 2007)

Ans. : A production function is a technological or an engineering relationship between inputs and output. A production function is usually written as :

$$Q = f(a, b, c, d \ldots)$$

where Q is the amount of output; and a, b, c, d, etc., are inputs.

Though product on function refers to a technological relationship, the concept is useful in economic theory as t is related to the costs of production of a unit.

Q.5. What is the difference between returns to an input and returns to scale?

Ans. : By returns to an input we mean the laws of change in output following a change in one or two inputs, keeping other inputs constant. Thus, this law remains valid in the short run. If all inputs are changed and output changes then we obtain laws of returns to scale which is a longrun phenomenon.

Q.6. What is meant by scale of production?

Ans. : In the long run there are no fixed inputs; all inputs are variable. A firm can instal a new machine or build up a new factory shade or switch over from one technique of production to another in the long run. This means that a firm can change its scale of operations or scale of output by changing all its inputs. This is called a change in scale of production.

Q.7. Define increasing returns to scale (IRS), constant returns to scale (CRS) and diminishing returns to scale (DRS).

Ans. : *IRS*: IRS is characterised by a situation where doubling or trebling of all inputs causes output to increase more than proportionately—then we say that the returns to scale are increasing.

CRS: If a given percentage increase in inputs causes output to increase by the same percentage, then CRS is said to have occurred. If output is doubled following the doubling of inputs then output growth is subject to CRS.

DRS: Output growth is subject to DRS if a given percentage increase in inputs leads to a smaller percentage increase in output. This means that doubling of inputs causes output to increase less than double.

Q.8. What is an isoquant?

Ans. : An isoquant shows different combinations of two inputs that produces a specified amount of output. On an isoquant, same level of output is obtained by using different combinations of two inputs. That is why an isoquant is called production indifference curve.

Q.9. Define marginal rate of technical substitution (MRTS).

Ans. : MRTS of labour for capital is the amount of capital that can be replaced by a 1 unit increase in labour, so that output remains constant. That is

$$MRTS_{K \text{ for } L} = -\frac{\Delta K}{\Delta L}$$

$$\text{or } MRTS_{L \text{ for } K} = -\frac{\Delta L}{\Delta K}.$$

Q.10. What is an isocost line?

Ans. : An isocost line shows various combinations of two inputs, say, labour and capital, that can be purchased for a given amount of expenditure. The slope of the isocost line is equal to the negative price ratio of two inputs.

Q.11. What do you mean by output expansion path?

Ans. : By joining various points of tangency between isoquants and parallely shifted isocost lines, one obtains output expansion path. It shows how input combinations change when output changes, keeping input prices constant.

Q.12. What do you mean by economies of large scale production?

Ans. : By scale of production we mean the size of a business or production unit. When a business unit expands its size of production (by increasing all the factors of productions), it secures certain advantages. These are known as economies of large scale production.

Q.13. Define internal and external economies of large scale production.

Or

What is the internal economy of a firm?

(C.U. 2008)

Ans. : Internal economies of production arise when the benefits or advantages of a firm's expansion are enjoyed by the firm itself. Thus, internal economies accrue only to the individual firm by its own organisational ability and effort. These are called internal because the scale economies are within the control of the firm.

External economies arise when an increase in a firm's expansion produces favourable effects on other firms. In other words, benefits of increased production spread to other firms in the industry or in the region. Thus, external economies are available to all firms in the industry, irrespective of their sizes. These are called external because the scale economies are outside the control of the firm.

Q.14. Name different types of internal and external economies of large scale production.

Ans. : Internal economies of large scale production can be grouped into (a) technological, (b) managerial, (c) marketing, (d) financial, and (e) risk distributional economies.

External economies are of the following types : (a) economies of localisation, (b) economies of research and information, and (c) economies of specialisation.

Q.15. What are diseconomies of scale?

Ans. : Economies of scale can never be unlimited. As a result, expansion beyond a certain stage will not cause costs to decline. Instead, it will rise as the firm expands. In other words, when the size of a firm becomes large, possibilities for economies get exhausted and diseconomies set in.

THE THEORY OF COST

Q.1. What is an opportunity cost?

Ans. : We know that resources are scarce. But they have alternative uses. A single plot of land can be used either for the production of paddy or wheat. When paddy is produced, the resources used in its production would not be used in the production of alternative goods, wheat. This means that the opportunity cost or alternative cost of paddy is the amount of output of wheat given up. So, the opportunity cost of anything is the next best alternative goods that is sacrificed.

Q.2. What are the fixed costs of a firm? Give examples.

Ans. : A firm uses two inputs—fixed inputs and variable inputs. Costs that arise due to the use of fixed inputs are called fixed costs. Whatever the level of output, fixed cost remains the same. Fixed costs are the following : (a) depreciation charges, (b) maintenance charge and rent for factory building, (c) interest cost on loans, (d) salaries of high ranking officials, (e) normal profit, etc.

Q.3. Explain why fixed cost does not enter into marginal cost of production.

Ans. : We know that

$MC_n = TC_n - TC_{n-1}$,

where n may be any number.

$$= (FC + VC_n) - (FC + VC_{n-1})$$

$$[\because TC = FC + VC]$$

$$= FC + VC_n - FC - VC_{n-1}$$

$$\therefore MC_n = VC_n - VC_{n-1}$$

Hence, MC is the addition to the total variable costs attributable to the addition of total output from n–1 units to n units of output.

Q.4. What are the variable costs of a firm? Give examples.

Ans. : A firm, while carrying production, employs both fixed and variable inputs. Costs that arise due to the use of variable inputs are known as variable costs (VC). It is dependent on the level of output. As output increases, VC increases. If output is zero, VC will be zero. VC includes (a) cost of buying raw materials, (b) wages of labour, (c) transport charges, (d) electricity charges, etc.

Q.5. Explain why does the minimum point of MC curve occur to the left of the minimum point of AC curve?

Ans. : Average cost or AC is the sumtotal of average fixed cost (AFC) and average variable cost (AVC). Thus, the shape of AC curve is determined by the shapes of AFC and AVC curves. On the other hand, shape of MC curve is determined only by the variable costs, and not fixed costs. For this reason, minimum point of AC lies to the right of the minimum point of MC.

Q.6. Is AFC curve U-shaped? If not, what is the possible shape of AFC curve?

What is the shape of the average fixed cost curve of a firm? (C.U. 2008)

Ans. : AFC curve is not U-shaped. Acutually, it is a rectangular hyperbola curve. As output increases, AFC continuously falls. But it is asymptotic to both the axes because AFC can never be zero (Fig. 17.10).

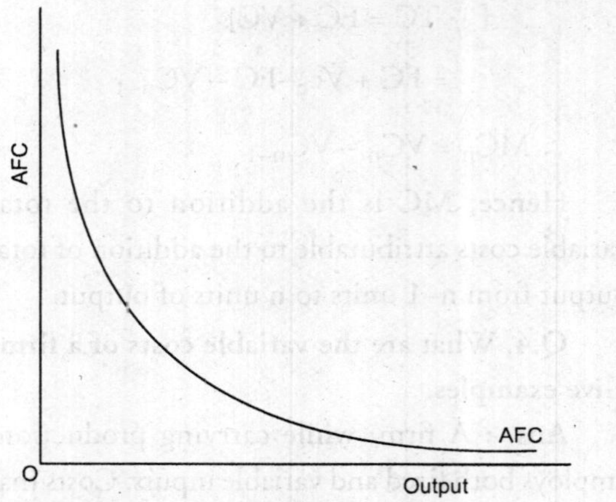

Fig. 17.10

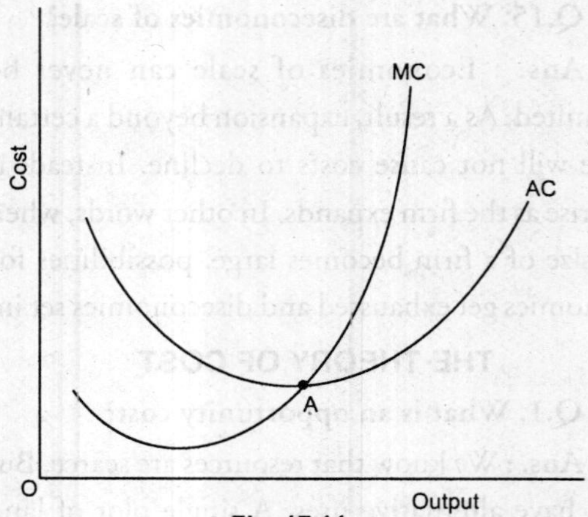

Fig. 17.11

Q.7. Will AC rise or fall when MC exceeds AC? If MC = AC, how will AC behave?

Ans. : The MC curve will always intersect at the minimum point of AC curve. This can be established by showing the relation between MC and AC. So long as the MC curve lies below the AC curve, the AC curve will be falling and, so long as MC lies above the AC, AC will be rising. At the point of intersection of the MC and AC curves, the AC curve reaches its minimum level. The slope of AC becomes zero at the minimum point of AC curve (Fig. 17.11).

Q.8. If all inputs are increased simultaneously will AC increase due to the law of diminishing marginal productivity?

Ans. : When all inputs are increased simultaneously, production is subject to the laws of returns to scale rather than the laws of returns to an input. If the rate of increase in output exceeds the rate of increase in inputs, production will be governed by the law of increasing returns to scale. On the other hand, if the rate of increase in input is greater than that of output we will experience law of diminishing returns to scale, and not law of diminishing marginal productivity. Consequently, in the long run AC will rise.

Q.9. All costs are variable costs in the long run. Explain.

Ans. : The long period refers to a period of time when the firm can change not only its variable factors of production but also fixed factors of production. In such a time period, the firm can construct a new building, or buy a new machine, or change its scale of production. Naturally, as in the long run all inputs are variable all costs are variable costs.

Q.10. Law of diminishing returns states that the marginal product gradually decreases, while total output increases. Do you accept this statement?

Ans. : This statement is partly correct. When total returns increase at an increasing rate, marginal returns increase. But after a while, when total returns increase at a diminishing rate, marginal returns gradually decline and it becomes negative when total returns decline.

Q.11. What do you mean by short period and long period in price theory?

Ans. : Short period is that period when a firm cannot change its fixed inputs. Fixed inputs are held constant in the short run. Further, it refers to that period when demand for a commodity can be adjusted with the supply of a commodity.

On the other hand, long period is that time period when the firm can change even its fixed inputs. In fact, in the long run all inputs are variable. In the long run, therefore, the firm can change its scale of production. Further, in the long run, supply of a commodity is adjusted to the demand.

PRICE DETERMINATION IN PERFECT AND IMPERFECT COMPETITION

Q.1. Clearly state what do you mean by 'market' in economics.

Ans. : In economics, market does not refer to a place. A market is an institution where buyers and sellers meet together to carry out their transactions i.e., purchase and sale of a commodity or an input.

Q.2. Define total revenue (TR), average revenue (AR), and marginal revenue (MR).

Ans. : Total revenue (TR) is the receipt that a firm earns from selling various amounts of its product at a given price. Thus, TR is the price per unit (p) multiplied by the number of goods sold (q). That is,

$$TR = p \times q$$

Average revenue is the income which a firm earns from the sale of goods. That is,

$$AR = \frac{TR}{q},$$

Marginal revenue is the change in total revenue resulting from a change in the number of goods sold or output. In fact, MR is the revenue earned for one unit of output or goods sold. So,

$$MR = \frac{\Delta TR}{\Delta q},$$

$$\frac{\Delta TR}{\Delta q} = \frac{\text{change in total revenue}}{\text{change in number of goods sold}}$$

Q.3. Under what condition demand curve, AR curve and price line are the same?

Ans. : Irrespective of the market situation, demand curve or AR curve and price line are same. AR is obtained by dividing total revenue by the total output sold. Total revenue is the price per unit of output multiplied by the number of units of output sold. Suppose, a seller sells 10 units of a goods at the rate of Rs. 5 per unit. Thus, total revenue is Rs. 50. Now by dividing total revenue by output we get AR. Thus, by definition, AR and price are identical. And, this AR curve is the demand curve which shows various quantities of a commodity that can be bought at various price. Thus, AR = P = Demand.

Q.4. Is the MR curve identical with the AR curve for an individual firm under perfect competition?

Or

What is the shape of the AR curve in a perfectly competitive market? (C.U. 2007)

Ans. : Under perfect competition, every buyer and seller behaves as a price-taker. That is why price and AR are identical. As in a competitive firm price remains the same, AR also remains unchanged. By MR we mean change in revenue resulting from a change in output. Thus, AR coincides with MR, i.e., AR = MR.

Q.5. When will the average revenue and marginal revenue be different?

Ans. : Under imperfect competition, since a seller can influence the price of a product, both average revenue and marginal revenue curves become downward sloping, but average revenue becomes greater than marginal revenue. In other words, under imperfect competition, AR curve lies above the MR curve, i.e., AR > MR.

Q.6. Suppose the average revenue curve of a firm is a horizontal straight line. Draw a total revenue curve in this situation.

Ans. : Under perfect competition as sellers behave as 'price-takers', they cannot influence the

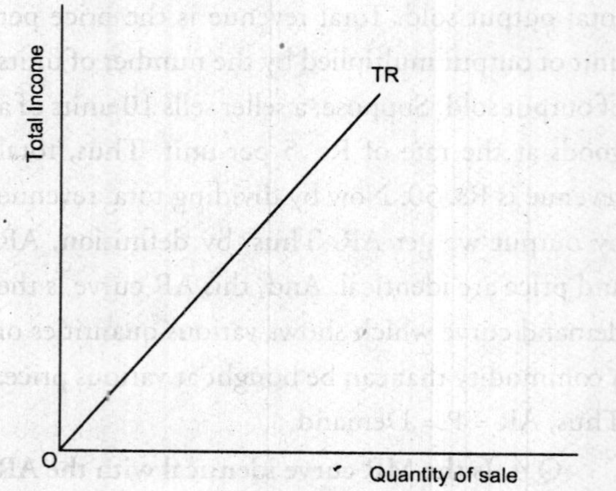

Fig. 17.12

price. At a given price, sellers can sell any amount as they like. In such a situation, total revenue rises proportionately with the increase in sales. This means that TR curve is a straight line rising curve starting from the origin, shown in Fig. 17.12.

Q.7. Mention the conditions of equilibrium of a firm.

Or

What are the conditions of profit maximisation of a firm? (C.U. 2008)

Ans. : Irrespective of the market conditions, a firm will be in equilibrium if two conditions are simultaneously fulfilled. *First* is the equality between MC and MR. This condition is known as necessary condition. *Second* is that MC curve must cut the MR curve from below. This condition is known as sufficient condition.

Q.8. What are the features of perfect competition?

Or

Write down four characteristics of perfect competition. (C.U. 2008)

Ans. : A product market is said to be a perfectly competitive one if the following conditions are fulfilled :

(a) There exists innumerable number of sellers and buyers. (b) Sellers behave as 'price-takers'. Buyers also cannot influence the price ruling in the market. Consequently, AR curve = price line becomes perfectly elastic. (c) Sellers sell homogeneous goods. (d) In the long run, there is perfect freedom of entry and exist. (e) Factors of production are perfectly mobile.

Q.9. Why would a firm under pure competition never want to spend any money on advertisement for his product?

Ans. : Under pure competition, sellers sell homogeneous goods. This means that to the buyers all the available goods in the market are perfect substitutes. Naturally, sellers are not willing to spend on advertisement for his product to buyers.

Q.10. Why does a firm in pure competition operate in the rising portion of its MC curve?

Ans. : A firm under perfect competition, in order to maximise profit, operates at the rising

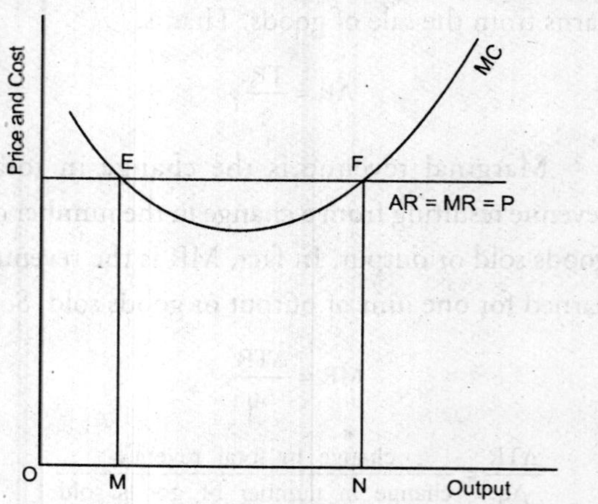

Fig. 17.13

portion of its MC curve. In terms of figure (17.13), a firm should operate at point F, rather than E where MC curve is falling. At E, profit can never be maximum by producing OM output. If a firm decides to raise output (up to ON) its revenue will increase than its cost. So a producer determines its output level at the rising portion of its MC curve.

Q.11. Is it possible for a competitive firm to earn supernormal profit or sustain loss in the long run?

Ans. : In the long run, a competitive firm enjoys only normal profit, because of free entry and free exit of firms in the industry. If some firms earn supernormal profit, other firms will join the industry and pull down the volume of supernormal profit. Similarly, sustenance of loss by some firms will cause them to leave the industry and, ultimately, loss will be eliminated.

Q.12. Is it correct to say that in the short run a profit-maximising firm under perfect competition may produce under a loss?

Ans. : In the short run, a perfectly competitive firm faces two types of cost—fixed cost and variable cost. If the firm fails to cover not only fixed cost but also a part of the variable cost it will shut down the business. But, if it covers up just the variable cost still then it will continue business with the hope of managing a part of the fixed cost in the near future.

Q.13. What is a shutdown point?

Ans. : If the price of the product of a competitive firm is just equal to the minimum average variable cost (AVC), the firm reaches shutdown point. When price becomes equal to minimum AVC, the firm covers up its variable cost only. So, when price = minimum AVC, the shutdown point emerges.

Q.14. Where does a competitive firm's breakeven point occur. (C.U. 2007)

Ans. : Breakeven point is that point where price of a product of a competitive firm becomes equal to minimum AC. This amounts to saying that the firm covers up total cost (both fixed cost and variable cost) including normal profit. So, at the breakeven point price or AR becomes equal to minimum AC.

Q.15. You know demand curves are negatively sloped. Then how do you reconcile it with horizontal demand curve under perfect competition?

Ans. : Negative sloping demand curve shows how the consumers demand larger (or smaller) quantities of a commodity at a lower (or high) prices. The market price is the result of the demand and supply of the commodity in the market or the industry. Once this price is determined, a competitive firm has to accept this price since the competitive firm behaves as a price-taker. A price-taker can sell any amount at the ruling price. That is why the demand curve faced by a competitive firm is a horizontal straight line.

Q.16. How is the short run supply curve of a competitive firm obtained?

Ans. : Short run MC curve that lies above the AVC curve is called the short run supply curve of a competitive firm.

Q.17. Is it possible to derive the long run supply curve of a competitive industry from the long run MC curves of all firms?

Ans. : In the long run, the supply curve of a competitive industry cannot be obtained by summing up the short run MC curves of firms. The shape of a supply curve in the long run is governed by the laws of production or cost conditions. If production is subject to the law of constant cost, the supply curve of an industry will be a straight line parallel to the horizontal axis. If increasing costs operate, the supply curve would be upward rising and downward sloping in the case of diminishing costs.

Q.18. When does a market become competitive and when it becomes imperfectly competitive?

Ans. : A competitive firm is characterised by (i) inumerable number of sellers, (ii) homogeneous goods; (iii) given price, and (iv) free entry and exit. If one of these features are absent the market becomes imperfectly competitive which has different variants, like monopoly, monopolistic competition and oligopoly.

Q.19. What is the shape of the total revenue curve under monopoly?

Ans. : Under imperfect competition or monopoly, if a firm intends to sell more it will have to cut down price. As price declines TR rises following an increase in sales. However, TR becomes maximum at a particular level of output sold. After that, TR declines and it reduces to zero (see Fig. 17.14).

Q.20. Why does not a monopoly producer operate at the inelastic range of his demand curve?

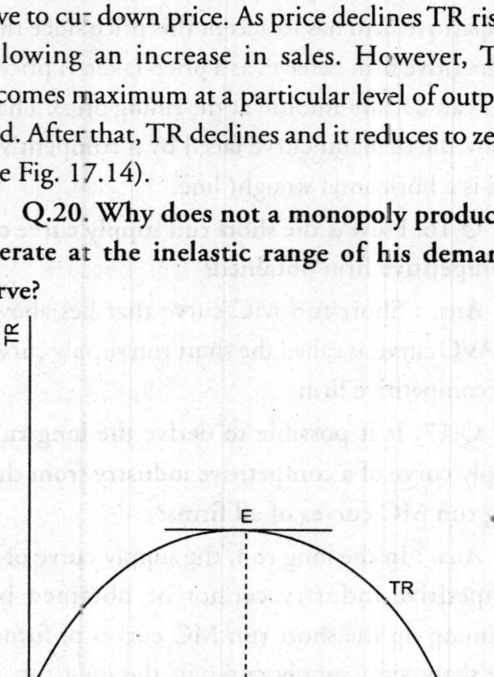

Fig. 17.14

Ans. : In the inelastic range of the demand curve, marginal revenue becomes negative. We know that marginal cost is always positive. As negative marginal revenue cannot be equated with the positive marginal cost, a monopolist does not operate at the inelastic range of his demand curve. Only at the elastic range of the demand curve marginal revenue is positive where he produces.

Q.21. What is the basic difference between the equilibrium of a competitive firm and monopoly firm?

Ans. : A competitive firm will be in equilibrium when MC = MR = AR. But, as monopolist's MR curve lies below the AR curve, he will be in equilibrium when MC = MR < AR.

Q.22. What is meant by price discrimination by a monopolist?

Ans. : Price discrimination is said to exist when sellers charge different prices to different buyers for his product. Price discrimination is possible under monopoly since a monopolist pursues an independent price policy.

Q.23. When is price discrimination profitable?

Ans. : Price discrimination will be profitable if two conditions are fulfilled. These are (a) elasticities of demand for a product at a given monopoly price must be different in different markets; and (b) marginal revenues in all markets must be the same.

Q.24. Could you discriminate between buyers while selling a product under perfect competition?

Ans. : Price discrimination is impossible under perfect competition since sellers behave as price-takers. Buyers also know the price of the product ruling in the market. Neither buyer nor seller can influence the price in any direction. Price discrimination is only possible under monopoly where a monopoly seller behaves as the price-setter.

Q.25. What is monopolistic competition?

Ans. : Monopolistic competition is an admixture of both perfect competition and monopoly. Here large number of sellers sell differentiated goods. Sellers also behave as price-makers.

Q.26. What is oligopoly?

Ans. : An oligopoly market is said to exist where the number of sellers is very few. Price rigidity is one of the characteristics of the oligopoly market.

Q.27. The monopolistically competitive firm may engage in non-price competition. Give two instances of such non-price competition.

Ans. : Product variation and selling costs are two important forms of non-price competition. According to Chamberlin, in monopolistic competition, sellers adopt non-aggressive price policies. They compete with each other just by varying the product and by altering the magnitude of selling costs than by changing prices.

Q.28. Why is monopoly price greater than marginal revenue under monopoly?

Ans. : Under monopoly, if the seller wants to sell a larger quantity he will have to lower down the price of his product. As a result, average revenue declines. As average revenue declines marginal revenue must decline and marginal revenue becomes less than average revenue or price (MR < AR = P).

Q.29. Why does a monopolistically competitive producer fail to operate at the minimum point of his AC curve? What is its economic significance?

Ans. : A monopolistically competitive firm faces a downward sloping demand curve which can never be tangential to the AC curve at its minimum point. Because of the nature of demand curve, the firm must operate somewhere to the left of the minimum point of the AC curve.

Operation in this range of AC curve implies that the firm fails to operate at optimum stage. An excess capacity develops resulting in a smaller output than perfectly competitive output and higher prices than competitive prices.

Q.30. What are the competitive elements and monopoly elements of monopolistic competition?

Ans. : Competitive elements of monopolistic competition are (a) existence of many competing firms; (b) free entry and exit in the long run; (c) P = AC in the longrun; (d) occurrence of only normal profit in the long run and supernormal profit, loss as well as normal profit in the short run.

Monopoly elements are the following: (a) negative sloping AR and MR curves; (b) equilibrium is attained when MC = MR < AR; (c) existence of monopoly of a producer due to differentiated products; (d) higher price and smaller output; (h) excess capacity.

Q.31. Why, instead of industry, is the word 'group' used in monopolistic competition?

Ans. : Industry refers to a collection of firms that produce homogeneous goods. But under monopolistic competition we have product heterogeneity. That is why Chamberlin preferred the word 'group' instead of industry. By 'group', he meant number of sellers whose goods are close substitutes.

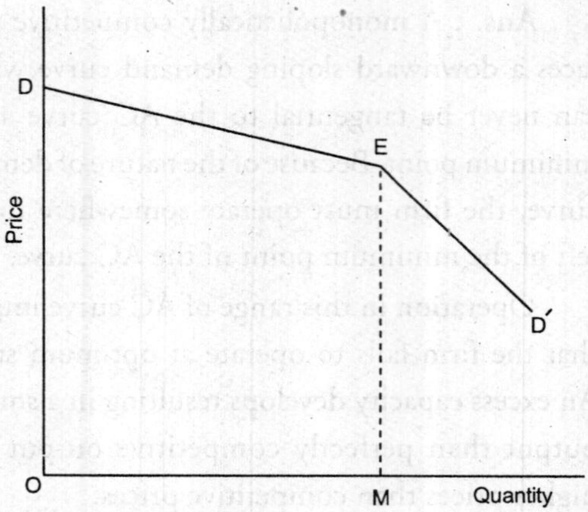

Fig. 17.15

Q.32. Why are selling costs or advertisement costs incurred in a monopolistically competitive market?

Ans. : In a monopolistic competitive market, sellers sell heterogeneous goods. These goods are treated as close substitutes to each other, but not perfect substitutes. That is why, sellers in order to attract customers to their own products spend money for advertisement. This advertisement cost is regarded as a part of the selling cost.

Q.33. Why is price higher under monopolistic competition?

Ans. : Under monopoly or monopolistic competition, AR diverges from MR and AR curve lies above MR curve. But, in perfect competition AR curve coincides with MR curve. That is why price is higher in monopoly or monopolistic competition than under perfect competition.

Q.34. Will a competitive producer, monopoly producer and monopolistically competitive producer earn supernormal profit in the longrun?

Ans. : Because of free entry, a competitive firm in the long run never earns supernormal profit. It earns only normal profit. That is why P = AR = MR = MC. Similarly, a monopolistically competitive producer also enjoys normal profit on the same ground i.e., free entry and free exit. Though P < MR, still then a monopolistically competitive producer earns normal profit in the long run. On the other hand, entry of new firms is blocked under monopoly.

Q.35. Draw a kinked demand curve and show that price is inflexible in the oligopoly market.

Ans. : Under oligopoly, demand curve is kinked at the ruling market price. If a seller cuts the price of his product, other sellers will follow him. That is why, in the range ED′, demand curve is inelastic (Fig. 17.15). On the other hand, if a seller increases the price of his product, other sellers will not follow him. That is why, in the range DE, demand curve is elastic. As price in this market remains unchanged, demand curve is kinked at the price ME

Q. 36. What is the absolute value of the price elasticity of demand, when marginal revenue is zero? (C.U. 2008)

Ans. : The absolute value of the price elasticity is unity when merginal revenue becomes zero and total revenue becomes maximum.

MARGINAL PRODUCTIVITY THEORY—FACTOR PRICING THEORY

Q.1. Define marginal physical product (MPP), value of the marginal product (VMP), and marginal revenue product (MRP) of a variable input.

Or

What is the difference between marginal physical product and marginal revenue product? (C.U. 2007)

Ans. : MPP is the change in total product attributable to a change in the use of a variable input. When MPP is expressed in money firms, we obtain VMP. MRP is the change in total revenue following a change in the employment of a variable input.

Q.2. Why is an input demand called 'derived demand'?

Ans. : An input demand is a derived demand in the sense that inputs are not directly demanded. We first demand goods. To meet the consumers' demand, producers demand inputs. Thus, first comes consumer demand and after that input demand. As an input demand is obtained from the consumption demand, demand for an input is a derived demand.

Q.3. Under what conditions value of the marginal physical product (VMP) of an input is equal to the marginal revenue product (MRP) of that input and VMP is not equal to MRP?

Ans. : If perfect competition in the product market exists, VMP = MRP. But under imperfect competition in the product market, VMP diverges from MRP, and VMP > MRP.

Q.4. How do you explain the demand curve of an input?

Ans. : We know that under perfect competition in the product market, VMP = MRP. If the prices of the product and of the inputs remain constant, then VMP = MRP curve of the variable input is the firm's demand curve for that input. It is a downward sloping curve indicating that at a lower price of the input more of that input will be demanded. But, under imperfect competition, MRP curve is the firm's demand curve for the variable input.

Q.5. What is economic rent?

Ans. : Economic rent is a producer's surplus beyond full cost of production. It is never fixed by contract. Economic rent is also defined as payments made for inputs whose supply is inelastic.

Q.6. Will economic rent arise if input supply is perfectly elastic and perfectly inelastic?

Ans. : Economic rent is the difference between actual earnings and the minimum supply price of an input. If input supply is perfectly elastic, rent will not arise since actual earnings and the minimum supply price of that input are the same. On the other hand, rent will arise in the case of perfectly inelastic supply since its minimum supply price is zero. The whole of its earning is the rent.

Q.7. Why do people demand money? On what factors these demand for money depend?

Or

What are the motives behind an individual's demand for money? (C.U. 2008)

Ans. : Liquidity preference or the demand for money to hold arises because of three motives—(a) transaction motive, (b) precautionary motive, and (c) speculative motive. Transaction demand for money as well as precautionary demand for money largely and directly depend on the individual's level of income. Speculative demand for money is a function of the rate of interest, increasing as the interest rate falls and decreasing as the interest rate rises.

Q.8. Distinguish between rent, wages, interest and profit.

Ans. : (a) As rent, wages and interest are contractual incomes, they can never be zero or negative. But profit may be zero, positive and negative.

(b) Rent, wages and interest are included in the cost of production. On the other hand, as profit is a surplus income, it cannot be included in the cost of production.

Q.9. What is meant by keeping money in hand for speculative purpose?

Ans. : Speculative motive for holding money refers to the desire of the people to hold cash balances to take advantage of market movements regarding the future changes in bond prices or its rate of interest. In other words, money kept for this purpose is used to make speculative gains by dealing in bonds whose prices fluctuate. Thus, money held for this purpose serves as a store of value.

Q.10. If the rate of interest declines in the market, what will be its effect on the holding of money by the public?

Ans. : When rate of interest falls people anticipate that it will rise in the future. Consequently, prices of securities go down and possibility of capital loss arises. In view of this uncertainty and anticipation regarding the future rate of interest, people will hold money in their possession. In this situation, cash becomes more attractive than securities.

Q.11. If the money income of the people go up, what will be the effect on their liquidity preference?

Ans. : Liquidity preference arises because of transaction purpose, precautionary purpose and speculative purpose. The first two types of demand for money (or liquidity preference) are directly related to the level of income. As income rises, demand for money for the said two purposes will rise.

Q.12. If the rate of interest decreases, what will be its effect on the prices of outstanding bonds in the market?

Ans. : There is an inverse relationship between the rate of interest of bonds and its prices. When the rate of interest on bonds decline people anticipate that it will rise in the future. Consequently, bond prices tend to decline.

Q.13. People demand money to satisfy 3 motives, e.g., transaction, precautionary and speculative motives. A man keeps some amount in a bank to pay his house rent. What kind of demand for money is it?

Ans. : Money is demanded for transaction, precautionary and speculative purposes. Obviously, when a man keeps some amount of money in a bank for paying house-rent it must be a transaction demand for money. It is neither a precautionary demand for money arising out of unforeseen phenomenon nor speculative demand for money (arising out of anticipation regarding the future rate of interest on securities).

Q.14. What is liquidity preference?

Ans. : Liquidity preference means desire of the public to hold cash. Of all the assets, the most liquid asset is cash. Therefore, people have the preference to hold cash rather than other assets which are less liquid than money.

Q.15. Can the rate of interest or liquidity preference fall to zero?

Ans. : Of all the assets, cash is the most liquid asset. People want to hold liquid money. As people have the preference for liquid money, liquidity preference and, hence, the rate of interest can never fall to zero.

Q.16. Can profit be zero?

Ans. : Gross profit is the difference between total revenue and total explicit cost. Once total revenue and total explicit cost becomes zero, gross profit becomes zero. But net profit is the difference between total revenue and both explicit and implicit costs. Thus, net profit can never be zero since it is the remuneration of the entrepreneur.

Q.17. What is an abnormal profit?

Ans. : If total revenue of a firm exceeds total costs of production then the profit that will emerge may be called as an 'abnormal' one.

Q.18. What is non-insurable risk?

Ans. : Risks that cannot be anticipated earlier or risks for which insurance companies never ask for insurance policy may be called non-insurable risk or uncertainty. It is uncertainty or non-insurable risk for which profit arises.

Q.19. What is pure profit?

Ans. : Profit is the differences between total revenue and total costs. Total costs include both explicit costs and implicit costs or opportunity costs. Pure profit is defined as the difference total revenue and explicit plus implicit costs.

Q.20. Distinguish between money wage and real wage. (C.U. 2008)

Ans. : Money wage or nominal wage is the wage that a worker earns after rendering his service in an office or a factory per day/week/month. The amount of goods and services which the labourer gets in exchange of his labour service is called real wage.

ECONOMIC GROWTH TRENDS IN INDIA

Q.1. What is macroeconomic environment?

Ans. : Macroeconomic environment of business has broad reference to the broad characteristics of the economic system in which firms attempt to carry out their activities. It refers to the institutional framework of the environment in which fundamental economic problems are solved.

Q.2. What are the essential elements of macroeconomic environment?

Ans. : The four essential components of macroeconomic environment are (i) economic system, (ii) anatomy of the economy, (iii) national economic planning, and (iv) economic policy instruments.

Q.3. What is meant by an economic system?

Ans. : An economic system includes laws, rules and regulations, to influence what is produced, how it is produced and who gets it. Thus, the economic system refers to the totality of arrangement that the members of the communities have to make for the satisfaction of their wants.

Q.4. What is meant by a mixed economy?

Ans. : A mixed economy is characterised by the existence of both public and private sectors. However, the growth of the private sector is controlled or regulated by the government; price mechanism also operates. At the same time, administered prices rule. As all these features are present in the Indian economy, it is called a mixed economy.

Q.5. What is meant by the structure of an economy?

Ans. : It refers to an interrelationship between different sectors of the economy, i.e., primary, secondary and tertiary sectors. These three sectors constitute the structure of an economy.

Q.6. What is meant by less developed country?

Or

Mention the features of an underdeveloped economy.

Or

Indicate four characteristics of a less developed country. (C.U. 2008)

Ans. : The term undeveloped economy is a relative concept. However, a less developed economy has the following distinguishing characteristics: (a) low per capita income; (b) significant dependence on the primary sector, mainly agriculture; (c) unutilisation or under-utilisation of resources; (d) rapid growth of population; (e) vast unemployment problem.

Q.7. Which country has the highest per capita income?

Ans. : The highest per capita income nation is Norway. Its per capita income was $ 66,530 in 2006.

Q.8. At present, how much is India's national income and per capita income?

Ans. : India's national income in 2007-08 stood at Rs 27,67,682 crore at 1999-2000 prices. Per capita income of an average Indian at that time came to Rs 24,321 p.a. or Rs 2,027 p.m.

Q.9. Which method is used to measure India's national income?

Ans. : To measure national income, the National Income Committee uses commodity flow approach and incomes received approach. In agriculture and industry, the former method and in other sectors, the last method is used. However, in certain sectors, such as small enterprises both the approaches are used.

Q.10. Mention the contribution of different economic sectors towards India's national income.

Or

What is the recent contribution of the service sector to India's national income ?

(C.U. 2008)

Ans. : The shares of primary sector, secondary sector and tertiary sector towards national income in 2007-08 were 19.5 p.c., 24.9 p.c. and 55.7 p.c., respectively.

Q.11. Mention the various causes responsible for the slow growth of national income in India.

Ans. : Following are the causes responsible for the slow growth of national income in India : (a) uncertainty in agricultural output due to natural calamities, like flood or drought; (b) sluggishness in industrial production due to acute power crisis; (c) faulty planning; etc.

Q.12. Define national income.

Ans. : National income is the aggregate money value of all goods and services produced in a year. Or it is the sumtotal of incomes of all factor owners.

Q.13. What is value added method? How is it calculated?

Ans. : To measure the contribution to current output, the value of the intermediate materials that a firm purchases must be subtracted from the value of its own, the difference being the firm's value added. Suppose, a farmer sells wheat of Rs 5 only to a flour mill owner. If the mill owner now sells flour to the bakery at Rs 8 only, then the mill's value added is Rs 3 only. Bread manufacturer, then sells it to the buyer at Rs 10 only, therefore, its value added is Rs 20 only. If all these value added of intermediate stages of bread production are summed up (i.e., Rs 5+ Rs 3 +Rs 2), the price of bread then becomes Rs. 10 only.

Q.14. What is transfer income?

Ans. : Transfer income is excluded from national income since such income does not represent payment for contributing the production of goods and services. It is just the transfer of income from one pocket to another pocket.

Q.15. What are the components of business environment in India? (C.U. 2007)

Ans. : The main components of Indian business environment are (i) mixed economic system where public and private sectors function; (ii) national economic planning known as indicative planning; (iii) replacement of inward-looking strategies of development pursued during 1950-91 by outward-looking strategy of development.

Q.16. What is poverty line? (C.U. 2008)

Ans. : If a person is unable to bear the expenditure required for maintenance of nutritional norms, say daily calorie intake of 2,400 per person in rural areas and 2,100 in urban areas then he is categorised as poor man living below the poverty line. This expenditure is officially estimated at Rs 228.9 per capita per month in rural areas and Rs 264.1 in urban areas at 1993-94 prices.

Q.17. Distinguish between GNP and GDP (C.U. 2007)

Ans. : GNP is a broader concept than GDP. GDP is the market value of all goods and services produced by factors of production located and paid for in the domestic economy, even if these factors are located abroad. GNP includes GDP plus net property income from abroad. It, thus, includes income that nations earn from abroad. On the other hand, GDP is concerned with incomes generated domestically even by the foreigners.

INDIAN AGRICULTURE—PROBLEMS, PERFORMANCE AND POLICIES

Q.1. How far is it true that the Indian economy is an agrarian economy?

Ans. : Occupational pattern and the contribution of agricultural sector towards national income indicate India's economy as an agrarian one. According to the 2001 census, of the total work force, 64 p.c. people were engaged in the agricultural sector and the rest in the secondary, and tertiary sectors. During 2007-08, agriculture contributed nearly 19.4 p.c. of our national income. In these senses, Indian economy is an agrarian one.

Q.2. Mention the causes of low agricultural productivity in India.

Ans. : Following factors are responsible for the low productivity in Indian agriculture : absence of adequate irrigation facilities, surplus agricultural labour whose marginal products are zero or negative, inadequate use of high-yielding varieties of seeds, chemical fertilisers, etc., use of old and hackneyed methods of production, inadequate use of non-farm services like finance, marketing, etc., small and fragmented land holding; reactionary land tenure system; etc.

Q.3. What measures would you recommend for improving agricultural productivity in India?

Ans. : Following measures may be suggested for improving India's agricultural productivity : extension of artificial irrigation facilities throughout the country, strengthening of the flood controlling measures, extensive use of HYV seeds, fertiliser, modern techniques of production, fallow land to be made cultivable; prevention of land erosion, liberal grant of loans to farmers, etc. Above all, structural and institutional changes must have to be made.

Q.4. Name the principal objectives of land reforms in India. (C.U. 2007)

Ans. : There are two fundamental objectives of land reform measures in India : *Firstly*, country's agrarian structure has to be rearranged in such a way that the relations between land and labour promote the growth of agriculture. *Secondly,* all feudalistic and semi-feudalistic elements of exploitation and social injustice must have to be eliminated. In sum, growth and social justice are the basic objectives of our land reform policies.

Q.5. Mention the institutional changes covered by the concept of land reforms.

Or

What are the basic steps to land reforms in India?

Ans. : The concept of land reform refers to changes in institutional factors which envisage distribution of land to the actual tillers of the soil, improve the size of farms, provide security of tenure and rent regulation, etc. Thus, the land reform measures are integral part of institutional reforms. It breaks the shackles of feudal or semi-feudal agricultural structure and distributes land-asset in favour of the landless cultivating classes.

Q.6. Mention the various measures adopted under the land reforms programme in India.

Ans. : To make the land reform policy a successful one, following measures were taken by the Government : (a) abolition of intermediaries, (b) tenancy reforms—(i) security of tenure for tenants, (ii) conferment of ownership on tenants, and (iii) regulation of rent, (c) ceiling on landholdings, (d) consolidation of scattered and fragmented land holdings, and (e) extension of cooperative farming.

Q.7. What is meant by green revolution? (C.U. 2008)

Ans. : The green revolution refers to a sudden large increase in agricultural production. The basic components of the New Agricultural Strategy are high-yielding varieties of seeds or miracle seeds, extensive application of chemical fertilisers, pesticides, etc., extension of irrigation facilities, improved agricultural machinery, etc.

Q.8. Since when has the green revolution been in operation in India?

Ans. : The result of the New Agricultural Strategy of 1966-67 is the green revolution. However, some experts of the Ford Foundation of America recommended for the introduction of the New Agricultural Strategy on an experimental basis in 1960-61.

Q.9. What is khariff crop?

Ans. : Agricultural practices in India are classified on the basis of season as khariff crop and rabi crop. Khariff crop refers to that crop which is harvested during the rainy season.

Q.10. What is rabi crop?

Ans. : Rabi crop refers to that crop which is harvested during the winter season. Examples of rabi crops are wheat, potato, etc.

Q.11. What is subsistence farming?

Ans. : Typically, Indian agriculture is based on the subsistence level. This means that farming is conducted just to meet consumption requirements of the cultivators. In other words, subsistence farming refers to that farming in which production equals consumption. No surplus foodgrain emerges.

Q.12. What is tenant farming?

Ans. : Under tenant farming, the farming society stands as the owner of large tracts of land which is divided into small holdings and is based among the member farms against the payment of a fixed rent. Each farmer can dispose off the produce the way he likes.

Q.13. What is share cropping?

Ans. : Under this, crops produced are determined in accordance with a specified norm between landowners and bargadars. The principle of share cropping will differ if the cost of cultivation is fully and/or partly borne by the landowner.

Q.14. What is 'operation barga'? (C.U. 2007)

Ans. : Bargadars are often evicted from land by the landowners. To preserve their rights on land and to improve their economic position, the West Bengal Government passed laws in this direction. Under it, the sharecropper must get legal sanction from his jotedar. This law suggests that (i) the name of the bargadars, (ii) quantum of crops produced, (iii) 'number' of the plot of land, etc., are to be given in the form of a receipt to the bargadar by the jotedar. This is known as 'operation barga'.

Q.15. Mention two sources of institutional credit in India. (C.U. 2008)

Ans. : The two sources of institutional credit provided to the agriculturists are public sector banks and cooperative banks.

INDIAN INDUSTRY—PROBLEMS, PROSPECTS AND THE ROLE OF THE GOVERNMENT

Q.1. How does agriculture promote industrial development?

Ans. : Agriculture and industry are interrelated sectors. Agriculture helps industry in the following way. In the *first* place, agricultural development means rising incomes of farmers. Increased income creates demand for industrial goods. *Secondly,* agriculture provides raw materials and intermediate goods to various industries. *Thirdly,* by exporting agricultural commodities, capital goods for industries can be imported.

Q.2. What does the term 'industrialisation' mean?

Ans. : The term 'industrialisation' refers to the setting up of capital goods industries and basic industries capable of ensuring a high rate of growth of the economy as a whole.

Q.3. What do you mean by industrial structure?

Ans. : By industrial structure we mean inter-relationship among various branches of industries—the relationship between small scale and large scale industries, the relationship between consumer goods industries and capital goods industries. In the process of industrial development, industrial structure undergoes a change.

Q.4. Which is the oldest industry in India?

Ans. : The cotton textile industry is the oldest industry in India.

Q.5. What is meant by 'public sector'?

Ans. : A public sector may be defined as that sector in which government owns and manages it fully on its own initiative.

Q.6. Point out the reasons for expansion of the public sector industries in India.

Ans. : In India, a great deal of importance is attached to the public sector to (a) prevent the growth of monopolies and concentration of economic power in the hands of a few small businessmen, and (b) to establish a socialistic pattern of society.

Q.7. Mention the major drawbacks of public sector industries in India.

Ans. : The major drawbacks of public sector enterprises in India are (i) unnecessary delay in the execution of a project and escalation of the cost of construction, (ii) problem of overcapitalisation, (iii) use of manpower resources in excess of actual requirements, (iv) underutilisation of capacity, (v) excessive stock in inventories, (vi) bureaucratic, corrupt and inefficient management, (vii) faulty price policy, etc.

Q.8. What do you mean by 'infrastructure'?

Ans. : Capital invested for the improvement of transport, communication, generation of power, and creation of public services like education, health, etc. are known as 'social capital'. By infrastructure we mean 'physical capital' and 'social capital'. To accelerate the process of economic development in a country, development of economic infrastructure is a pre-condition.

Q.9. Point out the causes of the problem of sickness in Indian industries.

Or

Mention two causes of industrial sickness in India. (C.U. 2007)

Ans. : Both exogenous and endogenous factors are responsible for industrial sickness. They are government policies pertaining to production, distribution and prices; change in the investment pattern due to the change in plan priorities, power shortage, scarcity of raw materials, unfavourable industrial relations, etc. Endogenous factors are the following : managerial inefficiency, diversion of funds, lack of provision for depreciation of machinery, excessive inventories, etc.

Q.10. Point out the symptoms of industrial sickness.

Or

Mention two causes of industrial sickness in India. (C.U. 2007)

Ans. : One of the important symptoms of industrial sickness is the liquidity crisis which develops if the industry fails to manage required amount of resources and money. Irrational capital structure is considered to be another symptom of industrial sickness.

Q.11. What is meant by privatisation?

Ans. : In India, privatisation refers to the selling of shares or equity to mutual funds, financial institutions and the private sector. So, it means disinvestment of the public sector industries.

Q.12. Mention two objectives of New Economic Policy.

Ans. : New Economic Policy has the two important objectives : (i) macroeconomic adjustment and balance that aims at reduction in fiscal deficit, establishing balance in foreign trade and stabilisation in prices; (ii) reorganisation of the Indian economy.

Q.13. In what forms private foreign capital comes to India?

Ans. : *Firstly,* foreign capital enters India in the form of equity capital. *Secondly,* it takes the form of equity participation by foreigner's and creditor's capital. That is to say, it can take the form of foreign collaboration. *Thirdly,* foreign capital may take the form of direct inter-government loans. *Fourthly,* loan from international financial institutions at concessional rate is another source of foreign capital.

Q.14. At present, which country dominates in the supply of foreign capital in India.

Ans. : The bulk of foreign private investment comes from Mauritius where tax laws are very lenient. However, the US FDI comes to India via Mauritius.

Q.15. What is 'industrial sickness'?

Ans. : An industry which has at the end of the financial year accumulated losses equal to or exceeding its entire net worth and has also suffered cash losses in such year and the financial year immediately preceding such financial year.

Q.16. Mention two elements of 'exit policy'.

Ans. : Exit policy refers to the (i) shedding of the load of excess workers in the public sector or popularly called the 'voluntary retirement scheme' (VRS), and (ii) disinvestment of public sector enterprises or the so-called privatisation.

Q.17. When were the First and the Latest Industrial Policies announced?

Ans. : The first Industrial Policy Resolution was adopted in April 1948. The current policy in respect of industries is governed by the Industrial Policy Statement of July 1991.

Q.18. Indicate two main obejectives of the Industrial Policy (1991) of the Government of India. (C.U. 2007)

Ans. : The 1991 Industrial Policy aims at deregulating the industrial economy so as to make it more competitive both internally and internationally. Another objective is the privatisation of the public sector.

INDIA'S FIVE YEAR PLANS

Q.1. What are the basic objectives of economic planning in India?

Ans. : The basic or long term socio-economic objectives of India's Five-Year Plans are the following : (a) a higher rate of economic growth by developing agriculture, industry, electricity, transport and communications and other sectors of the economy; (b) sizeable increase in national income and per capita income so as to raise the levels of standard of living of people; (c) removal of poverty and unemployment; (d) attainment of self-reliance; (e) reduction of social, economic and regional inequalities; etc.

Q.2. State two main objectives of the Eleventh Plan.

Ans. : The two most important objectives of the Eleventh Plan are—(i) faster growth in GDP and per capita income; and (ii) inclusive growth. This last objective says that the benefits of growth must reach the marginalised sections of population so that they are integrated to the processes of development.

Q.3. State three main objectives of the Ninth Plan.

Ans. : The focus of the Ninth Plan was on growth with social justice and equality. The specific objectives are—(i) accelerating the growth rate of the economy with stable prices; (ii) providing basic minimum services of safe drinking water, primary health care facilities, universal elementary education, shelter, etc., (iii) containing the growth of population.

Q.4. What are most important objectives of the Tenth Plan?

Ans. : The Tenth Plan aimed at achieving a higher growth rate (8 p.c. p.a.), a higher employment rate, reduction of gender gaps in literacy, and a significant reduction in poverty rate by 5 percentage points. It also aimed at ensuring access to basic services, like education, health, drinking water and basic sanitation.

Q.5. Indicate the average rate of growth of the Indian economy during the last decade.

Ans. : The decade of 1990s saw a growth rate of India's national income of 5.42 p.c. p.a.

Q.6. Which two States in India today has the per capita income highest and lowest?

Ans. : Available data indicates that Goa is the highest per capita income State in India. Chandigarh stands second.

Bihar, in terms of per capita income, is the poorest state in India. Next comes Orissa.

Q.7. Indicate two main causes for 'poverty' in India.

Ans. : The most immediate cause of mass poverty in India is the vast inequality in the distribution of income and wealth. *Second* is the economic backwardness. Economic backwardness has kept the Indian economy in a perpetual state of vicious circle of poverty. Besides these, terrific unemployment problem is also responsible for mass poverty.

Q.8. At present, how many Indians are living below the poverty line?

Ans. : The percentage of population below the poverty line has been estimated at 28 p.c. in 2004-05.

INTERNATIONAL ECONOMIC ENVIRONMENT

Q.1. What is meant by globalisation?

(C.U. 2008)

Ans. : Globalisation is a process of increasing integration and growing economic interdependence of countries. It is a process through which domestic economies are opened up. Thus, globalisation refers to the extension of economic activities across borders.

Q.2. What are the major dimensions of globalisation?

Ans. : There are four broad dimensions of globalisation. These are : international trade, international investment, international finance and multi-country network of multinational corporations.

Q.3. Name the major elements of international trading environment.

Ans. : The three crucial elements of international business environment are : (i) international trade policy, (ii) existing politico-economic situation or international power and influence, and (iii) international trading institutions.

Q.4. What is 'free trade' ?

Ans. : By 'free trade' we mean absence of restrictions on trade. Government does not intervene in trading activities. Thus, free trade eliminates tariffs and duties.

Q.5. Mention four important objectives of the International Monetary Fund.

Ans. : (i) To promote international monetary cooperation, (ii) to facilitate the expansion and balanced growth of trade, (iii) to promote exchange stability, and (iv) to assist in the establishment of a multilateral system of payments are the four major objectives of the IMF.

Q.6. What is "Bretton Woods System"?

Ans. : The first 25 years (1946-1970) of activity of the IMF is known as the "Bretton Woods System". The System provided exchange rate stability in the short run, but allows for the possibility of exchange rate adjustment when a country experiences fundamental disequilibrium in its BOP country.

Q.7. What are the main functions of the World Bank?

Ans. : The World Bank (i) assists in the construction and development of territories of its members; (ii) promotes private investment and long run balanced growth of trade and BOP equilibrium; (iii) provides finance to projects, etc.

Q.8. What are the principles of GATT?

Ans. : The three guiding principles of GATT are: reciprocity, transperancy and non-discrimination.

Q.9. Mention at least four functions of WTO.

Or

Indicate two major objectives of forming World Trade Organisation

Ans. : *First,* WTO facilitates the implementation, administration and operation of the WTO trade agreements. *Secondly,* it provides a forum for negotiation among member countries. *Thirdly,* it monitors national trade policies. *Fourthly,* it provides technical assistance and training to its members—developing countries.

Q.10. What is counter-trade?

Ans. : Countrer-trade is the direct or indirect exchange of goods for other goods in international trade. It is, thus, a form of barter in international trade when currency is not used for payments.

Q.11. What are the essential ingredients of globalisation of the Indian economy?

Ans. : The three essential ingredients of globalisation of India are—(i) privatisation of the public sector, (ii) dismantling of bureaucratic controls and regulations, and (iii) opening up and the closer integration of the Indian economy with the world economy through deregulation of trade and finance, etc.

APPENDICES

APPENDIX TO CHAPTER 1

1.1 REPRESENTING OBSERVATION WITH FUNCTIONS, GRAPHS

The discipline economics is subject to quantification. Running through the pages of economics book one can see graphs and tables, equations, etc., that illustrate economic relationships both in verbal and diagrammatic manner. Understanding of these tools does not mean that the knowledge of mathematics is essential. Students are not of homogeneous category having different abilities and adaptabilities. Graphs, tables, equations, etc., help students to understand and analyse economic events. However, in recent times, mathematical aspects have become more important than verbal, diagrammatic representation to understand and analyse the economic processes. This appendix, at this level of study of the subject economics, is devoted to familiarise students with the basic quantitative tools only, and not the technique of calculus—the specialised application of mathematics.

1.1.1 Variables and Functions

Economic theories are built on the basis of assumptions from which logical reasoning follows. This then leads to the formation of hypotheses about economic behaviour. Mathematics then comes to the picture to explain the logical chain of reasoning and, finally, it provides the basis for the (statistical) tests for the hypotheses drawn. In brief, economic theories are built on assumptions about how variables—the basic elements of theories—are related to each other.

We often encounter two kinds of quantities: constants and variables. A constant is such whose quantity or magnitude remains constant in spite of the variation of the variable. On the other hand, a variable is something whose magnitude or value changes from time to time or from observation to observation. Price, cost, revenue, profit, national income, consumption, etc., are the most frequently used macroeconomic and microeconomic variables in economics that take different values under different circumstances. There are different kinds of variables. Most important of these are: (i) exogenous and endogenous variables; (ii) stock and flow variables; etc., (iii) dependent and independent variables.

- **Exogenous and Endogenous variables:** Variables considered by the economic theorists may be explained by factors within and outside the theory. A variable that is determined by factors outside the theory is called exogenous variable. On the other hand, a variable that is explained within the theory is called endogenous variable.

Often many airline authorities make announcements to attract more fliers in their respective airlines—"Fly anywhere, at the lowest price". This induces some people to fly more frequently and in large numbers. Thus, the purchase of airline ticket depends on airfare. But journey by air depends on lot of things other than the airfare. One such important determinant is the weather condition during the winter season when fog disrupts air services. Such weather condition does not influence airfare. Weather is the exogenous variable not determined by any economic events. On the other hand, lower airfare causes people to fly more frequently. Thus, air journey—an endogenous variable—depends on airline ticket which is explained within the theory.

- **Dependent and Independent variables:** Variables that depend on something may be called dependent variables. For instance, your purchase of a cinema ticket in a multiplex depends largely on your pocket-money and the price of the ticket. Thus, purchase of a cinema ticket is a dependent variable; it is a function of two variables—pocket-money and the price of the ticket. But as these two variables do not depend on anything else these may be called independent variables. It is independent of anything else.

- **Stock and Flow variables:** Stock variables are measured *at a given point in time* whereas flow variables are valued *over a period of time.* Thus a stock variable has no dimension while a flow variable has a time dimension. To understand the difference between these two variables, one may consider a tub of water that contains 50 litres of water. This quantity is a stock of water at this instant in time. The amount of water that is released from the tub per 5 minutes is the flow variable.

A business firm owns a plant, machinery, building, etc., to produce some goods. These then may be called the capital stock of the firm at a given point in time. On the other hand, investment, say purchase of a new machine in the year 2010, is a flow concept. As it has a time dimension, investment is a flow variable. Again, income earned or expenditure incurred in a month or per day is a flow variable. But a deposit in your bank is a stock variable. Suppose, today an individual puts Rs. 50,000 in a bank for a period of 2 years with a promise that an annual 8 p.c. rate of interest will be given for the said deposit and such will be deposited in his savings account. However, the rate of interest earned by the individual is a flow variable. If the depositor keeps all or a portion of the interest payment in his account then both stock and flow variables will simultaneously grow.

Now, we intend to show the relationships, if any, between the variables. Such relationship is explained in terms of function.

1.1.2 Function and Its Classification

We define function terms of a general law. Let us consider the law of demand that shows a relationship between price and quantity demanded for a commodity at a particular time. This law then shows the relation between two variables: price and quantity demanded. The functional relationship between these two variables shows an inverse relationship: as price increases (decreases) quantity demanded falls (rises). Thus, price is an independent variable while quantity demanded is a dependent variable.

In the language of mathematics, this relationship between two variables (one dependent and another independent)—say x and y—can be written as

$x = f(y)$ [to be read as x is a function of y and $f(y)$ does not mean f times (y).]

Here 'f' may be viewed as a 'machine', y is the 'raw material' and 'x' or $f(y)$is the output. A function is a relation: x depends on y. Thus, x is a dependent variable, while y is an independent variable.

Likewise, the demand function used in economics and business is given as

$$q = f(p) = 160 - 4p$$

where q is the quantity demanded and p is the price. If we know the price, we will be able to quantify the volume of goods to be demanded.

Note that here the gradient or slope is -4. This means that the demand curve has a negative stope.

Again, $C = f(Y)$

This is macroeconomic consumption function that fixes the relation between aggregate consumption and aggregate income. Here Y is the independent variable.

In economics and business, we are more interested in showing relationships between the variables. It is argued that supply depends on price, total revenue depends on price, saving depends on income, price level depends on money supply, and so on. This means that one depends on other—given a y-number one can calculate the corresponding x-number. If so, we then say that x is a function of y. A function thus links one set of things to another set of things in which one is a dependent thing (or variable) and another is an independent thing (or variable).

Let us rewrite single-valued function as

$$x = f(y) \quad \text{or } x = \phi(y)$$
$$\text{or } x = g(y)$$
$$\text{or } x = F(y)$$

'f' is traditionally used as a notation for the word 'function'. Instead of 'f', other symbols like F, g, ϕ (Greek letter 'phi'), etc., are employed as functional notations.

It has been said that the quantity demanded depends on the price of a commodity alone. But it is also true that the quantity demanded for a commodity depends not only on its price, but also other factors, like income, tastes and preferences, advertisement, and so on. Under the circumstances, demand function can be written as

$$q = f(p, m, t, a)$$

This type of demand function is called multi-valued function of q.

Let us re-write a multi-valued demand function in the following form:

$$q = 100 - 4p + 0.2m + 0.9a$$

Here m, and a denote money income, and advertisement respectively.

This multi-valued demand function describes how does independent variable influence dependent variables or how does a change in independent variable bring about a change in dependent variables. In this equation q is inversely related to $p(-4p)$, and q is directly related to m and a.

It is to be kept in mind that these single-valued or multi-valued demand functions describe the relationship between the variables in a general way and not in a precise way. And for the purpose of linking these relationships we need equations. That is to say, an equation that specifies the link in which a dependent variable behaves in response to a change in independent variable. For example,

$q = 24 - 2p$ (demand equation)

$C = 50 + 0.72Y$ (consumption equation)

Here 'C' stands for aggregate consumption while Y stands for aggregate income.

- **Inverse function:** We have considered a demand equation like

$$q = f(p) = 24 - 2p$$

where p is the independent variable.

Let us for the moment assume that p is the dependent variable and q is the independent variable. Then demand equation can be rearranged as

$p = f(q)$ [read p is an inverse function of q]

or $p = 12 - q$

This is the inverse function of q = 24–2p.

- **Linear and non-linear functions:** Every functional relationship is represented by an equation. A linear function, when plotted, is one that gives a straight line. A linear function is one whose highest power is 1. For example:

$$y = c + mx$$

where 'c' is the intercept and 'm' is the slope or gradient and 'y' is a function of x. A linear demand function can be expressed as

$$q = a - bp$$

where 'a' is the intercept and 'b' is the gradient.

A linear consumption function is of the form: $C = a + bY$. Here 'a' is the intercept and 'b' is the slope or marginal propensity to consume (MPC). A linear demand function and a linear consumption function have been represented in Fig. 1.1(a) and 1.1(b).

In the demand function, quantity demanded (dependent variable) is measured on the horizontal axis and price (independent variable) is measured on the vertical axis in Fig. 1.1(a). Here point M is the intercept where the straight line cuts the vertical axis. This means that the quantity demanded reduces to zero when price is equal to Rs. 12. Further, the slope or the gradient may be positive or negative. This demand curve has a negative gradient $q - 2$.

In Fig 1.1(b), a linear consumption function has been shown on the basis of a linear consumption function.

$$C = a + bY \text{ or } C = 50 + 0.75Y$$

Here 'a' or the intercept is (20) and 'b' or the slope is 0.75. This means that MPC is $\frac{3}{4}$. In other words, people consume $\frac{3}{4}$th of their incomes. It starts from the vertical axis above the origin. This means that its intercept is positive. Intercept of a function may also be negative. Anyway, this positive intercept

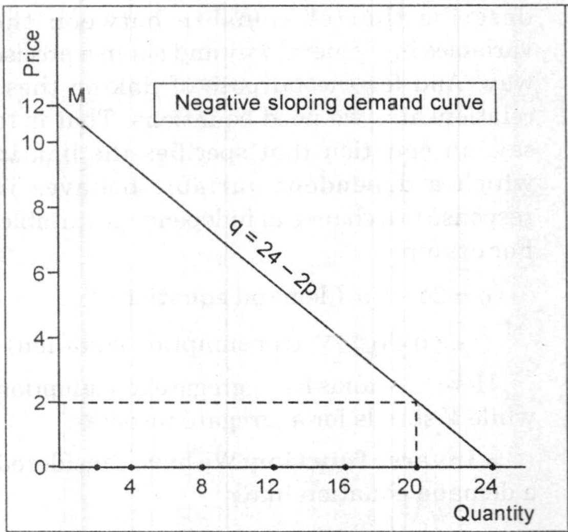

Fig. 1.1(a) A Linear Demand Function

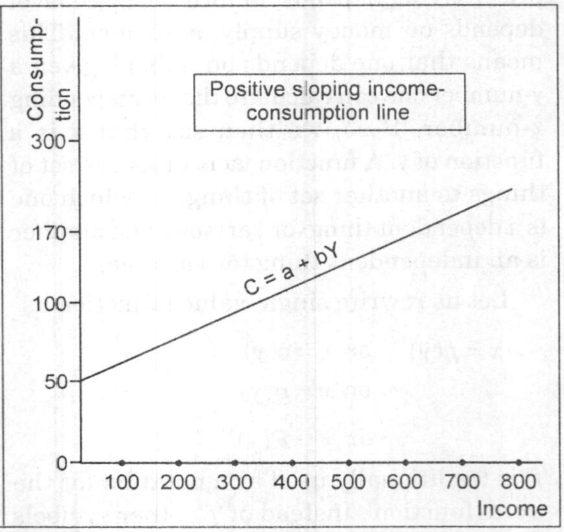

Fig. 1.1(b) A Linear Consumption-Income (in Rs. crore) Function

indicates that even if income is zero, consumption is positive. For a straight line function the gradient remains the same throughout the curve.

A non-linear function is one that does not produce a straight line one where the gradient changes along any section of the curve. Non-linear functions are usually represented by the short run total product curve, the short run U-shaped cost curves, etc.

Further, a function may be a quadratic one. A quadratic function is one whose highest power is 2. A quadratic function, when plotted, generates a parabola. Thus, in a quadratic equation, one obtains 'two solution values'. A quadratic demand function may be expressed as

$$q = 4 - p^2$$

A cubic function is one whose highest power is 3. The graph of a cubic function shows two 'bends'. A cubic function may be expressed as

$$x = a + by - cy^2 + dy^3$$

The equation of a short run total cost function of the third degree is

$$TC = a + bQ - cQ^2 + dQ^3$$

Here a is the total fixed cost having positive intercept and the rest is total variable cost.

1.2 SLOPE (OR GRADIENT)

We have already come across functions—given a y-number (x-number) corresponding x-number (y-number) is calculated. For every value of y(or x) there is corresponding value of x(or y). If the values of y and x are plotted one obtains either a straight line or a curve. Such a line or a curve demonstrates the inclination or the slope that may be positive, negative, zero or undefined/infinite.

The slope or gradient of a straight line or a curve suggests a relationship between pairs of values of two variables, x and y. Such relationship may be positive or negative or zero or undefined. The gradient of a line (i.e., a linear function) is calculated by the ratio of vertical distance to horizontal distance. In other words, the slope of a line between two points is the change in variable (say, y) measured on the vertical axis divided by the change in another variable (say, x) measured on the horizontal axis. The formula of gradient or slope is then

$$\text{Slope} = \frac{\text{change in variable as measured on the vertical axis}}{\text{change in variable as measured on the horizontal axis}}$$

$$= \frac{\text{change in } y}{\text{change in } x}$$

$$\text{or Slope} = \frac{y_2 - y_1}{x_2 - x_1}$$

This is shown in Fig. 1.2. In Fig. 1.2(a), a straight line AB with the positive direction has been drawn. The vertical distance between points M and N is $(y_2 - y_1)$ while the horizontal distance is $(x_2 - x_1)$. Thus, the slope of the line AB is

$$\frac{y_2 - y_1}{x_2 - x_1} = \frac{\Delta y}{\Delta x}$$

It is evident from the figure that as we travel along the line AB from point M to N the slope becomes a positive number since both x and y increase (or decrease) in the same direction.

A linear consumption function as shown in Fig. 1.1(b) generates a positive slope. Let the consumption be Rs. 275 crore and aggregate income be Rs. 300 crore. If income rises to Rs. 400 crore, consumption would then rise Rs. 350 crore. Thus, the slope of the line is

$$\frac{y_2 - y_1}{x_2 - x_1} = \frac{350 - 275}{400 - 300} = \frac{75}{100} = 0.75$$

Thus, the slope between points M and N of the line AB (assuming it as a consumption line) [Fig. 1.2(a)] can be thought of as +0.75.

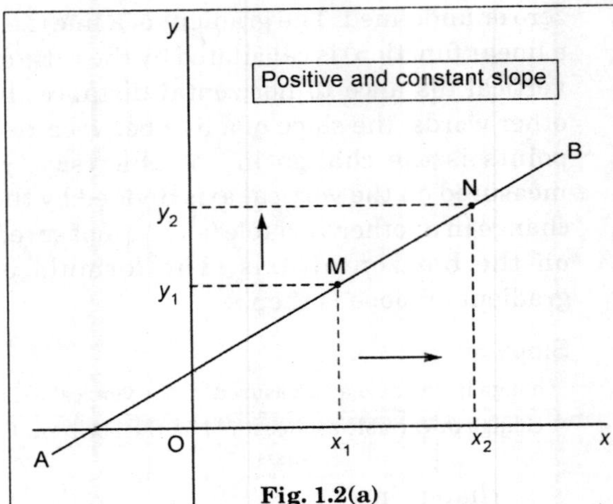

Fig. 1.2(a)

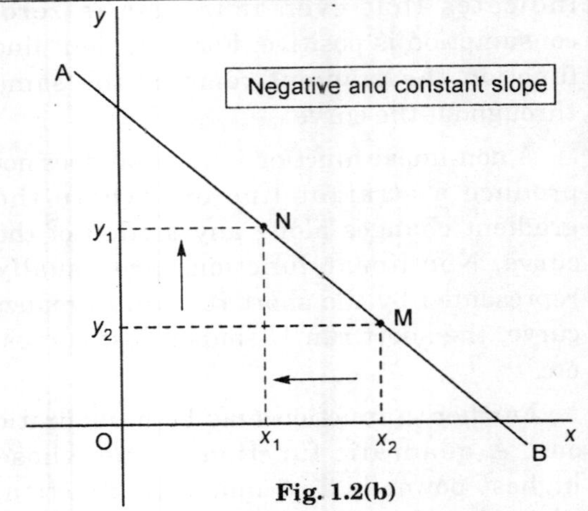

Fig. 1.2(b)

Slope of a Linear Function

In Fig. 1.2(b), the line AB has the negative direction of the x-axis. It is clear from the figure that, as we move from N to M, x increases from x_1 to x_2, while y decreases from y_1 to y_2. Thus, the negative number divided by the positive number (i.e. vertical distance/ horizontal distance) gives a negative quotient.

If the straight line AB is parallel to the x-axis or coincides with the y-axis [Fig 1.3(a)] its slope is then zero $(\Delta y = 0)$. This can be demonstrated by the fact that as one moves from M to N on the line AB, the x-number increases from x_1 to x_2 while y-number remains unchanged (that is, $y_1 = y_2$). Thus, the slope of the line AB is

$$\text{slope} = \frac{\Delta y}{\Delta x} = \frac{y_1 = y_2 = 0}{x_2 - x_1} = \frac{0}{\Delta x} = 0$$

If the AB line is parallel to the y-axis or coincides with the x-axis [Fig. 1.3(b)], its slope is then infinite or undefined. Fig. 1.3(b) shows that as we move from M to N, this time y-number increases (that is $y_1 \neq y_2$) while x-number is kept unchanged at $x_1 = x_2$. Thus, the slope of the line AB is

$$\text{slope} = \frac{\Delta y}{\Delta x} = \frac{y_2 - y_1}{x_1 = x_2 = 0} = \frac{\Delta y}{0} = \infty$$

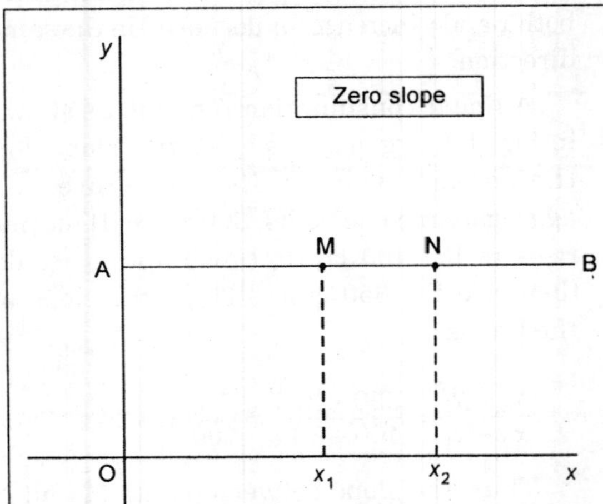

Fig. 1.3(a)

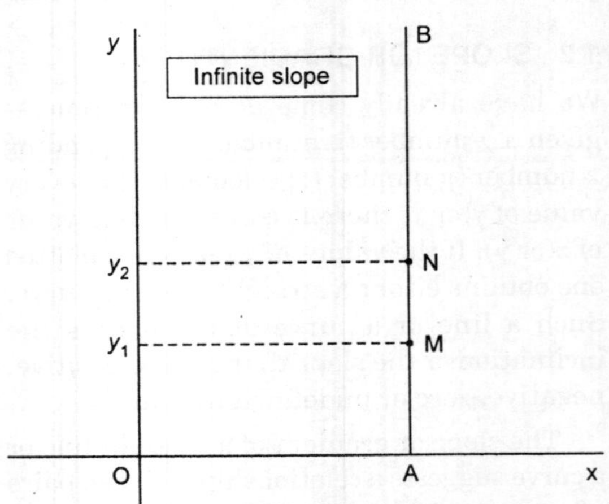

Fig. 1.3(b)

Slope of a Linear Function

Or the slope of a straight line may be defined as the tangent of the angle between the line and any line parallel to the x-axis. An upward sloping straight line has a positive slope since any tangents with the straight line illustrate a positive value. For a negative sloping straight line, tangents with the straight line will have a negative value.

The slope of a curve, on the other hand, does not remain invariant along the curve—it changes continually. It is non-linear. In Fig. 1.4, we have drawn as many as six curves whose slope changes.

Fig. 1.4(a) suggests that as one moves from y_1 to y_2 along the curve AB, x-value increases from x_1 to x_2. It then indicates a positive sloping curve. In this region, the curve AB is steep. But its steepness declines if one moves from y_2 to y_3 and from x_2 to x_3. The vertical distance $(y_3 - y_2)$ is rather a shorter one compared to the horizontal distance $(x_3 - x_2)$ for every x-number. Hence the slope diminishes. This means that slope indicates steepness or flatness of a line or a curve. For the obvious reason, the AB curve of Fig. 1.4(b) shows positive slope too but its steepness gradually increases if one moves from left to right. However, the AB curve of Fig. 1.4(c) shows a negative sloping curve with an increasing slope as we move from left to right.

In Fig. 1.4(d), AB curve shows negative slope but it continually decreases as we travel from left to right. Fig. 1.4(e) shows both

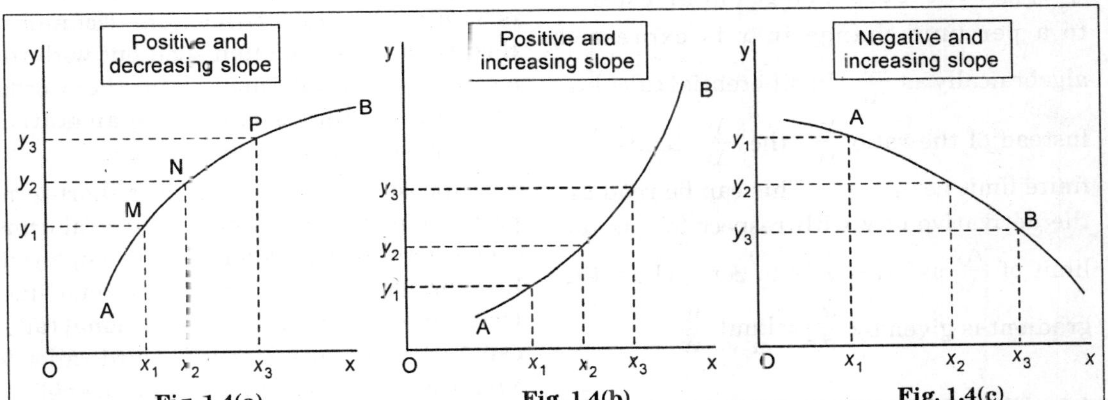

Fig. 1.4(a) **Fig. 1.4(b)** **Fig. 1.4(c)**

Changing Slopes along Curves

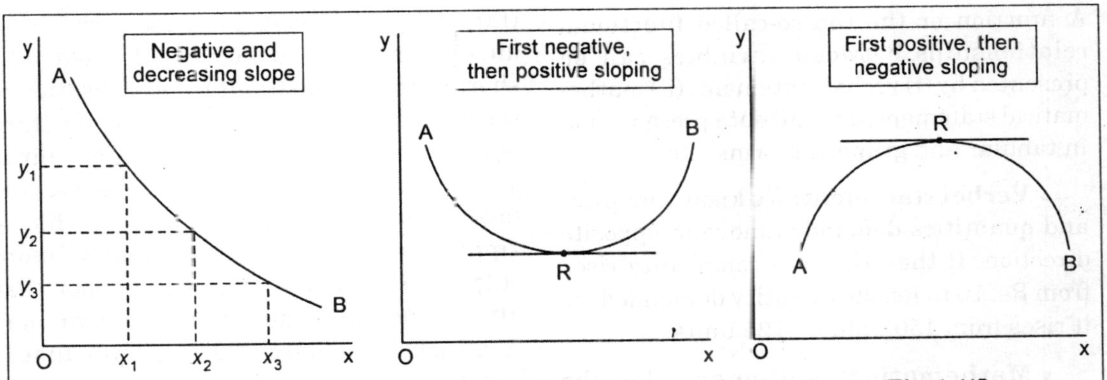

Fig. 1.4(d) **Fig. 1.4(e)** **Fig. 1.4(f)**

Changing Slopes along Curves

negative and positive slopes. As one moves from A to R, the slope becomes negative while the movement from R to B shows a positive slope. However, at point R, the slope becomes zero. The curve AB of [Fig. 1.4(f)] demonstrates that the slope is positive as we move in the x-direction. But after reaching R, the slope becomes negative. However, at point R in the last two figures the slope is zero since y-value does not change.

However, measuring the gradient or slope of a curved line which changes continually involves some difficulties. To overcome such difficulties economists use a mathematical tool called differential calculus. Better estimates by differential calculus involves in finding the rate of change of one variable (say, y) per unit change in another variable (say, x). Let the functional relationship be $y = f(x)$. The rate of change in y in response to a per unit change in x is expressed algebraically as $\frac{\Delta y}{\Delta x}$. In differential calculus, instead of the ratio $\frac{\Delta y}{\Delta x}$, the $\frac{\Delta y}{\Delta x}$ tends to a finite limit as $\Delta x \to 0$. This can be read as: the derivative of y with respect to x is the limit of $\frac{\Delta y}{\Delta x}$ as Δx tends to zero. Thus, the gradient is given by $\frac{dy}{dx} = \underset{\Delta x \to 0}{\text{limit}} \frac{\Delta y}{\Delta x}$.

1.3 UNDERSTANDING SCHEDULES AND GRAPHS

A function or the the so-called functional relationships between variables can be presented by (i) verbal statement, (ii) mathematical statement, and (iii) data presentation in tabular and graphical forms, etc.

• **Verbal statement:** We know that price and quantities demanded move in opposite direction. If the price of a commodity rises from Rs. 10 to Rs. 20, quantity demanded for it rises from 150 units to 125 units.

• **Mathematical statement:** Let the demand function for this commodity be:

$$q = 200 - 5p$$

Thus, at a price of Rs. 10, quantity demanded is 150 units but at a price of Rs. 15, quantity demanded declines to 125 units.

• **Data presentation in tabular and graphical forms**

Another basic quantitative tool is the data presentation in the form of a table or schedule. Quantitative data give non-numerical responses. It may be added here that data or information may be both quantitative and qualitative. Quantitative data give numerical information as information is presented in terms of numbers. If information is not given in terms of numbers then such is called qualitative data. Here we are interested in only quantitative data. Economics among all the social sciences, is subject to quantification. Economic theories/models are often spelt out with the aid of numerical information. In other words, economic statistics provide quantitative measures of economic phenomena.

Suppose you have been given a short-term production or output schedule of a tailoring shop where two tailor-masters are employed. But the owner owns two sewing machine. Under the circumstance, an additional tailor can give more output. If the third tailor is employed the shop owner will not be able to use this tailor unless another sewing machine is bought. However, the owner can utilise the third labour without purchasing or hiring another machine (which is ruled out in a short span of time) by efficient utilisation of the third labour force. For instance, the third one can be used for fixing buttons on shirts. This will cause output to grow. Likewise, the fourth labour can be employed in fixing zippers in trousers. Consequently, more output can be produced. It may happen that after some time adding more labour may cause no rise in output. This means that it has reached the saturation point beyond which output will not increase. Further, employment of tailor in a situtation of two sewing machines (fixed input) may cause output to decline.

Let this information be presented in the form of a table in which total, average and marginal product of labour schedules (keeping number of machines fixed at 2) have been shown. Such table illustrates the relationship between input changes and output changes in the short run. This table is known as the production schedule that catalogues different quantities of output of the tailoring shop when it increases tailors with a fixed number of two machines.

This schedule shows that, as number of workers with fixed capital increases, marginal product (A change in total product consequent upon a change in variable input, labour, is called the marginal product) initially rises, then falls to zero, and finally becomes negative. This schedule then generates the celebrated law of diminishing returns to a variable input. Many productive activities are associated with this output behaviour. It then suggests a signal to the producer once it reaches capacity level of production. The signal is: There is a limit to production. However, this situation can be averted by business managers if they decide to choose the right type of technology as there are alternative techniques of producing a commodity. For instance, capital intensive or labour saving technology may be employed.

Such schedules (output schedule, demand schedule, supply schedule, etc.,) can be represented more forcefully by graphical devices. As data or numerical figures may seem to be unispiring and less appealing to many people, we plot such schedules in the form of a graph. Graphical representation helps us to visualise the whole meaning of a numerical complex at a glance. In fact, graphical representation (i.e., visual aids) is not only simple and easily understandable but also helps in memorising the facts than mere numerical figures.

A function of one variable can be interpreted geometrically by means of a graph. Thus a graph is a two-dimensional representation of a data. However, if two variables, instead of a single one, are considered for representation by presenting two variables on two axes in the form of a graph, the cartesian coordinate system is used. However, in this book we have considered only the upper right quadrant of the coordinate system where only positive values of x and y are considered. Negative values of x and y of the coordinate system are ignored here. A linear function will generate a straight line figure.

To draw a demand graph, let us prepare a demand schedule for a commodity at different prices of an individual. The demand schedule for a commodity of an individual is

Table 1.1: Total, Average and Marginal Products of Labour Schedules (Capital is fixed)

No. of Tailors (L)	Total product (TP)	Average product $AP\left(=\frac{TP}{L}\right)$	Marginal product $MP\left(=\frac{\Delta TP}{\Delta L}\right)$
1	4	4	4
2	10	5	6
3	18	6	8
4	22	5.5	4
5	22	4.4	0
6	18	3	–4

a catalogue of different amounts of the commodity that he buys at different prices.

We can easily present this schedule (Table 1.2) in the form of a graph shown in Fig. 1.5. Here we measure price on the vertical axis and quantity demanded on the horizontal axis. Point 'a' shows that when price is Rs. 25 the quantity demanded is zero. Point 'b' shows as price drops to Rs. 20 quantity demanded is 2 kg. Points c, d, e, etc., are plotted in this way that represents other price-quantity combinations. Now, by connecting all these points, we get a continuous line. This may be called the demand line for good X. It is thus a graph that shows the quantity a buyer will buy at every possible price.

In other words, picturisation of the demand schedule, is given by a demand curve. A demand curve is thus a graph of the demand schedule.

Further, the demand curve that has been drawn here illustrates the law of demand, whose slope is negative—since price and quantity move in opposite direction.

1.3.1 Cross-section and Time-series Data

We have already learnt that numerical table is cumbersome and speaks less than graph.

Economic data are usually grouped into cross-section and time series data. Cross section data refers to statistical information of an individual (also firm) or a group of individuals (also industry) *at a single point in time*. Cross-Section data can be collected from several different firms or industries *at a single point in time*. Thus, this type of data may involve demand, income, price, cost, revenues, national income, aggregate consumption, etc., at a given time. This means that cross-sectional data may be used in analysing both microeconomic and macroeconomic phenomena.

Suppose the following cost-output data (Table 1.3) of seven cellular phone companies in the month of April 2010 have been obtained. Anyway, we are not interested here in estimating the relationship between cost and output of some firms at a given data.

Table 1.2: Mr. A's Demand Schedules for good X

Price (Rs. per kg)	Quantity demanded (kg per week)
25.00	0
20.00	2
15.00	4
10.00	6
5.00	8

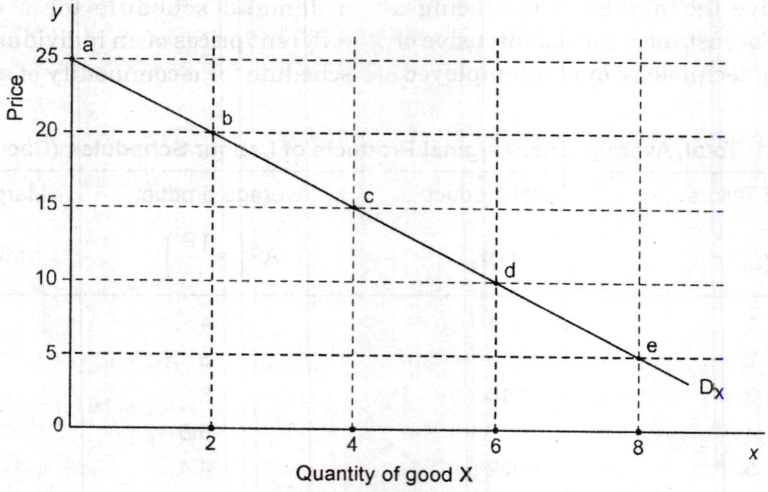

Fig. 1.5. Mr A's demand for X

A macroeconomic cross-sectional data may also be presented here. An example of this data has been shown in Table 1.4 in which aggregate income-consumption relationship has been described among some group of persons at a single point in time.

Likewise, time-series data is employed in both microeconomics and macroeconomics. Such data consist of historical records of firms/industries or macroeconomic phenomena with observations extending *over many periods of time*. For instance, month-wise or year-wise data of sales and advertising cost of Hindusthan Lever in Kolkata metropolitan area is an example of time-series data set at the microlevel.

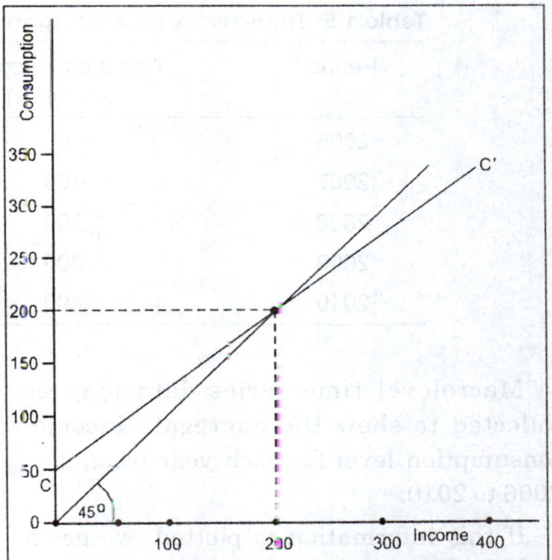

Fig. 1.6. Macroeconomic consumption function

Table 1.3: Cross-sectional Data of Seven Mobile phone Manufacturers in April 2010

Firm	Cost (Rs.) per unit	Output of phones (in numbers)
A	79	4,650
B	85	6,230
C	78	4,955
D	80	4,000
E	89	3,234
F	89	2,886
G	82	5,000

Table 1.4: Cross-sectional Data of Income and Consumption by Income Groups in the Year 2009

Income Group (Rs.)	Average aggregate income (Rs.)	Average aggregate consumption (Rs.)
0-999	450	600
1,000-1999	1,590	1,830
2,000-2999	2,630	2,700
3,000-3999	3,500	3,480
4,000-4999	4,560	4,200

Table 1.5: Time-series Data on Aggregate Income-Consumption (2006-10)

Period	Aggregate income (Rs. crore)	Aggregate consumption (Rs. crore)
2006	0	50
2007	100	125
2008	200	200
2009	300	275
2010	400	350

Macrolevel time series data may be collected to show the aggregate income-consumption level for each year from, say, 2006 to 2010.

If this information is plotted, we get a straight line consumption-income relationship. In Fig. 1.6, aggregate consumption is measured on the vertical axis while aggregate income on the horizontal axis. The line CC′ is the consumption line that cuts the vertical axis at some positive point, indicating that if aggregate income is assumed to be zero, consumption is positive (Rs. 50 crore). As income rises consumption rises. When income is Rs. 200 aggregate consumption is also worth Rs. 200 in 2008 and the CC′ line cuts the 45° line. Further, increase in income causes an increase in consumption and the CC′ line lies below the 45° line.

APPENDIX TO CHAPTER 3

3.1 DISTINCTION BETWEEN SLOPE AND ELASTICITY OF DEMAND

By slope of the demand function we mean change in price divided by the change in quantity. Let $P = f(Q)$ be the inverse demand function. Thus, the slope of the demand function

$$= \frac{\text{absolute change in price}}{\text{absolute change in quantity}} = \frac{\Delta P}{\Delta Q}$$

Again, slope refers to the steepness of the demand curve. In fact, slope of the demand function measures the steepness or flatness of the function.

On the other hand, elasticity of demand measures the relative change in price and quantity. Thus,

$$E_P = -\frac{\Delta Q}{\Delta P} \cdot \frac{P}{Q}$$

Elasticity of demand is the reciprocal of the slope of the demand function, multiplied by the price-quantity ratio, i.e.,

$$E_P = -\frac{1}{\frac{\Delta P}{\Delta Q}} \cdot \frac{P}{Q} = -\frac{\Delta Q}{\Delta P} \cdot \frac{P}{Q}$$

Thus, the slope and elasticity of demand are related but are not the same thing. Simply by studying the slope of the demand function one cannot determine the value of elasticity of demand, though it is said that steeper (latter) the demand curve lower (higher) is the elasticity of demand. This is a wrong conception. In fact, there is no connection between the slope and the elasticity of demand. It may happen that the two demand curves may have different slopes but the same elasticity or the two demand curves may have same slopes but different elasticities.

In Fig. 3.1, we have drawn two demand curves labelled as DA and DB. These two demand curves have the same intercept from the price axis, but they exhibit different slopes. In fact, the curve DA is steeper than DB. So elasticity of demand at any point on the DA curve should be less than that of the demand curve DB. But this is not so. This can be verified in the following way:

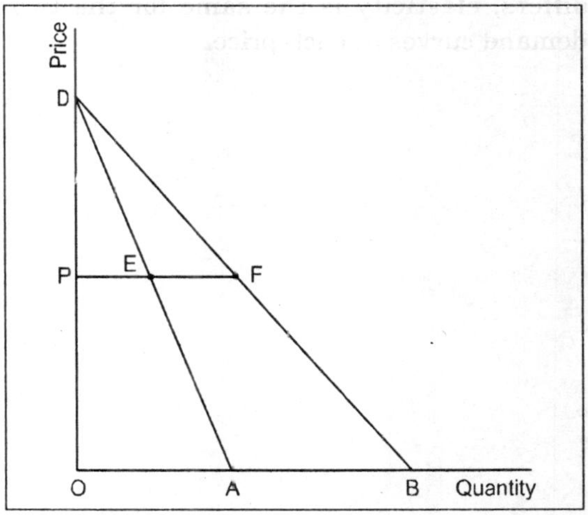

Fig. 3.1: Different Slopes but same Elasticity

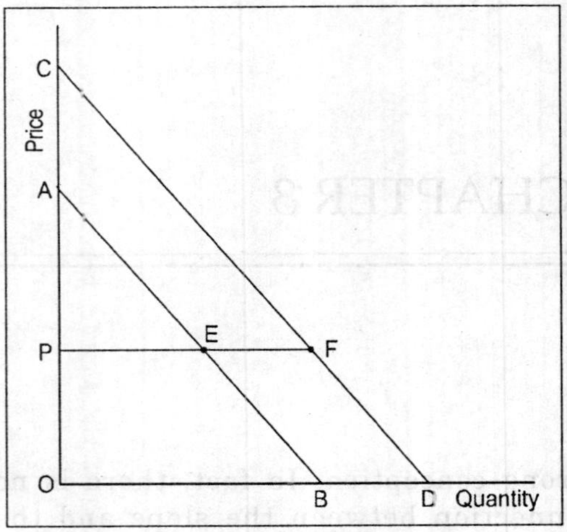

Fig. 3.2: Same Slope but different Elasticities

Consider two points E and F on the two demand curves having the same price OP. Elasticity of demand at point E on the curve DA is

$$\frac{EA}{ED} = \frac{OP}{PD}$$

Similarly, elasticity of demand at point F on the demand curve DB is

$$\frac{FB}{FD} = \frac{OP}{PD}$$

Thus, elasticity at point E = elasticity at point F. This suggests that though slope differs, elasticity is the same for the two demand curves at each price.

Fig. 3.2 shows that the two demand curves may have the same slope but different elasticities. Being parallel, two demand curves AB and CD have the same slope. Now consider points E on the demand curve AB and F on the curve CD. Now consider price OP. Then elasticity of demand at point E on the demand curve AB is

$$\frac{EB}{EA} = \frac{OP}{PA}$$

Again, elasticity of demand at F on the curve CD is

$$\frac{FD}{FC} = \frac{OP}{PC}$$

It is clear from the figure that since PC > PA

$$\frac{OP}{PC} < \frac{OP}{PA}$$

Thus, elasticity at point F on the curve CD is less than the elasticity at point E on the curve AB. Alternatively, in Fig. 3.2, point E may be assumed as the mid-point on the curve AB corresponding to the price OP. Thus, at that point, elasticity of demand is equal to one. But F on the demand curve CD at the price OP lies below its mid-point. So, elasticity at F must be less than one.

Thus, slope and elasticity of demand are not the same thing.

APPENDIX TO CHAPTER 10

10.1 THE LABOUR SUPPLY CURVE

So far we have considered two types of labour supply curve. One is perfectly elastic and the other is upward sloping curve. A perfectly elastic or a horizontal supply curve of labour is not found in reality. An individual labour supply curve is likely to be positive sloping—indicating larger supplies of labour at a higher wage rate. But this is not always so. That means, a worker may be induced to work less when his wage rate tends to rise. Thus, labour supply curve may be backward bending. How such individual supply curve of labour is derived may be described in terms of Fig. 10.1.

We know that an individual's supply of labour depends on the wage rate. Usually, as wage rate rises, an individual labour supplies more working hours than before. But there is another temptation on the part of the worker—the temptation of less work and more leisure. Once the optimum wage is earned by a labour, further increase in wage rate may induce him to work less and take more leisure. Leisure is attractive too. As a result, labour supply curve becomes backward bending. This has been shown in terms of indifference map between work (or leisure) and wage rate. A labour's indifference curve represents different combinations of work or leisure and wage that yield the same amount of utility to the labour. The level of

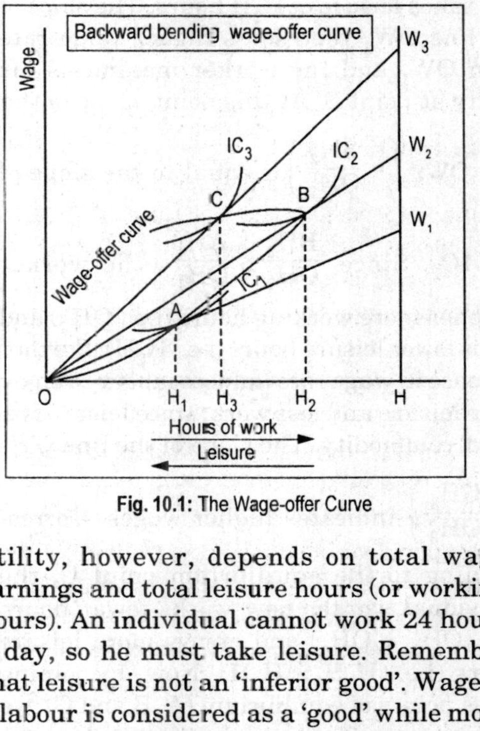

Fig. 10.1: The Wage-offer Curve

utility, however, depends on total wage earnings and total leisure hours (or working hours). An individual cannot work 24 hours a day, so he must take leisure. Remember that leisure is not an 'inferior good'. Wage to a labour is considered as a 'good' while more work is considered as a 'bad' commodity.

In Fig. 10.1, we measure working (or leisure) hours on the horizontal axis and wage rate on the vertical axis. Let us assume that an individual labour can work up to OH hours, rather than 24 hours. IC_1, IC_2, and IC_3 are three indifference curves. Higher indifference curve represents higher level of utility. We have drawn three straight lines OW_1, OW_2, OW_3 whose slopes represent different wage rates. These lines are called wage constraint line or simply, the budget lines. Higher the line, higher is the wage rate. The worker will reach equilibrium when the slope of the budget line equals the slope of the indifference curve. In other words, equilibrium occurs at that point where budget line becomes tangential to the indifference curve. The slope of the line OW_1 represents a wage rate equal to $\frac{AH_1}{OH_1}$. At this wage rate, an individual works OH_1 hours and takes leisure of H_1H hours. The slope of the line OW_2 represents higher wage rate than OW_1 and the worker maximises his utility at point B. At this point, slope of the line $OW_2 \left(=\frac{BH_2}{OH_2}\right)$ is equal to the slope of the IC_2. Since $\frac{BH_2}{OH_2} > \frac{AH_1}{OH_1}$, the worker supplies more working hours (i.e., OH_2) and takes fewer leisure hours (i.e., H_2H). Further increase in wage rate induces labour to enjoy more leisure and less work, since leisure is a 'good' commodity. The slope of the line OW_3 $\left(=\frac{CH_3}{OH_3}\right)$ indicates higher wages. Corresponding to the equilibrium point C, the individual worker now works fewer hours (i.e., $OH_3 < OH_2$) and enjoys more leisure hours (i.e., $H_3H > H_2H$). Now, by joining these points of equilibrium (A, B and C), we obtain wage-offer curve. Initially, this curve is upward rising but once point B is reached it takes a backward turn. This means that, in the initial stage, supply of labour rises as wage rate rises, but, ultimately, supply of labour declines as wage rate rises.

This backward bending wage-offer curve may be used to derive a backward bending labour supply curve. In this connection, we may use the concepts of income effect (IE) and substitution effect (SE of wage change). Higher wage rate induces a worker to work more instead of availing more leisure. To the worker, as leisure is now expensive, higher wage rate encourages a substitution of work for leisure. This is called substitution effect. Substitution effect is always positive. It is because of the positive substitution effect that an individual labour tends to work more when wage rate rises. This is evident from Fig. 10.2. As wage rate rises from OW_1 to OW_2, the supply of labour rises from OH_1 to OH_2. As wage rate rises, the worker substitutes extra hours of work for leisure.

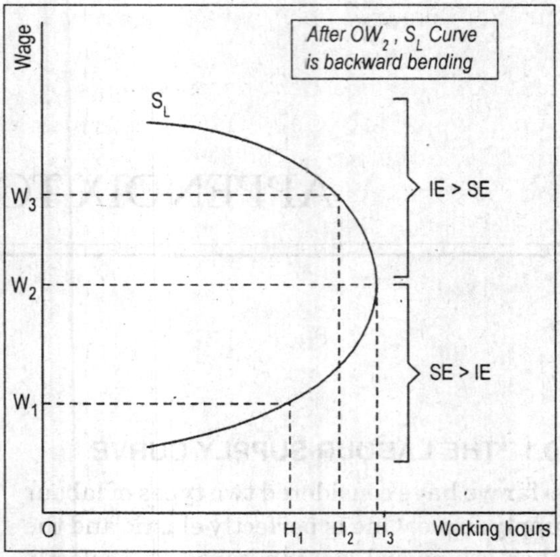

Fig. 10.2: The Labour Supply Curve

But as wage rate rises, individual worker's real income rises. This increased real income increases his demand for normal good, including leisure. (Leisure may be a normal or a superior commodity.) This is called income effect of wage rate changes. If the current wage rate becomes too high to an individual labour, he prefers to work less and take more leisure. In our example, if wage rate goes above OW_2, the individual labour may be tempted to work less from OH_2 to OH_3. As a result, his leisure hours increase.

Thus, between wage rates OW_1 and OW_2, substitution effect (SE) is stronger than income effect (IE), inducing individual labour to work more and take less leisure. The S_L

curve or labour supply curve slopes upward between wage rates OW_1 and OW_2, and it has a positive slope. Between wage rates OW_2 and OW_3, income effect outweighs substitution effect, inducing our worker to work less and take more leisure. The supply curve of labour, S_L, thus becomes backward bending. The S_L curve of labour now slopes downwards. The phenomenon of some reputed city doctors working only four hours a day and taking Saturdays and Sundays as absolutely free for themselves may be an evidence of backward bending supply curve of labour at high income levels.

APPENDIX TO CHAPTER 12

12.1 INTRODUCTION

More than three-quarters (5624 millions in 2008) of the world's population (6692 millions) live in developing countries where conditions of living are precarious. Here people live in abject poverty. Quite a large number of people do not have any shelter and spend their entire life on footpaths. Medical care is not meant for these people. That is to say, the basics of life—adequate food, clothing, and shelter—are not available to the vast majority of the population. In contrast, people in the developed counterparts enjoy decent living. These parts of the world are called affluent societies. We reproduce here two quotes to describe the glaring contrasts between the developing and developed countries:

"Most of the people of the world are poor, so if we knew the economies of being poor we would know how much of the economics that really matters."—Theodore Schultz.

"More than three-fourths of the world's people live in developing countries, but they enjoy only 16 per cent of the world's income—while the richest 20 per cent have 85 per cent of global income."—*Human Development Report, 1995*.

Even in the 21st century people die from starvation and 852 million people of the global South (i.e., LDCs) are malnourished. Hunger causes more than 18 million deaths per year worldwide: more than 18,000 a day. These people are unable to secure minimum nutritional requirements of food. Thus, these countries suffer from the problems of food insecurity, inaccessibility of basic education and primary health facilities, and so on.

Thus, the study of the 'poverty of nations', is more important than the study of 'wealth of nations', since poverty anywhere is a threat to poverty everywhere. The present chapter is devoted to the economic problems of developing or underdeveloped countries. But the process of economic development in these countries is an on-going process. These less developed countries (LDCs) are making sincere effort in raising their standards so as to catch the developed world. Some of these poor countries have moved to the ranks of middle income countries or newly industrialising countries, like South Korea, Taiwan, Singapore, and Hong Kong. In this chapter, we will trace out the causes of underdevelopment in these countries. Solution to the problems of backwardness will be discussed here. Before this, we must define economic growth and economic development.

12.2 GROWTH *vs* DEVELOPMENT

In ordinary discussion, people use these two words interchangeably. But economists argue that economic development is not identical with growth. These are two slightly different concepts.

The concept of economic development is broader than the concept of economic growth. Economic growth simply means an increase in per capita income of a country.

In the words of Simon Kuznets: "Economic growth may be defined as a sustained increase in its population and product per capita." But economic development is not the same thing as economic growth. Economic development implies progressive changes in the socio-economic structure of a country. Economic growth implies not only more output, but also more inputs and more efficiency, i.e., an increase in output per unit of input, or in other words, an increasing productive capacity of the economy. Development, however, is something more than that. It is 'growth plus change'. Development implies changes in the structure of output and in the allocation of inputs by sectors.

It follows from this definition that economic development encompasses social, political and cultural development of a country. Clearly, it is a value-based concept or a normative concept. It includes not only a sustained rise in gross (or net) per capita national product but also includes welfare of masses, reduction in income inequality, increase in employment opportunities, and so on. Thus, economic growth is a quantitative concept while economic development is a qualitative concept.

Economic development may be defined "as the process of increasing the degree of utilisation and improving the productivity of available resources of a country which leads to an increase of the economic welfare of the community by stimulating the growth of national income." Economic growth, indeed, is not concerned with the poverty-inequality reduction, unemployment situation and, above all, better quality of living. Thus, economic development is more than economic growth.

Economic growth = increase in per capita income—a quantitative expression

Economic Development = increase in per capita output + welfare of the masses — a qualitative expression

"Growth involves focussing on height or weight while development draws attention to the change in functional capacity", says C. P. Kindleberger.

12.2.1 Economic Growth—a Narrower Concept

Economic growth and economic development are, thus, not synonymous. Economic growth may be a necessary condition for economic development of countries, but it is not a sufficient condition. In fact, economic growth does not give us correct assessment of an economy for the following reasons.

- **Per capita income growth does not measure welfare:** *First*, economic growth is associated with an increase in GNP/GDP per capita. But per head GNP does not, by itself, constitute or measure welfare or success in development. This is because per capita income does not give any information about income distribution. It is observed that despite high rate of growth, some of the countries experience high incidence of poverty and unemployment.

Secondly, economic growth does not talk about the quality of life. Undernutrition, disease and the associated problems of lower life expectancy at birth and higher infant mortality rates, literacy rates, and many other indicators of health and education of different populations which comprise human development. In poor developing countries (i.e., global South), people end themselves at low level of literacy, low standards of health and nutrition, etc. Miseries arising from the lack of food and shelter do not get reflected in the concept of economic growth.

• **Growth ignores environmental issues:** *Thirdly*, economic growth does not deal with environmental issues. In the process of achieving higher economic growth, environmental considerations like depletion of renewable natural resources, air pollution, etc., are given little weightage. These aspects have an important bearing on the economic development of a country in the long run. Desire for higher and higher economic growth is associated with environmental damages. It is economic development that cares for environmental issues.

• **Economic development—'a multi-dimensional process':** It is, thus, obvious that economic development involves something more than economic growth. In fact, there are certain qualitative dimensions in the process of development that are conspicuous by their absence in the growth or expansion of an economy. Economic development implies both more output and changes in the technical, institutional arrangements by which it is produced, and a change in attitudes and values. "Development concerns not only man's material needs but also improvement of the social conditions of his life. Development is, therefore, not only economic growth but growth plus change—social, cultural and institutional as well as economic. Development is, thus, not purely an economic phenomenon; it has to be conceived of as a multi-dimensional process." Naturally, economic development is a value-based concept. It should include not only the acceleration of economic growth but also the reduction of inequality and eradication of poverty, increase in employment opportunities and welfare of the masses, etc.

• **Growth is silent about the quality of life and broad human development:** However, economic development may mean more. Economic development must encompass human development. Amartya Sen defines economic development in terms of 'entitlement' and 'capability'. Entitlement refers to the set of alternative commodity bundles that an individual can command through the totality of rights and obligations that he or she faces. Thus, entitlements of people generate 'capabilities'. Entitlements of people do not only depend on their incomes but also on a host of power relations in a society, the spatial distribution of resources in a society (like facilities of health care and schooling) and what individuals can accumulate from such supplied by the state. 'Capability' represents a person's freedom to achieve various functioning combinations. Thus, the notion of capability is essentially one of freedom—the range of options a person has in deciding what kind of life he or she wants to pursue.

Poverty, according to Amartya Sen, is a kind of 'capability deprivation'. Sen says that economic development should be interpreted as a process of expansion of the freedoms that people enjoy. Important areas of unfreedom that people face are famine and under-nourishment, mass illiteracy, poor state of health of people, lack of shelter and other basic needs, economic insecurity, denial of basic civil and political liberty, etc.

Through the policies of expansion of human capabilities, development processes can be initiated. That is why it is said that the basic objective of development is the process of expansion of entitlements and human capabilities. That is to say, how GNP growth is used to improve human capabilities and, in turn, how people utilise their capabilities is economic development.

Amartya Sen, thus, emphasises that, instead of concentrating on GNP or GDP, development economics should take into account both entitlements and capability expansion. He argues that income does not necessarily address the nature of entitlement. Taking a cue from the Chinese famine (1958-1961) as well as the Bengal famine (1943), he emphatically demonstrated that famines, in general, were to be attributed to the entitlement failure rather than the shortage of food. Despite abundant supplies in food, people had to suffer miserably from hunger and famine in Bengal due to entitlement failure in collecting food from the market. Famine is one source of unfreedom.

Sen says: "Development requires the removal of major sources of unfreedom." The basic condition for economic development are the freedoms from hunger and famine, malnutrition, deficient schooling, poverty, poor health, economic insecurity, denial of civil and political rights, social inequalities, etc. These human goals of economic development as emphasised by Amartya Sen have brought about a change in development thinking at least since the 1970s.

Amartya Sen, carrying on his value-loaded development economics, talks on social justice. He says that undernourishment of children, absence of opportunities of basic schooling, lack of entitlement of basic medical attention, particularly to the underprivileged of our society, etc., are nothing but social injustices. Since most of these facilities—meant for all Indians—crowd out the underdogs through the dominant class or partners of the society, injustices pile upon the vulnerable sections of the population. This kind of gross injustice is nothing but denial of development or 'exclusive development'. Thus, in the development discourse, social justice—a more normative concept—needs to be provided to all. And that is economic development.

How economic growth and economic development are interrelated can be known from the Fig. 12.1

12.3 MEANING OF UNDERDEVELOPMENT

Immediately after the industrial revolution (1750 onwards) some of the countries experienced a dramatic increase in their national outputs. Most of these countries are capitalist countries, like the U.K., the USA, etc., or the global North. As these countries enjoy high income as well as one of the best

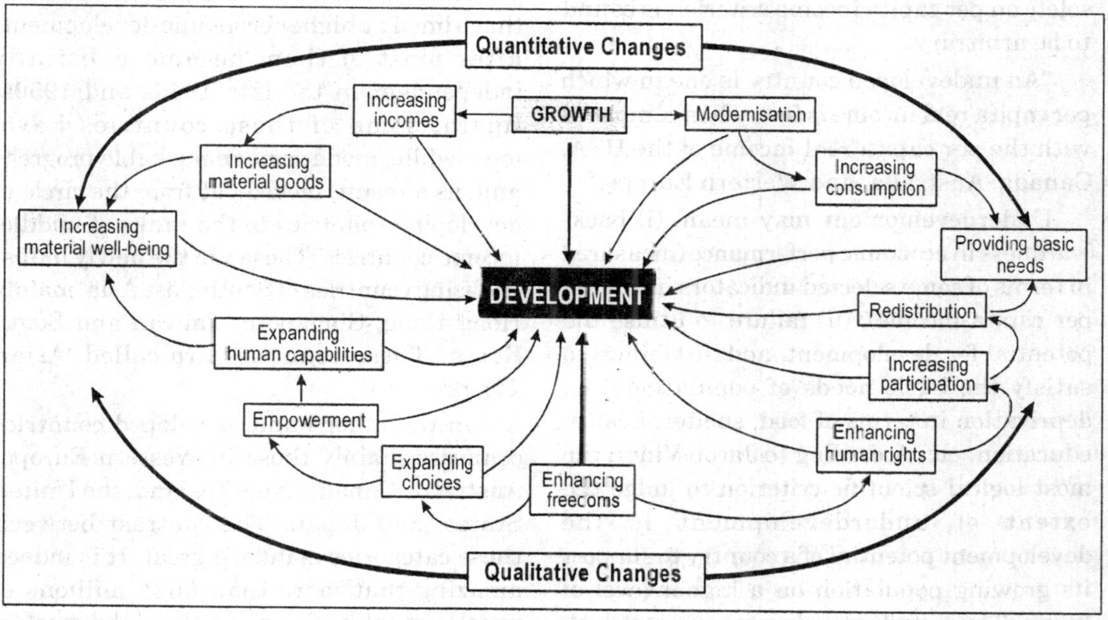

Fig. 12.1: Concepts of Growth and Development

living standards they are called 'First World' countries or the developed countries. Countries that experienced large economic growth in between the two World Wars (1914-18 and 1939-1945) are called 'Second World' countries or the socialist countries, like the erstwhile USSR. Newly independent but poor countries of Asia and Africa are making serious efforts to raise their living standards since the termination of the Second World War. These are called 'Third World' countries (or the global South). These countries, in economic literature, have earned various names. Other names are: 'backward', underdeveloped', 'developing', 'low income', 'less developed countries (LDCs), etc.

A country may be regarded as a developed one or an undeveloped one if per capita income of a nation crosses a limit. The World Bank classifies economies into four categories in accordance with the per capita gross national income measured in terms of US dollar. It will not be irrelevant here to reproduce Hla Myint's observation: "Definition of an underdeveloped country, relying solely on per capita income criterion is bound to be arbitrary."

"An undeveloped country is one in which per capita real income is low, when compared with the per capita real income of the USA, Canada, Australia, and Western Europe."

Underdevelopment may mean: (i) backwardness in economic performance (measured in terms of some selected indicators including per capita income), (ii) failure to utilise the potential for development, and (iii) failure to satisfy the basic needs of population, i.e., deprivation in terms of food, shelter, health, education, etc. According to Jacob Viner, the most logical scientific criterion to judge the extent of underdevelopment is the development potential of a country to support its growing population on a higher level of living. Thus, underdevelopment is just lack of development.

Further, development or underdevelopment needs to be measured not only in terms of per capita income (or economic indicators) but also in terms of non-economic social indicators like literacy, health conditions, shelter, etc. According to M. P. Todaro: "Underdeveloped economy is that economy in which there are low levels of living, absolute poverty, low per capita income, low consumption levels, poor health services, high death rates and dependence on foreign economies."

12.3.1 Key Indicators of Development/ Underdevelopment

No economy ever remains static; they grow over time. Industrialised countries of Europe first got their tastes of economic development. These countries of the North, or the so-called capitalist countries, are called 'First World' countries. Part of Western and Eastern European countries belong to the 'Second World' countries as their levels of development rose to a great height in-between the two World Wars. Poor, backward countries are called 'Third World' countries that aimed at higher economic development, after most of them became politically independent in the late 1940s and 1950s. Again, some of these countries have, meanwhile, made some remarkable progress and, as a result, moved out from the circle of developing countries to the ranks of middle-income countries. These are the newly industrialising countries of South East Asia, mainly Hong Kong, Singapore, Taiwan and South Korea. These countries are called 'Asian Tigers'.

On the other hand, developed countries comprise mainly those in Western Europe, Australia, Canada, New Zealand, the United States, and Japan. The contrast between these categories is indeed great. It is indeed amazing that more than 5624 millions of people, roughly three-fourth of the world's population 6692 millions—who live in the

Third World countries on less than one dollar a day. Developed countries or North had such living standards at least two centuries ago!

The economic distance between these two categories needs to be narrowed down as soon as possible to have a prosperous, healthy, and a competitive global economy. Otherwise, the North (First World countries) will politically and economically exploit the South (Third World countries) as it is used to do at the present time.

There are some key indicators (both economic and non-economic) of economic development/underdevelopment. These are: population growth, per capita GNP attained in a given year, average annual growth of GDP over a period of time, life expectancy at birth for male and female children, adult literacy/illiteracy, schooling, health conditions, and, above all Human Development Index (HDI). These indicators may be used as benchmark to gauze the nature of development/underdevelopment of different nations. Some of these countries are described as LIC (low income countries having per capita income less than $ 975), LMC (lower middle income countries with gross national or per capita income of $ 976-$3,855), UMC (upper middle income countries with gross national per capita income of $ 3,856-$ 11,905), and HIC (high income counries of per capita income higher than $ 11,906) according to 2008 GNI per capita. Table 12.1 shows some key indicators of development of a few selected nations and their relative standings in the level of development.

Table 12.1: Selected Indicators of Development

	Population (million) 2008	Per capita GNP ($, PPP) 2008	Life expectancy at birth (years) 2007		Adult literacy rate (%) 1999-07		HDI Ranking 2008
			Male	Female			
India (LMC)	1,140	1070	63	66	66	(Medium HDI)	134
China (LMC)	1,326	2,940	71	75	93.3	(Medium HDI)	92
Nigeria (LMC)	151	1160	46	47	72	(Low HDI)	158
Sierra Leone (LIC)	6	320	46	49	38.1	(Low HDI)	180
Vietnam (LIC)	86	890	72.3	76.1	90.3	(Medium HDI)	116
Russian Federation (UMC)	142	9,620	59.9	72.9	99.5	(High HDI)	71
Brazil (UMC)	192	7,350	68.6	75.9	90	(High HDI)	75
Sri Lanka (LMC)	20	1,790	70 3	77.9	90.8	(Medium HDI)	102
Korea Democratic Republic (HIC)	49	21,530	75.8	82.4	—	(High HDI)	26
United States (HIC)	304	47,580	76.7	81.3	—	(High HDI)	13
Japan (HIC)	128	38,210	79.0	86.2	—	(High HDI)	10
Norway (HIC)	5	87,070	78.2	82.7	—	(High HDI)	1

Source: *World Development Report 2010; Human Development Report, 2009*

NOTE: LIC : Gross national income per capita of $ 975 or less
LMC : Gross national income per capita of $ 976-$ 3,855
UMC : Gross national income per capita of $ 3,856-$ 11,905
HIC : Gross national income per capita of $ 11,906 or more in 2008

It is clear from this table that there are huge gaps between the low income and high income countries in terms of the above indices. In terms of population growth, India ranks second, next to China—a lower middle income country. Among the poor countries, population in Siera Leone is just 6 million, slighly ahead of Norway—a high income country. But, in terms of per capita GNP, neither Sierna Leone, nor India or China are comparable to Norway, or the United States or Japan. Life expectancy at birth in LICs is pretty low. Same is true about the adult literacy rate. Above all, one observes even wide differences among different LICs in respect of per capita GNP, life expectancy at birth, adult literacy rate, HDI, etc. In this table, countries have been ranked by their HDI value. Out of 182 countries, Norway is ranked first while Niger is at the bottom—the 182nd. Human development may be high (with an HDI of 0.800 or above), medium (with an HDI of 0.500-0.799), and low (with an HDI of less than 0.500). But a similarity among these countries exists—the similarity of underdevelopment—to which we will now turn.

12.4 COMMON CHARACTERISTICS OF LDCs

Just as there are large differences between developed and developing countries, so too there are great differences among the developing countries. Their differences may be observed in resource endowment, size and income of the country, political environment, dependence on external sources, levels of human development, etc. Some developing countries are better endowed with natural resources while some of them can boast of huge human resource. In this sense, every country is unique and that is why the structure of all developing countries is divergent. Thus, LDCs are a diverse group—their cultures, politics, and even their geography vary enormously. It is neither proper to treat them as belonging to a homogeneous group nor suggest the same strategy of development for each country. In fact, depending upon the nature and extent of underdevelopment, the development potential of these countries differ significantly.

But a close look reveals that in spite of their diversity, different LDCs of Asia, Africa and Latin America have some common characteristics. These common characteristics have been aptly summed up by M. P. Todaro. He says that most of the Third World nations have a set of common and well-defined goals. These are the reduction of poverty, inequality, and unemployment, the provision of minimum levels of education, health, housing and food for every citizen, and so on. Common problems that these countries face, of course in varying degrees, are widespread poverty, gross income inequality, massive unemployment, low level of agricultural and industrial output growth, absence of housing and sanitation facilities, high infant mortality rate, and low expectancy of life, prevalence of child labour, etc.

We now describe the most common characteristics of LDCs:

- **Low per capita income and widespread poverty:** The most important indicator of economic backwardness is per capita income. Per capita GNP of LDCs is very low. That is why most people in such countries live under severe hardships. They do not get sufficient food to eat, adequate medical care and minimum educational opportunities. About 40-50 p.c. people in such countries live below the poverty line. In terms of per capita income and living standards not only the gap between the developed and underdeveloped countries is large, but the gap is widening over the years. For example, in 2008, India's per capita GNP (in U.S. dollars) was a modest $ 1,070 compared to $ 47,580 of the USA, $ 87,070 of Norway. The average GNP per capita of low income countries in 2008 stood at $ 524 compared to $ 39,345 for high-income countries (Data Source: *World Development Report 2010*, Table 12.1).

• **Shortage of capital:** In LDCs like India, there is a shortage of capital of all varieties. There is shortage of not only private capital like structure, factories, steel mills, etc., but also shortage of social overhead capital such as roads, highways, railroads, hospitals, schools, etc. This is largely due to low per capita income and widespread poverty. Since most people are poor they cannot save much. In fact, poor people have a high propensity to consume (or a low propensity to save). Ragnar Nurkse has pointed out that most LDCs are caught in a vicious circle of poverty: 'A country is poor because it is poor.' Low per capita income leads to low saving. Low saving leads to low growth and low growth, in turn, leads to low per capita income. In fact, low per capita income is both the cause and the consequence of poverty.

• **Population explosion and high dependency:** Another major characteristic of LDCs is high rate of growth of population. The population bomb has exploded in most such countries, as has been predicted by T. R. Malthus in 1798. This is due to a two-fold reason: (a) a fall in the death rate, and (b) almost unchanged or constant birth rate. As a result, population has virtually exploded. Population in these countries is increasing annually at the rate of almost 2 p.c.

On the contrary, supply of inputs is inelastic. Consequently, land-labour ratio has become unfavourable leading to a growth of an army of surplus labour. These labourers are unproductive in the sense that they depend on productive labourers. In fact, due to lack of adequate employment opportunities, the dependency burden is very high.

• **Massive unemployment:** Another important characteristic of LDCs is the existence of a considerable amount of unemployment, underempolyment, and disguised unemployment. Traditional agricultural sector cannot cope with the rising population. As a result, the magnitude of disguised unemployment is mounting in these countries. Finding no alternative employment opportunities, rural people flock to the urban areas in order to survive. But the rate of industrial growth, again, is not encouraging to absorb rural masses. In addition to this, a large number of educated youth do not find employment in these countries.

• **Predominance of agriculture:** An underdeveloped economy is predominantly an agrarian economy. Predominance of agriculture is viewed from two angles—first is the contribution of this sector towards national income. In LDCs, agriculture contributes roughly 30-50 p.c. towards national income. On the other hand, in the developed countries, agriculture occupies a secondary position since 2-8 p.c. of national income comes from this sector. *Secondly*, LDCs mainly depend upon agriculture and extractive industries like mining, fisheries and forests. This means that the bulk of the population is engaged in agriculture and allied pursuits. About 55-75 p.c. of the people are engaged in agriculture. Only 10 p.c. are employed in the secondary sector, and the rest in the tertiary sector. In advanced countries, agriculture provides employment to a small fraction of the people (2 p.c. to 5 p.c.). All these explain the predominance of agriculture in LDCs. Though agriculture occupies a predominant position in LDCs, it is always in a backward condition leading to low productivity.

• **Unproductive investment:** It is anybody's knowledge that due to massive poverty people have very little power to save in LDCs. These countries are not capable of saving of more than 15 p.c. of GDP as compared to more than 35 p.c. of GDP saved by people of advanced countries. The small amount which is saved in LDCs is not invested properly. Some of it is used in hoarding, black-marketing and other unproductive activities—like decorating 'gods' in temples by gold ornaments. A large part is used to buy unproductive assets like gold and jewellery. This sort of unproductive investments cannot promote economic growth.

• **Low levels of productivity:** Another feature of an LDC is low productivity of land, labour and capital. The productivity of land is low for various reasons—institutional, technological, and natural.

Productivity of labour is also low for various reasons. Most workers are poor and do not get either sufficient food or adequate medical care. So they cannot work hard. They are most illiterate, unskilled and lack technical training. They do not have sufficient complementary resources such as land and capital to work with.

In short, low productivity of labour is both a cause and an effect of the low levels of overall productivity and living in these countries. Low levels of living and low productivity go hand in hand. It is really difficult, in practice, to identify the cause and the effect.

12.4.1 Vicious Circle of Poverty

Continuous and rapid economic growth is a historical abnormality. Therefore, any overall approach to development must take note of the reality, i.e., the various obstacles to growth as well as the persistence of stagnation over a long period of time. The most fashionable concept here is the vicious circle of poverty—a concept introduced by Ragnar Nurkse and others. A less developed country is caught in the vicious circle of poverty.

The vicious circle argument holds that conditions in LDCs are such that economic development is impossible. To explain this vicious circle argument, one often uses the notion of a poor man. A poor man, because of very low income, is underfed and undernourished. Underfeeding as well as undernourishment makes him weak and becomes susceptible to sickness and diseases. A poor man earns less as his capacity to earn is also low due to sickness or poor health. Thus, a man is sick because he is poor. Or a man is poor because he is sick. The implication is clear: It assumes that people of less developed countries save little or nothing since they are poor. Since savings are low, investment is low. Low investment means low productivity levels, and, with low productivity levels, people will always remain poor.

The basic logic of this vicious circle argument is that the greatest obstacle towards the development of an economy is poverty. The primary causes of underdevelopment are so intimately connected that they together form a circle which is vicious. Ragnar Nurkse explains that the vicious circle implies a circular constellation of forces tending to act and react upon one another in such a way as to keep a poor country in a state of poverty. The entire argument is summed up in Nurkse's words: "A country is poor, because it is poor." Or "Because it is poor, the country does not develop; because it does not develop, it remains poor."

Vicious circle argument is often explained from the supply side and demand side of capital. The supply of capital is governed by the ability and willingness to save, the demand for capital is governed by the incentives to invest. Nurkse says: "On both sides of the problem of capital formation in poor countries a vicious circle exists."

Let us first explain the supply side of capital. A poor country saves little because of poor income. As a result, it experiences shortage of capital for developmental activities. Lack of capital supports the labour-intensive technique of production. This technique of production is less productive. In other words, a poor country experiences low productivity. And low income is the result of low productivity. The supply side has been aptly summarised by P. A. Samuelson: "They (the underdeveloped countries) cannot get their heads above water because their production is so low that they can spare nothing for capital formation by which their standard of living can be raised." This sort of vicious circle may be represented diagrammatically (Fig 12.2).

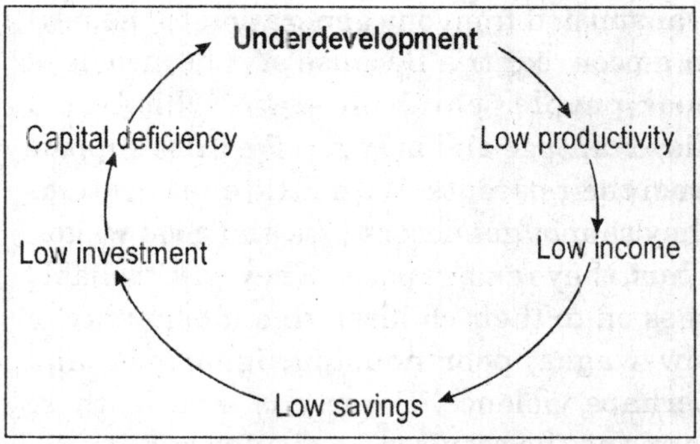

Fig. 12.2: The Vicious Circle: Supply side

Now from the demand side of capital, one can explain the vicious circle argument. The logic is as follows: In a poor country, demand for capital is less becuase of low investment which is the result of low purchasing power of masses. In other words, low income means limited market opportunities. Low purchasing power or limited market for goods tells on investment— which becomes low. Low investment now spells low income. Thus, underdevelopment perpetuates and the poor country is caught in low income equilibrium. This is shown in Fig 12.3.

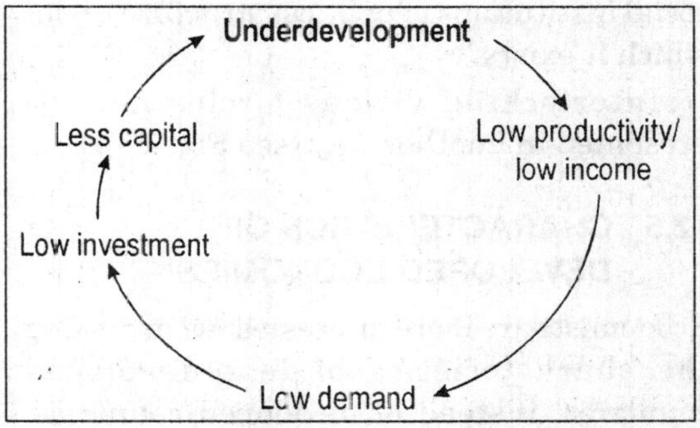

Fig. 12.3: The Vicious Circle: Demand side

It is thus clear that poverty is the cause of poverty and the entire logic is cumulative. In other words, poor countries are held down to their low levels of per capita incomes by "interlocking vicious circles". Self-perpetuating poverty and deprivation get

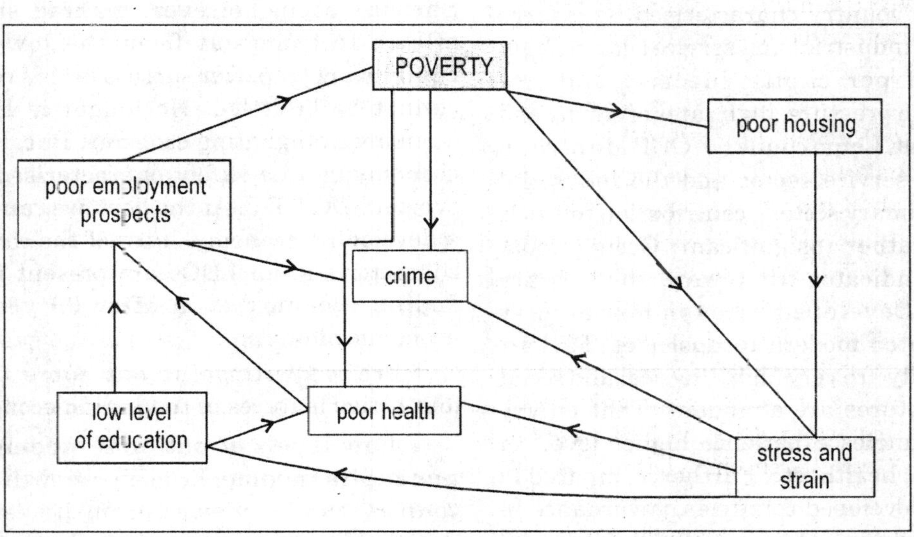

Fig. 12.4: The Vicious Circle

Source: *The Dictionary of Human Geography*, edited by: R. J. Johnston et. al, Blackwell Reference (1986)

transmitted from one generation to the next in a poor country. Because of poor income of poor people, children start school at a disadvantage and may receive little support from their parents. With little qualifications they cannot get decent jobs and good wages. Thus, they remain poor. "They will probably pass on to their children this inheritance of low wages, poor housing, ignorance and perhaps violence. Poverty is seen in these terms as the result of particular qualities of those in poverty, without reference to the social institutions of political structure under which it exists."

Interlocking vicious circles may be presented in another way (see Fig. 12.4).

12.5 CHARACTERISTICS OF DEVELOPED ECONOMIES

Economists are more interested in earmaking the characteristics of less developed countries, instead of developed countries. However, from our discussion made so far, we can define or point out some basic common features of the developed economies of Europe, North America, Japan, etc.

A developed economy is an economically advanced country characterised by a large growth of industrial and service sectors, high levels of per capita income, and low population pressure, high rates of saving and investment. Large chunks of GDP are derived from the service sector and the industrial sector. Primary sector's contribution towards GDP is rather insignificant. Occupational pattern indicates tilt toward the tertiary sector. Developed economies employ sophisticated modern technologies. Factors' productivity are very high. Physical and social infrastructures are abundant. That is why these countries experience higher levels of education, health, etc. Further, compared to the less developed countries, governance in developed countries is more strong, transparent and efficient. However, one sees a great deal of inequality in income distribution in these economies too, and, hence the problem of poverty must not be ignored.

If the world as a whole is to develop or progress, the gaps between these countries need to be minimised. Developing countries are required 'to race to the top' from their present status. Today, we see some pockets of remarkable achievements in some of these developing countries. However, performance needs to be boosted as some of the developing countries of Africa are sinking because of many well-known reasons, like weak governance. In this connection, G. E. Meier and J. E. Stiglitz's comment may be worth noting: 'People are not poor because they are poor, but because of poor policies.' In addition, developed countries must gear themselves to help developing economies to come out of the low level equilibrium trap.

12.6 FEATURES OF THE INDIAN ECONOMY

India got her independence in 1947. At that time she exhibited features of underdevelopment. Her economy during about 200 years' British rule (1757-1947) was a stagnant one. She has been, however, making sincere efforts to come out from the low level equilibrium trap. Her success in this respect cannot be belittled. No longer is Indian economy a stagnating economy. But, Indian economy can be safely characterised as a typical LDC/UDC. At the best, we can call it a developing economy. Most of the common characteristics of LDCs are present in the Indian economy even after 60 years of economic planning.

Here we will point out some of the distinctive features of the Indian economy:

- **Low levels of national income and per capita income:** Economic growth of any country can be viewed from its level of national income and per capita income. It is said that higher the level of national income, higher is the rate of economic growth. India's net national product (NNP) at factor cost in 2008-09 at 2004-2005 prices stood at Rs. 36,72,192 crore. Population in 2008-09 stood at 1164 million. This amounts to saying that per capita NNP came to Rs. 31,821 or Rs. 2,652 per month. Standards of living of masses are miserably low. Even the basic necessities are beyond the means of the majority of population. Comparing India's per capita income with the other countries of the world, one comes to the conclusion that India is one of the poorest nations of the world.

• **Vast inequalities in income and wealth:** Not only per capita income is low, but Indian economy is also marked by great inequalities in the distribution of income and wealth. In India, as years roll on, inequalities are on the rise. The logical corollary of this inequality is mass poverty. Nearly 60 p.c. of the total population share one-third of India's national income while only rich 5 p.c. of the total population enjoy the same amount of national income. This inequality widens the problem of poverty. Even in 1972-73, more than 50 p.c. of the total population lived below the poverty line. Thanks to some economic progress, it has come down from 36 p.c. in 1993-94 to about 27.5 p.c. in 2004-05, poverty estimate being based on Uniform Recall Period (URP). Recently, poverty data has been revised. After accepting the recommendations of S. Tendulkar Committee's Report, the number of people living below the poverty line in 2004-05 stands at 37.2 p.c. and not 27.5 p.c. In absolute terms, it is roughly 407 million in 2004-05. In short, Indian economy still reels under the vicious circle of poverty.

• **Predominance of agriculture:** LDCs live mainly upon agriculture and extractive industries like mining, fisheries and forests. Predominance of agriculture is explained from the viewpoint of sectoral composition of national income and occupational pattern. In India, in 1950-51, more than 55 p.c. of our GDP came from the agricultural sector or the so-called primary sector. In 2008-09, however, the contribution of this sector toward GDP came down to 18.9 p.c. Howerer, the *Economic Survey of 2009-10* presented in the Indian Parliament in late February, 2010 says that agriculture's contribution towards GDP in 2008-09 stands at 15.7 p.c. The contributions of the secondary and tertiary sectors were 23.8 p.c. and 57.3 p.c., respectively, during the same time. Thus, (1951-2010) agriculture has been losing its importance. It is suggestive of development. However, occupational structure tells a story of predominance of the agricultural sector and backwardness of the industrial sector.

• **High population pressure:** In LDCs, the rate of growth of population is very high. So far as the size of population is concerned, India ranks second next only to China (132 crores). India's population is now 1170 million in 2009-10. During the decade of 1991-01, the growth rate of population in India was 1.61 per cent per annum, as compared to 0.7 per cent growth rate of population of developed countries. High birth rate (28 per 1000) coupled with low death rate (7.4 per 1000 in 2008-09) is the genuine cause for population explosion in India.

• **Massive unemployment:** In LDCs, not only natural resources are underutilised but also a massive wastage occurs in the case of manpower resources. Slow economic growth rate on the one hand, and rapid growth of population on the other hand, has accentuated the problem of unemployment in India. Between 1971 and 1999, the number of unemployed in India increased by 10 times though the number of job-seekers increased by 2.5 p.c. annually; but the employment possibilities increased by a modest rate of 1.8 p.c. Number of registered job-seekers in December 2007 stood at 41.7 million. Unemployment rate has been rising persistently since the day of economic reforms began. It rose from 1.96 p.c. in 1993-94 to 2.39 p.c. in 2004-05. Rural unemployment rate, according to current daily status (CDS) method, in 2004-05 was as high as 8.2 p.c., as contrasted to 8.3 p.c. urban unemployment rate (*Economic Survey 2009-10*).

But employment growth in recent decades is not in comensurate with the labour force growth rate. What we experience now is the 'jobless growth'. The rate of growth of employment in the organised sector came to a negative of 0.03 p.c. p.a. during 1994-2007 as compared to 1.20 p.c. p.a. in 1983-1994. Some people prefer to call it 'job loss growth', instead of 'jobless growth'. Employment opportunities since 2008 have been badly affected by the recent global financial crisis and the consequent economic slowdown in India. However, the first six months of 2010 have been showing some gains in employment in many sectors—textiles, metals, etc.

It is somewhat tragic as well as paradoxical that, despite massive investment made during the plan period, unemployment problem has assumed a gigantic proportion. This amounts to huge wastage of human capital.

• **Scarcity of capital and low rate of capital formation:** As people in LDCs are poor, their capacity to save is low. This results in a low rate of capital formation. That is why development economists suggest that to break the vicious circle of poverty it is necessary to push up the rate of investment. Since India is a capital-poor country, capital per head is low. This scarcity of capital causes overall backwardness of the Indian economy. In 1950-51, net savings and net investments stood at slightly more than 5 p.c. of NDP and these two increased to 15 p.c. and 14.3 p.c., respectively, in 2001-02. The position, however, in recent times has improved a lot. The two figures increased to 30.1 p.c. and 31.7 p.c. in 2007-08. This is an encouraging development for the Indian economy.

Along with the low volume of physical capital, human capital formation is also low. As per 1951 Census, 34.62 p.c. of the total population at that time was illiterate. The literacy rate has gone up to about 64.8 p.c. by 2001—of course, by mathematical jugglery. Mass illiteracy acts as an impediment to India's economic development.

India has the dubious distinction of having the largest number of illiterate population (304 million) in the world (Source: *Eleventh Five Year Plan, Vol. 1*). The ground reality is more frightening. Close to one-half of the nation continue to be functionally illiterate, as said by Ashok Mitra. India has an adverse sex ratio with only 933 women per 1,000 men in 2001.

• **Underdeveloped infrastructure:** Being an LDC, India's infrastructural facilities or economic and social overheads of capital are inadequate. It consists of (a) transport and communications, (b) energy, (c) finance, housing and insurance, (d) science and technology, and (e) health, education, etc. Availability of these infrastructures creates the conditions for favourable growth. The superstructure of an economy largely depends on the availability of infrastructural facilities.

As far as social and economic overheads are concerned, India is poor. It is indeed true that her railway and road networks are comparable to the developed nations. But her demand for infrastructural facilities and services outpace their supplies. Per capita energy use (oil equivalent) of an Indian in 2005 was 491 kg *vis-a-vis* USA's 7,893 kg. Even China's per capita energy use was higher (1,316 kg) than India's. Compared to other countries, India is poor in information technology. In 2006, the use of personal computers per 100 Indians was as low as 2 as against 768 per 100 US people. India's health expenditure as a percentage of GDP was 1.39 p.c. in 2007-08 over the USA's 15 p.c of GDP. Thus, India's social infrastructural facilities are not only inadequate compared to the needs, but also awfully low compared to different countries of the world.

• **Low level of technology:** Due to illiteracy, use of advanced or sophisticated technology is rather an exception in India. Because of the limited growth of technological institutions, we are forced to use primitive methods of technology whose productivity is low. Though modern industrial sectors employ advanced technology, village industries still employ old and hackneyed methods even in the age of modern science and globalised world. This is nothing but technological dualism that persists in LDCs like India. Truly speaking, low productivity of Indian labour is explained in terms of low level of technology.

From the above discussion, we can conclude that all the characteristics of LDCs are found in India. No doubt, during the planning era (1951 to date) she has made progress in different directions. Still, considering the needs of the country, it is inadequate. Indian economy is characterised by low per capita income, widespread poverty, massive unemployment, gigantic rise in population, and so on. So, India is an underdeveloped country. India is one of the poorest nations of the world. Her position is worse compared to even some African countries !

12.7 IS INDIAN ECONOMY A DEVELOPING ECONOMY?

There is hardly any doubt that the present Indian economy is still a less developed economy because it exhibits all the characteristics of an LDC. But it is not a stagnant economy. It has achieved modest growth. It is also achieving some degree of modernisation. Moreover, some important structural changes have occurred in the economy in the post-independence period. All these made it clear that the Indian economy is gradually marching towards a distant but clearly visible goal, viz., the goal of a developed economy—after being locked in the vicious circle of underdevelopment and suffering from secular stagnation.

With the launching of the five year plans in 1951, a growth momentum appeared in the Indian economy. Over the passage of time, far-reaching changes have taken place in the economy. Here we group these changes into two broad categories—quantitative and qualitative. Here, first of all, we will describe quantitative changes and, finally qualitative changes.

• Quantitative Changes

• **Rising trend of national income and per capita income:** Economic growth of any country is measured by the increase in national and per capita output. During the plan period, national income of the country has certainly gone up. In 1950-51, net national product at factor cost or national income (at 1999-2000 prices) stood at Rs. 2,04,924 crore. It rose to Rs. 36,72,192 crore in 2008-09 (at 2004-05 prices). GDP growth rate in 2000s was unprecedented. It rose from 5.8 p.c. in 2001-02 to 7 2 p.c. in 2009-10.

However, the better measure of economic development is the per capita income. Per capita NNP rose to Rs 31,821 in 2008-09 (at 2004-2005 prices) as against Rs. 6,122 of 1950-51 at 1999-2000 prices. This means that during this period, compound annual growth rate of net per capita income rose by 2.5 p.c. p.a. Historically, it exhibits a better growth rate. Yet, it is inadequate compared to the needs of the country. The only encouraging aspect is that it shows a rising trend.

• **Increase in agricultural and industrial output:** Over the plan period, Indian economy experienced a higher growth rate in agriculture as well as in industry. Pre-plan period recorded an agricultural growth rate of 0.3 p.c while the plan period 1951-2009 showed a growth rate of 2.2 p.a. Performance of the industrial sector is certainly a better one. During the plan period, 1951-2009, the overall achievement in this sector is more than 4.7 p.c. p.a. India's growth trend of agriculture and industry shows India on the upward move.

• Qualitative Changes or Structural Changes

During the plan period, the Indian economy witnessed structural changes. By economic structure we mean interrelationship among the different productive sectors, i.e., agriculture and allied activities (known as the primary sector), manufacturing and industries (called the secondary sector), and trade and services (or the tertiary sector). At a low level of economic development, one finds predominance of the primary sector. The predominance of any sector can be viewed from the sectoral composition of national income and occupational structure. When, in an economy, primary sector is considered as the predominant one then it means that the contribution of this sector towards national income is the largest. Not only this, the bulk of the population derives their livelihood from this sector. On the other hand, in the sectoral composition of national income as well as in the occupational pattern, the contributions of the secondary and tertiary sectors stand lower. As economic development proceeds, the interrelationships among these sectors undergo a change. As economic development takes place, the primary sector (from the standpoint of sectoral composition of national income and occupational pattern) loses its importance and secondary as well as tertiary sectors gain in importance.

Thus, structural changes indicate economic development. This is what Colin Clark hypothesised.

We will see whether structural changes have taken place in India during the plan period:

• **Sectoral composition of national income:** In 1950-51, the contribution of the primary sector towards India's gross domestic product or GDP was nearly 55.9 p.c., while it was 14.9 p.c. for the secondary sector. Since then there has been a steady decline in the share of the primary sector in GDP and it declined to 18.9 p.c. in 2008-09. However, the *Economic Survey*, 2009-10 says that being the world's largest agrarian economy agricultural sector accounts for 15.7 p.c. of the GDP (at constant 2004-05 prices), in 2008-09, compared to 18.9 p.c. in 2004-05 (rather than 2008-09 as per the *SOI* data).

Table 12.2: GDP and its Sectoral Shares (1999-2000 prices)

Year	Agriculture and allied	Industry	Services
1950-51	55.9	14.9	29.2
1970-71	45.2	21.7	33.1
1980-81	39.1	23.6	37.3
1990-91	33.2	25.2	41.6
2006-07	20.6	24.6	54.8
2007-08	19.8	24.5	55.7
2008-09	18.9	23.8	57.3

Source: *Statistical Outline of India, 2008-09*

On the other hand, over the plan period, as the industrial sector expanded, its contribution to GDP has been on the rise and it rose to more than 25 p.c. in 1990-91. Since then, the contribution of this sector has been falling regularly but slowly. In 2008-09, its contribution towards GDP came to nearly 1980-81 level. However, one can observe consistency in the growth of the services sector particularly during the reform era. Along with the growth of the secondary sector, the services sector also registered a higher growth rate. In 2008-09, its contribution was 57.3 p.c. Thus, it is clear that, as economic development took place during about six decades of planning, the primary sector lost its pre-eminence. This, of course, is a sign of economic development.

Despite the green revolution in agriculture, the share of the primary sector to GDP has been continuously declining. Further, the secondary and tertiary sectors continously grew at a double rate than that of the primary sector during the first decade.

In the subsequent periods, the tertiary sector outstripped the growth of the secondary sector. Unfortunately, between 1990-91 and 2008-09, there has been a fall in the growth of the secondary sector from 25.2 p.c. to 23.8 p.c. Thus, the pattern of structural changes that has taken place in India has deviated from the pattern of developed economies.

Present growth trend is dominated by the services sector. Very aptly, it is called 'service-led growth'. But what we see in India is the 'excess growth of the service sector'. Possibly, India may display a new paradigm of development.

Another important aspect of sectoral composition of national income is the contribution of the public sector towards GDP. As time progresses, the contribution of this sector rises. In 1970-71, the public sector contributed 14.9 p.c. towards GDP, but it rose to 24 p.c. in 2001-02. However, following the introduction of new economic policy in 1991, the contribution of public sector enterprises towards GDP declined from 11.68 p.c. in 2004-05 to 11.12 p.c. in 2005-06.

Finally, one may notice a structural change by studying the contribution of the commodity sector and non-commodity or service sector in net national product. Between 1950-51 and 1976-77, the rate of growth of the service sector (4.90 p.c.) was satisfactory as compared to the growth of the commodity sector (2.90 p.c.). Furthermore, between 1980-81 and 1995-96, growth rate of the commodity sector came to 5.30 p.c., while that of the service sector rose to 6.50 p.c. Same story has been repeated during the period 1991-2008. Expansion of the tertiary sector is tantamount to modernisation. Yet, we must say that the growth of the service sector at the expense of the commodity sector is undesirable as it reflects some sort of 'structural retrogression'.

• **Occupational pattern:** In the light of structural change, one finds India's occupational structure as a static one. But we know that, as economic development takes place, occupational structure also undergoes a change.

Considering the development of the Indian economy in the last six decades (1951-2010), recently one finds some favourable changes in the occupational structure of India. Throughout the 20th century, the percentage of people engaged in agriculture had not fallen appreciably. Even in 2001, 57 p.c. of the total population were engaged in the primary sector, compared to 72.1 p.c. in 1951. However, between 2000 and 2004-05, people's dependence on agriculture has been showing a decelerating trend. In 2004-05, the percentage of people engaged in the agricultural and allied activities had fallen to 52.1 p.c. (*Economic Survey 2009-10*) for which many reasons (fall in arable land, global warming and the consequent drop in output, etc.) are advanced. On the other hand, between 1951 and 1981, the percentage of people engaged in the secondary sector increased marginally from 10.6 p.c. to 13.5 p.c. but it declined to 12.7 p.c. in 1991 and then again rose to 17.5 p.c. in 2001. The only sector that showed a steady rise in employment is the tertiary sector. It rose from 17.3 p.c. in 1951 to 23.8 p.c. in 2000. This is shown in Table 12.3.

Table 12.3: Distribution of Working Population (in percentage)

Sector	1951	1981	1991	2000
Primary	72.1	68.7	66.8	56.7
Secondary	10.6	13.5	12.7	17.5
Tertiary	17.3	17.8	20.5	25.8

Source: *Economic Survey 2008-09*

Thus, it is clear that the occupational pattern is not only a static one but also an unbalanced one. This, of course, is not a healthy sign and it explains underdevelopment. Only in 2004-05, there has been a drop in the number of people dependent on agriculture. It is around 52 p.c.

• **Economic and social capital formation:** By social capital we mean transport, irrigation, power, education, health, etc. Building up of social capital is one of the prerequisites of economic development. Infrastructural development helps quicker economic development. So, social capital formation is equivalent to economic development. During the plan period, we have made rapid strides in respect of construction of railway lines, irrigation, power, health and sanitation, education, etc.

Conclusion: If all these are considered as criteria of development, then we must say that the Indian economy has witnessed enormous changes which are not only synonymous with development. Despite these, black spots of underdevelopment are still prominent. At the same time, it is true that we have been able to come out of the 'low level equilibrium trap'. Signs of development are positive in nature. Thus, in India, we find both the pictures of development and underdevelopment. It thus exhibits pictures of contrast. The British economist Joan Robinson once remarked about India that whatever could be said about it, so could the opposite. Anyway, Indian economy can be labelled as an 'under-developed-developing economy'.

12.8 A PROFILE OF PROBLEMS OF INDIA'S GROWTH AND THE ROLE OF THE GOVERNMENT

The growth process started with the launching of the five year plan. Changes took place in several directions. India has now moved to a higher growth path. She has broken the 'syndrome of Hindu rate of growth' of 3.75 p.c. Anyway, from a state of underdevelopment, she has stepped into the status of a 'developing' economy or more aptly LIC. But all is not good. In many areas, achievements fall short of our expectations. The performance has been less impressive as compared with some of the developing countries, like China and other poor Asian countries. Some of them have excelled India and are called Asian Tigers.

Gains of economic growth have not been distributed in favour of the disadvantaged people, although we pledged that inequalities in the distribution of income and wealth have been reduced. One of the greatest evils of income inequality is poverty which has assumed a serious proportion in India. Poverty and inequality are the two sides of the same coin that abounds both in rural and urban areas. Most of the anti-poverty measures taken so for have benefitted little to the poor. That is why, more than one-third (37 p.c.) of the Indian population live below the poverty line (2004-05) thereby robbing of social justice. Poverty cuts human freedom and development means freedom. Since poverty and inequality are interrelated in a society, unfreedom limits development. In the present frame of Indian society, one cannot, however, eliminate poverty and inequality completely.

It is said that some people are poor because they are out of jobs and some people are unemployed because they are poor. As these two problems are considered simultaneously we find a kind of vicious circle of poverty and unemployment. In India, unemployment is a major social and economic problem as well as a great challenge to the authorities. In an economic sense, it is a loss of human capital. It is a big social issue as unemployed labour force tend to alienate themselves from the society in which they live. Finally, chronic unemployment results in political instability. Thus, our foremost task is the generation of productive and gainful employment so that the huge growing unemployed labour force can be absorbed. If we succeed then the goal of inclusive growth can be achieved. So far, our past record is rather miserable. What is striking in the liberalised regime is the case of 'jobless growth'

Here we will deal with these two great issues. In addition, the problem of parallel economy—that has assumed a serious proportion in recent times—will be discussed. Finally, the role of the government in tackling these problems of growth will also be dealt with.

12.9 WHAT IS MEANT BY UNEMPLOYMENT?

Unemployment eludes definition. Yet, in simple terms, it refers to lack of employment opportunities. It can be either voluntary, or involuntary. In economics, unemployment implies involuntary unemployment. A man is involuntarily unemployed if he is not employed but desires to be employed. It is the negative aspect of the economic process. Unemployment is a condition of the labour market in which the supply of labour is greater than the number of jobs available.

Unemployment is, thus, a serious evil. When large number of people remain unemployed, the situation poses a danger to the entire social set-up. It needs to be reduced. It is one of the principal aims of economic policy of any welfare government to completely eradicate unemployment.

12.9.1 Types of Unemployment

Involuntary unemployment may be of various types. A summary account is given:

- *Seasonal*: There are some industries where the same volume of employment cannot be maintained throughout the year, e.g., agriculture. Some people get jobs only for a part of the year and remain unemployed during the rest of the year.
- *Disguised unemployment*: This refers to those men who appear to be employed, but make no contribution to total output. It prevails in Indian agriculture where many people are said to be employed. But if some of them are removed from land, total agricultural productivity would remain unchanged. Suppose, there is a small plot of land owned by 5 men. They work on the land and produce 20 quintals of paddy per annum. Now, suppose one worker is taken away from the land and we see that there is no fall in production. In this sense, the fifth worker is said to be redundant and his marginal productivity is zero. Apparently, this fifth labour is engaged in land but does not help in production. This is called surplus labour or disguisedly unemployed.
- *Structural or technological unemployment*: This type of unemployment occurs due to changes in the techniques or methods of production. For example, when computers are introduced, manual workers are thrown out of employment. Thus, technology dismisses labour from jobs. This is then called structural or technological unemployment.
- *Frictional unemployment*: It occurs when some people are temporarily unemployed due to imperfection in the labour market. This may be due to breakdown of machinery, shortage raw materials industrial reorganisation, lack of knowledge regarding job availability, and the like.

12.9.2 India's Unemployment Problem: Extent and Magnitude

India's unemployment problem is a gigantic one. India's unemployment is mainly of two types: urban unemployment and rural unemployment. Urban unemployment can be classified into industrial unemployment and educated unemployment, while rural unemployment may be classified as open unemployment and disguised unemployment. In addition, India's agricultural sector is characterised by seasonal unemployment.

It is widely believed that reliable estimates of rural and urban unemployment are not available in India. In the period between 1950 and 1970, data or estimates of unemployment were available from the Planning Commission. In addition, the National Sample Survey (NSS) provided data on unemployment in its 9th Round (1955). In 1970, the National Sample Survey Organization (NSSO) was set up. Since the conventional estimates made by the Planning Commission were subject to same serious limitations, urgency was felt to develop good estimates of unemployment. In the light of long experience in field surveys and the recommendations of the Comittee of Experts on Unemployment Estimates, the NSSO has developed and standardised the concepts and definitions of labour force, employment and unemployment and adopted them in 5-yearly surveys on employment and unemployment since 1972-73 (27th Round).

Estimates of unemployment are available on the basis of three concepts:

- *Usual status*: A person is considered unemployed if he or she does not get job for a long period, usually one year. This sort of unemployment is measured in numbers or persons. It indicates chronic unemployment.
- *Current weekly status*: Here the reference period is week. A person is considered unemployed if he or she fails to get work for even one hour during a week. The estimates are made in terms of the average number of persons unemployed per week.
- *Current daily status*: A person who works for one hour but less than four hours a day is considered having worked for half a day. The estimates are given in terms of time rate.

Among these three concepts, the current daily status is the most comprehensive measure of unemployment. According to Raj Krishna: "The daily status flow rate is evidently the most inclusive, covering open as well as partial unemployment.....The weekly status rate can only be regarded as a rough measure of the proportion of workers remaining unemployed for a whole week and the usual status rate as a rough estimate of the 'chronic' unemployment rate."

During the First Five Year Plan (1951-56), the extent of unemployment stood at 5.3 million. This number rose to 34 million at the beginning of the Ninth Plan (1997).

The Planning Commission estimated the extent of unemployment on the basis of the 43rd Round of the NSS for 1987-88. Daily status unemployment—a comprehensive measure of unemployment—rose to 6 p.c. in 1993-94 as against 8.20 p.c. in 1983. As per the latest data the rate of growth of employment, on current daily status (CDS) basis, declined from 2.7 p.c. p.a. in 1983-94 to 1.87 p.c. p.a. in 1994-2005. The decline in the rate of growth of employment during 1990s *vis-a-vis* the higher growth rate in GDP suggests 'a decline in the labour intensity of production.'

Thus, despite plan interventions and commitment towards reduction of unemployment problem, the unemployment rates increase plan after plan. Sarcastically, an author has questioned that if unemployment problem grows in magnitude over time, then how many plans the country needs to make the whole country unemployed? This comment is suggestive of the high incidence of unemployment in India. The position has deteriorated further since 1990s when structural adjustment measures were undertaken. Exit policy, disinvestment, privatisation, etc., are the policies responsible for the slow growth of employment in the organised sector.

During the reform era, what emerges is the insignificant increase in aggregate employment but associated with the sharp shrinkage of employment opportunities in the agricultural sector. The 11th Plan (2007-2012) Document states that the agricultural sector cannot be expected to create additional employment, it can reduce the extent of underemployment. If it is so, incomes and wages of those employed in agriculture will most likely go up while surplus labour will move to non-agricultural sector. Incidently, it may be added that performance in this area is also disappointing. If sector-wise employment pattern is considered, dependence on the agricultural and allied sector as a source of employment has been declining in recent years. Consequently, the rate of growth of organised employment or the share of organised sector employment has increased during the period under consideration. But such increase is 'entirely on account of what is classified as informal employment in the organised sector, that is, workers who do not have the benefit of provident fund and social security. Whereas employment of this category expanded by over 42%, employment categorized as formal was more or less stagnant' (*11th Plan Document, Vol. 1;* p. 69).

Table 12.4: Rate of Growth of Population, Labour Force Employment and Unemployment

Period	Rate of growth of population (% p.a.)	Rate of growth of labour force (% p.a.)	Rate of growth of employment (% p.a.)	Unemployment rate (%)
1993-94—1999-2000	1.98	1.47	1.25	9.22 (1983)
1999-2000—2004-05	1.69	2.84	2.62	6.06 (1993-94)
1983—1993-94	2.11	2.28	2.61	7.31 (1999-00)
1993-94—2004-05	1.85	2.09	1.87	8.28 (2004-05)

Source: *Eleventh Five Year Plan*, Planning Commission, Vol. I, . . 65, Table 4.1

Employment in obsolute terms has increased from 334.20 million in 1993 to 419.65 million (i.e., 2.09 p.c.) in 2004-05.

It is clear from the above table that the population growth declined largely during the period 1993-94—2004-05 over the earlier period. However, employment growth also declined in the later period. As employment growth was lower than the rate of growth of labour force, unemployment rate rose from 6.06 p.c. in 1993-94 to 8.28 p.c. in 2004-05. It is feared that the unemployment rate might go up to 9.8 p.c. in 2006-07 and further to 10.6 p.c. in 2011-12.

The issue of unemployment has assumed a serious proportion consequent upon the global recession that we have been witnessing since 2008. Following such recession, we see drop in the industrial production—thereby adversely affecting mainly both software industry and export industry. One can also find negative employment growth in the construction industry, hotel and restaurant, transport and communications, tourism, etc. An unofficial estimate suggests that at least 2 million have lost work opportunities in India following global meltdown.

12.9.3 Causes of India's Unemployment Problem

Unemployment and underemployment are the two evils causing the greatest hardship to the people of our country. The major causes responsible for unemployment in the agricultural and non-agricultural sector may be explained here.

Bulk of unempolyment in India manifests itself in the rural areas. Such unemployment has two aspects—seasonal and perennial. Seasonal unemployment is caused by the seasonality of agricultural production.

The root cause of underemployment and disguised unemployment—the second aspect of rural unemployment—is the rapid growth of population, the prevalence of the then joint family system, and inelasticity of supply of land. This is also attributable to over-dependence on agriculture (today more than 50 p.c. of the total population) and our inability to develop the secondary sector at a rapid rate so as to have a strong manufacturing base in order to be able to absorb the surplus in agriculture.

Slow rate of capital formation is another reason for the unsatisfactory performance of the agricultural sector in expanding job opportunities. For instance, inadequate irrigation facilities (as a percentage of cropped area, gross irrigated area is estimated to be 42.9 p.c. in 2005-06); shortage of power and fertilisers, etc., have slowed down employment possibilities in the agricultural sector. It has been estimated that its employment elasticity has declined to 0.15 during 1993—2004-05. Thus, the most vital sector of India is shrinking, at least in terms of employment.

Now, let us turn to the problem of urban unemployment. It is of two kinds: (i) unemployment among industrial workers, and (ii) unemployment among the educated people. The first type of unemployment is caused by the fact that the rate at which the expansion of industries has been taking place is not keeping pace with the growth of industrial labour force.

The second type of urban unemployment exists due to a two-fold reason: (i) primarily because there are too many graduates and others relative to the number of job opportunities that require these qualifications. The fault lies partly with the educational system for not imparting technical and vocational education, and partly with educated individuals themselves for preferring white collar jobs to manual and industrial occupations as in Japan. (ii) It is also partly the result of a slower rate of industrial expansion which has failed to absorb these unemployeds in vocational or technical jobs. These two forces complement one another and are often indistinguishable so that one cannot disentagle their separate influences.

The above analysis of unemployment in India suggests that this problem is mainly structural in this country. Here we discuss the major structural causes that have resulted in a massive wastage of human resources over the last 5 decades (1951-2010).

In the *first* place, as economic growth in India is inadequate, the growth of employment is very slow. No doubt, over the plan period, all the sectors of the economy have expanded but not in commensurate with the country's requirements and plan targets. Job opportunities could not be expanded in adequate numbers. Higher growth rate of the Indian economy and the lower growth rate of employment may be attributed to declining employment elasticities in almost all the major sectors of the economy.

Secondly, the growth of population at the rate of 2.2 p.c. p.a. is followed by a corresponding growth of labour force at the rate of 1.9 p.c. Due to a variety of demographic and social factors strong in this country, population grows at a high rate. This results in the growth of labour force in the labour market. On the other hand, the additional labour force does not get employment in view of the slow and inadequate growth of the economy.

Thirdly, inappropriate technology is another reason. Being labour-surplus and capital scarce country, India should have used labour-intensive technologies. On the contrary, expansion of capital-intensive industries during the plan period as well as adoption of the capitalist farming in India have resulted in the number of unemployed persons both in urban and rural areas. Further, industrialists, attracted by higher profit motive, make attempt for rationalisation and labour-saving technology. This is one of the greatest weaknesses in our planning techniques. Virtually, there was no employment planning before the Fifth Plan.

Finally, the faulty educational system is also responsible for the high growth rate of unemployment, especially among the educated people. In other words, the weak manpower planning, i.e., balance between demand and supply of labour force, has failed to deliver the goods in the right manner. Without considering the needs and requirements of the economy, opportunities for education, mainly higher education, have been widened extensively. Bleak employment possibilities encourage people to opt for higher education. In fact, higher education has become an alternative to employment in India. Thus, the education system of our country has made the situation of unemployment an explosive one. The immediate social cost of unemployment and poverty is the increase in crime and criminal activities.

12.9.4 Government Policies and Measures for Removing Unemployment

Usually, one finds two measures of solving any problem. One is the short-run or temporary measure and other is the long-term measure. One of the major objectives of planning in India is the creation of additional employment opportunities in the country and the mitigation of the problem of unemployment. But, long-term or permanent solution of India's unemployment problem had never been spelt out. In the mathematical models on which five year plans are built, 'employment' variable in the first 20 years of planning received very scant attention. Planning authority placed great importance to the development of basic and heavy industries in the Second Five Year Plan (1956-1961). It was argued at that time by the planners that once these industries are developed automatically next category of industries (such as, small scale and cottage industries) would develop. Ultimately, growth and employment would be automatic. This is the essence of the Mahalanobis Strategy of Planning.

But hopes were belied; trickle-down mechanism did not work. As a result, employment possibilities could not increase in the industrial sector. The policy emphasis was changed in the Fifth Plan (1974-1979) when government for the first time attached importance to the growth of employment. Employment policy under the Sixth Plan (1980-1985) had two major goals: reducing unemployment by increasing the rate of growth of the gainfully employed and reducing unemployment on the basis of open unemployment. The Seventh Plan (1985-1990) had also almost the same objective with added emphasis on technological upgradation, modernisation, etc.

Government measures: Since the nature of unemployment in India is different from those of advanced countries, the nature of solution of the problem is different and varied. Since economic growth is not a guarantee to jobs for all, government resorts to direct intervention in employment generation through programmes of asset building, income generation and wage employment. Most of these measures are indeed ad hoc in nature; but are directed towards the disadvantaged or poor persons of mainly rural areas.

Following are the important measures taken by the government to alleviate underemployment and create extra employment opportunities in rural areas:

- *Employment Guarantee Scheme of Maharashtra*: In 1972-73, the Maharasthra Government introduced this novel scheme for the first time to give recognition to the 'right to work' included in the Constitution. Its basic objective was to provide gainful and productive employment to an individual in approved rural works which would raise the productivity of the economy.

Several other measures like Rural Works Programme, Small Farmers' Development Agencies and Marginal Farmers and Agricultural Labourers, Crash Programme for Rural Employment were introduced to provide employment and alleviate underemployment in the decade of 1970s. Results were miserable.

- *Integrated Rural Development Programme*: Since most of the above noted anti-unemployment programmes involved duplication, single integrated programme was the need of the hour. This programme has been named as the IRDP and was launched in 1980 with the aim of raising persons living below the poverty line by the creation of sustainable opportunities for self-employment in the rural sector. To support IRDP, National Rural Employment Programme, (NREP), Training of Rural Youth for Self-employment (TRYSEM), Development of Women and Children in Rural Areas (DWCA), Million Wells Scheme, etc., were launched mostly in the 1980s.
- *Jawhar Rozgar Yojana*: JRY was launched in 1989 (the last year of the Seventh Plan) after merging NREP and RLEGP with the objective of providing additional gainful wage employment during the lean agricultural season to rural poor.
- *Employment Assurance Scheme*: EAS was introduced in 1993 in backward districts situated in drought-prone areas, desert areas, tribal areas and hill areas to give a fillip to employment generation. It was restructured in 1999-2000 to make it a single wage-employment programme.
- *Swarna Jayanti Shahree Rozgar Yojana* (SJSRY): This Yojana came into operation in 1997. It replaced various programmes operated earlier for urban poverty alleviation. It aims at providing gainful employment to the urban unemployed or under-employed poor through encouraging the setting up of self-employment ventures or provision of wage employment.
- *Swarnajayanti Gram Swarozgar Yojana*: SGSY was introduced in 1999 by amalgamating IRDP, DWCRA, TRYSEM, MWS, etc., as a single self-employment programme. It aims at promoting micro-enterprises and helping the rural poor into Self Help Groups. The coverage of the scheme is very wide since it covers all aspects of self-employment. The target group of the scheme is the rural families/individual living below the poverty line. Since inception, total funds utilized under it were Rs. 3,497 crore to benefit 32.48 lakh Swarozgaris.
- *Jawhar Gram Samridhi Yojana*: JGSY was started in 1999 by restructuring the JRY with the main objective of creating durable productive community assets. Generation of wage employment for the rural unemployed poor is its secondary aim.
- *Sampoorna Grameen Rozgar Yojana*: SGRY launched in 2001 aims at providing wage-employment in rural area along with food security, the creation of durable community, social and economic assets and infrastructure development in the rural areas. EAS and JGSY have been integrated with SGRY in April, 2002.

In addition, Prime Minister's Gram Sadak Yojana, Indira Awas Yojana and the flagship programme of the UPA Government Mahatma Gandhi

National Rural Employment Guarantee Programme (MGNREGP) are important policy measures.

Conclusion: "It must be emphasised that the special employment programmes play only supplementary and short-term role, and the lasting solution to the problems of unemployment and poverty is faster generation of productive employment in the growth process. Slow employment growth in the past is partly due to the growth of capital-intensive methods of production which was, to some extent, induced by the protective labour laws. Other factors responsible for slow growth of employment are mismatch between skill requirements and employment opportunity, low productivity, occupational shifts from artisans to unskilled labour and declining trend of labour absorption in agriculture in the past. It is expected that the ongoing economic reforms with emphasis on private participation in the growth process and the expansion of investment and production would give a fillip to the growth of employment in the medium-term."

The failure of India to generate more jobs has been exacerbated by restrictive labour practices. The existence of underutilised capacity has also enabled output growth in many industries to be achieved through increasing the productivity and utilisation of existing labour rather than through hiring new workers. To absorb the natural growth of the labour force, India must create an additional eight million jobs annually. To eliminate open unemployment, employment growth must, therefore, rise even faster. Currently, new jobs are being created to absorb the growth in the labour force, but little progress has been achieved in clearing the backlog of unemployment.

12.10 SOCIAL INJUSTICES AND INCOME INEQUALITIES IN INDIA

One of the important objectives of India's five year plans is the equality in the distribution of economic growth among all persons so that social justice can be established. Economic growth alone cannot bring social justice as the trickle down meachanism did not work in India in the early years of planning. It is often found that the major gains of economic growth are enjoyed by the upper income brackets. Very little has gone to benefit the poor. As a result, social injustice has widened.

At the time of independence, India was one of the poorest nations of the world. Since then various rosy promises and determination to reduce poverty and inequality in the distribution of income and wealth have been made by our political leaders. But nothing much has changed. Rather, like the population growth, inequality has also the tendency to 'grow' in size. A large number of studies made by different economists and institutions confirm this conclusion.

12.10.1 Estimates of Income Inequality in India

In India, the distribution of income is highly inequitable. Several estimates and studies will show that the top—constituting the minority of population—enjoy a sizable proportion of national income while the bottom—who constitute the majority of population—command a rather insignificant proportion of national income. The inequalities are widespread if one takes into account rural and urban distribution profile. Consumption expenditure also indicates the degree of inequality.

Various estimates of personal income distribution have been made during the 1950s by Lydall, Iyenger and Mukherjee, the RBI and the NCAER. Iyenger and Mukherjee estimated the extent of inequality for the period 1952-53 to 1956-57. According to their estimates, top 10 per cent and 5 per cent household cornered as much as 24 per cent and 14 per cent of the national income while the bottom 20 per cent shared only 7.5 per cent in 1952-53. The shares of the top 10 per cent are 17.5 per cent while the bottom 20 per cent had to live with as little as 8.5 per cent in 1956-57. The RBI's estimates for the 1953-54 to 1956-57 also show the similar trend. The NCAER estimates of inequality for 1960 also tell the same story.

However, we do not have any recent studies of income distribution in India to explain the glaring income inequalities that have widened more now. The World Bank in World Development Report 1978 had shown that the top 10 per cent had a share of 36.6 per cent of household income while the lowest 20 per cent had a share of more than 7 per cent of household income.

The distribution of consumption also shows a substantial degree of inequality. According to the NCAER estimate for 1959-60, bottom 20 per cent received 42.39 per cent of the total consumption expenditure. As per the Sixth Plan data, the share of the bottom 40 per cent rural population was only 21.6 per cent and that of top 20 per cent as big as 40 per cent in 1977-78. The inequalities were even worse in the urban sector for the same time period.

A recent NCAER (July, 2010) shows that India's number of rich people outstrips the number of poor people now.

Furthermore, land being the chief source of income in India, inequalities are equally prominent with reference to the distribution of land. Data provided in the Sixth Five Year Plan reveal that more than 10 hectares of land are enjoyed by only 3 per cent of the cultivating population, while less than 2 hectares are owned by 72.6 per cent of the total agricultural population. A survey of land ownership indicates that 5 per cent urban population are the owners of the property to the extent of 52 per cent, while 20 per cent city-dewllers do not have any property.

All these information lead us to conclude that in India over the planning period income inequality has assumed a serious proportion. Now it is our time to enquire why "indecent" income inequalities in India have increased rather than diminished.

12.10.2 Causes of Income Inequalities

Because of the inherent character of our economic system based on the institutions of private property, inequalities in India have widened. Here we will emphasise this point in greater detail.

Firstly, one observes the inequitable distribution of land holdings in the rural economy. The pattern of distribution of landholding as revealed in the NSS (26th Round) data of 1971-72 also showed that the top 5.44 per cent of the peasant households possessed ownership of land of about 40 per cent of the total agricultural land while 44 per cent marginal farmers (having land ownership below 1 acre) owned even less than 2 per cent land. More than 10 hectares of land are enjoyed by only 2 per cent of the cultivating population, while less than 2 hectares are owned by 6 per cent of total agricultural population. This means that land ceiling measures have made little impact to reduce inequality in the distribution of land.

Similarly, in the industrial field, one notices concentration of assets in the hands of a few small businessmen. Some of the large industrial houses have amassed huge wealth over the plan period. Not only this, there is grossly unsatisfactory asset distribution. Remember that the assets owned by the bottom section of the population are not income-yielding assets since it contains mainly huts, household goods and livestock. In the urban areas, according to the NCAER survey of 1975-76, 47 per cent of the total built-up property was in possession of the top 10 per cent property owners as against less than 12 per cent property being owned by the bottom 60 per cent of the population.

Apart from the above-said causes of income inequalities in India, there are other cooperating factors which have sharpened the already existing inequalities over time. These are:

Secondly, the most important cause of inequality and, hence, poverty, is the chronic unemployment and underemployment. This definitely has the potentiality of reducing output, and, hence, income. This means that the low rate of economic growth is the cause of the low level of income of the vast majority of the population.

Thirdly, tax structure of the country leading to tax evasion is another influencing factor in increasing inequality. Tax evasion has led to the growth of black money in a reckless speed. This black income is owned by the high income group people. Then there are government officials and business barons who untiringly devise schemes to cheat the government so as to earn huge rental income and endangers the lives of '*aam admi*'. This tax structure is contributing greatly to fuel the inflationary spiral. Inflation tends to worsen economic inequality.

Fourthly, it is argued by the leftist economists that markets marginalise people. Since 1991, the Indian economy has become more market-oriented rather than state-oriented. In a market economy, purchasing power of individual makes the distribution of goods. Larger the income greater is the purchasing power. Market expansion, on the one hand, and the reduction of state patronage on social sectors of health, education, etc., on the other hand, have forced low-income group of people to buy those commodities at an expensive price. Commercialisation of health and education have been marginalising poor people more—leading to an increase in income inequality.

Speculative hoarding and smuggling activities have taken a serious proportion. People engaged in these activities manage to enjoy a greater proportion of income.

Generally, the twin causes of poverty are underdevelopment and inequality of wealth. Both factors are equally responsible. Thus, our economy is caught in a vicious circle. The poor remain poor and do not earn enough to invest in any sector of the economy. This causes poor growth of the economy. Growth and inequality have to be tackled successfully.

12.10.3 Government Measures to Reduce Inequalities

One of the important objectives of India's five year plans is the reduction in inequality. And to reduce the undesirable income inequalities, the Government has taken a variety of measures. These are:

In the *first* place, the Government has tried to remove poverty and inequality in income distribution through five year plans by accelerating economic growth. It is argued that the average income could not be increased substantially only by redistribution. Hence, it is required that the total amount of goods and services produced by the country must increase substantially. In view of this, the Government has always hoped to raise the growth rate in various plans by allocating larger and larger resources in agriculture, industry, and other sectors. Further, it is to be taken into account that redistribution of income implies increasing the consumption of the poor. In this connection, P. Chaudhury argues that if any one believes that the possibilities of redistributing existing incomes or consumption is small then additional consumption can be made out of incremental incomes or output. Hence the necessity of accelerating economic growth—a right direction to eliminate or reduce income inequalities.

Secondly, a major cause of rural inequality is the unequal distribution of land ownership. To curb glaring inequalities in the land distribution, the Government has introduced various land reform measures. Through its land reform measures, like the abolition of the zamindary system, ceiling on rural landholdings, etc., the Government has brought about a great change in the country's agrarian structure. Surplus lands in excess of ceiling have been redistributed in favour of the small and marginal farmers. But, on close scrutiny, it appears that the land reform measures are yet to make any dent on rural poverty or inequality.

Thirdly, the cause of inequality is the lack of employment opportunities. Poverty or inequality and unemployment go hand in land. Thus, the creation of adequate employment opportunities is central to the issue of reducing inequality or poverty. But no significant progress has ever been achieved in this direction.

However, several employment-generating programmes have been undertaken by the Government to provide employment for the rural poor as anti-poverty measures. In addition, the encouragement of small-scale industries as well as concessions and technical help given to them have also helped to create more employment and self-employment opportunities.

Finally, the anti-monopoly policy of the Government of India is another and highly relevant policy for the reduction of the overall disparity of incomes and wealth in the economy. This policy has greater relevance than to raising the absolute levels of incomes of the very poor. To control the growth of large business houses in India, the Government of India has passed the Monopolies and Restrictive Trade Practices (MRTP) Act in 1969. However, this Act, has now been abolished.

Such policy continued till 1990. However, the Government placed the red carpet at the footsteps of large industrial houses in its industrial policy announced in 1991.

To sum up, all the aforesaid measures made little impact on inequality or poverty. Had these measures been effective to some extent, a vast majority of Indian population would not have lived below the poverty line.

On the other hand, various anti-poverty measures to lift the poor sections have hardly affected their fortunes. It was assumed by planners that a high growth rate would reduce inequalities and poverty and, hence, social injustice, rather automatically. But such 'trickle down hypothesis' did not work in India. That is why newer and newer schemes are launched almost regularly to raise the income level of poor persons. But again, nothing great has been achieved.

12.11 PROBLEM OF POVERTY—DEFINITION OF POVERTY LINE

Inequality and poverty are interrelated. Poverty may be a reflection of inequality. In general, a person is considered to live in poverty if his (her) income and other means of support are insufficient.

There is some controversy about the percentage of population living below the poverty line in India since measurement involves decisions relating to indicators, time trends, interpretation of data, etc. Whether one should use income or consumption as the criterion, whether to use indicators which are distribution-sensitive, whether to place emphasis on non-income indicators—are all important questions to address the problem of poverty.

Defining poverty line is the first step for estimating poverty. Nutrition-based norm may be used to identify the number of people below that norm. If a person is unable to bear the expenditure required for maintenance of nutritional norms then he is categorised as poor—living below the poverty line. Not only calories, but also the amount of protein intake should be considered as a criterion. But, generally, calorie intake norms are accepted as a simpler indicator of poverty.

12.11.1 Extent of Poverty

Economists make use of the concept of poverty line to gauge the extent of poverty—

the number of poor people living in the country. So far, various studies have been conducted by economists at different times since 1962. These studies are: Study Group of the Planning Commission headed by P.D. Ojha (1962), Dandekar and Rath, Pranab Bardhan, B. S. Mishra and so on. The latest one is the Tendulkar Committee. However, there is no uniformity in the estimates of poverty in India and almost all the official poverty estimates are criticised on various grounds.

The concept of poverty is associated with deprivation in respect of basic human needs—both material and non-material. Anyway, the concept of poverty is multidimensional. The Planning Commission appointed an Expert Group headed by D. T. Lakdawala in 1993. Prior to the acceptance of the Tendulkar Committee Report in 2010, the all-India official poverty lines were defined on the basis of recommended per capita calorie norms of 2,400 (rural) and 2,100 (urban) per day. This definition covered the consumption of all good services incorporated in the rural and urban reference poverty line baskets. As this measurement involved numerous problems, the Planning Commission set up an Expert Group under the Chairmanship of Suresh Tendulkar to examine the issue and suggest new poverty line and estimates.

Although the Expert Group estimates poverty based on private household consumption expenditure, it moves away from the caloric requirement. Further, it considers actual private consumption expenditure per capita on food, education, and health. In the earlier estimates based on calorie requirements, education and health remained out of consideration. In this sense, the present poverty lines are much broader. The revised poverty estimates made by the Tendulkar Committee in 1993-94 are 50.1 p.c. in rural areas, 31.8 p.c. in urban areas, and 45.3 p.c. in the country as a whole. The official estimates (even before the acceptance of the Tendulkar Committee Report) on poverty in 1993-94 for rural, urban areas, estimates and all-India level were respectively 37.2 p.c.; 32.6 p.c., and 36 p.c. The new poverty line based on head-count ratio as suggested by the Tendulkar Committee—is 41.8 p.c., 25.7 p.c. and 37.2 p.c. for rural, urban areas, and all-India, respectively in 2004-05. However, the old methodology used by the Planning Commission on the incidence of poverty yielded a poverty ratio of 28.3 p.c. in rural areas, 25.7 p.c. in urban areas, and 27.5 p.c. for the country as a whole in 2004-05.

Thus the recommendations and the acceptance of Tendulkar Committee Report suggest an increase in BPL coverage. In other words, it implies an automatic expansion of the PDS and other government schemes like the proposed National Food Security Bill where beneficiaries are to be decided on the BPL basis.

12.11.2 Causes of Increasing Poverty

Now we will mention some factors which are operating in India to widen economic inequality and poverty despite planned efforts to reduce them.

Table 12.5: Estimates of Poverty Based on Old Methodology and New Methodology (Tendulkar Committee)

	Old methodology		New methodology	
	1993-94	2004-05	1993-94	2004-05
Rural	37.2	28.3	50.1	41.8
Urban	32.6	25.7	31.8	25.7
All-India	36.0	27.5	45.3	37.2

In the *first* place, ownership of industries in the hands of a few small businessmen in India has made the distribution of income inequitable. These people have amassed huge profit, and, hence, wealth.

Secondly, in the initial stage of planning, planners placed a great deal of emphasis on growth objective as growth itself would take care of inequality or poverty. The Fifth Plan (1974-1979) stated that a higher rate of growth of national income would itself enlarge employment opportunities and, hence, standard of living of poor masses. But this did not happen. But in a society characterised by gross unequal distribution of assets, economic growth itself failed to reduce poverty. Thus the problem of poverty in India lies in the economic structure—"skewed distribution of the ownership of income-yielding assets".

Thirdly, same trend is observed in the rural economy where we find inequaitable distribution of land.

Fourthly, the most important cause of inequality and, hence, poverty is the chronic unemployment and underemployment. This definitely has the potentiality of reducing output and, hence, income. Despite several measures to reduce unemployment, the problem in recent times has assumed a gigantic proportion making the problem of poverty more acute as well as painful.

Fifthly, tax structure of the country leading to tax evasion is another influencing factor in increasing inequality and poverty. Tax evasion has led to the growth of black money in a reckless speed. This black income is owned by the high income group people. Black money fuels the inflationary spiral. Inflation tends to widen economic inequality.

Sixthly, high rate of population growth in India has also made the problem of poverty an acute one. Because of illiteracy, population growth among the poor masses is high. Above all, as they consider male child as an asset, they enlarge their size of families. Obviously, with little employment and bigger-sized families, incomes per head of the family are inadequate even to meet the basic food-need. This is one aspect of the 'vicious circle of poverty'.

Seventhly, continuous hike in procurement prices of foodgrains without a corresponding increase in wages is responsible for a rise in poverty, mainly rural poverty. Above all, benefits and subsidies given to the Indian population are mostly enjoyed by the richer sections of the community. For instance, fertiliser subsidy mostly serves the needs of the rich farmers. Subsidised foodgrains are supplied to all through fair price shops. Thus, inadequate subsidies given to the poorer people are responsible for increase in poverty ratio.

Finally, considering the extent of poverty, the anti-poverty measures taken by the government are grossly inadequate. As a result, a large number of people now live below the poverty line.

Generally, the twin causes of poverty are under-development and inequality of wealth. Both factors are equally responsible. Thus, our economy is caught in a vicious circle. The poor remain poor and do not earn enough to invest in any sector of the economy. This causes poor growth of the economy. Growth and inequality have to be tackled successfully to start removal of poverty.

12.11.3 Review of Poverty Alleviation Programmes

As per the new methodology used by the Tendular Committee, the total number of poor people in India has gone up to about 407 million in 2004-05. Earlier, the number of population below the poverty line was rather lower—403 million in 1993-94. In view of this, anti-poverty measures were taken in the Fifth Five Year Plan (1974-79). However, the planners believed that high economic growth would take care of poor people. That is why, planners laid greater emphasis on economic growth in the first four plans. They hoped that the trickle down theory would work. This means that, as growth rate rises automatically benefits of higher growth rate would be shared by all the members of society—thereby ensuring social justice. Unfortunately, hopes were belied and the poverty ratio went on increasing. An attempt was made in the Fifth Plan to correct this situation when an all-out effort was made to tackle the growing poverty and unemploy-ment. 'Garibi Hatao' objective is the hallmark of this plan. Investments are to be made in such a way that it not only ensures higher growth rate but also establishes social justice. In view of this, several poverty alleviation programmes were undertaken.

First is the employment-oriented programmes aimed at the target group to step up the purchasing power. As the incidence of rural poverty is high, various special employment programmes were launched in the 1970s and onwards. Some of the schemes are:

Swanajayanti Gram Swarozgar Yojana (SGSY), Sampoorna Grammin Rozgar Yojana (SGRY), Pradhan Mantri Gram Sadak Yojana (PMGSY), Indira Awas Yojana (IAY), Swarnajayanti Saharee Rozgar Yojana (SJSRY), National Rural Employment Guarantee Scheme (NREGS) or currently renamed Mahatma Gandhi National Rural Employment Guarantee Scheme (MGNREGS) , etc., are the most important. Some of these programmes may be briefly explained here.

• **SGSY/IRDP:** The Integrated Rural Development Programme (IRDP) was introduced in 1977 to promote self-employment by providing productive assets and inputs to the rural people living below the poverty line. To facilitate employment, the three sub-schemes under the IRDP were TRYSEM (Training of Youth for Self-Employment), DWCRA (Development of Woman and Children in Rural Areas), and MWS (Millions Wells Scheme). Reorganising these three sub-schemes the IRDP was replaced by the Swarnajayanti Gram Swarozgor Yojana (SGSY) in 1999. It is a self-employment programme for the rural people of the country. The basic objective is to bring the assisted Swarozgaris above the poverty line by providing them income- generating assets through bank loans and government subsidy. This scheme helps rural people in the formation of Self-Help Groups (SHGs). The cost for this scheme is shared by the Union and State Government on a 75 : 25 basis. Till December 2009, as many as 36.78 lakh SHGs had been formed and nearly 133 lakh Swarozgaris have been assisted.

• **SGRY:** By merging Jawahar Gram Sarmriddhi Yojana (launched in 1999) and Employment Assurance Scheme, the Government introduced Sampoorna Grammen Rozgar Yojana (SGRY) in September 2001 with the objective of providing employment in rural areas. The objectives of the scheme are manifold: providing food security to the poor disadvantaged people, creation of durable social and economic assets of the community and improvements in rural infrastructures so as to boost additional wage employment. In 2008, this Yojana has been merged with the NREGS or MGNREGS.

• **IAY:** The objective of Indira Awas Yojana is to provide financial assistance to the SCs and STs, free bonded labourers, non-SC/ST rural households, widows and physically challenged rural people living below the poverty. line in the rural areas for construction/upgradation of changes. During 2008-09, 21.05 lakh houses have been constructed.

• **PMGSY:** The Pradhan Mantri Gram Sadak Yojana was launched on December 2000 as a 100 p.c. centrally-sponsored scheme. The primary objective of this scheme is to provide all-weather connectivity to the unconnected rural areas. Till March 2009, a total road length of 2,14,280 kms have been constructed.

• **SJSRY:** Not only the rural poor, but also the urban poor households have been included so as to reduce the burden of poverty by expanding employment opportunities. Previously introduced many schemes for urban poor have been merged and a new scheme called Swarnajayanti Shaharee Rozgar Yojana was launched in 1997. The SJSRY has been revamped on April, 2009. The revamped scheme provides gainful employment to the unemployed and underemployed poor through encouraging the setting up of self-employment ventures by the urban poor. During the year 2009-10, about 29,000 urban poor were assisted to set up individual enterprises. About 13,500 urban poor women have been given help to set up group enterprises. The number of total beneficiaries under the scheme till March 2009 reached about 9.50 lakhs.

• **NREGP/MGNREGP:** The National Rural Employment Guarantee Act (NREGA) enacted in 2005 is undoubtedly a landmark legislation as far as the entitlement of 100 days of unskilled work in rural India is concerned. The Act came into force on 2 February 2006 in 200 backward districts of the country. In 2007, another 130 districts came under its purview and from April 1, 2008 the Act is in operation in all the districts of the country.

This is the largest social safety net scheme not found anywhere else in other developing countries. Being a pioneering legislator, the Act offers and provides legal guarantees of 100 days of employment to the vulnerables. It is a right-based framework for wage-employment programme. Being statutory in character, the government is accountable for providing unskilled work for 100 days at the minimum wage to each household for providing employment in a time-bound manner.

Features of the MGNREGA : At least one adult member of a rural family willing to do unskilled normal work is legally entitled for wage-employment. Wages will be paid in accordance with the minimum wages on a weekly basis. To get a job, one has to apply for registration to the local Gram Panchayat. The applicant, after receiving job card from the GP, will make a written application for employment. Employment will be given within 15 days after submission of the application. If employment is not provided, daily unemployment allowance will have to be paid; job will have to be provided within 5 km radius of the village At least one-third of persons must be women.

As is known to all that agricultural activities are seasonal in character, many poor landless and small and marginal farmers remain out of employment during off season. Thus the incidence of poverty is mostly among them. As soon as the scheme starts working unskilled employment gets a boost in rural India. Above all, this scheme helps in the creation of durable productive areas. Wage-employment programme under the scheme helps water conservation and harvesting, small irrigation, digging of pond, afforestation, road construction, flood and drought control works, etc. These rural works are expected to increase the yield of agricultural produce as well as help regeneration of natural and livelihood resource base.

The scheme has many areas of achievements and failures. Since its inception to 2009 August, as many as 12.27 crore rural households got employment against which a wage-income of more than Rs. 41,000 crore had been created. As far as wage-employment is concerned, priorities had been accorded to SCs and STs households and women. It is said that the scheme has been more successful in the creation of 100 days of employment in a year, but not in the creation of durable social assets of the rural districts. Many loopholes of the earlier anti-poverty scheme have been plugged under it. Leakages in respect of employment days and wage payments have been largely prevented by this scheme. These are wage payments through opening accounts in post offices and banks, social audit, use of Right to Information (RTI) Act, active participation of Gram Panchayat, etc. Because of its performance, some rich farmers have been complaining about the non-availability of farm labour during sowing season to carry out agri-cultural operations.

But its failures are nonetheless significant during 2008-09. For the 18 states 43 person-days of employment were provided against 42 person-days of 2007-08. Among the states, Rajasthan tops the list—nearly 80 days. Another disturbing fact is that during the last $3\frac{1}{2}/4$ years, as many 19.49 lakh jobs were taken up but only 14 p.c. of these had been completed by August 2009. This means that the scheme has largely failed in creating rural social productive assets. Another area of concern is the volume of corruption. Despite the provision of social audit, roughly Rs. 800-1,000 crore evaporated midway in the state of Rajasthan. Misappropriation of funds under this flagship programme in Uttar Pradesh has come to light in July 2010 when a chunk of more than Rs. 50 lakh was spent on buying tricycles, plastic balls and toys to keep labourers' children busy at work sites in the Sultanpur district of UP and Rs. 1 crore in Gonda of UP (*Times of India*, July 2010). Thus, the scheme has failed to arouse transparency and accountability to the minimum desired level.

Despite these shortcomings, everyone recognises the initiatives taken by the MGNREGS for the transformation of rural livelihoods in India. This scheme heralds a revolution in rural governance in India. This scheme will very surely help in attaining the goal of 'inclusive growth' by removing its deficiencies. The geography of rural India is expected to change more favourably if the scheme becomes more successful. It will not only bring improvement in the quality of life in villages but also help overall social and human development.

12.12 INFLATION

It is said that slight increase in the rate of prices is good for economic development. But, once the slight increase in prices threatens to be a larger one, fruits of economic development are minimised or lost. That is why price stability is considered as an essential condition for stability in the life of an economy as well as economic growth. In India, inflation is public enemy number one. It is playing havoc almost since the beginning of the Second Plan (1956-1961). As a result of high rate of inflation, India's economic growth in real terms seems to be unsatisfactory.

Except for the First Plan (1951-56), when there was a fall in the general price level, the Indian economy has been badly fighting the menace of rising prices of varying intensity till now.

The period from the early 70s to 2010 is a period of great inflationary pressure. During the two years of 1973-74 and 1974-75, the price rise was phenomenal. The official price index rose by 30 p.c. in 1973-74—an all-India record. However, the situation started looking up after 1975. The rate of inflation dropped down from 16.7 per cent in 1980-81 to 2.4 per cent in 1981-82. But this favourable situation was a short-lived one. During the Seventh Plan (1985-90), the average rise in price level was roughly 7 p.c. per annum. But the massive price rise occurred during the early years of 1990s for which the Government itself can be blamed. The inflationary spiral which began in October 1990 continued through 1991, with the rate of inflation peaking at 16.7 p.c. in August 1991. The annual inflation rate (as measured by the WPI) declined to a single digit level by August 1992. Average annual inflation rate (measured by WPI) in 2000-01, 2004-05 and 2008-09) hovered around above 5.5 p.c. However, the year 2008-09 witnessed a high inflation rate of 8.4 p.c. because of high global fuel prices and rise in food prices. As these prices started stabilising in the first half of 2009-10, inflation rate started declining. Again, from September 2009 onwards, WPI inflation started rising at a very fast rate because of the rise in price of food items specially and non-food agricultural items. Reason that is advanced for this development is the shortfall in agricultural production due to deficient rainfall all over the country. Average food inflation went up to 13.54 p.c. during fiscal 2008-09. Overall food inflation peaked at a high of almost 20 p.c. in December 2009.

12.12.1 Causes of Price Rise in India

Inflationary rise in prices can be caused by a rise in demand for goods and services or the failure of supply to increase correspondingly.

The following factors may be said to have caused inflation in India during the plan period:

- **Demand-pull factors:** During the plan period there has been a phenomenal growth of money supply. As supply of money exceedes the available goods, inflation appeares. Demand-pull inflation may be attributed to excessive money supply growth. The question is: Why did money supply grow in the plan period?

First, there has been a massive increase in government expenditure. Total expenditure of both Central and State governments that stood at 18.6 p.c. in 1960-61 rose to 44 p.c. in 1989-90. For the rest of the period, this figure has not shown any sign of decline. Thus government expenditure creates an increased demand for goods and services. When the government spends more, money ultimately reaches the hands of the people who spend more and thus increases inflationary pressures. Consequent upon the implementation of the Fifth Pay Commission's recommendations in 1998-99, government expenditure came to 30 p.c. of GDP. It is feared that this sum will go up now following the implementation of recommendations of the Sixth Pay Commission. The complete picture is yet to come out. Most importantly, most of the government expenditure in India is of non-developmental variety (e.g., interest burden on public debt , food subsidy, defence, etc.). It is estimated that more than 35 p.c. of government expenditure is non-developmental type. Rising volume of non-developmental or unproductive expenditure triggers inflation.

Secondly, rising government expenditure alone is not the cause of money supply. Deficit financing contributes greatly to the money supply growth. Fiscal deficit as a percentage of GDP increased from 5.9 p.c. in 1991-92 to a high of 6.2 p.c. in 2001-02. Since then it continued to fall to as low as 2.7 p.c. of GDP in 2007-08. But this trend reversed in 2008-09 and in 2009-10 it jumped to 6.8 p.c. To finance its expenditure, government borrows money. One point about the financing of fiscal deficit is the growing monetised deficit (i.e., borrowing from the RBI) and borrowing from the market at higher interest rates. The basic reason behind the high dose of fiscal deficit is the failure in mobilising financial resources in accordance with the expenditure needs of the government.

Thirdly, there is no denying the fact that unaccounted money is an important demand-pull factor that fuels inflation in India in a greater way. Black money or unaccounted money—i.e., income which is not declared to the tax authority—is a great menace to the Indian economy. Thus, tax evasion and black income go hand in hand. Black income or concealed income may be used for the creation of real assets like buildings and other properties. Black income is mainly spent for unproductive purposes. It has been estimated that the volume of black money accounts for 18-21 p.c. of GDP; to some researchers it is nearly 44 p.c. of GDP (in 1999). Black money created parallel economy that has grown in volume over the years is one of the important drivers of demand-pull inflation in India.

Finally, inflow of foreign capital (non-debt type) triggers demand-pull inflation in India. As inflows increase, market experiences more dollar inflow. This causes an appreciation of Indian rupee. This then forces the RBI to buy more dollars. As the volume of dollar increase, supply of Indian rupee and M_3 increase. Such money supply increase consequent upon the inflow of non-debt foreign capital ignites inflation.

• **Cost-push factors:** Inflation is not caused alone by demand-pull forces. Supply-side constraints in wage goods seem to be another good reason for inflation. Most important of the these are following.

First, a decline in aggregate supply—either due to a crop failure or restricted imports—can contribute towards inflation. Whenever agricultural production suffers, inflation follows suit. Consecutive low monsoons in the last three years has led to an unprecedented rise in food inflation to the extent of more than 19 p.c. in December 2009. The increase in price level since September 2009 is mainly due to the rise in the prices of mainly food articles caused by deficient monsoon and expectations of shortage.

High food inflation is observed in cases of onions, potatoes, other vegetables, pulses, rice, wheat, etc Except edible oils, inflation is found in non-administered mineral oils in the fuel group, sugar and oilcakes in manufactured groups. Sugar production has fallen significantly from 2007-08. India is a net importer of pulses leading to a shortage expectations. Thus domestic production constraints have been pushing prices of food items.

Rising domestic inflation gets incentives through world food inflation that has been rising since April 2008. This means there exists global and domestic price linkage. However, the impact of global prices on domestic prices can be lessened through appropriate domestic policy measures. However, apart from the linkage, jump in the minimum support price of various crops since 2007-08 has also contributed to inflationary tendencies. Large hoardings of foodgrains and speculative trading by black marketeers also stokes inflationary fire.

The same is true with the industrial and consumer goods which could not meet the gap between demand and supply—this has enabled producers to increase prices keeping in line with their profit motive. It may be added that infrastructural bottlenecks—particularly in respect of transport, power, etc.,—have been causing low output, thereby leading to a rise in the general price level.

Secondly, many agricultural crops and industrial products are subject to government regulations. Government sets procurement price and minimum support price for many agricultural products. There has been almost a regular upward revision in the prices of foodgrains. Regular upward revisions in the prices of coal, steel, cement, railway fares and freights are made as the prices of these products are called administered prices. Price set by the fiat of the government are called administered prices. Such prices are often raised to cope up rising production cost and/or compensating the losses incurred in the public sector industries. These prices then ultimately pulls costs upward and consequently inflation rate.

Thirdly, India's dependence on imported pretroleum products is too large. The country is forced to import more than 75 p.c. of its requirements. The inflation in non-administered petro-products is linked to international crude oil prices. An unprecedented jump in oil prices ($ 142 per barrel) was noticed in the first half of 2008. Average international crude oil prices increased from $44 in January-March 2009 to $ 80 per barrel in June-

July, 2010. Such price inflation in petro-products have a strong bearing on rising inflation. Anyway, inflation is thus imported.

Fourthly, India cannot remain insulated from what is happening in the global market. Whenever inflation threatens in other countries, India is supposed to purchase goods from these countries, of course at a higher price. Domestic inflation thus rises in sympathy with the global inflation. Further, the new economic policy encourages higher and higher exports. More exports means lesser domestic availability and, hence, price rise caused by demand-supply imbalances.

Finally, let us talk about sellers' inflation. Under it, everyone wants to have higher prices. Workers want higher wages, landlords more rent, traders more profit. The zeal for higher income means larger sharing of the national income. But all cannot get more—one gets more at the cost of the others. This means a drop in real national output but not in monetary terms. This is what we may call inflation from which the country cannot escape.

Thus, inflation in India is caused by the interplay of both demand-pull factors and cost-push factors. Which factors are more important is difficult to answer because the movements in the inflation rate reflect changes in both demand and supply conditions in the economy. Even then the outlook for inflation in the first half of 2010 is largely conditioned by the supply-side pressures, particularly in respect of food articles. The government is banking on good monsoon in the current year (2010). If weather variablility is stabilised one can expect a good khariff production that may bring down the current food inflation rate. But if it is belied, the country will experience a further spurt in inflation.

Inflation management thus involves controlling both the demand and supply situation as well as controlling inflationary expectations. Now we turn to anti-inflationary measures.

12.12.2 Anti-inflationary Measures

A number of measures have been adopted by the government and the RBI relating to money suppy, revenue-expenditure pattern and distribution of essential items. By contolling money, overall aggregate demand is controlled. That is why the RBI uses various monetary measures to control money supply growth. Likewise, government through the change in revenue-expenditure arrangements, attempt to regulate people's disposable income. This policy measure is called fiscal policy. In addition, direct measures are also used to reign price increases. In spite of these measures taken by the Government and the RBI, we occasionally see rising inflationary trends. Whenever such inflation reaches a critical high, emergency measures are taken.

Here we will present anti-inflationary policies grouped into: (i) monetary policy, (ii) fiscal policy, and (iii) direct measures—with special reference to the current decade's, anti-inflationary measures.

• **Monetary policy measures:** The monetary policy allows the Reserve Bank to use general and selective credit control measures. The stress has been on restricting bank credit against inflation-sensitive goods and to influence the cost and availability of commercial bank credit. In recent times, the RBI's reliance on bank rate and selective credit control as anti-inflationary measure is conspicously invisible. The RBI, prior to 1991, used the bank rate extensively as an anti-inflationary weapon. The last time the bank rate was raised in 1991 from 10 per cent to 12 per cent. The RBI in June 1997 lowered down the bank rate from 12 p.c. to 10 p.c. in two stages. As price stability in the later years of 1990s was achieved, the RBI went on lowering bank rate from time to time. It was lowered down to 6 p.c. in April 2003.

Since then (that is over the last 7 years), the bank rate has remained unchanged at 6 p.c. till June, 2010.

In fact, the RBI putting less emphasis on the bank rate places greater reliance on 'repo rate' (RR) and 'reverse repo rate' (RRR). RR is the rate at which commercial banks take loans from the RBI by depositing securities while RRR is the rate at which the RBI sells securities to the commercial banks. Increase in RR and RRR mean more control over the money supply. As price situation tended to be a problematic one to the common people during 2007-08, both RR and RRR were raised to 7.25 p.c. and 7.75 p.c. in October 2007 with the aim of reducing liquidity of cash so that the then inflationary tendencies could be curbed. As price situation eased marginally, RR was raised to 7.75 p.c. while RRR was lowered down to 6 p.c. in April 2008. By end-December 2008, both RRR and RR were kept pegged at 5 p.c. and 6.50 p.c. due to the development of recessionary tendencies both in the country and all over the globe.

In 2008-09, a policy challenge was to be faced: make a balance between higher growth path and price stability against the backdrop of global meltdown. Since then, the RBI has been trying to counter economic meltdown in India by reducing RRR to 3.25 p.c., RR to 4.75 p.c. in April 2009. However, with the recovery in the global economy in the last quarter of 2009, and the rising inflationary tendencies in the domestic economy, particularly in respect of food articles, the RBI again intervened so as to mop up excess liquidity from the market by raising both RRR and RR to 3.5 p.c. and 5 p.c., respectively in March 2010. As food inflation continued its upward thrust, the RBI again, in June 2010 raised these two short-term policy interest rates—the RR and the RRR—by 0.25 percentage point.

India's success in counteracting global meltdown is faster. This is a good sign. But inflation rate of double digit is definitely a great concern. As demand-pull inflationary pressures are still strong the RBI has again raised the repo rate (short-term lending rate) by 25 basis points form 5.5 p.c. to 5.75 p.c.; and the reverse repo rate (borrowing rate) by 50 basis points from 4 p.c. to 4.50 p.c. from July 27, 2010.

The RBI frequently uses cash reserve ratio (CRR) with a view to stabilising prices. Though CRR was raised to as high as 15 p.c. in March 1989, it was to be lowered down as per the recommendations of the Narasimham Committee. Since 1998, the RBI has been reducing it regularly as soon as price stability was achieved. By January 2007, it was lowered to 5.50 p.c. After that, as price situation worsened, CRR had been raised regularly. It was raised to 9 p.c. in September 2008 when inflation rate climbed up to almost 13 p.c. With the coming of global recession there had been a regular fall in CRR to 5 p.c. by April 2009. Now as inflation again appeared with ugly head, the RBI raised it to 5.75 p.c. in March 2010 and to 6 p.c. in April 2010.

Apart from the CRR, commercial banks are under obligation to invest certain amount of old and unencumbered government and other approved securities as secondary reserve. This is called statutory liquidity ratio (SLR). By 1990, it was raised to 38.5 p.c. As the statutory floor of SLR is at 25 p.c., it was reduced to 25 p.c. by 2006. However, with the removal of statutory limit of SLR at 25 p.c., the SLR stands reduced to 24 p.c. in November 2008. Since then, the SLR has not been changed by the RBI.

Finally, open market operations of the RBI has now become defunct.

• **Fiscal policy measures:** The three main planks of India's fiscal policy are taxation, expenditure, and borrowing. By raising various direct tax rates, government intends to curb disposable income to contain aggregate demand. However, as India was one of the highly taxed nations of the world, tax evasion was rampant. Tax evasion then causes inflation to flare up. To plug this loophole, there has been continuous and concerted effort to reduce tax burden leading to a greater compliance. Partly this objective has been fulfilled. Another reason for inflation generation in India is the increase in unproductive expenditure. But the impact on the government in this direction is rather minimal since there has been no let-up in the reduction of interest-defence-subsidy expenditures leading to a huge growth in fiscal deficit and increase in net RBI credit to the government. Fiscal deficit rose to 6.6 p.c. of GDP in 1990-91. It declined to 4 p.c. in 2004-05 and to 2.3 p.c. in 2007-08. Anyway, such reduction in fiscal deficit is ascribed to increase in tax revenues and reduction in non-interest expenditure of defence and subsidy as well as interest expenditures.

Government's efforts in curbing the menace of black money to contain inflation are rather limited. Black money is rather a villain of the piece.

• **Supply management:** In addition to the monetary policy and fiscal policy measures, it is necessary to have due attention on raising production and productivity even on a long-term basis of agricultural commodities, mainly wage goods. Efforts are on in increasing agricultural production and productivity since the days of green revolution. Success was achieved. But with the decline in public investment in agriculture in recent years, deficient rainfall caused by global warming, conversion of arable land in bio-fuel production and other commercial crops, etc., have resulted in a serious shortage of food crops. All these have cumulative adverse effect on agricultural food thereby fuelling food inflation to an unprecedented height. Since domestic output fell short of the country's requirement, the country had to import some agricultural crops. In addition, import duties on edible oil, pulses, sugar are revised from time to time.

A key component of supply management of essential foodgrains is the public distribution system (PDS). Since PDS is deemed to be inefficient poor people are hit hard and are often forced to commit suicide. Food insecurity and hunger loom large. This is because of the absence of storage facilities. Foodcrops worth Rs. 58,000 crore are wasted annually because of the lack of storage facilities. The impact of recent drop in agricultural output cannot be minimised through the PDS.

Conclusion: Inflation, as it stands today, is the number one villain in India. Policy makers are too much obsessed with higher economic growth. Further, global inflation is also responsible for India's recent price rise. But as the effort in raising agricultural production is limited, the major burden of inflation is felt by the poor masses. Government hopes that the present predicament can be overcome by September-October 2010, provided there is good monsoon.

Anyway, a judicious balancing of demand and supply would help in attaining the goal of price stabilisation. However, in the coming years, containment and reduction in the rate of inflation will depend largely on measures adopted to minimise the fiscal deficit so as to reduce the potential for monetary expansion. Furthermore, recovery of industrial production and management on the supply of foodgrains and the other key essential goods will also enable the Government to hold the price line.

12.13 PARALLEL ECONOMY

Black money is a great menace to the Indian economy. Hence both 'white money' and 'black money' operate simultaneously to finance various kinds of transactions. Money involved in black or unsanctioned transaction is so high that a parallel economy has emerged. This is also referred to as 'unaccounted economy', 'black economy', 'underground economy', 'unreported economy', etc.

Meaning: Black money refers to unaccounted money, i.e., income which is not declared to the tax authority. In other words, income earned from various sources are kept secret. Contrasted to this is the white money that is reported to the tax authorities. Thus, tax evasion and black income go hand in hand. Black income or concealed income may be utilised for the creation of real assets like buildings and other properties. When this black income is used in a rampant manner, parallel economy is established.

Magnitude: Though it is difficult to estimate accurately the volume of black incomes in India, some efforts have, however, been made in this direction. That is why these estimates are called guesstimates. The most reliable estimate of black economy in India has come from a study of the National Institute of Public Finance and Policy (NIPFP). Its estimate of black income for the period 1983-84 is: The aggregate black income generated is estimated to be in the range of Rs. 31,584 crore to Rs. 36,784 crore, i.e., 18 p.c. to 21 p.c. of GNP. It is said that this is an 'underestimate'. Suraj Gupta's data reveals that black income generation in India in 1980-81 was of the order of Rs. 50,977 crore (i.e., 41.7 p.c. of GNP). The figure went up to Rs. 85,208 crore (i.e., 45.8 p.c. of GNP) in 1983-84 and to Rs. 149,297 crore (i.e., 50.7 p.c. of GNP) in 1987-88. Average annual growth of black income for the period 1980-81 to 1987-88 came to about 16.54 p.c. Hence the name 'Parallel economy'. The Indian Merchant Chamber of Commerce estimated that black income generation in India had been about Rs 4 crore to Rs. 4.6 crore per hour. Thus, the figure of the black income is, indeed, staggering.

12.13.1 Causes

There is no doubt that the black economy or parallel economy is the most worrying aspect in India for quite a number of years. Its horizon is so wide that for most transactions black incomes are used. Thus, the so-called parallel economy generates and propagates within the existing economic structure. It is, therefore, necessary that we find out its sources or causes. The important ones are:

In the *first* place, faulty taxation system is responsible for this menace in India. Tax rates are high. Tax administration is not taxpayer-friendly. Tax laws are rigid. For all these reasons, people evade taxes.

Secondly, the regulatory mechanism of the government has enlarged the scope of generating black income. Indian economy is subject to a plethora of controls and regulations. Controls in the form of license-permit-quota have made the Indian economy subservient on bureaucrats. These people apply their own discretion and power and indulge themselves in interpreting laws and procedures that suit them most. All these lead to delay or red tapism in administration. Speed money can overcome this hurdle. Or clearance demands illegal payments. It is strongly argued that an over-controlled economy is an ideal breeding ground for corruption. In the process, black economy thrives.

Thirdly, another ideal ground for the generation of black income is the scarcity of goods and services. One finds large illegal transactions in urban real estate (like renting or buying and selling of land or buildings) as metropolitan cities like Kolkata or Mumbai chronically face housing problem. In Mumbai city, it is alleged that approximately 50 p.c. of black money is used for the purpose of purchase and sale of flats. Since these are unaccounted money, by definition, it generates further black money. Admission of wards in good schools and colleges (e.g., medical or engineering college) usually demands 'donations'. These are nothing but black money. It is the experience of an Indian that whenever the government comes forward with controls, black money shoots up. Earlier, we experienced scarcity of cement, steel, cooking gas, telephone, etc. Scarcity then led to the generation of black money. In recent years, these are not in short supply. Possibility of generation of black money diminishes once scarcity of goods and services vanishes. Since quality flat at prime location in a city is in short supply or good schools and colleges are few in number, black transaction comes into opration.

Fourthly, subscriptions or donations to the political parties by big businessmen and industrialists are considered to be another reason for the emergence of black money in India. Election and political propaganda in our country demands uses of black money. Political propaganda before election means huge expenditure on various heads, such as postering, publication of pamphlets and booklets, conduct of meeting, hiring of various types of workers. Most of these expenses incurred by political parties in India are financed by illegal payments.

Datt and Sundaharam remark: "The political instability witnessed in the country in various states has resulted in widespread horse-trading of the MLAs at the state level and MPs at the central level. In this process of buying political support, black money plays a crucial role. Consequently, the determination of the ruling political party to curb black money has become very weak."

Thus, black money in India operates in a variety of transactions. In the following transactions, black incomes are used: real estate transactions, film industry construction activity, investment in non-banking companies, hotels, restaurants, casinó games, video piracy, kickbacks on contracts, bribes, etc. For all these activities, black money is used or cash transactions are made. The liquid cash-GDP ratio (i.e., use of cash in making transactions) is roughly 10 p.c. as contrasted to 3 to 4 p.c. in advanced countries. Greater the use of cash, greater is the possibility of generation of black money. Anybody intending to purchase real estate is required to pay both in cash and cheque. Use of cash money for real estate transaction is absolutely black transaction.

12.13.2 Government Measures to Control Black Money

The Government of India has taken various measures to unearth black money in India. The principal measures adopted so far since independence include the following:

First, tax laws and tax administration are considered to be one of the great sources of black incomes in India. For these reasons, tax evasion is rampant. To check this tendency, loopholes in tax laws and administration are being constantly plugged by the Government. For instance, effective tax rates have been lowered. Lower the tax rate, higher is the tax compliance. Particularly after 1991, the Government of India is serious in reducing tax rates to prevent tax evasion. One of the recent measures to check the problem of tax evasion is the compulsory filing of tax returns by everyone with a taxable income, declaration of PAN (Permanent Account Number) while purchasing/selling real estate, cheque payment for transactions beyond Rs. 20,000, declaration of bank account number in various transactions, etc.

Secondly, demonetisation is another measure to control the menace of black money. Demonetisation was first made in 1946. And again in 1978 when high denomination notes of Rs. 1,000, Rs. 5,000 and Rs. 10,000 were demonetized. As it represents a small fraction of the total black income, it has failed to make any impact on unearthing black money.

Thirdly, Special Bearer Bond scheme was introduced in 1981 for canalising unaccounted money for productive purposes. Truly speaking, in January 1981, the Government of India officially recognised the existence of black money for the first time and announed various measures to unearth black money. The introduction of 'Special Bearer Bond' is a measure in this direction. This bond offered tax-free benefits to its owners. Above all, the buyer of the bond need not have to disclose the sources of income to the Government. Unfortunately, this scheme did not elicit enough response

Fourthly, voluntary disclosure scheme (VDS) introduced in the 1997-98 Budget is another attempt in this direction. It is true that unless a package of harsh economic and non-economic measures are introduced immediately, the black money menace will surely destroy the fabric of the Indian economy. New innovative schemes are required to be introduced. Such schemes were introduced in the 1990s. The first is the deposits with the National Housing Bank (NHB). The Budget for 1991-92 made such a step which involved making a deposit with the said bank. No authority can put question on such deposits, but 40 p.c. of the amount deposited will be deducted for utilisation in some socially productive projects, like slum-clearance and low-cost housing in semi-urban areas. The second is the foreign remittance scheme. The third is the Gold Bond Scheme introduced in March 1993. VDS is another important scheme. Under this scheme, the holders of black money have been permitted to convert it into white money by paying taxes at the rate of 30 p.c. for individuals and 35 p.c. for corporations. Black money holders are granted impunity—irrespective of their sources of black funds accumulated over time. The scheme yielded an unprecedented succes in terms of revenue gain. But against the vastness of the problem, such gain is nominal—just 3 p.c. of the total black money! This is just the tip of the iceberg.

Despite all these measures taken so far, the volume of black money shows no sign of abatement. Virtually, the distinction between real and illegal transactions has vanished. Possibly, the approach of the Government is half-hearted. Any serious commitment on the part of the Government to curb it is yet to come. As a result, mistrust and cynicism on the part of people have been growing. The credibility of the Government in this business is seriously at stake. It is true that it is very difficult to wipe it out completely since corruption has become a way of life from the top brass of the society to the people at the bottom level. No longer, corruption is an elitist phenomenon. Even then, government officials at the helm of affairs siphon off the large cake. Economic Adviser to the Prime Minister Dr. M. M. Singh recently stated that much of the wealth created comes from proximity to the government. Unfortunately, India is slipping into some sort of 'oligarchic capitalism'. Anyway, blackmoney, corruption, etc., are the outcomes of poor governance and ultimately a threat to the country's democracy.

APPENDIX TO CHAPTER 13

13.1 RURAL CREDIT

Any economic activity needs finances as finance is the lifeblood. Agricultural sector needs finance too. Financing of agricultural activities may be made through (a) disposition of the surplus agricultural produce, and (b) borrowing. Indian agriculture generates very little surplus produce because of many reasons. Thus the possibility of re-investment of savings, that is marketable surplus, is rather bleak. Finding no other alternative, farmers—both large and small—borrow money from many sources to carry out agricultural operations.

From time persective, Indian peasants need short-term, medium-term and long-term loans. Short-term loans required for the purchase of seed, fertilisers, etc., cover for a period not more than 15 months. For short-term loans farmers largely depend on private non-institutional persons, like village moneylenders, cooperative societies and nationalised banks. Medium term loan usually covers for a period not exceeding 5 years. Such loans are raised for the purpose of buying small implements and tools, cattle, pond renovation, etc. Moneylenders, relatives and friends cooperative societies, and commercial banks provide such loans. Finally, loans for the purchase of tractor and other heavy machines, permanent improvement of land provisions for irrigating land, etc., comprise long-term loans. These loans are usually met by land development bank and NABARD.

However, Indian peasents, being too poor, are forced to take even consumption loans or unproductive loans not required for agricultural operations (like marriage ceremony, shradh, etc.,) for which they depend on private moneylenders.

To sum up, Indian farmers need both production loans and consumption loans. As far as consumption loans are concerned, institutional credit-giving agencies remain shy. Anyway, production credit—short medium and long term—meets the resource gap of the farmers. Modern agricultural operations have become more expensive. Further, agriculture is now being diversified so as to meet the country's requirements. Greater the diversification, larger is the need for credit. Indeed, credit is an essential input without which agricultural production and productivity cannot be raised. There is a strong nexus between credit and agricultural development on a sustained basis.

13.2 SOURCES OF RURAL CREDIT

Rural credit includes not only credit provided to farmers but also credit extended to artisans, owners of small and medium enterprises (SMEs) in rural areas, small transport operators and so on. The sources of rural credit can be grouped into two: (i) private or non-institutional agencies; and (ii) institutional agencies. The former includes private moneylenders, traders and commission agents, relatives, and landlords or jotedars. The sources of institutional credit are: rural cooperatives, commercial banks—particularly the nationalised banks, the RBI, NABARD, regional rural banks, etc.

The aim of institutional credit is to replace the widely prevalent usurious exploitative moneylending. As far as the credit delivery is concerned, these traditional suppliers—because of proximity and informal distribution of credit to assetless rural peasants hold a dominant position in rural India. In recent years, institutional credit arrangements, to a considerable extent, have succeeded in achieving this aim. The interaction between informal and formal credit delivery arrangements over the period 1951-1991 has been presented below in the form of a table.

It is clear from the table that, in 1951, non-institutional sources provided the bulk of credit (93 p.c.) of the agriculturists while the institutional sources delivered credit as low as 7 p.c. of rural credit. Among the non-institutional sources, moneylenders occupied the pre-eminent position in the 1950s. The position, however, changed in 1981 when the share of institutional sources climbed up to more than 63 p.c. and the rest—that is 37 p.c. of rural credit—came from informal sources. This has become possible because of the commendable performance of the cooperative societies and nationalised commercial banks. However, between 1981 and 1991, cooperative societies fared badly. Its share in total credit declined from 30 p.c. to about 24 p.c. On the other hand, this decline in the share of rural credit had been compensated by commercial banks. Their share rose to 35.2 p.c. in 1991, to 54 p.c. in 2001-02 and as high as 69 p.c. in 2005-06.

The picture that emerges from the preceding discussion is that the informal sources were important in the realm of credit distribution in the early years of planning. Such dominance, according to the All-India Rural Credit Survey Committee, is attributed to the following factors—consumption loans

Table 13.1: Sources of Rural Credit (%)

	1951	1961	1971	1981	1991
1. **Institutional**	**7.3**	**18.7**	**31.7**	**63.2**	**69.4**
i. Government	3.1	15.5	7.1	3.9	5.7
ii. Cooperative societies/ Banks	3.3	2.6	22.9	29.9	23.6
iii. Commercial banks	0.9	0.6	2.6	29.4	35.2
iv. Others	—	—	0.2	0.7	4.9
2. **Non-institutional or Private**	**92.7**	**81.3**	**68.3**	**36.8**	**30.6**
i. Professional moneylenders	69.7	49.2	36.1	16.1	17.5
ii. Traders	5.5	8.8	8.4	3.2	2.2
iii. Friends, relatives, etc.	14.2	8.8	13.1	8.7	4.6
Iv. Landlords and others	3.2	14.5	10.7	8.8	6.3
3. **Total**	**100.0**	**100.0**	**100.0**	**100.0**	**100.0**

Source: *All-India Debt and Investment Survey 1991-92; RBI Bulletin, May 1999*

(not sanctioned by formal institutions) constitute l as high as 50 p.c. while running expenses and capital expenditures for agricultural farms comprised 10 p.c. only and 28 p.c., respectively.

Secondly, because of the change of policy of the government the contribution of village moneylenders, jotdars, etc., in credit distribution has been showing declining trend. Even then, the outreach of the formal institutional credit structure is a matter of serious concern. This is evident from the findings of the NSSO 59th Round (2003) data. This data revealed that 27 p.c. of the total number of cultivator households received credit from formal sources as contrasted to 22 p.c. sanctioned by informal sources. Small and marginal farmers had no credit outstanding. May be data an old one, but the 11th Plan Document laments that "It is unlikely that the situation has changed much since 2003".

We have already argued that as far as institutional sources of credit are concerned, there have been definitely some improvements in this area. The ground level credit flow to agriculture during 2005-06 registered an annual growth of 44 p.c., commercial banks made a growth of 54 p.c., cooperative banks 25 p.c., and regional rural banks (RRBs) 22 p.c. during the year.

Despite the disappearance of dual rural financial structure, moneylenders are still operating their businesses. There are many reasons for this sorry state of affairs. *First*, considering the credit needs of the agricultural sector, credit inadequacy, particularly the formal one, is an inducement on the part of moneylenders to continue business. Further, institutional sources are not offering finance to small and marginal farmers in right quantities at the right time. It has been our experience that cooperatives and commercial banks are finding difficulties in meeting the credit needs of the farmers. Above all, these institutions, while sanctioning loans, prefer large farmers because of creditworthiness. Small and marginal farmers still remain unworthy borrowers in the banking parlance.

Secondly, institutional finance is subject to complicated formalities and rigid repayment conditions. The moneylenders' method of sanctioning loans are highly simple and informal. Loans are often sanctioned not against asset mortgage. Above all, petty farmers badly need consumption loans, though these loans are highly expensive. Moneylenders do not hesitate in sanctioning such loans required for typical familial needs.

Thirdly, mounting overdues seem to be a common problem of all formal rural credit institutions. Such overdues not only weaken the financial position of these institutions but also chokes credit growth cycle. This is not only attributable to the existence of a large number of wilful defaulters, but also to wrong lending policies, inadequate supervision, ineffective recovery procedure, etc.

Finally, in recent years, a serious agrarian crisis has appeared in the economy. This crisis has also led to default by many farmers, and a consequent freeze on their ability to access institutional sources of credit. Meanwhile, an unfortunate development of farm suicides that set in motion in the late 1990s has been a pointer to the agrarian crisis. The ground reality is that the total number of farm suicides are rising within a declining farm population. The worst affected parts of the country are big 5 states of Maharashara, Andhra Pradesh, Karnataka, Madhya Pradesh and Chattisgarh. Suicides recorded in these states over the 12-year period (1997-2008) accounted for nearly 2 lakhs (1,99,132). The Government of India introduced the loan waiven scheme in 2008 to give some relief to the farmers. About 3.68 crore farmers have been benefited from the debt waiver scheme and debt relief of Rs. 65,318 crore. However, the scheme covered only institutional sources. Farm ers—small and marginal farmers—getting loans from private moneylenders remain outside the purview of the scheme. Although the loan waiver is not a bad thing, the agrarian crisis that erupted with the liberalisation of the Indian economy remains unaddressed by the government.

As credit is an essential requirement for revitalising agriculture, it is of urgent need to have an effective rural credit structure so that access to institutional credit can be harnessed. We talk about 'inclusive growth'—that is, growth needs to be broad-based and ensure equality of opportunity for all. But the existence of the private institutional sources of rural credit and their continual exploitative business practices and, above all, the current agrarian crisis will definitely make agricultural peasants poorer and deprived ones—thereby leading to a classic situation of 'exclusive growth'..

13.2.1 A Profile of Formal/Institutional Agencies Catering Rural Credit

Institutional credit, both short-term and long-term, has played a pivotal role in the delivery of credit to the agricultural sector. However, over the years, demand for credit has far exceeded the supply. To meet the credit needs various institutions have been created. Most important among them are: cooperative societies/banks, commercial banks, regional rural banks, NABARD, etc.

• **Cooperative societies:** The cooperative societies are supposed to be the cheapest and the most important source of rural credit. The cooperative credit societies were set up first in 1904 with the aim of combating rural indebtedness caused by exploitative role played by the village moneylenders. As they played a positive role in the sphere of rural credit, the All-India Rural Credit Survey Committee or Gorwala Committee in 1951 remarked that its purpose had been totally defeated, but it must succeed. It made several recommendations for the better functioning of the cooperative societies. Anyway, performance of these societies remained far below the desired level. The Agricultural Credit Review Committee or Khusro Committee of 1989 lamented that, despite the disappearance of the dual financial arrangements to a great extent, money-lenders were still occupying the agricultural credit turf. Since then, the situation has improved marginally.

The basic objective of setting up cooperative credit system in India was to protect the farmers from the exploitation of the village moneylenders and to provide loan at a concessional rate of interest. The major sources of (short and medium-term) cooperative credits are: (i) primary agricultural credit societies (PACs), (ii) district or central cooperative banks, and (iii) state cooperative bank—the apex bank.

This apex bank functions as the connecting link between the RBI from which it obtains loanable funds and the cooperative central (or district) banks and PACs.

Cooperative societies have achieved both successes and failures. But there is a feeling that it has largely failed and is yet to achieve its declared objectives.

In 1950-51, cooperatives provided 3.3 p.c. of the total agricultural credit, far below the desired level. Against this backdrop, the RBI and the Government of India came forward to help expansion of cooperative societies in a great measure. In 1950-51, the number of agricultural cooperative societies stood at 1.05 lakhs that covered as little as 9 p.c. of the rural families. Total credit granted by cooperatives was just Rs. 23 crore. Such volume of credit went up to Rs. 2,125 crore in 1989-81 and Rs. 23,604 crore in 2001-02. Credit growth by the cooperatives during the 10th Plan period (2002-2007) picked up rather quickly. By 2006-07, the volume of credit sanctioned by cooperatives increased to 42,480 crore. It is argued that almost 100 p.c. villages of the country are now covered by cooperative societies. Thus, cooperatives work as a great 'means for widening and deepening access to institutional credit' to the poor rural peasants.

After green revolution in Indian agriculture and bank nationalisation in 1969, several initiatives and policies were introduced so that cooperative societies/banks could meet the increasing credit requirements of the agricultural sector. For instance, one notices diversification in the activities of cooperatives. No longer cooperatives link their loans to production only. Food processing industries, investment in agriculture, rural infrastructure development, and then in cases of consumption loans, cooperatives come forward. In other words, cooperative loans have now been integrated with the total development of the agricultural sector.

However, the growth of cooperatives have been slow and sporadic throughout the plan period. This is evident from the Table. In 1981, the total volume of advances made by cooperative societies/banks amounted close to 30 p.c. But it declined to slightly less than 24 p.c. by 1991. This means that cooperatives have failed to touch most of the poor, deprived and exploited rural peasants.

One of the major causes of slow growth of cooperatives is heavy overdues. Truly speaking, like all other institutions, cooperatives too suffer from large volume of non-performing assets (NPAs), although in recent years it has declined. Managerial problems seem to be a patent reason for large overdues.

Secondly, as one-third of finance goes to small and marginal farmers for the purchase of agricultural inputs, this is considered to be grossly inadequate to meet the essential production needs. What is worse is that the share of the poorest of the weaker sections such as the artisans, sharecroppers, tenants, landless workers, etc., continue to be in the range of 3 to 5 p.c., even after six decades of planning.

Thirdly, the rural community is largely dominated by powerful landlords-jotedars. These rich farmers succeed in obtaining a disproportionate share of loan and other assistance. The poor and the genuinely needy ones suffer from all types of deprivation. As a result, most cooperatives suffer from managerial deficiency. Most cooperatives have failed due to lack of manpower development.

Fourthly, there is regional disparity in the distribution of financial resources. Some states have received more than the national average and others less.

Anyway, cooperatives are now at crossroads. The ground reality, as said by the Prime Minister Monmohan Singh, is that cooperatives that exist in rural India just survive without any real usefulness. Although autonomous and democratic in character, elections of office-bearers are not being held in most societies—thereby hampering managerial efficiency. In a true sense, cooperative societies are run by bureaucrats and ministers rather than the members of the societies. Accounts of the societies are not even audited. Accountability of higher-ups is a matter of serious concern. All these call for serious action so that cooperative structure can be revitalised without any delay. It may be noted here that the speedy restructutring of the cooperative societies is in progress in accordance with the recommendations made by the Vaidyanathan Committee. It may be added at the end that it is necessary to take steps in depoliticising the system immediately.

• **Commercial banks:** One of the major objectives of bank nationalisation in India in 1969 was to change the pattern of credit allocation in adequate quantities in favour of the priority sectors, like agriculture, small industry, and exports. This demanded branch expansion so as to improve the availability of banking facilities in rural areas.

To provide extension of credit to small borrowers, banks have drawn up many schemes. Total priority sector advances by the public sector banks increased from Rs. 44 crore (14.6 p.c.) in 1969 to Rs. 720,083 crore (42.5 p.c.) in March 2009, of which both direct and indirect finance to the agricultural sector comprised more than 17.6 p.c., and small scale industries accounted for 11.3 p.c. It may not be irrelevant to point out here that, in March, 2008, priority sector advances rose as high as 45 p.c. This suggests that the pace of granting credit to the priority sectors has recently been slowed down slightly.

Despite these failures are worth noting. It is because of accumulation of NPAs in the nationalised banks, the issue of viability became a matter of concern a few years back. The position in recent times has improved. But this prevented banks from extending credit to the borrowers of the priority sectors and thus poor landless peasants, artisans, etc.

Further, state-owned banks have now been showing apathy towards priority sectors as is evident from the volume of personal consumption loans granted by these banks (for buying cars, computers, housing loan, etc.) In March 2009, agricultural advances accounted for 17.6 p.c. as contrasted to personal consumption loans to the extent of 9.3 p.c. (Rs. 156,590 crore) of the total bank advances. This is attributed to the development of 'plastic money culture' with the opening of the Indian economy in 1991. Middle-income and high income groups have developed the habit of using credit card, debit card, etc., to buy consumption goods, but at the cost of poor rural agriculturists. Above all, village moneylenders have been taking advantage of this unhealthy development in the banking industry.

• **Regional rural banks:** The basic purpose of setting up Regional Rural Banks (RRBs) in 1975 was to make credit and other services readily available to the small and marginal farmers, landless workers, agricultural labourers, rural artisans and owners of small-scale and cottage industries. Even after nationalisation, commercial banks did not find much interest in penetrating rural areas as it found rural banking business petty, cumbersome and unrewarding. Further, cooperative societies lacked competence needed for the steadily growing rural industries and tertiary sectors of the rural economy. As it is, the cooperative system has hardly touched the small traders and shopkeepers, repair workshops, artisans. These gaps were most likely to be filled up by the RRBs. Another objective of setting up RRBs was to curb the influence and dependence of rural moneylenders.

RRBs are scheduled banks in which nationalised banks are authorised and empowered to sponsor RRBs. Since the inception of these banks in 1975, the number of branches operating in 23 states rose from 5 (1975) to 196. The volume of credit in 2007-08 increased to Rs. 57,417 crore from Rs. 18,000 crore in 2001-02.

No doubt the RRBs have been incurring losses since their inception. Reasons behind this sorry state of affairs are: poor quality of lending, bad management, and large scale defaults, etc. The Agricultural Credit Review Committee headed by A. M. Khusru in 1989 recommended the merger of RRBs with the commercial banks as the former suffers from built-in non-viability. As its NPAs are huge, in recent years some of these banks have been wound up. Despite the fact, as the RRBs act as alternative agencies to provide institutional credit in rural areas, it is expected to minimise the activities of moneylenders in the long run. If we are interested in keeping this service as a poverty alleviation strategy, losses of these RRBs need to be shouldered by the Government. Winding up their businesses may not augur well.

• **NABARD:** In the late 1970s and early 1980s, it was felt that the provision of credit to the agricultural sector remained inadequate and growth, in its supply, did not commensurate with the growth of its demand. That is why the government set up a specialised financial institution—the National Bank for Agriculture and Rural Development (NABARD) in July 1982. Specified as 'an organisational device for providing undivided attention, forceful direction and pointed focus' to the credit problems of the rural sector, NABARD now functions as an apex bank for rural credit (a function which had so long been performed by the RBI).

It provides short term credit (for a period not exceeding 18 months to State Cooperative Banks; medium term credit (for a period of 18 months and maximum period of 7 years) to State Cooperative Banks and RRBs; and long-term credit for a period not beyond 25 years to State Cooperative Banks, Land Development Banks, RRBs, and commercial banks. Thus NABARD does not deal with farmers and other rural people.

A very important and a very novel approach initiated by the NABARD is the provisioning of credit to poor households as a tool to combat poverty. This approach has come to be known as 'micro finance', that is, 'banking with the poor'. This has led to the evolution of Self-Help Groups (SHGs)-Bank Linkage model so as to provide credit delivery to the hitherto large number of unreached and under-served poor outside the banking fold.

Unfortunately, NABARD also suffers from huge overdues. Its unrecovered loans in the last 3-4 years (2003-07) constituted nearly 40-42 p.c. If it continues, we are afraid that cooperative societies may be facing a serious credit crunch in the near future. Under the circumstance, we doubt how far this apex institution will succeed in delivering credit to poor households of the rural areas.

13.3 AGRICULTURAL MARKETING

Long ago, Alfred Marshall rightly commented: 'economic progress consists of marketing at a distance'. This statement holds even today and has validity in the context of Indian agriculture.

India is an agricultural country and the economic position of the farmer depends on the money that he can earn by selling his surplus produce. However, trading in agricultural commoditles is an example of pure competition. So an individual farmer has to act as a price-taker. He has hardly any control over the existing price of a particular crop. This price is basically determined by the impersonal forces of demand and supply. However, the revenue of the farmer can be raised through proper handling and better distribution of his produce and by reducing the margins acquired by a chain of intermediaries between the producer and the consumer. This necessitates an improvement in the agricultural marketing system. However, the sad truth is that the Indian farmer is handicapped by a number of factors, most of which are beyond his control. On most occasions, he has to sell his output at a wrong place, at the wrong time and at unfavourable terms.

An efficient and well-organised marketing system is a prerequisite for agricultural growth, employment, and economic prosperity of the rural areas. Agricultural development becomes self-sustaining when additional output can be sold in the market at a remunerative price. In India, agricultural development rests mainly on the private sector, though incentive and assistance to grow more output come from the government. However, the crucial incentive is, of course, profit. Emergence of profit induces farmers to produce more. Furthermore, the existence of an efficient marketing system induces cultivators to bring their produce in the market for sale. Thus, creation of a marketable surplus greatly depends on the marketing network of agricultural produce.

Because of the transition of the Indian economy during the plan period and the growing connection of Indian farmers with the global market following GATT/WTO agreement, agricultural marketing has assumed a great importance. But the present agricultural marketing system of India seems to be far from perfect. The major defects of the system are the following:

In the *first* place, a long chain of intermediaries in India play havoc since the marketing of the agricultural produce is conducted by these people and not the farmers themselves. The middlemen and intermediaries make fraudulent practices while purchasing and selling agricultural produce. In the process, they earn a huge margin. It has been estimated that the sellers-farmers earn as much as 53 p.c. of the sale price of rice, while 31 p.c. is managed by the intermediaries without performing any economic function. Moreover, false weights and measures are used and unnecessary deduction is made. Thus the farmer is exploited in more ways than one.

Secondly, because of the lack of well-organised or controlled markets in required quantities, farmers are often forced to make distress sale of their produce to the middlemen at a comparatively low prices at the wrong time and at a wrong place. Illiteracy and ignorance of the Indian farmers seem to be a great cause for this malady.

Thirdly, the average Indian farmer does not have adequate storage facilities. Moreover there is no warehousing facility in the market. As a result, foodcrops get wasted and often become unfit for human consumption. Such losses may, in some years, range between 1.5 p.c. and 2 p.c. One estimate suggests it to be 10 p.c. Anyway, the government has admitted that because of inadequate storage facilities about Rs. 58,000 crore foodgrains are wasted annually. From the economic point of view, this loss is scandalous.

Further, for perishable agricultural goods like vegetables cold storage units are grossly inadequate (roughly 9 p.c.). The market structure itself lacks even basic infrastructures like shops, godowns, and platform in front of shops, etc., at many places, given the needs of Indias' diversified agriculture. The basic facilities of internal roads, boundary walls, electric lights, weighing equipments are not available in about 20 p.c. of the markets. In addition, farmers are exposed to many non-transparent methods of price charges. Electronic auctioning has been introduced in some markets as merely an exception. Truly speaking, marketing infrastructure needs to be modernized immediately.

Fourthly, India's rail-road network is grossly inadequate compared to its needs. The road condition in rural areas is really pathetic. Virtually, most of the Indian villages are cut off from towns because of the absence of rail-road link. The problem gets multiplied during monsoon. Even the rich farmers, having a surplus to dispose off, are often not interested in going to the *mandis*.

Fifthly, Indian farmers do not usually get information about the prices that prevail in big and organised markets due to (i) illiteracy, and (ii) poor communication facilities. Actually speaking, it is the dishonest middlemen who provide price information to the sellers. For the most obvious reasons, such information is not only inadequate but also grossly incorrect. Poor farmers, as a result, suffer.

Finally, at present agricultural markets are regulated by a chain of institutions. These are State Agricultural Produce Marketing (Regulation) Acts (or APMC Act), Essential Commodities Act and Various Central Orders issued thereunder. "All these have created restrictive and monopolistic marketing structures, which have resulted in inefficient operation and high degree of marketing costs.

They have also had an adverse impact upon agricultural production and system, inefficient flow of commodities, and lack of competitiveness." (*11th Plan Document*).

• **Remedial measures:** The Government of India's measures in the area of agricultural marketing fall into three broad categories, *viz.*, setting up of appropriate marketing organisations, establishment of regulated markets and encouragement to cooperative marketing. We may now make a brief review of these three measures:

• **Setting up of marketing organisations:** The Government maintains marketing organisations both at the Centre and in the States to carry out three broad categories of functions: (a) investigation, (b) development, and (c) grading and standardisation.

The Government Marketing Organisation is really purposive. Firstly, it undertakes and publishes

i. marketing surveys of a large number of various agricultural commodities. These surveys bring into focus the diverse problems connected with agricultural marketing and put forward suggestions for their removal.

ii. The Government has also done much technical work to grade and standardise many agricultural goods. The Agricultural Produce (Grading and Marketing) Act was passed ten years before Independence, viz., in 1937. In pursuance of the Act, the Government has set up grading stations for several commodities like ghee, flour, eggs, etc. Such graded goods bear the Ag-Mark which helps the producer to sell more and more at higher prices.

iii. The contract terms for several commodities (wheat, groundnut, etc.,) have also been standardised. This has helped to widen their markets considerably.

iv. The Government has also taken steps to disseminate market information. The All India Radio and some TV channels broadcast the prices and stock position of such agricultural goods as rice, wheat, pulses, etc., on both daily and weekly basis.

v. The Agricultural Prices Commission (currently known as Commission for Agricultural Costs and Prices since 1985) fixes prices of foodgrains, pulses, cotton, jute, oilseeds, etc. Furthermore, Food Corporation of India (FCI) and Cotton Corporation of India exert considerable influence on the prices of their respective commodities by large scale involvement in these markets.

vi. Further, to promote the setting up of cold storages under cooperative sector, the National Cooperative Development Corporation has provided a sum of Rs. 80 crores for installation of 248 cold storages having an installed capacity of 7.39 lakh tonnes till the end of March 1996.

• **Establishment of regulated markets:** A very important measure adopted by the Government for improvement of agricultural marketing has been the establishment of a large number of regulated markets (7, 139 in 2009) in the country. With their establishment, the various malpractices in *mandis* have been largely removed and the market charges have been largely rationalised.

• **Encouragement of cooperative markets:** At the village end, the Government has rendered considerable help in the setting up of primary cooperative marketing societies. The Government has set up the Central Marketing Societies and State Marketing Societies for financing them and helping them in various other ways. In the absence of Central Marketing Societies, the State Bank of India has been entrusted with the responsibility of providing financial assistance to cooperative marketing and processing societies. The National Agricultural Co-operative Marketing Federation has also been set up at the national level.

- **Provision of warehousing facilities:** The Government has done some positive work in the field of warehousing. It has set up a large number of warehouses in villages and towns As early as in 1956 it set up the National Cooperative Development and Warehousing Board to perform comprehensive range of functions: planning and promoting programmes for the production, processing, marketing, storage, warehousing and importing and exporting of agricultural produce through marketing cooperative societies. Of late, most of the State Governments have set up State Warehousing Corporations. Their functions resemble closely those of the Central Warehousing Corporation.

- **Comprehensive crop insurance scheme:** With the objective of providing financial support to cultivators in the event of crop failure following drought or flood and to restore the credit eligibility for the next crop season, a Comprehensive Crop Insurance Scheme (CCIS) was introduced in April 1985 and, at present, covers wheat, paddy, millets, oilseeds and pulses in more than 20 States.

Conclusion: In short, various steps have been taken from 1951 to date to improve India's agricultural marketing system, *viz.*, standardisation of weights and measures, development of infrastructural facilities, introducing quality standards in respect of certain crops, and so on. The legal framework has also been strengthened through Agricultural Markets Act in many states. However, much remains to be done.

Agricultural trade in India is mainly carried out by private traders operating in organised markets/*mandis*. The role of the Government is limited to protecting the interests of producers and consumers and also promoting organised marketing of agricultural commodities in the country. Most of the State Governments and Governments of Union Territories endeavour to promote organised marketing of agricultural commodities in the country.

One final point. There is now a greater need for ensuring uniformity in the state-level tax structure throughout the country in respect of agricultural commodities so as to improve market efficiencies. This should also call for rationalisation of taxes on raw agricultural commodities and removal of restrictions on goods movement across state borders as well as provisioning of hassle-free collection of revenues at convenient points.

Above all, the country as a whole need to be conceptualized as 'a unified integrated national market'.

13.4. STATE OF INDIA'S FOOD SECURITY

As India was living from 'ship to mouth' in the 1950s and early 1960s, efforts were made to improve agricultural production and productivity via land reform measures and the technological change or the so-called green revolution. Indeed, the 'natural' limits to agriculture were broken and the country achieved self-sufficiency in foodgrains at least 30-35 years back. But in the reform era, fatigue in agricultural growth has again appeared and the per head food supply has been declining. Thus the attainment of food self-sufficiency is a myth. Almost 35 p.c. Indians (more than 35 crore people) go to bed in empty stomach everyday. Despite green revolution, these people remain food insecure.

- **What is food security?** The two words—food security (FS) and hunger—are used interchangeably. Hunger is a situation of without eating food over a period of time. Food security exists when all people have physical and economic access to sufficient, safe and nutritious food for a healthy and active life. FS is a dynamic concept. FS is interrelated to nutritional security. FS has three essential components. These are: food availability (dependent on production, stock of foodgrains, etc.), accessibility to food supply (dependent on food entitlement), and accessibility of basic needs to non-food elements, like health, education, etc.

The International Food Policy Research Institute (IFPRI) devised an index called Global Hunger Index (GHI) in 2006 to know the state of food security in the globe. India's position in 2009 was pathetic. She is ranked 65th in the world—slightly better placed than Bangladesh, but falls behind Cameroon, Kenya, Nigeria, Sudan, etc. It is rather paradoxical that the Indian economy in the current decade is food insecure despite the high GDP growth rate of 8-9 p.c.—mass-hunger amidst mounting stock of foodgrains rotting in godowns. Government candidly admits that food valued at Rs. 58,000 crore get wasted every year because of the virtual absence of supply chain from farm to other delivery branches.

There has been a general decline in the per capita net availability of foodgrains in recent decades. The per capita availability of cereals per day—that rose to 510.1 gm in 1991—declined to 436 gm in 2009. Further, the rate of growth of foodgrains is unsatisfactory in the reform era, particularly in the last 3-4 years (2007-2010).

• **Reasons for food insecurity:** In view of the recent stagnation in production and an increasing consumption need of the growing population, one must point out the reasons behind India's state of food insecurity:

First is the low agricultural productivity. This may be attributed to the 'natural limits' (such as the operation of law of diminishing returns) on agricultural growth. This is evident from the area, production and yield of farm products. As net sown area has been declining (due to conversion of land for bio-fuel production, diversion of land for non-agricultural uses, uncertain weather conditions, and global warming, etc.,) the immediate fallout is the larger dose of migrant farm labourers to cities and towns in search of employment. This has been compounded by the decline in public investment in agricultural infrastructures like irrigation, development of right type of technology, credit, agricultural research and development. Water scarcity as well as huge decline in water table consequent upon over exploitations of groundwater has hit Indian agriculture badly. Further, soil health has been showing gradual deterioration due to wrong policy of fertiliser subsidy. Non-availability of certified seeds in sufficient quantities have an adverse effect on crop productivity.

There has been a fall of foodgrains production in 2008-09. The year 2009-10 shows slowdown in agricultural production by about 2 p.c.—particularly due to unfavourable weather condition. All these have an impact on the prices of food grains and other food items, putting many of these items out of reach for a huge number of people. In other words, this puts a severe strain of the food security on people living below the poverty line (more than 37 p.c. of the total population in 2004-05).

Secondly, India's food management policy suffers from many deficiencies. The objectives of such food management policy are steady growth of per capita supply of foodgrains, self-sufficiency and maintenance of buffer stock of foodgrains for food security and price stability. The main FS safety net is the public distribution system (PDS).

The PDS operates through a network of fair price shops to ensure adequate supplies of essential consumer goods to weaker sections of the population at stable prices. It is also an important anti-poverty programme of the government. To benefit the move, the targeted TPDS—a two-tier, subsidised pricing system, one each for the BPL and another for the APL families—was introduced in June 1997. Currently, the allocation of foodgrains to the BPL families is 25 kgs of foodgrains at a price of Rs. 3.00 per kg per month. The objective of the scheme is to ensure FS.

But the PDS has come in for sharp criticisms. *First*, the government could not ensure adequate supplies of foodgrains to the poorest people leading to leakage of foodgrains in favour of the APL families and the free market. The actual off take of cereals is much larger reflecting better market access and narrowing down of PDS prices and open market prices. This leads to sale of substandard grains in FPSs and diversion of quality grains in open market by the ration dealers so as to get some fair return on their investments. In addition, errors in targetting the genuine poor people have aggravated the cards. This has been compounded by the existence of a huge number of ghost ration cards. It has been reported that in 2008, altogether 10.28 crore FPS cards had been issued against 6.52 crore BPL families. Finally, the country experiences off and on the phenomenon of huge foodstocks against shortfall in the supply of foodgrains in FPSs. Comfortable food stock position is yet to provide any kind of relief to the poor people. Thus, the country's food management has failed to provide FS to the masses.

To give relief to the poor, the Government of India has proposed National Food Security Act to provide 25 kg of wheat/rice per month at Rs. 3 kg per month to the families living below the poverty line in its Budget 2009-10.

Finally, global warming and global food price rise have also a strong bearing on FS. It is estimated by the FAO that for every one degree rise in temperature, 6 million tonnes of wheat will be lost in India. Progressive warming climate will expand dry land and cause larger incidence of droughts. All these have led to lower productivity and declining output below the requirement.

Measures required: Being a rural agriculture-dependent country, the solution to food security in India needs an improvement in agricultural production and productivity. For this what is immediately needed is the increase in public investment in agriculture. It is often said that agriculture is no longer the driver of India's higher economic growth. That is why there has been an exodus of agricultural labourers to the cities and towns to get employment there. However, improvement in agricultural production requires an increase in income of the rural farm and non-farm households by developing non-farm services so that migration from the rural economy can be combated. This will then increase income of the rural people and help them to maintain minimum dietary and nutritional requirements. Poverty removal is fundamental to improve access to food.

However, availability of food supplies through increased production is not the only one element of FS. Another element is the accessibility to food. Access to food to the rural families and hence the implementation of the National Food Security Act largely depends on the PDS mechanism for which targetting the poor is the most important. Further, buffer stocks of foodgrains need to be built up adequately so that hunger and malnutrition can be averted. As we know, over the last 12-13 years, nearly 2 lakh farmers were forced to commit suicides. To prevent further calamites, the National Food Security Bill needs to be introduced immediately.

In addition, environmental damages need to be combated so that India's agricultural system becomes a sustainable one.

The country must achieve sustainable food security system—a hunger-free India Adhocism is not the solution to this serious problem. All the stockholders—Government NGOs, panchayats, rural community—must work together so that a long term solution can be achieved.

APPENDIX TO CHAPTER 15

15.1 RATIONALE OF ECONOMIC PLANNING IN INDIA

• **Meaning of Economic Planning:** To most people, planning is often confused with socialism or communism. Therefore, economic planning means state intervention in economic affairs as contrasted to the 'invisible hand' of market forces. However, the state can intervene in the economy even without making a plan. In other words, economists do not describe any form of state intervention as economic planning. "Only if such intervention is concerted, deliberate and designed to achieve some specific desired goals is the term applicable."[1] "Economic planning may be described as a deliberate governmental attempt to coordinate economic decision making over the long run and to influence, direct, and, in some case, even control the level and growth of a nation's principal economic variables: income, consumption, employment, investment, saving, exports, imports, etc., to achieve a predetermined set of development objectives."[2]

Economic planning is often regarded as a technique of managing an economy. When the structure of an economy becomes complex and subject to rapid change and transformation, some sort of advance thinking becomes necessary to resolve that complexity and to prepare the economy for those changes. Such preparation is nothing but economic planning.

Most often than not, an economic plan is regarded as a programme of action. It may also be taken to mean an instrument for regulating a free private enterprise economy.

It should be remembered that as plan is just a programme of action; it is not a guarantee for action. In short, a good plan is one which makes adequate provision for and ensures that its targets are properly fulfilled. By definition, planning must be directed towards the attainment of some macro-economic objectives or goals such as high employment or poverty alleviation or improvement in the country's balance of payments situation.

• **Rationale of planning: Breaking vicious circle of poverty:** The basic task of economic planning in developed countries is one of controlling trade cycle fluctuations—the ups and downs of economic activity. But as LDCs confront the problem of low economic growth, planning in these countries is the way of securing higher growth by harnessing all kinds of resources available—

[1] Ajit K. Dasgupta (1979): *Economic Theory and the Developing Contries*, P. 45; ELBS

[2] M. P. Todaro and S. C. Smith (2003). *Economic Development*, P. 681; *Pearson Education Asia*.

natural, physical, and human—as far as possible. The task is one of securing economic development and, hence, this sort of planning is called development planning.

Generally, almost all LDCs experience a large number of obstacles in their development path. This is due to the fact that these countries reel under a circle called vicious. Economic planning is needed to break this circle. Uncontrolled market economy cannot handle this problem. It is a historically testified truth that it is never accomplished under free enterprise capitalistic economy. Herein lies the rationale of planning in LDCs like our own.

• **Compensates market failure:** It is argued with conviction that market (i.e., free competitive market) cannot ensure maximum social walfare. This means that markets fail to achieve social efficiency and equity. Markets cannot allocate resources over time for investment efficiently. Market failure, in ordinary sense, means that prices fail to provide proper signals to economic agents—consumers and producers.

In LDCs, various commodity and input markets are not perfect; rather these markets are not only distorted but also badly organised. This means that prices are distorted and do not give proper signals for resource allocation. Unless these markets are controlled or regulated by the appropriate authority they will deliver undesirable results in LDCs. State intervention is also sought in sectors like economic and social infrastructures where private players hesitate to invest. The remedy of all such problems lies in organised governmental efforts. Likewise, state investment is indeed important also in industrial products. Under the circumstances, the government comes forward in LDCs to undertake all these activities that adequately compensates market failure.

Again, market fails in distributing resources among people. Market brings in inequality in income distribution. A more equal income distribution is a desired goal and that can be achieved if economic planning is pursued.

Finally, economic planning is also needed to improve and strengthen market mechanism that works in LDCs imperfectly. The government regulates and controls the activities of the private sector so that scarce investible resources are allocated in accordance with the plan priorities. In India, industrial production and foreign trade were under government control before 1991. Truly speaking, there has been a great deal of intervention in the market mechanism in India to foster rapid economic development since the beginning of the Eighth Plan (1992-1997).

• **Balanced development:** Balanced development, again, is possible only under planning. Any kind of regional imbalances and inequalities are likely to appear in the process of development since historical inequalities are difficult to remove. Thus, planned intervention on the part of the government is required to ensure that regional imbalances do not recur. The Second Five Year Plan (1956-1961) expressed its concern for growing regional imbalances in India and stated that in any comprehensive plan of development special attention is required to be given to the needs of poor, backward states. The pattern of investment needs to be designed in such a manner that a balanced regional development can be made. This can be done by planning alone.

• **Provisioning of public goods and service:** There is no denying the fact that provisioning of public goods and services, human resource development (like, elementary education, primary health care, etc.) and promotion of the optimum use of environmental resources is possible only by government action or planning.

Today, the global economy is more integrated than ever before. Such integration has some serious costs that need to be minimised as far as practicable. 'India needs to switch over from a region of investment planning to that of policy planning'. Thus, in a liberalised frame, planning has a different role to play in the economic life of people in India. Despite problems associated with governmental intervention, planning cannot be given up at the altar of market mechanism. Planning needs to be continued—the content of planning has to change.

Some exciting gifts are up for grabs with this book!!

BUSINESS ECONOMICS AND INDIAN BUSINESS ENVIRONMENT

Debes Mukherjee

FREE Gifts Rs. 1000/-

Dear Readers

By now you must have gone through this book in the entirety. So we invite your assessment on this title with absolute impartiality and candid observations. After all, we publishers blindly depend on your benchmarking. Friends, please fill up the open spaces below with CAPITAL LETTERS. You may add some extra sheets of paper if the space provided is not sufficient for you.

i. What are the important topics of your syllabus which are not adequately covered in this book?

ii. In which chapters and on what topics the treatment of the subject-matter by the author is not satisfactory and why?

iii. Have you come across the typos, factual inaccuracies, inconsistencies, and other forms of mistakes in the book? If yes, then please specify the mistakes and page numbers.

iv. Name top three books on the same subject, which, in your consideration, are better than this book. Could you provide some reasons?

Your 1st Preference: ....

Your 2nd Preference: ....

Your 3rd Preference: ....

v. Any suggestion to improve the quality of illustrations, diagrams, etc.?

vi. How did you like the cover design? Any suggestion on colours?

vii. Suggestions for further improvement of production-standard:

viii. Who recommended you this book:

☐ Teacher ☐ Friend ☐ Parents ☐ Bookseller ☐ Librarian

ix. Name of the person who has recommended:

Designation: ....

Address: ....

Phone No.: ....

e-mail: ....

x. Name and address of the bookseller from whom you have purchased this book:

....

....

....

xi. Name and address of the library where you would like to find the book:

....

....

xii. Name and address of your institution (Please mention the University or Board):

....

....

xiii. Your name, e-mail, and complete postal address:

....

....

....

xiv. A few other titles published by us that you would like to read:

....

....

The best assessment will be rewarded half-yearly. The award will be in the form of our publications, as decided by the Editorial and Marketing Operations Division, amounting to Rs. 1000/- (Rupees one thousand) only.

....

Please mail the filled up coupon at your earliest to :

Editorial & Marketing Operations Division

NEW CENTRAL BOOK AGENCY (P) Ltd

8/1 Chintamoni Das Lane, Kolkata 700 009

West Bengal, INDIA

Phone + Fax: 033 + 2241 8411, 2241 8573, 2241 9094

e-mail: ncbapvtltd@eth.net, ncba@cal2.vsnl.net.in

Website: www.centralgroup.com